New Zealand Yearbook of International Law

# New Zealand Yearbook of International Law

(this *Yearbook* covers the period 1 January 2018 to 31 December 2018)

*General Editor*

Jan Jakob Bornheim (*University of Canterbury, New Zealand*)

*Associate Editor*

Christian Riffel (*University of Canterbury, New Zealand*)

*Book Reviews Editor*

Róisín Burke (*University of Canterbury, New Zealand*)

*Editorial Assistant*

Robert Brew (*University of Canterbury, New Zealand*)

VOLUME 16, 2018

The titles published in this series are listed at *brill.com/nzyb*

## Advisory Board

Philip G. Alston
*Professor, School of Law,*
*New York University, US*

Tony Angelo ONZM
*Professor, Faculty of Law,*
*Victoria University of Wellington, NZ*

Richard Barnes
*Professor, Law School, University of Hull, UK*

Neil Boister
*Professor, School of Law,*
*University of Canterbury, NZ*

Richard Burchill
*Director of Research and Engagement, TRENDS*
*Research Advisory, UAE*

Andrew Byrnes
*Professor, Faculty of Law, University of New*
*South Wales, Australia*

Roger S. Clark
*Professor, Rutgers School of Law,*
*New Jersey, US*

Alex Conte
*Executive Director, Child Rights Connect*
*Geneva, Switzerland*

Alberto Costi
*Professor, Faculty of Law,*
*Victoria University of Wellington, NZ*

James Crawford AC
*Judge, International Court of Justice,*
*The Hague, The Netherlands*

Scott Davidson
*Professor and Vice-Chancellor of*
*Newman University, UK*

Kevin Dawkins
*Professor, Faculty of Law, University of*
*Otago, NZ*

Treasa Dunworth
*Associate Professor, Faculty of Law,*
*University of Auckland, NZ*

Francesco Francioni
*Professor Emeritus of International Law,*
*European University Institute, Florence, Italy*

Caroline Foster
*Associate Professor, Faculty of Law,*
*University of Auckland, Australia*

Chris Gallavin
*Professor and Deputy Pro Vice Chancellor,*
*Massey University, NZ*

Kennedy Graham
*Director, New Zealand Centre for*
*Global Studies, NZ*

Mark Gobbi
*Parliamentary Counsel, Parliamentary*
*Counsel Office, NZ*

Michael Hahn
*Professor, Faculty of Law & Director,*
*World Trade Institute, University of Bern,*
*Switzerland and Honorary Professor,*
*Faculty of Law, University of Waikato, NZ*

W. John Hopkins
*Professor, School of Law,*
*University of Canterbury, NZ*

Amokura Kawharu
*Associate Professor, Faculty of Law,*
*University of Auckland, NZ*

Sir Kenneth Keith ONZ, KBE
*Faculty of Law, Victoria University of*
*Wellington, NZ*

Benedict Kingsbury
*Professor and Director of the Institute for*
*International Law and Justice, School of Law,*
*New York University, US*

Meredith Kolsky Lewis
*Associate Professor and Associate Director,
New Zealand Centre of International Economic
Law, Victoria University of Wellington
Law School, NZ*

Bill Mansfield
*Barrister, NZ*

Susan Marks
*Professor, Department of Law, London School
of Economics, UK*

Annick Masselot
*Professor, School of Law,
University of Canterbury, NZ*

Penelope Mathew
*Dean and Professor, Auckland Law School,
University of Auckland, NZ*

Campbell McLachlan QC
*Professor, Faculty of Law, Victoria
University of Wellington, NZ*

Joanna Mossop
*Associate Professor,
Faculty of Law, Victoria University
of Wellington, NZ*

Ray Murphy
*Professor, Irish Centre for Human
Rights, National University of Ireland
Galway, Ireland*

Roda Mushkat
*Professor, Johns Hopkins University,
The Paul H. Nitze School of Advanced
International Studies (SAIS), Hopkins-Nanjng
Centre, China*

Sir Geoffrey Palmer KCMG, AC, QC
*Barrister, Distinguished Fellow, Faculty of Law
and New Zealand Centre for Public Law,
Victoria University of Wellington, NZ*

Mere Pulea
*Judicial and Legal Training Consultant
in the Pacific Region, NZ*

Penelope Ridings MNZM
*Barrister, NZ*

Donald R. Rothwell
*Professor, ANU College of Law, Australia
National University, Australia*

Karen Scott
*Professor, School of Law, University of
Canterbury, NZ*

Tim Stephens
*Professor, Faculty of Law, University of Sydney,
Australia*

Stefan Talmon
*Professor and Director of the Institute for
Public International Law, University of Bonn,
Germany*

Li-ann Thio
*Professor, Faculty of Law, National University
of Singapore, Singapore*

Barbara von Tigerstrom
*Professor, College of Law, University of
Saskatchewan, Canada*

Nigel White
*Professor, School of Law, University of
Nottingham, UK*

# New Zealand Yearbook of International Law

*Volume 16, 2018*

*Edited by*

Jan Jakob Bornheim
Christian Riffel

BRILL
NIJHOFF

LEIDEN | BOSTON

Typeface for the Latin, Greek, and Cyrillic scripts: "Brill". See and download: brill.com/brill-typeface.

ISSN 1176-6417
ISBN 978-90-04-42325-1 (hardback)
ISBN 978-90-04-42326-8 (e-book)

Copyright 2020 by Koninklijke Brill NV, Leiden, The Netherlands.
Koninklijke Brill NV incorporates the imprints Brill, Brill Hes & De Graaf, Brill Nijhoff, Brill Rodopi, Brill Sense, Hotei Publishing, mentis Verlag, Verlag Ferdinand Schöningh and Wilhelm Fink Verlag.
All rights reserved. No part of this publication may be reproduced, translated, stored in a retrieval system, or transmitted in any form or by any means, electronic, mechanical, photocopying, recording or otherwise, without prior written permission from the publisher.
Authorization to photocopy items for internal or personal use is granted by Koninklijke Brill NV provided that the appropriate fees are paid directly to The Copyright Clearance Center, 222 Rosewood Drive, Suite 910, Danvers, MA 01923, USA. Fees are subject to change.

This book is printed on acid-free paper and produced in a sustainable manner.

# Contents

Preface    XI

## Articles and Commentaries

Investor-State Dispute Settlement in the *CPTPP*: Perspectives from Australia, Japan and New Zealand    3
   *Ashley Chandler*

Will the Anti-corruption Chapter in the *TPP11* Work? Assessing the Role of Trade Law in the Fight Against Corruption Through International Law    39
   *José-Miguel Bello y Villarino*

The Confluence of International Trade and Investment: Exploring the Nexus between Export Controls and Indirect Expropriation    76
   *Umair Ghori*

Subsidies and "New Industrial Policy": Are International Trade Rules Fit for the 21st Century?    118
   *Tracey Epps and Danae Wheeler*

Out with the Old Approach: A Call to Take Socio-Economic Rights Seriously in Refugee Status Determination    145
   *Imogen Little*

A Critical Re-analysis of *Whaling in the Antarctic*: Formalism, Realism, and How Not to Do International Law    174
   *James C. Fisher*

Jurisdictional Aspects of Dispute Settlement under the *UN Convention on the Law of the Sea*: Some Recent Developments    207
   *Gino Naldi and Konstantinos Magliveras*

State Immunity and the Application of Customary International Law in New Zealand: The *Young v Attorney-General* Litigation    241
   *Jared Papps*

The Human Rights Committee, the Right to Life and Nuclear Weapons: The Committee's *General Comment No 36 on Article 6 of the Covenant on Civil and Political Rights*   263
    *Roger S. Clark*

## The South Pacific

Pacific Islands Forum 2018   279
    *Tony Angelo*

## The Year in Review

International Human Rights Law   285
    *Cassandra Mudgway and Lida Ayoubi*

Indigenous Peoples' Rights under International Law   310
    *Fleur Te Aho*

International Economic Law   322
    *An Hertogen*

International Environmental Law   332
    *Vernon Rive*

Law of the Sea and Fisheries 2018   353
    *Joanna Mossop*

The Antarctic Treaty System   362
    *Alan D Hemmings*

International Criminal Law and Humanitarian Law   371
    *Treasa Dunworth*

International Law and Security   378
    *Anna Hood*

## New Zealand State Conduct

Treaty Action and Implementation    389
    Mark Gobbi

## Book Reviews

*International Human Rights Law in Aotearoa New Zealand* by Margaret Bedggood, Kris Gledhill and Ian McIntosh (eds)    439
    Cassandra Mudgway

*The Global Anti-Corruption Regime: The Case of Papua New Guinea* by Hannah Harris    445
    Neil Boister

*Legal Responses to Transnational and International Crimes: Toward an Integrative Approach* by Harmen van der Wilt & Christophe Paulussen (eds)    449
    Robert J. Currie

# Preface

The editors are pleased to publish this 16th volume of the New Zealand Yearbook of International Law covering the year 2018.

The first four articles are the result of a workshop by the International Economic Law Interest Group of the Australian and New Zealand Society of International Law that took place in February 2019 in Christchurch. The workshop revolved around current topical issues in international economic law. Chandler discusses investor-state arbitration in the CPTTP, while Bello y Villarino looks at the anti-corruption provisions of the same treaty. Ghori analyses the relationship between expropriation and export controls and investment treaties. Epps and Wheeler look ahead at the topic of the treatment of subsidies and new forms of industrial policies in international economic law.

Next, there a number of articles outside the international economic law subsection. Little looks at the consideration given to socio-economic rights in New Zealand refugee law. Fisher tells a cautionary tale about the *Whaling* case at the International Court of Justice, while Naldi and Konstantinos look at the UNCLOS dispute settlement mechanism. The general section concludes with two shorter notes. First, Papps discusses state immunity and *forum non conveniens* in the *Young* litigation in New Zealand. Second, Clarke discusses the Human Rights Committee's position on nuclear weapons.

This volume includes a regular update, this year by Angelo, on the activities and developments with respect to the Pacific Island Forum. Yearly, the Yearbook encourages submissions on issues of international law affecting the South Pacific Region.

The Year in Review section focuses inwardly and outwardly on New Zealand and its role in contemporary international law during the 2018 year. It covers international human rights law, indigenous peoples' rights under international law, international economic law, international environmental law, law of the sea and fisheries, the Antarctic treaty system, international criminal law and international humanitarian law, and international law and security. The commentators provide a brief overview and commentary on New Zealand's practice and developments with respect to each of these areas of international law during 2018. The Year in Review continues with a comprehensive report on New Zealand state conduct with respect to Treaty Action and Implementation in New Zealand for the 2018 period. The Yearbook ends with a number of book reviews.

The views of the authors throughout are naturally their own.

The Editors wish to extend their gratitude to the Advisory Board, the academics who continue to provide annual contributions to the Yearbook Year in Review, the authors contributing to this volume, and other academics, practitioners and government officials from New Zealand and globally who continue to support the development of this publication. A particular thank-you goes to members of the Advisory Board and others taking the time to review contributions.

Finally, we would like to thank a number of individuals, without whom the publication of this Volume would not have been feasible. We would like to thank our Book Reviews Editor, Dr Róisín Burke, and our Editorial Assistant, Robert Brew, for their valuable contributions and hard work in producing the Yearbook.

*Jan Jakob Bornheim*
Editor

*Christian Riffel*
Associate Editor

*Articles and Commentaries*

# Investor-state Dispute Settlement in the *CPTPP*: Perspectives from Australia, Japan and New Zealand

*Ashley Chandler*\*

**Abstract**

The *Comprehensive and Progressive Agreement for Transpacific Partnership* ("CPTPP") has come into force during a time of continued debate over the future of investor-state dispute settlement ("ISDS"). This paper seeks to examine the incremental approach to reform taken in its investment chapter in reference to the treaty practice and policy of three CPTPP countries: Australia, New Zealand and Japan. The analysis of these countries, selected for their potential to play a greater role in shaping international investment law, supports the conclusion that the CPTPP's approach is a balanced one, appropriately addressing common criticisms of ISDS while maintaining the merits of the mechanism. This approach may hold greater significance to the extent that it influences future large-scale regional initiatives. Importantly, however, this paper also argues that regardless of stated positions on ISDS, it remains simply one of many tools in the trade negotiator's toolbox, subject to compromise and concession when convenient.

## 1   Introduction

Although initially developed in the 1960s,[1] it is over the last two decades that the modern system for the settlement of disputes between investors and states under international investment agreements has come to have major impact.[2] There are currently over 2,500 international investment agreements ("IIAs") in

---

\*   Ashley Chandler is a lawyer based in Brisbane, Australia. She holds a Bachelor of Laws with Honours and Bachelor of Arts (Economics and Political Science) from the University of Queensland. Ashley spent two years working at Japanese law firm, Nishimura & Asahi, most recently in the international dispute resolution practice group. She now serves as the Associate to a Justice of the Supreme Court of Queensland.
1   *Convention on the Settlement of Disputes Between States and Nationals of Other States*, opened for signature on 18 March 1965, 575 UNTS 159 (entered into force 14 October 1966).
2   United Nations Conference on Trade and Development ("UNCTAD") records a cumulative total of 855 known ISDS cases: UNCTAD, *Investor–State Dispute Settlement: Review of Developments in 2017*, UN Doc UNCTAD/DIAE/PCB/INF/2018/2 (June 2018) 2.

force around the globe, including 2,354 bilateral investment treaties ("BITS") and 313 other treaties, such as free trade agreements ("FTAS"), containing investment provisions.[3] States typically enter into investment treaties for one or more of three reasons:[4] to protect the investments of nationals of the state in the territory of the counterparty; to stimulate inbound foreign direct investment ("FDI");[5] and/or, more generally, to facilitate investment liberalisation. At a broader level, investment agreements contribute to the stability of the international investment environment by providing substantive guarantees to foreign investors and their investments through placing enforceable obligations on states.[6] The prevailing method of such enforcement is investor-state dispute settlement ("ISDS"), whereby a foreign investor can bring a claim for breach of the investment treaty directly against the host state.[7]

Since the late 1990s, the number of ISDS claims has increased rapidly.[8] This has been accompanied by a rise in criticism, with the system being increasingly called into question and accused of lacking legitimacy. As Hindelang and Krajewski explain,[9]

> international investment law is facing serious challenges concerning the legitimacy of its underlying objectives and the mechanisms through which investment disputes are adjudicated: parts of civil society, some parliamentarians and the public more generally increasingly question the current – "traditional" – approach of foreign investment protection.

---

3   UNCTAD, "International Investment Agreements Navigator", *Investment Policy Hub* (Web Page) <https://investmentpolicy.unctad.org/international-investment-agreements>.
4   Kyle Dylan Dickson-Smith and Bryan Mercurio, "Australia's Position on Investor-State Dispute Settlement: Fruit of a Poisonous Tree or a Few Rotten Apples?" (2018) 40(2) *Sydney Law Review* 213, 217.
5   Ibid 217. The authors further note that "the increase of bilateral and regional FTAs is purported to create a self-reinforcing, or contagious, process that compels other states to follow and increase the standards of protections in investment agreements in order to remain competitive and attract FDI": at 218.
6   United Nations Commission on Trade Law Working Group III (Investor-State Dispute Settlement Reform), *Possible Reform of Investor-State Dispute Settlement (ISDS): Note by the Secretariat*, UN Doc A/CN.9/WG.III/WP.149 (5 September 2018).
7   This is in contrast to diplomatic efforts which had to be relied upon prior to the advent of ICSID and the modern international investment law regime.
8   Figure 1 shows the significant uptick in cases filed from the 1990s through present: *Investor-State Dispute Settlement: Review of Developments in 2017* (n 2) 2.
9   Steffen Hindelang and Markus Krajewski, "Conclusion and Outlook: Whither International Investment Law?" in Steffen Hindelang and Markus Krajewski (eds), *Shifting Paradigms in International Investment Law*, (Oxford University Press, 2016) 377.

Multiple solutions to these perceived problems have been proposed,[10] including a complete overhaul of the system and replacement with a standing investment court. Less radical is the suggestion to incrementally reform the current system. The *Comprehensive and Progressive Agreement for Trans-Pacific Partnership* ("CPTPP") stands as the preeminent example of the latter approach.

The CPTPP traces its origins to the original *Trans-Pacific Partnership* ("TPP"), which was hamstrung following the withdrawal of the United States ("US") in January 2017.[11] With Japan taking the lead,[12] the remaining 11 states[13] proceeded in the absence of the US and in March 2018 signed the CPTPP.[14] On 30 December 2018, the CPTPP entered into force following its ratification by six countries.[15] The CPTPP covers 13.3% of global gross domestic product ("GDP"), worth a total of USD10.6 trillion.[16] Although undoubtedly significant in both geographical scope and coverage of world gross domestic product, the CPTPP may yet be dwarfed by the *Regional and Comprehensive Economic Partnership* ("RCEP").[17] In the context of ongoing RCEP negotiations, in which an investment

---

10  This has been described by UNCTAD as an "Improved ISDS Procedure" approach, in contrast to other principal approaches ("No ISDS", "Standing ISDS tribunal", "Limited ISDS" and "Unreformed ISDS"): UNCTAD, *Reforming Investment Dispute Settlement: A Stocktaking*, UN Doc UNCTAD/DIAE/PCB/INF/2019/3 (March 2019) 2, figure 1.

11  The TPP was to enter into force when at least six parties accounting for 85 per cent of the combined GDP of the 12 member states ratified the agreement: *Trans-Pacific Partnership*, signed on 4 February 2016 (not yet in force) art 30.5.

12  Rintaro Tobita and Yuji Ohira, "Japan Rings in the Year of Mega Free Trade", *Nikkei Asian Review* (Web Page, 30 December 2018) <https://asia.nikkei.com/Economy/Trade-war/Japan-rings-in-the-year-of-mega-free-trade>.

13  In addition to the countries which are the subject of this article, the remaining countries are Brunei, Chile, Canada, Malaysia, Mexico, Peru, Singapore and Vietnam.

14  "Comprehensive and Progressive Agreement for Trans-Pacific Partnership (CPTPP): About the Comprehensive and Progressive Agreement for Trans-Pacific Partnership (CPTPP)", *Department of Foreign Affairs and Trade* (Web Page) <https://dfat.gov.au/trade/agreements/in-force/cptpp/pages/comprehensive-and-progressive-agreement-for-trans-pacific-partnership.aspx>.

15  *Comprehensive and Progressive Agreement for Trans-Pacific Partnership*, signed on 8 March 2018, [2018] ATS 23 (entered into force 30 December 2018) art 3 ("*CPTPP*").

16  Ministry of Foreign Affairs and Trade, "Comprehensive and Progressive Agreement for Trans-Pacific Partnership", *New Zealand Foreign Affairs and Trade* (Web Page) <https://www.mfat.govt.nz/en/trade/free-trade-agreements/free-trade-agreements-in-force/cptpp/cptpp-overview/>.

17  The Australian Department of Foreign Affairs and Trade ("DFAT") notes that "[t]he 16 RCEP participating countries account for almost half of the world's population, over 30 per cent of global GDP and over a quarter of world exports": "Regional Comprehensive Economic Partnership: About the RCEP Negotiations", *Department of Foreign Affairs and Trade* (Web Page) <https://dfat.gov.au/trade/agreements/negotiations/rcep/Pages/regional-comprehensive-economic-partnership.aspx>.

chapter has yet to be concluded, it will be interesting to observe what influence the *CPTPP's* incremental approach may have.[18]

This paper provides an analysis of that incremental approach to ISDS reform as informed by the experience of three *CPTPP* signatory states: Australia, New Zealand and Japan. These countries have been selected primarily for their potential to play a greater role in the development of international investment law in the region; Japan in its own right and Australia and New Zealand together. Japan is widely recognised as a key economic player in the Asia-Pacific region. It has the potential to exert significant influence on the trajectory of investment law policy, and for this reason its recent enthusiasm for ISDS warrants closer examination. It has also been suggested that Australia and New Zealand, sharing as they do similar economies and experience with ISDS, may be well placed to work in tandem in contributing to the development of investment law in the region. The two countries provide an interesting contrast to Japan, as they have both been more critical of ISDS and have taken concrete measures to insulate themselves from it. The experiences of the three countries also illustrate perceptions and concerns over ISDS which are held more widely and hence provide a solid foundation from which to assess the approach of the *CPTPP* in addressing these concerns.

Section 2 examines the investment policy and practice of these countries and considers the primary criticisms of ISDS by reference to the debates and discussions in each country. Section 3 will then examine how the *CPTPP* addresses three of the major concerns about ISDS drawn from that analysis. Finally, Section 4 concludes by considering the potential impact of the *CPTPP*, particularly in relation to ongoing reform discussions at the United Nations Commission on Trade Law ("UNCITRAL") and in the context of continuing *RCEP* negotiations.

## 2   ISDS: Attitudes and Experiences

This section seeks to contextualise the conclusion of the *CPTPP* by examining the investment policy, practice and negotiating position of Australia, New Zealand and Japan. In the experiences of these three countries, familiar criticisms and concerns over the use of ISDS come to light. These reflect the debates and

---

18   Markert and Ishido have noted that "[i]t would therefore not be surprising if the *CPTPP* Investment Chapter became an inspiration for other states seeking to modernise their investment agreements, in Asia and beyond".: Lars Markert and Shimpei Ishido, "The Comprehensive and Progressive Agreement For Trans-Pacific Partnership" in Barton Legum (ed), *The Investment Treaty Arbitration Review* (Law Business Research, 4th ed, June 2019) 402.

discussions taking place the world over and illustrate some of the key problems to which the *CPTPP* investment chapter attempts to respond. This section demonstrates the astute observation of the former Chief Justice of the High Court of Australia, Robert French, that "while international trade and commerce may be global, the politics that informs its law and practice is, in important respects, local".[19]

## 2.1   *Australia*
### 2.1.1   Background

> Since the First Fleet, Australia has been a country unashamedly reliant on foreign investment… As a big and sparsely populated continent with a thin domestic capital market … our reliance continues today.[20]

As this statement by Australia's first Minister for Investment suggests, Australia has long been a net foreign direct investment ("FDI")-importer.[21] This has in large part underpinned Australia's approach to ISDS and its conclusion of investment agreements more generally. Australia was involved in efforts to establish a multilateral agreement on investment ("MAI") at the Organisation for Economic Cooperation Development ("OECD") and the World Trade Organisation ("WTO"), but turned to bilateral initiatives when these failed.[22] Currently, Australia has in force 18 BITs containing ISDS provisions[23] and 17 treaties

---

19   Robert French, "Preface to International Investment Treaties and Arbitration Across Asia" in Julien Chaisse and Luke Nottage (eds), *International Investment Treaties and Arbitration Across Asia* (Brill Nijhoff, 2017) XI.
20   Andrew Robb, "Australia: A Land of Investment and Opportunity" (Speech, Credit Suisse Asian Investment Conference, 27 March 2014), quoted in David Uren, *Takeover: Foreign Investment and the Australia Psyche* (Black, 2015) 7, quoted in Dickson-Smith and Mercurio (n 4) 220.
21   "Australia has always been a net importer of capital": Frank Bingham, *Australia's Trade Since Federation* (Report, June 2016) 15.
22   Kawharu and Nottage note that "[l]ike New Zealand, after it became clear around 2000 that there was little scope to achieve a broadly multilateral agreement through the OECD or the WTO, Australia began focusing on comprehensive FTAs": Amokura Kawharu and Luke Nottage, "Foreign Investment Regulation and Treaty Practice in New Zealand and Australia: Getting it Together in the Asia-Pacific?" in Julien Chaisse and Luke Nottage (eds), *International Investment Treaties and Arbitration Across Asia* (Brill Nijhoff, 2017) 445, 469.
23   These are with: Argentina, China, Czech Republic, Egypt, Hong Kong, Hungary, Indonesia, Lao People's Democratic Republic, Lithuania, Pakistan, Papua New Guinea, Peru, Philippines, Poland, Romania, Sri Lanka, Turkey and Uruguay: UNCTAD, "International Investment Agreements Navigator: Australia", *Investment Policy Hub* (Web Page) <https://

containing investment provisions, seven of which include ISDS.[24] Under these agreements, Australia has successfully defended one claim, *Philip Morris v Commonwealth of Australia*,[25] and at the time of writing has one officially pending claim by a US investor,[26] and a further claim looming.[27] A number of Australian investors have also taken advantage of ISDS provisions to protect their overseas investments, with six known claims brought by Australian

---

investmentpolicy.unctad.org/international-investment-agreements/countries/11/australia?type=tips>.

[24] These are: CPTPP (n 15); *Free Trade Agreement between the Government of Australia and the Government of the People's Republic of China*, signed 17 June 2015, [2015] ATS 15 (entered into force 20 December 2015); *Agreement between Australia and Japan for an Economic Partnership*, signed 8 July 2014, [2015] ATS 2 (entered into force 15 January 2015); *Free Trade Agreement between the Government of Australia and the Government of the Republic of Korea*, signed 8 April 2014, [2014] ATS 43 (entered into force 12 December 2014); *Malaysia–Australia Free Trade Agreement*, signed 22 May 2012, [2013] ATS 4 (entered into force 1 January 2013); *Protocol on Investment to the New Zealand-Australia Closer Economic Relations Trade Agreement*, signed 16 February 2011, [2013] ATS 10 (entered into force 1 March 2013); *Agreement Establishing the ASEAN–Australia–New Zealand Free Trade Area*, signed 27 February 2009, [2010] ATS 1 (entered into force 1 January 2010) ("AANZFTA"); *Australia – Chile Free Trade Agreement*, signed 30 July 2008, [2009] ATS 6 (entered into force 6 March 2009); *Australia–Thailand Free Trade Agreement*, signed 5 July 2004, [2005] ATS 2 (entered into force 1 January 2005); *Australia–US Free Trade Agreement*, signed 18 May 2004, [2005] ATS 1 (entered into force 1 January 2005); *Agreement between the Government of Australia and the Government of Fiji on Trade and Economic Relations*, signed 11 March 1999, [1999] ATS 32 (entered into force 15 December 1999); *Trade and Economic Cooperation Arrangement between the Government of Canada and the Government of Australia* (entered into force 15 November 1995); *Energy Charter Treaty*, signed 17 December 1994, 2080 UNTS 95 (entered into force 16 April 1998); *South Pacific Regional Trade and Economic Cooperation Agreement with Schedules*, signed 14 July 1980, 1240 UNTS 65 (entered into force 1 January 1981); *Agreement on Trade and Commercial Relations between the Government of Australia and the Government of Papua New Guinea*, signed 6 November 1976, [1977] ATS 7 (entered into force 1977). "International Investment Agreements Navigator: Australia" (n 23).

[25] *Philip Morris Asia Limited v Australia (Award on Jurisdiction and Admissibility)*, (Permanent Court of Arbitration, Case No 2012-12, 17 December 2015) 186.

[26] "Power Rental Asset Co Two LLC (AssetCo), Power Rental Op Co Australia LLC (OpCo), APR Energy LLC v the Government of Australia, UNCITRAL", *italaw* (Web Page) <https://www.italaw.com/cases/5687>; Jarrod Hepburn, "A Second US Investor Tries to Arbitrate under Australia-US FTA, despite Absence of an Investor-State Arbitration Mechanism", *Investment Arbitration Reporter* (Web Page, 24 April 2017) <https://www.iareporter.com/articles/a-second-us-investor-tries-to-arbitrate-under-australia-us-fta-despite-absence-of-an-investor-state-arbitration-mechanism/>.

[27] Jarrod Hepburn, "US Investors Mired in Australian Dispute Contend that State-to-State Consultations, if Launched, Must Be Followed by Investor-State Arbitration" *Investment Arbitration Reporter* (Web Page, 1 December 2015) <https://www.iareporter.com/articles/us-investors-mired-in-australian-dispute-contend-that-state-to-state-consultations-if-launched-must-be-followed-by-investor-state-arbitration/>.

investors. As at July 2019, three have been finalised: *White Industries v India*[28] and *Tethyan Copper v Pakistan*[29] decided in favour of the investor, and *Churchill Mining and Planet Mining v Indonesia*,[30] decided in favour of Indonesia.[31] There are also currently the following pending claims brought by Australian investors: *Kingsgate v Thailand*;[32] *Munshi v Mongolia*;[33] and *Emerge Gaming and Tantalum International v Egypt*.[34]

2.1.2 Origins of ISDS Opposition

Despite this largely positive experience of a successfully defended claim and reasonable uptake by Australian investors, the Productivity Commission, in its review of Australia's treaty practice in 2010,[35] concluded that Australia should avoid entering into treaties with ISDS provisions.[36] A detailed review of the report and its findings is beyond the scope of this paper.[37] For present purposes, it is sufficient to note that the Productivity Commission's rejection of ISDS was based on concerns including "regulatory chill", inconsistency in tribunal determinations, arbitrator bias and conflicts of interest, and a lack of transparency.[38] On the point of inconsistency, the Productivity Commission

---

28 *White Industries Australia Limited v India (Final Award)* (Ad Hoc Tribunal, 30 November 2011).
29 "Tethyan Copper Company Pty Limited v Islamic Republic of Pakistan, ICSID Case No. ARB/12/1", *italaw* (Web Page) <https://www.italaw.com/cases/1631>.
30 *Churchill Mining Plc v Indonesia (Decision on Jurisdiction)* (ICSID Arbitral Tribunal, Case No ARB/12/14 and 12/40, 24 February 2014); *Planet Mining Pty Ltd v Indonesia (Decision on Jurisdiction)* (ICSID Arbitral Tribunal, Case No ARB/12/40 and 12/14, 24 February 2014); *Churchill Mining PLC and Planet Mining Pty Ltd (Award)* (ICSID Arbitral Tribunal, Case No ARB/12/14 and 12/40, 6 December 2016); *(Decision on Annulment)* (ICSID Arbitral Tribunal Case No ARB/12/14 and 12/40, 18 March 2019).
31 As an aside, both India and Indonesia have reformed their ISDS practice, partly in response to such claims.
32 "Kingsgate Consolidated v Thailand", *italaw* (Web Page) <https://www.italaw.com/cases/5572>.
33 "Mohammed Munshi v Mongolia, SCC CASE No 2018/007", *italaw* (Web Page) <https://www.italaw.com/cases/6656>.
34 UNCTAD, "Investment Dispute Settlement Navigator: Emerge Gaming Ltd and Tantalum International Ltd v Arab Republic of Egypt (ICSID Case No ARB/18/22)", *Investment Policy Hub* (Web Page, 31 December 2018) <https://investmentpolicy.unctad.org/investment-dispute-settlement/cases/867/emerge-gaming-and-tantalum-international-v-egypt>.
35 Kawharu and Nottage, "Foreign Investment Regulation and Treaty Practice in New Zealand and Australia: Getting it Together in the Asia-Pacific?" (n 22) 469.
36 Productivity Commission, *Bilateral and Regional Trade Agreements* (Research Report, November 2010) 276.
37 For such a detailed analysis, see Dickson-Smith and Mercurio (n 4).
38 Ibid 225–226.

noted that the absence of a binding system of precedent results in tribunals reaching disparate conclusions on cases with similar or identical facts.[39] The Productivity Commission also concluded that ISDS offered little benefit to Australia because there is no clear evidence that it significantly increases inbound FDI and also because Australian investors overseas do not rely on the provisions and have other options, such as political risk insurance, available to them.[40]

The report has been widely criticised, with Dickson-Smith and Mercurio identifying the following key methodological errors: conflation of trade and investment issues; lack of analytical depth; failure to adequately engage with the benefits of ISDS; and failure to consider the circumstances of current and potential treaty counterparties.[41] Former US trade negotiator and WTO Deputy Director-General, Professor Andrew Stoler, who was appointed as an ad hoc associate commissioner, issued a strong dissent.[42] Notably, Stoler stated that arguing that investors have recourse to insurance is akin to arguing against the need for a fire department because homeowners can buy property insurance.[43] Despite such criticism, the Productivity Commission largely reiterated its views in an updated report in 2015,[44] albeit with some engagement with empirical data.[45] The Productivity Commission's report has had a profound influence on Australian policy, providing the bedrock upon which much subsequent opposition to ISDS has been based. Most significantly, in 2011, in reliance on this report, the centre-left Gillard Labor Government established a trade policy which expressly stated that Australia would no longer conclude agreements providing for ISDS.[46]

While this policy was in force, Australia became subject to its first claim. The claim was brought by Phillip Morris Asia (Hong Kong) in the wake of an unsuccessful constitutional challenge to Australia's tobacco plain packaging legislation.[47] The claim was ultimately dismissed at the jurisdictional stage as an abuse of rights.[48] Although this decision and indeed the merits decision in

---

39  *Bilateral and Regional Trade Agreements* (n 36) 273, box 14.5.
40  Ibid 270.
41  Dickson-Smith and Mercurio (n 4) 226–228.
42  Kawharu and Nottage, "Foreign Investment Regulation and Treaty Practice in New Zealand and Australia: Getting it Together in the Asia-Pacific?" (n 22) 472.
43  *Bilateral and Regional Trade Agreements* (n 36) 320.
44  Productivity Commission, *Trade & Assistance Review 2014–15* (Annual Report, July 2016).
45  Dickson-Smith and Mercurio (n 4) 233.
46  DFAT, *Gillard Government Trade Policy Statement: Trading Our Way to More Jobs and Prosperity* (Policy Statement, April 2011) 14.
47  *JT International SA v Commonwealth of Australia* (2012) 250 CLR 1.
48  *Philip Morris Asia Limited v Australia (Award on Jurisdiction and Admissibility)* (n 25).

the *Philip Morris v Uruguay*[49] case arguably show the system functioning as intended, it continues to be cited by opponents of ISDS in Australia as an example of how foreign companies can take advantage of rights they are accorded over and above Australian citizens who are unable to arbitrate against the government.

### 2.1.3 Political Context

Following its election in 2013, the centre-right Liberal-National coalition government led by Prime Minister Tony Abbott revoked the *Gillard Government Trade Policy Statement* and instituted a policy of case-by-case consideration of ISDS.[50] It has been noted that although the policy appears superficially attractive, it can prove challenging for treaty partners, foreign investors and domestic interests. Trakman and Sharma explain that the approach assumes that the government will be able to determine in advance the nature of the disputes likely to eventuate and consider whether it ought to negotiate for ISDS, but conclude that there is simply insufficient evidence to make such predictions with any confidence.[51]

In spite, or perhaps because, of Australia's official policy, several challenges were mounted to ISDS over the proceeding years, primarily through legislation and parliamentary reviews of treaties.[52] Most relevantly, the Parliament's Joint

---

49  *Philip Morris Brands Sàrl, Philip Morris Products SA and Abal Hermanos SA v Uruguay* (*Award*) (ICSID Arbitral Tribunal, Case No ARB/10/7, 8 July 2016).
50  This remains the policy to date. See DFAT, "Investor-state Dispute Settlement (ISDS)", *About Foreign Investment* (Web Page) <https://dfat.gov.au/trade/investment/Pages/investor-state-dispute-settlement.aspx>.
51  Leon E. Trakman and Kunal Sharma, "Jumping Back and Forth between Domestic Courts and ISDS: Mixed Signals from the Asia-Pacific Region" in Steffen Hindelang and Markus Krajewski (eds), *Shifting Paradigms in International Investment Law: More Balanced, Less Isolated, Increasingly Diversified* (Oxford University Press, 2016) 316, 323.
52  See for example, Joint Standing Committee on Treaties, Parliament of Australia, *Report 142: Treaty tabled on 13 May 2014* (Report, 4 September 2014); Foreign Affairs, Defence and Trade Committee, Parliament of Australia, *Report: Korea-Australia Free Trade Agreement*, (Report, 1 October 2014); Foreign Affairs, Defence and Trade Committee, Parliament of Australia, *The Commonwealth's treaty-making process* (Report, 25 June 2015); Foreign Affairs, Defence and Trade Committee, Parliament of Australia, *Proposed China-Australia Free Trade Agreement* (Report, 6 November 2015); Joint Standing Committee on Treaties, Parliament of Australia, *Report 165: Trans-Pacific Partnership Agreement* (Report, November 2016); Joint Standing Committee on Treaties, Parliament of Australia. These are discussed in Luke Nottage, "Investment Treaty Arbitration Policy in Australia, New Zealand – and Korea?" (2015) 25(3) *Journal of Arbitration Studies* 185, 195–208. More recent reviews include *Comprehensive and Progressive Agreement for Trans-Pacific Partnership* (Report 181, August 2018); Joint Standing Committee on Treaties, Parliament of Australia, *Report 180: Peru FTA; EU Framework Agreement; Timor Treaty-Maritime Boundaries; WIPO Australian Patent Office; Scientific Technical Cooperation: Italy and Brazil* (Report, August

Standing Committee on Treaties ("JSCOT") undertook a review of the *CPTPP*. In addition to primary concerns about constraints on regulatory capacity, its final report noted that a number of submissions had identified the lack of precedent in ISDS and the resulting lack of consistency in arbitral awards as an issue.[53] In consideration of such submissions, JSCOT concluded that Australia should advocate for a system of precedent, which would provide a degree of clarity as to what to expect from tribunal decisions.[54] The report also recommended the introduction of an appellate mechanism and a code of ethics for arbitrators.[55]

Within these parliamentary reviews and debates, the battle lines have usually been drawn along the party-political divide: the economically liberal, socially conservative side of politics generally support ISDS, while the more socially progressive, left-leaning parties tend towards opposition. This has manifested most recently in the introduction of the A Fair Go for Australians in Trade Bill 2018. This bill, which was introduced into the Senate in October 2018, seeks to legislate a prohibition on the inclusion of ISDS provisions in Australia's international investment agreements,[56] and passed its second reading stage in November 2018.[57] The second reading speeches reveal that the main concern continues to be with the right to regulate,[58] but that concerns over

---

2018); Joint Standing Committee on Treaties, Parliament of Australia, *Report 183: Aspects of the Peru-Australia Free Trade Agreement Revisited* (November 2018).

53 Joint Standing Committee on Treaties, Parliament of the Commonwealth of Australia, *Comprehensive and Progressive Agreement for Trans-Pacific Partnership* (Report No 181 , August 2018) 41 [4.93].

54 Ibid 42 [4.98].

55 Ibid 43 [4.104].

56 "The Commonwealth must not, on or after the commencement of this Act, enter into a trade agreement with one or more other countries or a bilateral investment treaty that includes an investor-state dispute settlement provision".: *A Fair Go for Australians in Trade Bill 2018* (Cth) s 4.

57 "A Fair Go For Australians in Trade Bill 2018 [No 2]", *Parliament of Australia* (Web Page) <https://www.aph.gov.au/Parliamentary_Business/Bills_Legislation/Bills_Search_Results/Result?bId=s1146>.

58 See, for example, Labor Senator Carr's statement, during the second reading, that the bill is aimed at ensuring that Australians are not disadvantaged by trade agreements with other nations, that we do ensure we are able to maintain access to engagement in the international trading system without losing sovereignty for this nation and undermining the living conditions of our own people.
Commonwealth, *Parliamentary Debates*, Senate, 12 November 2018, 7683 (Kim Carr).

transparency and the privileging of foreign investors are also present.[59] The national Labor Party platform clarifies that this prohibition was not only intended to operate prospectively, but that a team of negotiators from the Department of Foreign Affairs and Trade ("DFAT") would be assembled and tasked with the duty of renegotiating pre-existing agreements containing ISDS provisions.[60] In light of the current composition of Parliament following the May 2019 election,[61] there is a strong possibility of further agitation of these issues, though the extent to which this impacts Australia's ISDS policy remains to be seen.[62] For the moment with the re-election of the Liberal-National Coalition to government, the current case-by-case approach, which saw Australia agree to ISDS in the *CPTPP*, can be expected to remain.

## 2.2  New Zealand

### 2.2.1  Background

There are significant parallels between Australia's experience and that of New Zealand. However, differences must also be noted. The most basic of these is the difference between the two economies. Australia's economy is larger than

---

59  See the remarks of Greens Party Senator Hanson-Young who raises concerns about a lack of transparency, privileging of multinational companies over locals and constraints on capacity to regulate for progressive environmental and labour standards: Commonwealth, *Parliamentary Debates*, Senate, 12 November 2018, 7691 (Sarah Hanson-Young).

60  Australian Labor Party, *A Fair Go for Australia* (Policy, 2018) 32 [132]–[133].

61  As at 26 May 2019, the Liberal-National Coalition is predicted to take 78 seats in the House of Representatives (76 required to form government): "Federal Election 2019 Results", *Australian Broadcasting Corporation* (Web Page, 2019) <https://www.abc.net.au/news/elections/federal/2019/results>. As for the Senate, votes counted thus far indicate that the Coalition will take 34 of 76 seats up for election, with Labor, the Greens and the Centre Alliance expected to take 26, eight and two, respectively: "Senate Results", *Australian Broadcasting Corporation* (Web Page) <https://www.abc.net.au/news/elections/federal/2019/results/senate>. The position of the Coalition, Labor and the Greens are discussed in the main text. The minor party Centre Alliance may be expected to be more resistant to ISDS on the basis of election policies advocating tightening of Australia's foreign investment regulations (for example, "Australia needs a strategic approach to foreign investment, rather than the inconsistent approach we have now. Foreign investment would be much lower if there were greater incentives for Australians to invest in their own country"): "Policies", *Centre Alliance* (Web Page) <https://centrealliance.org.au/policies/>.

62  Although speaking in regard to the previous administration, Kawharu and Nottage note that the Liberal-National Coalition government may need to compromise with Labor to secure passage of key agreements containing ISDS and suggest a number of forms such compromise could take: Kawharu and Nottage, "Foreign Investment Regulation and Treaty Practice in New Zealand and Australia: Getting it Together in the Asia-Pacific?" (n 22) 484.

that of New Zealand,[63] and has both higher inbound and outbound FDI.[64] Although the position on a per capita basis is not so stark, these economic foundations may go some way towards explaining New Zealand's less active treaty programme since both countries signed their first BIT with China in 1988.[65] As Nottage and Kawharu note, Australia has also been more active in concluding standalone BITs, in light of considerably more outbound FDI,[66] while New Zealand has focussed on promoting its trade agenda through FTAs.[67] This difference in practice is also evident in the number of investment agreements New Zealand currently has in force: two BITs, both of which provide for ISDS,[68] and 14 treaties with investment provisions, of which 10 contain ISDS provisions.[69]

---

63   Australia has a GDP of USD1.4 trillion while NZ's GDP is New Zealand's GDP is USD0.2 trillion (based on current GDP for 2017): UNCTAD, "General Profile: Australia", *UNCTADStat* (Web Page, 16 April 2019) <https://unctadstat.unctad.org/CountryProfile/GeneralProfile/en-GB/036/index.html>; UNCTAD, "General Profile: New Zealand", *UNCTADStat* (Web Page, 16 April 2019) <https://unctadstat.unctad.org/CountryProfile/GeneralProfile/en-GB/554/index.html>.

64   USD46.37 billion and USD4.88 billion for Australia as compared with USD3.57 billion and USD5.88 billion for New Zealand: ibid.

65   Kawharu and Nottage, "Foreign Investment Regulation and Treaty Practice in New Zealand and Australia: Getting it Together in the Asia-Pacific?" (n 22) 468.

66   Ibid 446.

67   "However, once it became clear from around 2000 that further liberalisation was not going to be readily forthcoming through the WTO, both countries started to expand their bilateral and regional FTA programs, overwhelmingly concentrated on the Asia-Pacific": ibid 446.

68   *Agreement on the Promotion and Protection of Investments (with Exchange of Notes), New Zealand–China*, signed 22 November 1988 (entered into force 25 March 1989) and *Agreement between the Government of Hong Kong and the Government of New Zealand for the Promotion and Protection of Investments*, signed 6 July 1995 (entered into force 5 August 1995): UNCTAD, "International Investment Agreements Navigator: New Zealand", Investment Policy Hub (Web Page) <https://investmentpolicy.unctad.org/international-investment-agreements/countries/150/new-zealand>.

69   CPTPP (n 15); *Free Trade Agreement between New Zealand and the Republic of Korea*, signed 23 March 2015, [2015] NZTS 10 (entered into force 20 December 2015); *Agreement between New Zealand and the Separate Customs Territory of Taiwan, Penghu, Kinmen and Matsu on Economic Cooperation*, signed 10 July 2013, [2013] NZTS 11 (entered into force 1 December 2013); *Protocol on Investment to the New Zealand–Australia Closer Economic Relations Trade Agreement* (n 24); *New Zealand–Hong Kong, China Closer Economic Partnership Agreement*, signed 29 March 2010, [2011] NZTS 1 (entered into force 1 January 2011); *Free Trade Agreement between the Government of New Zealand and the Government of Malaysia*, signed 26 October 2009 (entered into force 1 August 2010); *AANZFTA* (n 24); *Free Trade Agreement between the Government of New Zealand and the Government of the People's Republic of China*, signed 7 April 2008, [2008] NZTS 19 (entered into force 1 October 2008); *Trans-Pacific Strategic Economic Partnership Agreement*, signed 18 July 2005, [2006] NZTS 9 (entered into force 28 May 2006); *Agreement between New Zealand and Singapore on a*

Despite these differing approaches, there have also been some striking similarities in the experiences of the two countries. For example, parliamentary reviews also became an outlet for ISDS opposition, as demonstrated by the FTA with South Korea. The Foreign Affairs, Defence and Trade ("FADT") parliamentary committee undertook a review of this agreement which contains ISDS provisions.[70] The majority view of the FADT committee, reflecting the position of the incumbent National government which had negotiated the treaty, emphasised that no claim had been brought against New Zealand under existing FTAs and that the risks to New Zealand were low.[71] The Labour party representatives noted concerns over sovereignty and took the view that ISDS was of little benefit in agreements with countries with robust judicial systems,[72] while the two minor parties represented were both highly critical of ISDS. The Greens party argued that ISDS does not meet jurisprudential standards and is contrary to democratic principles,[73] while New Zealand First was particularly critical of the lack of transparency.[74] New Zealand First referred to arbitration as "a black box process where deliberations are often held in secret with no information provided publicly as to why and how a decision was reached".[75] Ultimately, ISDS was included in the agreement as concluded, with media reporting that it was a bottom-line requirement for Korea.[76] Nottage notes that the ISDS risk

---

*Closer Economic Partnership*, signed 14 November 2000, [2001] NZTS 1 (entered into force 1 January 2001); *Trade and Investment Agreement between the Government of New Zealand and the Government of the United Mexican States (with Annex)*, signed 14 April 1994, [1996] NZTS 19 (entered into force 21 October 1996); *Agreement between the Government of New Zealand and the Government of the United States of America Concerning a Framework of Principles and Procedures for Consultations Regarding Trade and Investment Relations, with Annex*, signed 2 October 1992 (entered into force 2 October 1992); *South Pacific Regional Trade and Economic Cooperation Agreement with Schedules* (n 24): "International Investment Agreements Navigator: New Zealand" (n 68).

70 Foreign Affairs, Defence and Trade Committee, New Zealand Parliament, *International Treaty Examination of the Free Trade Agreement between New Zealand and the Republic of Korea* (Report, 22 May 2015).
71 Ibid 6.
72 Ibid 10–11.
73 Ibid 12.
74 Ibid 13.
75 Ibid.
76 Business News, "Questions Raised over Korea FTA", *Radio New Zealand* (Web Page, 27 March 2015) <www.radionz.co.nz/national/programmes/businessnews/audio/20172599/questions-raised-over-korea-fta>, cited in Kawharu and Nottage, "Foreign Investment Regulation and Treaty Practice in New Zealand and Australia: Getting it Together in the Asia-Pacific?" (n 22) 445, 457.

was likely outweighed by other benefits of the FTA given the low levels of Korean investment in New Zealand.⁷⁷

Shortly following the report's publication, New Zealand First mounted a legislative challenge to ISDS through its private member's bill, the Fighting Foreign Corporate Control Bill 2015, which ultimately lapsed.⁷⁸ The parallels with developments in Australia, right down to the emotive titles, is clear. Another commonality is seen in the election of a centre-left government which ushered in an era of strong ISDS opposition. Jacinda Ardern became Prime Minister of New Zealand in 2017, after her Labour Party entered into a coalition with New Zealand First. This brought an end to a decade of rule by the more conservative National Party. We see some similarities here with the approach taken by the Gillard Labor government in Australia in 2011, though New Zealand has notably stopped short of issuing an official, publicly available government policy against ISDS.⁷⁹ The absence of an official policy, however, has not stopped New Zealand from advocating against ISDS. Indeed, the total removal of ISDS from the CPTPP was one of New Zealand's key goals in CPTPP negotiations.⁸⁰

### 2.2.2 CPTPP Negotiations

New Zealand did have some limited success in this regard. The Ministry of Foreign Affairs and Trade ("MFAT") currently notes on its website that "outcomes that were of concern to New Zealanders the first time around [in the TPP] in the areas of investment, intellectual property and health will not apply".⁸¹ This refers to the fact that New Zealand was able to negotiate the exclusion of ISDS claims based on investment contracts, meaning that companies which enter into an investment contract with the New Zealand government, rather than

---

77  Kawharu and Nottage, "Foreign Investment Regulation and Treaty Practice in New Zealand and Australia: Getting it Together in the Asia-Pacific?" (n 22) 445, 457.
78  Ibid 460.
79  Note, however, the Foreign Affairs, Defence and Trade Committee's comment that it had been advised that the government will not include ISDS in future agreements: Foreign Affairs, Defence and Trade Committee, New Zealand Parliament, *International Treaty Examination of the Comprehensive and Progressive Agreement for Trans-Pacific Partnership (CPTPP)* (Final Report, 24 May 2018) 6.
80  Prime Minister Ardern was reported as saying, in relation to negotiations, that "[w]e are going in with the explicit intent to try and remove New Zealand from these clauses": Derek Cheng, "Ban on Foreign House Buyers by Early 2018 – but Aussie Buyers Exempt", *New Zealand Herald* (online, 31 October 2017) <https://www.nzherald.co.nz/business/news/article.cfm?c_id=3&objectid=11939067>.
81  Ministry of Foreign Affairs and Trade (n 16).

relying on the treaty, will not have recourse to ISDS for any dispute arising thereunder. New Zealand has also excluded ISDS claims against decisions not to grant approval to a foreign investment under its *Overseas Investment Act 2005*,[82] as Australia has also done for its foreign investment-screening legislation.[83] One wonders about the prospect of amending that act to include as a condition for approval of a foreign investment a requirement that an investor enter into an investment contract with the government. While perhaps a remote possibility, it is one that would be open to New Zealand and allow it to further insulate itself against ISDS claims.

As might have been expected, New Zealand was not successful in achieving a total exclusion of ISDS. However, New Zealand was able to secure side letters excluding the operation of ISDS with five countries: Australia, Brunei Darussalam, Malaysia, Peru and Vietnam. Similar measures were already in place between Australia and New Zealand.[84] The executed side letters take two separate approaches; a total exclusion of ISDS as with Australia and Peru;[85] and the institution of a tiered dispute resolution process, agreed with Brunei, Malaysia and Vietnam.[86] The tiered process requires the investor and the state to first attempt to resolve the dispute amicably through consultations, which may include the use of non-binding third party procedures such as good offices, conciliation and mediation. If such consultations do not resolve the dispute within six months, it may then be submitted to arbitration, provided that the state consents (and in the case of Vietnam, "specifically consents") to the application of the investment chapter to the dispute. Where such consent is not provided, the other contracting state may request consultations with the host state.

---

82    *CPTPP* (n 15) annex 9-H.4.
83    Consisting of the *Foreign Acquisitions and Takeovers Act 1975* (Cth), *Foreign Acquisition and Takeovers Regulations 1985* (Cth), *Financial Sector (Shareholdings) Act 1998* (Cth) and associated Ministerial Statements by the Treasurer of the Commonwealth of Australia or a minister acting on his or her behalf on whether or not to approve a foreign investment proposal: *CPTPP* (n 15) annex 9-H.1.
84    For example, under the AANZFTA (n 24). The *Protocol on Investment to the New Zealand–Australia Closer Economic Relations Trade Agreement* (n 24) also does not provide for ISDS.
85    Side Letter to the *CPTPP* from David Parker to Eduardo Ferreyros Küppers, 8 March 2018; Side Letter to the *CPTPP* from David Parker to Steven Ciobo, 8 March 2018.
86    Side Letter to the *CPTPP* from David Parket to Dato Erywan Pehin Yusof, Side Letter to the *CPTPP* from David Parker to HE J Jayasiri, 8 March 2018; Side Letter to the *CPTPP* from David Parker to Tran Tuan Anh, 8 March 2018.

Through these side letters, New Zealand has quarantined 80 per cent of its inbound FDI from potential ISDS claims.[87] This is largely due to the fact that Australia accounts for over 50 per cent of all of New Zealand's inbound FDI.[88] In addition to the side letters, New Zealand has also signed a *Joint Declaration* with Canada and Chile.[89] The *Joint Declaration* has been described by a Labour parliamentarian as "an acknowledgement of public concerns about ISDS" and a pledge to work alongside the other signatory countries to promote transparency.[90] The *Joint Declaration* can also be seen as indication of concerns by New Zealand about the conduct of arbitrators. It records the parties' intention[91]

> to promote transparent conduct rules on the ethical responsibilities of arbitrators in ISDS procedures, including conflict of interest rules that prevent arbitrators from acting, for the duration of their appointment, as counsel or party appointed expert or witness in other proceedings.

An interesting aspect of New Zealand's opposition to ISDS is that it has yet to have any significant negative experience with the mechanism. New Zealand has never been a respondent to an arbitration claim instituted under an investment treaty. It was subject to a claim arising out of an energy project contract by Mobil Oil Corporation in 1987, which was settled following an adverse liability finding.[92] This is consistent with the recent trend of opposition from developed states to ISDS absent any particularly adverse experiences. This is the case in the EU, and to an extent with Australia, who, despite having been subject to the Philip Morris claim, was successful in that case. New Zealand's

---

[87] Ministry of Foreign Affairs and Trade (n 16). However, as noted by Markert and Ishido, despite requiring the specific consent of the host state, investors from Brunei, Malaysia and Peru, may still be able to pursue an ISDS claim against New Zealand under the AANZFTA without New Zealand's consent: Markert and Ishido (n 18) 401.

[88] NZD2,935 million out of NZD5,027, or approximately 58%: "Investment Statistics: Key Data at a Glance", *New Zealand Trade & Enterprise* (Web Page) <https://www.nzte.govt.nz/investment-and-funding/investment-statistics>.

[89] *Joint Declaration on Investor State Dispute Settlement*, Canada–Chile–New Zealand, signed 8 March 2019.

[90] New Zealand Government, "New Zealand Signs Side Letters Curbing Investor-State Dispute Settlement" (Media Release, 9 March 2018).

[91] *Joint Declaration on Investor State Dispute Settlement* (n 89).

[92] *Mobil Oil Corporation and Others v New Zealand* (*Findings on Liability, Interpretation and Allied Issues*) (ICSID Arbitral Tribunal, Case No ARB/87/2, 4 May 1989). For a discussion of the claim and related domestic proceedings, see Amokura Kawharu and Luke Nottage, "The Curious Case of ISDS Arbitration Involving Australia and New Zealand" (2018) 44(2) University of Western Australia Law Review 32, 43–48.

position is also no doubt underscored by its lower rates of outbound FDI. While the trade-off for many states in exposing themselves to potential claims is the reciprocal protection they obtain for their investors abroad, this is clearly less relevant in light of fewer New Zealand investors overseas. There is, however, evidence of one known claim brought by a New Zealand investor. The claim was brought under the *Netherlands-Macedonia BIT*, on the basis of the company's ownership structure, but the New Zealand investor, Guardian Fiduciary Trust Ltd, was ultimately unable to surmount the jurisdictional hurdle.[93] In this regard, it is not difficult to comprehend New Zealand's assessment that the risk of ISDS outweighs any potential reward.

Nonetheless, questions remain about the approach taken by New Zealand. As in the case of Australia, it appears that there has thus far not been any rigorous analysis of the costs and benefits of ISDS to New Zealand. Commentaries on Australia's earlier eschewal of ISDS observed that Australia would have been better served by remaining a "crafter, drafter and mere participant" of the evolving investment law system than by withdrawing entirely.[94] Such observations are applicable now to New Zealand. In light of New Zealand's concerns about the current ISDS system, it seems that participation in incremental reform efforts would serve its interests, and those of the international community, better than a total refusal to engage. New Zealand's ultimate agreement to the *CPTPP*, following the achievement of certain changes to the ISDS mechanism, is a promising development to the extent that it indicates a willingness to do this. As posited by Kawharu and Nottage,[95] with the commonalities in their investment policies, New Zealand and Australia may be well placed to potentially emerge as a collective "middle power" and influence the ongoing development of international investment law in the Asia-Pacific region.

## 2.3 *Japan*
### 2.3.1 Background

Similarly, Japan may also be able to shape the trajectory of regional policy. It is recognised as one of the economic powerhouses of the Far East, a region which is increasingly a focal point for international investment law.[96] Japan's

---

93   *Guardian Fiduciary Trust Ltd, f/k/a Capital Conservator Savings & Loans, Ltd v Former Yugoslav Republic of Macedonia* (Award) (ICSID Arbitral Tribunal, Case No ARB/12/31, 22 September 2015).
94   Dickson-Smith and Mercurio (n 4) 230.
95   Kawharu and Nottage, "Foreign Investment Regulation and Treaty Practice in New Zealand and Australia: Getting it Together in the Asia-Pacific?" (n 22) 445.
96   Stephen Schill, "Changing Geography: Prospects for Asian Actors as Global Rule-Makers in International Investment Law" (2016) 177 *Columbia FDI Perspectives* 1.

influence could reasonably be expected to be far more ISDS-friendly. In contrast to Australia and New Zealand, Japan has much greater incentive to conclude IIAs that contain investor protections as a net capital exporter,[97] especially given the active and increasing presence of Japanese investors internationally, in developing countries throughout Southeast Asia in particular.[98] This can be seen as the underlying rationale behind Japan's increased enthusiasm for concluding investment treaties over the past decade or so.

These activities have stemmed from the 2014 "Revitalising Japan Strategy", a strategy for global outreach, based principally on building strategic trading relationships and promoting economic partnerships.[99] The strategy stated that the government would accelerate the conclusion of investment agreements in order to promote the development of Japanese companies operating overseas.[100] The Keidanren (Japan Business Federation) and other industry bodies have strongly advocated for such measures,[101] though the extent to which this has influenced government policy has been questioned.[102] The "Revitalising Japan Strategy" was followed in 2016 by an "Action Plan for the Improvement

---

97   Shotaro Hamamoto and Luke Nottage, "Foreign Investment In and Out of Japan: Economic Backdrop, Domestic Law, and International Treaty-based Investor-State Dispute Resolution" (2011) 8(5) *Transnational Dispute Management* 1. This is a point supported by Hunt and Trehearne, who note that it has further been identified that for Japan, as a resource-poor investor into other TPP nations and a nation historically receiving limited inbound investment, the protections take on increased significance: Christopher Hunt and Colin Trehearne, "Japan in the Pacific Century: Opportunities and Challenges Arising from the TPP" (2015) 12(1) *Transnational Dispute Management* 5.

98   For example, a survey conducted by the Japan External Trade Organization found that 55.1% of respondents expect to further expand business in Southeast/Southwest Asia and China: "Results of JETRO's 2018 Survey on Business Conditions of Japanese Companies in Asia and Oceania", *Japan External Trade Organization* (Web Page, 13 February 2019) <https://www.jetro.go.jp/en/news/releases/2019/6980a2e6ad84b745.html>.

99   Government of Japan, *Japan Revitalization Strategy: Japan is Back* (Policy Strategy, 14 June 2013) 128.

100  Ibid 129.

101  See, for example, "Calling for Accelerated Conclusion of Investment Agreements – Toward Establishment of 21st-Century International Investment Rules (Provisional Translation)", *Keidanren: Japan Business Federation* (Policy Proposal, 15 December 2015) <https://www.keidanren.or.jp/en/policy/2015/119.html>; Keidanren, Japan Chamber of Commerce and Industry, Japan Association of Corporate Executives and Japan Foreign Trading Council, "Seeking the Swift Conclusion of the TPP11", *Keidanren: Japan Business Federation* (Web Page, 23 October 2017) <http://www.keidanren.or.jp/en/policy/2017/085.html>.

102  See, eg, Hamamoto and Nottage (n 97) 19–20.

of the Investment Environment Including the Promotion of IIAs",[103] which included the key goal of concluding investment agreements with 100 countries or regions by 2020.[104] It is interesting to note that 2020 is also the target date for an increase in inward FDI stock to JPY35 trillion, on which the Japan External Trade Organization notes there has been steady progress.[105] One wonders whether another motivation for Japan in its accelerated conclusion of IIAs is to "future-proof" against growing inbound FDI and the associated exposure to ISDS.

Since the publication of the 2016 "Action Plan", nine agreements have been signed.[106] At this stage, it seems unlikely that Japan will reach the century, but the statement still stands as a clear indication of the Japanese government's position on the desirability of international investment treaties. In any event, as Stoel, Ishikawa and Jacobson observe, "Japan's list of IIA negotiating partners continues to grow and to be varied, roughly corresponding with Japanese companies' most important locations for foreign investment".[107]

### 2.3.2  Position on ISDS

Strong support from the Japanese government can also be perceived for ISDS itself, albeit less equivocal than that for investment agreements generally. For example, Japanese ministry officials have previously been reported

---

103  "投資関連協定の締結促進等投資環境整備に向けたアクションプラン" [Action Plan to Promote the Conclusion of Investment-Related Agreements to Consolidate the Investment Environment], *Ministry of Foreign Affairs of Japan* (Web Page, 11 May 2016) http://www.mofa.go.jp/mofaj/ecm/ec/page24_000606.html.

104  Ibid.

105  As at the end of 2017, inward FDI stock in Japan was JPY28.55 trillion, an increase of JPY322.7 billion (1.1%) in annual terms, seeing the fourth successive year of record high (Chart 1-1). Inward FDI stock as a proportion to nominal gross domestic product ("GDP") remains 5.2%, the same as the previous year: Japan External Trade Organization, *JETRO Invest Japan Report 2018* (Report, November 2018) 2.

106  Japan has six BITs with Kenya, Israel, Armenia, United Arab Emirates, Jordan and Argentina (signed, but not in force) alongside the *TPP*, the *CPTPP* and the *Agreement between the European Union and Japan for an Economic Partnership*, signed 17 July 2018 (entered into force 1 February 2019) (the latter without an investment chapter): UNCTAD, "Country Navigator: Japan", *Investment Policy Hub* (Web Page) <https://investmentpolicy.unctad.org/country-navigator/107/japan>.

107  Jonathan T Stoel, Tomoko Ishikawa and Michael G Jacobson, "Japan's Ambitious International Investment Agreement Policy – Laying the Groundwork for Future Disputes?" (2015) 12(1) *Transnational Dispute Management* 7.

as favouring investment arbitration as essential.[108] Further, of all of the investment agreements Japan has concluded, there are only two which do not contain arbitration provisions, one of which is the *Japan–Australia Economic Partnership Agreement* ("JAEPA"). It has been reported that Japan pushed hard for the inclusion of ISDS but was not willing to offer enough in return to elicit Australia's agreement.[109] Though JAEPA explicitly provides for review of the ISDS position in January 2020, this is of little relevance given that ISDS is now in force between the two countries by virtue of the *CPTPP*.

Despite this capitulation, Japan has been resolute in its desire for ISDS in other contexts, most notably in negotiations with the European Union ("EU"). Although the *Agreement between the European Union and Japan for an Economic Partnership* entered into force on 1 February 2019, it currently has no investment chapter. The EU's website implies that this is due to Japan's refusal to agree to the former's proposal for an investment court system, stating unequivocally: "Anything less ambitious, including coming back to the old Investor-to-State Dispute Settlement, is not acceptable. For the EU ISDS is dead".[110] Japan's scepticism over the EU's proposed investment court system has also been apparent in the ongoing discussions at UNCITRAL's Working Group III, which has been tasked with reviewing ISDS.[111] While some participants have expressed a desire to look closely at a multilateral investment court system, Japan has been steadfast in its view that the solution to problems identified must not be prejudged.[112] Japan's delegation has also stated its strong preference for incremental reform within the current system and emphasised that the Working

---

108   In the context of the *Energy Charter Treaty*, for example, the two ministries leading Japanese IIA negotiations and implementation, the Ministry of Economy Trade and Industry and Ministry of Foreign Affairs, saw their officials publicly favour investment arbitration as "essential" and state that it was simply expected that Japanese companies would use these tools to resolve disputes: Tatsuo Sato, "Opening Remarks" (Speech, Energy Charter Forum, 21 November 2014) and Nobuaki Ito (Speech, Energy Charter Forum, 21 November 2014) cited in Hunt and Trehearne (n 97) 6.

109   Kawharu and Nottage, "Foreign Investment Regulation and Treaty Practice in New Zealand and Australia: Getting it Together in the Asia-Pacific?" (n 22) 473–474.

110   European Commission, *A New EU Trade Agreement with Japan* (Report, July 2018) 6 <http://trade.ec.europa.eu/doclib/docs/2017/july/tradoc_155684.pdf>.

111   The mandate contains three stages: (a) to identify and consider concerns regarding ISDS; (b) to consider whether reform was desirable in light of any identified concerns; and (c) if the Working Group were to conclude that reform was desirable, to develop any relevant solutions to be recommended to the Commission: *Report of the United Nations Commission on International Trade Law*, UN Doc A/72/17 (2017) 264.

112   Listen to the Japanese delegate's remarks at 10:53:00–11:01:46 of the audio recording from the 36th session of the UNCITRAL Working Group III (29 October 2018).

Group should not consider criticism which is merely perception-based, but should focus on facts.[113]

### 2.3.3 Political Context

This is not to say that ISDS has received widespread and unwavering support in Japan. Indeed, the TPP was a catalyst for debate and discussion over ISDS in Japan's parliament. Hamamoto summarises the criticisms raised as dealing with the constitutionality of ISDS in Japan, issues of state sovereignty and regulatory capacity, a perception that ISDS is biased towards the US and a view that ISDS is only acceptable in relation to developing states.[114] In his analysis, Hamamoto concluded that many of these criticisms were unfounded and often resulted from an underlying anti-American sentiment.[115] Interestingly, in contrast to the situation in Australia and New Zealand, where the issue of ISDS has tended to fall along party lines, Hamamoto posits that ISDS criticism served as a pretext for criticising the incumbent government.[116] He notes that not only did critics continue to vote to approve investment treaties but also that "every anti-ISDS orator becomes silent when his/her party comes to power".[117]

Nonetheless, the responses from the current incumbent government have demonstrated little concern over the potential risks ISDS might pose to Japan. Then-Minister for Foreign Affairs Fumio Kishida has stated that the government did not expect Japan to be subject to a claim,[118] and Prime Minister Shinzo Abe has gone even further, stating that even if Japan were to have a claim brought against it, it would not lose.[119] This bravado is no doubt bolstered by the fact that Japan has never been subject to an ISDS claim. Hamamoto notes that this position might change were Japan to become the subject of an ISDS claim, though he predicts that it may just lead to the anti-ISDS discourse becoming even more hypocritical: "[n]o problem with treaties by which Japanese

---

113    Ibid.
114    Shotaro Hamamoto, "Recent Anti-ISDS Discourse in the Japanese Diet: A Dressed-up but Glaring Hypocrisy" (2015) 16(5–6) *Journal of World Investment & Trade* 931, 934.
115    Ibid.
116    Ibid 951.
117    Ibid.
118    Fumio Kishida (Statements, 192nd Session of the Diet, 27 October 2016) cited in Yuka Fukunaga, "ISDS Under the CPTPP and Beyond: Japanese Perspectives", *Kluwer Arbitration Blog* (Blog Post, 30 May 2018) <http://arbitrationblog.kluwerarbitration.com/2018/05/30/isds-cptpp-beyond-japanese-perspectives/>.
119    Shinzo Abe (Statements, 192nd Session of the Diet, 11 November 2016) cited in Fukunaga (n 118).

companies sue foreign governments, but down with treaties by which foreign companies sue the Japanese government".[120]

Interestingly, in terms of the former category of treaties, these have thus far rarely been invoked by Japanese investors. There are currently four known claims brought by Japanese investors on foot: *JGC v Spain*,[121] *Eurus Energy v Spain*,[122] *Itochu v Spain*[123] and *Nissan v India*,[124] the former three under the *Energy Charter Treaty* regarding Spain's renewables policy and the latter relating to payments claimed under an agreement to establish a car manufacturing plant.[125] However, there have been other cases brought by foreign subsidiaries of Japanese companies, including the well-known *Saluka v Czech Republic*[126] and, more recently, *Bridgestone v Panama*.[127] There have also been reports of investment treaty claims by Japanese investors settling upon the threat of arbitration.[128] In light of the government's continued promotion and accelerated

---

120 Shotaro Hamamoto, "Debates in Japan over Investor-State Arbitration with Developed States" (Paper, Centre for International Governance Innovation, 5 June 2016) 11.

121 UNCTAD, "Investment Dispute Navigator: JGC Corporation v Kingdom of Spain (ICSID Case No ARB/15/27)", *Investment Policy Hub* (Web Page, 31 December 2018) <https://investmentpolicy.unctad.org/investment-dispute-settlement/cases/638/jgc-v-spain>.

122 UNCTAD, "Investment Dispute Navigator: Eurus Energy Holdings Corporation and Eurus Energy Europe BV v Kingdom of Spain (ICSID Case No ARB/16/4)", *Investment Policy Hub* (Web Page, 31 December 2018) <https://investmentpolicy.unctad.org/investment-dispute-settlement/cases/703/eurus-energy-v-spain>.

123 UNCTAD, "Investment Dispute Settlement Navigator: Itochu Corporation v Kingdom of Spain (ICSID Case No ARB/18/25)", *Investment Policy Hub* (Web Page, 31 December 2018) <https://investmentpolicy.unctad.org/investment-dispute-settlement/cases/865/itochu-v-spain>.

124 UNCTAD, "Investment Dispute Settlement Navigator: Nissan Motor Co., Ltd. v Republic of India (PCA Case No 2017–37)", *Investment Policy Hub* (Web Page, 31 December 2018) <https://investmentpolicy.unctad.org/investment-dispute-settlement/cases/828/nissan-v-india>.

125 Aditi Shah and Sudarshan Varadahn, "Exclusive: Nissan Close to Settling Dispute with India over Unpaid Incentives", *Reuters* (Web Page, 1 August 2018) <https://www.reuters.com/article/us-nissan-india-arbitration-exclusive/exclusive-nissan-close-to-settling-dispute-with-india-over-unpaid-incentives-idUSKBN1KM544>.

126 UNCTAD, "Investment Dispute Settlement Navigator: Saluka Investments BV v The Czech Republic", *Investment Policy Hub* (Web Page, 31 December 2018) <https://investmentpolicy.unctad.org/investment-dispute-settlement/cases/57/saluka-v-czech-republic>.

127 UNCTAD, "Investment Dispute Settlement Navigator: Bridgestone Americas, Inc and Licensing Services, Inc v Republic of Panama (ICSID Case No ARB/16/34)", *Investment Policy Hub* (Web Page, 31 December 2018) <https://investmentpolicy.unctad.org/investment-dispute-settlement/cases/750/bridgestone-v-panama>.

128 Stoel, Ishikawa and Jacobson refer to *Nusa Tenggara v. Republic of Indonesia* and *Nippon Asahan Aluminium v Indonesia* as examples: Stoel, Ishiwaka and Jacobson (n 107) 20. See UNCTAD, "Investment Dispute Settlement Navigator: Nusa Tenggara Partnership BV and

conclusion of investment agreements, however, this could reasonably be expected to change. Consistent with the trend in domestic dispute resolution and international commercial arbitration, changing attitudes among Japanese companies who have traditionally been more dispute adverse[129] can also be expected to contribute to a growing number of claims by Japanese investors.

## 2.4    Common Themes Across Jurisdictions

### 2.4.1    Potential to Influence Regional Policy

Trakman and Sharma note that domestic policies and international accord in relation to ISDS have a direct impact on trade and investment, both within the region and globally. They further posit that "countries within the Asia Pacific region have the capacity to influence each other's investment regimes, as well as having an impact on investment practice outside the region".[130] Each of the focus counties has the potential to play a greater role in influencing the trajectory of international investment law in this region: Japan in its own right, and Australia and New Zealand in collaboration.[131] To this end, it is worth analysing the preceding sections to discern the commonalities between the approaches of the three focus countries and what this may mean for the future of international investment law in the region.

It is important to preface the discussion of similarities by first addressing the most obvious differences and what they imply about the countries. Japan

---

PT Newmont Nusa Tenngara v Republic of Indonesia (ICSID Case No ARB/14/15)", *Investment Policy Hub* (Web Page, 31 December 2018) <https://investmentpolicy.unctad.org/investment-dispute-settlement/cases/584/nusa-tenggara-v-indonesia>; Mark Smith and Louise Browning, "Indonesia and Nippon Asahan Aluminum Consortium Reach Settlement", *Ashurst* (Web Page, 1 February 2014) <https://www.ashurst.com/en/news-and-insights/legal-updates/indonesia-and-nippon-asahan-aluminium-consortium-reach-settlement/>.

129   Nottage and Weeranmantry offer five theories of the traditional dispute aversion: a cultural thesis; institutional barriers; the elite management thesis; the economic rationalist thesis; and hybrid theories: Luke R Nottage and Romesh Weeranmantry, "Investment Arbitration for Japan and Asia: Five Perspectives on Law and Practice", (Panel Paper, Asian Society of International Law Conference, 1–2 August 2009, 4 March 2009) [8] <http://asiansil-jp.org/wp/wp-content/uploads/2012/07/weeramantry.pdf>, cited in Stoel, Ishikawa and Jacobson (n 108) 18.

130   Trakman and Sharma (n 52) 318.

131   Nottage, Chaisse and Thanitcul refer to Japan as a "big player" and the potential for Australia and New Zealand to collectively emerge as a "potential middle player" for the future development of international investment law in the wider Asian region: Luke Nottage, Julien Chaisse and Sakda Thanitcul, "International Investment Treaties and Arbitration Across Asia: A Bird's Eye View", in Julien Chaisse and Luke Nottage (eds), *International Investment Treaties and Arbitration Across Asia* (Brill Nijhoff, 2017) 1, 42.

has been significantly more enthusiastic about ISDS than either Australia or New Zealand. This is likely to be simply a reflection of the economic reality of each country. It is understandable that Japan, as a net FDI-exporter, has a greater interest in the conclusion of investment protection agreements than does Australia or New Zealand, who are net FDI-importers. It must also be acknowledged that despite one of the underlying purposes of an investment agreement being to attract the flow of capital into the signatory's territory, empirical evidence on whether ISDS actually increases FDI flows is uncertain.[132]

Notwithstanding the basic structural differences in the economies of Australia, New Zealand and Japan, there have been some similarities in their experiences. An important one is that each country has proceeded from an original preference for multilateral initiatives.[133] This perhaps underlies the approach of each country to the CPTPP and the ultimate ratification of that agreement by all three. This, along with each country's involvement in the ongoing RCEP negotiations, demonstrates a commitment to regional solutions and a harmonisation of trade and investment law throughout the Asia Pacific.

2.4.2   Common Concerns – and Concessions?

In light of this potential, the congruence in the criticism raised against ISDS in each country is significant in indicating the potential for a convergence in approach to international investment law within the region. Consistent with the international trend in which ISDS is increasingly called into question, the primary concern raised in the focus countries is that it impinges on the state's right to regulate and thereby infringes state sovereignty. In addition to this, complaints about the legitimacy of the system, particularly in terms of its lack of transparency, were also at the forefront. Concerns regarding the lack of consistency and coherence across investment law jurisprudence were also raised and so too concerns about the integrity and qualifications of arbitrators.

These concerns notwithstanding, each of these countries has acceded to the CPTPP. This demonstrates that regardless of the domestic debate and a country's stated position on ISDS, it in fact remains simply one of many tools in the trade negotiator's toolbox and continues to be subject to the overall trade-offs

---

132   See, generally, Shiro Armstrong and Luke Nottage "The Impact of Investment Treaties and ISDS Provisions on Foreign Direction Investment: A Baseline Econometric Analysis" (Research Paper No 16/74, Sydney Law School, 15 August 2016),.

133   Tomoko Ishikawa, "A Japanese Perspective of International Investment Agreements: Recent Developments" in Julien Chaisse and Luke Nottage (eds), *International Investment Treaties and Arbitration Across Asia* (Brill Nijhoff, 2017) 513, 515; Kawharu and Nottage, "Foreign Investment Regulation and Treaty Practice in New Zealand and Australia: Getting it Together in the Asia-Pacific?" (n 22) 445, 446.

involved in any negotiation. This is most clear in the case of New Zealand. Despite its strong anti-ISDS stance and its undeniably ambitious attempts to exclude ISDS from the *CPTPP*, New Zealand was ultimately willing to agree to ISDS with those countries with which it could not secure a side letter. New Zealand was successful in securing some changes which the Prime Minister stated made the agreement "a damn sight better than what we started with",[134] but that simply reinforces the point. With the modifications that New Zealand secured, alongside key benefits,[135] the upside ultimately outweighed New Zealand's conscientious objection. It was willing to compromise in order to secure significant market access and to not be left out of the major regional agreement. This may also underpin New Zealand's decision not to formalise its opposition to ISDS in government policy or binding legislation; allowing "wriggle room" for compromise where necessary.

The give-and-take of international investment law can also be seen to inform the approach of Australia's current government. Assessing ISDS on a case-by-case basis allows Australia to keep its cards up its sleeve and use ISDS as a bargaining chip to achieve its desired trade and investment outcomes. The same is true of Japan, even as a rather strong proponent of ISDS. The final *JAEPA* agreement is the perfect illustration of this trade off. It is widely known that Japan sought ISDS but seemingly did not "offer enough in return"[136] for its inclusion in *JAEPA*: likely, greater access to the Japanese market for Australian agricultural exports.[137] By its refusal, Australia was able to signal that it expected better trade-offs in its other ongoing negotiations.[138] As Trakman notes, Japan's willingness to exclude ISDS "shows at best that the economic and political advantages of securing a trade and investment agreement with Australia were greater than insistence on ISDS".[139] Both countries were also

---

134 "Jacinda Ardern Says Re-Branded TPP 'Not a Perfect Agreement but It Is a Damn Sight Better than What We Had'", *New Zealand Herald* (online, 12 November 2017) <https://www.nzherald.co.nz/nz/news/article.cfm?c_id=1&objectid=11943127>.
135 See Ministry of Foreign Affairs and Trade (n 16).
136 Kawharu and Nottage, "Foreign Investment Regulation and Treaty Practice in New Zealand and Australia: Getting it Together in the Asia-Pacific?" (n 22) 445, 473–474.
137 "In the FTA negotiations with Australia, the Japanese government may also have not wanted to press too hard to secure ISDS protections because this would probably have involved conceding even more access to Japan's politically sensitive sectors such as agricultural markets".: Nottage, "Investment Treaty Arbitration Policy in Australia, New Zealand – and Korea?" (n 52) 40.
138 Luke Nottage, "Investor-State Arbitration: Not in the Australia-Japan Free Trade Agreement, and Not Ever for Australia?" (2014) 19(38) *Journal of Japanese Law* 37, 41.
139 Trakman and Sharma (n 51) 324–325.

likely satisfied of adequate protection for investors given their generally well-developed and well regarded legal systems.[140]

These observations reflect the point made by the Japanese delegation at UNCITRAL that investment agreements are always the product of a negotiation informed by the economic, foreign policy and development priorities of the negotiating parties.[141] In addition to demonstrating that rather trite proposition, the country-by-country analysis has also provided insight into the approach of the CPTPP. The principal significance of that approach is in standing as an alternative to more radical calls for complete structural overhaul. In the ongoing climate of debate, the CPTPP provides an example of how concerns such as those which became apparent from the foregoing analysis can be addressed within the existing framework. The precise manner in which the CPTPP seeks to address concerns about the right to regulate, consistency, and transparency and accountability are examined in the next section.

## 3  The Approach Under the CPTPP

This section does not seek to provide a comprehensive analysis of the CPTPP as a whole or even the investment chapter in its entirety. Instead, it will focus on the CPTPP's approach to three areas of concern about ISDS which were identified in the examination of Japan, Australia and New Zealand in the preceding section. Although concerns over regulatory freedom have dominated discussion in each of the three countries, concerns about a lack of consistency in arbitral decisions, and over a lack of transparency and the conduct of party-appointed arbitrators have also arisen. These concerns are also being considered in the parallel reform initiative currently underway in the form of the International Centre for Settlement of Investment Dispute ("ICSID") Rules and Regulations Amendment Process. Discussion of those developments is beyond the scope of this work.

### 3.1  *Regulatory Freedom*

As can be seen from the foregoing discussion, states' primary concern with ISDS is its potential to encroach on their freedom to regulate as they see fit. This remains so despite recognition by various commentators that to the extent this is an issue, it can be addressed at the drafting stage through the text

---

140  Nottage, "Investor-State Arbitration: Not in the Australia-Japan Free Trade Agreement, and Not Ever for Australia?" (n 138) 41; Trakman and Sharma (n 51) 325.

141  Listen to the Japanese delegate's remarks at 16:21:54–16:26:22 of the audio recording from the 34th session of the UNCITRAL Working Group III (30 October 2017).

of the treaties themselves.[142] Indeed, it is this approach that has been adopted under the CPTPP. Similar to other modern investment agreements, the CPTPP emphasises throughout its text the state's right to regulate and includes provisions designed specifically to protect that right.

Article 9.16, dealing with "Investment and Environmental, Health and other Regulatory Objectives" is significant in this regard. This provision states:

> Nothing in this Chapter shall be construed to prevent a Party from adopting, maintaining or enforcing any measure otherwise consistent with this Chapter that it considers appropriate to ensure that investment activity in its territory is undertaken in a manner sensitive to environmental, health or other regulatory objectives.

This would appear to address the chief concerns expressed by Australia, namely in relation to health measures such as tobacco, as well as the pharmaceutical subsidy schemes in operation in both Australia and New Zealand.[143] Of itself, however, this provision is hardly revolutionary and it could be argued that it does not significantly alter the position already prevailing under most investment treaties. For example, the *Singapore–Australia FTA* also contains a provision specifically protecting tobacco and health measures from attack by way of ISDS arbitration.[144] Further, the merits decision in Phillip Morris' action against Uruguay demonstrates that even in the absence of such specific protection, a state's pursuit of legitimate policy objectives is unlikely to constitute a breach of an investment treaty.

---

142    Indeed, this was noted in a letter from the Australia Council of Chief Justices to the Attorney-General in November 2014, as cited in Robert French, "ISDS – Litigating the Judiciary" (Speech, Chartered Institute of Arbitrators Centenary Conference, 21 March 2015). It was likewise noted by James Allsop, Chief Justice of the Federal Court of Australia, "Commercial and investor-state arbitration: The importance of recognising their differences" (Speech, International Council for Commercial Arbitration Council Congress, 2018).

143    Such systems "selectively restrict public access to some pharmaceuticals while subsidising others": Trakaman and Sharma (n 51). In the context of Australia, see, "Pharmaceutical Benefits Scheme", *Department of Health* (Web Page) <http://www.pbs.gov.au/pbs/home>. In the context of New Zealand, see "Providing Funded Access to Pharmaceuticals for New Zealanders", *PHARMAC* (Webpage) <https://www.pharmac.govt.nz/>.

144    See art 22 of the investment chapter of the *Singapore–Australia Free Trade Agreement*, signed 17 February 2003, [2003] ATS 16 (entered into force 28 July 2003), amended most recently by the *Agreement to Amend the Singapore–Australia Free Trade Agreement*, signed 13 October 2016, [2017] ATS 26 (entered into force 1 December 2017), titled "Tobacco Control Measures". This article states that "No claim may be brought under this section in respect of a tobacco control measure of a Party", which is defined at footnote 29.

The CPTPP also addresses these concerns in other ways. The discussion of Australia and New Zealand above noted the exclusion of decisions under their respective foreign investment regulatory schemes. This is not new to the CPTPP. Australia and New Zealand both have a longstanding practice of carving out exceptions to their FDI screening regimes, showing that regulatory freedom can be protected at the time of drafting. This point is also demonstrated in the curtailment of some of the most frequently invoked substantive protections under the CPTPP,[145] and through the introduction of annex 9-G. That annex exempts measures taken in regard to public debt restructuring from the investment protections provisions. This is not directly relevant to the focus countries given the current state of their economies, but is a significant step. The significance is seen, for example, in the controversy that arose regarding the arbitral awards rendered about public debt restructurings by states in dire financial straits, most notably the aftermath of the Argentine financial crisis.[146]

Even if these steps are not revolutionary, they may still go some way toward addressing perceptions that ISDS impinges on state sovereignty. Given that the perception of ISDS is a large part of the problem,[147] such an effect is not to be understated. Importantly, in pursuing an approach more sensitive to states' concerns, the CPTPP has been careful not to let the pendulum swing too far in the other direction. Hindelang and Krajewski argue that the approach is a balanced one which not only focuses on the rights of the investor, but also on the obligation of the state to regulate economic activities in the public interest.[148]

### 3.2 Consistency

The Argentine cases mentioned above are often cited in support of alleged inconsistency in ISDS decisions. They serve as the prime example of this inconsistency as the decisions involved tribunals applying the same treaty to the same fact scenario, but ultimately reaching disparate outcomes. Inconsistency

---

145  Markert and Ishido (n 18) 396.
146  See, eg, *CMS Gas Transmission Company v Argentina (Award)* (ICSID Arbitral Tribunal, Case No ARB/01/18, 12 May 2005) [331] and *LG&E Energy Corp, LG&E Capital Corp and LG&E International Inc v Argentina (Decision on Liability)* (ICSID Arbitral Tribunal, Case No ARB/02/01, 3 October 2006) [245]. The former tribunal held that Argentina could not rely on the defence of necessity under Article XI of the US-Argentina BIT, while the latter held that the defence fully exempted Argentina from liability.
147  This acknowledgment by the delegate for Australia can be heard in the comments at 11:39:50–11:43:00 of the audio recording from the 36th session of the UNCITRAL Working Group III (29 October 2018).
148  Hindelang and Krajewski (n 9) 381–382.

of decisions, and the lack of a mechanism to address it, has been identified by the UNCITRAL Working Group as one of the current concerns with ISDS.[149] Such concerns over consistency, and a resulting lack of certainty, persist despite counterarguments that much of the perceived inconsistency can be explained by a closer examination of awards and differences in the underlying treaty texts. As noted above, concern over inconsistency in arbitral decisions was noted in Australia's Senate review of the *CPTPP*, which recommended the adoption of a system of binding precedent and an appellate mechanism as methods to address this.[150] This proposed solution reveals that part of the concern in Australia no doubt stems from the fact that a binding system of precedent is a key pillar of Australia's common law legal system. However, Trakman states that, notwithstanding the absence of judicial precedent as common lawyers conceive of it, ISDS is still likely to be "more coherent than a multiplicity of different state laws applied by local courts to foreign investment".[151]

In addition to those who argue against the charge of inconsistency, there are also those who question its desirability. Japan has been particularly vocal on this point in the discussions of UNCITRAL's Working Group III. A member of the Japanese delegation strongly cautioned against attempting to promote inter-treaty consistency in the name of ensuring the predictability of outcomes.[152] The delegate acknowledged that the perceived inconsistency arises from the fragmented nature of the underlying treaty provisions and accepted that there is wide variation in the standards of investor protection provided under different treaties.[153] However, Japan questioned whether this is a negative, emphasising that treaties are the result of resource-intensive negotiation between the contracting states and that the so-called fragmentation reflects a deliberate diversification by states.[154] Japan's position as enunciated at UNCITRAL is properly understood not as an opposition to consistency in arbitral decisions, nor as an argument that consistency should never be pursued, but rather an exhortation that the issue be given nuanced consideration.

The provisions under the *CPTPP* can be seen as an example of an approach that stems from such consideration. The aim is to ensure consistency in the interpretation of the *CPTPP* itself within the confines of the current system

---

149   United Nations Commission on Trade Law Working Group III (Investor-State Dispute Settlement Reform) (n 6) 3, 15.
150   Joint Standing Committee on Treaties (n 53) [4.104].
151   Trakman and Sharma (n 51) 333.
152   Japanese delegate's remarks at 16:21:54–16:26:22 of the audio recording from the 34th session of the UNCITRAL Working Group III (30 October 2017) (n 141).
153   Ibid.
154   Ibid.

rather than through the establishment of an appellate mechanism or binding system of precedent. In this regard, the *CPTPP* takes two notable steps. First, the parties have explicitly confirmed their shared understanding of certain terms. For example, annexes 9-A and 9-B respectively set out the shared understanding of the terms "customary international law" and "expropriation". The common understanding also reinforces the provisions in relation to the right to regulate that were discussed above. Annex 9-B.3(b) states that "non-discriminatory regulatory actions by a Party that are designed and applied to protect legitimate public welfare objectives, such as public health, safety and the environment, do not constitute indirect expropriations, except in rare circumstances". Perhaps in a nod to Australia and New Zealand's respective pharmaceutical benefits schemes,[155] greater certainty is provided by way of a footnote that "regulatory actions to protect public health include such measures with respect to the regulation, pricing and supply of, and reimbursement for, pharmaceuticals ...".[156]

Second, in addition to these interpretations which have been included in the text of the treaty itself, provision was also made for the establishment of a Commission, composed of government representatives of each party at the ministry or senior official level.[157] The Commission is empowered to issue interpretations of the provisions,[158] which are binding on tribunals and with which tribunals' decisions or awards must be consistent.[159] It remains to be seen how effective this is in practice as a means of promoting consistency in decisions.

In the current climate, particularly in relation to ongoing discussions about the necessity and form of reform to the ISDS system, these provisions are significant as an example of an incremental approach in place of a complete overhaul of the current infrastructure. While the extent to which such mechanisms will achieve consistency in decisions remains to be seen, the same could be said of any court that may be established. The experience of other international courts has certainly shown that the existence of a standing body alone is no guarantee of consistent decisions.

The introduction of an appellate body to deal with substantive questions (rather than the more limited grounds currently available for ICSID annulment proceedings, for example) has also been mooted as a solution to

---

155   "Pharmaceutical Benefits Scheme" and "Providing Funded Access to Pharmaceuticals" (n 143).
156   *CPTPP* (n 15) annex 9-B, footnote 36.
157   Ibid art 27.1.
158   Ibid art 27.2.2(f).
159   Ibid art 9.25.3.

inconsistency.[160] Examination of the merits of that argument is beyond the scope of this paper, save to note that this is not a step that was taken in the *CPTPP*. However, the agreement has explicitly left open the potential adoption of an appellate mechanism should one be developed.[161] Article 9.23.11 imposes no obligation on the parties to actively work towards developing such a mechanism, but simply states that parties shall consider whether awards rendered under the *CPTPP* investment chapter should be subject to an appellate mechanism developed in the future. Lastly, art 9.23.11 states that the parties shall strive to ensure that any such appellate mechanism they consider adopting provides for a similar level of transparency of proceedings to that established under the *CPTPP*.

## 3.3   *Transparency and Arbitrator Ethics*

### 3.3.1   Transparency

Another major concern about the ISDS system has been a perception that it operates from behind closed doors. This argument was made most strongly by the New Zealand First party, now in coalition government in New Zealand.[162] This is clearly illustrated by the example of the challenges to Australia's tobacco plain packaging legislation. In the domestic constitutional challenge, the hearings before the High Court of Australia were public and the submissions of the parties and full transcripts of the hearings are publicly available.[163] In contrast, hearings of Philip Morris' arbitral claim at the Permanent Court of Arbitration were closed, and while the *Award on Jurisdiction and Admissibility* and the *Final Award on Costs* have been released, they are partly redacted and the parties' submissions are not available.[164] Although this is standard practice

---

160   Note that this was rejected by ICSID member states when proposed by the ICSID Secretariat in 2014: Hindelang and Krajewski (n 9) 389.
161   *CPTPP* (n 15) art 9.23.11.
162   See above Section 2.2.
163   All hearings of the High Court of Australia are public. The High Court of Australia publishes a broad range of documents related to cases, including parties' submissions and transcripts of all hearings: "Information Publication Plan", *High Court of Australia* (Policy, 2013) <http://www.hcourt.gov.au/assets/corporate/policies/information%20publication%20plan%20feb%202013.pdf>. For the documents related to *British American Tobacco Australasia Ltd and ors v The Commonwealth of Australia*, see "Case S389/2011: British American Tobacco Australasia Limited and Ors v The Commonwealth of Australia", *High Court of Australia* (Web Page) <http://www.hcourt.gov.au/cases/case-s389/2011>.
164   Those materials are available at "Philip Morris Asia Limited (Hong Kong) v The Commonwealth of Australia", *Permanent Court of Arbitration* (Web Page) <https://pca-cpa.org/en/cases/5/>.

in international commercial arbitration, it is not appropriate in ISDS. As van Harten explains, "... secrecy is fundamentally misplaced in investment treaty arbitration where arbitrators regularly review decisions of legislatures, governments, and courts on matters of public interest and where they award compensation from public funds".[165]

To respond to this, the transparency provisions in the CPTPP set, as the norm, a similar level of public disclosure as is provided for under Australian domestic law. Article 9.24 provides for public hearings as the default position and also mandates the disclosure of the notice of intent, the notice of arbitration, pleadings, memorials and briefs submitted to the tribunal by a disputing party, minutes or transcripts of hearings and orders, awards and decisions of the tribunal. Of course, art 9.24 also makes provision for the protection and non-disclosure of certain classes of sensitive information. This is a significant step and one which appropriately reflects the public interest factors that are at play in investor-state arbitration. These provisions provide greater transparency than under many of the existing agreements concluded by the focus countries. For example, while some Japanese treaties concluded post-2012 contain very basic rules on transparency of ISDS procedures that allow, but do not require, the state to make documents available to the public,[166] Ishikawa notes that the addition of public hearings, not currently present in other Japanese treaties, will have a practical and significant impact on arbitral proceedings.[167]

New Zealand's Ministry of Foreign Affairs and Trade has also recognised that these transparency requirements will help to ensure integrity of the ISDS process.[168] Australia too is an enthusiastic supporter of increased transparency, having noted as much in its submission to the ongoing ICSID review by welcoming the institution of open hearings and the publication of recordings and transcripts.[169] Australia was also the first Asia-Pacific state to sign the *United Nations Convention on Transparency in Treaty-based Investor-State Arbitration*

---

165  Gus van Harten, "The European Commission and UNCTAD Reform Agendas: Do They Ensure Independence, Openness, and Fairness in Investor-State Arbitration?" in Steffen Hindelang and Markus Krajewski (eds), *Shifting Paradigms in International Investment Law: More Balanced, Less Isolated, Increasingly Diversified* (Oxford University Press, 2016) 128, 137.
166  Hamamoto (n 120) 7.
167  Although referring to the TPP, the observation remains applicable: Ishikawa (n 134) 529.
168  Ministry of Foreign Affairs and Trade, *Comprehensive and Progressive Agreement for Trans-Pacific Partnership* (National Interest Analysis, February 2018) 38.
169  Submission from Camille Goodman and Patricia Holmes to Meg Kinnear, 22 January 2019, 3 <https://icsid.worldbank.org/en/amendments/Documents/Australia_Comments_1.22.19.pdf>.

("*Mauritius Convention*").[170] Although there are many concurrent initiatives aimed at improving transparency, the efforts of CPTPP are currently the most significant as they are already in force between 11 countries and cover a large proportion of the global economy. This is in contrast to the *Mauritius Convention* which, at the date of writing, has only entered into force in respect of five countries.[171]

### 3.3.2 Arbitrator Ethics

Another step which the CPTPP has taken to address legitimacy concerns is in relation to the selection and conduct of arbitrators. Concerns continue to be raised about the impartiality of arbitrators, for example, by Australia's Productivity Commission[172] and New Zealand's *Joint Declaration*,[173] in relation to arbitrators who determine one arbitral claim while acting as legal counsel in others. This has been one of the major underlying factors behind the call for a permanent multilateral investment court.[174] However, the CPTPP demonstrates that steps can be taken to address these issues within the current system. Article 9.22(6) required the parties to provide guidance on the application of a code of conduct for arbitrators selected to serve on ISDS tribunals. The Commission described above met for the first time in January 2019 in Tokyo and issued a decision in which it established the *Code of Conduct for Investor-State Dispute Settlement Proceedings* ("*Code of Conduct*").[175]

One of the most significant provisions of the *Code of Conduct* is its prohibition of "double hatting", in which practitioners act concurrently as counsel and arbitrator in different cases. This practice has given rise to significant concerns about the legitimacy of the system, particularly in regard to arbitrator integrity

---

170  On 18 July 2017: Kawharu and Nottage, "Foreign Investment Regulation and Treaty Practice in New Zealand and Australia: Getting it Together in the Asia-Pacific?" (n 22) 481.
171  United Nations Commission on International Trade Law, "Status: United Nations Convention on Transparency in Treaty-based Investor-State Arbitration (New York, 2014)" (Web Page, 2019) <https://uncitral.un.org/en/texts/arbitration/conventions/transparency/status>.
172  *Bilateral and Regional Trade Agreements* (n 36) 274.
173  *Joint Declaration on Investor State Dispute Settlement* (n 89).
174  Though there are those who argue a standing court where appointments are made by the state is unlikely to resolve this issue. See, eg, the arguments in Charles Brower and Jawad Ahmad, "Why The "Demolition Derby" That Seeks To Destroy Investor-State Arbitration?" (2018) 91(6) *Southern California Law Review* 1139, 1156.
175  Commission of the Comprehensive and Progressive Agreement for Trans-Pacific Partnership, *Decision by the Commission of the Comprehensive and Progressive Agreement for Trans-Pacific Partnership regarding ISDS Code of Conduct*, Doc No CPTPP/COM/2019/D004, 19 January 2019 <https://dfat.gov.au/trade/agreements/in-force/cptpp/news/Documents/cptpp-com-2019-d004.pdf>.

and conflicts of interest. One of the guiding principles under the *Code of Conduct* is that, "upon selection, an arbitrator shall refrain, for the duration of the proceeding, from acting as counsel or party-appointed expert or witness in any pending or new investment dispute under the CPTPP or any other international agreement".[176] The *Code of Conduct* also imposes stringent requirements for independence and impartiality, as well as disclosure obligations on arbitrators, and arbitrators are required to sign an initial disclosure statement form, declaring their compliance.[177] Another interesting point to note is that the *Code of Conduct* imposes responsibilities on experts, assistants and staff to comply with certain of the provisions regarding disclosure obligations, performance of duties, duties of former arbitrators and maintenance of confidentiality.[178]

### 3.4  Impact of the CPTPP and these Changes

It is important to consider the possible impact that the CPTPP may have, both in relation to its approach to the three areas addressed above and more broadly. This is because it has the potential to influence the continued development of international investment law within the region and perhaps further afield. As Hindelang and Krajewski note:

> mega-regional agreements with investment protection including ISDS would have a significant impact on international economic law simply because of the sheer magnitude of investment relations... It would be difficult for other countries to ignore them completely. They would certainly provide a new driver for regulating investment protection by means of public international law.[179]

This is of particular relevance in light of the ongoing ISDS reform discussions at UNCITRAL's Working Group III. During the most recent meeting of the Working Group in April 2019, significant time was devoted to discussing whether the Working Group should look toward systemic or incremental reform in

---

176  Commission of the Comprehensive and Progressive Agreement for Trans-Pacific Partnership, *Code of Conduct for Investor-State Dispute Settlement under Chapter 9 Section B (Investor-State Dispute Settlement) of The Comprehensive and Progressive Agreement for Trans-Pacific Partnership*, Doc No Annex to CPTPP/COM/2019/D004, [3(d)] <https://dfat.gov.au/trade/agreements/in-force/cptpp/news/Documents/annex-to-cptpp-com-2019-d004.pdf>.
177  Ibid appendix.
178  Ibid [9].
179  Hindelang and Krajewski (n 9) 383.

the third phase of its mandate.[180] Throughout these discussions, Australia and Japan have made repeated reference to the approach taken under the CPTPP. This demonstrates that the CPTPP, though still very much in its infancy and thus far entirely untested, is already being seen as something of a model.

One of the earliest tests for the CPTPP as a "model agreement", and indeed the most relevant considering the focus countries of this paper, will be the extent to which it influences the outcome of ongoing RCEP negotiations. Australia, Japan and New Zealand are all taking part in these negotiations as well as other CPTPP member states, with the important addition of China. Alongside China, Japan, as the world's third-largest economy, must also be seen as one of the most influential players in RCEP negotiations.[181] Ishikawa notes that the draft text of the RCEP investment chapter leaked in 2016 indicates that provisions proposed by Japan largely reflect the evolution of Japanese IIAs towards more sensitivity to public interests.[182] Whether the more balanced approach of the CPTPP or a more pro-state approach prevails will be one of the key outcomes to watch in the RCEP negotiations, in addition to the general shape that the investment chapter takes.

## 4  Conclusion

As will be evident from the foregoing discussion, much of the CPTPP's approach is found in other modern investment agreements. However, the fact that CPTPP is not in all respects ground-breaking does not deprive it of significance. Given the size of the area it covers and the number and diversity of its parties, one of its true achievements is in providing an unprecedented level of consistency across the trans-pacific region. It should also be noted that the sheer size and scope of the CPTPP means that it will have far greater potential to influence future treaty development than individual bilateral agreements – particularly regionally, but also further afield.

The extent to which the CPTPP does ultimately influence the development of other international investment agreements will be the true test of its significance. An even more fundamental development to observe will then be whether its incremental approach to ISDS reform prevails over the competing

---

180  UNCITRAL Working Group III (Investor-State Dispute Settlement Reform), *Annotated Provisional Agenda*, UN Doc A/CN.9/WG.III/WP.148 (30 July 2018).
181  Ishikawa (n 133) 542.
182  Ibid.

suggestion of systemic overhaul and comes to dominate the international investment law landscape.

## Acknowledgements

The author would like to thank Dr Lars Markert, Foreign Law Partner at Nishimura & Asahi, for his encouragement and support for this endeavour, being the author's first work of this kind. All errors and opinions are the author's own.

# Will the Anti-corruption Chapter in the *TPP11* Work? Assessing the Role of Trade Law in the Fight Against Corruption Through International Law

*José-Miguel Bello y Villarino**

## Abstract

The Comprehensive and Progressive Agreement for Trans-Pacific Partnership, also known as CPTPP or TPP11, entered into force on 30 December 2018. The TPP11, a revival of the defunct *Trans-Pacific Partnership Agreement* ("*TPP*"), signed in 2016, kept one of its (claimed-to-be) biggest achievements of the original text: Chapter 26 on Transparency and Anti-Corruption.

This article assesses the actual value of that chapter, comparing its plausible effects to the track record of existing anti-corruption conventions. The author concludes that the wording of the clauses in Chapter 26 will undermine most of the benefits derived from incorporating anti-corruption clauses in a trade agreement.

To do this, the article relies on previous research by the author on anti-corruption conventions and their shortcomings and demonstrates that most of the defects identified in those conventions have been transplanted to the *TPP* and, subsequently, to the *TPP11*.

## 1  Introduction: Corruption and the *TPP11*

Located at the intersection of philosophy, sociology, law, economics and political science, corruption is a multidimensional[1] and elusive

---

* Ministry of Foreign Affairs of Spain (on leave) and Ph.D. Candidate at the University of Sydney.
1 It can be approached from the disciplines of ethics and philosophy (see eg, John Stuart Mill, *The Collected Works of John Stuart Mill, The Later Letters of John Stuart Mill 1849–1873 Part 1* [*1849*], eds Francis E Mineka and Dwight N Lindley (University of Toronto Press, 1972); Plato, "Laws", *The Internet Classics Archive* (Web Page) <http://classics.mit.edu/Plato/laws.html>; Jeremy Waldron, "Legislating with Integrity" (2003) 72(2) *Fordham Law Review* 373); sociology (see, eg, Hussein Alatas, *The Sociology of Corruption: The Nature, Function, Causes and Prevention of Corruption* (D. Moore Press, 1968); Peter Hodgkinson, "The Sociology of Corruption- Some Themes and Issues" (1997) 31(1) *Sociology* 17; Barry Hindess, *Corruption and Democracy in Australia* (Democratic Audit of Australia, ANU, 2004)); anthropology or ethnography (see, eg, Dieter Haller and Cris Shore, *Corruption: Anthropological Perspectives* (Pluto Press, 2005); Davide Torsello, "The Ethnography of Corruption: Research Themes in Political Anthropology"

concept,² with strong cultural connotations.³ Discussions about corruption tend to go beyond the individual "objective" term and involve an element of

---

in Peter Hardi, Paul M Heywood and Davide Torsello (eds), *Debates of Corruption and Integrity* (Palgrave Macmillan, 2015) 159); education (see, eg, Stephen P Heyneman, "Education and Corruption" (2004) 24(6) *International Journal of Educational Development* 637); economics (see, eg, Nathaniel Leff, "Economic Development through Bureaucratic Corruption" (1964) 8(3) *The American Behavioral Scientist* 8; Susan Rose-Ackerman, *Corruption: A Study in Political Economy* (Academic Press, 1978); Paolo Mauro, "Corruption and Growth" (1995) 110(3) *The Quarterly Journal of Economics* 681); as well as political sciences (see, eg, JS Nye, "Corruption and Political Development: A Cost-Benefit Analysis" (1967) 61(2) *American Political Science Review* 417; Samuel P Huntington, *Political Order in Changing Societies* (Yale University Press, 1968); Francis Fukuyama, "Corruption as a Political Phenomenon" in Kaushik Basu and Tito Cordella (eds), *Institutions, Governance and the Control of Corruption* (Springer, 2018) 51); and, obviously, law, whether international (see, eg, United Nations Office for Drug and Crime, *Travaux Préparatoires of the Negotiations for the Elaboration of the United Nations Convention against Corruption* (2010)); domestic (see, eg, Celia Wells, "Enforcing Anti-Bribery Laws against Transnational Corporations – A UK Perspective" in Peter Hardi, Paul M Heywood and Davide Torsello (eds), *Debates of Corruption and Integrity* (Palgrave Macmillan, London, 2015) 59 in the context of the United Kingdom; Daniele Canestri, "The 2012 Italian Anti-Corruption Law in Light of International Best Practices" (2014) 21(3) *Journal of Financial Crime* 264 in the context of Italy; Roger P Alford, "A Broken Windows Theory of International Corruption Symposium: The FCPA at Thirty-Five and Its Impact on Global Business" (2012) 73 *Ohio State Law Journal* 1253 in the context of the United States; Britta Bannenberg and Wolfgang Schaupensteiner, *Korruption in Deutschland: Portrait einer Wachstumsbranche* (Taschenbuch, 2004) in the context of Germany; Hualing Fu, "Building Judicial Integrity in China" (2016) 39(1) *Hastings International and Comparative Law Review* 167 in the context of Hong Kong and China; AJ Brown, *Whistleblowing in the Australian Public Sector: Enhancing the Theory and Practice of Internal Witness Management in Public Sector Organisations* (ANU Press, 2013) in the context of Australia; or Perfecto Andrés Ibáñez, *Corrupción y Estado de Derecho: El Papel de La Jurisdicción* (Trotta, 1996) in the context of Spain); or at the intersection of both (see, eg, Andreas F Lowenfeld, "U.S. Law Enforcement Abroad: The Constitution and International Law" (1989) 83(4) *The American Journal of International Law* 88). It can also be approached from any combination of the above, which is indeed the most common way of analysing the topic (see, eg, Monique Nuijten and Gerhard Anders, *Corruption and the Secret of Law: A Legal Anthropological Perspective* (Ashgate Publishing, 2007); Alina Mungiu-Pippidi, "Corruption: Good Governance Powers Innovation" (2015) 518(7539) *Nature* 295; Susan Rose-Ackerman and Bonnie J Palifka, *Corruption and Government: Causes, Consequences, and Reform* (Cambridge University Press, 2016)). Many other authors from other disciplines have also shown an interest in corruption, such as history (see, eg, Ronald Kroeze, André Vitória and Guy Geltner, *Anti-Corruption in History: From Antiquity to the Modern Era* (Oxford University Press, 2018)) or medicine (see, eg, Robert Jay Lifton, "Advocacy and Corruption in the Healing Professions" (1973) 39(12) *Connecticut Medicine* 803).

2   In the words of Avinash Dixit, an emeritus economics professor at Princeton: "Corruption is a complex, multidimensional problem. Even its definition is elusive and a matter of disagreement among those studying it": Avinash Dixit, "Anti-Corruption Institutions: Some History and Theory" in Kaushik Basu and Tito Cordella (eds), *Institutions, Governance and the Control of Corruption* (Springer, 2018) 15.

3   Akhil Gupta, "Blurred Boundaries: The Discourse of Corruption, the Culture of Politics, and the Imagined State" (1995) 22(2) *American Ethnologist* 375; Martin Paldam, "The

judgment – often distaste – that escapes the act to embrace and judge society as a whole.[4] As one author has put it, "corruption is not ... simply a matter of law; rather it is fundamentally a matter of morality".[5]

This article, however, leaves morality intentionally aside and focuses narrowly on how a legal instrument, the *Comprehensive and Progressive Agreement for Trans-Pacific Partnership* ("*TPP11*"),[6] cutting through very different cultural settings – New Zealand and ten other Pacific states – deals with corruption. Further, it aims to assess the expected effects of the *TPP11* in the wider fight against corruption, even if the agreement has barely been in force for a few months. Concretely, it discusses the expected effectiveness of Chapter 26 ("*Transparency and Anti-Corruption*") of the *TPP11* in delivering one of its objectives: namely, to "eliminate bribery and corruption in international trade and investment among its parties".[7]

This chapter can be a cornerstone for international anti-corruption efforts, having the *potential* to revolutionise the way in which international law is used against corruption. Although the effects of such a small intervention, in such a limited field, could never be expected to "solve" corruption for the signatories to the agreement, it could bring one of the most powerful tools in international law – trade-law agreements – into the fight. This approach can change *how effective* international law could be at reducing large-scale corruption and bringing to the legal surface corrupt activities without ever resorting to criminal law.

In that sense, although this is an article about legal clauses – the anti-corruption articles in the *TPP11* – in order to assess its potential, it requires a discussion in policy terms (including, inter alia, its effectiveness, impact and expected changes) that draw from the lessons of 40 years of academic work on corruption from several of the disciplines mentioned in footnote one.

As the reader can imagine, the main restriction to successfully performing this assessment is the brief amount of time which has elapsed since its entry into force. To analyse Chapter 26 of the *TPP11* with non-legal tools, a preferred approach would be to wait a few years and then focus on concrete outputs – i.e., performing an *ex post* analysis.

However, if one wants to explore what could be done to fight corruption through international trade law in the coming years, one cannot wait and see.

---

Cross-Country Pattern of Corruption: Economics, Culture and the Seesaw Dynamics" (2002) 18(2) *European Journal of Political Economy* 215; Abigail Barr and Danila Serra, "Corruption and Culture: An Experimental Analysis" (2010) 94(11) *Journal of Public Economics* 862.

4 Laura S Underkuffler, *Captured by Evil* (Yale University Press, 2013) 223.
5 Seumas Miller, "Corruption" in Edward N Zalta (ed), *The Stanford Encyclopedia of Philosophy* (Metaphysics Research Lab, Stanford University, 2011).
6 *Comprehensive and Progressive Agreement for Trans-Pacific Partnership*, signed 8 March 2018, [2018] ATS 23 (entered into force 30 December 2018) ("*TPP11*").
7 Ibid art 26.6.1.

Performing this assessment *now* requires instead a legal approach which learns from the findings extracted from analogous experiences. The tools used for this *ex ante* analysis are based on methods of legal reasoning (justiciability, sanctions, redress, binding obligations, etc.), which place the arguments closer to an "exegetical" doctrinal piece. The conclusions are not factual findings derived from concrete observations, but rather "exploratory assessments", which can inform drafters and negotiators of future trade agreements which include anti-corruption clauses.

To successfully and soundly deliver this mix of policy and doctrinal approaches, the article builds its argument through four steps. First, it provides a brief summary of the author's previous work on the effects of existing anti-corruption conventions. Second, it guides the readers through the common traits of those anti-corruption measures in international law and puts forward a few ideas on what can work, and what has worked, and what does not. Third, it applies those ideas to international trade law in general and Chapter 26 of the *TPP11* in particular. From there, in a final fourth step, it derives certain observations on how likely it is that Chapter 26 will have a noticeable effect in the corruption levels of its parties. It concludes by answering the question in the title in the negative: Chapter 26 of the *TPP11* is not likely to significantly reduce perceptions[8] of corruption among its signatories. Nonetheless, it may have set the template for future trade agreements that will.

## 2  Fighting Corruption through International Law

International law is one among many tools available to fight corruption. As a broad area of law, international law could be used in many different ways, take different approaches and employ different legal tools. However, despite this wide span of available tools *within* international law to fight corruption, we have largely seen the same approach repeated again and again since the adoption of the *OECD Convention on Combating Bribery of Foreign Public Officials in International Business Transactions* ("the OECD Convention");[9] namely, addressing corruption by engaging signatories of international treaties to align

---

8   The argument here restricts itself to discussing the effects of international law on "perceptions of corruption" as a reliable proxy to the "prevalence of corruption". For a detailed discussion on the issue of measurement, see José-Miguel Bello y Villarino, "Measuring Corruption: a Critical Analysis of the Existing Datasets and Their Suitability for Transnational Comparative Research" [2020] (forthcoming).

9   *OECD Convention on Combating Bribery of Foreign Public Officials in International Business Transactions*, signed 17 December 1997, 37 ILM 1 (entered into force 15 February 1999).

domestic legislation to certain treaty standards. I call this "conventional anti-corruption law", not only because it is formalised in "conventions", but also because it lacks creative thinking.[10]

A notable exception is conditionality. By this term, I am referring to a set of agreed requirements that need to be fulfilled by one party before the other party grants some kind of preferential treatment.[11] This kind of approach is commonly found in the context of development aid,[12] which usually operates at the margins of international law. If it is captured at all by international law,[13] it is through *softer* law instruments such as memoranda of understanding ("MoUs")[14] of limited (international) legal value.[15] However, it is also used neatly within the scope of international law, when some well-defined (and higher) standards are to be met in order to gain accession to integration regimes such as the European Union.[16]

---

10   Bello y Villarino (n 8).
11   A similar definition, although restricted to grants, is provided in Alina Mungiu-Pippidi, *The Quest for Good Governance: How Societies Develop Control of Corruption* (Cambridge University Press, 2015) 191.
12   See, eg, Doug Johnson and Tristan Zajonc, "Can Foreign Aid Create an Incentive for Good Governance? Evidence from the Millennium Challenge Corporation" (Working Paper No 11, Center for International Development at Harvard University, April 2006) where it is discussed in the context of the Millennium Challenge Corporation.
13   Often the restrictions ("conditionality") are included in the domestic legislation creating the assistance mechanism of the party offering the preferential treatment, as was the case with the Millennium Challenge Corporation: see, eg, *Millennium Challenge Act of 2003*, 22 USC (2004).
14   *New Zealand – Fiji Development Cooperation Arrangement between the Ministry of Foreign Affairs and Trade (MFAT) New Zealand and the Ministry of Foreign Affairs (MFA) of the Government of the Republic of Fiji*, signed 17 February 2016 (Memorandum of Understanding).
15   Anthony Aust, *Handbook of International Law* (Cambridge University Press, 2010) 54. A good example of this limited legal value can be found in the recent MoU between Indonesia and Australia on cyber security, which expressly denies any legal value to the agreement:
> This MOU does not create any legally binding obligations, and does not alter or effect any existing agreements between the Participants. ... The Participants acknowledge that this MOU is not an international agreement and will not create legal obligations governed by their respective domestic law or international law.

*Memorandum of Understanding between the Government of the Republic of Indonesia and the Government of Australia on Cyber Cooperation*, signed 31 August 2018, [10]. This MoU also forbids any kind of intervention of third parties in the settlement of disputes: at [7].
16   Consider, for example, Romania's creation of a "to do list" encompassing 39 measures and almost 140 concrete actions demanded of Romania by the European Union as part of the progress required for accession to the European Union: Bogdan Aurescu, *Final Negotiations Opening the Way for Romania's Accession to the EU. Council of Europe's Influence on Domestic Reforms* (Report, 21 October 2005) 5.

Another notable exception is the sanctions mechanism of the World Bank used against certain firms when the Office of Suspension and Debarment gathers evidence of the existence of corrupt practices in existing or previous contracts with the Bank.[17] This system exists in other international organisations[18] and some countries.[19] Cross-debarment among international financial institutions – i.e., not being able to participate in initiatives funded by any of the participating development banks if debarred by one of them – could be a powerful tool to modify the conduct of certain international corporations.[20]

Also on the margins of "formal" international law, we could find a third soft-law track in the context of public-private initiatives, such as the Extractive Industries Transparency Initiative ("EITI") standards.[21] These kinds of initiatives rely intensively on the goodwill of the parties[22] or the expected reputational benefits of participating,[23] and their track record is mixed.[24] However, it seems to be a good solution for certain specific areas of work, such as forestry,[25]

---

17   The system now has a long record and is generally considered to be an efficient (although narrow) way to deal with the problem at the World Bank level: Sope Williams, "The Debarment of Corrupt Contractors from World Bank-Financed Contracts" (2007) 36(3) *Public Contract Law Journal* 277; Tina Soreide, Linda Groning and Rasmus Wandall, "An Efficient Anticorruption Sanctions Regime? The Case of the World Bank" (2015) 16(2) *Chicago Journal of International Law* 523.

18   For an overview of other financial institutions, see Stuart H Deming, "Anti-Corruption Policies: Eligibility and Debarment Practices at the World Bank and Regional Development Banks" (2010) 44(2) *International Lawyer* 871; Christopher R Yukins, "Cross-Debarment: A Stakeholder Analysis Suspension and Debarment" (2013) 45(2) *George Washington International Law Review* 219.

19   For a comparison with the US framework, see Pascale Helene Dubois, "Domestic and International Administrative Tools to Combat Fraud & Corruption: A Comparison of US Suspension and Debarment with the World Bank's Sanctions System Combating Corruption" [2012] *University of Chicago Legal Forum* 195.

20   Cross-debarment "could result in global sanctions for prohibited practices in a single country": Norbert Seiler and Jelena Madir, "Fight Against Corruption: Sanctions Regimes of Multilateral Development Banks" (2012) 15(1) *Journal of International Economic Law* 5, 28.

21   EITI International Secretariat, *The EITI Standard 2016* (Report, 24 May 2017).

22   As the United States' withdrawal in 2017 clearly illustrates: see Letter from Gregory J Gould to Fredrik Reinfeldt, 2 November 2017.

23   Elizabeth David-Barrett and Ken Okamura, "Norm Diffusion and Reputation: The Rise of the Extractive Industries Transparency Initiative" (2016) 29(2) *Governance* 227, 227–228.

24   Compare the results in transparency and perceptions of corruption described by Kerem Öge, "Which Transparency Matters? Compliance with Anti-Corruption Efforts in Extractive Industries" (2016) 49 *Resources Policy* 41, 48.

25   Nalin Kishor and Richard Damania, "Crime and Justice in the Garden of Eden: Improving Governance and Reducing Corruption in the Forestry Sector" in J Edgardo Campos and Sanjay Pradhan, *The Many Faces of Corruption: Tracking Vulnerabilities at the Sector Level* (Publication, 1 January 2007) 89.

where international and national actors – public and private – can cooperate to close gaps in global and national regulation.[26]

Authors often also include among the international anti-corruption tools other international initiatives which are not necessarily designed to fight corruption as such, but which are aimed at dealing with ancillary practices.[27] Among these, the most commonly mentioned are (i) the Financial Action Task Force ("FATF"), an evaluation system designed to assess compliance with international standards of the anti-money laundering legislation of the assessed countries,[28] and (ii) the Stolen Assets Recovery ("StAR") Initiative, a joint effort of the World Bank and United Nations Office on Drugs and Crime to facilitate the return of the proceeds of corruption to their country of origin.[29] Despite the importance of these initiatives, their link to the reduction of corruption levels is tenuous at best. The FATF was established to deal with the illicit profits of the drug trade[30] and, subsequently, with the financing of terrorism. Corruption is mainly an afterthought, which can be traced back to a document produced by the INGO Global Witness in 2009,[31] although its importance cannot be understated.[32]

The StAR Initiative was created as a "support system for international efforts to deter the illicit flow of the proceeds of corruption".[33] In that sense, it deals with the aftermath of corruption; i.e., once an instance of corruption has been identified and the need for some legal redress has been established. It may indirectly affect perceptions of corruption or levels of actual corruption, as it makes it more challenging for the corrupt to place the stolen assets in a safe haven, but it does not create a deterrent for corrupt practices.

Other alternative approaches mentioned in the literature are configuring the fight against corruption as a human rights-based issue,[34] the insertion of

---

26   David-Barrett and Okamura (n 23) 243.
27   See, eg, Mungiu-Pippidi (n 11) 188.
28   Financial Action Task Force, *Procedures for the FATF Fourth Round of AML/CFT Mutual Evaluations* (Report, June 2019).
29   Stolen Asset Recovery Initiative, *StAR Annual Report 2017* (Report, May 2018).
30   D Chaikin and J Sharman, *Corruption and Money Laundering: A Symbiotic Relationship* (Springer, 2009) 7, 15–16.
31   Global Witness, *Undue Diligence: How Banks Do Business with Corrupt Regimes* (Report, March 2009) 108.
32   For a good case in support of its value, see JC Sharman and David Chaikin, "Corruption and Anti-Money-Laundering Systems: Putting a Luxury Good to Work" (2009) 22(1) *Governance* 27, 34–35.
33   Mark V Vlasic and Jenae N Noell, "Fighting Corruption to Improve Global Security: An Analysis of International Asset Recovery Systems Spotlight on Security" (2010) 5(2) *Yale Journal of International Affairs* 106, 114.
34   Martine Boersma, *Corruption: A Violation of Human Rights and a Crime Under International Law?* (Intersentia, 2012); Matthew Murray and Andrew Spalding, *Freedom from*

corruption-related clauses in investment treaties,[35] and/or preventing corruption through international commercial contracts.[36] Some authors have gone even beyond this framework and proposed initiatives – yet to materialise – such as the establishment of an international anti-corruption court[37] and targeted individual sanctions.[38]

This brief description of the international anti-corruption norms illustrates the panoply of tools available within international law. Yet the conventional approach has overwhelmingly dominated that landscape, namely through the *United Nations Convention Against Corruption* ("UNCAC").[39] In the next paragraphs, I explore its effectiveness.

### 2.1 Conventional Anti-corruption Law: How Effective Has It Been?

The UNCAC is a significant success in terms of reach, being one of the most widely ratified United Nations ("UN") treaties of the 21st century. Yet, fourteen years after its entry into force, a feeling is settling in that the – already not very

---

*Official Corruption as a Human Right* (Report, January 2015); Cecily Rose, "The Limitations of a Human Rights Approach to Corruption" (2016) 65(2) *International & Comparative Law Quarterly* 405; Anne Peters, "Corruption as a Violation of International Human Rights" (2018) 29(4) *European Journal of International Law* 1251.

35  Joost Pauwelyn, "Different Means, Same End: The Contribution of Trade and Investment Treaties to Anti-Corruption Policy" in Susan Rose-Ackerman and Paul D Carrington (eds), *Anti-Corruption Policy: Can International Actors Play a Constructive Role?* (Carolina Academic Press, 2013) 247.

36  Abiola Makinwa, "Private Remedies for Corruption: Towards an International Framework" (PhD Thesis, Erasmus University Rotterdam, 2012); Michael Joachim Bonell and Olaf Meyer, "The Impact of Corruption on International Commercial Contracts" in Martin Schauer and Bea Verschraegen (eds), *General Reports of the XIXth Congress of the International Academy of Comparative Law Rapports Généraux du XIXème Congrès de l'Académie Internationale de Droit Comparé* (Springer Netherlands, 2017) 195.

37  Mark L Wolf, "The World Needs an International Anti-Corruption Court" (2018) 147(3) *Daedalus* 144.

38  In line with the system established by the *Global Magnitsky Act*, which could be used to freeze assets and ban travel on (United States-designated) persons considered to be essential to grand corruption schemes. See the relevant legislation and its use: *Global Magnitsky Human Rights Accountability Act*, Pub L No 114–328 (2016); *Executive Order Blocking the Property of Persons Involved in Serious Human Rights Abuse or Corruption*, EO 13818 of 20 December 2017 (2017); "United States Sanctions Human Rights Abusers and Corrupt Actors Across the Globe" (Press Release, United States Department of the Treasury, 21 December 2017).

39  *United Nations Convention Against Corruption*, opened for signature 9 December 2003, 2349 UNTS 41 (entered into force 14 December 2005) ("UNCAC").

high[40] – expectations are not being met.[41] Alas, beyond the internal evaluations conducted within the organisation,[42] there has been limited evidence to support either this pessimistic view[43] or the opposite one (namely, that things are actually improving).[44]

However, my use of the term "conventional anti-corruption law" covers much more than the UNCAC. It includes any international anti-corruption norm which follows an analogous approach, namely the *OECD Convention*, the *Inter-American Convention against Corruption ("IACAC")* and the *African Union Convention on Preventing and Combating Corruption ("AUCPCC")*.[45]

---

40   Philippa Webb, "The United Nations Convention Against Corruption. Global Achievement or Missed Opportunity?" (2005) 8(1) *Journal of International Economic Law* 191; R Rajesh Babu, "The United Nations Convention Against Corruption: A Critical Overview" (Scholarly Paper, 1 March 2006).

41   Hannes Hechler et al, *Can UNCAC Address Grand Corruption? A Political Economy Analysis of the UN Convention against Corruption and its Implementation in Three Countries* (Report No 2011:2, October 2011); Antoine Martin, "Implementation as the Best Way to Tackle Corruption: A Study of the UNCAC and the AUC 2003" (Working Paper No 07/2011, Surrey Law School, 1 February 2011).

42   United Nations Office for Drug and Crime, *Mechanism for the Review of Implementation of the United Nations Convention against Corruption – Basic Documents* (Collection of Documents, 2011).

43   Tim Daniel and Tim Maton, "Is the UNCAC an Effective Deterrent to Grand Corruption" in Jeremy Horder and Peter Alldridge (eds), *Modern Bribery Law: Comparative Perspectives* (Cambridge University Press, 2013) 293, 294.

44   John Sandage, *Keynote Speech: Global Corruption and the Universal Approach of the United Nations Convention against Corruption* (2015) 53(1) Osgoode Hall Law Journal 7, 29.

45   *Inter-American Convention against Corruption*, opened for signature 29 March 1996, 35 ILM 724 (entered into force 6 March 1997) ("*IACAC*"); *African Union Convention on Preventing and Combating Corruption*, opened for signature 1 July 2003, 43 ILM 5 (entered into force 5 August 2006) ("*AUCPCC*"). Other international instruments, also formalised in conventions, are not covered in the 2019 article nor in the present one, namely those focused on the alignment of legislation. See, eg,, the Group of States against Corruption ("GRECO") instruments: the Council of Europe's *Criminal Law Convention on Corruption*, opened for signature 27 January 1999, ETS No 173 (entered into force 1 July 2002); *Civil Law Convention on Corruption*, opened for signature 1 November 1999, ETS No 174 (entered into force 1 November 2003) and its recommendations (Council of Europe, *Recommendation No R (2000) 10 of the Committee of Ministers to Member States on Codes of Conduct for Public Officials* (11 May 2000) and Council of Europe, *Recommendation Rec(2003)4 of the Committee of Ministers of Member States on Common Rules against Corruption in the Funding of Political Parties and Electoral Campaigns* (8 April 2003)). See also the actual mandates of international organisations, such as the *Convention Drawn Up on the Basis of Article K.3 (2) (c) of the Treaty on European Union on the Fight against Corruption Involving Officials of the European Communities or Officials of Member States of the European Union* [1997] OJ C 195/2; *Convention Drawn Up on the Basis of Article K.3 of the Treaty on European Union, on*

In a forthcoming piece, I use aggregated data on corruption from several datasets[46] and treaty ratification dates to argue that if commonly used indicators are accepted as reliable, basic statistical analysis seems to prove that the world overall is no less corrupt today than in 1997 (the year of signature of the first of these conventions). Further, I contend there that conventional anti-corruption law has not had a statistically significant impact on the levels of perceived corruption in the countries ratifying those conventions.[47]

This research confirms the findings of other statistical or econometric analyses. Against the intuition of Sandholtz and Gray that greater degrees of international integration – such as the ratification of international conventions against corruption – would lead to lower levels of corruption,[48] the studies of Friedman,[49] Mungiu-Pippidi et al[50] and Cole[51] point in the opposite direction.[52]

---

the Protection of the European Communities' Financial Interests [1995] OJ C 316/49; Directive (EU) 2017/1371 of the European Parliament and of the Council of 5 July 2017 on the Fight against Fraud to the Union's Financial Interests by Means of Criminal Law [2017] OJ L 198/29.

46   Namely, the Worldwide Governance Indicators and the Corruption Perception Index: Daniel Kaufmann, Aart Kraay and Massimo Mastruzzi, "The Worldwide Governance Indicators: Methodology and Analytical Issues" (Policy Research Working Paper No 5430, World Bank, September 2010) 32; World Bank, *Worldwide Governance Indicators 2017* (2018) <http://info.worldbank.org/governance/wgi/#home>; Dan Hough, "The Corruption Perceptions Index (CPI); Much Ado about Nothing?", *Sussex Centre for the Study of Corruption* (Web Page, January 2017) <https://scscsussex.wordpress.com/2017/01/25/the-corruption-perceptions-index-cpi-much-ado-about-nothing/>; "Corruption Perceptions Index 2017", *Transparency International* (Web Page, 2018) <https://www.transparency.org/news/feature/corruption_perceptions_index_2017>.

47   A detailed methodological explanation about the use of the data and the tools used provides the reader with the necessary qualifications for those findings (in general, they are more reliable in aggregate terms than as a country-based analysis) and how much they can be extrapolated to levels of actual corruption (with certain caveats, my claim is that measures of perceptions are a fairly good proxy to measures of prevalence of corruption). José-Miguel Bello y Villarino, "*On the Effectiveness of Conventional Anti-Corruption Law or How Not to Deal with Tyrant Banderas*" (2020) (forthcoming).

48   Wayne Sandholtz and Mark M Gray, "International Integration and National Corruption" (2003) 57(4) *International Organization* 761.

49   Alexandra Monica Friedman, "Can We Change Corruption from the Outside in? An Assessment of Three Anti-Corruption International Treaties" (PhD Thesis, University of Texas, 2010).

50   Alina Mungiu-Pippidi, "Contextual Choices in Fighting Corruption: Lessons Learned" (Research Paper, Norwegian Agency for Development Cooperation, 7 January 2011).

51   Wade M Cole, "Institutionalizing a Global Anti-Corruption Regime: Perverse Effects on Country Outcomes, 1984–2012" (2015) 56(1) *International Journal of Comparative Sociology* 53.

52   It should be noted here, that the finding that these treaties do not have a (statistically relevant) positive impact on perceptions of corruption does not exclude the possibility

In that sense, international law is not delivering on what it was created to do. The law may have different functions, but, above all, it is designed to shape behaviour according to certain rules, following a tridimensional structure of facts, norms and values.[53] Success, in legislative terms, should be primarily determined in relation to the declared objective of the norm. In the case of conventional anti-corruption law, for instance, art 1(a) of the UNCAC states that its purpose is "[t]o promote and strengthen measures to prevent and combat corruption more efficiently and effectively".

Commonly this kind of evaluation is done through *ex post* impact assessments, which allow us to say whether the norm has achieved the desired results or not.[54] If a norm is established to influence the conduct of its addressees (i.e. for individuals or entities not to be involved in corrupt practices) with the intention of fulfilling certain societal values (i.e., to reduce corruption, which is *considered to be* bad by society)[55] and there is no change in the conduct (i.e., no noticeable change in the prevalence of corruption), then that norm is not achieving its objective. It may have other positive effects (or not), but those are not the main reason for the creation of the conventional anti-corruption norm.

As mentioned earlier, the declared objective in Chapter 26 of the TPP11 is that the "[p]arties resolve to eliminate bribery and corruption in international trade and investment".[56] Once the TPP11 has been ratified and entered into

---

that a country can increase its level of perceived corruption while there is a decrease of actual corruption.

53  Miguel Reale, *Teoria Tridimensional do Direito* (Saraiva, 1994).
54  Irmgard Anglmayer, *Evaluation and Ex-Post Impact Assessment at EU Level* (Briefing, 14 September 2016).
55  Some authors have disagreed about this statement. The original works in this domain (Michael McMullan, "A Theory of Corruption" (1961) 9(2) *The Sociological Review* 181; Edward Shils, "Political Development in the New States" (1960) 2(3) *Comparative Studies in Society and History* 265) have been amplified by very influential pieces such as Huntington (n 1); JS Nye, "Corruption and Political Development: A Cost-Benefit Analysis" (1967) 61(2) *American Political Science Review* 417. We can consider this perspective to be held by a colourful minority today.
56  TPP11 (n 6) art 26.6.1. It could be argued that this is not an "objective" as such – art 26.6.1 is titled "scope" – particularly if compared to similar articles in other chapters, such as art 18.2 of the "Intellectual Property" chapter, whose headings actually contain the word "objectives". However, from a substantive point of view, the statement in art 26.6.1. frames the final objective – the ultimate intention of the parties, in relatively concrete terms, "to eliminate bribery and corruption", in the same way that art 18.2 establishes the final intent of the parties in relation to the protection of intellectual property. In contrast, art 15.2, in the procurement chapter – also titled "scope" – establishes which actions are covered by the TPP11 procurement rules, thus respecting the more conventional meaning of "scope" in legal documents. The strong wording of art 26.6.1. when compared to other free trade

force, Chapter 26 became legally binding for the parties. If it does not show in the future a reduction of the incidence of corruption in the international trade and investment among the parties, it will have failed to deliver this objective. As we will immediately see in the next subsection, there could be many possible explanations for this, but the main conclusion would still be that the desired result has not been achieved.

### 2.2 Possible Explanations for the Limited Effect of Conventional Anti-corruption Law

There are three overarching explanations for the lack of noticeable effect on levels of perceived corruption after the ratification of conventional anti-corruption norms. First, the conventions may actually have an effect on actual levels of corruption, but this effect cannot be reflected by the methods used to assess it. Second, they may have an effect, but there could be concurrent factors with equal (or stronger) opposite effect cancelling out the corruption-reduction impact derived from conventional anti-corruption law. Third, there may be no actual effect. I contend that the latter of the three is the most likely explanation.

In order to demonstrate this, the section establishes certain hypotheses about the assumed causality between the introduction of international law measures and the reduction in overall levels of measured corruption. On this basis, I suggest that conventional anti-corruption law is not *sufficient* to overcome factors at play that affect the prevalence of perceptions of corruption, because it does not include the appropriate legal mechanisms that could actually affect corruption (and not just perceptions of corruption). As Daniel and Maton eloquently wrote, "it is like expecting a burglar to hand himself in to the police after committing a crime, with the further requirement that he should hand over his swag. It does not happen".[57]

This argument is supported by a study of six possible reasons for the lack of impact of conventional anti-corruption law, summarised in Table 1. They are all connected to the idea of effectiveness but respond to two different sets of

---

agreements ("FTAs"), also supports seeing this as an objective. For example, in the equivalent article of the *United States-Korea FTA*, the parties simply "recognize the importance of regional and multilateral initiatives to eliminate bribery and corruption in international trade and investment. The Parties shall endeavor to work jointly to encourage and support appropriate initiatives in relevant international fora": *Free Trade Agreement between the United States of America and the Republic of Korea* , signed on 30 June 2007, 46 ILM 642 (entered into force 15 March 2012) art 21.6.5 (*"US-Korea FTA"*).

57  Daniel and Maton (n 42) 322.

TABLE 1    Possible explanations for the limited effect of conventional anti-corruption law

| Possible explanations for the limited effect of conventional anti-corruption law | |
|---|---|
| Related to the mechanisms to ensure the fulfilment of international compromises | Related to the substance and content of the existing conventions |
| Lack of systematic domestication | Lack of punitive effects |
| Lack of external enforcement mechanisms | Implementation by the subjects of the norms |
| Other issues related to domestication and enforcement | Compliance with the "letter" but not the "spirit" of the law |

limitations. On the one hand, there are those related to the existing mechanisms to ensure the fulfilment of international compromises, which we can call "mechanical". On the other hand, there are those specifically related to the substance and content of conventional anti-corruption law, which we can call "substantial".

### 2.2.1    Mechanical Limitations

#### 2.2.1.1    *Lack of Systematic Domestication*

Within the mechanical explanations, the lack of consequences for the non-fulfilment of obligations or compromises established in international law is a doctrinal area in itself.[58] Here, however, I focus narrowly on what happens when the standard anti-corruption obligation, such as the requirement that the parties make foreign bribery a crime, is not fulfilled.

In public international law terms, this is a problem of domestication, i.e., one of not effectively incorporating the international obligation into the national law of the signatory country. In my view, the prevailing international anti-corruption regime is not adequately designed to address ineffective domestication or the absence of domestication altogether.

The type of obligations determined by conventional anti-corruption law is, as described above, the establishment of certain standards that a country must adhere to. This often entails a modification of its domestic legislation, without

---

58   See the introductory part of Andrew T Guzman, "A Compliance-Based Theory of International Law" (2002) 90(6) *California Law Review* 1823.

any direct obligations affecting the signatory's relationships with third parties. Consequently, the non-fulfilment of the international obligation only has an internal dimension within the jurisdiction of the relevant state party.

For example, if state party A does not criminalise foreign bribery, no international consequence will be attached besides negative comments in the peer-review mechanisms[59] or a loss of a reputation of compliance.[60] The effects of the non-fulfilment will only be felt by companies which have bribed public officials abroad, as they will not be prosecuted in their domestic jurisdictions.

### 2.2.1.2  *Lack of External Enforcement Mechanisms*

Similarly, one can look at this limitation from the perspective of the other parties. What can the other signatories do if one party does not comply with an anti-corruption convention? The conventions, in general, do not create any mechanism for country B to force or even put on the public record that state party A has not fulfilled its obligation. Conventional anti-corruption law lacks teeth in terms of external coercion.

The exception to this statement is the UNCAC, which, at least on paper, opens up that possibility. Article 66 allows state parties to request the settlement of disputes between two or more state parties concerning the interpretation or application of the convention to arbitration, and, if no agreement on the arbitration is reached, to the International Court of Justice ("ICJ"). However, given the internal nature of the obligations under the convention, there are limited incentives and high political costs in pursuing this option.[61]

One can, however, imagine a party taking another to the ICJ in cases of lack of cooperation regarding asset recovery (Chapter V of the UNCAC). Regretfully, many of the jurisdictions which would have been relevant in recent cases of asset recovery have made a reservation to art 66. For example, among the parties that have issued a reservation one can find China, the United States ("US"), Panama, United Arab Emirates, Singapore and the Bahamas. Switzerland is probably the only one of the usual suspects[62] that has fully accepted a binding system for resolution of this differences and seems to be committed to the process.[63] Other countries that have indeed accepted the jurisdiction have been sheltering certain territories from the application of the convention altogether.

---

59  Edmund Bao and Kath Hall, "Peer Review and the Global Anti-Corruption Conventions: Context, Theory and Practice" (2017) 35 *Australian Yearbook of International Law* 67.
60  See, eg, the reasoning of Guzman (n 58).
61  Pauwelyn (n 35) 4.
62  George Turner, "Switzerland, USA and Cayman Top the 2018 Financial Secrecy Index", *Tax Justice Network* (Web Page, 30 January 2018) <https://www.taxjustice.net/2018/01/30/2018fsi/>.
63  United Nations Office for Drug and Crime, *Country Review Report of Switzerland* (Report, 2012).

For example, the United Kingdom was an early ratifier of UNCAC, but only extended its application to Bermuda on 4 June 2018.[64]

Dispute settlement mechanisms ("DSMs") are paramount for any treaty where there could be a misalignment between the interests of officials and the state. This is exacerbated if elected officials and public servants have an incentive to act as free riders, i.e., assuming that other countries will follow the agreed rules whilst they choose whether or not to follow the rules themselves. The relevance of DSMs in anti-corruption efforts is considerable if one looks at the impact of cases based on international investment law in bringing to the surface and publicising cases of corruption. Probably the *World Duty Free* affair is the best-known one, as it made public that the then-President of Kenya had received a bribe from the World Duty Free company,[65] but there are many others.[66] In the end the issue of corruption has attracted so much attention in the area of international investment law in recent years because in order for corruption to matter in terms of compensation for investors, it had to be litigated and discussed openly.[67]

### 2.2.1.3    *Other Issues Related to Domestication and Enforcement*

Finally, resolution of differences is impossible if there is no deadline to fulfil a commitment. Conventional anti-corruption law has no deadlines built into the wording of the treaties for domestication. This is particularly relevant in those cases where the obligation is a modification of internal legislation. It is unreasonable to expect that state party A will immediately modify its internal legal system just after ratification of the conventional anti-corruption law, but it is equally unreasonable not to build into the obligations any indication about when the other parties can expect that country to fulfil its obligations.[68] The same could be said about infra-state entities with legislative powers, as

---

64    "United Nations Convention against Corruption", *United Nations Treaty Collection* (Web Page, 2019) <https://treaties.un.org/Pages/ViewDetails.aspx?src=IND&mtdsg_no=XVIII-14&chapter=18&clang=_en>.

65    *World Duty Free v Kenya* (*Award*) (2006) 46 ILM 339; Andrew Brady Spalding, "Deconstructing Duty Free: Investor-State Arbitration as Private Anti-Bribery Enforcement" (2015) 49(2) *UC Davis Law Review* 443.

66    See the examples provided in Jason Webb Yackee, "Investment Treaties and Investor Corruption: An Emerging Defense for Host States?" (2012) 52(3) *Virginia Journal of International Law* 723. More recently, see, eg, *Georg Gavrilović and Gavrilović DOO v Croatia* (*Award*) (ICSID Arbitration Tribunal, Case No ARB/12/39, 26 July 2018).

67    Yackee (n 66); Aloysius P Llamzon, *Corruption in International Investment Arbitration* (Oxford University Press, 2014); Alina Mungiu-Pippidi, *Fostering Good Governance through Trade Agreements: an Evidence-Based Review* (Workshop Report, 28 March 2018).

68    Interestingly, the Organisation for Economic Co-operation and Development ("OECD") had built this kind of time limit (one year) when its Council, on 23 May 1997, adopted its

exist in federally organised countries. The lack of consequences for the federal government – the entity responsible under public international law for the lack of domestication by the sub-entities of the international obligation – creates no incentive for the federal government to push those sub-entities to complete the domestication process. This will be the case, for example, in Australia in the context of regulations for officials elected to state positions.

### 2.2.2 Substantive Limitations

The second track of limitations regarding the effectiveness of conventional anti-corruption law relates to the substance and content of the existing conventional anti-corruption law. This has less to do with the choice of conventions as the vehicle to create international anti-corruption law, and more to do with the wording actually used in these conventions.

#### 2.2.2.1 *Lack of Punitive Effects.*

The first, and probably the most evident of such limitations is the lack of punitive responses to violations of the obligations contained in the convention. Although this is related to the limitations presented before, it would be possible to imagine a convention that allows for some mechanism to penalise a party that does not fulfil its obligations, even without a DSM. As noted above, there are no complaint mechanisms attached to these conventions. However, theoretically speaking, punishing breaches could still be possible through, for example, self-enforcement by the aggrieved party. However, none of the anti-corruption conventions allow for any form of retaliatory mechanism.

Although this is not unusual in international law, other conventional instruments could rely on the assumed principle that other parties will not honour their commitments towards to a party that has not fulfilled its own.[69] Yet, in the context of conventional anti-corruption law, it is difficult to imagine how this could operate in practice. As was noted above, most of the obligations in these conventions have an internal dimension, and not a reciprocal one. The idea that state party B may not incorporate the crime of foreign bribery in its

---

*Revised Recommendation on Combating Bribery in International Business Transactions* (No C(97)123/FINAL, 30 May 1997): Giorgio Sacerdoti, "The 1997 OECD Convention on Combating Bribery of Foreign Public Officials in International Business Transactions" (1999) 3:1 *International Business Law Journal* 3, 7. Time limits, however, did not appear in the Convention.

69 Eric A Posner and Alan O Sykes, "Efficient Breach of International Law: Optimal Remedies, 'Legalized Noncompliance', and Related Issues" (2011) 110(2) *Michigan Law Review* 243, 245.

domestic legislation, or may change its legislation to decriminalise it[70] as a response to the violation of state party A of the same obligation, sounds preposterous.

#### 2.2.2.2  *Implementation by the Subjects of the Norms*
Second, the conventions rely mainly on legislative obligations. This means that a party is bound to domesticate its anti-corruption legal standards, aligning them to the global or regional standards set by the conventions. This is insufficient. Without implementation and enforcement, domestic legislation is not worth the paper it is written on. Not only will it fail to serve its purpose of creating an enforceable mechanism to prevent and punish corruption; it will also not be seen as a credible declaration of political will – i.e. a statement that a party will not accept corrupt behaviours – by the government domesticating the relevant obligation.[71]

Regretfully, conventional anti-corruption law relies on those who can benefit the most from the non-implementation or enforcement of the obligations – i.e., public or elected officials in a situation to receive a bribe – to enforce those norms. Police officers, elected officials, administrative authorities and judges and magistrates are commonly identified by the population among the people most commonly involved in corruption.[72] Given that these are the same individuals that should be identifying the cases of corruption, for those who are already corrupt there is no incentive to effectively enforce the international obligations.

#### 2.2.2.3  *Compliance with the "Letter" but Not the "Spirit" of the Law.*
Third, even if a state party fulfils its obligations by incorporating these conventional anti-corruption standards *and* creates the mechanisms to enforce them, the way the conventions are drafted make it easy to comply with the black letter of the law and not the spirit. In other words, the declared common objectives of the conventions are – amalgamating the wording of the relevant

---

70   UNCAC (n 39) art 16.
71   In the already classic words of Koskenniemi, "in the end, legitimizing or criticizing state behaviour is not a matter of applying formally neutral rules but depends on what one regards as politically right, or just". The ratification of an international norm stating that foreign bribery should be criminalised is a way of saying that that foreign bribery is wrong or unjust: Martti Koskenniemi, "The Politics of International Law" (1990) 1(1) *European Journal of International Law* 4, 31. Yet, ratification without a commitment to implement the norm sends a very different message.
72   "Global Corruption Barometer 2015/16/17", *Transparency International* (Web Page, 2018) <https://www.transparency.org/research/gcb/gcb_2015_16/0>.

articles to the UNCAC – "to promote and strengthen measures to prevent and combat corruption more efficiently and effectively",[73] as well as to facilitate cooperation between the parties in corruption matters.[74]

Focusing on the former, any domestication and enforcement of the obligations contained in the conventions that would not help in combatting corruption more efficiently or effectively would meet the legal requirements of the conventions but not fulfil their spirit, as captured in the articles stating their objectives. An example of this would be the domestication of the obligations stated in conventional anti-corruption norms through the enactment and enforcement of laws that meet the conventions' standards, but which are not real deterrents for corruption because they are accompanied by procedural rules that make prosecutions impossible, a lack of interest by prosecutors or an executive practice of amnesties for those crimes.

### 2.2.3  Preliminary Conclusion on the Set of Explanations

Overall, for the six reasons detailed above, it seems plausible that conventional anti-corruption law will keep failing in its objective to effectively fight corruption. It is not a matter of giving more time to these conventions to develop their full effect. The argument here is that this lack of effectiveness is linked to an intrinsic flaw in their design. Section 3 looks at what else could be done within international law, namely international trade law, using the example of the anti-corruption chapter in the TPP11.

## 3  Fighting Corruption through International Trade Law: The Anti-corruption Chapter in the TPP11

The TPP11 is a free trade agreement ("FTA") between Australia, Brunei Darussalam, Canada, Chile, Japan, Malaysia, Mexico, Peru, New Zealand, Singapore and Vietnam. It was signed by those 11 countries on 8 March 2018 in Santiago, Chile, and entered into force on 30 December 2018, 60 days after achieving six ratifications (Australia, Canada, Japan, Mexico, New Zealand and Singapore). On 14 January 2019, Vietnam joined the countries bound by the agreement. Brunei Darussalam, Chile, Malaysia and Peru are, at the time of writing, in the process of ratification. The TPP11 will extend its geographical application to those countries 60 days after they complete their respective ratification processes.

---

73   UNCAC (n 39) art 1(a); AUCPCC (n 45) art 2.1; IACAC (n 45) art II.1.
74   UNCAC (n 39) art 1(b); AUCPCC (n 45) art 2.2; IACAC (n 45) art II.2.

The *TPP11*, as the revival of the *Trans-Pacific Partnership Agreement* ("*TPP*"), is meant to be more than an FTA. Some authors have gone as far as to say that the original *TPP* was a "unique" type of agreement designed "to reach further behind the border than any previous free trade or investment agreement".[75] This fanfare – encouraged by public declarations of the then US Trade Representative[76] and the former US Foreign Secretary[77] – supported the view that the *TPP* was also a political tool.[78] The same officials saw the agreement as one prong of the bi-dimensional pivot (in terms of both trade relations and military presence) to Asia of the US. Its final objective would be to attract countries to a regulatory regime[79] that would counter the "spectre of geopolitical and economic competition from China".[80] All these statements seem more difficult to sustain in regards to the *TPP11*, as (i) it does not count the US as a party,[81] and (ii) it has removed many of the US-imposed clauses from its final text.[82]

In any case, the *TPP11* is, as an heir to the *TPP*, an ambitious agreement,[83] covering new grounds[84] through the creation of new "rules to deal with the

---

75 Jane Kelsey, "The Trans-Pacific Partnership Agreement: A Gold-Plated Gift to the Global Tobacco Industry?" (2013) 39(2–3) *American Journal of Law & Medicine* 237, 237, 241.

76 "The Trans-Pacific Partnership: Strengthening Good Governance", *United States Trade Representative* (Fact Sheet, May 2016) <https://ustr.gov/sites/default/files/TPP-Strengthening-Good-Governance-Fact-Sheet.pdf>.

77 Lauren Carroll, "What Hillary Clinton Really Said about TPP and the 'Gold Standard'", *Politifact* (Web Page, 13 October 2015) <https://www.politifact.com/truth-o-meter/statements/2015/oct/13/hillary-clinton/what-hillary-clinton-really-said-about-tpp-and-gol/>.

78 In the same line, see Ian F Fergusson and Bruce Vaughn, *Trans-Pacific Partnership Agreement* (Publication, 7 November 2010) 2.

79 Ibid 6.

80 Kelsey (n 75) 239.

81 Donald J Trump, "Presidential Memorandum Regarding Withdrawal of the United States from the Trans-Pacific Partnership Negotiations and Agreement", *White House* (Presidential Memorandum, 23 January 2017) <https://www.whitehouse.gov/presidential-actions/presidential-memorandum-regarding-withdrawal-united-states-trans-pacific-partnership-negotiations-agreement/>.

82 *TPP11* (n 6) art 2 establishes that the clauses and footnotes listed in its annex (many of them addressing important issues for the United States) are suspended "until the Parties agree to end suspension of one or more of these provisions".

83 Peter A Petri and Michael G Plummer, "The Trans-Pacific Partnership and Asia-Pacific Integration: Policy Implications" (Policy Brief, Peterson Institute for International Economics, 15 June 2012) 2–3.

84 In the words of the editors of a recent book on the *Trans-Pacific Partnership*, the agreement will have "improved and enhanced rules on traditional issues already covered by the WTO, such as goods, services and intellectual property rights, but also the carefully-designed rules in areas which have never been addressed or so widely addressed in the WTO or even other FTAs, such as state-owned enterprises, electronic commerce and labor

challenges in many key areas".[85] For the purpose of this article, I will only discuss Chapter 26, titled "Transparency and Anti-Corruption", here.

### 3.1   Overview of Chapter 26 of the TPP11

Chapter 26 is a remarkable achievement. Compared to other regional trade agreements, the anti-corruption provisions in the TPP figure prominently.[86] The Office of the US Trade Representative claimed at the time of the release of the text that the TPP "set a new high standard for action against corruption through a trade agreement".[87]

Given that no official documents about the negotiations were released,[88] it is difficult to understand how and when it was decided to incorporate these clauses into the agreement. A 2010 US congressional report does not include any reference to transparency or corruption in the issues open to discussion, but it does hint at the intention of expanding to areas beyond the normal scope of FTAs.[89] Some have linked it to a push by Transparency International to include similar wording in the (now defunct) *Transatlantic Trade and Investment Partnership* ("TTIP"),[90] but this seems like a bit of a stretch given the lack of traction of those clauses in the TTIP. However, in the TTIP, a US-originated proposal, based on the US *Foreign Corrupt Practices Act*,[91] was indeed discussed.[92]

---

and environmental issues." Julien Chaisse, Henry Gao and Chang-fa Lo (eds), *Paradigm Shift in International Economic Law Rule-Making* (Springer Berlin Heidelberg, 2017) 3.

85   Ibid. For a similar argument, see Jeffrey J Schott, Barbara Kotschwar and Julia Muir, *Understanding the Trans-Pacific Partnership* (Peterson Institute, 2013) 61.

86   Chang-fa Lo, "Anti-Corruption Provisions in the TPP: Innovation, Effectiveness and Prospects" in Julien Chaisse, Henry Gao and Chang-fa Lo (eds), *Paradigm Shift in International Economic Law Rule-Making: TPP as a New Model for Trade Agreements?* (Springer Singapore, 2017) 205, 206.

87   "The Trans-Pacific Partnership: Strengthening Good Governance" (n 75) 1.

88   Kelsey ( n 76) 240.

89   Fergusson and Vaughn (n 78) 8.

90   Kaitlin Beach, "A Trade-Anticorruption Breakthrough?: The Trans-Pacific Partnership's Transparency and Anticorruption Chapter", *The Global Anticorruption Blog* (Web Page, 23 November 2015) <https://globalanticorruptionblog.com/2015/11/23/the-trans-pacific-partnerships-transparency-and-anticorruption-chapter/>.

91   Bundesverband der Deutschen Industrie, "Anti-Corruption in TTIP" (Position, 22 September 2016) 2 <https://english.bdi.eu/media/.../TTIP/.../BDI_Position_Anti-Korruption_englisch.pdf>.

92   European Commission, "The Transatlantic Trade and Investment Partnership (TTIP) – State of Play" (Summary, 27 April 2016) 9 <trade.ec.europa.eu/doclib/docs/2016/april/tradoc_154477.pdf>.

This may suggest a will of the US negotiators to incorporate anti-corruption clauses in trade agreements as a broader policy position.

Chapter 26 is followed by annex 26-A regarding transparency and procedural fairness for pharmaceutical products and medical devices. Especially when compared to Chapter 26, this annex has received a surprising amount of attention by scholars on both sides of the Pacific Ocean.[93] Based on its position in the treaty, its numbering, and the titles of both sections, it would be reasonable to assume that annex 26-A establishes a subset of rules for pharmaceutical products and medical devices, deriving its more general principles from Chapter 26. However, despite the similar names and consecutive positions, the areas regulated are completely different. Annex 26-A's main objective is to set certain guidelines for the rules regarding reimbursement by national health care authorities of pharmaceutical products. This concept of transparency departs from the way it is normally used in anti-corruption norms and, consequently, from the scope of this article.

Chapter 26 is divided into three sections: definitions, transparency and anti-corruption. Section A ("definitions") is surprisingly short, especially when compared to the legislative verbosity of other parts of the treaty. In line with other international agreements on the issue of corruption,[94] it does not define "corruption", dwelling instead on the concept of "public official" and their "acts", whilst also establishing what is an administrative ruling of general application.[95]

Section B, "transparency", follows the structure and meaning of similar sections in other FTAs signed by the US ten years earlier, notably Chapter 21 (titled "Transparency", although having one article on anti-corruption) of the *US-Korea Free Trade Agreement*.[96] It covers two separate issues. One falls in

---

93   Erik Monasterio and Deborah Gleeson, "Pharmaceutical Industry Behaviour and the Trans Pacific Partnership Agreement" (2014) 127(1389) *New Zealand Medical Journal* 6; Brook K Baker and Katrina Geddes, "Corporate Power Unbound: Investor-State Arbitration of IP Monopolies on Medicines-Eli Lilly v. Canada and the Trans-Pacific Partnership Agreement" (2015) 23(1) *Journal of Intellectual Property Law* 1; Ronald Labonté, Ashley Schram and Arne Ruckert, "The Trans-Pacific Partnership: Is It Everything We Feared for Health?" (2016) 5(8) *International Journal of Health Policy and Management* 487; Brook K Baker, "Trans-Pacific Partnership Provisions in Intellectual Property, Transparency, and Investment Chapters Threaten Access to Medicines in the US and Elsewhere" (2016) 13(3) *PLoS Medicine* e1001970; Joel Lexchin and Deborah Gleeson, "The Trans Pacific Partnership Agreement and Pharmaceutical Regulation in Canada and Australia" (2016) 46(4) *International Journal of Health Services* 597.

94   Martin (n 41) 5.

95   Bonell and Meyer (n 36); *TPP11* (n 6) art 26.1.

96   *US-Korea FTA* (n 56).

what is commonly understood as transparency in other international instruments[97] – even if it is difficult to find a generally accepted definition of transparency.[98] Articles 26.2 (publication), 26.3 (administrative proceedings) and 26.5 (provision of information) fall within this group. These articles establish certain requirements from the parties focusing on the *final result* of applying transparency to the issues referred to. The guiding principle here is that the enactment of norms, administrative proceedings and information-sharing should be conducted in a way that make available to the interested persons or state parties all the information relevant for evaluating these institutional acts.[99]

Article 26.4 (review and appeal), on the other hand, points to a more procedural aspect. It requires (using the word "shall") a "prompt review ... of a final administrative action with respect to any matter covered by this Agreement"[100] by tribunals which are "impartial and independent of the office or authority entrusted with administrative enforcement and [with no] substantial interest in the outcome of the matter".[101]

Finally, Section C includes provisions on more traditional anti-corruption matters. Several have argued that they are the "most detailed anti-corruption provisions in all FTAs and other trade agreements".[102] The next paragraphs look at these provisions in detail and assess them against the explanations offered in Section 2 of this article on how to increase the effectiveness of international law in the fight against corruption.

The anti-corruption section of Chapter 26 opens with an ambitious declaration, in which "the Parties affirm their resolve to eliminate bribery and corruption in international trade and investment",[103] tempered by the following paragraph, which limits the scope of the section "to measures to eliminate bribery and corruption with respect to any matter covered by this Agreement".[104] This

---

97   One recent attempt to offer a holistic concept – "Transparency, as broadly defined, relates to the full flow of information within a polity" (James R Hollyer, B Peter Rosendorff and James Raymond Vreeland, "Measuring Transparency" (2014) 22(4) *Political Analysis* 413, 413) – can probably cover the concept of transparency as conceived by a majority of academic authors, but does not help much in understanding what transparency actually means.

98   Monika Bauhr and Naghmeh Nasiritousi, "Resisting Transparency: Corruption, Legitimacy, and the Quality of Global Environmental Policies" (2012) 12(4) *Global Environmental Politics* 9, 11; Kerem Öge, "The Limits of Transparency Promotion in Azerbaijan: External Remedies to 'Reverse the Curse'" (2014) 66(9) *Europe-Asia Studies* 1482; Öge (n 24).

99   Bauhr and Nasiritousi (n 98) 11.

100  *TPPII* (n 6) art 26.4.1.

101  Ibid art 26.4.1.

102  Lo (n 86) 206; see also Mungiu-Pippidi (n 67) 22.

103  *TPPII* (n 6) art 26.6.1.

104  Ibid art 26.6.2.

is a logical approach. It would not be reasonable to expect the anti-corruption section to extend to other trade and investment issues outside of the scope of the *TPP11*. Hence, the rules in Section C only cover the relations between the parties (*ratione personae*) and are limited to those issues not excluded from its subjective scope (*ratione materiae*).

From a positive point of view this means that the rules in Section C of Chapter 26 extend to government procurement matters (Chapter 15, an area where corruption can severely affect trade, as addressed already by the World Trade Organization's ("WTO") *Agreement on Government Procurement*),[105] but it also covers investment matters, regulated in Chapter 9 of the *TPP11*, as well as other trade-related matters such as temporary entry for business persons (visas notably, in Chapter 12), competition (Chapter 16) and state-owned enterprises (Chapter 17).[106]

From a negative perspective, art 26.6.2 entails, for example, that a party which fails, on a recurring basis, to effectively enforce its laws or other measures to combat corruption in relation to investment affecting a company from a country not covered by the *TPP11* would not be in violation of art 26.9.1. *A contrario*, if its inaction were affecting an entity of a state party to the *TPP11*, it would be a violation of that article.[107] Also from a negative perspective, but in reference to the subjective scope covered by the agreements, corruption in the context of areas covered by *TPP11* exceptions (such as trade in arms and ammunitions between *TPP11* parties) would not be protected by the anti-corruption clauses.[108]

---

105  See *Marrakesh Agreement Establishing the World Trade Organization*, opened for signature 15 April 1994, 1867 UNTS 3 (entered into force 1 January 1995), annex 4(b) ("*Agreement on Government Procurement*"); *Marrakesh Agreement Establishing the World Trade Organization*, opened for signature 15 April 1994, 1867 UNTS 3 (entered into force 1 January 1995), annex 4(b) ("*Revised Agreement on Government Procurement*"); see also Krista Nadakavukaren Schefer, "Will the WTO Finally Tackle Corruption in Public Purchasing? The Revised Agreement on Government Procurement", *American Society of International Law* (15 April 2013) <https://www.asil.org/insights/volume/17/issue/11/will-wto-finally-tackle-corruption-public-purchasing-revised-agreement>; Chang-fa Lo, "Anti-Corruption Provisions in the New GPA" (2016) 7(1) *Trade, Law and Development* 21.

106  Lo (n 86) 211 makes a similar argument referring to other parts of the agreement.

107  Although in light of the wording of art 26.9.1, one could argue that even the lack of implementation in relation to non-parties of anti-corruption measures could discourage trade and investment and, hence, violate the "spirit" of the agreement. This point about "the letter and the spirit" in trade agreements is discussed below.

108  Lo makes a more sophisticated argument, which disagrees with this literal reading. The former WTO panellist and current constitutional judge in Taiwan believes that if there are corruptions involved in such trade activities, a possible issue is whether such exempted trade matters are still within the scope of "any matter covered by this Agreement" as

Once these limits are clear, we can look at the concrete obligations established by Section C of Chapter 26 of the *TPP11*. Table 2 provides a (very simplified) summary of the different obligations. At first sight, most of the obligations incorporated in the *TPP11* are basically the transposition of obligations already existing in the context of the Organisation for Economic Co-operation and Development's (OECD) anti-corruption framework or the UNCAC (marked in grey). The *TPP11* includes an obligation to ratify (or accede) to the UNCAC (art 26.6.4), with limited practical value as all eleven members of the agreement have already done so.[109] It could become relevant if other countries were to join the *TPP11* in the future, but as we have seen before, almost all countries in the Pacific region are already parties to the UNCAC, the only exception being the Democratic People's Republic of Korea. In that sense, art 26.6.4 is better understood as being a strong declaration by the signatories of their adherence to the objectives of the United Nations instrument.

Among the "new" obligations, art 26.9.1, transcribed below, appears to be the cornerstone of the chapter:

> Article 26.9: Application and Enforcement of Anti-Corruption Laws 1. In accordance with the fundamental principles of its legal system, no Party shall fail to effectively enforce its laws or other measures adopted or maintained to comply with Article 26.7.1 (Measures to Combat Corruption) through a sustained or recurring course of action or inaction, after the date of entry into force of this Agreement for that Party, as an encouragement for trade and investment.

The importance of this clause cannot be overstated. Even if it is qualified by making an allowance for discretion in its implementation through a footnote (number eight)[110] and the following paragraph (art 26.9.2, referring to the discretion of authorities on enforcement and allocation of resources),[111] the

---

provided by Article 26.6.2. ... [Lo] would argue that the measures which are subject to TPP's exceptions are still those "matters" covered by the TPP. It is merely that some "obligations" are exempted from the obligations under the TPP for the Parties. A bribery provided in connection with trade in arms and ammunitions should still be the "matter covered by the TPP" and hence regulated by the anti-corruption provisions in Chapter 26 of the TPP. Lo (n 86) 212.

109 "United Nations Convention against Corruption" (n 64). At the time of the drafting of the original *TPP*, some countries had not yet ratified the UNCAC.

110 Footnote 8 explains that "[f]or greater certainty, the Parties recognise that individual cases or specific discretionary decisions related to the enforcement of anti-corruption laws are subject to each Party's own domestic laws and legal procedures".

111 The second paragraph of the article establishes that:

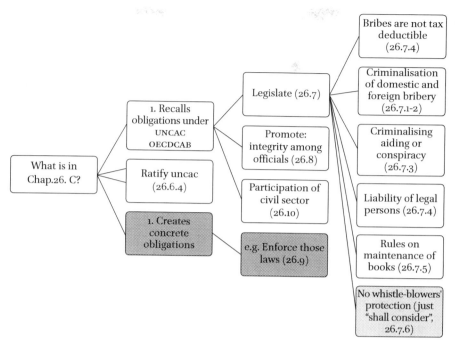

TABLE 2    Obligations in Section C of Chapter 26 of the *TPP11*

obligation to actually enforce the anti-corruption legislation means that parties shall actively prosecute corruption in matters related to the *TPP11*.

This article closes with a cryptic reference linking this obligation to being "an encouragement for trade and investment". Although this final clause could be interpreted as a restriction to its scope – i.e., that only failures to implement which are tantamount to a deterrent to trade or investment would be a violation of art 26.9.1 – a contextual reading would support a more expansive understanding and an assumption that any failure to effectively enforce the relevant laws or other measures in an issue related to the treaty will not "encourage trade and investment" and hence meet the threshold of the article. One can then imagine the potential impact of such a clause, for example, in regard to customs, often identified as a major hindrance for trade:[112] all plausible

---

"[i]n accordance with the fundamental principles of its legal system, each Party retains the right for its law enforcement, prosecutorial and judicial authorities to exercise their discretion with respect to the enforcement of its anticorruption laws. Each Party retains the right to take bona fide decisions with regard to the allocation of its resources ...."

112   As one author put it, "each step of the customs chain can present an opportunity for a corrupt act": Irène Hors, "Fighting Corruption in Customs Administration: What Can We

complaints regarding corrupt practices in customs processes must be actively investigated.

In counterpoint to this break-through clause, the lack of agreement to bind the parties to pass legislation granting protection to whistle-blowers is remarkable. Article 26.7.6, which could be seen as a compromise between diverging views, simply mandates that parties

> shall consider adopting or maintaining measures to protect, against any unjustified treatment, any person who, in good faith and on reasonable grounds, reports to the competent authorities any facts concerning [the offences that must be incorporated into the domestic legislation according to article 26.7].

### 3.2 How Does Chapter 26 of the *TPP11* Address the limitations of Conventional Anti-corruption Law

To assess how effective Chapter 26 can be in preventing corrupt practices – within its scope – in *TPP11* signatory countries, I revisit here the six limitations for the effectiveness of existing conventional anti-corruption law outlined in Section 2.2 above. I analyse how the *TPP11* addresses these shortcomings. When it does not provide a solution for those limitations, I distinguish whether this is due to the specific wording of the *TPP11* or to the way in which international trade law operates.

#### 3.2.1 Mechanical Limitations

##### 3.2.1.1 *Lack of Systematic Domestication*

The first possible explanation was the lack of systematic domestication of the obligations. This was the main limitation among those related to the mechanisms used in international law. Theoretically speaking, international trade law would suffer the same problem as conventional anti-corruption law. As with most international obligations, the rules established in the *TPP11* lack direct effect over individuals.[113] This, in turn, requires a process to incorporate these obligations into domestic law. In general, this is the logical consequence

---

Learn from Recent Experiences?" (Working Paper No 175, OECD Development Centre, April 2001) 15; see also Dean Yang, "The Economics of Anti-Corruption: Lessons from a Widespread Customs Reform" in Susan Rose-Ackerman (ed), *International Handbook on the Economics of Corruption* (Edward Elgar Publishing, 2006) 512.

113  See Andrea K Schneider, "Democracy and Dispute Resolution: Individual Rights in International Trade Organizations" (1998) 19(2) *University of Pennsylvania Journal of International Economic Law* 587, 596–600.

of having the same addressees as anti-corruption conventions: i.e,. state parties and not individuals. However, a significant number of trade law norms ultimately intend to create rights for individual companies or persons, such as a right to be protected against discrimination on the basis of the origin of the goods, or a right to receive analogous treatment to local providers of services.[114]

This creates a strong incentive for domestication, as local companies interested in enjoying those rights abroad would push their own legislators to incorporate those obligations in their domestic jurisdictions. Trade law therefore creates an incentive for local stakeholders to push for the domestication of international norms, with the advantage that those stakeholders normally enjoy a certain degree of economic power. The *TPP11* is no exception, with companies lobbying their governments to continue the process after the withdrawal of the US from the original TPP.[115] In countries with monist systems which are part of the *TPP11* – such as Chile, Mexico or Peru – this problem is partially avoided. The agreement became part of their domestic law immediately after ratification, opening the door for a certain degree of direct effect of its provisions. In broad terms, I contend that parties are likely to be more inclined to domesticate trade law agreements – and hence the corruption clauses built into them – than conventional anti-corruption law, notably in two cases. Firstly, this is likely to be the case in countries where civil society groups pushing for anti-corruption measures lack the political clout to influence legislators, as the push will also come from economic operators and their lobbies. Secondly, this also applies to countries appearing to be more reluctant to effectively fight corruption;[116] there would be a push also coming from within governments, particularly by the ministries with economic-related portfolios (agriculture, industry, trade, etc.).

---

114  Ibid 598–599.
115  See, eg, in Australia: "TPP-11", *Parliament of Australia* (Web Page) <https://www.aph.gov.au/Parliamentary_Business/Committees/Joint/Treaties/TPP-11/Submissions?main_0_content_1_RadGrid1ChangePage=3_20>; and, particularly, Business Council of Australia, Submission No 35 to Senate Foreign Affairs, Defence and Trade References Committee, Parliament of Australia, *Inquiry into the Proposed Comprehensive and Progressive Agreement for Trans-Pacific Partnership (TPP-11)* (May 2018).
116  Peru and Mexico, two monist countries, are ranked respectively at 105 and 138 in the "Corruption Perceptions Index 2018", *Transparency International* (Web Page, 2018) <https://www.transparency.org/cpi2018>, which contains data in respect of 180 countries. Australia, an identified decliner in the index, could also benefit from an adequate domestication of the *TPP11* obligations: see José-Miguel Bello y Villarino, "What Does Australia's Ranking in the Corruption Perception Index Mean?", *Australian Institute of International Affairs* (Web Page, 5 February 2019) <http://www.internationalaffairs.org.au/australianoutlook/australias-orange-ranking-corruption-perception-index/>.

#### 3.2.1.2 Lack of External Enforcement Mechanisms

Secondly, as mentioned before, the obstacles to domestication of the anti-corruption conventions have been exacerbated by the lack of external enforcement mechanisms. This problem is eliminated if the anti-corruption clauses are subject to the DSMs built into trade agreements. In the case of the *TPP11*, there are two distinct DSMs: investor-state (Chapter 9) and – WTO-type – state-state (Chapter 28) mechanisms.

The application of the investor-state mechanism to rights established in Chapter 26 could only take place in very limited circumstances. In case of a violation of the substantive rights established in Chapter 26, Section C, it seems reasonable to strictly interpret art 26.12 in a way that those violations can only be litigated according to the rules of Chapter 28 and not under Chapter 9. Article 26.12 states that "Chapter 28 (Dispute Settlement), as modified by this Article, shall apply to this Section", excluding *a contrario* bringing a claim under Chapter 9. Article 9.19.1(a)(i), establishing the concrete requirements for submission of investment claims to arbitration, clearly supports this interpretation.

Nevertheless, it could be possible for an investor to file a complaint against a state for the violation of one of the substantive rights established in Chapter 9 in connection to the procedural rights established in Chapter 26. Nothing in Chapter 26 precludes this possibility.[117] For example, a violation of the rights under art 9.4 (national treatment) without allowing for "a *prompt* review … of a final administrative action" (art 26.4). This would happen, for example, if the foreign incorporation of the investor was causing an unreasonable delay in the review process, when compared to a national investor. The wording of that article opening it "to any matter covered by this Agreement" seems to point in that direction.

Yet, this would be a rather exceptional case. Corruption matters are more likely to be subjected to the DSM established in Chapter 28. The risk of being dragged to a panel has the potential of creating a significant incentive for state-parties to comply with their obligations, as there is no possibility here – in contrast with what is happening in the *UNCAC* context detailed above – to introduce any reservations to Chapter 28.

However, as Lo previously pointed out, in relation to the *TPP*,[118] the dispute settlement mechanism can only be applied to anti-corruption matters (Chapter 26, Section C) in a limited manner. Article 26.12.3 excludes "strong" obligations connected to individual enforcement – i.e., those imposed through

---

117  Lo (n 105) 211.
118  Lo (n 86) 219.

"shall": 26.9.1 (effective enforcement) or 26.9.2 (discretionary enforcement) – from the DSM. Substantive "shall" obligations, actually covered by Chapter 28, refer mainly to legislative enactment of anti-corruption measures, which suffer from the same shortcomings identified above in relation to conventional anti-corruption law (see, for example, art 26.7) or are not likely to create a litigable offence – one cannot imagine violations of art 26.2, which establishes the obligation to promptly publish laws, regulations, procedures and administrative rulings of general application, ever being put to a panel.

Contrarily, art 26.4 (review and appeal), as explained before, may be a better candidate for litigation. This article not only establishes the right to a "prompt review ... of a final administrative action with respect to any matter covered by this Agreement", but also that the tribunals reviewing those actions "shall be impartial and independent of the office or authority entrusted with administrative enforcement and shall not have any substantial interest in the outcome of the matter". This is the type of anti-corruption clause that creates a substantive obligation with incisive teeth, even if was not negotiated as an anti-corruption clause as such. If state-state DSM covered more substantive clauses than this one – note here that art 26.4 (in Section B) is outside of the scope of 26.12.3, which refers to articles in that section (Section C) – we could expect the *TPP11* to become a powerful anti-corruption tool.

Finally, one can imagine a very contentious example of possible application of the investor-state DSM to 26.9.1 (effective enforcement) or 26.9.2 (discretionary enforcement). It could happen that a substantive right from Chapter 9 could be violated in connection to a procedural right of Chapter 26 Section C (anti-corruption). For example, a discretionary enforcement of an anti-corruption clause without *bona fide* because of the origin of the investor would fit that description. Such a decision would be excluded from the state-state DSM (Chapter 28) but it could potentially be subjected to the investor-state DSM (Chapter 9). In my view, although a literal interpretation of the text would allow investor-state litigation in this case, the intent of the parties appears instead to exclude art 26.9 from litigation, as one of the most intrusive obligations of the chapter in the sovereignty of the parties. The logic of art 26.12.3 seems to be the parties' desire to preserve their margin of appreciation in relation to enforcement of anti-corruption measures.

In relation to this discussion, one further appreciation is necessary. Trade law-style DSMs are better suited to deal with corruption than investment-related arbitration due to their different nature: investor-state disputes involve litigations for compensation, whereas trade-related state-state or private-state litigations not only seek redress of the wrong, but also aim to establish a rule of law in trade relations. This is manifested, for example, in the principle of transparency often linked to decisions on trade disputes.[119] Despite an increasing tendency to open an increasing number of investment arbitration procedures and awards to greater public scrutiny, the default position in investment tribunals remains confidentiality.[120] Trade DSMs provide a significant advantage in terms of their potential ability to adequately place blame. The DSM of the *TPP11* will make its decisions public, following the WTO practice.[121] This opens the possibility of having clearly detailed decisions, accessible to all, which will establish certain facts and the norm violated (or not). The objective of these decisions will be to impose an end to the corrupt practice as it hinders trade or investment among the parties, and not merely to grant compensation.

Further, if the DSM of Chapter 9 of the *TPP11* were to follow the *Methanex* precedent in the context of the *North American Free Trade Agreement ("NAFTA")*,[122] DSM procedures could provide civil society and the population at large with an independent forum where their opinion could be heard and taken into consideration, even in investment-related disputes.[123] In the context of a comprehensive agreement such as the *TPP11*, it is not difficult to imagine how clauses on corruption, procurement and protection of foreign investment could all be applicable to the same factual situation. In this context, a final decision on corruption claims in procurement procedures covered by the *TPP11* would not have a criminal value, but it would provide a legal space for accountability. It could establish relevant facts, which the media could amplify, allocating responsibility for corrupt practices to organs, even if not to individuals. Without reaching the level of Carrington's proposal[124] to allow private companies or other victims of corruption to claim compensations from perpetrators (private actors or government officials), creating an independent forum

---

119 For more on the case of the WTO, see Michael Ioannidis, "Can International Trade Law Promote Legitimacy? The Participatory Dimension of WTO Law" in Sinthiou Buszewski, Stefan Martini and Hannes Rathke (eds), *Freihandel vs Demokratie* (Nomos Verlagsgesellschaft mbH & Co KG, 2016) 183.

120 Azhaham Perumal Saravanan and Subramanian Ramamurthy Subramanian, "Transparency and Confidentiality Requirements in Investment Treaty Arbitration Comments" (2018) 5(4) BRICS *Law Journal* 114, 116.

121 *TPP11* (n 6) art 28.18.2.

122 *Methanex Corporation v United States of America (Decision of the Tribunal on Petitions from Third Persons to Intervene as "Amici Curiae")* (25 January 2001). See *North American Free Trade Agreement*, signed 17 December 1992, 32 ILM 289 (entered into force 1 January 1994).

123 This is likely to be the case: see *TPP11* (n 6) art 9.23.3.

124 Paul D Carrington, "Enforcing International Corrupt Practices Law" (2010) 32(1) *Michigan Journal of International Law* 129, 162.

where corruption issues connected to the scope of the *TPP11* are aired, is a promising approach.

#### 3.2.1.3  Other Issues Related to Domestication and Enforcement.

Moving now to the other "mechanical limitations" discussed above, the lack of clear deadlines for Chapter 26 are remarkable, especially when compared to the hard negotiations for tariff schedules. On this basis, any insufficiency of the legislative framework of a state party to meet the standards set in the transparency and anti-corruption chapter would be a violation of the agreement from the day after the entry into force of the *TPP11* (i.e., according to art 3, 60 days after ratification of the sixth party or 60 days after ratification for the seventh and following signatories). Yet, as noted above, it is unlikely that those obligations would ever be a cause of a dispute submitted to a panel. Given the novelty of the chapter, the best approach would be to understand this obligation in line with similar ones in environment or labour chapters in other trade agreements, although these are often drafted as justifications to impose certain restrictions on other treaty obligations.[125]

Regarding the issue of the implementation of the obligations by subnational entities, there is no doubt about the responsibility of the central government for all decentralised levels, as is the case in general with international trade law. The *TPP11* includes an annex 1A to Chapter 1, clearly identifying specifically which entities are to be considered as central and regional levels of government. In any case, the WTO experience has sufficiently clarified that, regardless of the origin of the violation, the responsibility is clearly allocated to authorities at the national level,[126] which will suffer any potential consequence, such as retaliatory measures. This, in turn, creates a strong incentive for the central level of government to ensure that all entities within the state's structure comply with their obligations.

Looking at these three limitations together, it appears that the *TPP11* has not sufficiently exploited all the potential of international trade law to address the mechanical shortcomings identified in conventional anti-corruption law. The

---

125  See, eg, *TPP11* (n 6) arts 20.3.2, 20.3.6.

126  See a discussion of the issue in connection to the attribution of responsibility in Santiago M Villalpando, "Attribution of Conduct to the State: How the Rules of State Responsibility May Be Applied Within the WTO Dispute Settlement System" (2002) 5(2) *Journal of International Economic Law* 393. Hayes offers, however, an interesting (although dated) take on the issue: see Edward T Hayes, "Changing Notions of Sovereignty and Federalism in the International Economic System: A Reassessment of WTO Regulation of Federal States and the Regional and Local Governments within Their Territories" (2004) 25(1) *Northwestern Journal of International Law & Business* 1.

*TPP11* has, however, addressed in a slightly more effective manner the limitations related to the substance and content of the existing conventions.

### 3.2.2 Substantive Limitations

#### 3.2.2.1 *Lack of Punitive Effects*

Firstly, although the *TPP11* opens the door to punitive measures, there are significant problems in how that would operate in practice. In principle, the offended party, after resorting to the DSM of Chapter 28, could be authorised to suspend the benefits that the party in violation of the agreement enjoys (art 28.20.2). However, it is difficult to imagine how it could do it in the "same subject matter" (art 28.20.4(a)) or take into account the factors listed in art 28.20.4(c)[127] for suspension in a different subject matter. A possible solution would be requesting a monetary assessment (art 28.20.7). Yet this option is conditioned to the acquiescence of the offender and limited by strict deadlines.

From a more philosophical point of view, this system of punitive measures points to a second problem: it creates a misalignment between the ultimate culprit of a violation of Chapter 11 (a private person or an individual official) and the entity having to compensate for that behaviour (the state), which has already suffered the economic consequences of the corrupt practices – in terms of an unfair procurement, a deviation of funds and/or restrictions to economic activity, for example. In a way, a trade law-style compensation for a corrupt practice represents a double punishment for the offending State.

#### 3.2.2.2 *Implementation by the Subjects of the Norms*

Secondly, regarding the implementation of the *TPP11* anti-corruption clauses, nominally there is no difference with conventional anti-corruption law. Implementation of the legislative obligations and enforcement of the anti-corruption norms included in the *TPP11* are equally entrusted to the real final addressees of Chapter 26: namely, legislators and public officials of a state party in their different capacities. Yet there is an essential difference in international trade law, as the state of origin of the entity suffering the effects of the violation has an incentive – protecting its own nationals, whether an individual

---

127 Namely, "(i) the trade in the good, the supply of the service or other subject matter in which the panel has found the nonconformity or nullification or impairment, and the importance of that trade to the complaining Party; (ii) that goods, all financial services covered under Chapter 11 (Financial Services), services other than such financial services, and each section in Chapter 18 (Intellectual Property), are each distinct subject matters; and (iii) the broader economic elements related to the nullification or impairment and the broader economic consequences of the suspension of benefits."

person or a company – to discuss the issue with the state in violation of the anti-corruption norm. The latter has also an incentive to discuss and solve the issue as it could always be taken to a DSM and suffer the consequences of a potentially adverse decision.

Furthermore, implementation can also be pushed from within the country. In general, the individuals conducting trade-related implementation talks (such as prime ministers' offices or foreign affairs and trade ministries) are not likely to be the same as those receiving bribes or allowing corrupt practices, except for in cases of state capture. Thus, there is a higher likelihood of top-down implementation and enforcement. Yet, in the context of the *TPP11*, the actual incentives to implement and enforce these anti-corruption clauses may be limited. As mentioned before, only legislative reform is a real obligation ("shall"), whilst proving trade-related damage to entities from other countries as a result of the lack of legislative reform may prove impossible. This eliminates the threat of a negative DSM resolution.

3.2.2.3    *Compliance with the "Letter" but Not the "Spirit" of the Law.*
Thirdly, trade law offers a relatively solid jurisprudence affirming that it is not sufficient to nominally comply with the "letter" of the law if the effects of the measures established in compliance with the relevant trade agreement are not in accordance with the more general objectives of the agreement. For instance, a domestic norm allowing companies to deduct expenses incurred for operations in a foreign country in relation to payments to any individual working in a customs office from their tax obligations, as far as those payments have not been established as bribery in the courts of the relevant foreign country, would, strictly speaking, satisfy the requirements set in art 26.7.4 of the *TPP11*. In practice, however, such a norm would not discourage foreign bribery and would undermine the parties' resolution "to eliminate bribery and corruption in international trade and investment", as stated in art 26.6.

In this sense, the jurisprudence of the WTO and other trade agreements which addresses this issue specifically is enlightening.[128] It is not sufficient to meet on paper the requirements of the norms if their effect does not achieve the objectives set in the treaty.

Finally, there is another substantive issue in the *TPP11* that may affect how effective Chapter 26 can be if a dispute ever makes it to a DSM panel. Article 26.11 includes a cryptic clause stating that nothing in this chapter should affect

---

128    Appellate Body Report, *European Communities – Regime for the Importation, Sale and Distribution of Bananas – Recourse to Article 21.5 of the DSU by Ecuador*, WTO Doc WT/DS27/AB/R,W/USA; WT/DS27/AB/RW2/ECU (26 November 2008) [142].

the rights and obligations of the parties under UNCAC, the OECD *Agreement* or the IACAC. One could then argue that any violation of a norm of the TPP11 aligning with obligation established in those conventions should be resolved through the mechanisms envisaged in those conventions and not those in the trade agreement. Such an interpretation would undermine any effective application of the anti-corruption clauses included in the TPP11, which can also be found in conventional anti-corruption law. As we saw before, the majority of the obligations to pass anti-corruption legislation in the TPP11 are just a reproduction of the ones existing already in the UNCAC, the OECD *Agreement* and IACAC. In a similar line, the TPP11 includes certain modifications[129] to the consultation process required before bringing a dispute to a panel[130] that allow (i) for other Parties to be involved in the process and (ii) for anti-corruption authorities to participate in it. These modifications seem to have been inserted to bring the consultation process closer to the logic of the peer-review mechanisms existing in conventional anti-corruption norms,[131] as they promote a dialogue between several TPP11 parties, rather than an adversarial confrontation between just two parties in court.

## 4 Conclusion: Expected Impact of the TPP11 Anti-corruption Clauses

It appears, from an exegetic analysis of Chapter 26, that the "new high standard for action against corruption through a trade agreement" has been drafted to only marginally raise the bar of previous agreements, which were actually quite low, limiting itself to vague references to existing commitments[132] without creating any real actionable obligations. Nonetheless, there are three aspects that could engender a certain degree of optimism.

Firstly, the lack of any published negotiation documents or *travaux préparatoires* only allows for conjectures about the negotiation dynamics. From a transactional point of view, it would be reasonable to assume that among the

---

129 TPP11 (n 6) art 26.12.4.
130 Ibid art 28.5.
131 United Nations Office for Drug and Crime (n 42).
132 Before February 2018, four countries (and, hence, their counterparts) had inserted anti-corruption clauses into some of their bilateral investment treaties and trade-related agreements: Japan, Austria, Canada and the United States of America. The European Union and European Free Trade Area have included some corruption-related provisions as well in some of their investment-related agreements. For a detailed analysis of this area, see Yueming Yan, *Global Anti-Corruption Efforts in a New Era of International Investment Agreements: From the Perspectives of the EU and China* (2020) (provisional title, forthcoming).

negotiating parties some wanted an agreement with powerful anti-corruption clauses and that some did not. The final text reflects this possible disagreement, as it includes strongly-worded clauses but removes their teeth. This could be an unsettling precedent for future attempts to include substantive anti-corruption clauses in trade agreements. The European Commission, for example, has declared a goal of including in all ambitious anti-corruption provisions in its future trade agreements.[133] This ambition could be expected to face pushback from less enthralled negotiation partners.

An optimistic observer could see Chapter 26, contrarily, as a necessary first step to overcoming the reluctance of these unwilling countries. In this view, the *TPP11* is a precedent, although a modest one, for including anti-corruption clauses in a multilateral treaty.

Secondly, this article has stressed several times the way in which Chapter 26 has been undermined by intentionally restricting DSMs in regard to matters of corruption matters. The wording inserted in art 26.12.3 placing "strong" obligations connected to individual enforcement of anti-corruption legislations outside of the scope of Chapter 28, severely limits the teeth of the substantive obligations. Although some leading authors, such as Lo, have high expectations about the practical effects of this chapter,[134] particularly about the application of DSM in the *TPP* (the treaty he discussed) to corruption matters, I believe that the actual wording and scope of the clauses subjected to DSM would severely curtail those expectations. In my view, we are unlikely to witness any litigation linked to the anti-corruption section of Chapter 26 in the coming years.

On a slightly more positive note, however, the incapacity of the *TPP11* to address the shortcomings identified in conventional anti-corruption law highlights that this incapacity is mainly due to the specific wording of this treaty. The limitation of its anti-corruption norms is not of an institutional nature, but is just a matter of incorporating more incisive drafting. This could come as a result of a stronger negotiating position for the parties pushing for their inclusion. This illuminates the way to effectively address corruption in future international trade law agreements.

Thirdly, there is already some space for optimism in the text, although outside Section 3 (anti-corruption) of Chapter 26. In art 26.4, "review and appeal" in Section 2 (transparency) is a promising – and innovative[135] – clause to effectively address corruption. Its potential lies in four different elements.

---

133   Mungiu-Pippidi (n 67) 6.
134   Lo (n 86) 221.
135   Although *US-Korea FTA* (n 56) art 21.4 is similar.

Firstly, it is covered by the DSM mechanism of Chapter 28. Although a narrow reading of art 26.12, establishing that "[C]hapter 28 (Dispute Settlement), as modified by this Article, shall apply to *this Section* [the corruption one]" could lead to the interpretation that Section 2 (Transparency) is excluded from the scope of Chapter 28 and that only Section 3 is covered, a better understanding of art 26.12 would place the stress on its inclusion of the phrase "as modified by this Article", which means that the whole of Chapter 26 is covered by the DSM except for art 26.9.

Secondly, it establishes concrete obligations such as the need for a "prompt review" by tribunals "impartial and independent" from the administrative authority involved in the decision under appeal. It also demands that those tribunals do not have "any substantial interest in the outcome of the matter". These are standards which can be analysed by a panel and assessed against precise factual events.

Thirdly, any case of corruption likely to end in an international DSM in matters covered by this agreement, will have been first litigated in domestic courts and, hence, covered by the scope of art 26.4.

Finally, a company from a state party which is denied a prompt impartial and independent review of an administrative decision which may be tainted by corruption – imagine, for example, one-off cases such as merger control in competition law or large-scale procurements – may have the size and economic power to push its state to bring the other one to the DSM. One can think, for example, of aviation or satellite providers, large construction companies or big internet firms which tend to have access to the relevant trade authorities in their countries of origin.

Taking these factors into account, art 26.4 could be the first building block for the creation of an effective trade anti-corruption mechanism. Regretfully, considering the pace of justice in these cases – especially if related to big procurements, competition rules or significant investments – this is a hypothesis which will take many years to test. For the time being, one should not expect much change in corrupt behaviours in trade-related matters as a result of ratification of the *TPP11*.

### Acknowledgements

The author thanks the participants of the workshop of the ANZSIL International Economic Law Interest Group (Christchurch 2019), with special gratitude to Tracey Epps, for their very useful comments; as well as Ramona

Vijeyarasa and the editors and anonymous reviewers of the *New Zealand Yearbook of International Law*. All errors remain the author's. The views expressed in this article do not represent a position of any of the organisations the author is affiliated with.

# The Confluence of International Trade and Investment: Exploring the Nexus between Export Controls and Indirect Expropriation

*Umair Ghori**

**Abstract**

Export controls have received little attention in international trade law. Considering recent decisions in trade disputes involving Chinese control of exports, the area has received renewed interest. This article explores the effect of export controls and their connection with indirect expropriation, especially where export controls are imposed by host states to alleviate shortages. Such controls may prevent a foreign investor from earning revenue through resource exports. The article posits that, in certain situations, export controls can be deemed expropriatory and, therefore, in the settlement of investment disputes between host states and foreign investor, the interpretation of *General Agreement on Tariffs and Trade ("GATT")*/World Trade Organization ("WTO") jurisprudence on the area may play a useful role because of the ad hoc nature of investor-state dispute settlement ("ISDS") arbitration and due to the lack of precedent in international investment law. However, this role can at best be an initial point, and that space must be reserved for international investment jurisprudence to develop more organically.

## 1  Introduction

This article explores the overlap between international trade and investment laws in an area which has begun to receive increased attention. The *General Agreement on Tariffs and Trade ("GATT")*[1]/World Trade Organization ("WTO") framework is mainly oriented towards controlling the import behaviour of WTO Members. This is in line with the prevailing wisdom during various

---

\*  LLB (Hons), LLM, PhD. Assistant Professor, Faculty of Law, Bond University, Robina QLD 4229 Australia. E-mail: ughori@bond.edu.au.

1  See *General Agreement on Tariffs and Trade*, signed 30 October 1947, 55 UNTS 194 (entered into force 1 January 1948); *Marrakesh Agreement Establishing the World Trade Organization*,

rounds of multilateral trade negotiations, where the overarching objective was to cut import tariffs in order to foster increased trade amongst nations.

Export controls received little attention during the phased construction of the WTO system. It was thought that since countries would be eager to export their outputs for monetary gain, export controls would be limited to circumstances such as national emergencies, natural disasters, famine or times of war. The inadequacies of the GATT/WTO system regarding export controls recently emerged following China's imposition of export restrictions on rare earths and certain raw materials.[2] However, in the not too distant past, United States ("US") and European textiles interest groups approached their governments to counter India's export controls on cotton because the restrictions were affecting their members' business.[3] Similarly, Pakistan took extensive efforts to prevent export of cotton yarn in 2009–10 after the local apparel industries complained about a lack of availability of cotton yarn domestically.[4] In 2018, the then Australian Prime Minister Malcolm Turnbull threatened to impose export quotas in order to convince gas companies to divert part of their output for domestic reserves.[5] The measures by the Australian government were meant to reduce domestic gas prices, in light of a possible phase out of coal-fired power plants and their substitution with gas-fired power stations.[6]

---

opened for signature 15 April 1994, 1867 UNTS 3 (entered into force 1 January 1995) annex 1A (*"General Agreement on Tariffs and Trade 1994"*).

2   Appellate Body Report, *China – Measures Related to the Exportation of Rare Earths, Tungsten and Molybdenum*, WTO Doc WT/DS431/AB/R; WT/DS432/AB/R; WT/DS433/AB/R (7 August 2014); Appellate Body Report, *China – Measures Related to the Exportation of Various Raw Materials*, WTO Doc WT/DS394/AB/R (30 January 2012).

3   "Global & Indian Textile Industry Locks Horn Over Cotton Exports", *The Economic Times* (online, 27 October 2010) <https://economictimes.indiatimes.com/industry/cons-products/garments-/-textiles/global-indian-textile-industry-locks-horn-over-cotton-exports/articleshow/6821998.cms>.

4   Ahmed Abdullah, "Pakistan: Export Yarn Duty Removed", *just-style* (Web Page, 27 July 2010) <http://www.just-style.com/news/export-yarn-duty-removed_id108416.aspx?1k=dm>.

5   Fleur Anderson, "Malcolm Turnbull Slaps Export Controls on Recalcitrant Gas Exporters", *Australian Financial Review* (Web Page, 26 April 2017) <https://www.afr.com/politics/malcolm-turnbull-slaps-export-controls-on-recalcitrant-gas-exporters-20170426-gvsuh4>; Louise Yaxley, "Malcolm Turnbull Says Government Will Restrict Gas Exports in Attempt to Lower Power Prices", *ABC News* (Web Page, 20 June 2017) <http://www.abc.net.au/news/2017-06-20/government-will-intervene-to-restrict-gas-export:-turnbull/8634674>; see also Henry Belot, "Gas Export Controls on Hold as Government Strikes Deal with Suppliers", *ABC News* (Web Page, 27 September 2017) <http://www.abc.net.au/news/2017-09-27/gas-export-controls-on-hold-amid-government-agreement/8993254>.

These measures indicate changing times. Governments appear inclined to use export controls to alleviate local shortages and to achieve domestic policy objectives. The scenario envisaged in this article is based on the large, multinational resource companies that invest in a country to mine, process and export products such as liquefied natural gas ("LNG"), liquefied petroleum gas ("LPG"), fuels and oils. If the government of the host state restricts the ability of the companies to export their output, that may undercut the profit margins of the investor, thereby indirectly expropriating the investment by the foreign investor. Of course, the question of whether indirect expropriation has occurred or not depends on the underlying free trade agreement ("FTA") or bilateral investment treaty ("BIT") which may have led to the initial investment. With this conceptual background, the article explores the larger theme of export controls and their expropriatory effects. The debate cannot be limited to natural resources and commodities only. As the global population grows, trade in agricultural products, food and livestock can be potentially affected by the application of export controls as well. Furthermore, policymakers in resource-exporting countries may be tempted to enact export controls in the form of higher tariffs when the economies graduate to higher value-added sectors. The aim behind such controls is to inwardly divert resources towards nascent value-added sectors in order to enhance their productivity and competitiveness in the international market. When industrial transition towards higher value-added sectors occurs, economies previously reliant on exports of primary production shift their economic policies towards exporting finished goods instead. At this stage, control of exports may assume greater importance and the economic interests of the host countries may conflict with those of existing foreign investors.

This article proceeds as follows: Part 2 of this article briefly covers the use of export controls. Part 3 summarises the WTO rules and jurisprudence on export controls, along with *GATT* art XX(j), which refers to the powers of the WTO member to adopt measures in order to secure or distribute products that are in short supply nationally or locally. Even though the discussion of *GATT* art XX(j) is in the context of the *India – Solar Cells*[7] case (a dispute concerning government subsidies), the treatment of art XX(j) by the Appellate Body provides us with useful insights of how the WTO treats the question of local or general short

---

6   Ian Verrender, "Gas, Not Coal, the Key to Fixing Australia's Electricity Mess", *ABC News* (Web Page, 11 September 2017) <http://www.abc.net.au/news/2017-09-11/gas-not-coal-the-fix-to-australias-soaring-electricity-prices/8890818>.
7   Appellate Body Report, *India – Certain Measures Relating to Solar Cells and Solar Modules*, WTO Doc WT/DS456/AB/R (16 September 2016) ("*India – Solar Cells,* Appellate Body Report").

supply, which may be one of the possible rationales for the imposition of export controls. Part 4 explores the possible connection between investment and export controls. In addition to briefly discussing various doctrines explaining indirect expropriation, this part constructs simulated scenarios to illustrate the premise that when foreign investors particularly invest in a country with a view to exporting the output of their operations, any governmental measures interfering with exports become expropriatory in nature. The aim behind simulated scenarios is to illustrate the use of export controls vis-à-vis foreign investments in the absence of no known disputes and/or cases on the area.

Taken on a basic plane, foreign investment based on the export-driven model presumes that the function of the investment is to generate profits through the process of export. Any restriction by the host state that undercuts the profitability of the venturers may amount to indirect expropriation. Part 5 of the article offers an analysis based on the question of what role GATT/WTO jurisprudence will play in the adjudication of future investment disputes arising based on export controls. To answer this question, Part 5 explores two paths, the first path involving parallel actions in the realm of international trade and international investment law, and the second path involving consideration of importing interpretative norms and standards from the GATT/WTO jurisprudence in settlement of any future investment disputes on export controls. Part 6 concludes.

Overall, this article surmises that any future investment disputes involving export controls will borrow heavily from GATT/WTO jurisprudence in the settlement of disputes and WTO Dispute Settlement Body ("DSB") decisions such as *India – Solar Cells* may play an important interpretative role if export controls have been imposed to alleviate a local or general short supply of materials.

## 2  When Do States Impose Export Controls?

Countries may use export controls to alleviate shortages of essential food and raw materials during testing times. In the past, the food price increased internationally whenever major supplier countries restricted its export to meet domestic demand. For example, the US imposed export controls on grains and fodder in 1973 to maintain domestic prices for animal feed. The flow-on effects of export controls were felt in Japan, which was dependent on such imports from the US.[8]

---

8   Mitsuo Matsushita, "Export Controls of Natural Resources and the WTO/GATT Disciplines" (2011) 6(2) *Asian Journal of WTO & International Health Law & Policy* 281, 284.

Export controls are also used to prevent proliferation of weapons and military technology.[9] Importers and exporters must be aware of any international sanctions, controls and monitoring mechanisms. Another example can be the export control of nuclear materials, which makes the export of nuclear weapons-related materials difficult.[10] The idea behind such control is not outright banning or prevention, but, rather, to increase the opportunity cost behind the transaction.

Another application of export control is prevention of trade in resources that result from exploitation such as slavery or that come from conflict zones.[11] Such controls make commerce and transactions difficult so that costs become prohibitively high. Export controls may also used in order to conserve archaeological and/or cultural artefacts or the environment, or in relation to trade affecting endangered species.[12] These are all specialised applications of export controls. The focus of this article, however, is on the economic aspect of export controls as manifested in international trade and investment law. In international trade, export controls may appear as quotas or increased export taxes. Export controls can also be achieved indirectly through reduced production of materials, which automatically leaves little for export. If there is little or no domestic consumption of the material in question, then there is effectively no export control. Price maintenance and affecting the availability and management of resources can also be potential uses of export controls. Governments often

---

9   See, eg, "Materiel Export Control", *Department of Defence* (Web Page) <http://www.defence.gov.au/CASG/DoingBusiness/Internationalengagementandexportsupport/Materiel%20export%20control.asp>; see also "Strategic Export Control in 2016: Military Equipment and Dual-Use Items", *Government Offices of Sweden* (Web Page, 3 November 2017) <http://www.government.se/legal-documents/2017/11/strategic-export-control-in-2016/>.

10  Lynn E Davis, "Arms Control, Export Regimes and Multilateral Cooperation" in Zalmay Khalilzad, John White and Andy Marshall (eds), *Strategic Appraisal: The Changing Role of Information in Warfare* (RAND Corporation, 1999) 361, 364–365; see generally Ian Anthony, Christer Ahlström and Vitaly Fedchenko, *Reforming Nuclear Export Controls: The Future of the Nuclear Suppliers Group* (SIPRI Research Report No 22, 2007).

11  Organisation of Economic Co-operation and Development, "Regulatory Transparency in Multilateral Agreements Controlling Exports of Tropical Timber, E-Waste and Conflict Diamonds" (Trade Policy Paper No 141, 10 December 2012).

12  See, eg, Nordic Council of Ministers, *Illicit Trade in Cultural Artefacts: Stronger Together – How can the Nordics Join Forces to Stop the Illegal Import and Export of Cultural Objects* (Report, 2017) 49–51; see also Neil Brodie and Isber Sabrine, "The Illegal Excavation and Trade of Syrian Cultural Objects: A View From the Ground" (2017) 53(1) *Journal of Field Archaeology* 74, 82; Rosalind Reeve, *Policing International Trade in Endangered Species: the CITES Treaty and Compliance* (Earthscan, 2002) 549.

resort to restrictions on exports to ensure availability of materials and goods at a certain price level. Another aspect of price maintenance is when states or groups of states that have common interests in trading in a commodity impose export controls to regulate prices (for example, countries in the Organization of the Petroleum Exporting Countries ("OPEC") frequently meet to discuss production and exports of petroleum to maintain pricing levels).

## 3    The GATT/WTO Framework and the Use of Export Controls

### 3.1    Overview

Export controls were largely ignored during negotiations for the GATT 1947 (the predecessor of GATT 1994) because of the singular attention given to the reduction of trade barriers and the cutting of high import tariffs[13] Export controls appear within GATT 1994 rather esoterically as a "prohibition on quantitative restrictions" (GATT art XI). Therefore, the GATT/WTO framework treats export quotas similarly to import quotas in that it prohibits quotas in its application to both imports and exports. However, the specified prohibition on quotas under art XI is qualified by several exceptions. GATT art XI(2)(a) allows WTO members to restrict exports temporarily in order "to relieve critical shortages of foodstuffs" or other "essential" products, while GATT art XI(2)(b) allows the WTO Members to apply technical standards for the classification, grading or marketing of commodities in international trade.

Export controls are further affected by GATT art XX, which enables WTO members to adopt exceptional measures. GATT art XX exceptions are further qualified by an additional requirement appearing in the *chapeau* to the said provision. The *chapeau* states that any measures adopted by WTO members in line with the general exceptions shall not be arbitrary or discriminatory "between countries where the same conditions prevail". The *chapeau* clearly states that the exceptions provided under art XX must not be employed as a "disguised" form of restrictions on international trade.

Export controls are also permissible under GATT art XXI(b)(iii), which enables WTO Members to maintain trade restrictions in times of war or national emergencies. Some commentators allude to the ineffectiveness of the GATT art

---

13    Mitsuo Matsushita, "Export Control of Natural Resources: WTO Panel Ruling on the Chinese Export Restrictions of Natural Resources" (2011) 3(2) *Trade, Law & Development* 268, 270; Bin Gu, "Mineral Export Restraints and Sustainable Development: Are Rare Earths Testing the WTO's Loopholes?" (2011) 4(4) *Journal of International Economic Law* 765, 784.

XI prohibition on export quotas by pointing out the high number of accompanying exceptions.[14]

Export tariffs can constitute an additional element of export controls. However, export tariffs are different from import tariffs because of *GATT* art II(1)(b), which imposes a limitation on the tariff levels which WTO members may place on imports above the concession rates. By comparison, export tariffs do not usually have such restrictions. Hence, WTO members can impose tariff-based export restraints.[15] Export tariffs as export controls are not prohibited *per se* under WTO law unless the tariffs are prohibitively high.[16] Effectively, this means that export tariffs can be used for actual export control or revenue generation by countries. However, if export duties reach a prohibitive level, then this essentially translates into zero-export quotas which falls within the coverage of *GATT* art XI's prohibition on quotas.[17]

*GATT* art XX is another provision that affects export controls. This provision allows WTO members to derogate from their obligations. In availing the exceptions, the foremost issue for the party invoking exceptions under *GATT* art XX is to satisfy the standard of proof. Cases such as *EC – Tariff Preferences* and *US – Shrimp* demonstrate that the standard of proof rests on the invoking party (the WTO member adopting export controls).[18] The country maintaining controls must demonstrate upon challenge that the justification for imposing the measure meets the exceptions outlined in *GATT* art XX. Additionally, the requirement of the *chapeau* must also be satisfied. The order of the burden of proof was clarified by the WTO Appellate Body in the *US – Shrimp* case. Firstly, the country maintaining the impugned measures must demonstrate that the measures fall within one of the *GATT* art XX exceptions. Secondly,

---

14   John H Jackson et al, *Legal Problems of International Economic Relations* (West Publishing, 3rd ed, 1995) 946, cited in Matsushita, "Export Control of Natural Resources: WTO Panel Ruling on the Chinese Export Restrictions of Natural Resources" (n 13) 272 and Matsushita, "Export Controls of Natural Resources and the WTO/GATT Disciplines" (n 8) 288.

15   Matsushita, "Export Control of Natural Resources: WTO Panel Ruling on the Chinese Export Restrictions of Natural Resources" (n 13) 273.

16   Ibid; see also Julia Ya Qin, "Reforming WTO Discipline on Export Duties: Sovereignty over Natural Resources, Economic Development and Environmental Protection" (2012) 46(5) *Journal of World Trade* 1147, 1153.

17   Matsushita, "Export Control of Natural Resources: WTO Panel Ruling on the Chinese Export Restrictions of Natural Resources" (n 13) 273; Ya Qin (n 16) 1153.

18   Appellate Body Report, *European Communities – Conditions for the Granting of Tariff Preferences to Developing Countries*, WTO Doc WT/DS246/AB/R (7 April 2004) [95] ("*EC – Tariff Preferences*, Appellate Body Report"); Appellate Body Report, *United States – Import Prohibition of Shrimp and Certain Shrimp Products*, WTO Doc WT/DS58/AB/R (12 October 1998) [158] ("*US – Shrimp*, Appellate Body Report").

the requirement of the *chapeau* must be fulfilled. Therefore, the order of application is to satisfy one of the exceptions under GATT art XX and then the *chapeau*.[19]

GATT art XX exceptions (b) and (g) have been the subject of the most usage and disputes in the WTO. Exceptions (b) and (g) are not the subject of discussion in this article, because where a country is attempting to alleviate shortfall of materials or resources, exception (j) becomes relevant, especially where export controls are concerned.

Exception (j) is the emerging category that has seen use only once as a defence in WTO dispute settlement proceedings. This occurred in the *India – Solar Cells* case, where India cited exception (j) along with exception (d) in defence of its solar panel subsidy measures which were challenged by the US.[20]

### 3.2 The India – Solar Cells *case and Exception (j)*

The case did not actually broach the question of export controls. Rather, it concerned government subsidies for solar industries. The case becomes relevant here for two reasons. Firstly, it is the only case in WTO jurisprudence where the question of securing or distributing products in short supply is discussed. Secondly, GATT art XX(j) may form the basis of exceptional arguments that WTO members can adopt when imposing export controls to secure or distribute products in short supply.

The Appellate Body, in determining the question of "short supply", stated that due regard must be given to the total quantity of imports that may be available to meet the necessary supply in a particular geographical area or market.[21] This may mean assessing whether international supply of the product is stable, which in turn considers "distance between a particular geographical area or market and productions sites" and "the reliability of local or transnational supply chains".[22]

---

19  *US – Shrimp*, Appellate Body Report (n 18) [118]–[121].
20  Panel Report, *India – Certain Measures Relating to Solar Cells and Solar Modules*, WTO Doc WT/DS456/R (24 February 2016) [7.3.1]–[7.3.2] ("*India – Solar Cells*, Panel Report").
21  The Appellate Body held that art XX(j) reflects a balance of different considerations that must be considered in assessing the question of "general or local short supply". Such considerations include the level of domestic production of the product in question, the nature of products in "general or local short supply", geographical market, price fluctuations, the purchasing power of domestic and foreign consumers and the role played by domestic and foreign producers in the market including "the extent to which domestic producers sell their production abroad": *India – Solar Cells*, Appellate Body Report (n 7) [6.4].
22  Ibid.

The Appellate Body further clarified that whatever factors are relevant depends on the peculiarities of each case.[23] Regardless of the factors that may be applicable, the party adopting the measure must demonstrate that "available" supply, from both domestic and international sources, is insufficient to meet demand.[24]

Note that the criteria from *India – Solar Cells* must be balanced with GATT art XI 2(a)–(b), GATT art XX(j) and its *chapeau* or GATT art XXI(b)(iii). The criteria seem open and adaptable enough to be applied to potential situations encountered in the future. However, the Appellate Body has not elaborated on the relative importance of the factors vis-à-vis each other. The question of importance is left open to be determined on a case-by-case basis. The risk with such an approach is that it may leave policymakers in a rather tricky position when constructing export controls, because factors that are deemed as essential domestically might not be perceived as such internationally.

## 4  Linking Export Controls to Indirect Expropriation

### 4.1  *Background*

FTAS and BITs have long included definitions that deal with the risks of nationalisation or expropriatory actions by host governments. Attitudes of arbitral tribunals have been consistent as far as the basic conceptualisation of expropriation is concerned. For example, in *Amoco International Finance Corp v Iran*, it was held by the Iran – US Claims Tribunal that "[e]xpropriation, which can be defined as a compulsory transfer of property rights, may extend to any right which can be the object of a commercial transaction".[25]

Furthermore, the Iran – US Claims Tribunal noted in *Phillips Petroleum Co Iran v Iran* that expropriation gives rise to liability for compensation regardless of "whether the expropriation is formal or de facto and whether the property is tangible, such real estate or a factory, or intangible, such as the contractual rights involved in the present case".[26]

Tribunals have also held that duty to compensate cannot be evaded by the host state on the grounds of any narrow meaning accorded to the term "expropriation" under municipal law.[27]

---

23  Ibid.
24  Ibid.
25  *Amoco International Finance Corp v Iran* (Partial Award No. 310-56-3) (1987) 15 Iran–US CTR 89, [108].
26  *Phillips Petroleum Co Iran v Iran* (Award No. 425-39-2) (1989) 21 Iran–US CTR 79, [76].
27  *Southern Pacific Properties (Middle East) Ltd v Egypt* (Award on the Merits) (ICSID Arbitral Tribunal, Case No ARB/84/3, 20 May 1992) [168].

Indirect expropriation, however, has eluded a specific definition. Arbitral tribunals have often referred to the analysis of indirect expropriation as being driven by the facts of each claim.[28] For example, in *Amco Asia Corporation v Indonesia*, the withdrawal of investment authorisation by a government body was treated as an expropriation.[29] In *Southern Pacific Properties (Middle East) Limited v Arab Republic of Egypt*, the cancellation of a tourist development project in order to protect antiquities was considered to be an "unquestionable attribute of sovereignty" and hence unchallengeable because of public interest.[30] However, the tribunal specifically stated that if expropriation is for a legitimate purpose, then it must be accompanied by fair compensation, otherwise it will amount to confiscation.[31] The definition of indirect expropriation depends on "the specific facts and circumstances of the case, particularly the gravity and length of interference, the rights of the parties under a contract, or general legislation, and even cultural elements that define shared expectations".[32] It is also noteworthy that expropriation and indirect expropriation are predicated on the fact that there must be a substantial deprivation of benefits or loss of value of investments as a result of governmental action.

In the oft-cited *Metalclad v Mexico* dispute, the arbitral tribunal explained that expropriation may encompass "covert or incidental interference with the use of property" which may deprive the owner of "use or reasonably-to-be expected economic benefit of property".[33] Similarly, some arbitral awards recognise restrictions on property rights, enhanced taxation, alteration of contractual rights or the suspension or withdrawal of licenses and/or regulatory permits as measures amounting to indirect expropriation.[34] This, however, must be contrasted with the proposition that regulatory takings or expropriatory actions by states is justified, with or without compensation, if

---

28  Yvette Anthony, "The Evolution of Indirect Expropriation Clauses: Lessons from Singapore's BITS/FTAS" (2017) 7(2) *Asian Journal of International Law* 319, 325.
29  *Amco Asia Corporation v Indonesia (Award)* (1984) 1 ICSID Rep 413, [244]–[250].
30  *Southern Pacific Properties (Middle East) Ltd v Egypt (Award on the Merits)* (n 27) [58]–[129].
31  Ibid [163].
32  Francisco Vicuna, "Carlos Calvo, Honorary NAFTA Citizen" (2003) 11(1) *New York University Environmental Law Journal* 19, 28, cited by Anthony (n 27) 325.
33  *Metalclad Corporation v Mexico (Award)* (ICSID Arbitral Tribunal, Case No ARB(AF)/97/1, 30 August 2000) [103].
34  For example, in *Compania del Desarrollo de Santa Elena SA v Costa Rica*, the tribunal observed that lapse of time can be a relevant factor in determining whether expropriation has occurred. This may be of immediate effect (like an outright seizure) or through a series of interconnected measures that gradually amount to a loss of ownership: *Compania del Desarrollo de Santa Elena SA v Costa Rica (Final Award)* (ICSID Arbitral Tribunal, Case No ARB/96/1, 17 February 2000) [76]–[77]. In determining indirect expropriation, some

the measures are taken in the "public interest" or pursuant to the "police powers" of a state.³⁵ However, what amounts to "police powers" of a state may vary from country to country, according to their municipal systems.

According to analysis by Yvette Anthony, the "police powers" of the state and the exercise of powers for "public purpose" or in the "public interest" are two different concepts.³⁶ Anthony cites awards in *Chemtura, AWG* and *Too v Greater Modesto Insurance Associates* to stress that the exercise of "police powers" by the host state does not constitute expropriation.³⁷ Anthony further observes that the US position on this issue is that a state is not responsible for any economic disadvantage incurred by the foreign investor that results from the exercise of the state's *bona fide* "police powers". Factors such as the discriminatory application of governmental measures, the extent of deprivation or loss of control over investment and the circumstances of each case may be considered when determining whether "police powers" degenerate into expropriation. Such factors are balanced with indicators such as the protection of public morality, public welfare, health and the environment to determine what constitutes "public interest", "public purpose" or "police powers".³⁸

Therefore, the question becomes, even where states are exercising legitimate "police powers" to achieve a "public welfare" aim or the preservation of the environment, whether the duty to compensate the foreign investor is then triggered or not. This is a question that continues to receive extensive academic attention but which exceeds the scope of this article. Suffice here to say that no clear answers have emerged from ISDS jurisprudence, and recourse is made

---

awards have indicated that the effect of state measures and the degree of loss suffered by foreign investor is the operative factor, rather than the intent behind the state measures: Anthony (n 28) 325; see also *Fireman's Fund Insurance Company v Mexico (Award)* (ICSID Arbitral Tribunal, Case No ARB(AF)/02/1, 17 July 2006) [176(f)]. The tribunal in *Spyridon Roussalis v Romania* declared that the effect of actions of the state is the key to determine whether indirect expropriation has occurred or not: *Spyridon Roussalis v Romania (Award)* (ICSID Arbitral Tribunal, Case No ARB/06/1, 7 December 2011) [327]–[328].

35  See, eg, the discussions in Andrew Newcombe and Lluis Paradell, *Law and Practice of Investment Treaties: Standards of Treatment* (Kluwer Law International, 2004) 341, 358; see also Anthony (n 28) 319, 327; James Crawford, *Brownlie's Principles of Public International Law* (Oxford University Press, 8th ed, 2008) 624; Surya Subedi, *International Investment Law: Reconciling Policy and Principle* (Hart Publishing, 2nd ed, 2012) 79, 119, 124.

36  Anthony (n 28) 332.

37  *Chemtura Corporation v Canada (Award)* (Permanent Court of Arbitration, Case No 2008-01, 2 August 2010) [266]; *AWG Group v Argentina (Decision on Liability)* (ICSID Arbitral Tribunal, Case No ARB/03/19, 30 July 2010) [139]; *Too v Greater Modesto Insurance Associates* (1989) 23 Iran–US CTR 378.

38  Anthony (n 28) 332; see also American Law Institute, *Restatement (Third) of Foreign Relations Law of the United States* (1987) § 712 cmt (g) ("*Third Restatement*").

to a case-by-case approach to determine the question of whether compensation is payable or not.

In addition to the "police powers" arguments, disputes such as *Tecmed v United Mexican States*[39] and others[40] highlight the approach of "legitimate expectations" that foreign investors may have considered when making the decision to invest.[41] The doctrine of legitimate expectations has gradually morphed

---

39   See generally *Técnicas Medioambientales Tecmed SA v Mexico (Award)* (ICSID Arbitral Tribunal, Case No ARB(AF)/00/2, 29 May 2003) [154] (*"Tecmed"*).
40   Other disputes following the *Tecmed* line of argument include *LG&E Energy Corp, LG&E Capital Corp and LG&E International Inc v Argentina (Decision on Liability)* (ICSID Arbitral Tribunal, Case No ARB/02/1, 3 October 2006) [127]; *Occidental Exploration and Production Company v Ecuador (Final Award)* (London Court of International Arbitration, Case No UN 3467, 1 July 2004) [185]; *CMS Gas Transmission Company v Argentina (Award)* (ICSID Arbitral Tribunal, Case No ARB/01/08, 12 May 2005) [279]; *Sempra Energy International v Argentina (Award)* (ICSID Arbitral Tribunal, Case No ARB/02/16, 28 September 2007) [298]. The *Tecmed* standard is criticised by Zachary Douglas as an example of "perfect public regulation in a perfect world, ...which all states should aspire but very few (if any) will ever attain": Zachary Douglas, "Nothing if Not Critical for Investment Treaty Arbitration: *Occidental, Eureko* and *Methanex*" (2006) 22(1) *Arbitration International* 27, 28.
41   Academics have highlighted the varied nature of the concept of legitimate practice. For example, Michele Potesta highlights the utility of using legitimate expectations in situations where an investor is induced on the basis of informal representations by the host country: Michele Potesta, "Legitimate Expectations in Investment Treaty Law: Understanding the Roots and the Limits of a Controversial Concept" (2013) 28(1) *ICSID Review* 88, 103–110, 121–122. Christopher Campbell, however, is more critical of the concept and terms it as an "invention of arbitrators", stating, moreover, that arbitral tribunals are grounding their decisions by citing other arbitral awards that do not carry precedent value and, hence, the doctrine should be rejected as providing any basis on which to judge state conduct: Christopher Campbell, "House of Cards: The Relevance of Legitimate Expectations under Fair and Equitable Treatment Provisions in Investment Treaty Law" (2013) 30(4) *Journal of International Arbitration* 361, 378–379. Elizabeth Snodgrass, on the other hand, is more accepting of the doctrine. She argues that the doctrine of legitimate expectations should be recognised as a general principle of law on the basis of a comparative survey of various European Union jurisdictions: see Elizabeth Snodgrass, "Protecting Investors' Legitimate Expectations: Recognizing and Delimiting a General Principle" (2006) 21(1) *ICSID Review – Foreign Investment Law Journal* 1, 56–58. Christoph Schreuer and Ursula Kriebaum offer a more balanced view, arguing that not every expectation upon which a foreign investor makes a business decision can form the basis of an expropriation claim against foreign investor. Schreuer and Ursula point out that the application of the legitimate expectation's argument is quite situational, especially in complex transactions. In order for foreign investors to rely on legitimate expectations, the foreign investor must have knowledge and basis on which reasonable expectations can take a business decision. These bases can be grounded in general regulatory framework or through governmental assurances: see Christoph Schreuer and Ursula Kriebaum, "At What Time Must Legitimate Expectations Exist?" in Jacques Werner and Arif Hyder Ali (eds), *A Liber Amicorum: Thomas Wälde. Law beyond Conventional Thought* (CMP Publishing, 2009) 265, 269–270, 273–276.

from its initial beginnings as an obiter dictum in the *Tecmed* award. Within the larger framework of ISDS, the doctrine of legitimate expectations occupies an uneasy posture when juxtaposed with a host state's right to regulate in the public interest. The doctrine of legitimate expectation views the stability and predictability of the regulatory system as a function of the fair and equitable treatment to be accorded to the foreign investor. In doing so, the foreign investor may have a legitimate expectation that, during the subsistence of the investment, the domestic regulatory framework would not be altered or modified in any way.[42]

Clearly, the expectation by foreign investors that there will never be regulatory intervention or legislative reform is unrealistic and problematic. Indeed, this proposition has received some recognition, for example in *Impregilo v Argentina*, where the dispute settlement tribunal stated that the legitimate expectations of foreign investors cannot be that the state will not modify its legislation. However, foreign investors are entitled to protection from *unreasonable* modifications of the legislative framework.[43]

Another aspect of the legitimate-expectations argument is that the government of the host state will be bound by any undertakings or representations given to the foreign investor prior to the foreign investment being made.[44] In *Thunderbird v Mexico*, the tribunal tackled the question of legitimate expectations based on a legal opinion rendered by a governmental department. Interestingly, the tribunal held that legal advice cannot constitute the basis for legitimate expectations unless the foreign investor discloses the full and complete nature of the investment in advance.[45] Even when the advice is of a more informal nature, tribunals have been cautious in classifying such

---

42    CMS *Gas Transmission Company v Argentina (Award)* (n 40) [274]–[276].

43    *Impregilo SpA v Argentina (Award)* (ICSID Arbitral Tribunal, Case No ARB/07/17, 21 June 2011) [291]–[292]; see further arguments in Potesta (n 41) 117.

44    See, eg, the discussion in Rudolf Dolzer and Christoph Schreuer, *Principles of International Investment Law* (Oxford University Press, 2nd ed, 2012) 148–149; see also Aniruddha Rajput and Sarthak Malhotra, "Legitimate Expectations in Investment Arbitration: A Comparative Perspective" in Mahendra Pal Singh and Niraj Kumar (eds), *The Indian Yearbook of Comparative Law* (Springer, 2018) 297, 302–303.

45    *International Thunderbird Gaming Corporation v Mexico (Award)* (North American Free Trade Agreement Chapter 11 Tribunal, 26 January 2006) [145], [147]–[148], [155], [166]. Thomas Wälde's separate opinion in the *Thunderbird* case highlights that the "quite high" threshold for assurances and specific representations can only be met if the assurances visibly display an official character: *International Thunderbird Gaming Corporation v Mexico (Separate Opinion of Thomas Wälde)* (North American Free Trade Agreement Chapter 11 Tribunal, 26 January 2006) [32]; See also Potesta,(n 41) 105–107.

representations as specific enough to give rise to a breach the fair and equitable standards under the legitimate expectations argument.[46]

Disputes involving indirect expropriation have also received attention under the proportionality principle, which entails evaluating a range of possible regulatory measures and opting for the least intrusive course of action.[47] Recent arbitral awards have also considered the interplay between proportionality and reasonableness. Detailed treatment of this issue, however, is beyond the scope of this article. Here, proportionality is being briefly discussed as an alternative approach to the sole effects or police powers doctrine.

Proportionality seeks to achieve a balance between the competing imperatives of governmental regulations and the commercial interests of foreign investors. It does so by posing four interlinked queries which must be satisfied: (i) the measure must be seen to achieve a legitimate aim; (ii) the measure must be suitable to the achieve that aim; (iii) the test of necessity must be applied;[48] and (iv) the measure must be balanced against competing interests,

---

46  This is seen in the high profile *Metalclad* case as well as in *White Industries v India*, where a governmental official made a statement describing the Australian and Indian legal systems as similar. The tribunal termed such a statement as too broad and non-specific to trigger legitimate expectations: *White Industries Australia Limited v The Republic of India (Final Award)*, (Ad Hoc Tribunal under the UNCITRAL Arbitration Rules, 30 November 2011) [5.2.6], [10.3.17].

47  See, eg, Caroline Henckels, *Proportionality and Deference in Investor-State Arbitration* (Cambridge University Press, 2015) 23–26; see also Caroline Henckels, "Indirect Expropriation and the Right to Regulate: Revisiting Proportionality Analysis and the Standard of Review in Investor-State Arbitration" (2012) 15(1) *Journal of International Economic Law* 223, 224–228; see also Benedict Kingsbury and Stephen W Schill, "Public Law Concepts to Balance Investors' Rights with State Regulatory Actions in the Public Interest: The Concept of Proportionality" in Stephen W Schill (ed), *International Investment Law and Comparative Public Law* (Oxford University Press, 2010) 75, 77–88.

48  The "necessity" test under the proportionality principle has a peculiar overlap with the equivalent term in WTO jurisprudence. Mitchell and Henckels consider the necessity analysis conducted by the arbitral tribunals to be more fragmented than the WTO jurisprudence on the area. One particularly relevant argument by Mitchell and Henckels is that WTO jurisprudence provides a useful source for guiding investment tribunals in determining necessity because WTO panels have displayed appropriate institutional sensitivity and deference to national autonomy in their analysis: Andrew Mitchell and Caroline Henckels, "Variations on a Theme: Comparing the Concept of "Necessity" in International Investment Law and WTO Law" (2013) 14(1) *Chicago Journal of International Law* 93, 126–137, 160,163; see also Mads Andenas and Stefan Zlepting, "Proportionality: WTO Law in Comparative Perspective" (2007) 42(3) *Texas International Law Journal*, 371, 383.

by weighing and balancing the social importance of achieving the measure's aims against the social importance of harm avoidance.[49]

Similar to the doctrine of legitimate expectations, arbitral practice shows a mixed usage of the proportionality principle. For example, *Saluka v Czech Republic* shows an early attempt to use proportionality in order to explain the failure by the Czech Republic to extend fair and equitable treatment to foreign investment by the claimant (Saluka).[50] On closer inspection, the *Saluka* award seems more in the line of "police powers" rather than setting a new standard.[51] The *Saluka* rule is succinctly summarised by Prabhash Ranjan as providing that "a bona fide, non-discriminatory measure adopted for public welfare objective is not expropriation, notwithstanding the economic impact on foreign investment".[52]

The proportionality doctrine, in terms of the lawfulness of a state action, received more attention in the *American Silver v Bolivia* dispute, which concerned a Bolivian governmental action of ordering the revocation of mining licences and the reversion of land ownership to the land's indigenous owners.[53] The tribunal explained that, contrary to the assertion by the claimant (American Silver), social benefit cannot be equated with purely economic benefit, seen through the lens of the expected economic benefit for the local communities, while ignoring the surrounding political and socio-economic situation in the region.[54]

The tribunal also interpreted the strict proportionality standard and stipulated that the economic loss for the investor cannot have more weight than the protection of the interests of the indigenous people.[55] For the tribunal in the

---

49   See, eg, a summary of the proportionality approach in Henckels, *Proportionality and Deference in Investor-State Arbitration* (n 47) 24–26; see also Aharon Barak, *Proportionality* (Cambridge University Press, 2012) 131, 357, 484.

50   *Saluka Investments BV v Czech Republic (Partial Award)* (Ad Hoc Tribunal under the UNCITRAL Arbitration Rules, 17 March 2006); see further discussion in George S Georgiev, "The Award in Saluka Investments v Czech Republic" in Guillermo Aguilar Alvarez and W Michael Reisman (eds), *The Reasons Requirement in International Investment Arbitration* (Nijhoff, 2008) 149, 150.

51   Prabhash Ranjan, "Police Powers, Indirect Expropriation in International Investment Law, and Article 31(3)(c) of the VCLT: A Critique of Philip Morris v Uruguay" (2019) 9(1) *Asian Journal of International Law* 98, 114–115.

52   Ibid 115.

53   *South American Silver Ltd v Bolivia (Award)* (Permanent Court of Arbitration, Case No 2013-15, 22 November 2018) [169]; see also the discussion in Lasse Langfeldt, "Proportionality in Investment Treaty Arbitration and the Necessity for Tribunals to Adopt a Clear Methodology" (LLM Thesis, Uppsala University, 2019) 24–26.

54   *South American Silver Ltd v Bolivia (Award)* (n 53) [578].

55   Ibid [578].

*American Silver* dispute, the initial point of investigation for the purposes of meeting the proportionality standard was to investigate whether the FTA or BIT that drove the investment (in this case, the *United Kingdom–Bolivia BIT*)[56] mentioned the proportionality standard or not. In this dispute, the *United Kingdom–Bolivia BIT* did not specifically address the standard of a proportionate response in relation to expropriation.[57] In fact, the very reason that the tribunal discussed proportionality was because the parties addressed the reversion as an issue from the perspective of proportionality.[58] In *RREEF v Spain*, the tribunal considered proportionality as being closely connected to reasonableness,[59] which is somewhat distinct from the earlier *Tecmed* characterisation of a regulatory measure as not being expropriatory where a reasonable relationship of proportionality can be established between the burden imposed by regulatory measures on foreign investors and the aims that the challenged measures are designed to achieve.[60] Regardless of the approaches and arbitral practices which have developed for explaining direct and indirect expropriation, the older generation of BITs and FTAs were more circumspect about the question of expropriation. Such BITs and FTAs included broadly worded provisions which mentioned the duty of prompt and adequate compensation but did not include specific mechanisms in the texts. Prominent examples include the *North American Free Trade Agreement* ("*NAFTA*") art 1110,[61] the *Australia–Thailand FTA* art 912,[62] the *Indonesia–Thailand BIT* art VI[63] and the *Singapore–China BIT* art 6.[64]

---

56   *Agreement between the Government of the United Kingdom of Great Britain and Northern Ireland and the Government of the Republic of Bolivia for the Promotion and Protection of Investments*, signed 24 May 1988, [1990] UKTS 34 (entered into force 16 February 1990).
57   *South American Silver Ltd v Bolivia (Award)* (n 53) [570].
58   See Langfeldt (n 53) 26.
59   *RREEF Instructure Ltd and RREEF Pan-European Infrastructure Two Lux Sàrl v Spain (Decision on Responsibility and on the Principles of Quantum)* (ICSID Arbitral Tribunal, Case No ARB/13/30, 30 December 2018) [463]–[468].
60   See *Tecmed* (n 39) [121]–[122]; see also the discussion in Ranjan (above n 51) 116.
61   See *North American Free Trade Agreement*, Canada–Mexico–United States, signed 17 December 1992, 32 ILM 289 (entered into force 1 January 1994).
62   See *Australia–Thailand Free Trade Agreement*, signed 5 July 2004, [2005] ATS 2 (entered into force 1 January 2005).
63   See *Agreement between the Government of the Republic of Indonesia and the Government of the Kingdom of Thailand for the Promotion and Protection of Investments*, signed 17 February 1998 (entered into force 5 November 1998).
64   See *Agreement on the Promotion and Protection of Investments (with Exchange of Letters)*, China–Singapore, signed 21 November 1985 (entered into force 7 February 1986).

The newer generation of FTAS and BITs now prescribe detailed expropriation provisions, including "carve outs", which expressly exclude public welfare objectives from the competence of the arbitral tribunals examining expropriation claims. Some examples of such provisions in the "new wave" of FTAS and BITs that include greater details and specificity are the *ASEAN Comprehensive Investment Agreement* ("*ACIA*") annex 2,[65] the *Comprehensive and Progressive Trans-Pacific Partnership* ("*CPTPP*") annexes 9-B and 9-C,[66] the Canada–European Union ("EU") *Comprehensive and Economic Trade Agreement* ("*CETA*") art 8.12,[67] the *EU–Vietnam Investment Protection Agreement* art 2.7 and the accompanying Annex 4 (Understanding on Expropriation).[68] These new wave FTAS and BITs contain greater details instructing future arbitral panels (or in case of *CETA* and the *EU–Vietnam FTA*, the newly constituted bilateral investment courts) on the factors which cause government conduct to amount to a legitimate exercise of governmental "police powers". In doing so, countries are eliminating the possibility of arbitral tribunals introducing their own interpretations in the dispute. However, even in the new wave FTAS and BITs, the concepts of "public purpose" and "legitimate public policy" are neither clarified nor defined. Hence, challenges by foreign investors can be mounted against state measures by questioning their legitimacy.

### 4.2 Underlying Assumptions: Can Export Controls by a Host State Amount to Indirect Expropriation?

Certain assumptions will be made for the purposes of the subject query. These are necessary to connect two otherwise unrelated concepts (export control is a trade measure, whereas indirect expropriation is an investment concept). However, both concepts spring from governmental action. The assumptions are summarised hereinbelow:

> Assumption 1: An investment being expropriated is controlled by a foreign investor and is made under an existing FTA or bit;
>
> Assumption 2: The main aim behind an investment is the processing and export of certain product(s). The services sector is excluded. Exports constitute a major share of the revenue of the investor;

---

65  See *ASEAN Comprehensive Investment Agreement*, signed 26 February 2009 (entered into force 24 February 2012) ("*ACIA*").
66  See *Comprehensive and Progressive Agreement for Trans-Pacific Partnership*, signed 8 March 2018, [2018] ATS 23 (entered into force 30 December 2018).
67  *Comprehensive Economic and Trade Agreement*, signed 30 October 2016 (not yet in force).
68  EU – Vietnam Investment Protection Agreement, signed 30 June 2019 (not yet in force).

Assumption 3: Export controls are imposed pursuant to a governmental policy and cause revenue-based damages to the foreign investor, due to the price difference between domestic and international sales; and

Assumption 4: Export controls are applied across the board and affect local and foreign-owned businesses equally. Therefore, violation of national treatment ("NT") norms is not at issue.

## 4.3   *Simulated Scenarios*

An overlap between the GATT art XX exceptions and the commonly cited public welfare and environmental grounds is immediately apparent. One particularly relevant exception, discussed above, is GATT art XX(j), pursuant to which a WTO member can adopt measures restricting exports in order to alleviate "general or local short supply". Using GATT art XX(j), and the assumptions outlined above, the following simulated scenarios are constructed to explain the proposition that export controls may amount to indirect expropriation.

The first scenario is based on Country X, a resource-based economy with a shrinking manufacturing base, that attracts foreign direct investment into the resources sector. The government of Country X grants concessions and tax breaks for foreign investors who wish to engage in development and exploration in the natural resource sector. In one case, Corporation A (a large, multinational gas company owned by foreign investors based in a BIT state party) heavily invests in the exploration for, and refining of, natural gas in Country X. Corporation A's business strategy is to export the bulk of output to Asia, where there is high demand for gas. Country X is facing high domestic energy prices. The prices in the Asian export markets, however, are lower than the price in Country X. The government of Country X notices the price differential and sees establishment of new gas-fired power plants as the solution for securing energy needs and bringing down the domestic price of gas. Accordingly, Country X systematically imposes export controls on gas to increase domestic supply. Country X justifies the new policies on the grounds of energy security, price stabilisation, the rights of people over their own resources, social license and acting in the larger public interest. The export controls are introduced in the form of quotas, which results in a reduction in the volume of refined gas that Corporation A can export. Resultantly, Corporation A's projected revenue decreases for the duration of export controls, while this news further affects the stocks of Corporation A. Has Country X indirectly expropriated Corporation A's investment through its export controls?

The second scenario is based on Country Y, a highly populated, developing country that is increasingly penetrating the developed markets with its cheaply-produced consumer goods. Country Y launches an ambitious plan to advance its manufacturing sectors and create additional job opportunities within the economy. The government imposes a five-year export control over certain raw materials and rare earths. The plan is to inwardly divert raw materials for use in the domestic manufacturing of value-added products for export. The export controls come in the form of increased tariffs added to the free-on-board ("FOB") price. The increased tariffs will be phased out over a five-year period. Resultantly, the export prices of rare earths increase, which consequently affects the price in the world market as well. In one case, Corporation B (an international mining business, incorporated as a company under the laws of Country Y) is engaged in mining and processing rare earths, which are exported in the form of ingots to specialised businesses overseas. Corporation B has invested in significant infrastructure for mining, processing and exporting rare earths. The measures by Country Y are forcing Corporation B to reduce its exports and divert its sales into the domestic market. Corporation B is further prevented from pursuing additional supply opportunities due to export controls. Corporation B believes that supplying domestic industries is not lucrative enough in the long run, and that the loss of additional business opportunities overseas has seriously affected the revenues of the business. Has Country Y indirectly expropriated Corporation B's investment through its export controls?

The third scenario is a deliberately constructed situation involving a mix of regulatory intervention and confiscatory actions. In this scenario, the government of Country Z, a least developed country ("LDC") that is a venue for outward production processing ("OPP")-based investment by overseas apparel companies, exceeds the scope of proportionality and necessity while purportedly acting in the public interest. The OPP businesses working in Country Z engage a vast number of employees in order to export their finished apparel. The export-oriented commercial and manufacturing activity is a valuable source of revenue for Country Z's economy. The apparel and textiles businesses in Country Z often source cotton yarn from domestic cotton yarn manufacturers, who in turn rely on cotton growers in Country Z to supply them with raw cotton. The cotton yarn manufacturers primarily supply their products domestically and any surplus is exported. Due to a sudden and unforeseen shortage of cotton yarn internationally, cotton yarn manufacturers see a spike in demand from overseas buyers and begin exporting yarn to maximise their profits, leading to domestic yarn shortages which affect local apparel manufacturing. Several delivery orders are delayed or cancelled because the manufacturers were unable to source cotton yarn domestically. The representative association of apparel manufacturers approach the government of Country Z and demand that export controls be imposed on cotton yarn manufacturers. The cotton yarn manufacturers resist these demands. The crisis spirals out of control and results in rioting and protests. In one instance, a mob burns a warehouse owned by Corporation C (a company registered under the laws of Country Z, but with a majority shares owned by foreign shareholders through a local holding company). Corporation C runs a vertically integrated operation, which involves feeding cotton yarn into its textiles and apparel facilities. The final outputs are then exported as value-added items. Under increasing pressure from the apparel industries and labour unions, the government of Country Z imposes export controls on cotton yarn until domestic supplies are stabilised. The government further confiscates all cotton yarn in port warehouses that is destined for exports. Corporation C feels aggrieved by the actions of Country Z and the foreign investors (the shareholders of Corporation C) view this action as expropriatory. Has Country C indirectly expropriated Corporation C's investment through its export controls and confiscatory actions?

With the above simulations summarising the basic positions of the imposing countries, potential arguments on export controls qualifying as indirect expropriation will now be discussed.

### 4.4   *Arguments*

The simulated scenarios illustrate instances where government actions have affected foreign investors' ability to export and earn profits. The decision to control exports can either be classified under the broader category of "police powers" of the state or actions taken in the "public interest" or for "public welfare". Alternatively, the expropriatory actions can be viewed through the lens of proportionality or the legitimate expectations of the foreign investor. The classification is important because the result may alter the outcome of the ISDS process, and may well affect the terms of compensation available to the foreign investors. Also, the expressions "police powers", "public interest" and "public welfare" have no universally accepted legal definition. Therefore, the only indicators are treatment of the issue under the principles of customary international law, in academic literature and/or by various arbitral tribunals constituted under FTAS and BITS.

The question of indirect expropriation and its difference from non-compensable taking under an exercise of "police powers" of the state is equally important to both foreign investors and governments. According to Dolzer and Stevens, for the foreign investor:[69]

---

69  Rudolf Dolzer and Margrete Stevens, *Bilateral Investment Treaties* (Martinus Nijhoff Publishers, 1995) 98, quoted in Organisation on Economic Co-operation and Development, "'Indirect Expropriation' and the 'Right to Regulate' in International Investment Law" (Working Paper on International Investment No 2004/04, September 2004) 5.

[t]he line of demarcation between measures for which no compensation is due and actions qualifying as indirect expropriations (that require compensation) may well make the difference between the burden to operate (or abandon) a non-profitable enterprise and the right to receive full compensation (either from the host State or from an insurance contract). For the host State, the definition determines the scope of the State's power to enact legislation that regulates the rights and obligations of owners in instances where compensation may fall due.

Sornarajah considers that governmental measures related to "anti-trust, consumer protection, securities, environmental protection, land planning are non-compensable takings since they are regarded as essential to the efficient functioning of the state".[70] However, any powers of the state that are exercised must be non-discriminatory.[71] Arbitral awards such as *Chemtura Corporation v Government of Canada* hold that the exercise of states' police powers must be linked to imperatives such as the protection of human health and the environment.[72] In *Saur International SA v Argentina*, the tribunal stipulated that in certain situations, the legitimate exercise of police powers of the state does not give rise to an obligation to compensate.[73]

Adding to the problem of legitimacy is the fact that any state can view its actions in the public realm as "necessary" to achieve a stated public purpose. The problem of necessity featured in several WTO cases such as *Korea – Beef*,[74]

---

70   Muthucumaraswamy Sornarajah, *The International Law on Foreign Investment* (Cambridge University Press, 1994) 283, cited in ibid 4–5.

71   See, eg, Robert Jennings and Arthur Watts (eds), *Oppenheim's International Law* (Oxford University Press, 9th ed, 1992) 919–920; *BP Exploration Company (Libya) Ltd v Libya* (1973) 53 ILR 297, 329 ("*BP Exploration*"); *Methanex Corporation v United States (Final Award on Jurisdiction and Merits)* (2005) 44 ILM 1345, 1456 ("*Methanex (Final Award)*"); Veijo Heiskanen, "The Contribution of the Iran-United States Claims Tribunal to the Development of the Doctrine of Indirect Expropriation" (2003) 5(3) *International Law Forum* 176, 179, 185; Ben Mostafa, "The Sole Effects Doctrine, Police Powers and Indirect Expropriation under International Law" (2008) 15(15) *Australian International Law Journal* 265, 272–274.

72   *Chemtura Corporation v Canada (Award)* (Permanent Court of Arbitration, Case No 2008-01, 2 August 2010) [266], cited in Anthony (n 28) 329.

73   *SAUR International SA v Argentina (Decision on Jurisdiction and Liability)* (ICSID Arbitral Tribunal, Case No ARB/04/4, 6 June 2012) [398], cited in Anthony (n 28) 329.

74   Appellate Body Report, *Korea – Measures Affecting Imports of Fresh, Chilled and Frozen Beef*, WTO Doc WT/DS161/AB/R; WT/DS169/AB/R (11 December 2000) ("*Korea – Beef*, Appellate Body Report"). In *Korea – Beef*, the Appellate Body held that the term "necessary", within the meaning of GATT art XX(d), requires a weighing and balancing of several factors which include the contribution of the compliance measure in enforcement of the law in question, the importance of common interests or values protected by the law and the impact of law on "imports or exports": at [164].

*EC – Asbestos*,[75] *EC – Tariff Preferences*,[76] *US – Gambling*[77] and *Brazil – Retreaded Tyres*.[78] In *Brazil – Retreaded Tyres*, for example, the Appellate Body

---

75   Appellate Body Report, *European Communities – Measures Affecting Asbestos and Asbestos-Containing Products*, WTO Doc WT/DS135/AB/R (12 March 2001) ("*EC – Asbestos*, Appellate Body Report"). In *EC – Asbestos*, the Appellate Body analysed the interpretation of "reasonably available" alternatives in order to determine whether French import restrictions were "necessary" within the meaning of *GATT* art XX(b): at [170], [173]–[175].

76   Appellate Body Report, *European Communities – Conditions for the Granting of Tariff Preferences to Developing Countries*, WTO Doc WT/DS246/AB/R (7 April 2004) ("*EC – Tariff Preferences*, Appellate Body Report"); Panel Report, *European Communities – Conditions for the Granting of Tariff Preferences to Developing Countries*, WTO Doc WT/DS246/R (1 December 2003) ("*EC – Tariff Preferences*, Panel Report"). The *EC – Tariff Preferences* case demonstrates that interpretation of "necessary" must be coupled with proven "effectiveness" of the trade measures (in this case, the EU's European Generalised System of Preferences ("GSP") scheme). The EU justified the scheme on the grounds that GSP tariff preferences promoted the "development of alternative economic activities to replace illicit drug production and trafficking" which, therefore, satisfied the standard under *GATT* art XX(b). The dispute settlement panel disagreed, and stated that the scheme was developmental in nature, with an emphasis on promotion of sustainable development in developing countries, which would mean that EU's defence under *GATT* art XX(b) was invalid. The panel cited the declining utility of GSP schemes due to global tariff reduction under WTO obligations, along with a lack of monitoring and compliance mechanisms for measuring "effectiveness" of the GSP scheme and the availability of less trade restrictive options. The panel concluded that the part of the EC GSP schemes relating to drug arrangements was not "necessary" to protect human life or health: [4.92]–[4.99], [7.211], [7.219]–[7.223]. The valuable takeaway for policymakers from the *EC – Tariff Preferences* case is that if a country adopts export controls and then seeks to justify them under the "necessary" standard, the measures must be factually proven as effective to achieve the stated goals.

77   The case concerned *Marrakesh Agreement Establishing the World Trade Organization*, opened for signature 15 April 1994, 1867 UNTS 3 (entered into force 1995) annex B ("*General Agreement on Trade in Services*") art XIV(a), which is identically worded to *GATT* art XX(a). The meaning of the term "necessary" was pinned to earlier jurisprudence (ie, assessing the "relative importance" of the interests or values promoted by the challenged measure, contribution of the measure to the achievement of the aims pursued by it, restrictive impact of the measure on international trade, weighed and measured with the interests or values, and, finally, a comparison between the challenged measure and possible alternatives available): Appellate Body Report, *United States – Measures Affecting the Cross-Border Supply of Gambling and Betting Services*, WTO Doc WT/DS285/AB/R (7 April 2005) [291], [304]–[309] ("*US – Gambling*, Appellate Body Report"). The Appellate Body also noted that "it is not the responding party's burden to show ... that there are no reasonably available alternatives to achieve its objectives" and that "a responding party need not identify the universe of less trade-restrictive alternative measures and then show that none of those measures achieves the desired objective": at [309]. Instead, the responding party must make a case that its measures are "necessary" by adducing evidence that allow the dispute settlement panels to assess the challenged measure in the light of the relevant factors to be "weighed and balanced" in a case: at [310]–[311].

78   Appellate Body Report, *Brazil – Measures Affecting Imports of Retreaded Tyres*, WTO Doc WT/DS332/AB/R (3 December 2007) ("*Brazil – Retreaded Tyres*, Appellate Body Report");

recognized the fundamental principle that WTO members have the right to determine the level of protection necessary to achieve a public policy goal.[79] In the first scenario (discussed above), the government of Country X can justify its measures as "necessary" under GATT art XX(d) by pointing to a short supply of gas which is leading to high energy prices within the country. To do so effectively, the challenge for Country X is to construct the export controls under the *Korea – Beef* approach by considering the possible alternatives which are reasonably available and then to further ensure that the "effectiveness" criteria is met, as highlighted in the *EC – Tariff Preferences* case.

Alternatively, Country X can consider pursuing an argument under GATT art XX(j), by claiming that export controls are "essential" to the distribution of products in "general or local short supply". To do so, the government of Country X must consider two factors: firstly, the "essential" criterion, and then the meaning of the term "general or local short supply" in the *India – Solar Cells* case.[80] In determining the meaning of "essential", the Appellate Body in *India – Solar Cells* endorsed a test similar to the "necessary" test under GATT art XX(d)

---

[79] Panel Report, *Brazil – Measures Affecting Imports of Retreaded Tyres*, WTO Doc WT/DS332/AB/R (12 June 2007) ("*Brazil – Retreaded Tyres,* Panel Report"). The term "necessary" received further treatment in *Brazil – Retreaded Tyres*, where the subject was Brazil's ban and penalties on the import and marketing of, and dealing with, retreaded tyres. Brazil's regional trading partners in the Mercosur regime received exemptions. Brazil cited the "necessary" argument under GATT art XX(b) and (d). The case illustrates an acknowledgment by the WTO that WTO Members have the right to determine the appropriate level of protection as per their public policy. The Appellate Body endorsed the panel's finding that the import ban on retreaded tyres can be provisionally justified: *Brazil – Retreaded Tyres*, Appellate Body Report (n 78), [145]. The panel "weighed and balanced" the contribution of the import restrictions in the context of the stated objective of the Brazilian policy. The panel then considered alternatives suggested by the complainant, and held that the suggested measures did not constitute "reasonably available" alternatives to the import restrictions: *Brazil – Retreaded Tyres*, Appellate Body Report (n 78), [157]; See also *Brazil – Retreaded Tyres,* Panel Report (n 78) [7.159]. The Appellate Body further noted that even where the contribution of the measures is not immediately observable, the measure could still be considered "necessary" encourages policymakers to closely scrutinise factors that contribute to the overall objective of the trade restrictive measure: *Brazil – Retreaded Tyres*, Appellate Body Report (n 78), [210]–[212]. The WTO seems to be endorsing a position where the expectation is that the imposing Member has undertaken a comparative analysis of the measure in light of possible, less-trade restrictive alternatives, while at the same time, the complaining WTO Member, is afforded the opportunity to identify possible less-trade restrictive measures that the responding Member could have taken.

[80] The term "essential", according to the Appellate Body, ranks closer to the "indispensable" end of the continuum than the word "necessary": *India – Solar Cells*, Appellate Body Report (n 7) [5.62].

which involves "weighing and balancing" a series of factors.[81] Secondly, Country X must consider the meaning of the term "general or local short supply" as enunciated by the Appellate Body in *India – Solar Cells*. The Appellate Body stated that in settling the question of "general or local short supply", regard must be given to:[82]

> [t]he total quantity of imports that may be available to meet demand in a particular geographical area or market. It may ... be relevant to consider the extent to which international supply of a product is stable and accessible, including ... distance between a particular geographical area or market and production sites, as well as reliability of local or transnational supply chains. Whether and which factors are relevant necessarily depend on the particularities of each case.

The Appellate Body held that, regardless of the occurrence of factors in each case, the responding party (namely, the party imposing the export control) has the burden to demonstrate that the quantity of available supply, from both domestic and international sources, to the relevant geographical market is insufficient to meet demand.[83]

No country has so far faced an accusation of expropriation in relation to export controls. If policymakers in a developing country design an investment policy, considerations that have been highlighted in *India – Solar Cells* provide a workable template in dealing with any future "general or local short supply" issue. Looking ahead, if these considerations are satisfied, a host country can adopt a "police powers"-based approach to argue that export controls are not expropriatory in nature and that the government had acted to alleviate "general or local short supply".

Indirect expropriation is usually connected to imperatives such as health and the environment. Devaluing the investment of a foreign investor(s) is often a by-product of governmental measures, which then leads to a claim of indirect expropriation by the affected foreign investor(s). Therefore, for Country X, the challenges in constructing export controls is to not only satisfy the GATT obligations owed to other countries (where importers are based), but also to ensure that any investor who may be damaged by export controls is unable to lodge a claim under any BIT or FTA signed by Country X. Hence, the origin of the foreign investor is an important factor to consider before imposing

---

81 Ibid [5.63] (emphasis added).
82 Ibid [6.4].
83 Ibid.

the export control. For example, assuming that Country X is already in a BIT with another country (Country D) and that investors (Corporation A) based in Country D have invested in the gas sector of Country X with the aim of extracting, refining and exporting gas from Country X, then any measures that restrict the Corporation A's stated rationale for investment can become the basis of a claim against Country X for indirect expropriation. Country X may be liable to pay compensation to Corporation A, however, this finding depends on a series of inter-connected factors such as legitimate expectations, the terms of the BIT, the proportionality and necessity of the adopted measures, and how the expropriation clauses are constructed within the underlying BIT. In any ISDS setting, Country X will most likely demonstrate that actions were undertaken pursuant to the police powers of the state, in order to ensure stable gas supply in the country, while Corporation A's strategy will be to claim compensation for indirect expropriation due to lost revenue and loss of share value. Alternatively, the government of Country X will seek to adopt an argument based in the proportionality, legitimacy and necessity analysis highlighted in more recent disputes such as *RREEF v Spain* and *American Silver*.[84]

One argument which may work in the favour of Country X is that if products are considered in "general or local short supply" under GATT art XX(j), then this automatically boosts the public interest argument which, by implication, can settle the issue of the police powers of the state as well. In simpler terms, states have the right to ensure that their people have access to the basic resources needed for living (such as access to food, water, affordable energy and security, etc). Resultantly, the claim by Corporation A of indirect expropriation based on export controls may stand on a weak basis.

In the case of Country Y (the second scenario discussed above), the outcome might be somewhat different. In this scenario, export controls are being used by the government of Country Y to boost economic activity in the country by diverting critical materials inwards through prohibiting their export. Like the first scenario, Country Y may face allegations of indirect expropriation if the wording of any underlying FTA or BIT enables Corporation B (the investor) to initiate ISDS proceedings. For this to happen, Corporation B must demonstrate that it is owned, in terms of shares, by a party and/or shareholder based in an FTA or BIT partner country. However, where Corporation B has an advantage, where claims are concerned, is that powers exercised by the government of Country Y are not likely to be interpreted as police powers of the state or regulatory powers exercised in the public interest or for public welfare.

---

84  In this respect, see the arguments above 4.2.

One can make the argument that governments have the right to adopt economic initiatives that result in economic advancement and the creation of jobs, but this argument may be on weak footing when it comes to the prejudice suffered by the foreign investor. Hence, Corporation B, in the second scenario, will have a stronger claim against Country Y for indirect expropriation. But what if Corporation B's investment was not under any FTA or BIT that Country Y has signed? In such a situation, Corporation B's efforts to protect its investment under an FTA or BIT will be difficult.[85] From the experience of Phillip Morris's claim against Australia's tobacco plain-packaging regulations, any *post facto* restructuring in order to bring an expropriation claim will likely not succeed.[86] Therefore, as long as Country Y treats investment in a non-discriminatory manner between domestic and foreign investors in the rare earths sector, it may be able to evade a claim of expropriation under any FTA or BIT.

One of the common themes in the first and second scenarios is that they both concern natural resources (gas and rare earths). In the second scenario, the changes introduced by Country Y are driven largely by economic and political motivations, whereas in the first scenario, the governmental measures are driven by a concern for ensuring stable gas supply. Both scenarios, however, hamper the ability of the foreign investors in question to carry out their business activity. A pre-emptive solution to the problem may be the incorporation of an economic equilibrium clause into the project agreement.[87] The economic equilibrium clause enables stabilisation of the economic return to the investor, instead of stabilisation of the legal framework.[88] Under economic equilibrium clauses, host states may be entitled to issue changes that can potentially affect the project, but will be bound to consult the foreign investor in order to

---

85 Russell Thirgood, Michael Roche and Erika Williams, "Australia: Proposed LNG Export Restraints and Australian Liability Under International Trade Law", *mondaq* (Web Page, 20 June 2017) <http://www.mondaq.com/australia/x/603326/Inward+Foreign+Investment/Proposed+LNG+export+restrictions+and+Australian+liability+under+international+trade+law>.

86 Phillip Morris attempted to restructure its investment in Australia to take advantage of the BIT between Hong Kong and Australia. This was ultimately unsuccessful and held to be an abuse of process by the tribunal: ibid.

87 For a brief discussion of the "economic equilibrium clause", see David Clinch and James Watson, "Stabilisation Clauses: Issues and Trends", *Lexology* (Web Page, 30 June 2010) <https://www.lexology.com/library/detail.aspx?g=c5976193-1acd-4082-b9e7-87c0414b5328>.

88 Stabilisation clauses are contractual protections incorporated within long term investments between foreign investors and states. Majority of stabilisation clauses appear in investment agreements in the oil, gas and resources sector. They can also be found in infrastructure and transport projects as well: ibid.

determine the impact of the proposed changes.[89] The parties usually discuss a renegotiated framework of investment or, alternatively, the state will pay appropriate compensation to the foreign investor. Moreover, any ISDS proceedings will be subject to the host states discussing the governmental measures with the foreign investors if an economic equilibrium clause has been included in the investment framework. However, if parties disagree on the remedial measures or the compensation payable, then the foreign investors can weigh in on whether to claim indirect expropriation by initiating ISDS proceedings. The feasibility of negotiating economic equilibrium clauses by the foreign investor may be influenced by a variety of factors, which include but are not limited to: the appetite of the government of the host country to enter into pre-investment negotiations; the quantum and nature of foreign investments; the size and frequency of profit remittance from the host country; the sociopolitical sensitivity of the sector in which the foreign investor has invested; and the investor's own understanding of the regulatory standards in the host economy as well as under the FTA or BIT umbrella.

In contrast to the first two scenarios, the third scenario has been deliberately constructed to explain a situation where the conduct of the host country is composite of direct takings (confiscation), accompanied by export controls that make the export of goods unattractive. Confiscation is a clear instance of direct expropriation, but export controls, as argued above in the first and second scenarios, may only be found to constitute indirect expropriation provided that certain conditions are met. This may involve the foreign investor showing that the exercise of power by the state did not meet the reasonableness standard, which in turn, may involve considering factors such as the legitimacy of the state measure's purpose, its proportionality and necessity, and the suitability of the measure to achieve public welfare.

In the third scenario, a government imposes export controls due to pressure from interest groups. The governmental motives are a mixture of factors ranging from unforeseen developments in the international market, economic factors and its responsibility to maintain employment levels in the country. However, not all of the aforementioned factors can become grounds for defence against a claim for indirect expropriation. For example, in the first and second scenarios, exercising police powers or acting in the public welfare can give the host state an excuse to resist indirect expropriation claims by foreign investors. In the third scenario, the confiscatory action was aimed at placating labour unions and local apparel businesses, which is clearly not a public welfare

---

89  Ibid.

objective. However, there may be a way out for Country Z. It is common knowledge that for many developing countries and LDCs, textiles and clothing are often the main value-added industries in their economy. If Country Z can satisfy the art XX(j) standard, it can basically argue that it is acting to alleviate "general or local short supply" in the country. If the measures are adopted in a non-discriminatory manner and are applied uniformly to all locally- and foreign-owned businesses, then there can be little doubt that such powers are part of the police powers of the state, which makes it difficult for the foreign investor to claim compensation.

Thus, can it be said that the government of Country Z in the third scenario is acting to control exports in order to alleviate "general or local short supply"? This query seeks to apply the Appellate Body's art XX(j) reasoning in *India – Solar Cells*, whilst also determining the broader question whether Country Z's actions are in the public interest. For example, what was the total quantity of imports available to meet demand in Country Z? The answer to this query is clearly obvious: due to an international shortage, the sourcing of cotton yarn through imports was impossible and Country Z's cotton yarn producers emerged as top suppliers (both domestically and internationally). Therefore, this factor works in the favour of Country Z's export controls. Further, the extent to which international supply of a product is stable and accessible is to be considered. Again, the answer is similar to the previous query. The supplies are largely from domestic sources which also happen to be proximate to the market and production sites within the country. The Appellate Body explained in *India – Solar Cells* that, when determining "general or local short supply", the relevant factors are peculiar to each case.[90]

Also, the extent to which domestic producers sell their production abroad is a relevant factor which was identified by the Appellate Body.[91] In the third scenario, cotton yarn producers were inclined to export their yarn rather than sell them domestically. These factors indicate that unless Country Z adopts export control measures, the domestic clothing sector will suffer immeasurably and may lead to rises in unemployment and business losses. Therefore, with the proviso that the measures are applied in a non-discriminatory manner, the export controls imposed by Country Z can potentially be considered as valid under art XX(j) and could give grounds to resist any ISDS claims that Corporation C may bring against Country Z for indirect expropriation. Note, however, that Corporation C must distinguish confiscation from export controls. Export controls that may have been imposed by Country Z do not impose an outright ban

---

90  *India – Solar Cells,* Appellate Body Report (n 7) [6.4].
91  *India – Solar Cells,* Appellate Body Report (n 7) [5.71].

on the exports of cotton yarn. Instead, like the export tariffs on the FOB price of rare earths discussed in the second scenario, they raise the export duty, with the aim of making exports unattractive for some exporters. Confiscation of property, on the other hand, is an outright taking which may be classified as direct expropriation. Therefore, if Country Z has confiscated any cotton yarn owned by Corporation C from the port warehouses, this may give rise to a claim for compensation even if the action was for a public purpose.

## 5    Analysis

### 5.1    *The Two Paths*

The challenge confronting any reader of this analysis is explaining the state actions from the several, and oft-competing, standpoints of "legitimacy", "necessity", "proportionality", "legitimate expectations", "public welfare" and/or "police powers". Are the three presented scenarios explained by the state exercising its regulatory powers, and/or is the state acting pursuant to a legitimate public purpose?

To answer this query, the exceptional grounds mentioned in *GATT* art XX have to be holistically considered, since they share a conceptual similarity with common grounds of public regulation by states. Investment disputes such as the *Methanex* case indicate that "non-discriminatory regulation for public purpose" can be deemed by arbitral panels as falling within the doctrine of police powers.[92] This is not different from public interest imperatives that the newer generation of FTAs and BITs refer to, while also constructing "carve out" clauses to make room for public welfare exceptions.[93]

The taxonomy of an export control is also important because there is a convincing line of arbitral cases that designate the exercise of police powers of state as non-compensable if done in a non-discriminatory manner. Conversely, the exercise of regulatory powers in order to promote public welfare objectives is recognised in some modern FTAs and BITs as not amounting to indirect expropriation. Hence, the actual procedure and the perception of the measure as being, or not being, in the public interest assumes greater importance.

---

92   See discussion in *Methanex (Final Award)* (n 71) 1456, cited in Mostafa (n 71) 272–274.

93   By way of illustration, ACIA (n 65) annex 2 (4) specifically provides for carve outs for "measures ... designed and applied to protect legitimate public welfare objectives such as public health, safety and the environment", which will not be considered to constitute expropriation.

As far as export controls are concerned, the Appellate Body in the *India – Solar Cells* case clarifies the meaning of "general or local short supply". Assuming the restrictions in question are applied uniformly and in a non-discriminatory manner, the claim of a foreign investor for compensation may be on weak grounds. One possible solution suggested hereinabove was the incorporation or negotiation of stabilisation and/or economic equilibrium clauses in investment agreements, which will allow foreign investors to have their say in managing the fallout of any governmental measures. The first and second scenarios discussed previously illustrate that the application of export controls in this context will likely not be construed as expropriatory. However, such a simplistic approach creates some challenges.

Firstly, actual disruption must be proven by the host state. This may well become a key determinant connecting export controls and the foreign investor's claim for compensation for expropriation. In absence of a defined criterion, the government of the host state and the foreign investor may end up arguing their subjective interpretation of what is, or should be, the disruption that justifies the export controls. Whilst disruptions in the context of international trade can be handled under the GATT/WTO framework, no centrally agreed definitions exist in the realm of international investment law. Furthermore, FTAS/BITS may consider defining what a disruption may look like, but again there are no known FTAS or BITS that define disruption in a foreign investment context, particularly where the aim behind foreign investment in the host state is to enable foreign investors to export resources or goods.

Secondly, action in response to anticipated shortages or market disruptions may be difficult to justify, politically motivated or, quite simply, speculative in nature. Should a host state wait until actual disruption occurs, or is a risk assessment of impending shortage sufficient to impose export controls? This is a moot point, because foreign investors will argue that no actual disruption and/or shortage has occurred, and hence that the imposition of export controls is expropriatory. Since there are no agreed formulae in international investment law to determine imminent market disruption, any attempt to speculate about the possible effects of market disruption in the absence of an actual one will likely be rejected by arbitral panels, as was the case with the Appellate Body's treatment of India's argument in *India – Solar Cells* case.[94] Additionally, foreign investors and arbitral panels may attempt to interpret questions of public

---

94 *India – Solar Cells*, Appellate Body Report (n 7) [5.76]. The panel in *India – Solar Cells* held that India "had not identified any actual disruptions", and that solar power developers ("SPDS") in India have not "experienced an actual disruption in supply": *India – Solar Cells*, Panel Report (n 20) [7.262].

interest when determining whether an "actual disruption" has occurred, or is likely to occur – a truly unsavoury proposition for most governments indeed. It is clear, from Australia's jousting with Phillip Morris, that well-endowed, multinational corporations ("MNCS") can exert substantial influence on governmental authorities, thereby resulting in regulatory chill. States and governmental authorities consider such fettering of their regulatory discretion an unwelcome prospect.[95]

Furthermore, there is a lack of general reporting mechanisms that enable the reporting of export controls to parties or countries affected by such measures.[96] The ubiquitous means of notification are the news and electronic media that may be relied upon by business interests. While the WTO does maintain a Trade Policy Review Mechanism ("TPRM"), which records any export restrictions or controls in place, TPRM Reports usually come at a four-year interval for some countries (and six years for countries identified as LDCS).[97] Clearly, this mechanism is not useful for the affected parties in circumstances where a government announces an export control, which may affect businesses dependent on goods or commodities that are subject to such controls. Considering the argument that export controls affecting MNCS owned by foreign investors may be subject to future disputes, it becomes worthwhile at this stage to discuss two possible paths for redress that may be chosen strategically by claimants.

### 5.2   The First Path: WTO Dispute Settlement as a Parallel Action to ISDS

Recourse to WTO dispute settlement by a foreign investor is based on the premise that export controls have breached GATT/WTO obligations owed to the country in which the foreign investor is based. This alternative poses several challenges. Firstly, the exact breach of WTO obligations must be ascertained, and the export controls in question must have violated the terms of the GATT/WTO framework (ie, the Most-Favoured-Nation ("MFN") or National Treatment ("NT") obligations, or the factors under GATT arts XI and XX, as explained through the WTO dispute-settlement jurisprudence). Secondly, the country in which the foreign investor is based must establish *locus standi* to bring about the complaint in the WTO. Thirdly, the WTO must grapple with a

---

95   Thirgood, Roche and Williams (n 85).
96   Matsushita, "Export Controls of Natural Resources and the WTO/GATT Disciplines" (n 8) 309.
97   See generally "Uruguay Round Agreement: Trade Policy Review Mechanism (TRPM)", *World Trade Organization* (Web Page) <https://www.wto.org/english/docs_e/legal_e/29-tprm_e.htm>.

breach of obligations that, quite possibly, may be owed under a different bilateral FTA.[98] This is where the foreign investor must assess its prospects of success, by investigating whether the underlying FTA contains a "fork-in-the-road"[99] clause, which requires the investor (claimant) to select whether to lodge a claim for compensation in the domestic courts or opt for international options.[100] However, "fork-in-the-road" clauses only enable selection between

---

[98] This is a challenging proposition, as is illustrated by the *Mexico – Soft Drinks* case in the WTO. See Appellate Body Report, *Mexico – Tax Measures on Soft Drinks and Other Beverages*, WTO Doc WT/DS308/AB/R (6 March 2006) ("*Mexico – Soft Drinks*, Appellate Body Report"); Panel Report, *Mexico – Tax Measures on Soft Drinks and Other Beverages*, WTO Doc WT/DS308/R (7 October 2005) ("*Mexico – Soft Drinks*, Panel Report"). In *Mexico – Soft Drinks*, the US argued that domestic taxes imposed by Mexico on drinks using non-cane sugar breached the NT obligations that Mexico owed the US under GATT. Mexico justified its measures because the measures were in response to the US breaching its market access commitments negotiated under NAFTA on trade in sugar, while the US-origin high-fructose corn syrup ("HFCS") (a sugar alternative used as input in manufacturing of beverages) enjoyed continued preferential access to the Mexican market. Furthermore, Mexico claimed that the US continuously refused to submit to the NAFTA dispute settlement process. Resultantly, Mexico viewed the measures as falling within the scope of the GATT art XX(d) exception, which permits a WTO Member to derogate from a GATT/WTO obligation to secure compliance with laws or regulations. The panel concluded that the tax breached the WTO NT obligation, but that the WTO has no jurisdiction to adjudicate on obligations owed under NAFTA: *Mexico – Soft Drinks*, Panel Report [4.70], [4.72], [8.193], [8.199]. The panel's conclusions were upheld on appeal by the Appellate Body. The Appellate Body disagreed with Mexico's argument on GATT art XX(d), and stated that the term "laws or regulations" in GATT art XX(d) referred "to the rules that form part of the domestic legal order of the WTO Member invoking the provision and do not include the international obligations of another WTO Member": *Mexico – Soft Drinks*, Appellate Body Report [75], [79]–[80]. See also detailed discussions in Sergio Puig, "The Merging of International Trade and Investment Law" (2015) 33(1) *Berkeley Journal of International Law* 1, 23–27; Roger Alford, "The Convergence of International Trade and Investment Arbitration" (2014) 12(1) *Santa Clara Journal of International Law* 35, 46–47.

[99] "Fork-in-the-road" clauses enable foreign investors to bypass the standard rule of public international law that requires parties to exhaust domestic remedies before lodging an international claim: see, eg, discussion in Deborah Ruff and Trevor Tan, "Fork-in-The-Road Clauses: Divergent Paths in Recent Decisions", *Norton Rose Fulbright* (Publication, October 2015) <http://www.nortonrosefulbright.com/knowledge/publications/132586/fork-in-the-road-clauses>; see also the discussion in Christoph Schreuer, "Calvo's Grandchildren: The Return of Local Remedies in Investment Arbitration" (2005) 4(1) *The Law & Practice of International Courts and Tribunals* 1, 3–5; Christoph Schreuer, "Travelling the BIT Route: Of Waiting Periods, Umbrella Clauses and Forks in the Road" (2004) 5(2) *Journal of World Investment and Trade* 231, 239–249.

[100] Puig, above n 89, 36; Schreuer, above n 90, 239–249; See further Norton Rose Fulbright, "Fork-in-the-Road clauses: Divergent Paths in Recent Decisions" (October 2015) <https://www.nortonrosefulbright.com/en/knowledge/publications/obd10ad8/fork-in-the-road-clauses> (accessed 11 July 2019).

enforcement alternatives, and do not concern treaty selection.¹⁰¹ Hence, the options for investors will be limited to local courts or redress under the operative FTA or BIT.

In the simulated scenarios discussed above, governmental actions were prompted by domestic compulsions in all three instances. If the act of imposing export controls is deemed a sovereign act, local courts will then be required to extend constitutional cover to cover the measures. Foreign investors will understandably be reluctant to approach domestic courts for redress. In the first and third scenarios especially, the government of the host state can refuse to pay any compensation by arguing that measures restricting exports were sovereign actions to alleviate "general or local short supply". If the matter proceeds to arbitration, the government can take up the plea that its export controls were an act of state.¹⁰²

As stated above, the WTO dispute-settlement system can only be pursued as an alternative if there is a prima facie violation of GATT/WTO norms in the imposition of export controls. On rare occasions, and if the investors have enough financial resources along with significant influence, the aggrieved investor can pursue parallel claims under ISDS and WTO dispute settlement proceedings.¹⁰³ Parallel proceedings may sometimes become necessary to secure comprehensive relief for the investors. For example, in the *Mexico – Soft Drinks* case, an action was pursued in the WTO alongside ISDS proceedings under NAFTA. Alford notes that in the case of Mexico imposing unlawful taxes on soft drinks, the WTO and NAFTA systems complemented each other in securing

---

101  Puig (n 98) 36.
102  This was recently illustrated in *Reliance Industries Ltd and BG Exploration & Production India Ltd v India*, in which the claimants (Reliance Industries and BG Exploration) lodged an arbitration claim against the respondent government (India) for unpaid sums due on production sharing contracts. After the tribunal found that it lacked jurisdiction to determine the question of legality of the government ordering its subordinate departments to withhold payments, the matter was appealed to the Queen's Bench Division, Commercial Court in England. Popplewell J held that the issues in question were covered under the foreign-act-of-state doctrine and were thus non-justiciable before the court and non-arbitrable before the tribunal. This decision underscores the application of act of state doctrine in arbitration as well as court proceedings. The implication of the decision is that a state party intending to avoid performance under a contract can easily issue executive orders, ordinances or legislation and then invoke the act-of-state principle in any proceedings where the seat of arbitration is in England: see generally *Reliance Industries Ltd and BG Exploration & Production India Ltd v India* [2018] EWHC 822 (Comm); see also Lucia Raimanova and Matej Kosalko, "Act of State Doctrine Applies in Arbitration", *Allen & Overy* (Web Page, 21 June 2018) <http://www.allenovery.com/publications/en-gb/|Pages/Act-of-State-doctrine-applies-in-arbitration.aspx>.
103  Puig (n 98) 44.

both prospective and retroactive relief for the investors.[104] If the WTO had been the only system used to adjudicate the dispute, then the WTO Appellate Body's direction to Mexico, to repeal the unlawful taxes, would have been the end of the matter. However, parallel claims under arbitration enabled the aggrieved investors to collectively receive approximately USD170 million in damages in three separate claims.[105]

Another recent example concerns the action launched by Cuba, Indonesia, Ukraine, Honduras and Dominican Republic against the Australian tobacco plain-packaging legislation in the WTO, alleging violation of the WTO's *Agreement on Trade-Related Aspects of Intellectual Property Rights*.[106] This action was launched in parallel to ISDS proceedings instituted by Philip Morris under the *Hong Kong–Australia BIT*.[107] Sergio Puig terms this behaviour of MNCs as "party shopping", whereby private parties strategically select a state party to espouse a claim on their behalf in the WTO.[108]

---

104   Alford (n 98) 47.
105   Three claims cited by Alford (n 98) 47 are: (i) *Archer Daniels Midland Co et al v Mexico* (*Award*) (ICSID Arbitral Tribunal, Case No ARB(AF)/04/05, 21 November 2007), where the tribunal awarded USD33 million in damages to the Claimant; (ii) *Corn Products International Inc v Mexico* (*Decision on Responsibility*) (ICSID Arbitral Tribunal, Case No ARB(AF)/04/01, 15 January 2008), where the tribunal awarded USD58.4 million in damages; and (iii) *Cargill Inc v Mexico* (*Award*) (ICSID Arbitral Tribunal, Case No ARB(AF)/05/02, 18 September 2009), where the tribunal awarded USD77.3 million in damages.
106   See generally Panel Report, *Australia – Certain Measures Concerning Trademarks, Geographical Indications and Other Plain Packaging Requirements Applicable to Tobacco Products and Packaging*, WTO Doc WT/DS435/R; WT/DS441/R; WT/DS458/R; WT/DS467/R (28 June 2018). In this case, the WTO panel endorsed Australia's plain packaging laws by holding that they contributed to improving public health by reducing and discouraging use of tobacco products: [7.228]–[7.232], [7.1725], [7.1731], [7.2794]–[7.2795]; see also "Australia Wins Landmark World Trade Organisation Ruling on Tobacco Plain Packaging Laws", *ABC News* (Web Page, 28 June 2018) <http://www.abc.net.au/news/2018-06-29/australia-wins-landmark-wto-ruling-on-tobacco-plain-packaging/9921972>.; *Marrakesh Agreement Establishing the World Trade* Organization, opened for signature 15 April 1994, 1867 UNTS 3 (entered into force 1 January 1995) annex 1C ("*Agreement on Trade-Related Aspects of Intellectual Property Rights*") ("*TRIPS Agreement*").
107   See generally *Philip Morris Asia Ltd v Australia* (*Award on Jurisdiction and Admissibility*) (Permanent Court of Arbitration, Case No 2012-12, 17 December 2015); *Agreement between the Government of Australia and the Government of Hong Kong for the Promotion and Protection of Investments*, signed 15 September 1993, [1993] ATS 30 (entered into force 15 October 1993).
108   Puig (n 98) 36; Alford observes that one of the complainants in the WTO case (Ukraine) had not exported tobacco to Australia in recent years: Alford (n 98) 50. British American Tobacco was known to be assisting Ukraine with its legal costs in the WTO claim because MNCs currently have no standing to lodge a WTO claim. Ukraine eventually dropped the

Parallel proceedings usually involve MNCs with significant resources engaging in a protracted dispute-resolution process. Pursuing such a strategy is based on a careful study of costs and benefits. In the simulated scenarios, all three affected businesses will have to determine whether they wish to pursue a strategy based on ISDS coupled with a WTO claim. For the parallel action strategy to work, the MNCs in question will have to lobby their governments to bring about a state-based response in the WTO, which is a difficult proposition due to the largely self-regulating nature of WTO dispute-settlement system.[109]

### 5.3 The Second Path: ISDS Adapting WTO Dispute-Settlement Jurisprudence as an Interpretative Aid (*Convergence*)

Given the challenges of adopting the approach outlined above, investors may consider "borrowing" arguments from WTO jurisprudence when pursuing their ISDS claim against the host state. *China – Rare Earths* and *China – Raw Materials* have demonstrated that the WTO remains interested in promoting the fair and equitable allocation of resources between domestic users and importers. However, the challenge in cross-implementing the WTO standards in investment disputes is a grey area. If disputes on export controls remain within the realm of international trade, GATT/WTO norms may provide a prospective solution (ie, the WTO DSB recommending that the offending WTO member brings its impugned measures in line with its WTO obligations). It is only when the export control disputes encroach into the field of international investment law that there are no clear characterisations of the issue, primarily because there are no international agreements addressing the relationship between export controls and expropriation. The meaning of expropriation has been left to individual BITs and FTAs and the interpretation of arbitral tribunals. Decisions issued in the past by the ISDS tribunals have done little to resolve the question of whether the host country remains the master of their natural resources or becomes subject to the requirement of an equitable distribution of resources after signing BITs and/or FTAs.

---

claim against Australia, citing hopes of finding a mutually agreed solution with Australia: "Ukraine Drops Lawsuit against Australia over Plain-Packaging Tobacco Laws, WTO Says", *ABC News* (Web Page, 3 June 2015) <http://www.abc.net.au/news/2015-06-04/plain-pac kaging-tobacco-ukraine-drops-lawsuit-against-australia/6520160>.

109 Puig (n 98) 36–37, citing Appellate Body Report, *Mexico – Anti-Dumping Investigation of High Fructose Corn Syrup from the United States – Recourse to Article 21.5 of the DSU by the United States*, WTO Doc WT/DS132/AB/RW (22 October 2001) [73]–[74], wherein the Appellate Body deemed that the request for establishment of panel by a WTO Member is premised on good faith and an exercise of sound judgment regarding the utility of dispute settlement process under the WTO system.

Future arbitral panels confronted with the question of export controls and indirect expropriation may consider "importing" or "transplanting" the interpretation of the concept of a local or general short supply of materials from GATT/WTO norms.[110] The interpretation of GATT art XX(j) by the Appellate Body in *India – Solar Cells* (especially in para [6.4]) may provide a useful initial point. The concluding comment in para [6.4], namely, "whether and which factors are relevant necessarily depend on the particularities of each case", can be termed as a control valve for the application of the standard to determine whether an export control can be justified based on "local or general short supply" similar in spirit to the *chapeau* of GATT art XX. This is just a starting point. The remaining development of the concept will then, it is hoped, assume a more organic trajectory in the form of arbitral panel decisions and their impacts on future BITs and FTAs. The adoption of GATT art XX(j) reasoning can further enable policymakers in host states to construct WTO- and/or BIT-compliant export controls in a manner that limits the possibility of challenges by foreign investors.

The approach of importing from WTO jurisprudence has not only been considered by arbitral panels in the past, but has received growing academic attention in recent years, resulting in a "convergence" of international trade and investment law.[111] This is not to suggest that the convergence approach finds total approval. It is merely a course of action which can be considered as an initial point in international investment dispute resolution where there are ambiguities in law or an absence of jurisprudence on an issue.

---

110   The underlying assumption is that export controls were imposed for alleviating local shortages or for domestic price stabilisation. Puig terms this approach as "transplantation", whereby disputing parties may import a rule from one trade treaty to another investment treaty. Puig cites the example of the strategy employed by Philip Morris, linking Australia's obligations under the *Hong Kong–Australia BIT* with Australia's WTO obligations under the *TRIPS Agreement* and the *Agreement on Technical Barriers to Trade (Marrakesh Agreement Establishing the World Trade Organization*, opened for signature 15 April 1994, 1867 UNTS 3 (entered into force 1 January 1995) annex 1A ("*Agreement on Technical Barriers to Trade*")): Puig (n 98) 41–44.

111   Jurgen Kurtz, "The Use and Abuse of WTO Law in Investor-State Arbitration: Competition and its Discontents" (2009) 20(3) *European Journal of International Law* 749, 751–759, 770–771; Robert Howse and Efraim Chalamish, "The Use and Abuse of WTO Law in Investor-State Arbitration: A Reply to Jurgen Kurtz" (2010) 20(4) *European Journal of International Law* 1087, 1088–1090; Alford (n 98) 37; Frank Garcia et al, "Reforming the International Investment Regime: Lessons from International Trade Law" (2015) 18(4) *Journal of International Economic Law* 861, 864; Brooks Allen and Tommaso Soave, "Jurisdictional Overlap in WTO Dispute Settlement and Investment Arbitration" (2014) 30(1) *Arbitration International* 1, 28; Andrea Bjorklund, "Convergence or Complementarity" (2013) 12(1) *Santa Clara Journal of International Law* 65, 68–70; Puig (n 98) 4–5.

By way of illustration, ISDS proceedings on NT issues show that dispute-settlement tribunals are hesitant to adopt WTO jurisprudence to explain NT in an FTA and/or BIT context. For example, in *Pope and Talbot v Canada*, the respondent (Canada) attempted to base its arguments on the NT standard under WTO law and import the same understanding in its dispute regarding softwood lumber with a US-based investor under *NAFTA*.[112] Canada specifically claimed that even where the foreign investor was awarded a lower quota than domestic producers, there was no discrimination because foreign investors were not disadvantaged disproportionately as a group.[113] Kurtz observes that Canada's arguments imply that the impact of a measure must be determined by comparing two basic groups (local producers and foreign investors) to assess any disproportionate impact on foreign investors as a whole.[114] In its analysis, the tribunal rebutted Canada's argument that the disproportionate disadvantage test was grounded in WTO jurisprudence.[115] The tribunal specifically pointed out that the disproportionate disadvantage test was unwieldy and posed practical obstacles in its implementations. In particular, the tribunal stated that if Canada's arguments were adopted, this would mean that the foreign investor would have to undertake the mammoth task of tracking the quota details of US-owned companies in Canada and then consider the treatment being accorded to those companies as a whole in contrast with domestic companies operating in like circumstances.[116] The tribunal concluded that, were this the approach to be taken, "only in the simplest and most obvious cases of denial of national treatment could the complainant hope to make a case for recovery".[117] Based on *Pope and Talbot v Canada* alone, and contrasting the three alternative scenarios provided in this article, a foreign corporation could consider making parallel arguments based on WTO laws, alongside an ISDS claim, that export controls by host states are discriminatory and amount to indirect expropriation, if it can be demonstrated that local actors are being advantaged.

Note, however, that this strategy may encounter practical difficulties for the aggrieved investors. The example being discussed here shows the potential possibilities, but not necessarily a practical strategy. Other disputes where the convergence approach was considered encountered cautious responses by the relevant dispute settlement tribunals. For example, in another *NAFTA* dispute,

---

112   See *Pope & Talbot Inc v Canada* (*Award on the Merits of Phase* 2) (Ad Hoc Tribunal under the UNCITRAL Arbitration Rules, 10 April 2001) [43]–[44] ("*Pope & Talbot v Canada*").
113   Kurtz (n 111) 761.
114   *Pope & Talbot v Canada* (n 112) [46]–[63].
115   Ibid.
116   Ibid [71]–[72]; Kurtz (n 111) 762.
117   *Pope & Talbot v Canada* (n 112) [71]–[72]; Kurtz (n 111) 762.

*SD Myers v Canada*, the tribunal cited the Appellate Body's treatment of "like" circumstances in *Japan – Taxes on Alcoholic Beverages*, wherein the Appellate Body had commented that:[118]

> [T]here can be no one precise and absolute definition of what is "like". The concept of "likeness" is a relative one that evokes the image of an accordion. The accordion of "likeness" stretches and squeezes in different places as different provisions of the WTO Agreement are applied.

The tribunal observed that similar to the GATT treatment of "like", the overall legal context provided by the FTA (in this case *NAFTA*) and any other treaties must be considered carefully.[119] The tribunal pointed out that all three NAFTA countries are also part of the Organisation of Economic Co-operation and Development ("OECD") and hence, the *OECD Declaration on International and Multinational Enterprises* becomes relevant as well in determining the question of "like" circumstances.[120]

In the well-known Methanex dispute, the tribunal considered the wto concept of NT in order to determine the connection between "like circumstances" and "like products".[121] The tribunal in Methanex specifically observed that "if the drafters of NAFTA had wanted to incorporate trade criteria in its investment chapter by engrafting a GATT-type formula, they could have produced a version of Article 1102".[122]

---

118   Appellate Body Report, *Japan – Taxes on Alcoholic Beverages*, WTO Doc WT/DS8/AB/R; WT/DS10/AB/R; WT/DS11/AB/R (4 October 1996) 21 ("*Japan – Alcoholic Beverages*, Appellate Body Report"), cited in *SD Myers v Canada (Partial Award)* (North American Free Trade Agreement Tribunal under the UNCITRAL Arbitration Rules, 13 November 2000) [244] ("*SD Myers v Canada*").
119   *SD Myers v Canada* (n 118) [245], [248].
120   The *OECD Declaration on International and Multinational Enterprises* dealt with the "like situation" test by affirming that
      [T]he comparison between foreign-controlled enterprises is only valid if it is made between firms operating in the same sector. More general considerations, such as the policy objectives of Member countries could be considered to define the circumstances in which comparison between foreign-controlled and domestic enterprises is permissible inasmuch as those objectives are not contrary to the principle of national treatment ...
      Ibid [249], citing the 1993 version of Organisation for Economic Co-operation and Development, *OECD Declaration on International Investment and Multinational Enterprises*, 21 June 1976.
121   Kurtz (n 111) 763–765; *Methanex (Final Award)* (n 71) 1447–1448.
122   *Methanex (Final Award)* (n 71) 1447–1448.

More specifically, the tribunal noted that it was apparent from the text that the drafters of NAFTA were careful about the inclusion of the terms such as "like goods", "any like, directly competitive or substitutable goods" and "like circumstances".[123] The tribunal observed that "like goods" is not used within the context of Ch 11 (investment), while "like circumstances" (which is used as an expression in art 1102, within Ch 11) is used for investment, with respect to standards related to measures constituting technical barriers to trade ("TBTs"), only in relation to services but not in relation to goods.[124]

Roger Alford comments that regardless of whether the tribunals in *Pope and Talbot*, *SD Myers* and *Methanex* reached the correct result, these leading cases presumed the relevance of WTO jurisprudence and that comments that the "pull toward reliance on WTO as persuasive authority appears almost irresistible".[125] Alford also cites comments by a dissenting arbitrator in *UPS v Canada*, who argued that the wording of NAFTA art 1102 suggests a close connection to NT standards in GATT and the *General Agreement on Trade in Services* ("GATS"), as well as other international trade and investment treaties.[126] The dissenting arbitrator views this as a reading consistent with precedent under GATT and WTO.[127]

It is noticeable that the NAFTA cases discussed above are based on the issue of NT between domestic industries and foreign investor-owned businesses aggrieved by governmental measures. The simulated scenarios in this article differ significantly, in that they deal with export controls which curtail foreign investors' ability to export. The scenarios have assumed that the export controls due to "local and general short supply" have equally affected the local industries, hence, a breach of NT can be set aside as a non-issue. Since export controls are not mentioned in any FTA or BIT specifically, in the absence of any express provisions, the standard discussed by the Appellate Body in *India – Solar Cells* can be considered as a close guide as to how they will be treated by an international investment tribunal.

The convergence approach, however, brings its own complications. According to some commentators, the approach of borrowing GATT/WTO

---

123   Ibid.
124   Ibid.
125   Alford (n 98) 42.
126   Alford (n 98) 42 n 27, citing comments by Dean Ronald Cass in *United Parcel Service of America Inc v Canada (Award on the Merits)* (*Separate Statement of Dean Ronald Cass*) (North American Free Trade Agreement Chapter 11 Tribunal, 24 May 2007) [57]–[61] <https://arbitrationlaw.com/sites/default/files/free_pdfs/UPS%20v%20Canada%20-Merits.pdf>.
127   Ibid.

jurisprudence requires sophisticated analysis by qualified individuals in the area, in order to minimise any inconsistencies in awards.[128] Kurtz opines that "serious, real-world implications" result from the cross-application of GATT/WTO jurisprudence in investment disputes without a proper understanding of the underlying norms. He cites Argentina's liability of millions of dollars due to "objective evidence of legal error" on the part of tribunals, which eventually resulted in the Latin American backlash to the International Centre for Settlement of Investment Disputes system.[129]

The attempt to connect WTO law with international investment disputes has received some criticism as well. In the context of the *US–Argentina BIT* and the claims for compensation by investors thereunder, the practice of drawing from WTO jurisprudence carries the merit of applying an internationally used standard which may be preferable to the prospect of applying domestic law of the host state to the dispute.[130] However, there were no reasons to assume that drafters of the *US–Argentina BIT* intended to connect modern WTO law to BIT disputes.[131] This is mainly because the meaning of "necessary" in

---

128  Kurtz cites the instance of the presiding arbitrator in *Continental Casualty Company v Argentina* who had served on the WTO Appellate Body: Kurtz (n 111) 771, citing *Continental Casualty Company v Argentina (Award)* (ICSID Arbitral Tribunal, Case No ARB/03/9, 5 September 2008), 85–89, [193]–[199]; see also Puig (n 98) 29; Alec Stone Sweet, "Investor-State Arbitration: Proportionality's New Frontier" (2014) 4(1) *Law & Ethics of Human Rights* 48, 49, 69–75 (Sweet terms the analysis by the tribunal in *Continental Casualty* as a "rich piece of jurisprudence, far more sophisticated than the awards produced in ... previous cases"). In *Continental Casualty*, Argentina defended its regulatory measures as necessary and relied upon the comparative definition of the term "necessary" under GATT art XX for explaining the effect of art XI in the *Treaty between United States of America and the Argentine Republic Concerning the Reciprocal Encouragement and Protection of Investment*, signed 14 November 1991 (entered into force 20 October 1994). The arbitral panel applied the WTO jurisprudence regarding GATT art XX from previous cases such as *Korea – Beef* and *Brazil – Retreaded Tyres* in explaining the terms "necessary" and "necessity".

129  For example, the leading economy in Latin America (Brazil) has refused to ratify the *Convention on the Settlement of Investment Disputes between States and Nationals of Other States*, opened for signature 18 March 1965, 575 UNTS 159 (entered into force 14 October 1966) ("ICSID Convention"). Other resource-rich developing economies in Latin America such as Bolivia, Ecuador and Venezuela withdrew from the ICSID Convention and Argentina threatened to withdraw (but has not withdrawn) from the ICSID Convention: see also Kurtz (n 111) 771; Jurgen Kurtz, "Adjudging the Exceptional at International Law: Security, Public Order and Financial Crisis" (Working Paper 06/08, Jean Monnet Program, 2008) 25–29.

130  See the discussion in José E Alvarez and Kathryn Khamsi, "The Argentine Arisis and Foreign Investors: a Glimpse into the Heart of the Investment Regime" (Working Paper 2008/5, Institute for International Law and Justice, 2008) 54–55.

131  Ibid.

GATT art XX is linked to a balancing test, implied in the preamble of that provision, which is missing from art XI of the *US–Argentina BIT*.[132] The thrust of this criticism seems to be that importing GATT/WTO norms into a BIT dispute is not merited, because the underlying treaty framework is affected by how operative clauses are interpreted in light of its substantive content.

## 6    Final Thoughts

Regardless of the two paths taken in resolving investment disputes on export controls, the field remains open to different interpretations and independent variables that may affect the outcome of disputes in the future. Multiple perspectives can determine the validity of export controls, which can affect the legality of the measures challenged in an ISDS setting. For host states, the question of imposing export controls must be looked at by policymakers through the lens of legitimacy and necessity. The experience of GATT/WTO jurisprudence and various arbitral awards is particularly illustrative for policymakers in constructing measures that remain within the GATT/WTO framework, while also remaining true to any applicable norms set by bilateral FTAs and/or BITs. It is fully possible that the resolution of points of contention in investment disputes may involve adjudication through transplanted norms from the GATT/WTO system. Additional complications can also stem from the selective citation of arbitral awards in previous investment disputes. The task of constructing legitimate and justifiable export control measures is, therefore, a difficult one for host states.

Conversely, the foreign investors can approach the process of challenging export controls from both a trade and investment angle. The obvious proviso is that foreign investors must possesses enough resources along with influence to trigger a state-based espousal on their behalf in the WTO. Investment arbitration can never be assumed to be fully self-contained system, even when modern FTAs and BITs are becoming increasingly prescriptive. ISDS panels cannot ignore the general norms and rules of international law in the arbitral process.[133] Additionally, the arbitral process suffers from a lack of any precedent-creating systems which could assure consistency for users of the

---

132    Ibid 55.
133    Margie-Lys Jaime, "Relying Upon Parties" Interpretation in Treaty-Based Investor-State Dispute Settlement: Filling the Gaps in International Investment Agreements' (2014) 46(1) *Georgetown Journal of International Law* 261, 272–277.

system.[134] With state-based espousal in the WTO a difficult proposition, the aggrieved foreign investor may wish to consider importing parallel arguments from the realm of international trade to reinforce their claims. For policymakers in host states, this means that design of export controls must be such that it remains compatible with trade and investment obligations.

### Acknowledgements

The author wishes to thank Emeritus Professor Mary Hiscock (Bond University) for her mentorship, guidance and feedback on several drafts of this research article. I also thank Professor Muthucumaraswamy Sornarajah (National University of Singapore) and Associate Professor Pasha L Hsieh (Singapore Management University) for their useful comments and feedback. I further thank two anonymous reviewers for their useful suggestions that have greatly improved the article. All errors are mine.

---

[134] Ibid 277–278; see generally the discussion in Alain Pellet, "Annulment Faute de Mieux: Is there a Need for an Appeals Facility?" in N Jansen Calamita, David Earnest and Markus Burgstaller (eds), *The Future of ICSIBID and the Place of Investment Treaties in International Law: Current Issues in Investment Treaty Law* (British Institute of International and Comparative Law, 2013) bk 4 255.

# Subsidies and "New Industrial Policy": Are International Trade Rules Fit for the 21st Century?

*Tracey Epps and Danae Wheeler**

**Abstract**

This article reviews the interaction between international rules and governments' provision of subsidies to support industrial policy. It does so in the light of the challenges that many governments are facing in today's "turbulent times" and an associated renaissance in their use of industrial policy to increase competitiveness and encourage economic growth.
Subsidies are disciplined under the World Trade Organisation's SCM *Agreement*, but there are concerns that the rules are not effectively curtailing the use of trade-distorting subsidies, and, at the same time, not providing governments with sufficient flexibility to adopt economic development policies.
This article finds that the case for disciplining subsidies is as strong as ever, but that the rules are not as constraining as some commentators have suggested. Nevertheless, the time is ripe for the rules to be reviewed to provide governments with greater certainty as to what is and is not allowed.

## 1  Introduction

This article reviews the interaction between international rules and governments' provision of subsidies to support industrial policy. It does so in the light of growing claims that globalisation has not been the unequivocal success story that many had hoped for, and in the light of the challenges that many governments are facing in today's "turbulent times" (a combination of consequences caused by factors including the global financial crisis, climate change, growing inequality, trade wars, a backlash against globalisation and the rise of populism).

We are seeing increased interest in the role that industrial policy, including through provision of subsidies, can and should play in a modern economy, and an associated debate on the extent to which World Trade Organization ("WTO") rules strike an appropriate balance in disciplining subsidies while

---

\*  Chapman Tripp, Wellington, New Zealand.

offering member states sufficient flexibility to promote economic and social development.

Industrial policy is largely disciplined in the WTO through the fundamental obligations in the *General Agreement on Tariffs and Trade ("GATT")*[1] (including disciplines on tariffs, the non-discrimination rule and the prohibition on quantitative restrictions), disciplines on subsidies in the *Subsidies and Countervailing Measures ("SCM") Agreement*[2] and on performance requirements in the *Agreement on Trade-Related Investment Measures ("TRIMS")*.[3] The *SCM Agreement* prohibits export and import substitution and subsidies, and makes other state measures "actionable" if they cause "adverse effects" to the domestic industries of other members. It is these rules that will be the main focus of this article.

Following negotiation of the *SCM Agreement* in 1994, governments generally moved away from assistance targeted at specific industries, and towards providing public support for economic development on a horizontal basis – incentivizing research and development (*"R&D"*) and training, providing general infrastructure and tailoring economic framework policies to promote growth. Such support has been largely considered consistent with the *SCM Agreement*, which focuses its disciplines on subsidies that are "specific" to certain sectors or enterprises.

Despite this, there is widespread concern that the *SCM Agreement* has not been as effective as necessary to curtail the use of trade-distorting subsidies.[4] There are also gaps which mean that certain types of subsidies are not fully captured at all, including subsidies to unsustainable fisheries and energy industries. At the same time, as governments are starting to look at what "new industrial policy" might entail, some have questioned whether the *SCM Agreement* actually gives governments sufficient flexibility to adopt economic development policies. This questioning arises from an increasing recognition, in the wake of the 2008 global financial crisis, that globalisation has not resulted in

---

1 *Marrakesh Agreement Establishing the World Trade Organization*, opened for signature 15 April 1994, 1867 UNTS 3 (entered into force 1 January 1995) annex 1A (*"General Agreement on Tariffs and Trade 1994"*).
2 *Marrakesh Agreement Establishing the World Trade* Organization, opened for signature 15 April 1994, 1867 UNTS 3 (entered into force 1 January 1995) annex 1A (*"Agreement on Subsidies and Countervailing Measures"*) (*"SCM Agreement"*).
3 *Marrakesh Agreement Establishing the World Trade* Organization, opened for signature 15 April 1994, 1867 UNTS 3 (entered into force 1 January 1995) annex 1A (*"Agreement on Trade-Related Investment Measures"*).
4 See, eg, European Commission, "WTO Modernisation: Introduction to Future EU Proposals" (Concept Paper, September 2018) <http://trade.ec.europa.eu/doclib/docs/2018/september/tradoc_157331.pdf>.

economic gains for everyone, and an associated consideration of the appropriate role of governments in the economy.

The debate then seems to be in a rather confused state – is the international trade regime too soft on industrial policy in the form of subsidies, too rigid, or is it a bit of both? The goal of this article is to assess and summarise the situation as it sits at this particular historical juncture. We adopt a perspective that recognises the importance of disciplining trade-distortive subsidies, but that also considers that the challenges facing governments today may require interventions which look different than the types of interventions contemplated when the SCM Agreement was negotiated.

We conclude that the case for disciplining subsidies remains strong, but that the rules are not as constraining as some commentators have suggested. Given the challenges facing governments, the time is ripe for a review of the rules to ensure a greater degree of certainty around what is and is not allowed. While it will never be possible (nor indeed desirable) to achieve complete certainty, it is important that governments know when they can act and take measures to ensure that the positive effects of globalisation are felt by all citizens in all parts of a country.

We structure our discussion as follows. Section II describes the concept of industrial policy and the rationales for and against disciplining subsidies. Section III identifies "new" challenges that governments are facing in the "turbulent times" of the 21st century, such as climate change, growing economic inequality and the rise of populism. Section IV considers the revival of "industrial policy" and the role of subsidies in this context. Section V asks whether international trade rules are fit for these 21st century challenges and the associated implications for "new industrial policy". Section VI concludes with four key observations.

## 2  Industrial Policy and Subsidies

The term "industrial policy" means different things to different people.[5] The Donor Committee for Enterprise Development defines it "as the strategic effort by the state to encourage the development and growth of a sector of the economy".[6] It refers to "any type of selective intervention or government policy

---

[5]  HJ Chang, Antonio Andreoni and Ming Kuan, *International Industrial Policy Experiences and the Lessons for the UK* (Review, October 2013) 1, 9.
[6]  The Donor Committee for Enterprise Development, *Industrial Policy* (Private Sector Development Synthesis Note, September 2017) 1.

that attempts to alter the structure of production toward sectors that are expected to offer better prospects for economic growth than would occur in the absence of such intervention".[7]

The notion of industrial policy began with the birth of capitalism itself, and with development of the "infant industry" argument.[8] The theory described the need for less developed countries to protect their new industries against competition from superior foreign producers. Alexander Hamilton, the first Treasury Secretary of the United States of America ("US"), argued in support of tariff protection along with other measures such as subsidies for strategic industries, tariff rebates on imported inputs used for exports, export bans on key raw materials and the imposition of mandatory product standards.[9]

Some authors distinguish between "hard" and "soft" industrial policy, with "soft" industrial policy encapsulating cooperation between government and industries. Ann Harrison and Andres Rodriguez-Clare write that "soft" industrial policy seeks to develop "a process whereby government, industry and cluster-level private organizations can collaborate on interventions that can directly increase productivity".[10] By contrast, "hard" industrial policy is epitomised by governments picking individual sectors or winners and using measures such as trade protection or selective subsidies.[11] Hard industrial policy was famously adopted by a number of governments in the post-World War II period as they sought to structurally transform their economies, including through creating national champions in industries deemed essential to the health of the national economy.

Industrial policy nevertheless took different forms in different countries, using various types of tools highlighted by Hamilton, including subsidies (whether through the direct provision of financial support or through the indirect provision of financial benefits, such as preferential tax policies or providing inputs at reduced prices).[12] Well-known examples include European

---

7   Ibid 1; see also Howard Pack and Kamal Saggi, "The Case for Industrial Policy: a Critical Survey" (Research Paper, Development Research Group of the World Bank, 16 January 2006) 2.
8   See, eg, Alexander Hamilton, "Report on Manufactures" (Speech, United States House of Representatives, 5 December 1791).
9   Ibid.
10  Ann Harrison and Andres Rodriguez-Clare, "Trade, Foreign Investment, and Industrial Policy for Developing Countries" in Dani Rodrik and Mark Rosenzweig (eds), *Handbook of Development Economics* (Elsevier, 2010) vol 5 4039, 4112.
11  Ibid 4113.
12  Harsha Singh and Rashmi Jose, "Industrial Policy and the WTO Rules-Based System" (Overview Paper, E15 Expert Group on Reinvigorating Manufacturing: New Industrial Policy and the Trade System, September 2016) 1, 3.

governments seeking to raise productivity closer to US levels by employing the technical and organisational innovations made by US companies before and during the war; Latin American countries introducing import substitution policies to develop local industries; and East Asian countries, such as Korea and Taiwan, focusing on export growth as both an objective and criterion that determined whether or not industries received state support.[13]

By the early 1990s, use of industrial policy had come to be viewed negatively in many quarters. The Washington Consensus focused on the key notions of macroeconomic discipline, a market economy, and trade and investment liberalisation. One author writes that, consequent upon the Washington Consensus, "industrial policy was regarded as antediluvian and the state began to largely withdraw from industrial intervention".[14]

With the conclusion of the Uruguay Round of trade negotiations in 1994, and the establishment of the WTO, tighter international discipline was placed on many industrial policy tools. With a changing policy environment and these new rules, the focus of interventionist industrial policy shifted in the 1980s to an approach of largely "horizontal" support, with an emphasis on incentives for R&D, training and opening markets to foreign competition. Horizontal subsidies are not explicitly industry-specific and instead are generally categorised by functions or objectives. These are often used to provide infrastructure, create incentives for investment and human capital development and tailor economic framework policies to promote growth.[15]

Free market orthodoxy emphasised the importance of disciplining industrial policy, and subsidies in particular. The rationale for disciplining subsidies has been well-traversed by many experts, and we simply note the key ones here, being their tendency to:
– distort trade, competition and investment by giving an artificial competitive advantage to exporters or import competing industries;
– lead to vast oversupply and the depression of world prices;

---

13   See Geoffrey Owen, "Industrial Policy in Europe since the Second World War: What Has Been Learnt?" (Occasional Paper No 1, The European Centre for International Political Economy, 2012) 5; Paul W Kuznets, "An East Asian Model of Economic Development: Japan, Taiwan and South Korea" (1988) 36(3) *Economic Development and Cultural Change* S11, S29; Joseph Stiglitz, "Some Lessons from the East Asian Miracle" (1996) 11(2) *The World Bank Research Observer* No 2 151, 169–170.

14   Keith Cowling and Philip Tomlinson, "Post the 'Washington Consensus': Economic Governance and Industrial Strategies for the Twenty-First Century" (2011) 35(5) *Cambridge Journal of Economics* 831, 834.

15   Dan Ciuriak and John Curtis, "The Resurgence of Industrial Policy and What it Means for Canada" (Research Paper No 2, IRPP Insight, June 2013) 1, 3.

- promote practices that are destructive to the environment, such as those leading to over-fishing or increasing greenhouse gas emissions;[16] and
- increase the economic disparity between nations.[17]

However, the other side of the coin is that there are also legitimate reasons to grant subsidies. Some of these reasons are as follows:
- to correct market failures, such as in health and education. This argument holds that policy space should be preserved to offer certain subsidies to tackle market failures. However, governments should undertake a cost-benefit analysis to determine if subsidies would create new distortions;[18]
- to shift profits in oligopolistic markets. In certain markets, high barriers to entry, such as high fixed costs and a high level of production required to recover initial costs, mean that only a few firms are present. Governments may wish to intervene to shift profit from competitors, for example, by subsidising domestic exporters, therefore inducing foreign competitors to contract their output;
- to provide social services. In New Zealand, for example, certain families are eligible for a "childcare subsidy", which is a payment that helps with the cost of pre-school childcare;[19] and
- for political economy reasons such as safeguarding jobs in declining industries or entering into new industries.[20]

In the late 1990s, the Washington institutions did begin to recognise that the state could play a complementary role in liberal economies, mostly to regulate financial markets and address some market failures. However, even during what some have labelled as a more progressive "post-Washington Consensus" phase, the state was largely subservient to the market.[21] Today, however, we see

---

[16] As *The Economist* writes, while there are big mistakes in economic policymaking, it would be "hard to find a worse one than energy subsidies": "Energy Subsidies: A Costly Mistake", *The Economist* (online, 19 May 2015) <https://www.economist.com/news/2015/05/19/a-costly-mistake>.

[17] The World Bank and organisations such as Oxfam argue that doing away with agricultural subsidies and protectionism in industrialized nations would significantly reduce poverty in the developing world: Nancy Birdsall, Dani Rodrik and Arvind Subramanian, "How to Help Poor Countries" (2005) 84(4) *Foreign Affairs* 136, 139.

[18] Dominic Coppens, *WTO Disciplines on Subsidies and Countervailing Measures* (Cambridge University Press, 2014) 8.

[19] "Childcare Subsidy", *Work and Income* (Web Page) <https://www.workandincome.govt.nz/products/a-z-benefits/childcare-subsidy.html>.

[20] World Trade Organization, *World Trade Report 2006: Exploring the Links between Subsidies, Trade and the WTO* (Report, 24 July 2006) 55.

[21] Cowling and Tomlinson (n 14) 834.

that other reasons for subsidisation have started to play a greater role, in light of the turbulent times the world is facing.

## 3   Turbulent Times

The term "turbulent times", used in the trade policy context by the current New Zealand Minister for Trade and Export Growth, David Parker, describes a confluence of various factors that, together, have come to define and shape the early years of the 21st century.[22] These include most prominently the 2008 global financial crisis, growing inequality, displacement caused by technological advancements, and increasingly imminent and serious threats presented by climate change. Alongside these factors, we have seen a backlash against globalisation in many countries, a rise in populism and sustained trade tensions following the imposition of various tariffs by the US in 2018.[23] We are also witnessing the massive disruption on business models and services caused by digitalisation.

While globalisation has decreased inequality between states, it has contributed to rising inequality within states.[24] Since 1980, the top 1% richest individuals in the world have captured twice as much wealth as the bottom 50% of individuals.[25] Growing economic inequality over the past four decades and the pushback against globalisation was a factor in the United Kingdom's popular vote to leave the European Union ("EU") and the election of the protectionist Donald Trump to the US presidency. Moreover, right-wing populism is on the rise in democracies of the developed world. In a recent survey conducted by the Ifo Institute in Munich, 64% of economic experts from 120 countries indicated that populism had increased in their countries over the previous five years, including in Asia and in Europe (with the exceptions of Ireland, Portugal and Norway).[26] Although right-wing populist parties have experienced mixed

---

22   See, eg, David Parker, "Speech at the 24th Nikkei Forum, Tokyo" (Speech, 24th Nikkei Forum, 11 June 2018) <https://www.beehive.govt.nz/speech/speech-24th-nikkei-forum-tokyo>.

23   "Debating the Great Disruption" (Project Syndicate, 18 December 2018) <https://www.project-syndicate.org/podcasts/debating-the-great-disruption>.

24   See, eg, Thomas Piketty, *Capital in the Twenty-First Century* (Harvard University Press, 2014); Thomas Piketty, *The Economics of Inequality* (Harvard University Press, 2015).

25   Facundo Alvaredo et al, *World Inequality Report 2018* (Report, 14 December 2017) 11.

26   Populism looks different in different countries. As noted here, in Europe it tends to be associated with right-wing politics, whereas in Latin America, populism tends to be associated with the left: see Dorine Boumans, "Does Populism Influence Economic Policy

electoral successes since 1980, evidence suggests that they are experiencing a resurgence in several countries.[27] In recent elections, around a fifth of Europe's electorate – almost 56 million people – voted for a left- or right-wing populist party. The support for right-wing populists peaked in 2016 at 12.3% of all votes across Europe's democracies.[28] The Ifo institute survey found mixed reports regarding the extent to which populism has impacted economic policy, with the impact considered stronger in some countries than others. Among the key economic outcomes identified with populism were an increase in short-term spending and the spread of redistributive policies.[29]

Throughout the world, we are seeing massive disruption of business models and services caused by digitalisation. These technologies cannot be easily modelled, such that we are seeing the application of increasing returns to scale which leads to natural monopolies. This has a practical consequence of wealth concentration, job displacement and instability.[30] Governments and citizens are questioning how to encourage wealth distribution through policies targeted at inflation, labour markets, deregulation and taxation.[31] There is a growing call for trade and investment to benefit everyone. In 2015, for example, the EU announced a new trade policy known as "trade for all".[32] Its main goals include making trade policy more effective in delivering new economic opportunities. Similarly, the New Zealand government in 2018 adopted a goal of ensuring "trade delivers for all New Zealanders wherever or whoever they are".[33] Initiatives to be promoted include poverty reduction and inclusive regional economic growth.

---

Making? Insights from Economic Experts Around the World" (2017) 15(4) *ifo DICE Report* 40, 40.

27  Nick Galasso et al, *The Rise of Populism and its Implications for Development NGOs* (Report, 2017) 5.

28  Matt Browne, Dalibor Rohac and Carolyn Kenney, "Europe's Populist Challenge", *Center for American Progress* (Web Page, 10 May 2018) <https://www.americanprogress.org/issues/democracy/reports/2018/05/10/450430/europes-populist-challenge/>.

29  Boumans (n 26) 43.

30  "Debating the Great Disruption" (n 23).

31  Jathan Sadowski, "Why Silicon Valley is Embracing Universal Basic Income", *The Guardian* (online, 22 June 2016) <https://www.theguardian.com/technology/2016/jun/22/silicon-valley-universal-basic-income-y-combinator>.

32  "Trade for All: European Commission Presents New Investment Strategy", *European Commission* (Web Page, 14 October 2015) <https://trade.ec.europa.eu/doclib/press/index.cfm?id=1381>.

33  "New Zealand Trade Policy", *New Zealand Foreign Affairs & Trade* (Web Page) <https://www.mfat.govt.nz/en/trade/nz-trade-policy/>.

## 4    A Renaissance in Industrial Policy?

It might be argued that industrial policy never went away, and further, that "everyone uses industrial policy" (even if some countries are less open about doing so than others).[34] Nevertheless, it is fair to say that in many countries, open discussion of industrial policy has, for some time, been frowned upon. One author notes, for example, that in Canada for over three decades, the term "industrial policy" "was not to be uttered in polite company in federal government circles".[35] Joseph Stiglitz has said that the term industrial policy "was a word that had a bad odour, including within the walls [of the World Bank], not that long ago".[36] However, times are changing, as highlighted by *The Economist*:

> Angst over petro prices, confusion over Britain's relationship with the EU, bemusement at the American president's legal tangles: it feels like the 1970s in Europe again. In policy circles, too, talk of corporate "champions" and "industrial policy" is now heard nearly as freely as it was in the era of bell-bottoms and dodgy sideburns.[37]

Industrial policy has undergone something of a renaissance in recent years as governments have looked at how best to align and harness innovation and competitiveness.[38] It seems that this renaissance has in large part been stimulated by the events described above. In 2012, two former Chief Economists of the World Bank, Justin Lin and Joseph E Stiglitz, began promoting a renewed embrace of industrial policy.[39] In a 2012 blog, Christopher Colford explained the World Bank's "New Competitive Industries Practice", aimed at helping

---

[34]   Ciuriak and Curtis (n 15) 1.
[35]   Christyn Cianfarani, "Why Canada is Ripe for a New Industrial Policy", *The Globe and Mail* (online, 26 February 2017) <https://www.theglobeandmail.com/report-on-business/rob-commentary/why-canada-is-ripe-for-a-new-industrial-policy/article34138869/>.
[36]   See Christopher Colford, "From Old Taboo to New Consensus: 'Industrial Policy' and 'Competitive Industries' (Pt 1)", *World Bank Blogs* (Blog Post, 12 June 2012) <http://blogs.worldbank.org/psd/from-old-taboo-to-new-consensus-industrial-policy-and-competitive-industries-pt-1>.
[37]   The *Economist*, "The EU's Industrial-Policy Fans Want to Go Back to the '70s", *The Economist* (online, 18 December 2018) <https://www.economist.com/europe/2018/12/22/the-eus-industrial-policy-fans-want-to-go-back-to-the-70s>.
[38]   Scott Vaughan, "A New Generation of Trade and Industrial Policy" (Commentary, International Institute for Sustainable Development, January 2017) 3.
[39]   Joseph Stiglitz and Justin Lin Yifu, *The Industrial Policy Revolution I: The Role of Government Beyond Ideology* (Palgrave Macmillan, 2013).

countries focus investments in their areas of potential comparative advantage within the global value chain.[40] Today, industrial policy is being used to increase competitiveness, through a variety of active policy instruments, and to encourage growth in certain sectors of the economy, such as high-tech manufacturing, artificial intelligence, additive manufacturing, driverless automobiles, big data and quantum computing.[41]

In 2015, John Weiss identified a shift in thinking since the mid-2000s. Many governments began contemplating the implications of a declining manufacturing sector for the globalised world economy.[42] He writes that "much of the previous focus on horizontal policies is now combined with efforts to stimulate innovation and the growth of small and medium enterprises ('SMES')".[43] Governments are looking at how to increase competitiveness across different sectors. In this regard, it seems that we are now witnessing a change in view among even "stalwart adherents to the free-market framework".[44] In June 2018, Angela Merkel, the German chancellor, said that European competition law "does not help us sufficiently to build" European champions.[45] In order to increase competitiveness, some governments are re-evaluating their industrial policy and in some cases we are seeing an increased use of subsidisation. In this regard, John Weiss has identified three notable types of industrial policy being practiced by developed states. These are "defensive industrial policy", "catch-up industrial policy" and "innovation-based industrial policy".[46] It is important to note that where the use of subsidies is involved, it is not always the case that the subsidies will have adverse effects on other countries' industries.

### 4.1    *Defensive Industrial Policy*
Defensive industrial policy involves governments addressing the problems of declining sectors, or lagging of regions or areas where those sectors are based.

---

[40]   See Christopher Colford, "From Old Taboo to New Consensus: 'Industrial Policy' and 'Competitive Industries' (Pt 2)", *World Bank* (Blog Post, 14 June 2012): <https://blogs.worldbank.org/psd/from-old-taboo-to-new-consensus-industrial-policy-and-competitive-industries-pt-2>.

[41]   "The Great Disruption" (Project Syndicate, 25 December 2018) <https://www.project-syndicate.org/videos/the-great-disruption>.

[42]   John Weiss, "Industrial Policy in High-Income Economies" (Think Piece, E15 Expert Group on Reinvigorating Manufacturing: New Industrial Policy and the Trade System, February 2015) 1.

[43]   Ibid 1.

[44]   Cianfarani (n 35).

[45]   "The EU's Industrial-Policy Fans Want to Go Back to the '70s" (n 37).

[46]   Weiss (n 42) 1.

Examples include auto-industry bailouts in the US provided to General Motors and Chrysler, worth USD80 billion,[47] or the bailout of American International Group for USD180 billion. In Europe, the EU Cohesion Funds support backward regions to raise income levels to support the further expansion of the internal market. In New Zealand, a NZD3 billion "Provincial Growth Fund" has been established to bring development to provincial New Zealand over three years.[48] The scheme has the goal of funding projects that will accelerate regional development, increase regional productivity, and contribute to more, better-paying jobs.[49] For example, Tairāwhiti has been allocated NZD150 million, most of which will be used for road infrastructure as its road network has suffered from "historical under-investment and recurring extreme weather events".[50] Aspects of this investment could be seen as "catch-up" policy; however, the focus on funding to lagging regions and sectors also means it might be better categorised as "defensive industrial policy". Investments in the Provincial Growth Fund are not made to enable industries to become global leaders, though that would be a desired outcome; the focus, instead, is on decreasing economic inequality in New Zealand by funding regions and sectors that are faced with higher unemployment and lower productivity. A recent example of the operation of this fund was the announcement of a NZD140 million package to the West Coast, which included an investment of a NZD9.9 million loan to Westland Milk Products,[51] which, in its 2017 annual report, held a debt of NZD254 million. It was reported that the New Zealand Treasury advised against giving Westland Milk Products the loan, as Westland had had problems obtaining a loan from its own bank on acceptable terms. Therefore, the Government would be acting as a lender. This NZD9.9 million would likely

---

47   Lauren Silva Laughlin and Richard Beales, "AIG's Big Debt to US Taxpayers", *The New York Times* (online, 26 January 2010) <https://www.nytimes.com/2010/01/27/business/27views.html?auth=login-email>.

48   Ministry of Business, Innovation and Employment, "The Provincial Growth Fund", *Grow Regions* (Web Page) <https://www.growregions.govt.nz/about-us/the-provincial-growth-fund/>.

49   "Provincial Development Unit", *Ministry of Business, Innovation and Employment* (Web Page) <https://www.mbie.govt.nz/business-and-employment/economic-development/regional-economic-development/provincial-development-unit/>.

50   Lucy Bennett, "Tairāwhiti Region Gets $150 in Provincial Growth Fund Money", *The New Zealand Herald* (online, 7 September 2018) <https://www.nzherald.co.nz/nz/news/article.cfm?c_id=1&objectid=12121050>.

51   Andrea Fox, "Govt Calls Off $10m Loan to Westland Milk following Sale News", *The New Zealand Herald* (online, 19 March 2019) <https://www.nzherald.co.nz/business/news/article.cfm?c_id=3&objectid=12214142>.

constitute an actionable subsidy, although at the time of writing it looked as if it would not go ahead, as Westland Milk Products had signed a conditional agreement to sell to Hong Kong Jingang Trade Holding.

## 4.2   Catch-Up Industrial Policy

Catch-up industrial policy involves policies designed to raise productivity in identified sectors to the levels of global market leaders. Impetus for this type of policy may come from China's growth which has caused governments to reflect and, in some cases, conclude that they need stronger state capacity. In the EU, during the annual State of the Union address in 2017, in which he presented a new "Industrial Policy Strategy", European Commission President Jean-Claude Juncker stated that "I want to make our industry stronger and more competitive. The new Industrial Policy Strategy we are presenting today will help our industries stay or become the world leader in innovation, digitalisation and decarbonisation".[52] In Germany, a "National Industrial Strategy 2030" was released in February 2019, in which consideration was given to the state taking stakes in strategically important companies vulnerable to falling under foreign control.[53] President Macron has similarly "nudged" French firms into deals with other European groups, dubbing them "European champions" to, arguably, "soften the blow of losing national icons".[54] A test case is the merger of the rail arms of Germany's Siemens and France's Alstom. The aim is to create a "Railbus" to compete globally, much as Airbus does in aircraft. Supporters say that "Europe needs a titan to compete with China's rail giant, CRRC".[55]

Aspects of New Zealand's Provincial Growth Fund also seem better categorised as "catch-up" industrial policy. For example, NZD40 million has been

---

[52]   "State of the Union 2017 – Industrial Policy Strategy: Investing in a Smart, Innovative and Sustainable Industry", *European Commission* (Web Page, 18 September 2017) <https://ec.europa.eu/growth/content/state-union-2017-%E2%80%93-industrial-policy-strategy-investing-smart-innovative-and-sustainable_en>.

[53]   Zaki Ladi, "Europe is Starting to Turn French", *The Financial Times* (online, 27 February 2019) <https://www.ft.com/content/f3940254-3907-11e9-9988-28303f70fcff>.

[54]   "The EU's Industrial-Policy Fnas Want to Go Back to the '70s" (n 37). One factor driving the mergers is Europe's declining significance as a home of big global companies. A decade ago, 28 of the world's 100 most valuable firms were based in the European Union. That figure is down to 17, and will shrink to 12 when Britain leaves the bloc. The youngest company worth over USD100 billion that was founded in an European Union country is SAP, a German software giant launched in 1972. Mergers may be the only way for Europe to bulk up. he *Economist*",.

[55]   "The EU's Industrial-Policy Fans Want to Go Back to the '70s" (n 37).

invested to improve digital connectivity in regional areas, so that New Zealanders living there can experience benefits of faster broadband.[56]

A further example of "catch-up" industrial policy is New Zealand's film industry subsidy scheme. In 2018, the New Zealand Treasury called for a review of the scheme that has seen NZD1 billion paid to Hollywood producers since 2004.[57] The policy has resulted in around NZD130 million being paid out annually,[58] with studios obtaining up to 25% of their spending in New Zealand. The goal was to place New Zealand amongst the most desirable international film- and television-production locations. The Treasury noted that claimed tourism boosts from film-making were "impossible to measure", but that, in any event, it might be better to divert the grant into explicit tourism promotion.[59] However, in response, the Minister for Economic Development said that without this, the film industry would not exist.[60]

### 4.3   *Innovation-Based Industrial Policy*

Innovation-based industrial policy includes horizontal measures related to the business environment, infrastructure provision, support for cluster development, training, and improvements to financial intermediation. These kinds of measures are often combined with specific measures to support innovation, including state funding for research as well as credit for higher-risk innovative investment. In addition, some countries are going beyond general horizontal support to highlight priority areas for innovation initiatives.

Examples can be seen in Canada, where the Minister of Finance's Council on Economic Growth stated that "the need for a focused, sector approach to economic development is particularly acute".[61] The Council recommended the unleashing of growth in high potential sectors such as agri-food, advanced manufacturing, energy and renewables, health care and life sciences.[62] In its 2017 report, the Council recommends establishing "business-led innovation",

---

56   "PGF to Improve Regional Digital Connectivity" (Media Release, New Zealand Government, 15 November 2018).

57   Matt Nippert, "Treasury Warnings over Billion-Dollar Film Subsidies Ignored", *The New Zealand Herald* (online, 3 November 2018) <https://www.nzherald.co.nz/business/news/article.cfm?c_id=3&objectid=12153268>.

58   Ibid.

59   Ibid.

60   "Government Backs Down on Film Subsidy Cap", *Radio New Zealand* (Web Page, 29 September 2018) <https://www.radionz.co.nz/news/political/367551/government-backs-down-on-film-subsidy-cap>.

61   Cianfarani (n 35).

62   Advisory Council on Economic Growth, *The Path to Prosperity: Resetting Canada's Growth Trajectory* (Report, 1 December 2017) 6.

such as through the development of superclusters, and leveraging government procurement to help "innovators".[63] Similarly, in Australia, there has been a move away from lower-skilled and highly labour-intensive industries towards more knowledge-intensive and internationally-focused industries, especially in services and advanced manufacturing.[64] Industrial policy has shifted to help businesses become internationally competitive by providing subsidies and investments in areas of new technology and R&D, such as online markets for consumer, property and business services, and smart phone app development.[65] Yet "innovation-based industrial policy" is not constrained to these new areas of growth. Manufacturing arguably remains a highly innovation-intensive sector. Arguably, "no country can be an innovation leader without the ability to apply innovation in manufacturing", as manufactured goods account for over two thirds of world merchandise trade.[66]

### 4.4 *Green Economy-Based Policy*

A fourth category might usefully be added to those identified by Weiss, namely, that of "green economy-based policy". Many governments are looking at the use of subsidies not simply to mitigate negative externalities due to climate change or to induce behavioural change, but also to help industries adapt. For example, Australia has an Emissions Reduction Fund, which supports businesses and farmers to adopt new practices and technologies to reduce Australia's greenhouse gas emissions.[67]

In New Zealand, the government has announced a Green Investment Fund ("GIF").[68] According to the New Zealand Productivity Commission, a green investment fund could stimulate some of the technology and infrastructure needed to achieve the low emissions transition; however, the size of the GIF (NZD100 million) may make it less suitable to large-scale infrastructure

---

63   Ibid 6.
64   Eugenia Karanikolas, "Industry Policy in an Open Economy", *Parliament of Australia* (Web Page) <https://www.aph.gov.au/About_Parliament/Parliamentary_Departments/Parliamentary_Library/pubs/BriefingBook44p/IndustryPolicy>.
65   Ibid.
66   Jim Stanford, "Manufacturing (Still) Matters: Why the Decline of Australian Manufacturing Is Not Inevitable, and What Government Can Do About it" (Briefing Paper, Centre for Future Work at the Australia Institute, June 2016) 1.
67   "Climate Solutions Fund – Emissions Reduction Fund", *Department of Environment and Energy* (Web Page) <http://www.environment.gov.au/climate-change/government/emissions-reduction-fund>.
68   New Zealand Productivity Commission, *Low-Emissions Economy* (Report, August 2018) 188–189; see also "$100 Million Investment Fund Launched to Invest in Reducing Emissions" (Media Release, New Zealand Government, 5 December 2018).

projects.⁶⁹ The Productivity Commission states that it may be able to provide smaller-scale, low-emissions infrastructure if the GIF has a wide degree of flexibility in its scope or financing approach.⁷⁰

This brief overview highlights that the use of industrial policy, including through provision of subsidies, is alive and well. Some of the statements noted above suggest that the rationale behind some policies may not be too different from that which underlay industrial policy during the post-war era. The category of "innovation-based" policy raises interesting questions about whether such policies are really horizontal in nature, or whether they are in fact targeted at specific types of industries and sectors (for example, those that support industries facing particular types of risks).

## 5 Are International Rules Fit for the 21st Century?

To summarise the situation so far: we are seeing industrial policy being widely talked about as governments scramble to respond to turbulent times and find ways to ensure that the benefits of trade and investment are available to everyone. Subsidies form a fundamental pillar of any industrial policy. This raises some key questions around whether the international trade rules that govern subsidies are fit for the 21st century.

### 5.1 *The Rules*

As noted, the relevant rules are found for the most part in the *SCM Agreement*.⁷¹ At its outset, the *SCM Agreement* had three classifications for subsidies: prohibited; actionable; and non-actionable.

Subsidies that are contingent upon export performance or on the use of domestic inputs fall within the category of *prohibited* subsidies and therefore may not be used by WTO Members. These subsidies are treated more harshly than others because they are considered to have greater trade-distorting effects than other types of subsidies. Export subsidies can harm foreign competition in global markets, while domestic content subsidies limit foreign companies'

---

69 New Zealand Productivity Commission (n 68) 189.
70 Ibid 189.
71 We do not address here the rules found in the WTO's *Agreement on Agriculture*, which details specific rules to deal with subsidisation in the agriculture sector.

access to a member's domestic market and promote the use of domestic inputs.[72]

The second category is that of *actionable* subsidies. These are subsidies that produce certain negative trade effects (namely: injury to the domestic industry of another member; nullification or impairment of benefits; or serious prejudice to the interests of another member). Where the existence of such effects is shown, then the subsidies will violate the *SCM Agreement*.

A third category expired in 2000. It was for subsidies deemed *non-actionable* and included those for R&D, those providing assistance to disadvantaged regions and those ensuring compliance with environmental regulations. Since 2000, R&D subsidies have been actionable, either by dispute settlement or unilateral countervailing duties, subject to a demonstration of their injurious effects on another WTO Member.

While export subsidies can sometimes be difficult to identify (the subsidy must be "contingent" on exports), the most difficult type of subsidy to address tends to be those that are known as "domestic subsidies". These are, as John Jackson explained, "clearly the most perplexing, because they involve a vast range and number of government policies, many of which are perfectly justifiable as exercises of sovereign activity within a country".[73] As highlighted above, the *SCM Agreement* deals with this reality only by disciplining those subsidies which are "specific", and, even then, only by allowing action by WTO Members if they cause negative effects to the domestic industries of other countries.[74]

## 5.2 *Do the Rules Strike an Appropriate Balance?*

As to whether this regime strikes an appropriate balance in the current environment, there is a diversity of views, which can create uncertainty as to whether the rules give countries sufficient flexibility to implement desired policies. But equally, there is widespread condemnation of the rules for their failure to adequately discipline certain subsidies, particularly those handed out by China to various industries, as well as those which are proving to be catalysts for environmentally destructive behaviour (such as fossil fuel subsidies and fisheries subsidies).

---

72  Simon Lester, Bryan Mercurio and Arwel Davies, *World Trade Law: Text, Materials and Commentary* (Hart Publishing, 3rd ed, 2018) 472.
73  John H Jackson, *The World Trading System: Law and Policy of International Economic Relations* (The MIT Press, 2nd ed, 2000) 280.
74  *SCM Agreement* (n 2) art 5.

### 5.2.1 The Rules Are Not Flexible Enough

One of the strongest proponents of the view that WTO rules are not sufficiently flexible is Dani Rodrik. He has written that the WTO regime is "dysfunctional", because it was predicated on the idea that economic practices in different nations would converge.[75] The rules have, he argues, "over-reached", and do not recognise the diversity in economic models.[76] Instead, Rodrik argues that there is no good reason for states' economic practices to converge to accommodate economic diversity, but rather that each country may wish to pursue their own paths as they did so prior to the WTO.[77] To this end, he writes that the criticism of China is misguided.[78]

Rodrik concludes that when "trade threatens to undermine domestic labour standards, fiscal systems or investments in advanced technology, rich nations should be just as entitled to privilege these concerns over imports and foreign investment".[79] He suggests that a fair trading system would recognise the value of diversity in economic models and seek a way of accommodating diversity rather than seeking tighter rules.[80] It has been suggested that it is important that the state can nurture new industries and help uncompetitive industries exit, and that effectively designed sectoral policy can enhance rather than harm competition.[81] For example, tax-subsidy schemes can decrease concentration in the targeted sector and enhance incentives for firms to innovate.[82]

### 5.2.2 The Rules are Biased

Robert Wade and Linda Weiss both suggest that the problem is not just with over-reach, but rather with a lopsided approach that disciplines the types of subsidies used by developing countries, but not the types of schemes favoured by rich developed countries. Wade, in a response to Rodrik, argues that Rodrik

---

75 Dani Rodrik, "The WTO Has Become Dysfunctional", *The Financial Times* (online, 5 August 2018) <https://www.ft.com/content/c2beedfe-964d-11e8-95f8-8640db906oa7>.
76 Ibid.
77 Ibid.
78 Rodrik notes that China's industrial policy is similar to the US's practices in the 18th and 19th centuries. These have brought about significant domestic economic growth and greatly reduced poverty while serving as a market for western exports and investments: ibid.
79 Ibid.
80 Ibid.
81 Phillippe Aghion et al, "Industrial Policy and Competition" (2015) 7(4) *American Economic Journal* 1, 3.
82 Ibid.

"misses an important point".[83] Wade writes that the global playing field is level only from the perspective of the West:[84]

> Western states have crafted WTO rules to enable them to use industrial policy instruments appropriate for frontier industries and to prohibit or make actionable instruments appropriate for developing country industries and companies well within their frontier (such as local content requirements).

Both Wade[85] and Weiss[86] argue that the WTO rules diminish developing countries' ability to adapt to the current economic climate by prohibiting industrial policy measures such as those favouring labour- and capital-intensive manufacturing. In addition to the *SCM Agreement*, they single out the *TRIMS Agreement*. The authors take issue with the prohibitive requirements on foreign companies regarding local content, trade balancing, export performance, technology transfer and domestic sales. At the same time, WTO rules do not expressly prohibit the pursuit of industrial policy in technology-intensive industries, such as venture-capital financing of high-tech start-ups or strategic financing for product development.

Weiss argues that the developed countries have carved out a multilateral order which "best suits their current developmental trajectory", which simultaneously diminishes space for promoting the more labour- and capital-intensive industries critical to development and, on the other hand, increases space for knowledge-intensive industries.[87]

### 5.2.3 The Rules are Sufficiently Flexible for All Countries

On the other side of the coin, Joel Trachtman argues that the rules do not overreach, and do in fact provide sufficient flexibility.[88] He contends that Rodrik

---

83  Robert Wade, "Global Playing Field is Level but Only for the West", *The Financial Times* (online, 9 August 2018) <https://www.ft.com/content/c7cd567e-999e-11e8-9702-5946b ae86e6d>.
84  Ibid.
85  Robert Wade, "What Strategies are Viable for Developing Countries Today? The World Trade Organization and the Shrinking of 'Development Space'" (2003) 10(4) *Review of International Political Economy* 621.
86  Linda Weiss, "Global Governance, National Strategies: How Industrialized States Make Room to Move under the WTO" (2005) 12(5) *Review of International Political Economy* 723, 724.
87  Ibid 724, 729.
88  Joel Trachtman, "The Domain of WTO Dispute Resolution" (1999) 40(2) *Harvard International Law Journal* 333, 364; see also Singh and Jose (n 12) 4.

has misunderstood the WTO model.[89] Instead of requiring a specific type of economic model, the WTO is a system for interface: it allows member states with different economic models to trade, while partially insulating themselves from excessive policy externalities caused by differences in their economic models. Complete flexibility has been argued to arise in the case of horizontal subsidies based on general objective criteria or conditions for subsidies provided to services and for subsidies to agriculture that are specified in annex 2 of the WTO Agreement.[90] Moreover, even though subsidies to certain industries or enterprises would be deemed actionable and subject to WTO disciplines, only a few WTO members have been subject to complaints under the WTO's dispute settlement system for these reasons.

In a similar vein, Aggarwal and Evenett, in a study of various national and sectoral contexts, refute the "exaggerated" claim that WTO membership rules out the use of industrial policy.[91] In fact, much industrial policy in fact emerges unscathed from WTO obligations. They give the example of Brazil, which faced WTO complaints in response to its *Plano Brasil Maior (Great Brazil Plan)*, an industrial policy announced in 2012 aimed at improving local industry competitiveness to sustain growth and job creation during periods of economic uncertainty.[92] The Brazil–US Business Council highlighted aspects of the Plan that were prima facie inconsistent with WTO rules, including subsidies tied to local content requirements as well as discriminatory taxation that applies to Brazil's "New Automotive Regime".[93] In December 2013, the EU initiated a WTO complaint against Brazil concerning these automobile sector-related fiscal incentives, amongst other matters.[94] Argentina, Japan, and the US later joined this dispute as complainants. The Panel in 2017, and subsequently the

---

[89] Joel Trachtman, "Trachtman comments on Dani Rodrik FT Op-ed, August 5, 2018, 'THE WTO has become dysfunctional'", *World Trade Law* (Blog Post, 6 August 2018) <https://worldtradelaw.typepad.com/ielpblog/2018/08/trachtman-comments-on-dani-rodrik-ft-op-ed-august-5-2018-the-wto-has-become-dysfunctional.html>.

[90] Singh and Jose (n 12) 4. *Marrakesh Agreement Establishing the World Trade Organization*, opened for signature 15 April 1994, 1867 UNTS 3 (entered into force 1 January 1995) annex 1B ("General Agreement on Trade in Services"); Marrakesh Agreement Establishing the World Trade Organization, opened for signature 15 April 1994, 1867 UNTS 3 (entered into force 1 January 1995) annex 1A ("*Agreement on Agriculture*").

[91] Vinod K Aggarwal and Simon J Evenett, "Do WTO Rules Preclude Industrial Policy? Evidence from the Global Economic Crisis" (2014) 16(4) *Business and Politics* 481, 482.

[92] Brazil–US Business Council, *A Greater Brazil? Industrial Policy, Competiveness and Growth* (Report, November 2015) 1.

[93] Ibid 7.

[94] *Brazil – Certain Measures Concerning Taxation and Charges*, WTO Doc WT/DS472/1, G/L/1061; G/SCM/D100/1, G/TRIMS/D/39 (8 January 2014) (Request for Consultations by the European Union); see generally "DS472: Brazil – Certain Measures Concerning

Appellate Body in 2018, found that Brazil's tax measures concerning automobiles and ICT products were inconsistent with its national treatment obligations (Articles III:2 and III:4 of the *General Agreement on Tariffs and Trade 1994* (*GATT 1994*) and Article 2.1 of the *Agreement on Trade-Related Investment Measures* (*TRIMs Agreement*)).[95] The Appellate Body found that certain tax measures in these sectors are inconsistent with Article 3.1(b) of the *SCM Agreement*, but reversed the Panel's finding that the tax benefits for exporting companies were inconsistent with Article 3.1(a) of the *SCM Agreement*.[96] Nevertheless, the Appellate Body's decision was delivered five years after the inception of the Great Brazil Plan, and, as Aggarwal and Evenett write, "much of [the] Plan [has] managed to fall outside of WTO rules or [has] exploited the considerable leeway in those WTO rules that allow for the imposition of protectionism".[97]

Another example of a national industrial policy that has gone unchallenged in the WTO comprises interventions in the wind sector undertaken by various governments. One of the more popular policies in the wind-energy sector is a feed-in tariff. This provides a fixed price for power generated from a renewable energy source over a set time period. Payment is often administered by the utility company or the grid operator and is derived from an additional per-kWh charge for electricity. By 2010, 61 countries and 26 states had feed-in tariffs in place.[98] Canada and China have been challenged on their schemes, but these are the exception rather than the rule.

Furthermore, the use of bailouts, public procurement measures and quantitative restrictions on imports would all likely constitute subsidies under the *SCM Agreement*. For instance, in 2009, General Motors and Chrysler received substantial bailouts (worth an estimated USD80 billion), yet these bailouts were not challenged under the *SCM Agreement* for a variety of reasons. One reason for this is because the bailout might not have caused adverse effects. On this account, the *SCM* rules are likely sufficiently flexible, with a narrowed understanding of what constitutes an adverse effect. Another competing explanation for a lack of willingness to enforce the rules is that countries, in a general

---

Taxation and Charges", *World Trade Organization* (Web Page) <https://www.wto.org/english/tratop_e/dispu_e/cases_e/ds472_e.htm>.

95    Panel Report, *Brazil – Certain Measures Concerning Taxation and Charges*, WTO Doc WT/DS472/R, WT/DS497/R (30 August 2017) para 7.63.

96    Appellate Body Report, *Brazil – Certain Measures Concerning Taxation and Charges*, WT/DS472/AB/R, WT/DS497/AB/R (13 December 2018) para 6.21.

97    Aggarwal and Evenett (n 91) 497–498.

98    Joanna I Lewis, "Industrial Policy, Politics and Competition: Assessing the Post-Crisis Wind Power Industry" (2014) 16(4) *Business and Politics* 511, 524. *Renewables 2011 Global Status Report* (REN 21, 2011) 1, 13.

environment of economic slowdown or recession, will be reticent to mount a claim if they want to pursue a similar policy in the near future. Perhaps, too, bailout programmes and the like are widespread such that there is little motivation for a member to mount a challenge unless there is a serious material injury.[99]

There are other ways of providing subsidy-like support to local firms. For example, countries are allowed to reimburse firms for the taxes they pay on imported goods that are later used in exports. These reimbursements, known as "drawbacks", constitute direct payments to producers but are not defined as subsidies under the WTO, and countries may set their own rules and programmes.[100] Alvaro Santos argues that strategic lawyering, pursuing policy objectives by changing rule interpretation and adjusting to the rule in the most favourable way, creates additional flexibility in the rules.[101] As an example, Santos refers to the US successfully expanding the scope of Article XX of GATT so that it could ban the importation of products originating from countries that did not adopt its environmental standards.[102] In the *US – Tuna* cases,[103] the US adjusted its measures and then defended its adjustment whenever it was challenged. Santos writes that "along the way, the United States also took advantage of the procedural vulnerabilities of the system, by delaying the measure adjustment as much as the procedural mechanism allowed".[104] Perhaps the use of "strategic lawyering" could also be characterised as a subset of strategic realpolitik calculations.

Some countries manoeuvre under the WTO system through strategic realpolitik calculations rather than by adopting international norms and playing by the "spirit of the WTO rules".[105] For example, Seung-Youn Oh characterises China's liberal use of industrial policy measures, only to remove them once

---

99   John Paul MacDuffie and Paul Eisenstein, "The Auto Bailout 10 Years Later: Was it the Right Call?", *Knowledge at Wharton* (Web Page, 12 September 2018) <http://knowledge.wharton.upenn.edu/article/auto-bailout-ten-years-later-right-call/>.
100  Kenneth C Shadlen, "Exchanging Development for Market Access? Deep Integration and Industrial Policy Under Multilateral and Regional-Bilateral Trade Agreements" (2006) 12(5) *Review of International Political Economy* 750, 758.
101  Alvaro Santos, "Carving Out Policy Autonomy for Developing Countries in the World Trade Organization: The Experience of Brazil and Mexico" (2012) 52(3) *Virginia Journal of International Law* 551, 571.
102  Ibid, 571.
103  Panel Report, *United States – Restrictions on Imports of Tuna*, WTO Doc DS21/R (3 September 1991); Panel Report, *United States – Restrictions on the Import of Tuna*, WTO Doc DS29/R (16 June 1994) [5.24].
104  Santos (n 101) 584–585.
105  Rodrik (n 75).

a WTO dispute is brought against them, as "convenient compliance".[106] Oh writes that China crafts protective industrial policy in a way that enables it to stay ahead of WTO enforcement. China will then comply with the WTO ruling (which may take months or a year to come to fruition given the four-stage formal WTO dispute-settlement process), thereby demonstrating its ability to act as a responsible WTO member. At the same time, China no longer needs the industrial policy as it has already largely achieved its desired goals. On the other hand, developing countries are more likely to concede to rules relating to foreign direct investment, capital liberalisation and labour and environmental standards when negotiating regional trade agreements while opposing the same measures in WTO. Accordingly, Gallagher[107] Shandlen[108] and Haque[109] claim that regional trade agreements and international supply chains have intensified attendant policy trade-offs more than traditional WTO commitments.

5.2.4 The Rules are not Strong Enough as There is a Failure to Adequately Discipline Certain Subsidies

The flip side of the discussion about whether or not the rules afford countries sufficient flexibility is the concern that not all subsidies are adequately disciplined because the rules are not strong enough. Alan Sykes argues that the *SCM Agreement* rules do not identify subsidy practices that ought to be discouraged or identify market-distorting subsidies with accuracy.[110] He cites the WTO case *United States – Measures Treating Export Restraints as Subsidies* as an example.[111] In that case, Canada challenged the US determination of Canadian export restraints as constituting a "financial contribution" by government, and hence an actionable subsidy.[112] The Panel found in Canada's favour because, even if the export restraints resulted in lower input prices for Canadian

---

106   Seung-Youn Oh, "Convenient Compliance: China's Industrial Policy Staying One Step Ahead of WTO Enforcement" (Working Paper, East Asia Institute, May 2015).
107   Kevin Gallagher, "Understanding Developing Country Resistance to the Doha Round" (2008) 15(1) *Review of International Political Economy* 62, 70.
108   Shadlen (n 100) 750–775.
109   Irfan ul Haque, "Rethinking Industrial Policy" (Discussion Paper No 183, United Nations Conference on Trade and Development, 2007) 1, 5.
110   Alan Sykes, "The Questionable Case for Subsidies Regulation: A Comparative Perspective" (2010) 2(2) *Journal of Legal Analysis* 473, 474.
111   See "DS194: United States – Measures Treating Export Restraints as Subsidies", *World Trade Organization* (Web Page) <https://www.wto.org/english/tratop_e/dispu_e/cases_e/ds194_e.htm>.
112   Ibid.

producers, there was no actual financial contribution.[113] Sykes questions whether any government regulation that arguably lowers input prices should be treated as a subsidy, but also asks why, if it is acceptable to ignore the effects of regulatory policies, one should bother with subsidies at all.[114]

At least three categories of subsidies which are not sufficiently disciplined can be identified: (i) those provided by or to state-owned enterprises (such as in China); (ii) those that encourage over-fishing; and (iii) those that encourage emissions of greenhouse gases.

In part, whether subsidies provided by or to state-owned enterprises violate the *SCM Agreement* is perhaps an issue with interpretation rather than the existence of rules per se. In the context of subsidies provided *by* state-owned enterprises, Jennifer Hillman argues that the term "public body" has been interpreted in too narrow a way, particularly in cases involving China where questions have been raised about whether state-owned enterprises or state-owned commercial banks are considered public bodies and thus capable of subsidising under the terms of the *SCM Agreement*.[115]

According to the United Nations Food and Agriculture Organization's *State of World Fisheries and Aquaculture* 2018 report, 33.1% of marine fisheries stocks were classified as overfished in 2015.[116] Harmful fishing subsidies that contribute to overfishing are estimated to be as high as USD35 billion.[117] In July 2016, the United Nations Conference on Trade and Development ("UNCTAD"), the

---

113  Panel Report, *United States – Measures Treating Export Restraints as Subsidies*, WTO Doc DS194/R (29 June 2001) 9.1.

114  Sykes (n 110) 510.

115  Jennifer Hillman, "Ensuring Global Fair Trade by 2030" (Presentation, WTO Public Forum, 16 October 2018). See, eg, Panel Report, *United States – Definitive Anti-Dumping and Countervailing Duties on Certain Products from China*, WTO Doc WT/DS379/R (22 October 2010); Appellate Body Report, *United States – Definitive Anti-Dumping and Countervailing Duties on Certain Products from China*, WTO Doc WT/DS379/AB/R (11 March 2011). The panel in this case recognised that was no clear definition for the term "public body", namely because jurisdictions define what constitutes a "public body" under their own law in different ways. The panel focused on the element of control as the distinguishing factor, whereas the Appellate Body focused on the functions and whether they would be considered governmental in nature. The panel pointed out that "[s]ome of these go well beyond government agencies or similar organs of government, and include, inter alia, government-owned or -controlled corporations providing goods and/or services".

116  Food and Agriculture Organization, The State of World Fisheries and Aquaculture: Meeting the Sustainable Development Goals (Report, 2018) 45.

117  "Next Month's Ocean Conference Eyes Cutting $35 Billion in Fisheries Subsidies – UN Trade Officials", *United Nations* (Web Page, 10 May 2017) <https://www.un.org/sustainabledevelopment/blog/2017/05/next-months-ocean-conference-eyes-cutting-35-billion-in-fisheries-subsidies-un-trade-officials/>.

Food and Agriculture Organization of the United Nations ("FAO") and the United Nations Environment Programme ("UNEP") issued a joint statement during the 14th session of UNCTAD, which emphasized the need to address harmful fisheries subsidies.[118] We note that work is ongoing in the WTO to conclude negotiations on fisheries subsidies.[119]

Fossil fuel subsidies are equally as harmful, but proving difficult to address, despite frequent calls by some WTO Members for work to be undertaken on addressing them. There is no uniform, internationally agreed methodology for monitoring fossil fuels. Recent estimates of the annual value of fossil fuel subsidies range from USD160 billion to USD333 billion.[120] The IMF estimates that the negative impact of fossil fuel subsidies on the global economy amounts to USD4.7trillion each year, or 6% of global gross domestic product ("GDP").[121] By contrast, renewable-energy subsidies amount to USD120 billion.[122] United Nations Secretary-General António Guterres has stated that by subsidising fossil fuels, humanity is "investing in its own doom".[123] Fossil fuel subsidies are, of course, different in nature from other types of subsidies that may cause adverse effects to the industries of other WTO Members. While fossil fuel subsidies may have this effect, the far greater concern is with their environmentally-damaging consequences which are leading to significant harm to the global commons.

### 5.2.5 The Rules are not Strong Enough because They are Incoherent

For rules to be strong, they need to be coherent so that governments know when an action is allowed, or, by contrast, when it is prohibited. Alan Sykes criticises the *SCM Agreement* for this very reason – not for the inadequacy of

---

118  Food and Agriculture Organization (n 116) 81.
119  At the Buenos Aires Ministerial Conference in November 2017 ("MC11"), WTO Members agreed to engage in negotiations on fisheries subsidies, with a view to adopting an agreement by the Ministerial Conference in 2019 to discipline certain forms of fisheries subsidies: *Fisheries Subsidies: Ministerial Decision of 13 December 2017*, WTO Doc WT/MIN(17)/64 WT/L/1031 (18 December 2017, adopted 13 December 2017) (Ministerial Decision).
120  United Nations "Measuring Fossil Fuel Subsidies in the Context of the Sustainable Development Goals" (United Nations Environment Programme, 2019) 9. (https://wedocs.unep.org/bitstream/handle/20.500.11822/28111/FossilFuel.pdf?sequence=1&isAllowed=y).
121  David Coady et al, "Global Fossil Fuel Subsidies Remain Large: An Update Based on Country-Level Estimates" (IMF Working Paper WP/19/89, International Monetary Fund, May 2019) 1, 27.
122  Friends of Fossil Fuel Subsidy Reform, "Fossil Fuel Subsidies and Business-Time to Get Involved" (2015) 1, 2.
123  António Guterres, "Remarks at One Planet Summit" (Speech, One Planet Summit, 12 December 2017).

the rules, but for what he considers to be inconsistency inherent in the rules, particularly with respect to the specificity requirement.[124]

The *Agreement*'s rules only apply to specific subsidies. Prohibited subsidies (for example, those contingent on exports or use of domestic inputs) are deemed to be specific.[125] Other subsidies are considered to be "specific" if one of the following three definitions is met: *enterprise specificity* (i.e., a situation in which a government targets a particular company or companies for subsidisation); *industry specificity* (i.e., a situation in which a government targets a particular sector or sectors for subsidisation); or *regional specificity* (i.e., a situation in which a government targets producers in specific parts of its territory for subsidisation).[126] These subsidies are only considered problematic if they cause adverse effects to another WTO Member. As Sykes writes, "the concept of an actionable subsidy is circumscribed by the specificity test, which turns in a murky way on the degree of industrial targeting".[127] Moreover, Sykes finds it problematic that when determining whether a subsidy is specific, regard must be given to "certain enterprises" and "group of enterprises or industries", both of which are undefined.[128] They can therefore be applied broadly or narrowly in ways that "reflect political considerations rather than economic principle".[129] Sykes uses the example that the US has "long held the view, for example, never challenged under GATT or the WTO, that government subsidy programs applicable to the agricultural sector as a whole are not specific".[130]

The specificity requirement is nevertheless important, and should remain in the rules. The basic principle that a subsidy that distorts the allocation of resources within an economy should be subject to discipline is important. Equally important is providing that where a subsidy is widely available within an economy, such a distortion in the allocation of resources is presumed not to occur. The specificity requirement is key for excluding broadly based general welfare programmes, such as aid to the poor, from regulation. Such subsidies are considered less likely to have trade-distorting effects and, even if they do, broad-based subsidies are more likely to be considered necessary to promote

---

124   Alan Sykes, "The Questionable Case for Subsidies Regulation: A Comparative Perspective" (2010) 2(2) *Journal of Legal Analysis* 473, 482.
125   World Trade Organization, "World Trade Report 2006 Exploring the Links Between Subsidies, Trade and the WTO" 1, 199.
126   World Trade Organization, "Subsidies and Countervailing Measures, Overview" (Web Page) <https://www.wto.org/english/tratop_e/scm_e/subs_e.htm>.
127   Sykes (n 124) 482.
128   Ibid 482.
129   Ibid 512.
130   Ibid 512.

legitimate policy goals. However, there is no obvious "bright line" test for specificity, and there are several problems with application of the rule. A determination of specificity requires identifying the industry that is the beneficiary of the grants. Inconsistencies can arise. For example, while a grant for the development of hydrogen fuel cells might not be considered specific, R&D subsidies to improve the efficiency of photovoltaic panels are likely targeted at solar panel companies, and are thus specific.[131] Additionally, smaller economies will likely have fewer industries than bigger economies ones and therefore certain programmes may appear more specific.

Keith Markus similarly argues that it would be useful to clarify what the concept of specificity means, so that governments know what sort of policies they can pursue without fear of challenge.[132] He states, for example, that for an R&D subsidy to provide fiscal support to a horizontal competitor within a prescribed industry would be inappropriate; however, subsidies for infrastructure and laboratory buildings and equipment that aim to develop or modernize industrial activities around the adoption of a general purpose technology should not be held specific in the SCM sense.[133]

There are those that argue the rules are not strong enough as there is a failure to adequately discipline certain subsidies, and there are also those that argue that the rules are not strong enough because the specificity requirement lacks coherence. These arguments are likely related. For example, because there is not sufficient clarity about whether a subsidy is specific, there is a failure to adequately discipline those subsidies.

## 6  Conclusion

Based on the discussion above, we can reach four general conclusions.

*There is a renaissance in industrial policy*: Governments around the world are facing turbulent times in the wake of forces that have led to disruption on various fronts and a palpable sense of public dissatisfaction with globalisation and domestic responses to it. The need to respond to the challenges of these times has prompted a renaissance of sorts in industrial policy and, with it, the

---

131  Ilaria Espa and Sonia Rolland, "Subsidies, Clean Energy, and Climate Change" (Think Piece, E15 Task Force on Rethinking International Subsidies Disciplines, February 2015) 1, 5.
132  Keith Maskus, "Research and Development Subsidies: A Need for WTO Disciplines?" (Think Piece, E15 Task Force on Rethinking International Subsidies Disciplines, July 2015) 1, 9.
133  Ibid 9.

use of subsidisation. Whether all industrial policy being discussed is in fact "new", or whether it is a minor variation of the industrial policy of "old", is a subject for another discussion. But what we have identified here is a trend for the term "industrial policy" to be used, and various examples of policy tools being discussed and used by governments. Industrial policy is much broader than simply growing "national champions", and it can play an important role in how economies change and evolve. There must, however, be parameters to how it is used if it is not to result in harm or perverse outcomes, a topic which again is beyond the scope of this article.

*Criticism of a lack of flexibility in the WTO rules is overblown*: Criticism that WTO rules do not provide sufficient flexibility for governments to adopt innovative policies to respond to new challenges is exaggerated. The rules in the *SCM Agreement* prohibit export subsidies, but allow other subsidies to be used, subject to action by other WTO Members whose domestic industries of like products suffer material injury as a result of the subsidies.

*Some egregious subsidies remain unaddressed*: International trade rules do not address some of the most egregious subsidies that form part of some industrial policy. As noted above, disciplines on fisheries subsidies are currently under negotiation in the WTO, although it is proving more difficult to get serious traction on addressing fossil fuel subsidies.

*There are uncertainties and inconsistencies in the rules which should be addressed*: There are uncertainties and inconsistencies in the rules which raise questions about what governments can do to respond to new challenges. It is these uncertainties and inconsistencies, looked at through the lens of the need for governments to respond to the challenges of today's turbulent times, which suggest that the time is ripe for countries to look at reviewing the rules. We have not taken on this task here, our goal being instead to document the present state of affairs. Ideas for reform are already being considered, including reinvigoration of the non-actionable subsidies category,[134] development of an agreement (or waiver) around subsidies to promote a green economy-based policy[135] and addressing the role of state-owned enterprises. All are worthy endeavours which should be actively pursued – the more certainty that governments can have in these uncertain times, the better.

---

134   See for example Mark Wu, "Re-Examining 'Green Light' Subsidies in the Wake of New Green Industrial Policies" (Think Piece, E15 Expert Group on Reinvigorating Manufacturing: New Industrial Policy and the Trade System, August 2015) 1, 9.

135   Robert Howse, "Climate Change Mitigation Subsidies and the WTO Legal Framework: A Policy Analysis" (Paper, International Institute for Sustainable Development, June 2010) 24.

# Out with the Old Approach: A Call to Take Socio-Economic Rights Seriously in Refugee Status Determination

*Imogen Little*

**Abstract**

The misconception that those fleeing from socio-economic rights abuses are necessarily economic migrants – and not refugees – has been pervasive from the outset in international refugee law. In 2005, New Zealand decisively rejected any hierarchy of human rights in its application of the *Refugee Convention*, and similar jurisdictions have since followed suit. Yet, in canvassing recent decisions of New Zealand's appellate refugee body, the Immigration and Protection Tribunal, it becomes clear that a hierarchical approach to human rights still invades New Zealand's refugee jurisprudence, seeping in through the interpretation of the requirement of serious harm in socio-economic claims. The unfortunate result has been perplexing and inconsistent outcomes for those fleeing from socio-economic rights abuses.

## 1   Introduction

Ideas and assumptions as to who is, and who is not, a refugee are constantly evolving. Previously narrow assumptions have, in the past few decades, broadened: the traditional image of a male fleeing imprisonment or torture based on his political or religious beliefs is now recognised as just one, and not the only, form a refugee may take. One initial idea about refugees that has since been challenged and rejected is that refugees are necessarily fleeing from breaches of their civil and political, rather than socio-economic, rights.

The distinction between these two classes of rights relates back to the historical context in which refugee jurisprudence developed. The *United Nations Convention relating to the Status of Refugees* (the "*Convention*") was adopted by the United Nations ("UN") General Assembly in 1951.[1] This was the first time that a general definition to denote refugee status was used to set out countries' rights and obligations relating to refugees. Heavily influenced by the

---

[1] *Convention relating to the Status of Refugees*, signed 28 July 1951, 189 UNTS 137 (entered into force 22 April 1954).

events of the Second World War ("World War II") and the Cold War, the *Convention* was restricted to a Eurocentric focus: the refugee's flight had to have been prompted by a pre-1951 event in Europe.[2] So, although in 1967 the scope of the *Convention* was expanded by removing these geographical and temporal limitations,[3] the refugee definition applied today was drafted with the Western political refugee in mind. And, as refugee jurisprudence developed, it continued to undervalue socio-economic rights compared to their civil and political counterparts.

However, in New Zealand, the Refugee Status Appeal Authority ("RSAA") rejected the hierarchal approach to human rights in refugee jurisprudence in 2005,[4] becoming a frontrunner and leader in this issue for the rest of the world.[5] In 2009 the Immigration and Protection Tribunal ("IPT") succeeded the RSAA,[6] and in 2012 the IPT confirmed its rejection of the hierarchical approach.[7] Today, New Zealand jurisprudence accepts that refugee status can arise from socio-economic claims – those based on breaches of socio-economic, rather than civil and political, rights. Yet an examination of recent case law from the IPT calls into question how genuine this rejection of the old approach, and how effective the implementation of a new approach, have been. I will argue that the traditional hierarchical approach still very much influences the IPT's application of the definition of a "refugee", leading to the undervaluing of socio-economic rights, and thus generating perplexing and inconsistent results in socio-economic refugee claims.

To start by giving context to this argument, the human rights framework in which refugee law operates will be laid out. Human rights became relevant to

---

2   *Convention relating to the Status of Refugees* (n 1) art 1(B).
3   *Protocol relating to the Status of Refugees*, opened for signature 31 January 1967, 606 UNTS 267 (entered into force 4 October 1967).
4   *Refugee Appeal Nos 75221 and 75225* (Refugee Status Appeals Authority, Member Burson, 23 September 2005) 20 [81].
5   Within international refugee jurisprudence, it is increasingly recognised that consistency in interpretation across jurisdictions is desirable, and those interpreting the definition tend to carefully consider, and sometimes adopt, legal reasoning of other jurisdictions: see James C Hathaway and Michelle Foster, *The Law of Refugee Status* (Cambridge University Press, 2nd ed, 2014) 4.
6   Under the *Immigration Act 2009* (NZ), the IPT replaced four specialist immigration-related appellate bodies, including the Refugee Status Appeals Authority ("RSAA"). In one of the first refugee and protection decisions of the IPT, the Tribunal emphasised the persuasive value of RSAA decisions, despite their non-binding status under the new *Immigration Act*. I will refer to the Immigration and Protection Tribunal as either "the IPT" or "the Tribunal". Also note that, in New Zealand, refugee status is first determined by the Refugee Status Branch, and appeals are then heard by the IPT.
7   *BG (Fiji)* [2012] NZIPT 800091, [90].

refugee law through the concept of "being persecuted", and so I will firstly explain the development and application of the human rights approach in New Zealand. Next, I will specifically address the place of socio-economic rights within this framework, explaining the application of the traditional hierarchical approach and its later rejection. This section will also describe the forms of socio-economic refugee claims as they tend to appear in the IPT today.

Third, three case studies from appeals decided by the IPT will demonstrate how remnants of the traditional hierarchical approach can still be seen to linger in the Tribunal's response to socio-economic claims. It is in the Tribunal's assessment of the level of "serious harm" resulting from breaches of socio-economic rights that this puzzling approach emerges. Finally, I will take a closer look at the serious harm threshold in refugee jurisprudence to confirm that the concept of serious harm is being misapplied in relation to socio-economic claims. As will be seen, this misapplication is leading to troubling and confusing outcomes.

## 2  A Human Rights Approach to Persecution

### 2.1  *The Development of the Human Rights Approach*

To understand the position of socio-economic rights in refugee status determination, it is first helpful to look to the broader development of human rights law within refugee jurisprudence. The *Convention* defines a refugee as someone who:[8]

> [O]wing to well-founded fear of being persecuted for reasons of race, religion, nationality, membership of a particular social group or political opinion, is outside the country of his nationality and is unable or, owing to such fear, is unwilling to avail himself of the protection of that country; or who, not having a nationality and being outside the country of his former habitual residence as a result of such events, is unable or, owing to such fear, is unwilling to return to it.

The requirement to demonstrate a well-founded fear of "being persecuted" is central to the refugee definition. However, due to the impossibility of foreseeing all forms of mistreatment that could justify international protection, the

---

8   *Convention relating to the Status of Refugees* (n 1) art 1(A)(2).

*Convention* left the concept of persecution undefined.⁹ It was thus for domestic decision-makers, guided by scholars and judges, to interpret this term;¹⁰ and, from the outset, persecution was seen to involve two essential limbs: serious harm and a failure of state protection.¹¹ In 1991, James Hathaway, whose textbook *The Law of Refugee Status* is internationally regarded as the seminal text on the *Refugee Convention*, reformulated this test as the "sustained or systemic violation of basic human rights demonstrative of a failure of state protection".¹² This human rights approach has since been endorsed by the UN High Commissioner for Refugees ("UNHCR") and widely applied across common law jurisdictions, and is becoming increasingly adopted in the civil law world.¹³

It is largely agreed, both in New Zealand and international refugee jurisprudence, that the human rights relevant to persecution should be identified by reference to international treaties,¹⁴ the most central and authoritative being the *International Covenant on Civil and Political Rights* ("ICCPR")¹⁵ and the *International Covenant on Economic, Social and Cultural Rights* ("ICESCR").¹⁶ These covenants (the "*Covenants*") both derived from the *Universal Declaration of Human Rights* ("UDHR").¹⁷

### 2.2 Application of the Human Rights Approach in New Zealand

From the beginning, New Zealand refugee decision-makers adopted this human rights approach.¹⁸ In the case *Re MN*, the RSAA concluded that

---

9  Guy S Goodwin-Gill and Jane McAdam, *The Refugee in International Law* (Oxford University Press, 3rd ed, 2007) 90; and James C Hathaway, *The Law of Refugee Status* (Butterworths, 1991) 102.
10  Hathaway and Foster (n 5) 4.
11  Hathaway (n 9) 105. See also *Refugee Appeal No 71427/99* (Refugee Status Appeals Authority, Chairperson Haines and Member Tremewan, 16 August 2000) [67].
12  Hathaway (n 9) 104–105.
13  Hathaway and Foster (n 5) 185.
14  See *Refugee Appeal No 74665/03* (Refugee Status Appeals Authority, Chairperson Roche, Member Haines and Member Murphy, 7 July 2004) 27 [65].
15  *International Covenant on Civil and Political Rights*, opened for signature 16 December 1966, 999 UNTS 171 (entered into force 23 March 1976).
16  *International Covenant on Economic, Social and Cultural Rights*, opened for signature 16 December 1966, 993 UNTS 3 (entered into force 3 January 1976).
17  *Universal Declaration of Human Rights*, GA Res 217A (III), UN GAOR, UN Doc A/810 (10 December 1948).
18  *DS (Iran)* [2016] NZIPT 800788, [114]; see also *Refugee Appeal No 11/91 Re S* (Refugee Status Appeals Authority, Chairperson Haines, Member Lombard and Member Priestley, 5 September 1991); *Refugee Appeal No 135/92 Re RS* (Refugee Status Appeals Authority, Chairman Nicholson and Member Haines, 18 June 1993).

"New Zealand refugee jurisprudence accepts that refugee law ought to concern itself with actions which deny human dignity in any key way and that the sustained or systemic denial of core human rights is the appropriate standard".[19]

In the 2016 case *DS (Iran)*, the Tribunal clarified that Hathaway's formulation does not fully encapsulate the persecution element of the *Convention*.[20] Instead, the sustained and systemic violation of human rights must still lead to *serious harm*, in order for the claimant to be recognised as a refugee, as per the original two-limb approach for persecution (serious harm and a failure of state protection).[21] Hathaway's formulation must be regarded as epexegetic of "being persecuted", rather than a replacement term, and thus serious harm is still a necessary component.[22] This involves looking at the "severity of impact" of the anticipated breach of human rights on the claimant,[23] thus making the underlying breach of human rights and the question of serious harm related, but separate, issues.[24] Thus, the Tribunal created a four-step test for the serious harm limb of persecution, encompassing the human rights approach:[25]

(a) Does the claimant's predicament, as found, indicate there will be an interference with a basic human right or rights in the form of a restriction on its exercise or enjoyment? (the question of scope).

(b) If there will be interference, does the right in principle permit any restriction? (the question of nature).

(c) If restriction is in principle permitted, is the restriction at issue lawful in terms of the relevant limitation or derogation clause? (the question of legality).

(d) If the restriction is not permitted in principle, or is permitted but applied unlawfully, will the breach of the right cause some form of serious harm to the claimant? (the question of impact).

This test embodies Hathaway's human rights formulation in its first three steps, while also demanding a separate serious harm inquiry in the fourth step.

---

19  *Refugee Appeal No 2039/93 Re MN* (Refugee Status Appeals Authority, Chairman Haines and Member Gutnick, 12 February 1996) [40].
20  *DS (Iran)* (n 18) [127].
21  Ibid.
22  Ibid [116]–[124].
23  Ibid [128].
24  Ibid [131].
25  Ibid [203]. Note that the first three steps of this test reflect the analysis advocated for by Hathaway and Foster: see Hathaway and Foster (n 5) 204–206.

The test was subsequently confirmed and slightly rephrased by the Court of Appeal.[26]

It is here that New Zealand jurisprudence has slightly departed from dominant ideas in academic literature: the second edition of *The Law of Refugee Status*, co-written by Hathaway and Michelle Foster, suggests that it should only be in "exceptional cases", where the rights violation amounts to "*de minimis* harm", that this requirement would not be satisfied.[27] Guy Goodwin-Gill and Jane McAdam acknowledge that the approach to persecution across different states is inconsistent, and canvas several varied interpretations, rather than putting forward one recommended approach.[28] However, Goodwill-Gill and McAdam do suggest that whether or not less extreme forms of persecution, such as denial of access to employment or the professions, suffice will depend on various factors including "(1) the nature of the freedom threatened, (2) the nature and severity of the restriction, and (3) the likelihood of the restriction eventuating in the individual case".[29] This does not seem to impose an additional requirement of resulting serious harm to the applicant.

The IPT's explanation of the fourth step of the *DS (Iran)* test suggests that New Zealand has adopted a more stringent serious harm inquiry than that endorsed by dominant refugee law academia.

In *DS (Iran)*, the IPT defined serious harm as "harm arising from breaches of human rights as codified under international human rights law which, due to their nature, intensity and/or duration, are appropriately categorised as serious".[30] It acknowledged that, given the non-hierarchical approach to human rights, serious harm can encompass a broad range of harm,[31] and can result from non-physical forms of harm, such as "loss of liberty, restrictions on conduct or psychological forms of harm".[32] The form that this harm takes will be shaped by the aspect of human dignity relevant to the breached right or bundle of rights, to be considered in light of the context of the claim and the

---

26  *Refugee and Protection Officer v CV and CW* [2017] NZLR 585, 606–607 [82] (Winkelmann J for the Court) (New Zealand Court of Appeal). Although the *DS (Iran)* test is laid out slightly differently by the Court of Appeal, there is no substantive difference to the inquiry under the Court of Appeal's test and the *DS (Iran)* test. Therefore, I will continue to refer to this as the *DS (Iran)* approach. This is also how the IPT have subsequently referred to the approach.
27  Hathaway and Foster (n 5) 206.
28  Goodwin-Gill and McAdam (n 9) 91.
29  Ibid 92.
30  *DS (Iran)* (n 18) [179].
31  Ibid [177].
32  Ibid [181].

circumstances of the claimant.[33] Serious harm can arise from a single act or omission, or from repetitive or systematic acts or omissions.[34] It was acknowledged that serious harm can arise from an accumulation of breaches of rights where none of these breaches, in isolation, would constitute serious harm.[35]

The human rights approach to the question of persecution requires scrutiny of the particular circumstances of the claimant, meaning that an abuse of rights may amount to serious harm for one claimant due to their personal attributes, where it would not for another.[36] This includes, for example, the claimant's age, gender and standard of health.[37] The Tribunal noted in *DS (Iran)* that standard of health includes both mental and physical health, as per ICESCR art 12(1).[38] Importantly, the Tribunal in *DS (Iran)* did not seem to consider it was altering the serious harm threshold, but seemed to consider instead that it was laying out and clarifying the approach already being taken.[39] This indicates that cases decided before *DS (Iran)* should still have relevance to an examination of the serious harm threshold.

This fourth step of the *DS (Iran)* test is crucial when examining the interaction between socio-economic rights and the definition of a "refugee". Although, as will be seen, the relevance of socio-economic rights is increasingly being acknowledged in refugee jurisprudence, this serious harm threshold proves to be the biggest stumbling block for socio-economic claims.

## 3  Socio-Economic Rights within the Human Rights Framework

### 3.1 *The History and Development of Socio-Economic Rights in Refugee Jurisprudence*

The divisive history of socio-economic rights sheds light on the slow recognition of their equal importance with civil and political rights in refugee

---

33  Ibid [179].
34  Ibid [181].
35  Ibid.
36  Ibid [182].
37  *AC (Syria)* [2011] NZIPT 800035, [102].
38  *DS (Iran)* (n 18) [171].
39  See ibid [170]–[183]. The Tribunal refers to past decisions in laying out these points about serious harm – for example, *Refugee Appeal No 2039/93 Re MN* (n 19) is authority for the proposition that non-physical harm is able to constitute persecution: at [170]; *AC (Syria)* (n 37) is provided as authority for the proposition that the seriousness of the harm will be shaped by the personal characteristics of the claimant: [170]; and *BG (Fiji)* (n 7) is provided as authority for the proposition that serious harm can incorporate a broad range of harms: [177].

jurisprudence. Both internationally-binding human rights standards and the *Refugee Convention* were products of World War II;[40] both were thus heavily influenced by the ideological split between the East and West leading to the Cold War.[41] Civil and political rights were favoured by the West, while the East focused on the importance of economic, social and cultural rights. Despite the acknowledgement at the 1993 Vienna World Conference on Human Rights of the equal value of the two sets of rights,[42] this Western preference for civil and political rights is still visible today.[43] And, as Kate Jastram, a senior research associate to the Refugee Law Initiative and previously a legal advisor to the UNHCR, pointed out, the ideas of civil and political protection and the *Refugee Convention* are so interwoven that refugee status is frequently labelled "political asylum".[44] The refugee definition itself was drafted from a Eurocentric, liberal-rights lens, and its interpretation has traditionally been informed by such notions.[45]

Thus, socio-economic refugee claims, meaning those that are based on breaches of socio-economic, rather than civil and political, rights, do not fit this traditional refugee mould. Furthermore, the *ICCPR* and *ICESCR* have not always been given equal value in refugee jurisprudence. In 1991, Hathaway laid out the distinct types of obligations within the *UDHR* relevant to refugee law, in the form of a hierarchy.[46] First were non-derogable rights which were immediately binding with the passing of the *ICCPR*, such as freedom from arbitrary deprivation of life and the prohibition of torture. Failure to guarantee such rights would, according to the hierarchy, always amount to persecution. Second-level rights were those contained in the *ICCPR* from which derogation is permitted during emergency, such as freedom from arbitrary arrest and due

---

40  Ed Bates, "History" in David Moeckli, Sangeeta Shah and Sandesh Sivakumaran (eds), *International Human Rights Law* (Oxford University Press, 3rd ed, 2018) 3, 18–19.
41  Ibid.
42  *Vienna Declaration and Programme of Action*, UN Doc A/CONF.157/123 (12 July 1993) [5].
43  For example, the United States, initially leading the West in its preference for civil and political rights, has not yet ratified the *ICESCR*.
44  Kate Jastram, "Economic Harm as a Basis for Refugee Status and the Application of Human Rights Law to the Interpretation of Economic Persecution" in James C Simeon (ed), *Critical Issues in International Refugee Law: Strategies toward Interpretative Harmony* (Cambridge University Press, 2010) 143, 143.
45  Bonny Ibhawoh, "Defining Persecution and Protection: The Cultural Relativism Debate and the Rights of Refugees" in Niklaus Steiner, Mark Gibney and Gil Loescher (eds), *Problems of Protection: The UNHCR, Refugees, and Human Rights* (Routledge, 2003) 61, 67.
46  Hathaway (n 9) 108–112. This hierarchy involved four levels of obligation, but only the first three are discussed here. Fourth level rights are those which were not codified in either the *ICCPR* or the *ICESCR*, and will not usually be sufficient to claim the failure of state protection.

process rights. Failure to ensure these rights would generally be a breach of a state's duty of protection, unless the derogation was due to emergency, was not inconsistent with international law and was not applied discriminatorily. ICE-SCR rights ranked third, due to the progressive rather than immediate duties imposed by this covenant. Of this level, Hathaway stated:[47]

> While the standard of protection is less absolute than that which applies to the first two categories of rights, a state is in breach of its basic obligations where it either ignores these interests notwithstanding the fiscal ability to respond, or where it excludes a minority of its population from their enjoyment.

Significantly, Hathaway discussed this hierarchy in relation to the extent of a state's duty, rather than the seriousness of a breach of the duty. This is why it is appropriately viewed as a hierarchy of obligation, rather than a hierarchy of rights in which civil and political rights are attributed a higher normative value than their socio-economic counterparts.[48] This model addresses the question of whether a right has actually been breached, by examining the different levels of obligation imposed on parties by the *Covenants*.[49] It relates to the first step of the *DS (Iran)* test, as to whether or not the right in question had been breached, and not to the question of serious harm per the fourth step. Therefore, the correct interpretation of this hierarchy is that a state that is not ensuring socio-economic rights will not automatically be in breach of its obligations, as would be the case for first-level rights. Instead, a state will only breach third-level obligations if it either has the economic means to provide such rights, yet without reasonable justification chooses not to, or if the state discriminates against a section of society in offering these rights.

However, the United Kingdom, Canada, and New Zealand incorrectly applied this model as a hierarchical categorisation of the normative value of rights, and thus implemented a hierarchy of rights rather than of obligation.[50] Foster, in her highly regarded book on socio-economic rights and refugee status, explains that this hierarchy was used by courts to assess how "fundamental" a particular right was, and thus whether the type of harm could constitute persecution.[51] The ranking of socio-economic rights in third place in this

---

47  Ibid 111.
48  Michelle Foster, *International Refugee Law and Socio-Economic Rights: Refuge from Deprivation* (Cambridge University Press, 2007) 113–114 (*"Refuge from Deprivation"*).
49  Ibid 113.
50  Ibid 120.
51  Ibid.

hierarchy was actually intended to demonstrate the idea that measuring the necessary implementation, and consequently the breach, of socio-economic rights is less straightforward, not that they had any less normative value.[52] Yet, case law from these jurisdictions demonstrated "a pervasive conflation of the two conceptually distinct issues".[53] Notably, Hathaway makes no mention of his hierarchy in the second edition of *The Law of Refugee Status*, instead stressing the equality of these two sets of rights.[54]

New Zealand refugee law long accepted and applied this hierarchy in its decision making: a form of "sliding scale" was used whereby the higher on the hierarchy the relevant right fell, the more likely a breach was to constitute serious harm and therefore persecution.[55] Case law from the RSAA referred to socio-economic rights as being "secondary in importance",[56] "low in the hierarchy of rights",[57] and "only a third-level right ... not a basic or core human right".[58] Unsurprisingly therefore, refugee claims founded on the ICESCR, rather than the ICCPR, met with little success due to being seen as not severe enough to constitute persecution.[59]

However, from the 2000s the RSAA began to question this hierarchical approach,[60] and in 2005 it definitively rejected the notion of categorising rights into hierarchies.[61] In 2012 the IPT confirmed this position, rejecting the "hierarchical perspective in which civil and political rights take precedence over, or are a superior form of rights to, their economic, social and cultural

---

52  Ibid.
53  Ibid.
54  Hathaway and Foster (n 5) 203.
55  Bruce Burson, "Give Way to the Right: The Evolving Use of Human Rights in New Zealand Refugee Status Determination" in Bruce Burson and David James Cantor (eds), *Human Rights and the Refugee Definition: Comparative Legal Practice and Theory* (Brill Nijhoff, 2016) 25, 35.
56  *Refugee Appeal No 1/92 Re SA* (Refugee Status Appeals Authority, Chairman Nicholson, Member Haines and Member Priestley, 30 April 1992) 49.
57  *Refugee Appeal No 732/92 Re CZZ* (Refugee Status Appeals Authority, Chairman Haines and Member Domzalski, 5 August 1994) 9.
58  *Refugee Appeal No 71163/98* (Refugee Status Appeals Authority, Member Plunkett, 31 March 1999) 10.
59  See, for example, *Refugee Appeal No 70863/98* (Refugee Status Appeals Authority, Chairperson Shaw and Member Plunkett, 13 August 1998); and *Refugee Appeal No 76043* (Refugee Status Appeals Authority, Member Murphy, 7 December 2007).
60  See *Refugee Appeal Nos 72558/01 and 72559/01* (Refugee Status Appeals Authority, Chairperson Haines and Member Lawson, 19 November 2002) [114]; *Refugee Appeal No 74665/03* (n 14) 34 [80].
61  *Refugee Appeal Nos 75221 and 75225* (n 4) [81].

counterparts".[62] This rejection has since been accepted and advocated for by influential academics, with Foster stating that New Zealand has "displayed the most pronounced leadership on this issue".[63] It is now understood that the progressive implementation of socio-economic rights does not make them less important than their counterparts, but rather recognises the longer length of time inevitably needed to implement them.[64] The Tribunal has furthermore confirmed that breaches of the *ICESCR* "may, in principle, be relied on to found a refugee claim as rights *in themselves*".[65]

### 3.2    Forms of Socio-Economic Claims

Of course, valuing socio-economic rights equally is not to say that any socio-economic issue can suffice for refugee status. Economic hardship cannot in itself meet the threshold of "being persecuted", and those who migrate only to build a more economically secure life are not refugees.[66] Due to the refugee definition requirements, socio-economic claims almost always involve the discriminatory denial of socio-economic rights to certain marginalised groups, where this discrimination is for a reason covered by the *Convention*.[67] Such cases meet the lack-of-state-protection limb of persecution, as the state will either be complicit in, or unwilling or unable to stop, the discrimination. They also satisfy the first three steps of the *DS (Iran)* test, because a discriminatory denial of rights is unlawful by default: non-discrimination is "an immediate and cross-cutting obligation" of the *ICESCR*.[68] However, socio-economic claims tend to fail on the fourth step of the *DS (Iran)* test: namely, the question of whether the breach of the right actually resulted in "serious harm".

---

62   *BG (Fiji)* (n 7) [90].
63   Michelle Foster, "Economic Migrant or Person in Need of Protection? Socio-Economic Rights and Persecution in International Refugee Law" in Bruce Burson and David James Cantor (eds), *Human Rights and the Refugee Definition: Comparative Legal Practice and Theory* (Brill Nijhoff, 2016) 229, 248 ("Economic Migrant or Person in Need of Protection?").
64   Hathaway and Foster (n 5) 203. Goodwin-Gill and McAdam do not discuss in detail the issue of socio-economic rights in refugee status. However, they do acknowledge that "the value of certain economic and social rights is increasingly accepted", and that this is an area for future development within refugee law: Goodwin-Gill and McAdam (n 9) 134.
65   *BG (Fiji)* (n 7) [90] (emphasis in original).
66   Ibid [88].
67   I will use the term "socio-economic claims" to refer to this type of refugee claim.
68   Committee on Economic, Social and Cultural Rights, *General Comment No 20: Non-Discrimination in Economic, Social and Cultural Rights (Art 2, Para 2, of the International Covenant on Economic, Social and Cultural Rights)*, UN Doc E/C.12/GC/20 (2 July 2009) [7].

The harm faced in socio-economic claims involving work and education is generally a denial of dignity and harm to wellbeing, caused by the severe, systemic and ongoing discrimination, rather than harm in the form of tangible effects of that discrimination.[69] For example, the IPT has recognised "the importance of assuring the individual's right to freely chosen decent work as a fundamental aspect of individual dignity",[70] and the fact that education has not only practical purposes but is also "one of the joys and rewards of human existence".[71] Similarly, in discussing the right to work, Foster asks, "[s]hould we be concerned only with pure economic impact or is there something more fundamental about work (and other socio-economic rights), relating to dignity, identity and self-worth?"[72]

However, some socio-economic claims also result in economic proscription: the complete inability to earn a livelihood.[73] The serious harm that arises from a claim involving economic proscription is of a tangible nature, in the form of complete economic deprivation, potentially leading to a threat to one's basic survival. Hathaway's hierarchy of obligations, although supposedly no longer in effect, is a useful tool for recognising the difference between these outcomes in socio-economic claims. In describing third-level rights, Hathaway stated:[74]

> Moreover, the deprivation of certain of the socio-economic rights, such as the ability to earn a living, or the entitlement to food, shelter, or health care will at an extreme level be tantamount to the deprivation of life or cruel, inhuman or degrading treatment, and hence unquestionably constitute persecution.

Thus, under the traditional hierarchy, a third-level socio-economic claim involving economic proscription actually becomes a first-level claim. It is no longer truly viewed as a socio-economic claim but is elevated to the status of civil and political claim, due to the consequences of economic proscription on the claimant's right to life or to not be subjected to cruel, inhuman or degrading

---

69   Another line of socio-economic claims involves the denial of health care, and the health issues that result from this. I will not address this line of cases, instead focusing on denial of work and education.
70   *AZ (Turkey)* [2018] NZIPT 801224, [138].
71   Ibid [137], quoting Committee on Economic, Social and Cultural Rights, *General Comment No 13: The Right to Education (Article 13 of the Covenant)*, UN Doc E/C.12/1999/10 (8 December 1999).
72   Foster, *Refuge from Deprivation* (n 48) 101.
73   Ibid 90.
74   Hathaway (n 9) 111.

treatment. For this reason, even from its outset and while the hierarchy of rights was being applied, the *Refugee Convention* was in fact intended to cover claims involving economic proscription.[75] Of course, under today's non-hierarchical approach to human rights, this economic proscription element, elevating a socio-economic claim to a "first-level" claim, should no longer be crucial for finding refugee status in socio-economic claims.

Yet, as is always the case, a theoretical understanding of equality is not guaranteed to seamlessly transfer into practice. Examining how the IPT is applying this supposedly non-hierarchical approach reveals the complexities and issues still present in the intersection of socio-economic rights and refugee jurisprudence.

## 4  New Zealand Case Studies

To gain an understanding of the IPT's current approach to socio-economic rights in refugee determination, we will now explore three telling case studies. The first two cases demonstrate problematic aspects of the IPT's assessment of socio-economic claims, and the third case reveals the worrying results of such an approach.

### 4.1  AC (Egypt)

The 2011 appeal *AC (Egypt)* involved a citizen of Egypt who faced discrimination on account of his oculocutaneous albinism (a condition which affected his pigmentation and hair, and also rendered him partially blind).[76] These effects meant he was classified as disabled under Egyptian legislation. The Tribunal found that the appellant had been harassed, discriminated against and socially marginalised his whole life on account of his albinism. He faced ostracism from peers in school and university, occasional physical violence, and denial of consent to marriage from the parents of the woman he loved. After obtaining his undergraduate degree, the appellant's master's proposal was rejected, seemingly on discriminatory grounds. The appellant was turned down for every job for which he applied, despite Egyptian laws ensuring disabled persons' employment in government roles. His business, started with his father's assistance, also failed due to customers not wanting to buy from a person with albinism.[77]

---

75  Foster, *Refuge from Deprivation* (n 48) 90.
76  *AC (Egypt)* [2011] NZIPT 800015.
77  For a full description of these facts see ibid [4]–[27].

### 4.1.1 The Tribunal's Approach

The Tribunal found that this appellant was "denied the very core of the right to work ... [he] *exhaustively* sought to enjoy this right but has been effectively shut out or refused access to employment".[78] Yet the serious harm the appellant had faced from this was not as a result of the economic deprivation he suffered, as is the case for claims involving economic proscription.[79] The financial support the appellant received from his parents meant that he had not suffered serious harm from this economic deprivation. Instead, in assessing the question of whether the appellant had suffered serious harm *in the past*, the Tribunal held:[80]

> Individually, the discrimination the appellant has encountered in his education, employment and the isolated physical violence and intended hit and runs may not have caused the Tribunal to consider his past predicament amounted to his being persecuted. However, when the cumulative effect of these matters is weighed the Tribunal finds that the appellant has suffered serious harm within the meaning of the Refugee Convention. The net effect of these matters has been to deny the appellant any chance of a meaningful life through gaining any form of employment and self-worth.

Thus, the IPT found that the psychological effect of the systemic discrimination, denying the appellant his dignity and the "chance of a meaningful life", was sufficient to constitute serious harm.

Interestingly, however, the Tribunal fell back on harm in the form of economic deprivation to ultimately decide the case. When assessing the appellant's risk of serious harm *in the future*, the Tribunal found that he would remain completely reliant on his parents for financial support, and because his parents were now retired and had used a significant portion of their pension as start-up capital for the appellant's failed business, they would not be able to continue to assist him financially in the long term.[81] The IPT concluded that this financial deprivation, considered in accumulation with the denial of

---

78  Ibid [83].
79  Note that this case was decided five years before *DS (Iran)*, and so does not use the four-step test for serious harm. However, serious harm was always a necessary element of persecution.
80  Ibid [88].
81  Ibid [93].

dignity and worth, discrimination, social isolation, depression, and occasional physical threats suffered by the appellant, amounted to serious harm.[82]

### 4.1.2 The Issue Raised

At first glance this appeal appears to be a positive acknowledgement of the equal value of socio-economic rights – the discrimination faced by this appellant was largely in his employment, education and social opportunities, and this was recognised to constitute serious harm. However, this appeal also hints at the idea that the Tribunal still seems to prefer to rely on economic proscription to find serious harm in socio-economic refugee claims.

The facts of this case clearly indicate that the predominant harm the appellant was fleeing from was the attack to his dignity, worth, and wellbeing caused by the systemic discrimination. The appellant suffered "considerable depression" from this discrimination, and during his final year in Egypt the appellant lived a "hermit's life" where he rarely ventured outside[83] – a fact that the Tribunal obligingly chose to "not overlook" in its assessment of serious harm.[84] The certain denial of "any chance of a meaningful life" should be, and was, enough to reach the serious harm threshold,[85] and yet the Tribunal felt the need to rely on the uncertain risk of economic proscription in finding refugee status.

The appellant had not suffered economic proscription in the past (because of his parents' support), whereas he *had* suffered serious harm through the denial of dignity caused by systemic discrimination in his socio-economic rights. The Tribunal's reasoning indicates a reluctance to allow an appeal based on this ground, despite recognising its validity and ability to meet the threshold. The Tribunal preferred to view this claim through an economic proscription lens, even though by its own reasoning the case could have succeeded without this extra element. And, through the lens of the traditional hierarchy, this economic proscription element would have shifted this from a third-level to potentially a first-level claim. Perhaps this indicates that lingering sentiments as to the inferiority of socio-economic or third-level claims still remain in the Tribunal's assessment of serious harm in the fourth step of the *DS (Iran)* test.

---

82  Ibid [92]–[95].
83  Ibid [94].
84  Ibid.
85  Ibid [88].

## 4.2 AL (South Korea)

Remnants of this hierarchy are again seen in the 2016 appeal *AL (South Korea)*, decided three months after *DS (Iran)*.[86] This appeal concerned a North Korean defector who had gained citizenship in South Korea. Defectors from North Korea are frequently subject to prejudices and discrimination by South Koreans, and this animosity seems to be growing.[87] However, the state recognises North Koreans as protected persons and has a legislative framework to protect and support defectors: the *Korean Refugees Protection and Settlement Act 1997* provides North Korean defectors with support such as settlement services, academic recognition, social adaptation education, vocational training, accommodation support, financial support in settlement and support and protection in employment.[88]

Thus, the appellant had received subsidised accommodation, a sum of money to assist with his resettlement, and a pathway to complete a vocational trade. However, after encountering discrimination and only being able to obtain part-time casual employment as a labourer, the appellant completed a Bachelor of Science degree in engineering. This tertiary education was free for the appellant due to his status as a North Korean defector. The appellant then applied for over 50 jobs but did not obtain even an interview, which he felt was because his applications indicated his North Korean ethnicity.

Socially, the appellant was ostracised by university peers and was once the victim of an unprovoked assault. He formed a romantic relationship with a South Korean woman, but her parents refused consent to marry him as he was from North Korea. This continual discrimination caused the appellant to become severely depressed, and on two occasions he was on the brink of suicide.[89]

### 4.2.1 The Tribunal's Approach

The Tribunal outlined the developing thought concerning economic proscription cases and refugee status, before concluding that:[90]

> While the law in relation to socio-economic rights as a basis for claiming refugee status is an evolving one, there appears to be consensus that mere financial hardship arising from workplace discrimination will not

---

86   *AL (South Korea)* [2016] NZIPT 800858.
87   Ibid [77]–[80].
88   Ibid [67]–[69].
89   For a full description of these facts, see ibid [5]–[18].
90   Ibid [44].

suffice, but that threats to the claimant's capacity to subsist through wholesale denial of access to the labour market on discriminatory grounds may do so. There is a large grey zone between these two poles, encompassing situations where the claimant is not wholly shut out of the labour market on discriminatory grounds to the point where their livelihood or capacity to subsist is threatened, but discrimination in accessing employment nevertheless impacts on them in some way which transcends simple financial hardship.

This is a curious approach because, as the facts clearly demonstrate, this was not a case about economic proscription at all. The appellant received financial help from the government,[91] and was able to earn some form of living through employment, although on a casual basis. In fact, the Tribunal only accepted that discrimination "at least played some part" in the appellant's issues in finding employment, but this problem could also be simply put down to a competitive society in which the appellant had only just obtained a qualification.[92] So, although the IPT accepted that the appellant would likely face some discrimination in finding employment in his chosen profession should he return to South Korea, it also expressly found that the appellant would likely continue to enjoy an adequate standard of living, through other employment he could find and by way of state support.[93]

Thus, this case was not so much about the appellant's economic prospects as it was about his mental and emotional wellbeing. The Tribunal described the particular importance of finding meaningful work for this appellant as an "antidote to the assaults on his dignity arising from his experiences in North Korea, and the discrimination and ostracism encountered in his private and work life following his defection".[94] Ultimately, the Tribunal found that the appellant was "particularly vulnerable to suffering serious psychological harm" from the discrimination he would face upon his return to South Korea, due to his existing precarious state of mental health.[95]

The Tribunal found that this harm would reach a severity amounting to degrading treatment under *ICCPR* art 7, thus constituting sufficiently serious

---

91    Note that despite the government's affirmative action and best efforts, the lack of state protection requirement was still met here as the state was unable to reduce the risk of persecution arising from non-state actors to below the "well-founded" level: see ibid [56].
92    Ibid [84].
93    Ibid [87].
94    Ibid [88].
95    Ibid [89].

harm under the *Refugee Convention*.[96] The appellant was recognised as a refugee.

### 4.2.2 The Issue Raised

The description of socio-economic claims laid out by the Tribunal in the above paragraph is exactly in line with Hathaway's original hierarchy. The reference to "threats to the claimant's capacity to subsist through wholesale denial of access to the labour market" is a reference to the type of situation in which socio-economic claims involve economic proscription and become first-level claims. Classifying socio-economic claims as falling somewhere within "a large grey zone between these two poles", depending on the economic consequences of discrimination" elevates the gravity of economic proscription claims, traditionally first-level, above that of standard socio-economic "third-level" claims.

Such an approach collapses two different forms of harm that result from socio-economic claims into one sliding scale, where "mere financial hardship" cannot meet the serious harm threshold. This completely ignores the fact that the serious harm in socio-economic claims not involving economic proscription is actually the harm to dignity and wellbeing caused by severe discrimination. If decision-makers automatically jump to questions of economic harm when faced with a case concerning the right to work or education, their reasoning will undoubtedly be influenced by this idea that the less serious the economic consequences are, the less serious the harm. Such an approach could surreptitiously raise the level of serious harm that these claimants would need to show in order to counter this assumption.

The fact that the Tribunal began its assessment by looking at financial deprivation, when this was not actually in issue, suggests an attempt from the outset to categorise these facts as "first-level", in order to find serious harm. If the Tribunal truly accepts that "third-level" claims, resulting in harm to dignity and wellbeing, could qualify for refugee status *in themselves*, surely the Tribunal would have begun its assessment by looking at the actual harm suffered rather than assessing the existence of economic proscription. This case involved strong evidence of other serious harm: the appellant was suicidal and had a psychiatric report diagnosing him with post-traumatic stress disorder and associated anxiety and depression. This ultimately allowed the claim to become "first-level", and thus succeed – the harm suffered by the appellant was enough to breach his right to not be subjected to degrading treatment under ICCPR art 7. However, if this undeniable psychological evidence had been missing, it seems likely that the Tribunal could have altogether missed the serious harm

---

96  Ibid.

clearly caused by such discrimination, due to the pervading influence of the traditional hierarchy.

### 4.3 AZ (Turkey)

This third case study demonstrates how the influence of the traditional hierarchy can have troubling consequences on the outcome of socio-economic claims. *AZ (Turkey)*, decided at the start of 2018, involved a 25 year old female Alevi Kurdish appellant from Turkey.[97] Alevism is a minority religion of Turkey, accounting for around 25–31% of the Turkish population.[98] After reviewing the country of origin information regarding the Alevi religion, the IPT concluded that "Alevis have long been marginalised and discriminated against in Turkey".[99] A similar finding was made as to people of Kurdish ethnicity in Turkey. In assessing the discrimination faced by the appellant on account of her gender, ethnicity, and religion, the IPT stated that:[100]

> The Tribunal accepts that the appellant has experienced instances of racial, religious and gender discrimination in access to, and enjoyment of, her rights to education and employment. Country reports confirm that discrimination continues to exist against Alevi, Kurds and women, and that these intersecting statuses possessed by the appellant both deepen and increase the likelihood of her encountering discrimination in these areas.

This discrimination affected the appellant in a variety of ways. She had been given her last choice of university, far from where she lived. She was unable to graduate from her tourism diploma and she could not transfer universities. If she started another course of study from scratch, there was every possibility she could encounter this same denial again. Throughout her education, from primary to tertiary levels, she was harassed both verbally and physically.

The appellant was repeatedly denied employment due to her Alevi Kurd status. Almost all short-term employment opportunities were only given to her due to internship programmes set up by her vocational high school and university course. Even these jobs only offered her half the remuneration that other workers of the same level and experience were given, due to her Alevi Kurd identity. She was forced to conceal her religious and ethnic status in this

---

97  *AZ (Turkey)* (n 70).
98  Ibid [83].
99  Ibid [85].
100 Ibid [183]–[184].

employment, and faced workplace harassment. The only work the appellant was ever able to obtain herself and receive adequate pay for was working for a friend's father in a school canteen for six months. The Tribunal found that conditions for minorities were worsening in Turkey, and that the appellant was likely to encounter similar conditions in the future. It also found that, in order to secure any employment in future, she may well have to conceal her ethnic and religious identity. The appellant's family members, especially the women, faced similar discrimination.

In discussing the issue of gender discrimination in Turkey, the Tribunal noted that "gender-related homicides and other forms of violence against women remain a serious challenge".[101] The appellant had been physically assaulted on two occasions, one of which led to her being hospitalised, and she was lucky to not have sustained a serious brain injury. The Tribunal found that gender discrimination limits opportunities for women in public and private life in Turkey and is a driver for gender-based violence against women, and that the appellant may continue to face harassment from men in her day-to-day life. In Turkey, the appellant would be unable to wear her hair blonde as she did in New Zealand, nor dress and present herself as she wished to, due to the risk of sexual harassment and abuse.[102]

### 4.3.1 The Tribunal's Approach

The Tribunal found that the nature and degree of the discrimination faced by the appellant, "even cumulatively assessed", did not reach the serious harm threshold.[103]

Clearly, the serious harm in issue here was a loss of dignity and harm to wellbeing. However, the entire analysis of serious harm was coloured by the appellant's economic prospects. In deciding whether the systemic discrimination the appellant encountered in employment constituted persecution, the Tribunal stated that:[104]

> [T]he evidence does not establish that the appellant has been precluded from employment on discriminatory grounds to such an extent in the past so as to indicate that there is a real chance she will be shut out of future employment sufficient to constitute a well-founded fear of being persecuted on this basis. ... The fact that she has been unable to

---

101   Ibid [121].
102   For a full account of these facts, see ibid [65]–[72] and [169]–[180].
103   Ibid [177].
104   Ibid [165].

graduate from her diploma may prevent her from finding work in her chosen field. However, this does not preclude her from seeking other opportunities.

This assessment seems to demand the appellant having suffered economic proscription in order to find serious harm, rather than looking to the cumulative effect of the appellant having to accept half-pay, hide her ethnicity and religion, and work menial jobs due to her inability to complete her qualification (and, potentially, any other qualification). The same could be said of the Tribunal's analysis of the effect of the discrimination in education. The Tribunal found only that this would "disadvantage her in her employment opportunities in this area".[105] While this is undeniably true, it also misses the crucial point that it is above all a denial of dignity and an attack on her sense of worth. The Tribunal first and foremost assessed the economic effects of the discrimination, and related it to the sliding scale proposed by *AL (South Korea)*, considering that these effects would fall near the "mere financial hardship arising from workplace discrimination" pole, which, as the Tribunal had held in that case, "will not suffice" as serious harm.

Therefore, the appellant was not recognised as a refugee, due to a lack of serious harm under the fourth step of the *DS (Iran)* test.[106]

### 4.3.2 The Issue Raised

The Tribunal's focus on economic proscription was again an attempt to elevate this to a "first-level" claim as per the traditional hierarchy – when this proved impossible, the claim failed. Without the first-level economic proscription element, the Tribunal simply held that, despite accepted evidence of severe, ongoing and systemic discrimination in multiple facets of the appellant's life, there was "no evidence to establish that, in accumulation, such instances will give rise to some form of serious harm, whether of a physical, economic, or psychological nature".[107] This worryingly mirrors the old approach, suggesting that socio-economic claims that cannot rise to first-level claims under the traditional hierarchy of rights are still viewed as not resulting in serious enough harm. In other words, this is not a rejection of the hierarchical approach to human rights at all – rather, it is the same old approach with new wording.

---

105  Ibid [162].
106  Ibid [183]–[187].
107  Ibid [185].

### 4.4 Conclusion from the Case Studies

As shown, the traditional hierarchical approach to human rights still infects New Zealand refugee determination, despite being firmly rejected over a decade ago. The IPT's preference for economic proscription cases indicates the continued valuing of "first-level" civil and political claims over socio-economic claims. At the root of this issue lies the interaction of socio-economic rights and the serious harm threshold – these case studies suggest that socio-economic claims are having a harder time meeting the fourth step of the *DS (Iran)* test, due to this misguided approach to socio-economic rights and the harm they produce. To understand how these cases should really be addressed, a closer look at the serious harm threshold is required.

## 5 Interpreting Serious Harm

It might be suggested that cases such as *AZ (Turkey)* fail not by reason of an overly high serious harm threshold for socio-economic claims, but because the harm in question is simply not serious enough to meet the threshold, even as it applies to civil and political claims. To complete my argument, I will demonstrate that this is not the case. The issue does in fact lie in the socio-economic aspect of these claims, rather than in the existing serious harm threshold. This calls for a rethinking of how socio-economic rights and the serious harm threshold should interact.

### 5.1 Serious Harm Defined in DS (Iran)

There is no prima facie reason why, based on the law as laid out in *DS (Iran)*, socio-economic claims not involving economic proscription cannot meet the serious harm threshold.

As discussed earlier, in *DS (Iran)* the Tribunal stressed the fact that non-physical harm, and an accumulation of less serious breaches of rights (where none in isolation would suffice), can meet the serious harm threshold.[108] It also suggested that, given the non-hierarchical approach to human rights, the relevant form of harm will be shaped by the aspect of human dignity relevant to the breached right or bundle of rights, and may arise from repetitive or systematic acts or omissions.[109] So, from the outset, the type of harm resulting from socio-economic claims lacking economic proscription is clearly a valid form of harm. Furthermore, the human rights-based approach to the question

---

108   *DS (Iran)* (n 18) [181].
109   Ibid.

of persecution requires scrutiny of the particular circumstances of the claimant, meaning that an abuse of rights may amount to serious harm for one claimant due to their personal attributes, where it would not for others.[110] This would be relevant, for example, to a claimant who is particularly vulnerable due to intersectional discrimination or societal marginalisation. These characteristics were present in *AZ (Turkey)* and are common to socio-economic claims. Similarly, the IPT proposed in *DS (Iran)* that the "ongoing and often life-long discrimination felt by members of marginalised groups in some societies such as women or LGBTQI individuals" will contribute to the duration and intensity factors when assessing harm.[111] Such a statement is directly relevant to the appellant in *AZ (Turkey)* who faced life-long intersectional discrimination on account of her gender, ethnicity and religion. Again, many socio-economic claims would share this characteristic.

Thus, the Tribunal's own definition of serious harm strongly suggests that systemic and severe discrimination against a member of a vulnerable and marginalised group, as was the case in the facts of *AZ (Turkey)*, could easily meet the fourth step of the *DS (Iran)* test.

This conclusion begs the question of whether the same puzzling application of the serious harm threshold takes place in civil and political refugee claims.

## 5.2 *The Serious Harm Threshold for Civil and Political Claims*

If it were simply that the Tribunal struggles to apply certain aspects of the serious harm test to both civil and political claims and socio-economic claims, this argument would perhaps be about questioning the legal reality of the threshold. However, an examination of civil and political claims and the serious harm threshold reveals that a higher threshold is in fact being applied in socio-economic claims.

### 5.2.1 New Zealand Case Law

New Zealand case law shows far greater acceptance of seeing discrimination and psychological harm as serious in claims involving civil and political rights. This point is particularly visible in cases concerning freedom of religion and the right to manifest one's religion. The 2011 appeal case *AH (China)* involved a female Muslim appellant, of Uighur ethnicity, from China.[112] The appellant claimed refugee status on the basis of systemic discrimination on account of

---

110  Ibid [182].
111  Ibid [172].
112  *AH (China)* [2011] NZIPT 800197.

her Uighur ethnicity, which resulted in her not being able to openly practise her Muslim faith in China. Islam requires Muslims to pray five times per day, but praying at school and university in China is not permitted.[113] Laws and general harassment meant that the appellant was not able to wear her head-covering outside the house, and the government prohibited females from attending the mosque. The Tribunal found that the appellant had a "sincere desire to develop her knowledge of her religion",[114] and that returning to China would impede her ability to practise her faith. It also found that practising her faith would subject her to discrimination and harassment in employment. The Tribunal's conclusion was that "the appellant would not be able to manifest her religion, in public or in private, alone or in community with others. This would amount to serious harm for the purposes of the *Refugee Convention*".[115] The Tribunal did not assess the question of serious harm beyond this statement – it was simply accepted that the inability to manifest her religion amounted to serious harm. This appellant was not under particular threat of physical harm, nor did she give evidence showing specific psychological or emotional harm. But, this denial of her right to manifest her religion was enough to meet this threshold.

This type of assessment is not a one-off, and it continues in cases decided after *DS* (*Iran*). Another example is the 2018 appeal *DJ* (*China*).[116] This case found that the institutional and familial pressure that a thirteen year old boy from China would face to abandon his Falun Gong religion, if he returned to China, could be "expected to cause serious emotional harm",[117] amounting to cruel, inhuman or degrading treatment in breach of ICCPR art 7.[118] Again, this boy was not at risk of physical harm, nor was there any evidence of specific psychological harm to support this.[119]

Thus, the IPT's application of the serious harm threshold to civil and political claims supports the contention that the issue is not that this form of harm, being serious emotional harm, cannot meet the threshold – rather, it is that where socio-economic claims are concerned, the threshold is raised.

---

113   Ibid [8].
114   Ibid [67].
115   Ibid [70].
116   *DJ* (*China*) [2018] NZIPT 801242.
117   Ibid [63].
118   Ibid [64].
119   The Tribunal did find that "some risk [of serious physical harm] may exist" to him in the future, but there was no "real chance" finding in relation to this. In any case, it appeared that in any case the psychological harm in itself was enough to establish serious harm.

## 5.2.2 Academic Analysis of this Inconsistent Threshold

The evidence that a more stringent serious harm test is being applied to socio-economic claims is not only found in New Zealand case law, but is also supported by academic analysis.

Foster, whose book focuses on refugee jurisprudence from Australia, Canada, New Zealand, the United Kingdom and the United States, argues that refugee decision-makers are unduly constraining the potential of the *Convention* to extend to claims based on socio-economic rights, when in fact the *Convention* is very capable of such extension.[120] Foster suggests this is due to their lack of understanding as to the equal importance of these rights with civil and political rights.[121] She explains that the tendency of decision-makers to apply an overly high test for serious harm to claims based on socio-economic rights, which is much higher than the test for serious harm which would usually be required for refugee determination, seems to be justified by the idea that due to the lower value of socio-economic rights, a much more serious violation is required in order to make out persecution.[122]

Foster notes that this high threshold is most often used by decision-makers where claims could have wide ramifications for groups of marginalised people, suggesting there may be a floodgates rhetoric underpinning the refusal to accept these claims.[123] According to Foster, this higher threshold has also led to "the frequent requirement that socio-economic aspects necessarily be buttressed by an accumulation of factors or by a more traditional type of claim, such as a fear of physical violence".[124] The fact that the IPT seems more accepting of socio-economic claims if they have the added element of economic proscription, as demonstrated by the previous case studies, is similar to such a requirement.

As of September 2018, Foster's book in which she makes these arguments has been cited by the IPT (and previously by the RSAA) as an aid to socio-economic rights assessments in ten separate appeals since its release in 2007.[125] This suggests that it is respected and considered to be authoritative by New Zealand decision-makers.

The tougher approach to serious harm in socio-economic claims is also pointed out by Jastram. After reviewing recently-decided socio-economic

---

120 Foster, *Refuge from Deprivation* (n 48) 15–16.
121 Ibid.
122 Ibid 123.
123 Ibid 135.
124 Ibid 167.
125 This number is taken from a search of the Ministry of Justice's database, and will not include decisions of which the publication was prohibited.

claims from Australia, Canada, New Zealand, the United Kingdom and the United States, Jastram concludes that almost all were decided with a "more exacting test" than that which is justified by the *Convention* and would otherwise be applied to civil and political claims.[126] In Australia and in certain United States courts, economic harm is specifically required to meet a higher standard, but even in Canada, New Zealand and the United Kingdom, where this is not the case, a more rigorous threshold still seems to be applied.[127]

Thus, despite the rejection of the traditional hierarchical approach to rights, the undervaluing of socio-economic rights is still a very real concern in refugee jurisprudence, and is affecting refugee status outcomes via the fourth step of the *DS (Iran)* test by way of a higher serious harm threshold. Perhaps this calls for a reassessment by the Tribunal into how it practically approaches the serious harm issue in socio-economic claims.

### 5.3   *A New Approach*

Although I do not purport to offer an easy solution to such a complicated and deeply-rooted issue, some form of change is undeniably necessary. The current approach to socio-economic claims and serious harm not only results in troubling inconsistencies between these claims and civil and political claims, but also leads to perplexing discrepancies within socio-economic claims themselves.

For example, In *AL (South Korea)* the appellant suffered far less active discrimination than the appellant in *AZ (Turkey)*. In the former case, the state was decisively assisting the marginalised group to which he belonged, whereas in the latter appeal the state was complicit in the discrimination. Yet, the appellant in *AL (South Korea)* met the serious harm threshold due to being able to produce clear evidence of depression and suicidal impulses. The appellant in *AZ (Turkey)*, on the other hand, did not produce compelling and undeniable evidence of the effects of the serious discrimination on her mental wellbeing. Without this evidence, the Tribunal found no risk of serious psychological harm existed.[128] Such an approach appears to require the applicant to become deeply depressed or suicidal before recognising any harm to dignity and wellbeing in socio-economic claims as sufficiently serious – to put it colloquially, this represents an "ambulance at the bottom of the cliff" approach.

---

126   Jastram (n 44) 148.
127   Ibid.
128   Relevant to this point is the fact that the Tribunal will take into account the personal characteristics of the applicant. However, both appellants were in especially vulnerable positions in these cases.

I submit that two small changes could alter the application of the serious harm test to socio-economic claims, so as to create more just outcomes and consistency with civil and political claims.

Firstly, a simple recognition that economic proscription – or any form of economic deprivation – is not necessarily the form of harm relevant to socio-economic claims, and is not essential for finding serious harm, would remove this initial hurdle currently facing socio-economic claims. Acknowledging this reality would stop decision-makers from being influenced by traditional hierarchical ideas concerning harm arising from certain breaches of rights that were not deemed "first-level".

Secondly, perhaps if a claimant produces accepted evidence of systemic, ongoing and severe discrimination, serious harm should be presumed to result. The decision-maker would then have to satisfactorily explain why, in any particular scenario, serious harm is in fact not present. Although this may appear to be a shift of the standard burden of proof, it is surely troubling for the Tribunal to dismiss such discrimination as not amounting to serious harm *without* any justification. In fact, as just demonstrated, this suggested approach is exactly the approach currently being applied in some civil and political discrimination cases.[129]

This presumption would also render New Zealand jurisprudence consistent with influential academic thought. On serious harm, Hathaway and Foster suggest that if there is a sustained or systemic violation of basic human rights demonstrative of a failure of state protection (in other words, if the first three steps of the *DS (Iran)* test are met), it should be a "rare exception" for this not to be deemed serious harm.[130] Therefore, they believe that "it is not sufficient simply to state that the harm is *de minimis*, there must be 'critical analysis' of why this is so".[131] This is, effectively, a shift of the burden of proof to the decision-maker.

Key to this presumption is its rebuttable nature: not all socio-economic discrimination cases will meet the serious harm threshold, as this would clearly be over-inclusive. It must be remembered that human rights law and refugee status determination, although integrally connected, are placed under independent and separate treaty regimes.[132] Human rights law is not a substitute for the terms of the definition of a refugee, but, rather, it informs the sorts of

---

129 For example, see the discussion on *AH (China)* and *DJ (China)* above 5.2.1.
130 Hathaway and Foster (n 5) 206.
131 Ibid (citations omitted).
132 Foster, "Economic Migrant or Person in Need of Protection?" (n 63) 252.

harm the international community considers illegitimate.¹³³ Thus, the answer to the issues I identify lies in striking a balance between ensuring that socio-economic and civil and political claims are treated with equal importance, while still requiring some form of serious harm and acknowledging that mere discrimination does not in itself constitute persecution.

## 6      Conclusion

I have sought to critically examine New Zealand's non-hierarchical approach to human rights in refugee status determination. Illustrating how the human rights approach developed, and the shifting place of socio-economic rights within that framework, sheds light on the reason behind a somewhat puzzling approach to socio-economic rights in New Zealand case law. The over-reliance on economic proscription and the reluctance to accept other forms of harm as serious enough in socio-economic claims reverts back to lingering sentiments from the traditional hierarchy of rights.

This influence produces confused and inconsistent results, and therefore cannot afford to be ignored. It is asylum seekers who bear the brunt of this misapplication of the law, and the consequences for the individuals bringing claims to the IPT are in actual fact life-changing. For the appellant in *AZ (Turkey)*, it seems that a correct approach to socio-economic rights and serious harm would have resulted in her resettlement as a refugee in New Zealand. Instead, she was refouled to Turkey where she will continue to face a denial of higher education, menial (if any) employment offering half-pay, societal marginalisation, sexual, verbal and possibly physical harassment, a restricted ability to express herself as she wishes to, and pressure to conceal her religion and ethnicity.

Although the RSAA, and later the IPT, were previously frontrunners across international refugee jurisprudence in accepting the equal value of socio-economic and civil and political rights, this does not ensure that the theory is being applied in practice. James Hathaway once stated that "[t]he New Zealand Refugee Status Appeal Authority is second to none in the world today for the clarity of reasoning, for its constant concern to reconcile principle to hard realities. It has provided leadership to the rest of the world on hard refugee issues".¹³⁴

---

133   Ibid 249.
134   Doug Tennent, Katy Armstrong and Peter Moses, *Immigration and Refugee Law* (LexisNexis, 3rd ed, 2017) 209, quoting direct correspondence between Hathaway and Tennent.

If the IPT were to reconcile its once-preeminent rejection of the hierarchical approach to human rights with the reality of its current misapplication, New Zealand could again lead the rest of the world in this cutting-edge but complicated field of refugee law.

### Acknowledgements

The author would like to thank, principally, Associate Professor Treasa Dunworth for her invaluable guidance, enthusiasm and support in the production of this article. The author would also like to thank Dr Anna Hood for her insights and encouragement.

# A Critical Re-analysis of *Whaling in the Antarctic*: Formalism, Realism, and How Not to Do International Law

*James C. Fisher*[*]

## Abstract

Commentators have tended to overlook the lack of legal rigour displayed by the ICJ decision in *Whaling in the Antarctic* out of enthusiasm for its substantive outcome, but political developments, such as Japan's impending withdrawal from the International Whaling Commission, compel scholars to re-evaluate the decision from both legal and political perspectives. This article suggests that concern for the consequences of its decision led the ICJ to contort the application of formal law. On the best evidence available, it was predictable that doing so would further entrench the Japanese position. *Whaling in the Antarctic* therefore inhabits an unsustainable position between formalist and realist approaches to public international law; it is unprincipled in that it perforates the conceptual boundary between legal and non-legal reasoning, and is simultaneously ineffective, in that doing so failed to ameliorate Japanese state policy. While not suggesting that instrumentalist considerations should never influence formalist reasoning, this article argues that this must be done selectively and intelligently, balancing whatever immediate advantages this may offer against the countervailing harms of departing from positive law in hard cases.

> Towards thee I roll, thou all-destroying but unconquering whale; to the last I grapple with thee; from hell's heart I stab at thee; for hate's sake I spit my last breath at thee.
> (From the last words of Captain Ahab)
> HERMAN MELVILLE, *Moby-Dick; or, The Whale* (1851)

## 1   Introduction

Readers of Herman Melville's magisterial *Moby Dick* seldom forget the unyielding obsession with which Ahab pursued his vendetta against the titular whale.

---

[*] University of Tokyo (Faculty of Law and Graduate Schools for Law & Politics).

One might expect whaling to have lost its power to incite such passions now that most former whaling nations have abandoned the values of Melville's era, when the oceans crawled with whaling vessels like the ill-fated *Pequod*. But while revival of the global whaling industry is now almost unthinkable, a minority of states, with Japan prominent among them, remain committed to commercial whaling. For decades, the Japanese government characterised its extensive and controversial whaling activities as marine research, which employed lethal sampling in pursuit of scientific knowledge, defying the foreign governments, environmental organisations and domestic activists who condemned this as covert commercial whaling in contravention of Japan's obligations under public international law. Japan recently stoked further controversy by announcing that it was to withdraw from the International Whaling Commission ("IWC") and resume explicitly commercial whaling in 2019.[1]

In 2010, Australia initiated proceedings against Japan before the International Court of Justice ("ICJ"), which obligingly declared Japan in breach of many its obligations under the *International Convention for the Regulation of Whaling* ("*ICRW*").[2] Most commentators applauded the ICJ's decision in *Whaling in the Antarctic (Australia v Japan: New Zealand Intervening)*,[3] either overlooking or forgiving the lack of legal rigour revealed by careful analysis of the Court's reasoning, presumably out of enthusiasm for its substantive outcome. Superficially at least, the decision seemed to vindicate the international rule of law in the context of environmental protection and herald the beginning of the end for Japanese whaling. However, developments since that decision, not least Japan's withdrawal from the IWC, reveal the hollowness of this apparent triumph, and international lawyers should respond by dispassionately reevaluating *Whaling in the Antarctic* from both legal and political perspectives. Commentators have correctly identified many factors that contributed to this regrettable parting of the ways, including the IWC's unwillingness to reach pragmatic compromises, Japan's poor negotiation tactics,[4] and (hypocritical)

---

1 Daniel Victor, "Japan to Resume Commercial Whaling, Defying International Ban", *The New York Times* (online, 26 December 2018) <https://www.nytimes.com/2018/12/26/world/asia/japan-whaling-withdrawal.html>.
2 *International Convention for the Regulation of Whaling*, opened for signature 2 December 1946, 161 UNTS 72 (entered into force 10 November 1948) ("*ICRW*").
3 *Whaling in the Antarctic (Australia v Japan: New Zealand Intervening)* (*Merits*) [2014] ICJ Rep 226 ("*Whaling in the Antarctic*").
4 Michael Cucek, "The Whaling Controversy: Harpooning the Gordian Knot", *Tokyo Review* (Web Page, 1 February 2019) <https://www.tokyoreview.net/2019/02/the-whaling-controversy-harpooning-the-gordian-knot/>; see also Geoffrey Palmer, "Whales and Humans: How Whaling Went from Being a Major Industry to a Leading Environmental Issue then Landed

foreign pressure. This article shows that international legal institutions also bear some responsibility, the impasse having been compounded by the ICJ's inexpert handling of this divisive issue.

The first part of this article demonstrates the legal flaws in the decision that have not received sufficient attention. Out of political sensitivity, the ICJ elected not to adjudicate on the central allegation – that Japan was deliberately misrepresenting its true motives in granting whaling licences – and retreated instead into an over-engineered interpretation of the *ICRW* with little basis in accepted principles of public international law, thus undermining the decision's fidelity to *formal legal* models of international adjudication. The second part shows that this was an unwise departure from formal law because it was unlikely to be redeemed by its substantive consequences. Commentators overlooked extensive prior scholarship that accounted for Japan's official commitment to this most controversial of industries, in light of which it should always have been clear that the ICJ's contorted *ratio* would only further entrench the Japanese government's position on whaling.

This article consequently locates *Whaling in the Antarctic* in an unprincipled and ineffectual no-man's-land between two competing understandings of the public international legal order. *Formalists* conceive of public international law as a norm-defined arena of adjudication by reference to rules logically separable from the political values and priorities that produce them. Conversely, *instrumentalists* at least partially collapse the notional boundary between international law and politics, treat international tribunals as just another means out of many for influencing state conduct, and therefore see formal legal logic not as a deontological good, but as valuable only to the extent that it advances the interests of the international order in particular cases. To respect the former understanding of public international law, the ICJ should have reasoned by reference to the duty of good faith in the discharge of treaty obligations, assessing directly whether Japan was misrepresenting its true reasons for granting whaling licences, irrespective of the repercussions for diplomatic efforts to change Japanese policy. To respect the latter, the best evidence available suggests that the ICJ should have ruled in Japan's favour, which would have weakened – or, at least, would not have intensified – the domestic political case for Japan's whaling initiatives, and would have facilitated Japan's continued membership of the IWC. Successive Japanese governments have understood themselves to be exploiting a loophole in the *ICRW* regime, but one that

---

Japan in the International Court of Justice for the First Time" (2015) 13 *New Zealand Yearbook of International Law* 107, 126.

is nonetheless formally lawful,[5] and Japan appears genuinely and with good reason to have expected victory in the ICJ.[6] It was only by being able to insist upon the legality of its research programme that Japan for so many years consented to remain within the IWC framework, rather than departing to recommence openly commercial whaling, as it has now found necessary to do.[7]

Declining to adopt either (i) the politically counter-productive but legally principled or (ii) a well-informed instrumentalist approach to the dispute, the ICJ chose the false economy of a *via media* that was both unprincipled and ineffective. It produced a decision that damages the integrity of public international law *qua* law, while doing nothing to bring Japanese whaling policy into line with prevailing international attitudes, and in fact making matters still harder to resolve. *Whaling in the Antarctic* is therefore a powerful example of *how not* to do international dispute resolution for formalists and instrumentalists alike.

## 2  Contextualising Japan's Departure from the IWC

The *ICRW*, concluded in 1946, superseded previous efforts towards the international regulation of whaling. It created the IWC, authorised to legislate for the whaling activities of its member states. The IWC is composed of representatives from each of the (presently) 89 contracting governments, assisted by its Scientific Committee, which comprises a panel of experts in relevant fields. The IWC regulates by amending the Schedule of the *ICRW*, which binds all states parties except those that formally object to a specific amendment.[8] Since its inception, the IWC has imposed various restrictions on whaling, most significantly the 1982 moratorium on all commercial whaling,[9] in light of which

---

5   For a summary of Japan's long-standing position, see Mari Koyano, "Whaling Issues: International Law and Japan" (2013) 63(5) *Hokkaidō Law Review* 201.
6   See Shirley V Scott, "Australia's Decision to Initiate Whaling in the Antarctic: Winning the Case versus Resolving the Dispute" (2014) 68(1) *Australian Journal of International Affairs* 1, drawing on internal communications from the then Foreign Minister, Okada Katsuya, released by Wikileaks: "Rudd Says Zero 'Commercial' Whaling in Southern Ocean by November of Else", *WikiLeaks* (Web Page, 19 February 2010) <https://wikileaks.org/plusd/cables/10CANBERRA118_a.html>.
7   Chris Burgess, "'Killing the Practice of Whale Hunting is the Same as Killing the Japanese People': Identity, National Pride, and Nationalism in Japan's Resistance to International Pressure to Curb Whaling" (2016) 14(8) *Asia-Pacific Journal: Japan Focus* 2, 6.
8   *ICRW* (n 2), art v.
9   The IWC set commercial catch limits at zero: *ICRW* (n 2) sch [10(e)].

the only whaling lawful under the ICRW is aboriginal subsistence whaling,[10] and whaling under licence granted by national governments "for purposes of scientific research".[11]

Japan initially objected to the moratorium, but capitulated in 1987 under strong international pressure, especially from the United States ("USA").[12] That same year, Japan announced an extensive programme of scientific whaling – Japan's Whale Research Program under Special Permit in the Antarctic ("JARPA"). This ran for 18 whaling seasons, initially taking around 330 minke whales annually, and around 440 annually after 1996, representing a total of approximately 6800 minke whales over the programme's lifespan.[13] In comparison, in the three decades before the launch of JARPA – during which time Japan was conducting overtly commercial whaling – it took a total of only 840 whales from international waters for scientific purposes.[14] *Whaling in the Antarctic* concerned JARPA's successor programme, JARPA II. This too involved extensive whale hunting, with catch targets dramatically increased to around 850 minke whales per year, as well as approximately 50 fin whales and 50 humpbacks. Hunts occurred principally in the Southern Ocean Sanctuary, utilising Japan's sophisticated factory whaling vessel, the *Nisshin Maru*, by a private company (Kyodo Senpaku) which exists solely for this purpose and is fully dependent on these government contracts.[15] The research itself was performed by the Institute for Cetacean Research, a semi-governmental agency – established simultaneously with Kyodo Senpaku – funded by and accountable to the Fisheries Agency, itself subordinate to the Ministry of Agriculture, Forestry and Fisheries ("MAFF"). After research, carcasses were sold direct to the Japanese state to be distributed to local governments, who in turn introduced the meat into the

---

10   Aboriginal subsistence whaling operates under a special quota regime: ibid sch [13].
11   Ibid art VIII.
12   See generally Andrew Siegel, "The US-Japan Whaling Accord: A Result of the Discretionary Loophole in the Packwood-Magnuson Amendment" (1985) 19(2) *George Washington Journal of International Law and Economics* 577; Kazuo Sumi, "The Whale War Between Japan and the United States: Problems and Prospects" (1989) 17(2) *Denver Journal of International Law and Policy* 356.
13   International Whaling Commission, *Resolution 2005-1: Resolution on JARPA II*, 57th annual mtg, 4 July 2005.
14   Ibid.
15   Certain local communities also engage in coastal whaling and dolphin-hunting. This has traditionally attracted less international attention, but such attention is intensifying, at least in part due to Western documentary-makers. See eg Louie Psihoyos' Academy Award-winning *The Cove* (Participant Media, 2009) and, for a more nuanced reflection on the same issues, Keiko Yagi's *Behind The Cove: The Quiet Japanese Speak Out* (2015).

local market.[16] The proceeds were used to fund the whale research programme itself, although this still required substantial subsidies.[17]

Despite occasionally acknowledging the scientific relevance of JARPA and JARPA II,[18] the general response of the IWC and international community at large was critical.[19] Echoing the views of its Scientific Committee, the IWC often urged Japan to abandon or at least dramatically downscale lethal sampling,[20] and in repeated Resolutions declared that JARPA, JARPA II and JARPN (a sister programme in the North Pacific) offered little of scientific utility, and nothing that could not have been achieved by non-lethal methods.[21] The manifest shortcomings of Japanese whaling as a scientific endeavour convinced many that science was never the real reason for these initiatives, and that they were really a smokescreen for illegal commercial whaling.

After the ICJ in *Whaling in the Antarctic* declared the JARPA II licences unlawful under the *ICRW*, Japan agreed to "abide by the Judgment ... as a State

---

16   Keiko Hirata, "Why Japan Supports Whaling" (2005) 8(2–3) *Journal of International Wildlife Law and Policy* 129, 135.

17   The Institute for Cetacean Research, prior to Japan's withdrawal from the IWC, received annual public funding of around JPY800,000,000 (approximately USD7.5 million): International Fund for Animal Welfare, *The Economics of Japanese Whaling: A Collapsing Industry Burdens Taxpayer* (Report, 11 February 2013) 2.

18   Gillian Triggs, "Japanese Scientific Whaling: An Abuse of Right or Optimum Utilisation?" (2000) 5(1) *Asia Pacific Journal of Environmental Law* 33, 36. In fact, the IWC Scientific Committee accepted that JARPA produced new and beneficial knowledge: International Whaling Commission Scientific Committee, *Report of the Scientific Committee* (Report No SC/48/Rep 1, 1998) 98, 100. See also Maya Park, "Japanese Scientific Whaling in Antarctica: Is Australia Attempting the Impossible?" (2011) 9 *New Zealand Journal of Public and International Law* 193, 195.

19   The scientific community broadly agrees that "Japan's lethal research programmes have generated data of negligible scientific value and fail to meet basic peer-review standards for publication": Richard Caddell, "Science Friction: Antarctic Research Whaling and the International Court of Justice" (2014) 26(2) *Journal of Environmental Law* 331, 334.

20   See also International Whaling Commission, *Resolution 2003-3: Resolution on Southern Hemisphere Minke Whales and Special Permit Whaling*, 55th annual mtg, 2003; International Whaling Commission, *Resolution 2007-1: Resolution on JARPA*, 59th annual mtg, 4 June 2007.

21   See, eg, International Whaling Commission, *IWC Resolution 1997-5: Resolution on Special Permit Catches in the Southern Ocean by Japan*, 49th annual mtg, 1997; International Whaling Commission, *IWC Resolution 1997-6: Resolution on Special Permit Catches in the North Pacific by Japan*, 49th annual mtg, 1997; International Whaling Commision, *IWC Resolution 1998-4: Resolution on Whaling under Special Permit*, 50th annual mtg, 1998; International Whaling Commission, *IWC Resolution 2000–5: Resolution on Whaling under Special Permit in the North Pacific Ocean*, 52nd annual mtg, 2000; International Whaling Commission, *Resolution 2003-2: Resolution on Whaling under Special Permit*, 55th annual mtg, 2003; *Resolution 2007-1: Resolution on JARPA* (n 20).

that places a great importance on the international legal order".[22] That did not indicate a commitment actually to terminate its whaling programmes, but only to "consider [its] concrete future course of actions carefully, upon studying what is stated in the Judgment".[23] Japan suspended its Antarctic whaling operations for the 2014–15 season but did not suspend JARPN, which was in principle outside the scope of the judgment. In November 2014, Japan announced its new research programme, the New Scientific Whale Research Program in the Antarctic Ocean ("NEWREP-A"), intended to run for twelve years and cover more of the Antarctic Ocean than JARPA II, but with a reduced total target lethal take of 333 individuals. Although NEWREP-A was conspicuously designed to show formal adherence to the ICJ judgment – taking much language *verbatim* from the ICJ ruling – international detractors were unappeased. In a joint statement, the USA, Australia, New Zealand and the Netherlands (with the support of 29 other governments) denied that Japan had "sufficiently demonstrated that it has given due regard to the guidance found in the…judgment", protested its resumption of allegedly scientific whaling and reiterated that "all information necessary for management and conservation of whales can be obtained through non-lethal methods".[24]

Japan subsequently sought unsuccessfully to change IWC procedures to allow a simple majority to overturn the moratorium on commercial whaling,[25] and more recently in September 2018 submitted an equally unsuccessful bid to lift commercial catch limits from zero for select abundant whale species.[26] Ultimately, on 26 December 2018, the Japanese government formally announced that it would leave the IWC effective June 2019, to resume explicitly commercial whaling the following month.[27] Such whaling would, however,

---

22  Chief Cabinet Secretary of the Government of Japan, "International Court of Justice: Whaling in the Antarctic (Australia v Japan: New Zealand Intervening)" (Press Release, Ministry of Foreign Affairs of Japan, 31 March 2014).

23  Ibid.

24  Governments of Australia, the Netherlands, New Zealand and the United States, "Joint Statement on Whaling and Safety at Sea" (Media Release, Government of the Netherlands, 12 January 2016) <https://www.government.nl/documents/media-articles/2016/01/12/joint-statement-on-whaling-and-safety-at-sea>. The main purpose of this statement, however, is the condemnation of direct-action groups.

25  Justin McCurry, "Japan Faces Backlash over Push to Resume 'Cruel' Commercial Whaling", *The Guardian* (online, 2 July 2018) <https://www.theguardian.com/world/2018/jul/02/japan-commercial-whaling-backlash>.

26  David Child, "IWC Rejects Japan's Proposal to Lift Commercial Whale Hunting Ban", *Al Jazeera* (Web Page, 14 September 2018) <https://www.aljazeera.com/news/2018/09/iwc-rejects-japan-proposal-lift-commercial-whale-hunting-ban-180913222708438.html>.

27  Justin McCurry, "Japan to Resume Commercial Whaling One Day after Leaving the IWC", *The Guardian* (online, 25 January 2019) <https://www.theguardian.com/world/2019/jan/25/japan-to-resume-commercial-whaling-one-day-after-leaving-the-iwc>.

be limited to Japan's Exclusive Economic Zone ("EEZ"), as required of a non-member of the IWC, and subject to sustainable quotas calculated using IWC data.[28]

## 3   The ICJ Judgment under Scrutiny

Australia alleged that Japan was in breach of the moratorium, as well as prohibitions against the use of factory ships and taking whales other than minke whales in the Southern Ocean Sanctuary.[29] In defence, Japan relied on *ICRW* art VIII, which provides that "[n]otwithstanding anything contained in this Convention any Contracting Government may grant to any of its nationals a special permit authorizing that national to kill, take and treat whales for purposes of scientific research".

Japan initially maintained that the discretion inherent in art VIII was subject only to the duty to exercise it in good faith,[30] a submission which entailed that Japan's granting of whaling licences would be lawful unless the ICJ concluded that Japan's stated motive for granting them (ie scientific research) differed from its true subjective motive. Although politically bold and a far from inevitable response to the evidence, this would be uncontroversial in terms of law; it is uncontentious that states are bound to perform all treaty obligations

---

[28]   Chief Cabinet Secretary of the Government of Japan, "Statement" (Ministry of Foreign Affairs of Japan, 26 December 2018) <https://www.mofa.go.jp/ecm/fsh/page4e_000969.html>. Initial quotas are explained in a communication from the Fisheries Agency: "Resumption of Commercial Whaling" (Fisheries Agency of Japan, 1 July 2019) <http://www.jfa.maff.go.jp/e/whale/attach/pdf/index-5.pdf>.

[29]   See *ICRW* (n 2) sch, [10(d)], [7(b)], respectively. Australia also alleged violations of Japan's procedural duties, with which this article will not engage, and duties under the *Convention on Biological Diversity*, opened for signature 5 June 1992, 1760 UNTS 79 (entered into force 29 December 1993) ("*CBD*"), arts 3, 5, 10(b). At least three other international treaties are potentially relevant to Japan's whaling activities in the Antarctic: *United Nations Convention on the Law of the Sea*, signed 10 December 1982, 1833 UNTS 3 (entered into force 16 November 1994); the *Convention on International Trade in Endangered Species of Wild Fauna and Flora*, signed 3 March 1973, 993 UNTS 243 (entered into force 1 July 1975); and the *Convention for the Conservation of Antarctic Marine Living Resources*, opened for signature 5 May 1980, 1329 UNTS 48 (entered into force 7 April 1982) ("*CCAMLR*"). However, Australia provided little support for its allegations with respect to the *CBD* and did not pursue claims under other instruments of international law, and the ICJ judgment devotes reasoned analysis only to the issue of JARPA II's compliance with the *ICRW*.

[30]   "Counter-Memorial Of Japan", *Whaling in the Antarctic (Australia v Japan: New Zealand Intervening)* (International Court of Justice, General List No 148, 9 March 2012) 18 [50], 325 [7.11].

in good faith.[31] However, the Court declined – at least explicitly – to investigate whether Japan's stated motive for granting whaling licenses was a credible account of its true intentions. Rather, it accepted the Japanese government's stated subjective motives as true for the purposes of the litigation.[32] The majority instead declared the JARPA II licences unlawful by applying an objective standard of review. In the judgment of the Court, whether licences were "for purposes of scientific research" involved two distinct, sequential questions: did the whaling programme comprise "scientific research", and were the licences on which the programme depended granted "for purposes" of scientific research?[33] This second question, the Court held, is an objective one whose answer "does not turn on the intentions of the individual government officials".[34] Both would have to be answered in the affirmative for JARPA II to be within the scope of art VIII *ICRW*.

After cursory analysis, the ICJ held that JARPA II did involve objectives and activities that could broadly be considered scientific research (the first question), but ultimately concluded that the licenses were nonetheless not *for purposes of* scientific research (the second question).[35] The Court set out to answer this second question using a novel formula not found in the text of the Convention, namely whether JARPA II's "design and implementation are reasonable in relation to achieving its stated objectives".[36] In answering this, the ICJ analysed in detail the specifics of JARPA II, in particular the use of lethal sampling rather than other research methods.[37] Although noting that the IWC's sustained opposition to lethal sampling did not alone affect its legality,[38] the ICJ was critical of the large and unexplained increase in catch quotas that marked the transition from JARPA to JARPA II.[39] It also noted the extensive sale of whale meat as research by-products,[40] although it accepted that this was permitted in principle. The Court also emphasised the disparity between

---

31    This principle of customary international law is now codified in the *Vienna Convention on the Law of Treaties*, signed 25 May 1969, 1155 UNTS 331 (entered into force 27 January 1980) art 26 ("VCLT").
32    *Whaling in the Antarctic* (n 3) 260 [97].
33    Ibid 254 [67].
34    Ibid 260 [97].
35    Ibid 293 [227].
36    Ibid 254 [67]; see also ibid 260 [97].
37    Ibid 269 [135], 271 [142].
38    Ibid 257 [83].
39    Ibid 274 [153], [156].
40    Ibid 259 [94].

the stated sample size and the typically much lower actual catch,[41] and the programme's open-ended structure.[42]

Most welcomed the decision in its immediate wake, although a minority observed that, while the decision "at headlines level was categorical in reinforcing the prevailing norm against commercial whaling", on deeper analysis it represented – diplomatically put – "less than a total victory either for the whales themselves or for the broader development of international environmental law".[43] Subsequent events have vindicated those sceptical of the decision's utility. Before considering the decision's impact on the whaling issue, it is important thoroughly to explore its "internal" dimension – the status of the ICJ's analysis as a matter of formal law.

### 3.1 Legal Support for an "Objective" Review

Over the course of oral argument, Japan retreated from its submission that the granting of whaling licences could be reviewed only in terms of good faith, conceding eventually that the attributes of JARPA II itself were in principle amenable to review.[44] Japan instead centred its case around the appropriate *standard* of that review, emphasising the need for deference to the Japanese Government's own appraisal of the programme's suitability.[45] This concession proved "significant, even fatal" for Japan's case.[46] It is a curious concession to have made, and one the ICJ failed adequately to rationalise as part of its own analysis. The actual language of art VIII – specifying only that licenses must be granted "for purposes of scientific research" – seems naturally to restrict only

---

41   Ibid 289 [212]. This is a curious point against the legality of JARPA II. The implication is that the programme would have been less objectionable if it had in practice killed *more* whales, rather than *fewer*, in order more faithfully to correspond with the programme's stated parameters.
42   *Whaling in the Antarctic* (n 3) 266 [119], 290 [214], [216].
43   Shirley V Scott and Lucia Oriana, "*Whaling in the Antarctic (Australia v. Japan: New Zealand Intervening)* Judgment of 31 March 2014: A Decisive Victory – but for Whom?" (2014) 29(3) *International Journal of Marine and Coastal Law* 547, 557.
44   "Verbatim Record", *Whaling in the Antarctic (Australia v Japan: New Zealand Intervening)* (International Court of Justice, General List No 148, 15 July 2013) 23 [20] (Payam Akhavan); Elana Geddis and Penelope Ridings, "*Whaling in the Antarctic*: Some Reflections by Counsel" (2013) 11 *New Zealand Yearbook of International Law* 143, 150.
45   "Verbatim Record", *Whaling in the Antarctic (Australia v Japan: New Zealand Intervening)* (International Court of Justice, General List No 148, 15 July 2013) (n 44) 24 [24] (Payam Akhavan).
46   Geddis and Ridings (n 44) 150.

the *reasons for which* a state may decide to issue whaling licences.[47] As Judge Owada noted in his compelling dissent, the majority failed to explain in legally relevant terms how this nonetheless gave the Court a power of objective review, or – assuming that objective review of some kind was legitimate – why the appropriate *intensity* for that review was "reasonableness" rather than some more or less invasive degree of scrutiny.[48] Although the Court did not reason expressly in these terms, it understood "purpose" as concerning not *motivation* but *suitability* when it insisted that "whether the killing ... of whales ... is for purposes of scientific research cannot depend simply on [Japan's] perception".[49] It was this unexplained interpretive choice that led to the transformation of intuitively simple treaty language into a structured series of enquiries whose derivation from art VIII itself was not justified by the ICJ using orthodox rules of public international law.

Although its official conclusion was that "neither a restrictive nor an expansive interpretation of Article VIII is justified",[50] the Court's subsequent approach nonetheless reflected New Zealand's assumption that, since the ICRW intended to replace uncoordinated whaling at the national level with collective regulation, art VIII could not logically entail an *unfettered* discretion to grant whaling licenses, but rather must be read as meaningfully restricting national autonomy.[51] It is obvious and uncontentious that international treaties exist to reduce state autonomy in some way, but the mere existence of treaty obligations does not indicate *in what way* that autonomy is to be restricted; that necessarily turns on the language of the particular instrument. To treat the mere existence of treaty obligations as a guide to their interpretation is to beg the question. The logical fallacy into which the majority fell here is carefully identified, and avoided, in Judge Xue's sounder separate judgment: while

---

47  Ibid 144; Eldon VC Greenburg, Paul S Hoff and Michael I Goulding, "Japan's Whale Research Program and International Law" (2002) 32(2) *California Western International Law Journal* 151.

48  *Whaling in the Antarctic* (n 3) 313–314 [32]; Sonia E Rolland, "Whaling in the Antarctic (Australia v. Japan: New Zealand Intervening)" (2014) 108(3) *American Journal of International Law* 496, 500. Even more creatively, the majority felt able to list the aspects of JARPA II that fell to be considered as part of a reasonableness review: *Whaling in the Antarctic* (n 3) 258 [88].

49  *Whaling in the Antarctic* (n 3) 253 [61].

50  Ibid 252 [58].

51  "Written Observations of New Zealand", *Whaling in the Antarctic (Australia v Japan: New Zealand intervening)* (International Court of Justice, General List No 148, 4 April 2013) 9–10 [22]–[23]; "Verbatim Record", *Whaling in the Antarctic (Australia v Japan: New Zealand Intervening)* (International Court of Justice, General List No 148, 8 July 2013) 19 [14] (Penelope Ridings).

"the Convention confers a discretionary power on the contracting parties with regard to scientific whaling", the ICJ's degree of control over the use of that discretion was "the very question that divides the Parties",[52] and could only be legitimately answered by legally supported construction of the text of art VIII.

### 3.2 Flawed Guides to Interpretation

The ICJ accepted New Zealand's submission that art VIII formed "an integral part of the Convention", and therefore fell "to be interpreted in light of… [its] object and purpose … taking into account [its] other provisions".[53] This "object and purpose", Australia submitted, was the conservation of whales, and interpreting art VIII in light of this meant that it should be understood as a narrow exception to the prohibitions contained in the Schedule, and therefore subject to a demanding standard of justification. Japan conversely submitted that the ICRW's object was the sustainability of whaling, no matter what other significance it may have retroactively acquired in the Western imagination. Consequently, art VIII should be interpreted as reflecting states' inherent right autonomously to conduct their own whaling policies, except as regulated by specific provisions of the ICRW Schedule.

Frustratingly, the ICJ accepted that art VIII must be interpreted in light of the object and purpose of the ICRW as a whole,[54] without declaring what that actually was. Attempting to reconcile the irreconcilable, the Court took the Convention's purpose as comprising *both* conservation and sustainable exploitation of whale stocks.[55] The ICJ's position here was political; there exists a conspicuous ideological division within the international community between states that consider whales a resource – albeit one in need of careful management – and those that present whaling as an intrinsic wrong that should be prohibited irrespective of the recovery of whale populations.[56] The Court was commended for refusing to decide between conservation and sustainability as the object of the ICRW.[57] But authoritative resolution of that

---

52 *Whaling in the Antarctic* (n 3) 421 [5].
53 Ibid 250–251 [55], recalling the "Declaration of Intervention (Article 63 of the Statute) of the Government of New Zealand", *Whaling in the Antarctic (Australia v Japan: New Zealand Intervening)* (International Court of Justice, General List No 148, 20 November 2012) 16 [26]. This shows the importance of procedural developments such as the admittance of New Zealand as an intervening party, which was central to the disposition of the case: Geddis and Ridings (n 44) 147.
54 *Whaling in the Antarctic* (n 3) 250–251 [55]. Attention to object and purpose is required by VCLT (n 31) art 31(1), although the ICJ did not invoke this.
55 *Whaling in the Antarctic* (n 3) 252 [58].
56 Geoffrey Palmer, "A Victory for Whales" [2014] (4) *New Zealand Law Journal* 124, 125.
57 Jacqueline Peel, "Introductory Note to Whaling in the Antarctic (Australia v. Japan: New Zealand Intervening) (I.C.J.)" (2015) 54(1) *International Legal Materials* 1, 2.

question cannot be avoided if a purposive interpretation of art VIII is to be legally coherent. Certainly, a single provision of a convention is to be interpreted wherever ambiguity arises in accordance with the purpose of the instrument as a whole, but this must proceed from a stated position as to what that purpose *is*, if such an interpretation is not to be hopelessly arbitrary.

Not content with presenting the logically opposite goals of exploitation and *non*-exploitation of whales as complementary purposes of the ICRW, the Court stated of its own motion that scientific research was an additional purpose in its own right.[58] This is deeply unconvincing. Article VIII is the direct successor to art X of the *International Agreement for the Regulation of Whaling* of 1937, which allowed contracting states to give licences to their own nationals to conduct lethal sampling for scientific purposes subject only to those conditions "as the contracting Government sees fit". The design of ICRW art VIII inherits and upholds this delegated approach, leaving the actual conduct of scientific whaling *outside* the Convention, in the hands of individual governments. Indeed, this aspect of the current IWC structure is frequently criticised by those aspiring instead to a more effective centralised regime under which the IWC, rather than individual states, would authorise whatever scientific whaling may be necessary.[59]

In declining to determine whether the ICRW's object was sustainability or conservation, the ICJ missed the opportunity to clarify an uncertain but important point of public international law – namely, how far and in what circumstances subsequent practice, particularly of an international body independent from states parties, can alter the authoritative meaning of international legal instruments. Japan's characterisation of the ICRW is irresistible on the basis of its stated goals at the time of enactment,[60] namely to "[safeguard] for future generations the great natural resources represented by the whale stocks", in the belief that "increases in the size of whale stocks will permit increases in the number of whales which may be captured without endangering these natural resources".[61] Australia's submission conversely "ignores the original overarching motivation",[62] and is credible only if the subsequent practice

---

58 *Whaling in the Antarctic* (n 3) 252 [58].
59 Dan Goodman, "Japanese Whaling and International Politics" (2013) 84 *Senri Ethnological Studies* 325, 327–328.
60 Gail Osherenko, "Environmental Justice and the International Whaling Commission: *Moby-Dick* Revisited" (2005) 8(2–3) *Journal of International Wildlife Law and Policy* 221, 224; Park (n 18) 206; Donald R Rothwell, "The Antarctic Whaling Case: Litigation in the International Court and the Role Played by NGOs" (2013) 3(2) *Polar Journal* 399, 400, 402.
61 ICRW (n 2) Preamble.
62 Park (n 18) 206; see also Rothwell (n 60).

of the IWC has authoritatively *changed* the object and purpose of the ICRW to conservation for its own sake – a very unconvincing suggestion.[63] Although much of the IWC's activity in recent decades suggests it now conceives of its own mission primarily in terms of conservation,[64] this is not uniformly the case.[65] Even the moratorium was at the time of adoption expressed as a temporary measure, until a sustainable approach to commercial whaling could be devised.[66] And while the *Vienna Convention on the Law of Treaties* ("*Vienna Convention*") permits "subsequent practice in the application of the treaty which establishes the agreement of the parties regarding its interpretation" to affect the construction of the treaty itself,[67] this simply expresses an intuitive, estoppel-like logic, preventing states opportunistically reneging on a particular understanding of international law that they have previously indicated they share. That hardly applies to Japan, which has consistently and ardently resisted any attempt to (re)characterise the ICRW as a conservationist text.[68] The Court did conclude that IWC Resolutions condemning lethal research could not alone affect the meaning of the ICRW,[69] which is surely correct. Adopted frequently without unanimity and with Japan's explicit objection, IWC Resolutions constitute neither a subsequent agreement nor state practice under the *Vienna Convention*.[70] More generally, though, the ICJ gave inadequate scrutiny to Australia's unwieldy assertion that the meaning of the ICRW had changed from that clearly contemplated in the text itself.

The ICJ's pusillanimous position on the ICRW's purpose suggests judicial unease about the logical implications of accepting Australia's characterisation of the Convention on the basis of post-ratification developments – namely, that

---

63  Malgosia Fitzmaurice, *Whaling in International Law* (Cambridge University Press, 2015) 91.
64  Tanya Wansbrough, "On the Issue of Scientific Whaling: Does the Majority Rule?" (2004) 13(3) *Review of European Community & International Environmental Law* 333, 333–334; Rothwell (n 60) 400–401.
65  Park (n 18) 207.
66  Shortly after this the Scientific Committee recommended a revised management procedure in replacement of the moratorium, but the wider IWC declined to incorporate this into the ICRW Schedule: see "The Revised Management Procedure", *International Whaling* Commission (Web Page) <http://iwc.int/rmp>; "The Revised Management Procedure (RMP) for Baleen Whales", *International Whaling Commission* (Web Page) <https://iwc.int/rmpbw>.
67  VCLT (n 31) art 31(3)(b). This may not even need a formal explicit agreement on meaning: Triggs (n 18) 48.
68  Maria Clara Maffei, "The International Convention for the Regulation of Whaling" (1997) 12(3) *International Journal of Marine and Coastal Law* 287, 303.
69  *Whaling in the Antarctic* (n 3) 257 [82].
70  VCLT (n 31) art 31(3)(a)–(b).

Japan would be bound by obligations to which it had neither in fact consented nor given other states the reasonable impression that it was undertaking. Yet conversely, in assessing "objectively" whether JARPA II licences were for purposes of scientific research, "the court was probably concerned that leaving states a wide 'margin of appreciation' in implementing the Convention would leave it toothless".[71] This might indeed be the result of a convention that imposed restrictions only as to subjective motivations on the exercise of national discretion. But the judicial role is to enforce the obligations that sovereign states *have in fact* undertaken, and which are inevitably sub-optimal – treaties being invariably the product of negotiation, compromise and *realpolitik* – rather than what the ICJ believes would be a more effective version of those obligations. The legally correct conclusion might be the unpalatable one that the states parties to the *ICRW* did indeed enact a (legally) toothless convention, such that control of "rogue" states' whaling policy remains a task for politics and diplomacy rather than judicial review. This is hardly surprising, since in order to be agreed and concluded at all, the *ICRW* had to be sufficiently malleable to appease a large number of states with very different priorities and interests in whaling. It is for that very reason that the *ICRW* itself imposed few substantive obligations and postponed most concrete regulation of the whaling industry, seeking for it instead to be addressed through the collaborative rule-making process in the IWC.

This raises another point relevant to the construction of art VIII that the ICJ did not address. Judge Yusuf would have preferred the Court to avoid "reviewing the design and implementation of a scientific research programme", which the *ICRW* squarely makes "the task of the scientific committee of the IWC",[72] and implicitly therefore *not* the task of a subsequent tribunal such as the ICJ. Even if, "in repeating that it would not undertake a qualitative examination of JARPA II objectives", the ICJ sought to "distinguish its review from the Scientific Committee's",[73] the majority of the Court nonetheless did what the *ICRW* entrusts to the IWC – scrutinising the methods by which Japan sought to fulfil scientific research objectives (even though the ICJ, unlike the IWC, did not evaluate the utility of those research objectives themselves). The ICJ did not consider how the central role of the IWC in making judgments of scientific merit should affect the proper construction of the scope of judicial review over

---

71  Remi Moncel, "Dangerous Experiments: Scientific Integrity in International Environmental Adjudications after the ICJ's Decision in Whaling in the Antarctic" (2015) 42(2) *Ecology Law Quarterly* 305, 341.
72  *Whaling in the Antarctic* (n 3) 388 [17].
73  Guillaume Gros, "The ICJ's Handling of Science in the Whaling in the Antarctic Case: A Whale of a Case?" (2015) 6(3) *Journal of International Dispute Settlement* 578, 604.

similar questions.[74] Determining the appropriate intensity of judicial review is a complex process familiar to domestic public lawyers. Courts often agonise over how much intervention into decision-making by other institutions is legitimate – in other words, where the legally correct balance lies between (i) enforcing the legal limits logically prior to exercises of administrative discretion, and (ii) respecting the autonomy of other decision-makers, which are often better equipped than courts to decide these matters effectively. These same concerns are relevant in the international legal context – and are supplemented by the sensitive issue of national sovereignty – but the ICJ is largely silent on all of them.[75]

Eminent commentators applauded the Court for having "struck an effective balance" between state autonomy and objective review,[76] treating Japan with a "high degree of deference",[77] and allowing "the state broad discretion in designing and implementing an Article VIII whaling program".[78] Supporters of the ICJ's approach emphasise that it "did its utmost to remain a legal, rather than a scientific, arbiter",[79] and "confine[d] itself to … the interpretation of the Convention – while avoiding the scientific controversies underlying the

---

74   Ibid.
75   Indeed, "during its first meeting in the aftermath of the decision, the Commission adopted a resolution drafted by New Zealand determining new guidelines regarding the assessment of the whaling programmes to be made by the Scientific Committee": ibid 613. This resolution required the Scientific Committee, in reviewing the scientific whaling programmes of state parties, to base its determination on "whether the design and implementation of the programme, including sample sizes, are reasonable in relation to achieving the programme's stated research objectives": International Whaling Commission, New Zealand, *Draft Resolution on Whaling under Special Permit*, Doc No IWC/65/14 Revl, 65th annual mtg, 2014, 2 ("*New Zealand Draft Resolution*"). This is the same reasonableness test used by the ICJ in its assessment of JARPA II. Indeed, the Committee is tasked with answering that enquiry, "having regard to the decision of the International Court of Justice, including the methodology used to select sample sizes, a comparison of the target sample sizes and the actual take … [and] the programme's scientific output": *New Zealand Draft Resolution* 2.
76   Caddell (n 19) 339; Brendan Plant, "Sovereignty, Science and Cetaceans: The *Whaling in the Antarctic* Case" (2015) 74(1) *Cambridge Law Journal* 40, 43.
77   Rolland (n 48) 499.
78   Ibid 498.
79   Ibid 500. But compare Gros, for whom "the distance that the Court sought to create with regard to the scientific nature of facts through the use of a reasonableness test … is too close and at the same time too far from the facts. Too close because the Court considers the contents of the programme in itself and not [only] the related decision, and too far because the Court limits itself to a 'logical' judgment through reasonableness that may lead to a result opposed to objective reality. Gros (n 73) 614.

dispute".[80] This is a surprising conclusion and requires careful scrutiny. The Court barely engaged with established jurisprudence on treaty interpretation, but devoted significant resources to assessing directly the appropriateness of JARPA II's design and implementation in light of the research outcomes that it was (allegedly) intended to pursue. It is true that the ICJ declined the invitation authoritatively to define "scientific research",[81] and it did not pronounce a view on the scientific usefulness of the information JARPA II ostensibly aimed to provide.[82] But it nonetheless intimately considered the programme's actual design. It asked, in effect, whether JARPA II constituted *good science*. It follows from the reasoning of the ICJ that JARPA II's manifold shortcomings rendered it not just a *bad* programme for the purposes of scientific research, but not a programme "for purposes of" scientific research *at all*, implying that investigations can be properly considered for purposes of science only if competently conducted. As Judge Xue protested, separating "scientific research" from "purposes of scientific research" is an artificial complication of the language of art VIII,[83] and the majority failed to explain how the language supported this counter-intuitive bifurcartion.

It is far from clear that the ICJ "developed an analytical approach that distinguishes the role of the judge from the role of the scientist, while respecting both".[84] Talk of discretion or respect is meaningful only if a reviewer to some extent upholds the original decision despite concluding that it is sub-optimal on the balance of relevant first-order considerations – if the mere fact that the decision was taken by the body in question forms a second-order reason to uphold it, independent of its substantive merits.[85] Assuming that the *ICRW* did indeed impose an objective standard of review, the ICJ might conceivably have held JARPA II to a stricter degree of scrutiny than it ultimately did. The ICJ decision indeed stops short of outright appeal against the Japanese government's designs for JARPA II, holding it instead only to a standard of reasonableness. But any deference in the *application* of the objective review is eclipsed by

---

80  Plant (n 76) 43.
81  *Whaling in the Antarctic* (n 3) 258 [86].
82  Ibid 269 [134].
83  Ibid 425 [16].
84  Cymie R Payne, "ICJ Halts Antarctic Whaling: Japan Starts Again" (2015) 4(1) *Transnational Environmental Law* 181, 193.
85  Where (i) some degree of judicial oversight is applied, but (ii) the court stops short of outright appeal against an administrative decision, the status of the original decision-maker is not an *exclusionary* reason for upholding it, but merely a "reweighting" reason. On the distinction, see Stephen R Perry, "Judicial Obligation, Precedent, and the Common Law" (1987) 7(2) *Oxford Journal of Legal Studies* 215.

the Court's decision – lacking a formally rational legal basis – to apply an objective review in the first place. *Whaling in the Antarctic* is not an example of judicial deference to states, but rather a bold arrogation of judicial oversight powers. Laudatory claims that the decision simultaneously protects states' scientific discretion and "ensures that the objective limits to states' discretionary entitlements are upheld" rather beg the question,[86] since the whole dispute hinges on whether "objective limits" (beyond the requirement of good faith) exist under art VIII at all.

### 3.3 A Confused and Inconsistent Review

Judicial scrutiny of political decision-making comes in many forms. Most fundamentally, lawyers distinguish between procedural review – which examines *how* decisions were taken, for instance by checking that proper factors were considered and improper ones were excluded – and substantive review, which asks whether the decision made or action taken was itself legitimate. Substantive review, in turn, describes a spectrum of intensities, from full *de novo* review – in which the court decides whether the original decision-maker reached the definitively correct answer and itself retakes the decision, if not – and total deference,[87] passing through such positions as rationality review, in which the court requires not that the decision was correct, but only that it was one a reasonable and competent decision-maker might have made. This article has already exposed the lack of legal support for the species of review that the ICJ claimed to apply. However, the Court was not even consistent in applying that standard of review. Throughout its judgment, it fluctuates between different species of review without rationalising or even acknowledging those transitions.

At times, the review focussed on the Japanese government's decision-making process. For instance, the ICJ called on Japan "to explain the objective basis for its determination",[88] and criticised its increasing the sample size on transition from JARPA to JARPA II without waiting for the former to be thoroughly reviewed.[89] It also criticised Japan's failure explicitly to consider relevant factors; the Court insisted that states had a fundamental duty to co-operate with the IWC, and therefore that Japan should have given "due regard" to the IWC's frequent condemnations of lethal sampling by seriously considering alternative

---

86   Plant (n 76) 43.
87   Gros (n 73) 591.
88   *Whaling in the Antarctic* (n 3) 254 [68].
89   Ibid 274 [156].

research methods.[90] These aspects of the ICJ's analysis suggest a review "base[d] ... on the decision to grant a special permit ... rather than on the programme, which is the subject of the licence".[91] But that is not consistent with the stated *ratio* for the finding that JARPA II was unlawful,[92] which proposed direct assessment of the qualities of the programme itself.[93]

As for the intensity of that substantive review, the ICJ purported to stop short of *de novo* review,[94] denying any intention "to second guess the scientific judgments made by individual scientists or by Japan".[95] This inescapably implies *some* degree of deference to Japan's conclusions and actions.[96] The Court's refusal to define scientific research is perhaps best understood as an attempt at deference – it is not otherwise clear why the ICJ thought defining this crucial term in convention terminology would be impossible or illegitimate.[97] But while discounting *de novo* review, the Court also rejected Japan's claim to any "margin of appreciation" in the design and implementation of JARPA II. The Court seems therefore to conclude that Japan's appraisal of JARPA II's design and implementation simultaneously *is and is not* to be awarded some unarticulated degree of respect, or deference, in the review process. It is welcome that the Court rejected Japan's invocation of the margin of appreciation doctrine as a general principle of international law.[98] As Australia argued, the doctrine is authoritative only in the jurisprudence of the European Court of Human Rights,[99] and despite strong support from those who see it as a reliable and theoretically sound means of navigating between *de novo* review and full discretion,[100] accepting it as a general principle of international law risks undermining many co-ordinated international environmental efforts.[101] It is for this reason important that the language of specific instruments remains

---

90  Ibid 271 [141].
91  Gros (n 73) 602.
92  Ibid 602–603.
93  Ibid 603.
94  Ibid 598.
95  *Whaling in the Antarctic* (n 3) 282 [185].
96  Gros (n 73) 598.
97  Makane Moïse Mbengue, "Between Law and Science: A Commentary on the *Whaling in the Antarctic* Case" (2015) 2 *Questions of International Law* 176, 181.
98  *Whaling in the Antarctic* (n 3) 253 [61]. Japan called the margin of appreciation doctrine an "axiom of international law": Counter-Memorial Of Japan (n 30) 415 [9.16].
99  "Verbatim Record" (n 51) 25 [33] (Penelope Ridings).
100 See, eg, Yuval Shany, "Towards a General Margin of Appreciation Doctrine in International Law?" (2005) 16(5) *European Journal of International Law* 908.
101 See, eg, Caroline Foster, *Science and the Precautionary Principle* (Cambridge University Press, 2011) 16.

paramount in determining the degree of deference states enjoy in the implementation of international environmental law.

### 3.4 Accounting for the Confusion

Australia had directly alleged bad faith on the part of Japan – that the "scientific" nature of JARPA II was a cynical veneer for what the Japanese government really understood to be commercial whaling[102] – but in oral argument retreated and claimed to have made this allegation only as an alternative basis for the illegality of JARPA II.[103] Japan forcefully rejected what it considered tantamount to an allegation that "Japan has lied ... systematically, as a matter of State policy for almost 30 years".[104] It is unclear how far the majority of the ICJ entertained this central allegation, with the dissenting judges, and those who offered separate opinions, conspicuously holding different interpretations of the extent to which the majority suspected bad faith.[105] In principle at least, the ICJ did not decide the case on bad faith grounds, accepting that Japan's subjective motivation behind granting the JARPA II licences was the pursuit of scientific knowledge. Yet in places the Court appeared moved by an enduring scepticism on this point. It noted that the shortcomings of JARPA II – particularly discrepancies between the declared sample size and the actual catch – "lent support" to Australia's central contention that JARPA II was a cynical evasion of the moratorium on commercial whaling.[106] The allegation of bad faith was in fact "essential to Australia's argument",[107] and to the disposal of the case on well-supported legal grounds. Sensitivity to this may explain the ICJ's references to bad faith, despite it holding that the relevant review was an objective one into the reasonableness of JARPA II's design and implementation. It is tempting to see the ICJ's enthusiasm for a textually spurious objective review as political – an "overly strained exercise meant to avoid

---

102 "Application Instituting Proceedings", *Whaling in the Antarctic (Australia v Japan: New Zealand Intervening)* (International Court of Justice, General List No 148, 31 May 2010) 6 [8]; see also "Memorial of Australia", *Whaling in the Antarctic (Australia v Japan: New Zealand Intervening)* (International Court of Justice, General List No 148, 9 May 2011) 253–256 [5.122]–[5.128].
103 "Verbatim Record", *Whaling in the Antarctic (Australia v Japan: New Zealand Intervening)* (International Court of Justice, General List No 148, 10 July 2013) 34 [2]–[3] (Justin Gleeson SC).
104 "Verbatim Record" (n 44) 25 [27] (Payam Akhavan).
105 See, eg, *Whaling in the Antarctic* (n 3) 308–309 [21] (Judge Owada), 327–328 [28]–[29] (Judge Abraham), 401–402 [54] (Judge Yusuf), 354 [17] (Judge Cançado Trindade), 416–417 [29] (Judge Greenwood), 436 [18] (Judge Sebutinde), 457–458 [13] (Judge ad hoc Charlesworth).
106 Ibid 274 [156].
107 Park (n 18) 205, 208–209.

adjudicating on the breach-of-good-faith arguments presented by Australia",[108] and to permit it to condemn Japanese whaling without stating Japan was systematically deceiving the international community. Understanding bad faith as the hidden engine behind the majority's judgment accounts for its lack of orthodox legal precision, particularly its fluid and unreasoned transitions between different kinds and intensities of review, and its general obfuscatory tenor.

### 3.5  Wider Impact: Judicial Handling of Scientific Disputes

Some saw *Whaling in the Antarctic* as a positive model for the future use of scientific evidence and expertise in international adjudication, with the ICJ responding to an acknowledged need for change in "the way in which international courts ... adjudicate on scientific and technical issues".[109] Observers noted the "streamlined process adopted by the ICJ for the presentation and examination of scientific evidence",[110] and the Court's success in "avoid[ing] two pitfalls: the refusal to consider the scientific evidence presented, which was the approach taken in the *Gabčíkovo-Nagymaros* case, and that of drawing for itself scientific conclusions based on evidence, as the court did in the *Pulp Mills* case",[111] with which *Whaling in the Antarctic* has been favourably compared.[112]

As noted above, it is not clear that the ICJ truly achieved a "clear separation of questions of legal interpretation from those of scientific expertise",[113] or reached a principled point of compromise between the above two "pitfalls". The case may have demonstrated some procedural improvements but that itself typifies how "international tribunals are creating ad hoc procedural rules with limited political legitimacy and accountability",[114] which reflects the vital need for organised reform. The ICJ judgment anyway left crucial aspects of both legal and scientific reasoning unarticulated and unresolved. For instance, it is unacceptable that the Court gave no reasoned statement about the required

---

108  Rolland (n 48) 500.
109  Philippe Sands, "Water and International Law: Science and Evidence in International Litigation" (2014) 44(1–2) *Environmental Law and Management* 161, 197.
110  Peel (n 57) 1. See also Payne (n 84) 190.
111  Gros (n 73) 619.
112  Especially with the poor handling of technical evidence in *Pulp Mills on the River Uruguay (Argentina v Uruguay)* (*Judgment*) [2010] ICJ Rep 14. For more on the procedural failings of this case, see eg Cymie R Payne, "Pulp Mills on the River Uruguay (Argentina v. Uruguay)" (2010) 105(1) *American Journal of International Law* 94; Moncel (n 71) 315–317.
113  Peel (n 57) 1.
114  Moncel (n 71) 329.

standard of proof, the question of who bore the burden of establishing the scientific facts on which the determinations of law should turn or – most fundamentally – which side bore the burden of establishing the (il)legality of JARPA II.[115] The decision involved "a possible reversal of the burden of proof",[116] in that the ICJ looked to Japan to "explain the objective basis" for its decision to grant licences,[117] but this *dictum* suggests review of Japan's decision-making process rather than the substantial suitability of JARPA II that putatively comprised the *ratio* of the decision. The Court's judgment assumes, rather than explains, that it was Japan's responsibility positively to establish the reasonableness of the design and implementation of JARPA II,[118] but the Court was "careful to not explicitly state that Japan failed to meet the burden of proof",[119] and did not even use that terminology. What Foster has identified as the Court's "informal and malleable approach to the burden of proof" is surely unacceptable.[120] Axiomatic structural elements of legal reasoning such as burdens of proof do not legitimately admit of informality.

### 3.6 Whaling in the Antarctic *and the International Rule of Law*

*Whaling in the Antarctic* is conspicuous among ICJ judgments for the acutely divided positions of the judges.[121] The fundamental cleavage has been correctly identified – while the majority "emphasizes factual determinations and downplays legal issues", the dissenters and especially the separate concurring judgments "view the case as hinging more squarely on legal issues".[122] This invites scrutiny of one of the more laudatory claims about this case, namely that it "elevates ... respect for international environmental law above realist political considerations",[123] vindicating the international rule of law by protecting the independence of legal analysis from external pressures. The implication is that a victory for Japan would conversely have represented the triumph of politics

---

115   Ibid 308.
116   Gros (n 73) 581. In his dissenting judgment, Judge Abraham disparaged how the majority burdened Japan with the duty positively to prove its liberties under international law: *Whaling in the Antarctic* (n 3) 328–329 [31].
117   *Whaling in the Antarctic* (n 3) 254 [68].
118   Gros (n 73) 616.
119   Ibid.
120   Caroline Foster, "Methodologies and Motivations: Was Japan's Whaling Programme for Purposes of Scientific Research?" in Malgosia Fitzmaurice and Dai Tamada (eds), *Whaling in the Antarctic: The Significance and the Implications of the ICJ Judgment* (Brill-Nijhoff, 2016) 9, 22.
121   Rolland (n 48) 499.
122   Ibid.
123   Moncel (n 71) 308.

over law, although it is not explained precisely why this would be the case. Certainly, the decision against Japan shows that a powerful state was not immune from the application of international law, but there is more to the rule of law properly so called than simply ensuring that rule-breakers get their comeuppance.[124] It is hard to accept the view that the majority deployed "[t]ight legal analysis",[125] and Judge Bennouna was scarcely exaggerating in condemning the majority's *ratio* as "unfounded in law".[126] It cites no case-law in its entire discussion of the merits of the dispute,[127] and there is almost no discussion of the law applicable to the interpretation of treaties, on which this case should surely have turned. The ICJ adopted an artificial *ratio* divorced from orthodox international jurisprudence, apparently in order sensitively to navigate the political controversies involved, which would predictably have intensified had the Court reasoned instead by assessing Japan's good faith (or lack thereof). This is hardly a vindication of law's autonomy or insulation from international political realities.

### 4    *Whaling in the Antarctic* as Ineffective Instrumentalism

*Whaling in the Antarctic* is an unsound decision in terms of formal law. Many nonetheless praised the ICJ's decision from an instrumentalist perspective, despite acknowledging its weak legal basis,[128] or even specifically because of its evasion of the directly appropriate *ratio*, namely the question of bad faith. Palmer, for instance, applauded this "clever and subtle" decision that "navigates around the political shoals that bedevil this emotionally charged area".[129] Subsequent developments, however, have vindicated the minority of commentators who, in the decision's immediate wake, perceived that it represented "little more than a temporary setback for Japan",[130] and was never likely to bring Japanese ocean whaling any closer to cessation.

With little to recommend the decision's legal logic and no practical success to mitigate these formalist shortcomings, the best that can be said of *Whaling*

---

124   See, eg, Hart, distinguishing legal rules properly so called from the mere condition whereby certain actions reliably provoke retribution: HLA Hart, *The Concept of Law* (Clarendon Press, 2nd ed, 1994) 11.
125   Palmer (n 56) 128.
126   *Whaling in the Antarctic* (n 3) 347.
127   In contrast, the Court cited three cases in its short discussion of its own jurisdiction.
128   Rolland (n 48) 500.
129   Palmer, (n 56) 124.
130   Phillip J Clapham, "Japan's Whaling Following the International Court of Justice Ruling: Brave New World – Or Business as Usual?" (2015) 51 *Marine Policy* 238, 238, 241.

*in the Antarctic* is that it represents adroit manoeuvring through an area of international political sensitivity. But if this does not in fact materially affect states' behaviour, *quaere* to what extent such manoeuvring, impressive though it may be, really matters. It is not clear that bad law can be redeemed by (apparently) good results – still less so when it fails actually to achieve those results. Occasionally, the unforeseeable contingencies of international politics mean that a sound, pragmatic decision will nonetheless fail to achieve the result that it had the potential to produce. *Whaling in the Antarctic* is not such a case – for the following reasons, it was always apparent that the litigation would entrench, rather than end, Japan's commitment to whaling, especially considering the artificial and obfuscatory *ratio* by which the ICJ procured its declaration of JARPA II's illegality.

Japan's recalcitrance over whaling "is not consistent with its internationally cooperative position on other environmental matters",[131] and calls for an explanation in comparison with the success of "international pressure ... in areas as diverse as trade, gender equality, indigenous people's rights, and child-custody".[132] Even the most expert of international lawyers confess themselves "mystified" as to why successive Japanese governments are committed to whaling.[133] It is regrettable that so many surveys of the whaling controversy look principally to the "great divide between the international norm and domestic [Japanese] cultural values".[134] This exemplifies how discussions of Japan in the legal context – both domestic and international – are plagued with empirically thin, reductionist invocations of "culture" as a putative explanation for all manner of phenomena, obscuring material analysis of Japan's political economy and institutions.[135] On this point, there is no need to remain mystified – a clear explanation emerges from an understanding of the Japanese political environment. International pressure in this context has been ineffective because whaling has been "reactively defined in the domestic debate not as an issue of conservation and environmental protection but as a symbol of national identity and pride".[136] While there are indeed differences in attitudes towards cetacean

---

131  Hirata (n 16) 129.
132  Burgess (n 7) 2. Nevertheless, the author perhaps over-estimates how thoroughly Japan has responded to international pressure in these areas, particularly concerning child custody.
133  Palmer (n 4) 127.
134  Hirata (n 16) 141.
135  Influential critiques of this culturalist literature include: John Owen Haley, "The Myth of the Reluctant Litigant" (1978) 4(2) *Journal of Japanese Studies* 359; J Mark Ramseyer and Minoru Nakazato, "The Rational Litigant: Settlement Amounts and Verdict Rates in Japan" (1989) 18(2) *Journal of Legal Studies* 263.
136  Burgess (n 7) 1.

life in Japan and much of the West – the result of comparatively recent changes in prevailing Western thought – Japanese state recalcitrance over whaling is a political, rather than "cultural" product. The apparently cultural commitment to whaling represents carefully cultivated discourse-management by the state bureaucracy with a political interest in its continuation.

As scholars of Japanese policymaking have demonstrated, what principally conditions the success or failure of foreign pressure in making Japanese state policy conform to new international norms is the extent to which that pressure serves domestic Japanese elements with an ideological or material interest in changing state practice.[137] "Foreign demands ... to stop whaling are not aligning with any powerful domestic constituencies",[138] whereas powerful bureaucratic interests are invested in its continuation.[139] Japanese policymaking is "dominated by bureaucratic actors",[140] and MAFF has both "hegemonistic control over decision making on this issue"[141] and a powerful interest in maintaining whaling – an important part of its own departmental docket – given the "intense interministerial rivalries in Japan".[142] Problematically for MAFF, Japanese consumption of whale meat is at an all-time low and in continuing decline, and the dying industry employs no more than a few hundred people,[143] mostly in economically deprived, depopulated regions. MAFF has adroitly weaponised foreign opposition to whaling, turning what would otherwise be a debate about public spending priorities and subsidies for an ailing industry – which the whaling lobby could not conceivably win – into a defence of the national interest and sovereignty.[144] It has successfully nurtured belief in a characteristically Japanese whaling culture and presented international criticism as cultural imperialism.[145] The former element is largely an invented

---

137 See generally Leonard J Schoppa, "Two-Level Games and Bargaining Outcomes: Why Gaiatsu Succeeds in Japan in Some Cases but not Others" (2003) 47(3) *International Organization* 353; Aurelia George Mulgan, "The Role of Foreign Pressure (Gaiatsu) in Japan's Agricultural Trade Liberalization" (1997) 10(2) *Pacific Review* 165.
138 Mike Danaher, "Why Japan Will Not Give up Whaling" (2002) 14(2) *Pacifica Review* 105, 116.
139 Burgess (n 7) 7.
140 Hirata (n 16) 141.
141 Ibid 148.
142 Ibid 146. Importantly, it is not the whaling industry directly militating for the continuation of Japanese whaling, since this small group "does not have sufficient resources to lobby the government or the economic weight to impose its views": ibid 140. There are other ministerial interests at work too – whaling occurs mostly in deprived rural areas, and it may simply be cheaper to subsidise the ailing industry than let it fail and increase the cost of social welfare.
143 Hirata (n 16) 130.
144 Danaher (n 138) 116. For examples, see Hirata (n 16) 143–144.
145 Hirata (n 16) 142.

tradition; although coastal subsistence whaling is part of the traditional rural lifestyle in some regions, intensive high seas whaling is a thoroughly modern practice, escalating in Japan only after the Second World War, when Occupation forces promoted industrial whaling as a solution to the continuing food shortages in the wake of the war.[146]

MAFF's story of cultural imperialism, in contrast, is easy to substantiate, with even foreign observers accepting that the issue "perpetuates patterns of domination in which hegemonic nations impose their values, preferences and worldviews on less powerful as well as racially, culturally, and ethnically different nations".[147] The USA, progenitor of the 1982 moratorium, compelled Japan's agreement by threatening to remove its fishing rights in the USA's EEZ – subsequently doing so anyway, for protectionist reasons, shortly after Japan assented to the moratorium. The creation of the Southern Ocean Sanctuary in 1994 was specifically intended to head off Japanese interest in the Antarctic region,[148] containing the world's greatest concentration of whales. Although there is criticism of European whaling states like Norway and Iceland, it is conspicuously less vociferous and lacks the Orientalist othering conspicuous in condemnations of Japan, especially in the very racist rhetoric of militant groups such as Sea Shepherd.[149] The Japanese position – that "it is hypocritical

---

146  For information on the development of Japanese whaling in English, see, eg, Hiroyuki Watanabe, *Japan's Whaling: The Politics of Culture in Historical Perspective*, tr Hugh Clarke (Trans Pacific Press, 2009); Anne Kalland and Brian Moeran, *Japanese Whaling: End of an Era?* (Curzon Press, 1992).

147  Osherenko (n 60) 224.

148  Robert L Friedheim, "Introduction: The IWC as a Contested Regime" in Robert L Friedheim (ed), *Toward a Sustainable Whaling Regime* (University of Washington Press, 2001) 3, 5.

149  "Japan has always closely identified with blood and slaughter. From the decapitations by the Samurai upon innocent peasants to the suicidal insanity of the Kamikaze, violence and self destruction have been a part of Japanese culture": this statement by Paul Watson, in the piece "The Truth About 'Traditional' Japanese Whaling" (2006), has been removed but was once available on Sea Shepherd's website, and is reproduced in Burgess (n 7). It is curiously and suspiciously ironic that Western states are much more supportive of cultural claims to whaling by first peoples in their own states than from non-Western national governments: Peter J Stoett, "Of Whales and People: Normative Theory, Symbolism, and the IWC" (2005) 8(2–3) *Journal of International Wildlife Law and Policy* 151, 164–168. Western states unself-consciously make universalist arguments against Japanese policies, seeing "efforts to abolish whaling ... [as] reflective of a new, global consciousness" that whaling nations cannot legitimately obstruct, but ignore the hard questions of domestic racial and cultural politics. Must national indigenous minorities likewise "overcome their insensitive urge to kill advanced mammals such as whales"? (at 167–168.). Western environmentalists typically celebrate – even romanticise – indigenous traditional subsistence lifestyles precisely because of their apparent mastery of measured, equita-

that Westerners consider it morally wrong to kill certain mammals such as whales but consider it acceptable to kill others",[150] is very hard to refute. Whaling has become central to Western environmentalist consciousness as a guide to humanity's ecological soteriology – a "symbolic construction of redemption",[151] according to which humanity "stared our own cruelty and selfishness in the face, were repulsed by the image, and ... reinvented ourselves".[152] This collective redemption myth has had little traction in Japan, and is anyway largely fictional. Whaling was restricted for self-preservation by whaling states who understood it was otherwise "doomed as a commercial activity because of a rate of diminishing return".[153] Much modern anti-whaling rhetoric is absurd, anthropomorphising and privileging cetaceans above other mammalian life to a degree out of all proportion to their objective zoological uniqueness, awarding them some ineffable "psychic connection to humanity".[154] Ideologues have even accused the Japanese people of having "cannibalized" whales hunted under JARPA and JARPA II.[155]

Sensitive to the narrative on which the domestic Japanese whaling lobby relies, Hirata explains that foreign pressure makes it less, rather than more, likely that the Japanese government will abandon whaling.[156] There is no group in Japan with the motive, resources and access to policy-making necessary to overcome MAFF's institutional interests in the continuation of whaling. But MAFF cannot guarantee the significant public subsidies on which whaling relies without the imperialist narrative, and an ICJ decision based more upon politics than upon law feeds that narrative superbly. *Whaling in the Antarctic* may have compounded the problem because the decision is so poorly grounded in accepted principles of public international law.

Even from the Australian perspective, the ICJ's attempts at political tact appear counterproductive and poorly informed in terms of the concrete political situation. As lawyers invested in "the classic legal model [of interstate litigation]",[157] the judges of the ICJ appear to have assumed like other

---

ble exploitation of wildlife, including through sustainable whaling (at 164–165) which is precisely what the Japanese government understands itself to be advocating.

150  Hirata (n 16) 142.
151  Stoett (n 149) 172.
152  Ibid 153.
153  Ibid 154.
154  Ibid 161.
155  Michael Tobias, *World War III: Population and Biosphere at the End of the Millennium* (Bear & Co, 1994) 316.
156  Hirata (n 16) 149.
157  Scott (n 6) 2.

commentators that "Australia's goal in bringing these proceedings ... [was] to put a stop to large scale scientific permit whaling by Japan",[158] in the genuine belief that "(1) Australia had a strong legal case; (2) the ICJ would therefore decide in its favour; and (3) Japan would comply with the ICJ ruling".[159] However, attention to the Australian political context problematises all these assumptions, much like the domestic Japanese political context makes clear that litigation was unlikely to end Japan's whaling activities. For the reasons described above, formalist legal analysis in advance of the case suggested that Australia was likely to lose, and it seems that at the time of filing the governments of all three states anticipated a Japanese victory.[160] For the same reasons that "the expenditure of enormous diplomatic energies ... had borne little fruit",[161] it should have been clear that Japan was unlikely actually to cease its whaling activities even in the event of an Australian victory. The Australian government cannot have been so inexpertly advised as not to have understood this prior to bringing its complaint before the ICJ. What, then, really explains Australia's decision to litigate? Rothwell attributes it to the efforts of non-governmental organisations, particularly the International Fund for Animal Welfare ("IFAW"), whose research panels led the "development of litigation strategies ... in contesting the legality of JARPA II before an international court".[162] Indeed, this work informed the way in which Australia conducted its case – its submissions closely echoed the conclusions of the IFAW panels, and the panel members formed part of Australia's legal team at the ICJ. But the prime cause of Australia's decision to litigate at all, rather than simply continue diplomatic pressure, is political.[163] Allee and Huth note that states frequently litigate not hoping for victory in the orthodox legal sense, but rather to have an international

---

158   Park (n 18) 221.
159   Scott (n 6) 2.
160   Scott & Oriana (n 43) 548. See also Andrew Darby, "US Warns of Risks in Australia's Whale Action", Sydney Morning Herald (online, 31 May 2010) <https://www.smh.com.au/environment/conservation/us-warns-of-risks-in-australias-whale-action-20100530-wnjo.html>; Phillip Dorling, "'Doomed' Whaling Fight Aimed at Saving Labor Vote", Sydney Morning Herald (online, 5 January 2011) <https://www.smh.com.au/environment/conservation/doomed-whaling-fight-aimed-at-saving-labor-vote-20110104-19f52.html>.
161   Scott (n 6) 1.
162   Rothwell (n 60) 408.
163   Rothwell accepts that Australia's decision to sue was intimately tied to domestic politics, and that the contribution of environmental NGOs must "be set against the political backdrop of the relative positions [of] the then Howard Coalition (Liberal/National) government, and the Labor Opposition" (ibid 410). Labor could "use their endorsement of the work of the Sydney Panel ... as a point of distinction from the then official government position that international litigation on this matter was not viable" (ibid 411). On its electoral victory, the Labor Party was committed to what had become an electoral promise.

court authoritatively impose a pragmatic and mutually satisfactory compromise to an ongoing dispute.[164] Although both governments may wish to make balanced concessions and reach a practical settlement, to do so may be politically compromising. Offering concessions is hard when an electorate expects its leaders to show strength in the face of international pressure,[165] or when other states might interpret concessions as evidence of weakness. When an international tribunal imposes a mandatory middle-ground, governments can compromise while externalising public dissatisfaction. This explains Australia's decision to litigate despite the prospective improbability of victory. As Scott explains, Australia probably expected the ICJ to vindicate the legality of Japanese whaling, which would "enable the Australian government to accept the advice of its Department of Foreign Affairs and Trade and agree to compromise with Japan, presenting this to the Australian people as the best it could achieve given international legal constraints".[166] After all, Australian politicians must be seen to honour the strong anti-whaling sentiment of their electorate, but will ultimately prioritise Australia's strategically indispensable relations with Japan.[167]

Intuitively, it might appear that the ICJ decision's problematic effects have been mitigated by Japan's withdrawal from the IWC. Japan's planned whaling activities are now certainly within its rights under public international law – it has declared, for instance, that it will end whaling in the Southern Ocean Sanctuary and the North Pacific, confining hunts instead to Japan's own territorial waters and EEZ. The new situation is in many respects ideal for the Japanese state, which is able to save the expense of distant ocean whaling expeditions while nonetheless preserving Japan's whaling "heritage" and signalling its independence from the pressure of Western cultural hegemony. Nonetheless, the whaling lobby remains in need of a spectre of cultural imperialism in order to

---

      Domestic party politics and external affairs of state explain Australia's decision to litigate far more than does genuine environmental concern.

164  Todd L Allee and Paul K Huth, "Legitimizing Dispute Settlement: International Legal Rulings as Domestic Political Cover" (2006) 100(2) *American Political Science Review* 219.

165  Scott (n 6) 8.

166  Ibid 11.

167  Paul Watson, head of the Sea Shepherd Conservation Society, has accused the Australian government of acting secretly in league with Japan, indirectly supporting whaling by obstructing Sea Shepherd's activities, for instance by aggressive handling of their vessels in Australian waters: "Really what it's all about is appeasing Japan. Trade deals take priority over conservation law": Ben Doherty, "Sea Shepherd Says It Will Abandon Pursuit of Japanese Whalers", *The Guardian* (online, 29 August 2017) <https://www.theguardian.com/environment/2017/aug/29/sea-shepherd-says-it-will-abandon-pursuit-of-japanese-whalers>.

justify underwriting an industry to which the public would otherwise have little attachment and which an unstimulated free market in cuisine could not support. And even if the international community will now be unable to oppose Japanese whaling on the grounds of its alleged illegality, Western governments will remain compelled by public sentiment to apply performative political pressure on the Japanese state to abandon the practice. The failure of the ICJ decision to halt Japanese whaling and Japan's subsequent departure from the IWC may also confirm to foreign activists the inability of legal institutional constraints to guarantee cetacean protection, thus re-galvanising extra-legal – and downright *il*legal – methods, such as the piratical actions of groups like Sea Shepherd.[168]

## 5   Reflections: *Whaling in the Antarctic* and the Formalist/Instrumentalist Divide

To instrumentalists, this litigation's (inevitable) failure to stop Japanese whaling might exemplify the alleged ineffectiveness of public international law *qua* law as a meaningful constraint on state behaviour,[169] confirming the naiveté of

---

[168]   See generally Anthony LI Moffa, "Two Competing Models of Activism, One Goal: A Case Study of Anti-Whaling Campaigns in the Southern Ocean" (2012) 37(1) *Yale Journal of International Law* 201, favourably comparing the effectiveness of direct militant action, which famously forced the 2011 whaling fleet home early, with the civil protests staged by groups like Greenpeace. These methods too, however, have experienced major setbacks in more recent times, with Sea Shepherd ultimately abandoning its piratical interference with Japanese whale hunts: Robin McKie, "How Sea Shepherd Lost Battle against Japan's Whale Hunters in Antarctic", *The Guardian* (online, 23 December 2017) <https://www.theguardian.com/environment/2017/dec/23/sea-shepherd-loses-antarctic-battle-japan-whale-hunters>.

[169]   Compare, eg, Jack Goldsmith and Eric Posner, *The Limits of International Law* (Oxford University Press, 2006), which employs game theory to suggest international law is deployed only cynically to advance national interests, with Jens David Ohlin, *The Assault on International Law* (Oxford University Press, 2015). The debate has reignited following the publication of Oona Hathaway and Scott Shapiro, *The Internationalists: How a Radical Plan to Outlaw War Remade the World* (Simon & Schuster, 2017), which claims that the Kellogg-Briand, or Paris Peace Pact of 1928 was the "beginning of the end" of wars of conquest, due to the altered status of war in public international law. Cf Stephen Walt, "There's Still No Reason to Think the Kellog-Briand Pact Accomplished Anything", *Foreign Policy* (Web Page, 29 September 2017) <https://foreignpolicy.com/2017/09/29/theres-still-no-reason-to-think-the-kellogg-briand-pact-accomplished-anything/>, and the original authors' riposte: Oona Hathaway and Scott J Shapiro, "What Realists Don't Understand About Law", *Foreign Policy* (Web Page, 9 October 2017) <https://foreignpolicy.com/2017/10/09/what-realists-dont-understand-about-law/>. The debate also rages with respect to

classical international lawyers who, in contrast to the "realist" tendencies of political scientists and scholars of international relations,[170] "assume the efficacy of legal solutions and ... bemoan evidence to the contrary".[171] Such positions understand international law as just one part of the apparatus for influencing state behaviour, whose (limited) utility depends on its alignment with the more important, principally political, parts of that apparatus. This invites international tribunals to decide disputes tactically, as required by the material international situation. Conversely, committed formalists cannot endorse international courts' prioritising political considerations over legal logic. From that perspective, there is little to be said in favour of the ICJ's decision in *Whaling in the Antarctic*, in which the ICJ should simply have asked the legally orthodox question – was Japan acting in bad faith? – rather than allowing political sensitivity to dictate an outlandish construction of the *ICRW* regulatory regime, declaring either that Japan had been deceiving the international community about its true motivations, or otherwise upholding the legality of the much-maligned JARPA II programme. A principled formalist must accept that, when the language of treaties is faithfully applied, sometimes objectionable state actions will slip through the regulatory net because positive law is invariably imperfect. If international law is to be *law*, its agents must be prepared to give legally correct but politically obstructive answers.

This article is neutral with respect to this most primordial of disputes about the nature and utility of public international law. Instead it tentatively identifies in the shortcomings of *Whaling in the Antarctic* a partial synthesis of these

---

international human rights law: cf eg Eric A Posner, *The Twilight of Human Rights Law* (Oxford University Press, 2014) with Kathryn Sikkink, *Evidence for Hope: Making Human Rights Work in the 21st Century* (Princeton University Press, 2017).

[170] See, particularly powerfully, John J Mearsheimer, "The False Promise of International Institutions" (1994–1995) 19(3) *International Security* 5, for whom international law and its institutions are merely "epiphenomenal" to the practice of international politics.

[171] Tom Ginsburg, "Political Constraints on International Courts" in Karen Alter, Cesare Romano and Yuvai Shany (eds), *Oxford Handbook of International Adjudication* (Oxford University Press, 2013) 483, 485–486. The debate is hard to disentangle from the changing place of international law in jurisprudential thinking at its most profound. Traditionally, international law has been understood as a peripheral rather than central example of the concept of law, a concept defined from the perspective of state-based legal systems. Increasingly the relationship is more bilateral, such that "if international law does not fit the criteria of the concept of law used at the domestic level, it may not (only) be a problem for the legality of international law, but (also) for those criteria themselves and hence for a given legal theory": Samantha Besson and John Tasioulas, "Introduction" in Samantha Besson and John Tasioulas (eds.), *The Philosophy of International Law* (Oxford University Press, 2010) 8.

perspectives. Governments may litigate in international tribunals to mitigate the political consequences of adopting a compromise position with which they were anyway substantially content. Fidelity to international law is more palatable to national electorates – and perhaps also to the pride of political leaders – than simple capitulation to the demands of another state. The "losing" side is "more ready to accept unpleasant decisions which appear to be the ineluctable result of rigorously logical deductions".[172] Unwelcome outcomes are easier to accept if they appear to flow from logically prior rules, rather than immediate and partisan human agency.[173] To the extent that public international law is useful in resolving international disputes and materially influencing state conduct is, therefore, intimately linked to the credibility of its status *as law* – that is to say, with decisions' actual or at least apparent fidelity to positive rules of law and insulation from political considerations. Legal formalism has an instrumentalist advantage, and abandoning it an instrumentalist cost. This is not to say that instrumentalist considerations should never be allowed to temper or influence formalist reasoning, only that whatever immediate advantages this may offer in terms of controlling the conduct of a defendant state must be balanced against the countervailing dangers of departing from rigorous fidelity to positive law.

This article's objection to *Whaling in the Antarctic* is not that the ICJ prioritised political and instrumentalist considerations over legal formalism, but that it did so *incompletely*. The ICJ was either too much, or too little, influenced by the probable consequences of its decision, and the unprincipled *via media* on which the majority settled represents the worst of both worlds. Influential interests within the Japanese state remain committed to commercial whaling in defiance of any amount of international censure – like Ahab, they are prepared to pursue the cetacean "round perdition's flames" rather than abandon the hunt. An ICJ minded actually to accelerate the end of Japanese whaling should, on the basis of all the available evidence, have found in favour of Japan, so as not to intensify the domestic enthusiasm for what is otherwise a zombie industry with little to justify its consumption of public funds.

The ICJ was moved by political sensitivity and concern for the consequences of its decision to massage the ordinary application of formal law, but in so doing produced a judgment that makes the desired consequences less, rather

---

172   Walter Murphy, *Elements of Judicial Strategy* (University of Chicago Press, 1964). See also Ginsburg (n 171) 493.
173   This is reflected in the practices of other international courts. See, eg, Olof Larsson et al, "Speaking Law to Power: The Strategic Use of Precedent of the Court of Justice of the European Union" (2017) 50(7) *Comparative Political Studies* 879.

than more, probable, and the political situation between the litigant states more, rather than less, difficult. Generally, little in public international legal discourse fails to divide commentators according to the primordial cleft between formalist and realist understandings of international law's nature and optimal operation. But both principled formalists and ends-focused realists will find ample material to criticise in the ICJ's legal reasoning and its political manoeuvring, and can for once be united in condemning this case as an example of how international legal adjudication should not be done. Even those invested in the ideal of the international rule of law as a normatively independent constraint on global politics are moved to temper or mitigate the apparently problematic consequences of a decision that loyally adheres to positive law. Such an impulse is not self-evidently illegitimate; Crawford notes how context-blind, dogmatic formalism can "help account for international norm fatigue", to which "backlash can be an appropriate response".[174] But this should be done sensitively on the basis of sound evidence about the actual consequences of particular substantive outcomes and, crucially, of the specific legal reasoning that is deployed to produce them. *Whaling in the Antarctic* represents a position on the line between formalist and realist approaches to public international law that combines the key critiques that each camp deploys against the other – it is *unprincipled*, in that it perforates the allegedly vital conceptual line between legal and non-legal reasoning and thus undermines the "rule of law" properly so called, and it is simultaneously *ineffective*, in that doing so failed to bring Japanese state policy into conformity with the general desires of the international community.

---

174   James Crawford, "The Current Political Discourse Concerning International Law" (2018) 81(1) *Modern Law Review* 1, 6.

# Jurisdictional Aspects of Dispute Settlement under the *UN Convention on the Law of the Sea*: Some Recent Developments

*Gino Naldi\* and Konstantinos Magliveras\*\**

## Abstract

The United Nations Convention on the Law of the Sea ("UNCLOS") contains a discrete section, pt XV, which is dedicated to dispute settlement and obligatory for states parties, and contains a mixture of voluntary and compulsory procedures. These provisions are complex and a determination of their precise meaning calls for authoritative interpretation. It does not seem unfair to state that the UNCLOS dispute settlement procedures have been relatively underutilised since its entry into force in 1994. Few early cases addressed contentious issues regarding compulsory jurisdiction, though one proved exceptionally controversial. Hence, many questions relating to the meaning and scope of the provisions on jurisdiction either remained unanswered or required further elucidation, a matter of academic speculation. However, since 2013, there has been a sudden increase in the number of cases submitted to the UNCLOS dispute settlement procedures. Many of these cases share features in common, namely, contested jurisdiction and even instances of non-appearance, which necessitated addressing a range of issues concerning the jurisdictional provisions of the UNCLOS dispute settlement system. The conclusions of the courts and tribunals on jurisdictional issues, many of them controversial, help to inform, clarify, develop and contribute to the debate on the interpretation and scope of the UNCLOS dispute settlement system.

## 1   Introduction

The *United Nations Convention on the Law of the Sea* ("*UNCLOS*")[1] makes detailed provision for the resolution of disputes concerning its interpretation or

---

\*   LLM, PhD (Birmingham), former university senior lecturer in Law, United Kingdom.
\*\*  LLB (Athens), LLM (Exeter), DPhil (Oxon), Professor in the Law of International Organizations, Department of Mediterranean Studies, University of the Aegean, Greece.
1   *United Nations Convention on the Law of the Sea*, opened for signature 10 December 1982, 1833 UNTS 3 (entered into force 16 November 1994) ("*UNCLOS*").

application, which importantly is obligatory for state parties,[2] an integral part of the *Convention*,[3] to be found in UNCLOS pt XV, arts 279–299 and annexes V–VIII. It has been described as establishing, "with limited exceptions, a compulsory dispute settlement regime".[4] The core principle at the heart of pt XV is that states must first seek to resolve their dispute by recourse to the voluntary procedures set out in Section 1 thereof, failing which the dispute may be submitted unilaterally by one of the parties to a court or tribunal having compulsory jurisdiction, thereby leading to a binding decision under Section 2 thereof.[5] Accordingly, under art 287(1), a state party may at any time make a declaration choosing a means of dispute settlement, namely the International Tribunal for the Law of the Sea ("ITLOS"), the International Court of Justice ("ICJ"), an arbitral tribunal under annex VII or a special arbitral tribunal under annex VIII (the latter two tribunals being ad hoc in nature). Where a state fails to select one of these bodies, the default procedure expressed in art 287(3) is that annex VII arbitration applies.[6] However, what appeared to have been a settled view has been thrown into question by the ICJ in the *Maritime Delimitation in the*

---

2   See generally RR Churchill and AV Lowe, *The Law of the Sea* (Manchester University Press, 3rd ed, 1999) 453; Natalie Klein, *International Dispute Settlement in the UN Convention on the Law of the Sea* (Cambridge University Press, 2005); Donald R Rothwell and Tim Stephens, *The International Law of the Sea* (Hart Publishing, 2nd ed, 2016) 479; JG Merrills, *International Dispute Settlement* (Cambridge University Press, 3rd ed, 1998) ch 8; Bernard H Oxman, "Courts and Tribunals: The ICJ, ITLOS, and Arbitral Tribunals" in Donald R Rothwell et al. (eds), *The Oxford Handbook of the Law of the Sea* (Oxford University Press, 2015) ch 18; Oxford University Press, *Max Planck Encyclopedia of Public International Law* (online at 16 September 2019) Law of the Sea, Settlement of Disputes ("*Max Planck Encyclopedia of Public International Law*, Law of the Sea, Settlement of Disputes"). Entities other than states may become parties to the dispute settlement procedures: ibid art 291(2). For example, the European Union acceded to UNCLOS on 1 April 1998.

3   *Philippines v China(Jurisdiction and Admissibility)* (Permanent Court of Arbitration, Case No 2013-19, 29 October 2015) [2] ("*Philippines v China Arbitration*"); *Arctic Sunrise Arbitration (Netherlands v Russia)(Award on Merits)* (2016) 55 ILM 5, 58 ("*Arctic Sunrise Arbitration*"); *Maritime Delimitation in the Indian Ocean (Somalia v Kenya)(Preliminary Objections)* [2017] ICJ Rep 3, 47 ("*Maritime Delimitation in the Indian Ocean Case*").

4   *Arctic Sunrise Arbitration* (n 3) 58.

5   In *Maritime Boundary (Barbados v Trinidad and Tobago)(Award)* (2006) 27 RIAA 147, 207 ("*Maritime Boundary Arbitration*"), the Arbitral Tribunal expressed the view that, in practice, the only relevant obligation upon parties under Section 1 is to seek to settle their disputes through negotiations. Cf *contra Land Reclamation by Singapore in and around the Straits of Johor (Malaysia v Singapore)(Provisional Measures)* (2003) ITLOS Rep 10, 53 (Judge Jesus) ("*Land Reclamation Case*").

6   As occurred in, inter alia: *Maritime Boundary Arbitration* (n 5); *Land Reclamation Case* (n 5); and *Enrica Lexie Incident (Italy v India)(Request for the Prescription of Provisional Measures)* (Permanent Court of Arbitration, Case No 2015-28, 29 April 2016) [52] ("*Enrica Lexie Case*").

*Indian Ocean Case*, where it held that it had jurisdiction based on a policy argument that if it declined jurisdiction, there was no guarantee that an arbitral tribunal would accept the case, which could thus result in a denial of justice.[7] Article 287(4) states that where the parties to a dispute have accepted the same procedure, that procedure applies unless otherwise agreed.[8] However, if they have not accepted the same procedure, art 287(5) provides that annex VII arbitration applies unless the parties otherwise agree.[9] Whereas this wide choice of courts and tribunals was designed to appeal to the predispositions of states on the question of judicial dispute settlement,[10] and has been described as reflecting "the need to establish a balance between the freedom to choose settlement procedures and the need to reach a binding settlement of the subject of the dispute",[11] it does raise the risk of the jurisprudence taking divergent paths. As will be seen, this fear is not without foundation.

The dispute settlement provisions of UNCLOS contain ambiguities of language, as do those of many other treaties. Some surround the meaning of phrases specific to UNCLOS, but others are familiar from other areas of international law. But any legal instrument can be expected to give rise to questions of interpretation, and UNCLOS should not be regarded as somehow unusual in this regard. Since UNCLOS came into force in 1994, a steady but small number of cases have come before the ITLOS and annex VII tribunals which necessitated discussion of the jurisdictional aspects of its dispute settlement provisions. Nevertheless, many issues still remained unaddressed or underexplored historically. However, the chance occurrence of a series of successive cases over recent years has provided opportunities to throw a spotlight on such jurisdictional questions. While some of the pronouncements may be considered to be in keeping with accepted international law, others have undoubtedly stirred controversy. Prior to 2013, there had been relatively few cases where the jurisdictional provisions of the UNCLOS dispute settlement system had played a

---

7   *Maritime Delimitation in the Indian Ocean Case* (n 3) 48–50. In a powerful dissent, Judge Robinson argued that this was improper speculation on the ICJ's part and that the outcome of its conclusion was to make the ICJ the default mechanism, contrary to the intent of art 287(3): at 77.
8   Cases where the parties subsequently agreed to transfer the case from an arbitral tribunal to the ITLOS include *M/V Saiga (No 2)(Saint Vincent and the Grenadines v Guinea)* (*Judgment*) (1999) ITLOS Rep 10, 30 [41] ("*M/V Saiga (No 2)*") and *M/V Virginia G (Panama v Guinea-Bissau)* (*Judgment*) (2014) ITLOS Rep 4, 38 [92] ("*M/V Virginia G Case*").
9   As occurred in *MOX Plant (Ireland v United Kingdom)(Provisional Measures)* (2001) 41 ILM 405, 413 ("*MOX Plant Case*").
10  Merrills, *International Dispute Settlement* (n 2) 173.
11  Anne Sheehan, "Dispute Settlement under UNCLOS: The Exclusion of Maritime Delimitation Disputes" (2005) 24(1) *University of Queensland Law Journal* 165, 168.

central role in the proceedings calling for their interpretation.[12] Many questions on the meaning, scope and interrelationship between the complex provisions on jurisdiction still remained to be answered or required explanation. But recent years have witnessed significant international litigation addressing a variety of issues on this subject. Many of these proceedings have proven contentious from the outset, involving contested jurisdiction and non-appearance, and have given rise to controversy, based, inter alia, on claims that the judicial bodies erred in law or sought improperly to expand jurisdiction. Nonetheless, the reasoning of the courts and tribunals in these and other cases on the interpretation of the UNCLOS provisions on compulsory jurisdiction make important contributions to the understanding and development of the dispute settlement system. These matters will be examined in the light of an array of relevant cases including the *Arctic Sunrise Case*,[13] the *Chagos Arbitration*,[14] the *Philippines v China Arbitration*,[15] and *Conciliation between Timor-Leste and Australia*, the first time the conciliation procedure has been used.[16]

## 2  The Interpretation of Part XV UNCLOS

### 2.1  *Non-appearance*

The respondents in three cases,[17] *Arctic Sunrise, Ukrainian Naval Vessels* and *Philippines v China*, refused to participate in the compulsory proceedings,

---

12   A notorious exception was *Southern Bluefin Tuna (Australia v Japan)(Jurisdiction and Admissibility)* (2000) 23 RIAA 1, 43–44 ("*Southern Bluefin Tuna Arbitration*"), where the Arbitral Tribunal controversially held that it lacked jurisdiction on the merits. See Barbara Kwiatkoska, "The Australia and New Zealand v Japan Southern Bluefin Tuna (Jurisdiction and Admissibility) Award of the First Law of the Sea Convention Annex VII Arbitral Tribunal" (2001) 16(2) *International Journal of Marine and Coastal Law* 239. For a negative assessment of this decision, see David A Colson and Peggy Hoyle, "Satisfying the Procedural Prerequisites to the Compulsory Dispute Settlement Mechanisms of the 1982 Law of the Sea Convention: Did the *Southern Bluefin Tuna* Tribunal Get it Right?" (2003) 34(1) *Ocean Development and International Law* 59.

13   *Arctic Sunrise (Netherlands v Russia)(Provisional Measures)*(2013) ITLOS Rep 230("*Arctic Sunrise Case*").

14   *Chagos Marine Protected Area (Mauritius v United Kingdom)(Award)* (UNCLOS Arbitral Tribunal, 18 March 2015) ("*Chagos Arbitration*").

15   *Philippines v China Arbitration* (n 3).

16   *Conciliation between Timor-Leste and Australia(Decision on Australia's Objections to Competence)* (UNCLOS Conciliation Commission, Permanent Court of Arbitration, Case No 2016-10, 19 September 2016) ("*Conciliation between Timor-Leste and Australia*").

17   In the first two cases, Russia was the respondent, while China was the respondent in the third.

claiming that the respective tribunals lacked jurisdiction. The first case arose from the fact that, in 2013, Russian authorities boarded and detained the Greenpeace vessel *Arctic Sunrise,* which flew the Dutch flag and had been conducting protests against a Russian oil platform located in Russia's exclusive economic zone ("EEZ"). The persons on board were arrested, detained and charged with various offences by the Russian authorities. The Netherlands, as the flag state, instituted arbitral proceedings against Russia pursuant to art 287 and annex VII UNCLOS, claiming, inter alia, that, absent flag state consent, Russia's actions were in violation of UNCLOS and customary international law. Pending the setting-up of the arbitral tribunal, the Netherlands, pursuant to art 290(5) UNCLOS, obtained an order for provisional measures from the ITLOS requiring the immediate release of the *Arctic Sunrise* and all detained persons.[18] Russia had challenged the jurisdiction of the ITLOS, asserting that it was excluded by the terms of the *Declaration* which it made when it ratified UNCLOS, stating that it did not accept pt XV, Section 2 procedures regarding disputes concerning law enforcement activities. It therefore refused to participate in the proceedings.[19]

The second case, the *Ukrainian Naval Vessels Case,* shared certain similarities with the above case. In March 2019, Ukraine instituted arbitral proceedings against Russia pursuant to art 287 and annex VII UNCLOS, claiming that the detention of three Ukrainian warships and their crew in disputed waters in the Black Sea violated their immunity under art 32 UNCLOS and customary law.[20] In May 2019, Ukraine obtained an order for provisional measures from the ITLOS, requiring the immediate release of the ships and their crew.[21] Russia refused to participate in the proceedings, claiming that the jurisdiction of the

---

18   *Arctic Sunrise Case* (n 13). See Alex G Oude Elferink, "The *Arctic Sunrise* Incident: A Multi-Faceted Law of the Sea Case with a Human Rights Dimension" (2014) 29(2) *International Journal of Marine and Coastal Law* 244, 246; Robin Churchill, "Dispute Settlement under the UN Convention on the Law of the Sea: Survey for 2013" (2015) 30(1) *International Journal of Marine and Coastal Law* 1, 14–22 ("Survey for 2013").

19   "Note Verbale of the Embassy of the Russian Federation in Berlin", *Arctic Sunrise (Netherlands v Russia)*(International Tribunal for the Law of the Sea, Case No 22, 22 October 2013).

20   *Detention of Three Ukrainian Naval Vessels (Ukraine v Russia) (Provisional Measures)* (International Tribunal for the Law of the Sea, Case No 26, 25 May 2019)("*Ukrainian Naval Vessels Case*"). The background to the dispute between Ukraine and Russia lies in Russia's annexation of the Ukrainian territory of Crimea in 2014 which resulted in Russian control of the waters in question. *Territorial Integrity of Ukraine,* GA Res 68/262, UN Doc A/RES/68/262 (27 March 2014) reaffirmed Ukraine's territorial integrity within its internationally recognized borders.

21   *Ukrainian Naval Vessels Case* (n 20).

ITLOS was excluded by the terms of its *Declaration*, and thus stated that it did not accept pt XV, Section 2 procedures regarding disputes concerning military activities.[22] Nevertheless, a *Memorandum* before the ITLOS set out the Russian position.[23]

The latter case, brought by the Philippines against China under annex VII UNCLOS, concerned maritime rights in a part of the South China Sea claimed by both states.[24] The origins of the dispute evidently lie in competing claims in the South China Sea,[25] aggravated by recent Chinese activities in the area.[26] However, in light of China's *Declaration* accepting the UNCLOS dispute settlement procedures which exclude, inter alia, issues of maritime delimitation and titles, the Philippines based its claims on maritime rights and entitlements. China considered that the subject-matter of the case was precisely one of territorial sovereignty and maritime delimitation,[27] areas in which it had not accepted compulsory dispute settlement under UNCLOS and which fell accordingly beyond the scope of UNCLOS, that the case was not concerned with the interpretation and application of UNCLOS, and further, that the case constituted an attempt to bypass the limitations in its *Declaration*.[28] In addition, any such disputes were in any case to be settled bilaterally by peaceful negotiations.[29] China claimed that the Tribunal did not therefore have jurisdiction.[30] The Arbitral Tribunal nevertheless held that it had jurisdiction to consider a number of the Philippines' submissions, but considered that others would have to be examined at the merits stage.[31]

---

22  Ibid [49].
23  Ibid [12].
24  Churchill, "Survey for 2013" (n 18) 25–28.
25  *Philippines v China Arbitration* (n 3) [152]. See generally Robert Beckman, "The UN Convention on the Law of the Sea and Maritime Disputes in the South China Sea" (2013) 107(1) *American Journal of International Law* 142; Jonathan I Charney, "Central East Asian Maritime Boundaries and the Law of the Sea" (1995) 89(4) *American Journal of International Law* 724; Florian Dupuy and Pierre-Marie Dupuy, "A Legal Analysis of China's Historic Rights Claim in the South China Sea" (2013) 107(1) *American Journal of International Law* 124.
26  See Yi-Hsuan Chen, "South China Sea Tension on Fire: China's Recent Moves on Building Artificial islands in Troubled Waters and Their Implications on Maritime Law" (2015) 1(1) *Maritime Safety and Security Law Journal* 1.
27  Chinese Society of International Law, "The South China Sea Awards: A Critical Study" (2018) 17(2) *Chinese Journal of International Law* 207, 251–259.
28  Ibid 247–248.
29  Ibid 274–306.
30  Ibid 48–374.
31  See Chris Whomersley, "The South China Sea: The Award of the Tribunal in the Case Brought by Philippines against China – A Critique" (2016) 15(2) *Chinese Journal of International Law* 239.

Article 288(4) UNCLOS states unambiguously that where the jurisdiction of a court or tribunal is challenged, that court or tribunal can decide on its own jurisdiction.[32] It therefore incorporates a fundamental principle of international law, which provides that where the jurisdiction of a court or tribunal is challenged, this body has the power to determine its own jurisdiction and rule on those objections (the so-called *Kompetenz-Kompetenz* principle).[33] The law set out in UNCLOS on non-appearing parties is clear, nonetheless: ITLOS Statute[34] art 28 and UNCLOS annex VII, art 9 declare, in identical terms, that failure of a party to appear before the tribunal or to defend its case does not block the proceedings.[35] The other party may therefore request the tribunal to continue with the case and make its award.[36] This is what occurred in these cases. At the provisional measures phase of the *Arctic Sunrise Case*, the ITLOS cited with approval the dictum of the ICJ in the *Nicaragua Case*[37] that the case continues without the non-appearing party, which remains a party to the case and is bound by the eventual judgment.[38] This was a point also made by the Arbitral Tribunal at the merits stage of the *Arctic Sunrise Arbitration*, where it stipulated that non-appearance "affects neither the jurisdiction of the tribunal ... nor the binding nature of any final decision".[39] The ITLOS further indicated

---

32  *Arctic Sunrise Arbitration* (n 3) 12, 58; *Philippines v China Arbitration* (n 3) [111].
33  *Nottebohm Case (Liechtenstein v Guatemala)(Preliminary Objection)* [1953] ICJ Rep 111, 119. In their Joint Separate Declaration in the *Arctic Sunrise Case* (n 13) 259 [8], Judges Wolfrum and Kelly commented forcefully that Russia could not rely on a "self-judging" approach to its declaration to justify its non-appearance since it is for ITLOS itself to determine its own jurisdiction based on the principle of *Kompetenz-Kompetenz*, as enshrined in UNCLOS art 288(4). See further *Border Dispute (Croatia v Slovenia)(Partial Award)* (Permanent Court of Arbitration, Case No 2012–04, 30 June 2016) [148]–[157].
34  UNCLOS (n 1) annex VI ("*ITLOS Statute*").
35  *Philippines v China Arbitration* (n 3) [11], [113]. See also *Philippines v China (Rules of Procedure)* (Permanent Court of Arbitration, Case No 2013–19, 27 August 2013); this was similarily the case in *Arctic Sunrise Arbitration(Netherlands v Russia) (Rules of Procedure)* (Permanent Court of Arbitration, Case No 2014–02, 17 March 2014) ("*Arctic Sunrise Arbitration (Rules of Procedure)*"). The position under UNCLOS is consistent with the constitutions of other international courts: see, e.g., *Statute of the International Court of Justice* art 53 ("*ICJ Statute*"). The ITLOS was able to rely on ample ICJ practice on this issue: *Arctic Sunrise Case* (n 13) 242 [48].
36  Unlike the rules under *ICJ Statute* (n 35) art 53(1), the court or tribunal is not called upon to decide the case in favour of the applicant or enter a default judgment: *Philippines v China Arbitration* (n 3) [12].
37  *Military and Paramilitary Activities in and against Nicaragua(Nicaragua v United States of America)(Merits)* [1986] ICJ Rep 14, 24 ("*Nicaragua Case*").
38  *Arctic Sunrise Case* (n 13) 242–243 [48]–[52]; *Ukrainian Naval Vessels Case* (n 20) [123]; *Philippines v China Arbitration* (n 3) [11], [114].
39  *Arctic Sunrise Arbitration* (n 3) 12 [10].

that the Netherlands should not be disadvantaged because of Russia's non-appearance, and that it therefore had to identify and assess the rights of the parties on the best available evidence, which, in the present instance, had been made more difficult by Russia's stance.[40] But art 9 of annex VII involved a balancing act, on the part of the Tribunal, in relation to the risks of prejudice that could be suffered by either party.[41] However, as the Tribunals were careful to point out, the tribunal must satisfy itself, before making its award, that it has jurisdiction and that the claim is well founded in fact and in law.[42] It cannot simply accept the appearing party's claims nor enter a default judgment.[43] The governing law, UNCLOS annex VII, art 5 and *Rules of Procedure* art 10, imposed an obligation upon the Tribunals to treat the parties equally, and they would therefore consider possible legal arguments that the absent parties may have submitted in support of their case, had they appeared.[44] The Tribunals proceeded to do this. In the *Philippines v China Arbitration*, China had made public its views in a *Position Paper* which the Tribunal, for all intents and purposes, treated as it entering a plea on its jurisdiction.[45] Nevertheless, the Tribunals' decision to proceed with the cases notwithstanding the non-appearance

---

40   *Arctic Sunrise Case* (n 13) 243 [54]–[57]; see also at 254 [2] (Judge ad hocAnderson). In *Philippines v China Arbitration* (n 3) [118], the Tribunal made the point that the Philippines' procedural rights had to be protected. See also*Ukrainian Naval Vessels Case* (n 20) [29].

41   *Philippines v China Arbitration* (n 3) [115]–[16].

42   *South China Sea Arbitration (Philippines v China)*(*Award*) (Permanent Court of Arbitration, Case No 2013-19, 12 July 2016) [119] ("*South China Sea Arbitration*"); *Philippines v China Arbitration* (n 3) [12]; *Arctic Sunrise Arbitration* (n 3) 12. Cf Douglas Guilfoyle and Cameron A Miles, "Provisional Measures and the MV *Arctic Sunrise*" (2014) 108(1) *American Journal of International Law* 271, 276–281, who argue that the ITLOS, seemingly motivated by a desire to address robustly Russia's stance, failed to conduct a proper detailed examination. However, it must be recalled that in provisional measures cases only a prima facie case needs to be made: *Ukrainian Naval Vessels Case* (n 20) [36].

43   *South China Sea Arbitration* (n 42) [12].

44   *Arctic Sunrise Arbitration* (*Rules of Procedure*) (n 35) art 25(2). Contrary to the previously outlined assertions of Guilfoyle and Miles (n 42), the better view seems to be that Russia's interests were properly protected: Massimo Lando, "Establishing the Existence of a "Dispute" under UNCLOS at the Provisional Measures Stage: the *Enrica Lexie Case*"(2015) 22(1) *Questions of International Law* 3, 13; Eugene Kontorovich, "Arctic Sunrise (Netherlands v Russia); In re Arctic Sunrise (Netherlands v Russia)" (2016) 110(1) *American Journal of International Law* 96, 100.

45   *Philippines v China (Procedural Order No 4)* (Permanent Court of Arbitration, Case No 2013-19, 21 April 2015) [1.1]; *Philippines v China Arbitration* (n 3) [14]–[15]. However, China has claimed that it was deprived of its procedural rights: "The South China Sea Awards: A Critical Study" (n 27) 620.

of a party has attracted considerable criticism of the cases as unfair and illegitimate.[46]

In the *Arctic Sunrise Case*, Judges Wolfrum and Kelly expanded on the question of non-appearance. In their view, *ITLOS Statute* art 28 was applicable to all procedures, including provisional measures, an argument the ITLOS had failed to make, although it had applied it in practice.[47] This position appears to have been attributable to an apparent inconsistency between UNCLOS art 290, governing provisional measures (in relation to which the court or tribunal need only establish prima facie jurisdiction), and *ITLOS Statute* art 28, which additionally requires that "the claim [be] well founded in fact and law". This highlights potential differences that may emerge as a consequence of the forum to which a state submits a dispute. The ITLOS seemed to be following the jurisprudence of the ICJ, but the *ITLOS Statute* is not identical to that of the ICJ in this respect, but, rather, has its own characteristic features.[48] However, the difficulty that existed was that there was no prior ITLOS practice on this point, this being the first time that the ITLOS was confronted with the problem of a non-appearing party. It therefore does not seem inappropriate for ITLOS to have relied on the ICJ's jurisprudence, as it has done in other areas,[49] as long as this is done with the necessary caution. Nevertheless, the judges were issuing a warning about the dangers of uniformly interpreting similar but differing provisions. But the judges made a more fundamental point – that non-appearance is not only contrary to the object and purpose of the UNCLOS dispute settlement system, but, moreover, that *ITLOS Statute* art 28 does not confer a right of non-appearance on parties but simply constitutes an acknowledgment of its possible occurrence.[50] This was an emphatic rejection of the view that no obligation exists under UNCLOS for states to participate in proceedings.[51]

Whilst non-appearance may be a tactical ploy by a recalcitrant state,[52] it is ultimately a self-defeating strategy. Although UNCLOS may not compel a party

---

46  "The South China Sea Awards: A Critical Study" (n 27); Peter Tzeng, "*Ukraine v Russia* and *Philippines v China*: Jurisdiction and Legitimacy" (2017)(1) *Denver Journal of International Law and Policy* 1, 15.
47  See also *Arctic Sunrise Case* (n 13) 273–275 [3] (Judge Paik).
48  Ibid 257 [4] (Judges Wolfrum and Kelly); 271–273 [2] (Judge Paik).
49  Alan Boyle, "UNCLOS Dispute Settlement and the Uses and Abuses of Part XV" (2014) 47(1) *Revue Belge de Droit International* 182.
50  *Arctic Sunrise Case* (n 13) 258 [6] (Judges Wolfrum and Kelly). Another judge expressed the view that non-appearance was detrimental to "the rule of law in international relations": at 254 [2] (Judge ad hoc Anderson).
51  *Arctic Sunrise Arbitration* (n 3) 58; Oxman (n 2) 399 n 15.
52  Shabtai Rosenne, *The World Court: What It Is and How It Works* (Martinus Nijhoff, 5th rev ed, 1995) 96.

to appear before a court or tribunal, it cannot prevent the court or tribunal from fulfilling its judicial function and thus adjudicating on the dispute.[53] Claims that the tribunals are undermining their own authority in these circumstances appear overstated. Moreover, the converse argument could be made that the tribunals, and by extension the international rule of law, would lose all credibility if they capitulated to bullying tactics by states. The proper response would be for the respondent to argue its case before the court to the best of its ability, trusting that the strength of its arguments will be persuasive. The law on non-appearance appears to have been properly applied.[54] Furthermore, in those instances where it has been argued that the reasoning of the Tribunals or ITLOS was not profound or extensive, it should be borne in mind that some of these proceedings concerned provisional measures where only a less reasoned, prima facie standard of inquiry is required. An immediate consequence of these findings was that states found themselves reluctant parties to litigation, a result that was rejected in forceful terms by China.[55] As has been repeatedly underlined, the non-participant is only likely to prejudice its own case[56] and leave itself open to being found in breach of its international obligations, as occurred with both China and Russia. And at the end of the day, the non-participant remains bound by any decision.[57]

### 2.2 Article 281 and the Procedure Where No Settlement Has Been Reached

It is a condition precedent of the UNCLOS dispute settlement procedures that a party wishing to have recourse to the binding procedures of Section 2 must initially satisfy the requirements of Section 1, subject specifically to the stipulations of art 281.[58] UNCLOS art 281(1) specifies that where the parties have agreed

---

53   *Arctic Sunrise Arbitration* (n 3) 58; see "The South China Sea Awards: A Critical Study" (n 27) 620.

54   John E Noyes, "In re Arbitration between the Philippines and China" (2016) 110(1) *American Journal of International Law* 102, 108. And see above n 44.

55   *South China Sea Arbitration* (n 42) [61].

56   *Arctic Sunrise Case* (n 13) 257–258 [5] (Judges Wolfrum and Kelly). See also *Nicaragua Case* (n 37) 544 (Judge Jennings); Boyle (n 49) 200–201; Mincai Yu, "China's Informal Participation in the Annex VII Philippines v China Arbitral Tribunal's Proceedings" (2015) 30(1) *International Journal of Marine and Coastal Law* 54, 64–65.

57   *Arctic Sunrise Arbitration* (n 3) 12. In 2017, the Tribunal awarded compensation to the Netherlands: *Arctic Sunrise Arbitration (Netherlands v Russia)(Award on Compensation)* (2018) 57 ILM 553.

58   *Southern Bluefin Tuna Arbitration* (n 12) 43–44; *Conciliation between Timor-Leste and Australia* (n 16) [50].

to seek settlement of the dispute by a peaceful means of their choice,[59] the procedures denoted in UNCLOS apply only if such other means prove fruitless and no other procedures are excluded by the parties.[60] In the *Philippines v China Arbitration*, the Arbitral Tribunal made a number of preliminary observations regarding art 281 and the procedures to be undertaken where no settlement has been reached between the parties. It stated initially that art 281 is dependent on the existence of a dispute concerning the interpretation or application of UNCLOS, and that absent such a dispute Article 281 has no relevance.[61] It could be said that this is a truism that applies throughout much of the UNCLOS dispute settlement system.

The Tribunal then considered whether the parties had "agreed to seek settlement of the dispute by a peaceful means of their own choice". But what if the parties cannot agree? Of significance is the fact that art 281 goes on to state, inter alia, that the compulsory procedures of Section 2 apply "only where no settlement has been reached by recourse to such means and [where] the agreement to seek a settlement does not exclude any further procedure". The language of this provision is open to the interpretation that agreed means, and the failure of a settlement conducted pursuant to such means, are preconditions before resort can be had to the compulsory procedures. Accordingly, failure by the parties to agree means that a breakdown in "talks about talks", so to speak, would block the applicability of the compulsory procedures. However, the Tribunal declared that lack of agreement "poses no obstacle to jurisdiction".[62] The reasons for this conclusion are not hard to discern. It would otherwise mean effectively handing either party a veto on making use of further settlement procedures through the simple expedient of ensuring that no initial agreement can be finalised.

Had the parties however, in fact reached agreement? The definition of "agreement" assumes a critical importance – is a binding or a non-binding, informal agreement envisaged? In its *Position Paper*, China argued that both it

---

59   In *Land Reclamation Case* (n 5) 20–21, Singapore argued that the ITLOS lacked jurisdiction, as recourse to UNCLOS had been excluded by Malaysia's acceptance of its proposal to negotiate. However, the ITLOS found that UNCLOS art 281 was inapplicable as Malaysia had accepted the proposal to negotiate subsequent to the initiation of proceedings under annex VII, and because it had been agreed that this was without prejudice to Malaysia's right to continue with the proceedings.

60   In the words of the Conciliation Commission, UNCLOS dispute settlement procedures are "subject to other procedures on which the parties may have agreed, providing that such procedures will prevail over the mechanisms created by [UNCLOS]": *Conciliation between Timor-Leste and Australia* (n 16) [49].

61   *Philippines v China Arbitration* (n 3) [194].

62   Ibid [195].

and the Philippines had, inter alia, committed themselves to resolving their disputes by negotiation only under a number of different instruments, namely, the *Declaration on the Conduct of Parties in the South China Sea*[63] (*"DOC"*) and a series of joint statements issued by China and the Philippines on the resolution of disputes via negotiation. The Tribunal also took into account *proprio motu* the *Treaty of Amity and Co-operation* (*"TAC"*),[64] and the *Convention on Biological Diversity* (*"CBD"*).[65] The question that arose was whether any of these instruments amounted to an agreement for the purposes of art 281 and did they exclude other procedures. According to China, the DOC, jointly adopted in 2002 with Association of Southeast Asian Nations (*"ASEAN"*) member states, including the Philippines, constituted an agreement to seek a settlement to the exclusion of other procedures, as envisaged by art 281. The Philippines challenged this interpretation, arguing, inter alia, that the DOC did not amount to a legally binding agreement, that even if it was, no settlement had been reached, and that it did not exclude resort to Section 2 procedures. The Tribunal's deliberation of this matter plainly presupposed that the term "agreement" in art 281 refers to a treaty as understood by international law; the actual question was whether the DOC itself could be classified as a legally binding agreement within the terms of art 281. The Tribunal concluded that the DOC was a political agreement which was not intended to create legal rights and duties,[66] confirmed by the parties' subsequent conduct. In relation to the joint statements, the Tribunal reached the similar conclusion that they were not meant to be legally binding, but were, rather, in the nature of political announcements. The Tribunal scrutinised the instruments in question and the circumstances in which they had been drawn up to determine whether they satisfied the necessary elements of a treaty in international law.[67] Its conclusion

---

63   *Declaration on the Conduct of Parties in the South China Sea*(signed October 17 2012).

64   *Treaty of Amity and Co-operation in Southeast Asia*, opened for signature 24 February 1976, 1025 UNTS 297 (entered into force 21 June 1976) (*"TAC"*).

65   *Convention on Biological Diversity*, opened for signature 5 June 1992, 1760 UNTS 79 (entered into force 29 December 1993).

66   *Philippines v China Arbitration* (n 3) [213]. The Tribunal's dismissal of the possibility of an estoppel arising out of the Philippines' adherence to the DOC has been criticised: Whomersley (n 31) 256–259.

67   *Dispute concerning Delimitation of the Maritime Boundary between Bangladesh and Myanmar in the Bay of Bengal (Bangladesh v Myanmar)*(*Judgment*)(2012) ITLOS Rep 4, 35; *Maritime Delimitation in the Indian Ocean Case* (n 3) 22–23; *Maritime Delimitation and Territorial Questions between Qatar and Bahrain*(*Qatar v Bahrain*) (*Jurisdiction and Admissibility*) [1994] ICJ Rep 112, 120–122; *Land and Maritime Boundary between Cameroon and Nigeria (Cameroon v Nigeria; Equatorial Guinea Intervening)* (*Judgment*) [2002] ICJ Rep 303, 429. The *Vienna Convention on the Law of Treaties*, opened for signature 22 May 1969, 1155 UNTS

that they did not appears to be correct. Of wider significance is the fact that an "agreement" for the purposes of art 281, was held to be a reference to a legally binding instrument, a conclusion that has met with criticism.[68] This finding was shared by the Conciliation Commission in *Conciliation between Timor-Leste and Australia*, which was confronted with Australia's argument that art 281 did not insist upon a legally binding agreement, and that an exchange of letters between the Prime Ministers of the two countries sufficed as an agreement for its purposes. The Conciliation Commission held that the letters did not amount to a legally binding agreement which was what was actually required. The Conciliation Commission found it compelling that art 282, in contrast, clearly contemplates a binding agreement and it would be illogical to expect associated articles to bear contradictory meanings. Moreover, the Conciliation Commission was of the view that it cannot have been intended for art 281 to permit the ousting of pt XV of *UNCLOS*, a binding agreement, by a non-binding one.[69]

By way of contrast, there was no question that the TAC and the CBD were treaties in international law. However, in relation to the TAC, it provides for consensual and "diplomatic" (that is, non-judicial or non-adjudicative) modes for the peaceful resolution of disputes.[70] Its framework led the Tribunal to conclude that the TAC does not constitute "a binding agreement to resolve disputes by negotiation or other chosen means" within the meaning of art 281; rather, it functions as a facilitator enabling the parties to a dispute to agree on the means of settlement. This analysis is shared by academic opinion.[71]

The Tribunal also found that, despite discussions over many years, no settlement had been reached under the DOC, that, if anything, matters had deteriorated and that negotiations could not proceed indefinitely.[72] In this instance, the Tribunal followed the view expressed in the *Southern Bluefin Tuna Cases*.[73] Neither the DOC nor the CBD exclude any other means of settlement, particularly of pt XV.[74] This was also true of the TAC, which explicitly permits

---

331 (entered into force 27 January 1980) art 2(1)(a) defines a treaty as "an international agreement concluded between states in written form and governed by international law".
68 "The South China Sea Awards: A Critical Study" (n 27) 360.
69 *Conciliation between Timor-Leste and Australia* (n 16) [56]–[8].
70 See Gino J Naldi, "The ASEAN Protocol on Dispute Settlement Mechanisms: An Appraisal" (2014) 5(1) *Journal of International Dispute Settlement* 105, 118–119.
71 Ibid.
72 *Philippines v China Arbitration* (n 3) [220].
73 *Southern Bluefin Tuna Arbitration* (n 12) 295.
74 *Philippines v China Arbitration* (n 3) [221]–[223], [283]–[289].

resort to other procedures as set out in *UN Charter* art 33(1),[75] and the joint statements.

The Tribunal's findings on this latter issue are important. It was generally agreed that the DOC did not contain an express exclusion, but the parties disagreed as to its significance. The Philippines argued that an intention to exclude any other procedures must be plain from the agreement itself. China by contrast, relied on the finding in the *Southern Bluefin Tuna Arbitration* that the exclusion need not be stated in express terms, but could be implicit. The Tribunal departed from the opinion in the *Southern Bluefin Tuna Arbitration* and expressed its belief that "the better view is that Article 281 requires some clear statement of exclusion of further procedures" which was in keeping with UNCLOS's object and purpose.[76] The Tribunal reiterated this conclusion regarding the Philippines' claim, along the similar grounds that the CBD's dispute settlement procedures did not explicitly exclude recourse to UNCLOS and that any intention to submit a dispute to another procedure must be stated expressly in the agreement. The *Southern Bluefin Tuna Arbitration* must now be regarded as bad law.[77]

The Tribunal sought to explain that the "exclusion of further procedures" requires states to "opt out" of the pt XV procedures rather than "opting in". "Opting in" applies, rather, to article 282, which contemplates situations where the parties have chosen an alternative agreement and recourse to the pt XV procedures can be had only if they "otherwise agree" – that is, if they opt back in.[78] The result of the Tribunal's interpretation of this clause is that the prevailing position is that states accept the applicability of other procedures unless they specifically reject them.

The question whether a treaty, *in casu* the *Treaty on Certain Maritime Arrangements in the Timor Sea* ("CMATS"),[79] excluded other means of settlement also arose in *Conciliation between Timor-Leste and Australia*. Upon examination, the Conciliation Commission concluded that CMATS was actually an agreement *not* to pursue means of dispute settlement and could not therefore be said to amount to a peaceful mode of dispute settlement of the Parties' own

---

75   TAC (n 64) art 17.
76   *Philippines v China Arbitration* (n 3) [223]–[225].
77   *Southern Bluefin Tuna Arbitration* (n 12) 53–57 (Justice Keith). There was a suggestion to this effect in the MOX *Plant Case* (n 9) 413: see Tullio Treves, "The International Tribunal for the Law of the Sea (2001)" (2001) 11 *Italian Yearbook of International Law* 165, 171.
78   *Philippines v China Arbitration* (n 3) [224].
79   *Treaty on Certain Maritime Arrangements in the Timor Sea*, opened for signature 12 January 2006, 2438 UNTS 359 (entered into force 23 February 2007).

choice as required by art 281.⁸⁰ However, on the assumption that a valid agreement is in place, the Conciliation Commission stated that the application of art 281 depends upon the arrangements for dispute resolution that the agreement makes and not its substantive content.⁸¹

## 2.3  Article 282 and Obligations under General, Regional or Bilateral Agreements

UNCLOS can defer to the dispute settlement means extant under other treaties in accordance with art 282.⁸² According to the Tribunal in the *Philippines v China Arbitration*, this provision contains four elements: (a) that the parties must have agreed through a general, regional or bilateral agreement that, (b) at the request of any party to the dispute, (c) the dispute shall be submitted to a binding procedure, and (d) that the parties have not agreed to "opt back in" to the Section 2 procedures.⁸³ The *ICJ Statute* comes within the scope of this prescription, given that UNCLOS art 282 "is broad enough to encompass an agreement to the jurisdiction of this Court that is expressed in optional clause declarations".⁸⁴

In the *Philippines v China Arbitration*, having already established that the DOC was a political rather than legal agreement, the Tribunal held that it was neither a legally binding agreement for the purposes of art 282, nor did it provide for procedures with a binding decision.⁸⁵ The latter was true also of the TAC.⁸⁶ In addition, the TAC failed to meet other conditions, since disputes could not be submitted at the request of *any* party but instead required the agreement of *all* parties,⁸⁷ nor did it provide for compulsory dispute resolution procedures in lieu of those under UNCLOS.⁸⁸ Regarding the CBD, the Tribunal

---

80  *Conciliation between Timor-Leste and Australia* (n 16) [59]–[64].
81  Ibid [85].
82  *MOX Plant (Ireland v United Kingdom)(Procedural Order No 3)* (2003) 42 ILM 1187, 1190 ("*MOX Plant Procedural Order*"); *Commission v Ireland* (C-459/03) [2006] ECR I-4635, [80]-[139] 4699–710. See Robin Churchill, "Dispute Settlement under the UN Convention on the Law of the Sea: Survey for 2006" (2007) 22(4) *International Journal of Marine and Coastal Law* 463, 468–470.
83  *Philippines v China Arbitration* (n 3) [291].
84  *Maritime Delimitation in the Indian Ocean Case* (n 3) 48–49. The ICJ relied on the *travaux préparatoires* to support its conclusion: at 48–49. This reliance was criticized by Judge Robinson as unsound: at 69–70. See also *MOX Plant Case* (n 9) 430 (Judge Treves); *Max Planck Encyclopedia of Public International Law*, Law of the Sea, Settlement of Disputes (n 2) [11]; Sheehan (n 11) 176–177.
85  *Philippines v China Arbitration* (n 3) [299]–[302].
86  Ibid [309].
87  Ibid [308].
88  Ibid [310].

had already held that it was not an agreement for the settlement of disputes concerning UNCLOS.[89] Nor did it stipulate agreement to submit a dispute to a compulsory procedure involving a binding decision.[90]

The effect of reservations to *ICJ Statute* art 36(2) was considered by the ICJ in the *Maritime Delimitation in the Indian Ocean Case*. The ICJ held that the phrase "or otherwise" includes optional clause declarations, and it therefore followed that an agreement to the ICJ's jurisdiction pursuant thereto, in the form of a valid reservation, comes within the scope of art 282 and applies "in lieu" of the procedures in Section 2.[91] A contrary interpretation would mean priority being given to the procedures in Section 2.[92] Judge Robinson, dissenting, faulted this broad approach (rightly, it is submitted), as it potentially negated the effect of reservations, with serious implications.[93]

### 2.4 Article 283 and Exchange of Views

Parties to a dispute must, according to art 283(1), "proceed expeditiously to an exchange of views regarding its settlement by negotiation or other peaceful means", an obligation that exists for both parties.[94] The rationale of this rule has been described as being "to solve the dispute without recourse to the mechanisms set out in Section 2".[95] It is settled law that these dealings cannot carry on indefinitely, and that a party is therefore under no obligation to continue to exchange views when it believes that no possibility of reaching agreement exists,[96] a position that has been upheld in the most recent cases.[97] Article 283 has been deemed to be of general application to all of UNCLOS and is a

---

89  Ibid [319].
90  Ibid [320].
91  *Maritime Delimitation in the Indian Ocean Case* (n 3) 49.
92  Ibid 50.
93  Ibid 70.
94  *M/V Norstar (Panama v Italy)(Preliminary Objections)* (International Tribunal for the Law of the Sea, Case No 25, 4 November 2016) [208], [213] ("*M/V Norstar Case*"); *Ukrainian Naval Vessels Case* (n 20) [88]; *M/T San Padre Pio (Switzerland v Nigeria) (Provisional Measures)*(International Tribunal for the Law of the Sea, Case No 27, 6 July 2019)[74] ("*M/T San Padre Pio Case*").
95  *M/V Louisa (Saint Vincent and the Grenadines v Spain)(Provisional Measures)* (2008–2010) ITLOS Rep 58, 85 (Judge Wolfrum) ("*M/V Louisa (Provisional Measures)*").
96  See e.g. *Maritime Boundary Arbitration* (n 5) 205–208; *Arctic Sunrise Case* (n 13) 247 [76]; *Guyana and Suriname Maritime Boundary Arbitration(Award)* (2007) 30 RIAA 1, 113–114 ("*Guyana and Suriname Arbitration*").
97  *Ukrainian Naval Vessels Case* (n 20) [87]; *M/T San Padre Pio Case* (n 94)[73].

procedural requirement, or "precondition",[98] that is applicable when the dispute first arises and there is "no controversy between the parties that a dispute exists".[99] The uncertainty surrounding the precise meaning of art 283(1) and the nature of its obligations has become a matter of contention. In the *Chagos Arbitration*, which concerned a dispute between Mauritius and the United Kingdom over the latter's creation of a Marine Protected Area ("MPA") around the 200 nautical mile zone of the Chagos Archipelago, over which Mauritius claims sovereignty,[100] the United Kingdom contended that the Arbitral Tribunal lacked jurisdiction on the grounds that Mauritius had failed to meet the requirement in art 283 to exchange views.[101] Specifically, it claimed that Mauritius had not articulated its views to the United Kingdom on the dispute in question or how it should be resolved. Mauritius, on the other hand, referred to the diplomatic correspondence between the two states regarding the MPA.[102] In the *Philippines v China Arbitration*, China's position was that the two countries had never entered into negotiations over their dispute and that "general exchanges of views" did not constitute negotiations.[103] The Philippines, alternatively, argued, inter alia, that an exchange of views on the general subject matter of the dispute sufficed, but that it was not necessary to discuss the substance of the dispute in detail. In the *Duzgit Integrity Arbitration*, São Tomé and Príncipe argued that Malta had failed to mention the prospect of arbitration and had also failed to specify the provisions of UNCLOS that it was relying upon.[104] The Tribunal stated in the *Chagos Arbitration* that the purpose of art 283 was to ensure that a state was "not taken entirely by surprise by the institution of compulsory proceedings".[105] It was of the view that art 283 does not impose an obligation on the parties to a dispute to engage in

---

98 *M/V Louisa (Saint Vincent and the Grenadines v Spain)*(*Judgment*)(2013) ITLOS Rep 4, 62–63 [24]–[27] (Judge Ndiaye) ("*M/V Louisa Case*").
99 *Maritime Boundary Arbitration* (n 5) 206; *Land Reclamation Case* (n 5) 18.
100 Malcolm Shaw, *Title to Territory in Africa* (Oxford University Press, 1986) 130–134.
101 *Chagos Arbitration* (n 14) [160]. "Exchange of views" has been described as a form of consultation: Office of Legal Affairs, *Handbook on the Peaceful Settlement of Disputes between States*, UN Doc OLA/COD/2394(1992) 10 [26].
102 *Chagos Arbitration* (n 14).
103 *Philippines v China Arbitration* (n 3) [324]–[325]; see further "The South China Sea Awards: A Critical Study" (n 27) 379–381.
104 *Duzgit Integrity Arbitration (Malta v São Tomé and Príncipe)*(*Award*) (Permanent Court of Arbitration, Case No 2014–07, 5 September 2016) [185] ("*Duzgit Integrity Arbitration*").
105 *Chagos Arbitration* (n 14) [382].

negotiations or other forms of dispute settlement on its subject matter.[106] Rather, its purpose is to require the parties to consult on the means of settling their disagreement.[107] The obligation is, therefore, procedural rather than substantive. Under UNCLOS, negotiations do not constitute a pre-condition to compulsory settlement.[108] The reading that the parties are not required to enter into substantive negotiations was subsequently endorsed.[109] All that is required is a sincere exchange of views on the modes by which the dispute can be resolved, not a resolution itself.[110] In this respect, art 283 constitutes a distinct feature of UNCLOS.[111] Nor is there an obligation, in the Tribunal's view on disputants to refer explicitly to UNCLOS, as long as a dispute had arisen with sufficient clarity that the parties were aware of the issues on which they disagreed.[112] UNCLOS does not require the parties to make known their legal claims in detail, only that the subject matter of the negotiations relates to the subject matter of the dispute.[113] The Tribunal in the *Chagos Arbitration* stated that art 283 was to be applied "without an undue formalism as to the manner and

---

106 Ibid [378]. But note the assertion that the better view is that the parties must make every effort to settle the dispute by negotiation or other peaceful means: *Arctic Sunrise Case* (n 13) 279 [7] (Judge Golitsyn). Negotiation is described as a "diplomatic procedure in which representatives of states, in direct personal contact or through correspondence, engage in discussing matters of mutual concern and attempt to resolve disputes": Robert L Bledsoe and Boleslaw A Boczek, *International Law Dictionary* (ABC-Clio, 1987) 302.

107 Or it is about "the expression of views regarding the most appropriate peaceful means of settlement" *Sunrise Case* (n 13) 254 [3] (Judge ad hoc Anderson); see *Maritime Boundary Arbitration* (n 5) 206–207. See also Sheehan who states that the obligation relates to the mechanism to be used in settling the dispute: Sheehan (n 11) 172.

108 *Chagos Arbitration* (n 14) [379]; *Philippines v China Arbitration* (n 3) [345]; *Land Reclamation Case* (n 5) 53 (Judge Jesus). No such obligation is imposed by general international law: *Land and Maritime Boundary between Cameroon and Nigeria (Cameroon v Nigeria) (Preliminary Objections)* [1998] ICJ Rep 275, 302–303 ("*Maritime Boundary between Cameroon and Nigeria*").

109 *Arctic Sunrise Arbitration* (n 3) 28; *Philippines v China Arbitration* (n 3) [333]. See also *M/V Norstar Case* (n 94) [208].

110 *Land Reclamation Case* (n 5) 18; *Philippines v China Arbitration* (n 3) [344], [350]; *M/V Norstar Case* (n 94) [215]. The view has been expressed that the procedural condition of UNCLOS art 283(1) would be met if a genuine attempt to exchange views was made: *M/V Louisa Case* (n 98) 62–63 [25]–[27] (Judge Ndiaye). Hence, a failure to exchange views would not result in a case being dismissed: at 159–160 [17]–[20] (Judge Lucky).

111 *Chagos Arbitration* (n 14) [378]. The point has been made that an obligation to negotiate may exist under treaty law or particular international law: *Philippines v China Arbitration* (n 3) [345]; JG Merrills, "The Means of Dispute Settlement" in Malcolm D Evans (ed), *International Law* (Oxford University Press, 2nd ed, 2006) 533, 536.

112 *Chagos Arbitration* (n 14) [382]; *Duzgit Integrity Arbitration* (n 104) [201].

113 *Philippines v China Arbitration* (n 3) [351].

precision with which such views were exchanged and understood", since an "overly formalistic approach" did not correspond to the reality of diplomatic negotiations where substantive and procedural negotiations could not be conveniently compartmentalised.[114] These pronouncements build upon an earlier finding that distinct negotiations are not required.[115] As had been previously suggested, the requirements of art 283 are not onerous,[116] and the *Chagos Arbitration* has been interpreted as making them even less demanding.[117] Nevertheless, a "degree of specificity" is called for.[118] In the *Philippines v China Arbitration*, the Tribunal found, inter alia, that the DOC had constituted an exchange of views between the Parties.[119]

Turning its attention to the adverb "expeditiously", the Tribunal in the *Chagos Arbitration* rejected the notion of imposing time limits on substantive negotiations or otherwise hurrying the parties.[120] But the Tribunal did not seek to define its meaning. However, in light of the possibility of delaying tactics, the Tribunal considered in the *Arctic Sunrise Arbitration* that its rationale was to discourage parties from improperly delaying or excluding resolution of the dispute.[121] Consequently, a ten-day limit was not deemed unreasonable in another case.[122] One commentator stressed that the importance of the use of the term "expeditiously" derives from the fact of the different procedures available to the parties.[123] Nevertheless, states are expected to enter into negotiations

---

114   Ibid. But this should not be an "empty formality": *Land Reclamation Case* (n 5) 39 (Judge Chandrasehkara Rao). This is in keeping with the ICJ's unceremonious approach to matters of form regarding jurisdiction: Malcolm Shaw, *International Law* (Cambridge University Press, 6th ed, 2008) 1070.
115   *Maritime Boundary Arbitration* (n 5) 206.
116   Ibid 206–207; *Bay of Bengal Maritime Boundary Arbitration (Bangladesh v India)(Award)* (Permanent Court of Arbitration, Case No 2010–16, 7 July 2014) [72].
117   Stefan Talmon, "The Chagos Marine Protected Area Arbitration: Expansion of the Jurisdiction of Part XV Courts and Tribunals" (2016) 65(4) *International and Comparative Law Quarterly* 927, 932.
118   Whomersley (n 31) 261.
119   *Philippines v ChinaArbitration* (n 3) [335]. However, according to one writer, the exchanges relied upon by the Philippines lacked the necessary specificity: Wholmersley (n 31) 261.
120   *Philippines v China Arbitration* (n 3) [378].
121   *Arctic Sunrise Arbitration* (n 3) 29. In *M/V Norstar Case* (n 94) [217], the ITLOS found that, by ignoring correspondence from Panama, Italy had precluded an exchange of views. See also *M/T San Padre Pio Case* (n 94)[72].
122   *Ukrainian Naval Vessels Case* (n 20) [86].
123   AO Adede, "The Basic Structure of the Dispute Settlement Part of the Law of the Sea Convention" (1982) 11(1–2) *Ocean Development and International Law* 125, 129.

"without delay".[124] In light of these pronouncements, the procedural requirements set out in art 283 cannot be said to be unduly burdensome.

## 2.5 The Existence of a Dispute Concerning the Interpretation or Application of UNCLOS

The exercise of jurisdiction by a court or tribunal under UNCLOS pt XV is predicated upon the existence of a dispute concerning the interpretation or application of UNCLOS. Phrases to this effect are to be found in several provisions of pt XV and arts 284–288.[125] Thus, under art 286, a party to a dispute concerning the interpretation or application of UNCLOS that has not been resolved under Section 1 can submit it to a court or tribunal having jurisdiction. Thus art 288, subject to the limitations in Section 3, confers jurisdiction *ratione materiae* on the aforementioned courts or tribunals concerning the interpretation or application of UNCLOS or any international agreement related to its purposes. The latter grant, in para(2), is said to be a source of "supplemental" jurisdiction, i.e., jurisdiction over non-UNCLOS claims.[126] It should initially be noted that the preposition "concerning" has been given a broad meaning.[127] The definition of a legal dispute in international law is long established and universally accepted,[128] and for that reason was adopted by the ITLOS in the *Southern Bluefin Tuna Cases*.[129] In addition, the ITLOS has also approved the statement

---

124  *Handbook on the Peaceful Settlement of Disputes between States*(n 101) 11 [28].
125  See also UNCLOS art 290 on provisional measures.
126  Peter Tzeng, "Supplemental Jurisdiction under UNCLOS" (2016) 38(2) *Houston Journal of International Law* 499, 506–507, 516–519.
127  *M/V Louisa Case* (n 98) 31 [83]; see "The South China Sea Awards: A Critical Study" (n 27) 314–318.
128  A legal dispute has been defined as "a disagreement on a point of law or fact, a conflict of legal views or of interests": *Mavrommatis Palestine Concessions (Greece v United Kingdom) (Jurisdiction)* [1924] PCIJ (ser A) No 2, 11; *Land and Maritime Boundary between Cameroon and Nigeria* (n 108) 314–315; see Manley O Hudson, *The Permanent Court of International Justice 1920–1942* (MacMillan, 1943) 454–456. Additionally, the claim of one party must be positively opposed by the other: *South West Africa Cases (Ethiopia v South Africa)(Preliminary Objections)* [1962] ICJ Rep 319, 328.
129  *Southern Bluefin Tuna Arbitration* (n 12) 293. The ITLOS has further accepted the ICJ's view that a dispute may exist by inference or stance: *M/V Norstar Case* (n 94) [99]–[102]; *Ukrainian Naval Vessels Case* (n 20) [43]; *M/T San Padre Pio Case* (n 94)[57], citing, inter alia, *Land and Maritime Boundary between Cameroon and Nigeria* (n 108) 315; *Application of the International Convention on the Elimination of All Forms of Racial Discrimination (Georgia v Russia)(Preliminary Objections)* [2011] ICJ Rep 70, 84 ("*Application of CERD Case*").

of the ICJ in the *Interpretation of Peace Treaties Case*[130] that whether a difference of opinion exists "is a matter for objective determination".[131] The criteria to be satisfied are not demanding.[132] In the *Philippines v China Arbitration*, the Tribunal reaffirmed this jurisprudence.[133] It therefore follows that the established principle of international law that a court or tribunal cannot decline to take cognisance of a dispute simply because it has other aspects, perhaps political,[134] has been adopted in the context of *UNCLOS*.[135]

If it has been established objectively that a dispute does exist,[136] it then becomes necessary for the court or tribunal to determine the actual issue in the case and the object of the claim,[137] and whether the case is properly concerned with the interpretation or application of *UNCLOS*. According to the ITLOS, this requires specificity from the applicant about the particular provisions of *UNCLOS* allegedly violated by the respondent, rather than the making of general or undefined statements.[138] In the *Philippines v China Arbitration*, the Tribunal pointed out the decisive nature of such findings for jurisdictional

---

130  *Interpretation of Peace Treaties with Bulgaria, Hungary and Romania (Advisory Opinion) (First Phase)* [1950] ICJ Rep 65, 74. See also *Fisheries Jurisdiction (Spain v Canada)(Judgment)* [1998] ICJ Rep 432, 447–449 ("*Fisheries Jurisdiction Case*").
131  *Southern Bluefin Tuna Arbitration* (n 12) 38–39.
132  In *Maritime Boundary Arbitration*, the Tribunal stated that the "fact that the precise scope of the dispute had not been fully articulated or clearly depicted does not preclude the existence of a dispute, so long as the record indicates with reasonable clarity the scope of the legal differences between the Parties": *Maritime Boundary Arbitration* (n 5) 204. In *Arctic Sunrise Arbitration(Netherlands v Russia)(Award on Jurisdiction)* (Permanent Court of Arbitration, Case No 2014-02, 26 November 2014) ("*Arctic Sunrise Arbitration (Jurisdiction)*"), the Tribunal found that it was apparent from the exchange of diplomatic notes between the parties that a dispute existed between them: at [61].
133  *Philippines v China Arbitration* (n 3) [149].
134  See, e.g., *United States Diplomatic and Consular Staff in Tehran (United States of America v Iran) (Judgment)* [1980] ICJ Rep 3, 19–20; *Military and Paramilitary Activities in and Against Nicaragua (Nicaragua v United States of America)(Jurisdiction and Admissibility)* [1984] ICJ Rep 392; *Accordance with International Law of the Unilateral Declaration of Independence in Respect of Kosovo(Advisory Opinion)* [2010] ICJ Rep 403, 415; Merrills, *International Dispute Settlement* (n 2) 155–159.
135  In the *Southern Bluefin Tuna Arbitration*(n 12) 293, Japan argued that the dispute was scientific rather than legal, but the ITLOS concluded that the differences between the parties also concerned points of law.
136  *Fisheries Jurisdiction Case* (n 130) 448.
137  Ibid 449; *Chagos Arbitration* (n 14) [208]; *Nuclear Tests (New Zealand v France)(Judgment)* [1974] ICJ Rep 457, 466.
138  *M/V Norstar Case* (n 94) [109]. This is required by *ITLOS Statute* art 54(2).

purposes, since failure to meet these requirements would result in a lack of jurisdiction.[139]

The characterisation of the dispute played a crucial role in the *Chagos Arbitration*. The United Kingdom objected to the Tribunal's jurisdiction to entertain Mauritius' claims regarding which state was, or was not, the "coastal state" for the purposes of UNCLOS, on the grounds that the issue at stake was actually one of sovereignty over the Chagos Archipelago and that that matter did not engage the interpretation or application of UNCLOS, as required by art 288(1). Mauritius's stance was that it was seeking an interpretation of the term "coastal state" as used in UNCLOS. But the British position more generally was that the Tribunal was being asked to interpret UNCLOS in such a manner as to broaden the scope of its compulsory jurisdiction.[140]

The Tribunal's view was that it was clear that a dispute existed between the parties as to territorial sovereignty over the *Chagos Archipelago*, and that disputes over territorial sovereignty exclusively did not concern the interpretation or application of UNCLOS.[141] However, the question arose whether UNCLOS art 288(1) confers jurisdiction on a court or tribunal over disputes concerning territorial sovereignty which are incidental to matters governed by UNCLOS, or mixed disputes.[142] It is important to note that territorial disputes are excluded by virtue of art 298(1)(a)(i), although there is a body of opinion which maintains that courts or tribunals can exercise jurisdiction over mixed disputes.[143] The Tribunal was of the opinion that it had not been envisaged that disputes over territorial sovereignty would come within the ambit of UNCLOS, or else an exclusion similar to that of art 298 could have been expected.[144] However, that did not mean that a court or tribunal would not be able to

---

139   *Philippines v China Arbitration* (n 3) [150]. Indeed, a link must exist between the alleged facts and UNCLOS: *M/V Louisa Case* (n 98) 34 [99]; *M/V Norstar Case* (n 94) [110]. However, China has disputed the Tribunal's conclusion:"The South China Sea Awards: A Critical Study"(n 27) 331–335.

140   In the *Duzgit Integrity Arbitration* (n 104) [125]–[131], [138], São Tomé and Príncipe raised a similar unsuccessful argument that Malta's claims were not based on specific provisions of UNCLOS but on extraneous legal norms.

141   *Chagos Arbitration* (n 14) [209]–[212], [215]–[217]. It appears that Russia is relying on this argument to resist the assumption of jurisdiction by the arbitral tribunal in the pending *Dispute Concerning Coastal State Rights in the Black Sea, Sea of Azov, and Kerch Strait (Ukraine v Russia)*: see Tzeng, "*Ukraine v Russia* and *Philippines v China*: Jurisdiction and Legitimacy" (n 46) 3–7.

142   It had previously been established that courts and tribunals enjoyed incidental jurisdiction: *Guyana and Suriname Arbitration* (n 96) 114.

143   See Talmon(n 117) 974 n 122.

144   *Chagos Arbitration* (n 14) [213]–[219].

address any issue of territorial sovereignty. As a general proposition, the Tribunal stated that where a dispute concerns the interpretation or application of UNCLOS, the jurisdiction of a court or tribunal under art 288(1) extends to making such findings of fact or ancillary determinations of law as are necessary to resolve the dispute.[145] However, where the "real issue in the case" and the "object of the claim" do not relate to the interpretation or application of UNCLOS, an incidental association between the dispute and a matter regulated by the UNCLOS is not enough to bring the dispute within the reach of art 288(1).[146] That a minor issue of territorial sovereignty could indeed be ancillary to the interpretation or application of UNCLOS could not be ruled out, but the Tribunal held that that was not so in the present case and that it therefore did not have jurisdiction over this particular claim.[147] The Tribunal therefore accepted a restrictive reading of this text, which met with criticism from the dissenting judges who argued for a less stringent approach, requiring only a "nexus" between the facts and UNCLOS.[148] The majority opinion is deemed by some scholars as the better view.[149]

While the adjectives "ancillary" and "incidental" may raise questions as to their precise meaning,[150] it should be observed that it has long been accepted in international law that the "interpretation of other international agreements is indisputably within the competence of the Court if such interpretation must be regarded as incidental to a decision on a point in regard to which it has jurisdiction".[151] This capacity had previously been sustained by the Tribunal in the *Guyana and Suriname Arbitration*.[152]

Similar considerations arose in the *Philippines v China Arbitration*. It will be recalled that China considered that the case was properly one of territorial

---

145  Alan E Boyle, "Dispute Settlement and the Law of the Sea Convention: Problems of Fragmentation and Jurisdiction" (1997) 46(1) *International and Comparative Law Quarterly* 37, 49–50; Tzeng, "Supplemental Jurisdiction under UNCLOS" (n 126) 562–563.
146  *Chagos Arbitration* (n 14) [220]. See *Application of CERD Case* (n 129) 183, 185 (Judge Koroma).
147  *Chagos Arbitration* (n 14) [221].
148  *Chagos Marine Protected Area* (*Mauritius v United Kingdom*)(*Dissenting and Concurring Opinion of Judges Kateka and Wolfrum*) (UNCLOS Arbitral Tribunal, 18 March 2015)[44]–[5]; see also Tzeng, "Supplemental Jurisdiction under UNCLOS" (n 126) 569–572.
149  Donald A Colson and Brian J Vohrer, "*In re* Chagos Marine Protected Area" (2015) 109(4) *American Journal of International Law* 845, 851; Alexander Proelss, "The Limits of Jurisdiction *Ratione Materiae* of UNCLOS Tribunals" (2018) 46(2) *Hitotsubashi Journal of Law and Politics* 46, 53–54.
150  Talmon (n 117) 935–936.
151  *Certain German Interests in Polish Upper Silesia* (*Germany v Poland*) (*Preliminary Objections*) [1925] PCIJ (ser A) No 6, 18; see Hudson (n 128) 649–650.
152  *Guyana and Suriname Arbitration* (n 96) 114.

sovereignty, which was excluded from the UNCLOS dispute settlement procedures by the terms of its *Declaration* when it ratified UNCLOS. In light of China's *Declaration*, the Philippines stressed that it was not submitting questions of sovereignty to be determined by the Tribunal.[153] Although the Tribunal accepted that the two parties were engaged in a dispute concerning territorial sovereignty over certain islands in the South China Sea, it did not follow that this was a true categorisation of the Philippine claim, which related primarily to other matters, pertaining to Chinese activities in the South China Sea and maritime features occupied by China, which did have to do with specific provisions of the UNCLOS.[154] It was possible for the Tribunal to rule on these aspects of the Philippines' submissions without necessarily addressing the question of sovereignty.[155] Notwithstanding that its jurisdiction would necessarily be constrained by China's *Declaration*, the Tribunal was not precluded from examining these issues, but it was careful to point out that it intended to ensure that its decisions did not impact on the parties' claims to sovereignty.[156] The Tribunal's findings have been criticised for failing to examine the Philippines' claims meticulously.[157] The Tribunal additionally rejected the Chinese categorisation of the dispute over the status of certain maritime features as being about the delimitation of maritime boundaries; rather, the dispute was about the existence of an entitlement to maritime zones, a separate issue.[158] This distinction has attracted criticism as being artificial and difficult to apply in actuality.[159]

While the Tribunals did not definitely come out in support of the proposition that jurisdiction could be exercised over mixed disputes, it is nevertheless noteworthy that they were receptive to these arguments and provided them with guarded endorsement.

### 2.6  *Provisional Measures*

A court or tribunal may prescribe provisional measures under art 290(1), whereas under art 290(5) the ITLOS is conferred a residual jurisdiction to order measures pending the constitution of an arbitral tribunal, described as "a

---

153   *Philippines v China Arbitration* (n 3) [153].
154   Ibid [151]–[153].
155   Ibid.
156   Ibid [153].
157   Whomersley (n 31) 248; "The South China Sea Awards: A Critical Study" (n 27) 279–287.
158   *Philippines v China Arbitration* (n 3) [155]–[157].
159   Whomersley (n 31) 248–252; see also Proelss (n 149) 53–56. It has been reiterated that the interpretation or application of UNCLOS was not at issue: "The South China Sea Awards: A Critical Study" (n 27) 336–340.

relative innovation".[160] An unusual aspect of this arrangement is that the ITLOS is required to make a judgment in relation to another body. However, it has been deemed that different procedures are envisaged and an arbitral tribunal is not bound by the ITLOS's prior measures where the subsequent request made to the arbitral tribunal is not simply a revision of these measures but is considered to be a new one.[161] Another feature is that before granting provisional measures, the ITLOS must satisfy itself that the arbitral tribunal would have prima facie jurisdiction.[162] The ITLOS has reiterated its previous jurisprudence on provisional measures, consistent with established international practice,[163] that it need not satisfy itself that it has jurisdiction on the merits and that its decision does not prejudge the question of jurisdiction or merits of the case.[164] But the view that, in its early jurisprudence, the ITLOS had set a low ceiling for establishing prima facie jurisdiction attracted criticism.[165] Indeed, one judge went as far as describing it as "perhaps virtually non-existent".[166] Nonetheless, this trend has continued, such as in the *Arctic Sunrise Case*[167] and the *Enrica Lexie Case*.[168] An overview of the cases suggests that the ITLOS's consideration of this issue can appear to lack coherence, its reasoning often being brief and subjectively based on the parties' submissions,[169] while at other times involving a deeper examination.[170] But the ITLOS is not isolated in its

---

160  Shabtai Rosenne, "The International Tribunal for the Law of the Sea: Survey for 1999" (2000) 15(4) *International Journal of Marine and Coastal Law* 442, 467.
161  *Enrica Lexie Case* (n 6) [72]–[74].
162  *M/V Saiga (No 2)(Saint Vincent and the Grenadines v Guinea) (Provisional Measures)* (1998) ITLOS Rep 24, 37 [29], 39 [46]; *M/V Louisa (Provisional Measures)* (n 95) 69.
163  See Thomas A Mensah, "Provisional Measures in the International Tribunal for the Law of the Sea (ITLOS)" (2002) 62(1) *Zeitschrift für ausländisches öffentliches Recht und Volkerrecht* 43, 43–44.
164  *Arctic Sunrise Case* (n 13) [100]; *Ukrainian Naval Vessels Case* (n 20) [37].
165  Rosemary Rayfuse, "The Future of Compulsory Dispute Settlement under the Law of the Sea Convention" (2005) 36(4) *Victoria University Wellington Law Review* 683, 696–697. Critics would feel vindicated in their admonition when the ITLOS ultimately held, contrary to its previous finding at the provisional measures phase, that it lacked jurisdiction: *M/V Louisa Case* (n 98).
166  *M/T San Padre Pio (Switzerland v Nigeria) (Provisional Measures) (Dissenting Opinion of Judge Lucky)* (International Tribunal for the Law of the Sea, Case No 27, 6 July 2019)[37].
167  *Arctic Sunrise Case* (n 13) 243 [58].
168  *Enrica Lexie Case* (n 6) [52]–[55].
169  See, e.g., *M/V Louisa (Provisional Measures)* (n 95) 67 [56]; *Arctic Sunrise Case* (n 13) 246 [68]; *Enrica Lexie Case* (n 6) [72]–[75]. See Churchill, "Survey for 2013" (n 18) 22; Guilfoyle and Miles (n 42) 279; Lando (n 44) 9, 19.
170  See e.g. *Southern Bluefin Tuna Arbitration*(n 12); *ARA Libertad (Argentina v Ghana)(Provisional Measures)*(2012) ITLOS Rep 332 ("*ARA Libertad Case*"); *Ukrainian Naval Vessels Case* (n 20) [36].

approach, as the low threshold has also been applied at times by the ICJ and much also seems to depend on the circumstances of the case, the degree of urgency or the extent of agreement between the parties.[171] And it should not be overlooked that the question of jurisdiction can be revisited at the merits stage.

### 2.7 Article 293(1) and Compatible Rules of International Law

Article 293(1) enables a court or tribunal to apply compatible rules of international law,[172] although these adjudicative bodies operate under restrictions as to the norms of international law or treaties which they can invoke,[173] with other treaties and customary law being but a necessary adjunct.[174] While UNCLOS fails to elucidate what these rules might be,[175] recourse has been had to customary law[176] and treaties.[177] And this trend has continued in recent cases. Thus, the principle of estoppel has been considered and applied,[178] as has that of due process.[179] In the *South China Sea Arbitration*, the Tribunal adopted the principle that states engaged in dispute resolution must refrain from aggravating and extending a dispute.[180]

Notwithstanding that an ordinary reading of this provision suggests that it does not confer jurisdiction on courts or tribunals,[181] a number of previous cases revealed that these bodies seemed willing to rely on general rules of

---

171  Churchill, "Survey for 2013" (n 18) 22; Lando (n 44) 7–8, 20–24. In order to assess the urgency of the situation, the ITLOS has resolved that the right to be protected must be "plausible": *Enrica Lexie Case* (n 6) [84]; *Ukrainian Naval Vessels Case* (n 20) [91]; *M/T San Padre Pio Case* (n 941) [77].

172  *Maritime Boundary Arbitration* (n 5) 210. See generally Michael Wood, "The International Tribunal for the Law of the Sea and General International Law" (2007) 22(3) *International Journal of Marine and Coastal Law* 351.

173  Günther Jaenicke, "Dispute Settlement under the Convention on the Law of the Sea" (1983) 43 *Zeitschrift für ausländisches öffentliches Recht und Volkerrecht* 813, 822; Merrills, *International Dispute Settlement* (n 2) 175.

174  Jaenicke (n 173) 816.

175  Its provisions being described as creating a "simple and imprecise formula": *Maritime Boundary Arbitration* (n 5) 210.

176  Thus, in *M/V Saiga (No 2)* (n 8) 61–62 [155] and *Guyana and Suriname Arbitration* (n 96) 119–126, the ITLOS and Tribunal respectively found the law on the use of force to be applicable. In *ARA Libertad Case* (n 170) 348 [95], the law on immunity of warships was applied.

177  Including the *Charter of the United Nations*: *Guyana and Suriname Arbitration* (n 96) 113.

178  *Chagos Arbitration* (n 14) [435]–[439]; see also *M/V Norstar Case* (n 94) [301].

179  *Tomimaru (Japan v Russia)(Judgment)*(2005–2007) ITLOS Rep 74, 96 [75]–[76].

180  *South China Sea Arbitration* (n 42) [1173].

181  Tzeng, "Supplemental Jurisdiction under UNCLOS" (n 126) 519–520.

international law that prima facie do not appear to have an obvious association with UNCLOS, in order to assert jurisdiction.[182] In later instances where claimant states have sought to rely on this jurisprudence, they have met with the assertion that art 293(1) is not intended to extend the jurisdiction of a court or tribunal.[183] In the *Chagos Arbitration*, the Tribunal observed that the parties more or less agreed that art 293(1) did not of itself constitute a basis of jurisdiction.[184] But UNCLOS does not exist in a vacuum, and in the *Arctic Sunrise Arbitration*, the Tribunal stated that in order to interpret and apply UNCLOS it may sometimes prove necessary to invoke general international law.[185] It explained that art 293 was not "a means to obtain a determination that some treaty ... has been violated, unless that treaty is otherwise a source of jurisdiction, or unless the treaty otherwise directly applies pursuant to the *Convention*".[186] In this case, the Netherlands had argued that the arrest and detention of the vessel and persons by Russia were in breach of a number of provisions of the *International Covenant on Civil and Political Rights*("ICCPR").[187] The Tribunal was of the view that it could take account of international human rights standards in interpreting and applying UNCLOS, but that it had the capacity neither to apply directly the ICCPR's provisions nor verify whether they had been violated.[188]

These dicta were cited with approval in the *Duzgit Integrity Arbitration*. The Tribunal endorsed the proposition that art 293 does not extend the jurisdiction of a court or tribunal, but that a court or tribunal may have to invoke general international law, such as the law of treaties, and that it further allows for relevant international law to be taken into account.[189] In this particular case, the principles of necessity and proportionality applied to the exercise of enforcement powers by a state.[190]

---

182  *Guyana and Suriname Arbitration* (n 963) 112–113. See also *M/V Saiga (No 2)* (n 8) 62–63 [155]; *M/V Virginia G Case* (n 8) 25–9 [54]. Cf contra *ARA Libertad Case* (n 170) 364–365[6]–[7] (Judges Wolfrum and Cot). See also Tzeng, "Supplemental Jurisdiction under UNCLOS" (n 126) 520–523; Wood (n 172) 357.
183  *Arctic Sunrise Arbitration* (n 3) 33; see Wood (n 172) 357.
184  *Chagos Arbitration* (n 14) [181].
185  *Arctic Sunrise Arbitration* (n 3) 33.
186  Ibid (citations omitted).
187  Ibid [140]. *International Covenant on Civil and Political Rights*, opened for signature 16 December 1966, 999 UNTS 171 (entered into force 23 March 1976); see also *Enrica Lexie Case* (n 6) [111]–[113]; *M/T San Padre Pio Case* (n 94) 7 [26].
188  *Arctic Sunrise Arbitration* (n 3) 34; see also *M/V Louisa Case* (n 98) 46 [155].
189  *Duzgit Integrity Arbitration* (n 104) [207]–[208].
190  Ibid [209].

The case law reveals an inconsistency.[191] In the later cases, the tribunals have reasserted the distinction between jurisdiction and the applicable law, and the fact that the latter is dependent on establishing the former.[192] Insofar as compatible international law is concerned, the tribunals have adopted a pragmatic approach and have necessarily and sensibly continued to resort to general international law as circumstances demand. While the finding that claims based *directly* on treaties other than UNCLOS are inadmissible[193] has been adhered to, its effect has to an extent been minimised by the readiness of the tribunals to interpret UNCLOS "by reference to relevant context"[194] in other treaties and, by extension, to shame wrongdoers. Previous findings that states had violated general international law rather than UNCLOS as such[195] may have caused some surprise,[196] but it is noteworthy that in the *South China Sea Arbitration* the Tribunal continued on this path when it held that China had breached its obligations under, inter alia, general international law not to aggravate or extend the dispute.[197]

### 2.8 *Article 295 and Exhaustion of Local Remedies*

The law heretofore applied on the exhaustion of local remedies was that, in conformity with customary law, the exhaustion of local remedies is a condition for the exercise of diplomatic protection but is inapplicable where a state is directly injured by the act of another state.[198] However, in those circumstances where elements of both situations are found (that is, injury to a state's indirect or direct rights), it becomes necessary to establish which part is "preponderant".[199] These tests were affirmed in the *Duzgit Integrity Arbitration*.[200]

---

191  The case law is adeptly analysed in Peter Tzeng, "Jurisdiction and Applicable Law Under UNCLOS" (2016) 126(1) *Yale Law Journal* 242.
192  Ibid 245–248; Proelss (n 149) 57.
193  *MOX Plant Procedural Order* (n 82) 1189–1190 [19].
194  *Arctic Sunrise Arbitration* (n 3) 34.
195  *M/V Saiga (No 2)* (n 8) 63 [159]; *Guyana and Suriname Arbitration* (n 93) 139.
196  Tzeng, "Jurisdiction and Applicable Law Under UNCLOS" (n 191); Wood (n 172) 358.
197  *South China Sea Arbitration* (n 42) [1203(B)(16)].
198  *M/V Saiga (No 2)* (n 8) 45–46[95]–[101]; *M/V Virginia G Case* (n 8) 53–54 [153]. See also *M/V Norstar Case*(n 95) [265]–[268].
199  *M/V Virginia G Case* (n 8) 54–55[157].
200  *Duzgit Integrity Arbitration* (n 104) [151]–[155]. In both cases, the Tribunals relied upon the International Law Commission Draft Articles on Diplomatic Protection as stating the correct law on this issue: see International Law Commission "Commentary on Article 14" reproduced in David Harris, *Cases and Materials on International Law* (Sweet & Maxwell, 7th ed, 2010) 529–530.

## 2.9 Exceptions to Compulsory Settlement under Articles 297 and 298

It will be recalled that certain categories of dispute may be excluded in accordance with arts 297 and 298, which have been held not to apply to the territorial sea.[201] Article 297(1) provides that disputes concerning the exercise by a coastal state of its sovereign rights or jurisdiction are subject to the compulsory procedures in three enumerated cases, relating principally to the EEZ. An important development in the *Chagos Arbitration* was the Tribunal's interpretation of art 297 to expand jurisdiction beyond that which would follow from an application of art 288(1) alone, on the basis that art 297(1) includes references to sources of law other than *UNCLOS*.[202] The ability to pass judgment over related legal instruments, including a number of multilateral treaties predating *UNCLOS*, would therefore be conferred on such courts and tribunals.[203]

The *Chagos Arbitration* Tribunal made another significant ruling concerning the situations specified in art 297(1). This provision had previously been interpreted as limiting the application of the dispute resolution procedures to "disputes concerning the exercise by a coastal state of its sovereign rights or jurisdiction in certain identified cases only".[204] However, this reading was explicitly rejected by the Tribunal, which stated that art 297(1) "is phrased entirely in affirmative terms and includes no exceptions to the jurisdiction the Tribunal may exercise".[205] The Tribunal reasoned that if art 297(1) meant that jurisdiction was conferred only in the cases listed therein, the exclusions of art 297(3) would be redundant, as they would already be excluded by virtue of their non-inclusion in art 297(1).[206] It concluded that[207]

> Article 297(1) reaffirms a tribunal's jurisdiction over the enumerated cases ... it does not restrict a tribunal from considering disputes concerning the exercise of sovereign rights and jurisdiction in other cases. Where a dispute concerns "the interpretation or application" of the [UNCLOS], and provided none of the express exceptions to jurisdiction set out in Article 297(2) and 297(3) are applicable, jurisdiction for the compulsory settlement of disputes flows from Article 288(1). It is not necessary that

---

201   *Philippines v China Arbitration* (n 3) [407], [410]; *South China Sea Arbitration* (n 42) [759], [928].
202   *Chagos Arbitration* (n 14) [316].
203   Ibid [321].
204   *Southern Bluefin Tuna Arbitration* (n 12) 44–45. See also Churchill and Lowe (n 2) 455.
205   *Chagos Arbitration* (n 14) [307]–[308].
206   Ibid [308].
207   Ibid [317].

the Parties' dispute also fall within one of the cases specified in Article 297(1).

A restrictive understanding of Article 297(1) has thus been replaced by an expansive one.[208]

One of the disputes that may be the object of exclusion under art 298(1)(a)(i) is one regarding the interpretation or application of UNCLOS in relation to sea boundary delimitations. In a general sense, art 298(1)(a)(i) has been understood as aiming to set the limits of what a party can exclude unilaterally from compulsory settlement of disputes, while simultaneously setting certain preconditions to the invocation of compulsory conciliation (ie, the exclusion of pre-existing disputes and the absence of a negotiated agreement).[209] That a dispute may have pre-existing elements may not result in its exclusion should the interpretation or application of UNCLOS also be at issue.[210]

In the *Philippines and China Arbitration*, the Tribunal had to address China's *Declaration* which excluded many of the exceptions in Article 298. One possible exclusion concerned the status of certain maritime features in the South China Sea and the overlapping entitlements to maritime zones they could create, which might necessitate a maritime boundary delimitation and would therefore not be allowed. However, the Tribunal found that the delimitation of maritime boundaries was not at issue but in actuality concerned the existence of entitlements to maritime zones. Disputes over entitlements need not imply delimitation, and consequently the exception did not apply to such cases.[211]

At the merits phase, the Tribunal considered the possibility of China claiming "historic rights" in the South China Sea, and whether these could come within the exclusion of "historic bays or titles". First, the Tribunal clarified that this exception to art 298(1)(a)(i) extends to disputes involving historic bays or titles generally and is not limited to disputes over delimitation.[212] The Tribunal then sought to elucidate and distinguish the terms "historic rights" and "historic titles". It defined the former as a general expression which can refer to any rights that a state may possess, which may include not only sovereignty but also rights not amounting to sovereignty such as fishing rights, whereas the latter refers to sovereignty over maritime areas derived from historical

---

208   Klein (n 2) 141; Talmon (n 117) 943.
209   *Conciliation between Timor-Leste and Australia* (n 16) [66].
210   Ibid [72].
211   *Philippines v China Arbitration* (n 3) [155]–[157]. See further above n 159. For criticism of this approach, see "The South China Sea Awards: A Critical Study" (n 27) 318–321.
212   *South China Sea Arbitration* (n 42) [215].

circumstances.²¹³ The Tribunal observed that art 298(1)(a)(i) was not intended to exclude jurisdiction over "a broad and unspecified category of possible claims to historic rights falling short of sovereignty", but was confined to disputes involving historic titles.²¹⁴

In the *Arctic Sunrise Arbitration*, the Tribunal had to interpret the scope of Russia's UNCLOS *Declaration*, which it claimed, in accordance with art 298, to have the effect of excluding compulsory procedures regarding disputes concerning law enforcement activities. Properly interpreted, art 298(1)(b) allows states to exclude only such disputes which are also excluded from the jurisdiction of a court or tribunal under art 297, paras (2)–(3), which concern disputes over marine scientific research and fisheries, and not every such dispute, as the Russian *Declaration* purported and which the Tribunal considered to be too broad in scope. Nevertheless, did the Russian *Declaration* apply to one of the permitted exceptions in art 297(2)–(3)? Clearly the dispute did not come within either category, and consequently the Russian *Declaration* was inapplicable.²¹⁵ The facts in this case presented the Tribunal with a relatively straightforward task of interpretation.

The exclusion of military activities in accordance with art 298(1)(b) was at issue in the *Ukrainian Naval Vessels Case*. Ukraine categorised the arrest and detention of its warships by Russia as law enforcement activities, whereas Russia claimed that its actions came within the "military activities" exception. The general principle set down by the Tribunal was that the distinction between the two activities rested on an objective evaluation of the nature of the activities in question, taking into account relevant circumstances.²¹⁶ The Tribunal found that the dispute focused on the parties' conflicting understanding of the right of passage in the Kerch Strait, which was not therefore of a military nature.²¹⁷

Article 298(1)(a)(i) refers to disputes arising "subsequent to the entry into force" of UNCLOS. The meaning of this phrase arose in the *Conciliation between Timor-Leste and Australia*. The question that was considered here was whether this constituted a reference to the entry into force of UNCLOS, 16 November 1994, or its entry into force as between the particular parties to the dispute.²¹⁸

---

213  Ibid [225]–[226].
214  Ibid [226], [229]. For criticism of this approach, see "The South China Sea Awards: A Critical Study" (n 27) 322–325.
215  *Arctic Sunrise Arbitration (Jurisdiction)* (n 132) [69]–[77]; *Arctic Sunrise Case* (n 13) 241 [45].
216  *Ukrainian Naval Vessels Case* (n 20) [66].
217  Ibid [72].
218  *Conciliation between Timor-Leste and Australia* (n 16) [73].

The Conciliation Commission reached the common sense conclusion that the ordinary meaning of the phrase supported the former interpretation, a conclusion also supported by the negotiating history.[219]

Article 298(1)(a)(i) proceeds to refer to disputes "where no agreement within a reasonable period of time is reached in negotiations between the parties". According to the Conciliation Commission, no prior negotiation between the parties is actually required, as such an obligation would in effect hand a party a veto to resort to compulsory conciliation by refusing to negotiate.[220]

## 2.10 Article 300 and Abuse of Rights

Article 300 enshrines the principles of good faith and abuse of rights, and has been held to apply to UNCLOS in its entirety and to be incapable of being "independently deployed".[221] The applicant must be specific about the rights and obligations that it believes a state to have failed to fulfil in good faith or that it alleges were exercised in an abusive manner, and not simply make general allegations about the conduct of a state.[222] Clearly the unilateral invocation of the dispute settlement procedure does not constitute an abuse of right.[223] In the *Duzgit Integrity Arbitration*, the Tribunal reaffirmed the previous pronouncements on art 300 that it was "an overarching provision" which applies to the whole of UNCLOS.[224] It stated that it may be invoked when "rights, jurisdiction and freedoms recognised in the *Convention* are exercised in an abusive manner".[225] Consequently, "a claim pursuant to art 300 is necessarily linked to the alleged violation of another provision" of UNCLOS,[226] and art 300 is therefore not a "stand-alone" provision.[227] The suggestion that art 300 could provide an independent cause of action in instances of "egregious" violations and "consequences of such gravity"[228] does not seem to have traction.

In the *Duzgit Integrity Arbitration*, the Tribunal had observed that there was little guidance as to the legal test to be satisfied to establish a breach of art 300.[229] Much will evidently be dependent on the facts and the available evidence. In light of the uncertainty surrounding the status of the doctrine in

---

219 Ibid [74]–[75].
220 Ibid [78]. Cf *contra* Sheehan (n 11) 179.
221 *M/V Louisa Case* (n 98) 43 [137].
222 *M/V Virginia G Case* (n 8) 109 [398]–[399].
223 *Maritime Boundary Arbitration* (n 5) 207–208; *Philippines v China Arbitration* (n 3) [126].
224 *Duzgit Integrity Arbitration* (n 104) [216]–[217].
225 Ibid [218].
226 *Chagos Arbitration* (n 14) [216]–[217].
227 *Duzgit Integrity Arbitration* (n 104) [216]; see also *Chagos Arbitration* (n 14) [303].
228 *Southern Bluefin Tuna Arbitration* (n 12) 46 [64].
229 *Duzgit Integrity Arbitration* (n 104) [262].

customary law, this was perhaps a missed opportunity to bring some clarity to the law.[230] However, in the *South China Sea Arbitration*, the Tribunal commented on the substantive content of the principle of good faith which may help provide some context. It stated that the principle of *pacta sunt servanda* was inherent in the principle of good faith, and that this obligation applied equally to treaties on dispute settlement.[231] This meant that the parties had to abide by the applicable procedure, including the final and binding nature of the award. Actions to aggravate or extend the dispute would be incompatible with states' good faith recognition and performance of their obligations.[232] It is noteworthy that, in both this case and the *Arctic Sunrise Arbitration*, the Tribunals found the respondents to have violated art 300.

A related proviso is to be found in art 294(1), which requires a court or tribunal to ensure that a case does not constitute, inter alia, an "abuse of legal process" when proceedings are initiated. This has been deemed suitable only in "the most blatant cases of abuse or harassment".[233]

3  Conclusion

Many of the cases discussed in this article have generated considerable controversy. The readiness of the judicial bodies to find a basis for establishing jurisdiction has met with criticism about a lack of restraint. Criticisms have extended from the suggestion that they should have exercised judicial caution and declined to proceed with the case[234] and that the cases may not have truly concerned the interpretation and application of UNCLOS,[235] to the contention that they ignored their mandate and extended the scope of their compulsory jurisdiction by engaging in judicial activism(or, in other words, that the UNCLOS courts and tribunals have been assigned compulsory jurisdiction, limited basically to the interpretation or application of UNCLOS, but that these judicial bodies have sinned by demonstrating a lack of restraint, taking account of international laws and matters extraneous to UNCLOS).[236] Underlying such a

---

230  John P Grant and J Craig Barker, *Encyclopaedic Dictionary of International Law* (Oxford University Press, 3rd ed, 2009) 3.
231  *South China Sea Arbitration* (n 42) [1171].
232  Ibid [1171]–[1172].
233  *Philippines v China Arbitration* (n 3) [128].
234  Whomersley (n 31) 254–256.
235  Proelss (n 149) 55–56; Natalie Klein, "The Effectiveness of the UNCLOS Dispute Settlement Regime: Reaching for the Stars" (2014) 108 *American Society of International Law Proceedings* 359, 361–362.
236  Talmon (n 117) 948–951; Proelss (n 149) 55–56.

stance can be the not unreasonable view that states may turn away from a system that is perceived as exceeding the boundaries of the powers granted it, thus undermining the international rule of law. But there is an alternative reading to the effect that, as a matter of principle, judicial bodies should exercise their judicial function unless there are sound objections to jurisdiction.[237] An excessively restrictive approach to jurisdiction could constrain their capacity to perform their judicial function and is just as likely to be damaging to a court's reputation as an overly expansive outlook. All these arguments are not unique to UNCLOS, but attach to any system of international and regional adjudication. The tribunals appear to have been aware of the fact that the ruling in the merits phase of the *Southern Bluefin Tuna Arbitration* that jurisdiction was absent had undoubtedly dealt a blow to the UNCLOS dispute settlement system, and ran counter to the intention that UNCLOS was designed to ensure that disputes were subject to some mode of dispute resolution. A restrictive interpretation of jurisdiction could lead, as in the *Southern Bluefin Tuna Arbitration*, to a situation where the dispute evaded judicial scrutiny, potentially amounting to a denial of justice. That seems to have been a motivating factor for the ICJ in the *Maritime Delimitation in the Indian Ocean Case*. That that particular aspect of the *Southern Bluefin Tuna Arbitration* has been reversed must be cautiously welcomed.

But one should be aware of another agenda, pursued by certain major powers and their stooges in the media, which calls for circumspection. And that agenda amounts to subverting the rules-based international order, or at the very least its institutions, and reverting to a pre-1919 system of power-politics.[238] Caution must be exercised that well-meaning criticism of international courts and their decisions are not hijacked by those with mal-intent.

The somewhat debatable position had been taken in earlier cases that UNCLOS does not establish a "truly comprehensive regime of compulsory jurisdiction entailing binding decisions".[239] However, Justice Keith's observations on the essential role of the peaceful settlement of disputes within UNCLOS appeared to be more persuasive,[240] and it is reassuring to note that ultimately this is the path followed in the instant cases.

---

237   *Continental Shelf (Libya v Malta)(Judgment)* [1985] ICJ Rep 3, 14.
238   Campbell McLachlan, "The Assault on International Adjudication and the Limits of Withdrawal" (2019) 68(3) *International and Comparative Law Quarterly* 499.
239   *Southern Bluefin Tuna Arbitration* (n 12) 45; Shigeru Oda, "Dispute Settlement Prospects in the Law of the Sea" (1995) 44(4) *International and Comparative Law Quarterly* 863, 866–871.
240   *Southern Bluefin Tuna Arbitration* (n 12) 55–57 (Justice Keith).

# State Immunity and the Application of Customary International Law in New Zealand: The *Young v Attorney-General* Litigation

Jared Papps*

### Abstract

In the *Young v Attorney-General* litigation, Ms Hayley Young pursued claims in New Zealand against the New Zealand and United Kingdom governments in relation to allegations that she suffered sexual harassment, assault and rape by United Kingdom Royal Navy and Royal New Zealand Navy officials. The litigation gave rise to issues of state immunity in relation to the United Kingdom, as well as the question of which forum was appropriate to hear the dispute. This case note explains the reasoning of the High Court, Court of Appeal and Supreme Court in addressing these issues. It then considers more broadly what this reasoning reveals about the approach of the New Zealand courts to customary international law, and suggests that this approach should be reconsidered. Finally, the note briefly discusses additional considerations the courts might have taken into account in deciding the appropriate forum.

## 1  Introduction

This case note discusses issues raised by the *Young v Attorney-General* ("*Young*") litigation. The case was concerned with allegations of sexual harassment, assault and rape of a Royal New Zealand Navy servicewoman, Ms Hayley Young, by United Kingdom Royal Navy and Royal New Zealand Navy officials. Ms Young has pursued claims against the New Zealand and United Kingdom ("UK") governments in the New Zealand courts for breach of their duties of care in relation to her safety, and for vicarious liability in relation to their employees' conduct. The case has garnered national interest.

The High Court held that Ms Young was entitled to pursue a claim against the Attorney-General of New Zealand ("AGNZ") on behalf of the New Zealand Defence Force. However, both the High Court and Court of Appeal held that Ms Young was barred from bringing her claim against the UK Ministry of Defence ("UK MoD") in the New Zealand courts due to the law of state immunity.

---

\* Solicitor, Chapman Tripp. This case note is written in my personal capacity.

Both of these courts also held that, in any event, the courts of England and Wales were the appropriate forum for the dispute. The Supreme Court denied Ms Young leave to appeal on both of these issues.

In Section 2, I summarise the judgments of the High Court, Court of Appeal and Supreme Court. In Section 3, I discuss the reason in relation to international law adopted (in particular) by the Court of Appeal, how that paradigm steered the court toward its conclusion on state immunity, and why the court ought to have adopted a more nuanced approach in applying immunity as a rule of customary international law[1] ("CIL"). Finally, in Section 4, I suggest that *Young* signals that the inquiry of which forum is appropriate to hear a dispute might be suitably widened to incorporate considerations of public policy, which appear in other areas of private international law, in the future.

## 2   The Proceedings

### 2.1   *The Facts*

While serving in the Royal New Zealand Navy, Ms Young accepted a secondment to the Royal Navy.[2] During her posting, she was under the command of both the Royal New Zealand Navy and the Royal Navy.[3]

Ms Young spent time in a British shore-based training facility and on two Royal Navy ships.[4] During that time, she claimed that she had been raped by a male naval officer, and sexually harassed and assaulted by a number of other male officers.[5] When she complained to superior officers about this conduct, the officers did not address her complaints.[6] She claimed that when she returned to the Royal New Zealand Navy, she continued to be sexually harassed

---

1  The proposition that state immunity operates as a rule of CIL was confirmed by the International Court of Justice in *Jurisdictional Immunities of the State* (*Germany v Italy: Greece Intervening*) (*Judgment*) [2012] ICJ Rep 99, 123 [56] ("*Jurisdictional Immunities*").
2  *X v Attorney-General* [2017] 3 NZLR 115, 119 [5] ("*X*") (Simon France J) (High Court of New Zealand). Although that proceeding was conducted in open court, interim name suppression was in place to protect the plaintiff and the subjects of the allegations. By the time of the Court of Appeal judgment, those suppression orders appear to have been removed: at 119 [5] n 2.
3  Ibid 119 [5].
4  Ibid 119 [5].
5  Ibid 119 [6]–[7].
6  Ibid 119 [7].

and assaulted by New Zealand officers and continued to receive no support from superior officers.[7] Ms Young resigned due to the stress of these events.[8]

Ms Young brought claims in relation to these allegations in the New Zealand High Court against the AGNZ, and against the UK MoD.

## 2.2    *In the High Court*

Ms Young claimed that the MoD had breached "a duty of care to take all reasonable steps to ensure [her] safety ... while in the United Kingdom", and that AGNZ had breached a similar duty (as well as contractual and statutory duties) in relation to her service in the Royal New Zealand Navy.[9] She also claimed that the AGNZ and UK MoD were jointly vicariously liable for the tort of battery for the assaults occurring outside New Zealand.[10] Ms Young claimed that the relevant conduct amounted to torture and/or cruel and degrading treatment.[11]

The UK MoD protested jurisdiction under r 6.29 of the High Court Rules 2016, on the basis that state immunity was applicable to Ms Young's claim against it, and that in any event the appropriate forum for the claim was the UK.[12]

AGNZ also protested jurisdiction.[13] It claimed that New Zealand was not the appropriate forum for the claim against it,[14] that a New Zealand court was not permitted to inquire into events that occurred on the warship of a foreign state,[15] and that the claim against it was excluded by sovereign immunity and the foreign act of state doctrine.[16] AGNZ's protest to jurisdiction was dismissed.[17]

Simon France J held that state immunity applied to the claim against the UK MoD.[18] He considered and rejected the argument that state immunity did not

---

7   Ibid 119–120 [8]–[10].
8   Ibid [11].
9   Ibid 132–133 [63].
10  Ibid 120 [12].
11  Ibid 124 [29].
12  Ibid 121 [15].
13  Ibid 118–119 [3].
14  Ibid 134 [68].
15  Ibid [77].
16  Ibid 135 [77].
17  Ibid 140 [101].
18  Ms Young argued that the issue of state immunity did not arise at all, on the basis that the MoD had submitted to New Zealand's jurisdiction by filing a joint memorandum agreeing to extend the time limit for filing its statement of defence. Simon France J rejected this argument, on the basis that the extension of time was a "minor and routine engagement

apply in cases where it would be contrary to New Zealand public policy, or in cases raising allegations of violations of fundamental human rights such as torture or cruel and degrading treatment. The existence of a public policy exception was discussed by the Court of Appeal in *Controller and Auditor General v Davison*,[19] where it was alleged that the Cook Islands government was complicit in a tax evasion scheme by issuing tax credits for use in New Zealand. These allegations were investigated by a Commission of Inquiry. The Cook Islands government sought to resist disclosure of relevant documents to the New Zealand Auditor-General on the basis of state immunity. While a (bare) majority of the Court of Appeal denied state immunity on the grounds that the Cook Islands' activities were private and commercial rather than sovereign, all judges also expressed varying degrees of support for a public policy exception.[20]

Simon France J held that *Davison* "did not empower the recognition of an exception for breaches of fundamental human rights", because the majority of the Court of Appeal dealt with the case under the established exception to state immunity for commercial activities. Moreover, the court was not dealing with allegations like those in *Young*.[21]

Simon France J also relied on the *Jurisdictional Immunities of the State (Germany v Italy)* judgment of the International Court of Justice. The case had emphasised that state immunity is a rule of CIL.[22] Simon France J held that this "undermine[d] the proposition that New Zealand, under the rubric of the common law, could develop its own contrary jurisprudence".[23] His Honour agreed with the observation in *Jurisdictional Immunities* that there was "a substantial body of State practice" rejecting an exception for fundamental breaches of human rights.[24]

Even if an exception to immunity existed, in Simon France J's view Ms Young's claims would not have engaged it. The conduct could be alleged as cruel and degrading treatment for interlocutory purposes, but he did not accept that all examples of such treatment would engage an exception. In his Honour's view, it was "likely that any exception would arise in circumstances

---

      with the Court" and not "only referable to accepting jurisdiction": ibid 122–124 [18]–[27]. His Honour also doubted the proposition that submission to jurisdiction would automatically lead to waiver of state immunity: at 123–124 [26].

19    *Controller and Auditor General v Davison* [1996] 2 NZLR 278 ("*Davison*").
20    See discussion: *X* (n 2) 125–127 [30]–[39].
21    Ibid 129–130 [47].
22    See *Jurisdictional Immunities* (n 1).
23    *X* (n 2) 127 [41].
24    Ibid 128 [42], citing *Jurisdictional Immunities* (n 1) 137 [84].

of more systemic state sponsored violations of human rights than that which was alleged here".[25]

Although Simon France J's view disposed of the claim against the UK MoD, his Honour discussed the appropriate forum for the claim against the UK MoD. He held that "the starting point for ascertaining where the most real and substantial connection lies is to look at what is said to have happened, who did it, and why the defendant is said to be liable".[26] In Ms Young's circumstances, the UK was held to be the appropriate forum. This was because the conduct had allegedly occurred in the UK, English law would be applicable to the claim and the subject matter required an inquiry better suited to the English courts.[27] Simon France J placed little weight on the difficulty of conducting proceedings in England because Ms Young had declined to make a complaint to the Royal Navy Police, who had offered to investigate if they received a complaint.[28]

### 2.3     In the Court of Appeal
#### 2.3.1     State Immunity

On appeal, Ms Young broadened her arguments against the application of state immunity to the claim against the MoD. Ms Young maintained that an "iniquity exception" to state immunity applied, whereby state immunity would not be upheld where the relevant conduct by the defendant "breaches a fundamental principle of justice or some deep-rooted tradition of the forum state".[29] She also argued that New Zealand owed her an obligation to provide her with an effective remedy:

(a)     as a matter of domestic law, under the *New Zealand Bill of Rights Act* 1990 ("*NZBORA*"); and

(b)     as a matter of international law, under jus cogens, CIL, and international instruments including the *International Covenant on Civil and Political Rights* ("*ICCPR*"), *Convention Against Torture* ("*CAT*") and *Convention on the Elimination of Discrimination Against Women* ("*CEDAW*").[30]

Ms Young argued that upholding state immunity would be a breach of the obligation to provide an effective remedy.

By way of preliminary comment, the court noted that state immunity is "a rule of international law which precludes the courts of the forum state from exercising adjudicative and enforcement jurisdiction in certain classes of case

---

25     *X* (n 2) 130 [49].
26     Ibid 131 [53].
27     Ibid 131–132 [55].
28     Ibid 132 [56].
29     *Young v Attorney-General* [2018] NZCA 307 [2] (Brown J for the Court) ("*Young (CA)*").
30     Ibid [2].

in which a foreign state is a party".[31] Its rationale was that, in such cases, "the exercise of jurisdiction is seen as incompatible with the dignity and independence of the foreign state".[32] Where state immunity applies, the court does not decline to exercise jurisdiction over the foreign state – rather, the court has no jurisdiction over the foreign state at all.[33] State immunity is "a mandatory rule of customary international law which defines the limits of a domestic court's jurisdiction".[34]

The court traced the development of the doctrine, observing that the commercial exception now applies in many states.[35] The court also noted that in recent decades there had been a range of cases challenging the applicability of state immunity where the foreign state is alleged to have breached a peremptory or *jus cogens* norm.[36]

2.3.1.1   *Obligation under NZBORA*

Ms Young's argument under the NZBORA was founded on the obligation in art 2(3) of the ICCPR to provide an effective remedy to any person whose rights or freedoms are violated, whether or not the violation has been committed by someone acting in an official capacity.[37] The general argument was that NZBORA affirmed the obligations of the ICCPR, including the obligation to provide an effective remedy.[38]

Significantly, the court held that acts performed abroad would be subject to NZBORA, provided that those acts are done by an entity falling within the scope of s 3 of NZBORA.[39] Section 3 states that NZBORA

applies only to acts done -
(a) by the legislative, executive, or judicial branches of the Government of New Zealand; or
(b) by any person or body in the performance of any public function, power, or duty conferred or imposed on that person or body by or pursuant to law.

---

31  Ibid [14].
32  Ibid [14], quoting *Governor of Pitcairn and Associated Islands v Sutton* [1995] 1 NZLR 426, 428 (Cooke P) (Court of Appeal of New Zealand).
33  *Young* (CA) (n 29) [24].
34  Ibid [27].
35  Ibid [16].
36  Ibid [18].
37  Ibid [35]; see *International Covenant on Civil and Political Rights*, GA Res 2200A, UN Doc A/6316 (23 March 1976, adopted 16 December 1966).
38  *Young* (CA) (n 29) [36]. Ms Young's statement of claim did not allege any specific breach of a NZBORA right, but the Court of Appeal proceeded on the basis that her claim could be amended if required: Ibid [37].
39  Ibid [40].

However, Ms Young's argument ultimately failed on the basis that the UK MoD was not an entity under s 3.[40] Her "rights under the *NZBORA* may indeed travel with her to foreign climes but the liabilities which can arise in respect of breaches of rights affirmed in the *NZBORA* do not expand to include other categories of person".[41] The "relevant obligation of the New Zealand state to provide an effective remedy in its courts relates only to liabilities which arise under the *NZBORA*", so she was not entitled to a *NZBORA* remedy from the UK MoD.[42]

### 2.3.1.2  Obligation under International Law

Ms Young argued, following the minority view in the decision of the European Court of Human Rights ("ECtHR") in *Al-Adsani v United Kingdom*[43] that upholding the claim of immunity would be a breach of her right to an effective remedy for breach of fundamental human rights under CIL.

The Court of Appeal responded by applying *Jones v Ministry of the Interior of the Kingdom of Saudi Arabia*.[44] In *Jones*, the House of Lords held that the minority ECtHR view simply assumed that the norm of the prohibition on torture conflicted with the rule of state immunity, and that the prohibition on torture, as a peremptory norm, accordingly overrode state immunity.[45] The House of Lords held that this approach was wrong, agreeing with Hazel Fox's view that "[s]tate immunity is a procedural rule going to the jurisdiction of a national court. It does not go to substantive law; it does not contradict a prohibition contained in a *jus cogens* norm but merely diverts any breach of it to a different method of settlement".[46]

Given that immunity was properly characterised as a procedural rule, it was necessary for the claimant to show that the prohibition on torture had generated an ancillary procedural rule entitling or requiring the forum state to assume jurisdiction over the defendant state.[47] Lord Hoffmann commented:[48]

---

40   Ibid [46]. The word "law" in s 3(b) of *NZBORA* referred to "the laws of New Zealand": ibid [45], citing *R v Matthews* (1994) 11 CRNZ 564, 566 (High Court of New Zealand).
41   *Young (CA)* (n 29) [48].
42   Ibid [53].
43   *Al-Adsani v United Kingdom* (European Court of Human Rights, Grand Chamber, Application No 35763/97, 21 November 2001) ("*Al-Adsani*").
44   *Jones v Ministry of the Interior of the Kingdom of Saudi Arabia* [2007] 1 AC 270 ("*Jones*").
45   *Young (CA)* (n 29) [57], citing *Jones* (n 44) 293 [43] (Lord Hoffmann).
46   *Young (CA)* (n 29) [74], citing *Jones* (n 44) 293 [44], citing Hazel Fox and Philippa Webb, *The Law of State Immunity* (Oxford University Press, 3rd ed, 2013) 525.
47   *Jones* (n 44) 293 [45].
48   *Young (CA)* (n 29) [58], citing *Jones* (n 44) 297–298 [63].

As Professor Dworkin demonstrated in *Law's Empire* (1986), the ordering of competing principles according to the importance of the values which they embody is a basic technique of adjudication. But the same approach cannot be adopted in international law, which is based upon the common consent of nations. It is not for a national court to "develop" international law by unilaterally adopting a version of that law which, however desirable, forward-looking and reflective of values it may be, is simply not accepted by other states.

Ms Young challenged the reasoning in *Jones* by arguing that the *jus cogens* prohibition on breaches of fundamental human rights entailed a correlative absolute right to an effective remedy. This right was an inherent part of, rather than being ancillary to, the prohibition.[49] The right was further evidenced by art 2 of the ICCPR and CEDAW. Ms Young submitted that this absolute right was also reflected in domestic law, where Ms Young had a "statutory or constitutional right to an effective remedy from within the New Zealand legal system, which [could not] be negatived by the common law".[50]

The Court of Appeal rejected these arguments. Even though the right to an effective remedy expressed in the cited treaty articles carried a procedural element, those articles did not provide evidence of an ancillary procedural rule requiring assumption of jurisdiction.[51] Relying on the UK Supreme Court's judgment in *Benkharbouche v Embassy of the Republic of Sudan*, the UK MoD submitted, and the court accepted, that the scope of the right to a remedy was to be interpreted in light of "any relevant rules of international law applicable in the relations between the parties".[52] The Court of Appeal agreed with the view in *Benkharbouche* that the rule of state immunity acted as a limit on the procedural right to a remedy found in art 47 of the *European Charter*, and held that this limit applied equally to the right expressed by ICCPR and CEDAW.[53]

Finally, the Court of Appeal agreed in full with Simon France J's reasoning regarding the existence of a public policy exception.[54] In particular, the court agreed that any comments supporting such an exception in *Davison* were

---

49   *Young* (CA) (n 29) [75].
50   Ibid [75].
51   Ibid [78].
52   *Young* (CA) (n 29) [80], citing *Benkharbouche v Embassy of the Republic of Sudan* [2017] 3 WLR 957, 977–978 [34] (Lord Sumption).
53   *Young* (CA) (n 29) [86].
54   Ibid [100].

obiter, given that the majority disallowed the immunity on the basis of the commercial exception.⁵⁵

### 2.3.1.3   *Extended Jurisdiction Argument*

Ms Young also argued that she remained subject to New Zealand jurisdiction when she was a service person abroad, and New Zealand had an obligation to provide her with an effective remedy.⁵⁶ However, the Court of Appeal held that this did not empower it to adjudicate upon the claim, because Ms Young and the relevant UK officers were beyond New Zealand's *territorial* jurisdiction.⁵⁷

### 2.3.2   Appropriate Forum

In relation to the issue of *forum conveniens* for an action against the UK MoD, Ms Young argued it would strongly disadvantage her to have to establish the extent to which each state had failed to discharge its obligations to provide her with a safe place of work, and the appropriate share of liability between each state, in two different jurisdictions.⁵⁸

The Court of Appeal agreed with Simon France J's reasoning leading to his conclusion that the UK was the appropriate forum. The court added that the AGNZ had proposed a "hybrid process" whereby the AGNZ would waive sovereign immunity in the UK, and undertake to be bound in respect of the claims against it by the factual findings of the English courts. The court said that that process was not available because Ms Young had indicated that she would only proceed against the UK MoD in the New Zealand courts – implying that Ms Young's unwillingness to take part in that process was a factor further weakening her claim that New Zealand was the appropriate forum.⁵⁹

## 2.4   *Application for Leave to Appeal to the Supreme Court*

Ms Young applied for leave to appeal to the Supreme Court. The court dismissed her application on the papers.

On state immunity, the court stated that Ms Young was not arguing that her claim fell into "one of the established exceptions to state immunity. She wishes to argue for a new exception …", referring to the obligation to provide an effective remedy that she had argued for in the Court of Appeal.⁶⁰ The court

---

55   Ibid [98].
56   Ibid [88]–[90].
57   Ibid [91].
58   Ibid [104].
59   Ibid [108].
60   *Young v Attorney-General* [2019] NZSC 23 [10] (Glazebrook, O'Regan and Winkelmann JJ).

accept[ed] that the issues related to the existence and/or scope of such a duty may be worthy of leave in a suitable case. But this is not that case. Even if the duty were found to apply in the present circumstances, it would then be necessary to establish that the duty would override state immunity and subject a foreign state to the jurisdiction of the New Zealand domestic courts.[61]

In relation to the appropriate forum issue, Ms Young argued that had the international human rights instruments she cited in the courts below been considered properly, the courts would have concluded that New Zealand was the appropriate forum. The court held that

> ...the place of international human rights instruments in the assessment of a claim of *forum non conveniens* may be an issue worthy of consideration in an appropriate case. But there is nothing in the material submitted by the applicant that provides an indication that the outcome in this case could be affected by that consideration.[62]

## 3 Mode of International Law Reasoning Applied by the New Zealand Courts

### 3.1 *Automatic Incorporation of CIL?*

*Young* is significant because it affirms New Zealand's commitment to a view of state immunity that applies even in cases of breaches of human rights or peremptory norms, or where domestic public policy is engaged. This confirms New Zealand's jurisprudence is aligned with that of the ICJ,[63] the ECtHR,[64] the US,[65] Canada,[66] and the United Kingdom,[67] among other international and domestic courts.

But *Young* is also significant because it provides insights into the New Zealand courts' approach to international law reasoning. Recall the Court of Appeal's endorsement of Lord Hoffmann's statement that "[i]t is not for a national court to 'develop' international law by adopting a version of that law which ...

---

61　Ibid [11].
62　Ibid [14].
63　*Jurisdictional Immunities* (n 1).
64　*Al-Adsani* (n 43).
65　See for example *Sampson v Germany*, 975 F Supp 1108 (Ill, 1997).
66　*Bouzari v Iran* (2004) 243 DLR (4th) 406 (Ontario Court of Appeal).
67　*Jones* (n 44).

is simply not accepted by other states".⁶⁸ This view had been previously endorsed by the High Court in *Fang v Jiang*,⁶⁹ but *Young* marks the first time it has been approved by a New Zealand appellate court.

The Court of Appeal is favouring what some commentators have called an *inductive* approach to determining and applying CIL.⁷⁰ This approach follows from art 38(1)(b) of the *Statute of the International Court of Justice*, which acknowledges "international custom, as evidence of a general practice as law" as a source of international law. CIL is to be determined only by reference to evidence of state practice, and evidence that states follow that practice out of a sense of legal obligation (*opinio juris*).⁷¹ Other domestic or international legal rules or principles, and moral or political values, do not play a role in this process. If a domestic court identifies a CIL norm through that process, it must follow state practice and apply the rule. Otherwise, the court is departing from established state practice and thereby "developing" international law in the way that Lord Hoffmann describes.

The International Law Commission's *Draft Conclusions on Identification of Customary International Law* confirm that the correct approach is inductive.⁷² A contrast is a *deductive* approach, which focuses on the external legal rules and principles, and moral and political values, referred to above.⁷³ The deductive approach derives specific CIL rules from these more general propositions.⁷⁴

The ILC has commented that "[t]he [approach to determining CIL] does not in fact preclude a measure of deduction as an aid, to be employed with

---

68  See above n 48. This view was also accepted by Simon France J in the High Court: see above n 9.
69  *Fang v Jiang* [2007] NZAR 420, 431 [51] (Randerson J) (High Court of New Zealand).
70  See Anthea Roberts, "Traditional and Modern Approaches to Customary International Law: A Reconciliation" (2001) 95(4) *American Journal of International Law* 757, 758; William Thomas Worster, "The Inductive and Deductive Methods in Customary International Law Analysis: Traditional and Modern Approaches" (2014) 45(2) *Georgetown Journal of International Law* 445; Nadia Bentaka, "A Theory of Constructive Interpretation for Customary International Law Identification" (2018) 39(3) *Michigan Journal of International Law* 301, 303.
71  Both state practice and *opinio juris* must be established for a CIL rule to arise: see *North Sea Continental Shelf (Federal Republic of Germany v Denmark)* (*Judgment*) [1969] ICJ Rep 3, 44 [77]. In the words of the International Law Commission, the test is whether there is a general practice that is accepted as law: International Law Commission, *Draft Conclusions on Identification of Customary International Law, with Commentaries*, UN Doc A/73/10 (2018) 125 [2] ("*Draft Conclusions*").
72  *Draft Conclusions* (n 71) 126 [5].
73  Roberts (n 70) 758; Banteka (n 70) 303; Worster (n 70) 455–456.
74  Banteka (n 70) 303.

caution ...".⁷⁵ Notably, this is particularly so "when considering possible rules of customary international law that operate against the backdrop of rules framed in more general terms that themselves derive from and reflect a general practice accepted as law, or when concluding that possible rules of international law form part of an 'indivisible regime'".⁷⁶ That context is arguably relevant when considering any exception to state immunity – both in terms of how the exception operates against the general rule of state immunity, and in terms of how the rule of state immunity operates against other external rules of customary international law (such as *jus cogens* prohibiting certain categories of breach of human rights).⁷⁷

In any event, the accepted inductive approach raises fundamental questions about the relationship between international law and New Zealand law – and the reasoning that New Zealand courts should apply in international law cases – that have not been fully considered. These questions have been the subject of attention in the context of treaty law, but less so in the context of CIL.⁷⁸ Even when a CIL norm is found to exist, there is a further question of what effect it should have in domestic law.

When considering the effect of treaties in New Zealand law, the accepted starting point is that the executive alone does not have constitutional authority to change New Zealand law through treaty-making.⁷⁹ This is why Parliament must legislate for treaties to have formal effect. In practice the situation is murkier, as treaty obligations have impacted on the reasoning in both common law and statutory interpretation cases.⁸⁰ There is a general presumption

---

75  *Draft Conclusions* (n 71) 126 (5).
76  Ibid.
77  The reasoning given in *Jones* and *Young* that an exception should not exist because a substantive *jus cogens* norm did not entail a corresponding procedural norm overriding immunity is an example of deductive reasoning. See, for example, Sévrine Knuchel, "State Immunity and the Promise of *Jus Cogens*" (2011) 9(2) *Northwestern Journal of International Human Rights* 149 for discussion of whether an exception to state immunity for breach of *jus cogens* norms should exist based on deductive reasoning.
78  A range of New Zealand cases have considered the role of unincorporated treaties in domestic law. See, e.g., *Tavita v Minister of Immigration* [1994] 2 NZLR 257 (Court of Appeal of New Zealand); *Sellers v Maritime Safety Inspector* [1999] 2 NZLR 44 (Court of Appeal of New Zealand); *Ye v Minister of Immigration* [2010] 1 NZLR 104 (Supreme Court of New Zealand) ("*Ye*"). But the New Zealand courts appear to have simply accepted that CIL is automatically incorporated into New Zealand law: see further discussion below.
79  *New Zealand Air Line Pilots' Association Inc v Attorney-General* [1997] 3 NZLR 269, 280–281 (Keith J for the Court) (Court of Appeal of New Zealand).
80  See Alice Osman, "Demanding Attention: The Roles of Unincorporated International Instruments in Judicial Reasoning" (2014) 12(2) *New Zealand Journal of Public and International Law* 345, 353–362, and the cases discussed therein.

that Parliament intends to legislate in accordance with its international obligations,[81] and those obligations are also "part of the values, norms and principles to be taken into account when developing the common law".[82]

Alice Osman has observed that, in such cases, treaty obligations are a source of "influential authority", "reducible neither to binding authority nor to the permissive extreme of purely persuasive authority".[83] While not automatically incorporated as an express rule of domestic law, the treaty obligation nonetheless informs how domestic law should be understood and developed.

What, then, of CIL? In *Trendtex Trading Corporation v Central Bank of Nigeria*, Lord Denning MR was of the view that CIL is automatically incorporated into English common law,[84] although the complexities of the application of CIL in the English courts have become more apparent over time.[85] The New Zealand courts have made no such explicit statement about the relationship between CIL and domestic law. However, in state immunity cases, the courts have simply assumed that state immunity takes effect as a rule of domestic law.[86] As Treasa Dunworth has identified, there are good reasons to question this assumption. Respect for international obligations ought to be balanced against New Zealand's own legal and moral values.[87] Further, CIL changes with new patterns of state practice, and may be difficult to determine.[88] It also, unlike treaty law, does not enter into domestic law through a democratic process.[89] These factors, as Dunworth argues, all suggest caution toward the

---

81  *Ye* (n 78) 125 [32] (Blanchard, Tipping, McGrath and Anderson JJ).
82  Susan Glazebrook, "Cross-Pollination or Contamination: Global Influences on New Zealand Law" 21 *Canterbury Law Review* 60, 67.
83  Osman (n 80) 350.
84  *Trendtex Trading Corporation v Central Bank of Nigeria* [1977] 2 WLR 356, 365–366 (Lord Denning MR, Stephenson and Shaw LJJ) (Court of Appeal) (*"Trendtex"*).
85  See for example *R v Jones (Margaret)* [2007] 1 AC 136, 155 (House of Lords) (Lord Bingham); *Belhaj v Straw* [2017] AC 964, 1158–1159 [252] (Supreme Court) (Lord Sumption) (*"Belhaj"*).
86  See *Reef Shipping Co Ltd v The Ship "Fua Kavenga"* [1987] 1 NZLR 550, 569 (Smellie J) (High Court of New Zealand). In that case, the Court accepted a statement by Lord Atkin in *The Cristina* [1938] AC 485, 490 that state immunity is a "proposition ... of international law engrafted into our domestic law". See generally Treasa Dunworth, "Hidden Anxieties: Customary International Law in New Zealand" (2004) 2(1) *New Zealand Journal of Public and International Law in New Zealand* 67, 70.
87  Dunworth (n 86) 79.
88  Ibid 79. See also further discussion of this instability as illustrated by discussion of state immunity in *Trendtex* (n 84) below n 94 and accompanying text.
89  Although, as discussed above, treaty law has an influential effect on New Zealand law even without direct incorporation through legislation.

automatic incorporation of CIL.[90] Instead, incorporation of a norm into CIL should depend on that norm's "pedigree" – if a norm is perceived by the New Zealand courts to be insufficiently legitimate, it should not be received into New Zealand law.[91]

If Osman's view that treaty obligations have influential authority is correct, then this view ought also to apply to CIL. Entertaining this view need not mean that courts will not afford CIL the consideration and authority it deserves. If CIL has influential authority, judges are still required to give it weight. As Osman comments, in justifying a decision the judge "must address the role of that authority in its justification or be found legally wanting".[92] International law's influential authority reflects its established role in interpreting legislation and developing the common law.

The assumption that states do not "develop" international law does not easily square with the reality that judicial decisions can be a source of novel state practice leading to new or modified CIL norms.[93] The history of the development of state immunity itself is a good example of this. In *Trendtex*, the English Court of Appeal held that immunity did not apply to state acts of a commercial or private character – the formulation commonly known as "restrictive immunity". Lord Denning MR observed that in the past, states never engaged in commercial activities, and states applied the rule that there were no exceptions to state immunity – known as "absolute immunity".[94] After economic and political transformation in the 20th century, it became commonplace for states to engage in commercial activities. To facilitate this development, many states shifted their view from absolute immunity to restrictive immunity. On one level, it could be said the states adopting new practice all breached an existing norm of absolute immunity. But those so-called "breaches" eventually led to the development of a new CIL norm providing a commercial exception to state immunity.

---

90   Dunworth also discusses the argument that it might favour the domestic constitutional balance for CIL to be received exclusively through treaties, so that the courts are not put in the position of deciding whether to breach New Zealand's international obligations: Dunworth (n 86) 80.
91   Ibid 81.
92   Osman (n 80) 350, citing Mayo Moran, "Authority, Influence and Persuasion: Baker, Charter Values and the Puzzle of Method" in David Dyzenhaus (ed) *The Unity of Public Law* (Hart Publishing, 2004) 389, 390.
93   Anthea Roberts, "Comparative International Law? The Role of National Courts in International Law" (2011) 60(1) *International & Comparative Law Quarterly* 57, 70.
94   *Trendtex* (n 84) 366.

If domestic courts generally were to adopt Lord Hoffmann's view, these new judicial currents of state practice would *never* arise, because courts would strictly follow the existing CIL norm, without considering modification of its scope.[95] Of course, the effect of CIL in domestic legal traditions can be expected to differ between monist and dualist traditions – one would expect that in monist traditions, where international law tends to take direct effect, courts would adhere to the CIL norm more strictly. But as a state that acknowledges a gap between international and domestic law, one would also expect that New Zealand can change its judicial state practice in response to emerging considerations such as breaches of developing *jus cogens* norms.

It is acknowledged that a human rights exception was rejected by a range of bodies and jurisdictions including the UK, Canada, the US, the European Court of Human Rights and International Court of Justice. That backdrop was undoubtedly an important consideration for the Court of Appeal when deciding whether to adopt such an exception. That is accepted. But it is submitted that the Court of Appeal was free to critically examine the reasoning of those jurisdictions in doing so, and whether the other jurisdictions' deference justified New Zealand following suit. Even if it is now indisputable that the rule of state immunity does not allow for a human rights exception or otherwise, that position will only ever change when an individual state decides to place itself in "breach".

The jurisprudence of the Italian courts in response to the *Jurisdictional Immunities* decision is an illustrative example of a state putting itself in that position. The decision had required Italy to, by enacting legislation or some other method, reverse previous Italian court decisions[96] declaring that Germany did not enjoy state immunity for atrocities it committed on Italian soil during World War II. In response, the Italian Parliament approved *Law No 5/2013*,[97] art 3 of which directly implemented *Jurisdictional Immunities* in Italian constitutional law. But in *Judgment No. 238/2014*, the Italian Constitutional Court held that this law, and the inclusion of state immunity for serious

---

95  Roberts (n 93) 72.
96  See *Ferrini v Federal Republic of Germany* (2006) 128 ILR 658; *Federal Republic of Germany v Giovanni Mantelli and others*, Corte Suprema di Cassazione [Italian Supreme Court of Cassation], Order No 14201, 29 May 2008; *Federal Republic of Germany v Liberato Maietta*, Corte Suprema di Cassazione [Italian Supreme Court of Cassation], Order No 14209, 29 May 2008.
97  *Adesione della Repubblica Italiana alla Convezione della Nazioni Unite sulle immunità giurisdizionali degli Stati e dei loro beni, fatta a New York il 2 dicembre 2004* [Accession of the Italian Republic to the United Nations Convention on the Immunity Courts of States and their Property] (Italy) 13 January 2013, Law No 5.

human rights breaches in Italian law, did not conform to the Italian Constitution.[98] This decision has been observed to be both "deferential and subversive", in the sense that while the court did not challenge the ICJ's ruling on the international law plane, it nonetheless held that the ruling could not be applied in Italian domestic law.[99] The court's rationale for doing so was that art 10 of the *Italian Constitution*, which provided that Italian law would comply with generally recognised rules of international law, did not incorporate those rules which conflicted with fundamental principles of the *Italian Constitution*.[100] The judgment demonstrates that the Italian courts were sensitive to the dynamic interplay between domestic and international legal principles. The *Young* decision may have been enriched by consideration of, and comparison with, the Italian example.

### 3.2  A Comparison with Private International Law

*Davison*, while being given short shrift by the High Court and Court of Appeal in *Young*, is an example of a New Zealand court showing sensitivity to the issues raised above. In *Davison*, Richardson J emphasised that "refusal of a claim to sovereign immunity could be justified only where the impugned activity, if established, breaches a fundamental principle of justice or some deep-rooted tradition of the forum state".[101] This appears to be a similar threshold for the application of *ordre public* in private international law. This doctrine holds that courts may disapply foreign law, or refuse to recognise or enforce a foreign judgment in exceptional circumstances. For the doctrine to apply, recognition or enforcement of the judgment, or application of the foreign law, must "'shock the conscience' of a reasonable New Zealander, or be contrary to New Zealand's view of basic morality or a violation of essential principles of justice or moral interests in New Zealand".[102]

While not a doctrine of public international law, *ordre public* is nonetheless concerned with comity and the appropriate boundaries between states in resolving disputes in that it decides when a state should defer to a foreign state's law or judgment. The high threshold for *ordre public* embodies a "tolerance of difference" to other states' laws (or, in the case of refusing to recognise

---

98   Corte costituzionale [Italian Constitutional Court], No 238, 22 October 2014 [1], [5] ("*No 238*").
99   Maria Elena Gennusa, "Constitutionalising the International Legal Order through Case Law – Judgment No. 238/2014 from the Italian Constitutional Court" 5(1) *Cambridge Journal of International and Comparative Law* 139, 143.
100  *No 238* (n 98) [3.1].
101  *Davison* (n 19) 305.
102  *Reeves v OneWorld Challenge LLC* [2006] NZLR 184, 195 [50], 198–199 [67] (Anderson P and O'Regan J) (Court of Appeal of New Zealand).

or enforce a foreign judgment, on the way they adjudicate disputes).[103] Similarly, there must be a high tolerance of difference in the exercise by states of their sovereign rights – other states should generally refrain from infringing those rights by adjudicating upon their actions.[104] But "high" does not mean "infinite".

The relationship between public and private international law is complex and beyond the scope of this note. But the basic point here is that just as the New Zealand courts acknowledge local values in matters of state relations in the sphere of private international law, there ought to be some scope to do so in public international law. Both systems of law delineate the appropriate boundaries of state authority, albeit in different (but often related) spheres of influence.[105] In both systems of law, then, there must be occasions where local values justify shifting these boundaries.

While it could be said that disapplying state immunity is a different matter from disapplying foreign law or foreign judgments because it involves the breach of a CIL norm rather than a departure from local rules reflecting comity, that contrast is tempered by the discussion in the previous section. Although the *ordre public* test may not translate directly into a public international law context, it provides a useful yardstick of the considerations that the New Zealand courts might take into account when deciding whether to stake out a different position to other jurisdictions on CIL matters. That yardstick could in future empower courts to follow the suggestion of an iniquity exception given in *Davison*.

Another potential benefit of this comparison is that it bolsters the idea that courts can make domestic value judgments when applying CIL, rather than solely framing the argument in terms of breaches of *jus cogens* or fundamental human rights. The distinction between the two was noted, in the context of the foreign act of state doctrine, in *Belhaj v Straw*. Lord Sumption observed that English courts were free to adjudicate on state acts which would otherwise fall within the foreign act of state doctrine if those acts offended English public policy.[106] He commented that the rule was one of *English* public policy, but

---

103 Alex Mills, *The Confluence of Public and Private International Law: Justice, Pluralism and Subsidiarity in the International Constitutional Ordering of Private Law* (Cambridge University Press, 2009) 258.

104 James Crawford, *Brownlie's Principles of Public International Law* (Oxford University Press, 8th ed, 2012) 488.

105 See generally Mills (n 103).

106 See *Belhaj* (n 85) 1157–1162 [249]–[257] (Lord Sumption); 1119–1120 [153]–[157] (Lord Neuberger). Lord Mance, rather than observing a public policy *exception*, considered that public policy considerations defined the scope of the act of state doctrine: at 1107–1109 [106]–[107] (Lord Mance).

that this domestic policy could be "informed by any relevant norms of international law binding on the United Kingdom".[107] While Lord Sumption was not speaking in the context of state immunity, the point is useful because it highlights an area of law, often operating closely alongside (but distinct from) state immunity, where states sometimes act on their own values rather than internationalist considerations. These values can be informed by rules and principles of international law, but those rules and principles are by no means exhaustive. Had the Court of Appeal in *Young* adopted a broad public policy or iniquity exception as recognised in *Davison*, rather than being required to strictly focus on whether a breach of *jus cogens* was established (which was not accepted to give rise to an exception to immunity), it would have been able to look at the alleged conduct broadly and decide whether it sufficiently engaged domestic concerns to justify disapplying state immunity.

### 3.3  *Relevance of Competing International Values*

Conversely, however, if domestic values ought to carry weight when applying CIL, then values of international law which align with those domestic values, and which may compete against the established CIL rule, should also carry weight. As noted in the previous section, public policy can be international in nature.[108] In *Young*, the principles and values which Ms Young relied upon were the force of *jus cogens* norms[109] and the international commitment to the right to an effective remedy in *ICCPR*, *CAT* and *CEDAW*. While the Court of Appeal sidestepped the tension between state immunity and these principles by holding that state immunity was a procedural norm, this does not eliminate the real moral and political tension at play. If *jus cogens* norms are to be more than mere aspirational statements, then arguably their especially heavy normative weight should be given weight in deciding whether to apply a CIL rule. If the effect of the CIL rule is inconsistent with the *jus cogens* norm, this may be a legitimate reason not to apply the CIL rule.

On this view, the strict demarcation of submissions into the right of access to a remedy at domestic law (under *NZBORA*) and at international law may not have been the most illuminating way to highlight the issues at play. For instance, the court's finding that s 3(b) of *NZBORA* does not regulate agents exercising public functions under foreign law, together with the fact that *NZBORA* affirms New Zealand's commitment to the *ICCPR*, might suggest that New

---

107  Ibid 1161–1162 [257].
108  See also Mills (n 103) 274–287.
109  These norms being the prohibition against torture and cruel and degrading treatment which Ms Young alleged were engaged.

Zealand does not consider its ICCPR obligations to include providing an effective remedy against agents of foreign states. The somewhat granular nature of the judgment obscures these possible linkages.

The purpose of this case note is not to articulate any particular view on the outcome that the court should have reached in *Young*. It is also acknowledged that the discussion above is brief, and only begins to address the complexities of the role of international law in New Zealand. But this note does contend that cases like *Young* raise important questions about a key pillar of New Zealand's constitutional order. State immunity undeniably has an enduring and important pedigree. As such, there is a significant tension between the doctrine and fundamental human rights or policy values. The Court of Appeal, by disregarding the possibility that courts may be independent and influential actors for the purposes of state practice, declined to engage with that tension. In applying state immunity the Court of Appeal should not merely have identified the absolute scope of state immunity, but gone a step further and justified *why* the immunity should apply at domestic law in that particular way.

## 4   A Note on Forum Conveniens

The discussion above also helps to provide insight into the issue of appropriate forum raised by *Young*.

Rule 6.28(5)(c) of the High Court Rules 2016 requires that, to grant leave to serve proceedings outside of the jurisdiction, the applicant must establish that New Zealand is the appropriate forum for the trial. This question is assessed by reference to the doctrine of *forum conveniens*. The doctrine is concerned with determining the court "in which the case may be tried more suitably for the interests of all the parties and the ends of justice".[110]

*Forum conveniens* has not historically been closely concerned with questions of human rights or public policy. The focus is on establishing the forum with which the proceeding has the most real and substantial connection.[111] In New Zealand, factors relevant to this question include "issues of convenience or expense, availability of witnesses, the law governing the relevant transaction and the places where the parties resided or carried on business".[112] If the

---

110   *Spiliada Maritime Corporation v Cansulex Ltd* [1987] AC 460, 474 (Lord Goff) (House of Lords) ("*Spiliada*"), citing *Sim v Robinow* (1892) 19 R 665, 668 (Lord Kinnear) (Court of Session).

111   *Wing Hung Printing Co Ltd v Saito Offshore Pty Ltd* [2011] 1 NZLR 754, 765 [45] (Randerson J for the Court) (Court of Appeal of New Zealand).

112   Ibid 765 [45].

connecting factors indicate that another forum appears to be more appropriate, the court will go beyond these factors to determine whether justice requires that the court should exercise jurisdiction regardless. At this second stage of the inquiry, a relevant consideration is whether the plaintiff will obtain justice in the foreign jurisdiction.[113] That consideration aligns with broader issues around how recognition of the right of access to justice intersects with *forum conveniens* principles.[114]

On orthodox *forum conveniens* principles, it is difficult to dispute that the courts of England and Wales had the most real and substantial connection with the dispute. But it may have been open to a court to conclude that the financial difficulty of bringing a claim in England, and the consequent risk of not obtaining substantial justice in that forum, overrode the factors favouring England as the appropriate forum – particularly at the broader second stage of the inquiry.[115] In the recent English case of *Lungowe v Vedanta Resources plc*, even though traditional connecting factors overwhelmingly favoured the claim being heard in Zambia, the UK Supreme Court nonetheless decided to exercise jurisdiction as the claimants were unlikely to obtain substantial justice in Zambia due to financial and institutional difficulties.[116] *Lungowe* emphasises that the broader question of substantial justice can take precedence over traditional connecting factors.

In terms of this question of substantial justice, if the Court of Appeal had decided that it should not apply state immunity due to overriding reasons of public policy, this might have suggested that the usual reference to connecting factors would be inadequate. It would be an odd result for a court to disapply state immunity and then decline to exercise jurisdiction because it was not the appropriate forum. Such a case would raise the question of whether the forum analysis could also be extended to include public policy grounds. The Supreme Court in its leave to appeal decision was attuned to this point. It acknowledged that whether human rights instruments can be incorporated into a *forum conveniens* analysis may be worthy of consideration.

---

113 *Spiliada* (n 110) 478.
114 The right of access to justice can be found in various human rights instruments, such as ICCPR art 14(1).
115 See, e.g. *Lubbe v Cape Plc* [2000] 1 WLR 1545 (House of Lords). Although Simon France J identified that the Royal Navy Police had offered to investigate the matter if she complained, it is understandable that Ms Young may not have wanted to pursue justice through a branch of the Royal Navy.
116 *Lungowe v Vedanta Resources plc* [2019] 2 WLR 1051, 1077–1083 [85], [88]–[101] (Lord Briggs JSC for the Court) (Supreme Court).

There is authority that, in the second stage of the inquiry, the forum can take into account the need to decide issues of public policy arising under its own law. In *E I Du Pont De Nemours & Co v Agnew*, a man in Illinois had developed necrosis in his legs due to an anti-coagulant drug administered by Du Pont and its subsidiary, Endo.[117] Du Pont and Endo were insured for product liability by various insurers, including Lloyd's underwriters based in England, and the English arm of a Swiss insurance company.[118] In separate proceedings in Illinois, the victim had been awarded punitive damages against Du Pont and Endo. A dispute arose between the insurers about whether they were required to indemnify Du Pont and Endo for their liability, given that a public policy exception precluding indemnification for awards of punitive damages might apply.[119]

The insurers based in England sought a stay on the basis that England was not the appropriate forum. A significant factor for the Court of Appeal in deciding that England was the appropriate forum was the importance of England having control of issues of English public policy arising under English law.[120] Given that the relevant insurance policies were governed by English law, the law to apply in deciding whether a public policy exception to indemnity applied under the policies would also be English.[121] This issue had not been decided in English courts before, and it was not "capable of fair resolution in any foreign Court, however distinguished and well-instructed".[122] This is an example of the second stage of the forum inquiry proving flexible and capable of evolution to address different factors.

It remains to be seen whether this type of reasoning would be applied in New Zealand, and in the context of violations of human rights. The interface between rules of jurisdiction and human rights is a developing one,[123] and *Young's* juxtaposition of this issue with state immunity provides much to think about.

---

117  *E I Du Pont De Nemours & Co v Agnew* [1987] 2 Lloyd's Rep 585, 586 (Court of Appeal of England and Wales) (Lord Bingham).
118  Ibid 587.
119  Ibid 587.
120  Ibid 594.
121  Ibid.
122  Ibid.
123  See Maria Hook, "Private International Law and Human Rights" in Margaret Bedggood, Kris Gledhill and Ian McIntosh (eds), *International Human Rights Law in Aotearoa New Zealand* (Thomson Reuters, 2017) Ch 20.

## 5     Concluding Remarks

*Young*, as the latest in a line of cases in New Zealand and overseas involving the application of state immunity in cases involving human rights breaches, reflects issues that have arisen before. But it shows that New Zealand, at the appellate level, is committed to a doctrine of state immunity that applies even when fundamental values or policies may favour disapplying the immunity. More broadly, *Young* serves as a reminder that New Zealand's conception of CIL in its legal and constitutional arrangements remains underdeveloped, and that there are persuasive arguments for holding that CIL should apply in a more nuanced way than mere incorporation. *Young* also raises interesting questions about the application of fundamental rights, policies and values to questions of jurisdiction. It is hoped that New Zealand authorities – Parliament, executive and judiciary alike – will engage further with these areas of development.

### Acknowledgements

I thank the anonymous peer reviewers for their comments.

# The Human Rights Committee, the Right to Life and Nuclear Weapons: The Committee's *General Comment No 36 on Article 6 of the Covenant on Civil and Political Rights*

*Roger S. Clark\**

Article 6 is the first substantive provision in the *International Covenant on Civil and Political Rights* ("*ICCPR*").[1] Its opening paragraph states, succinctly, that "[e]very human being has the inherent right to life. This right shall be protected by law. No one shall be arbitrarily deprived of his life".[2] Perhaps indicating the contemporary preoccupations of the drafters, this paragraph is followed by four, wordier, paragraphs cabining in the exercise of capital punishment.[3] In October 2018, the Human Rights Committee ("HRC") adopted a lengthy *General Comment No 36* ("*GC 36*") concerning art 6.[4] This Note deals primarily with the portion of the *GC* dealing with nuclear weapons. It reads:

> 66. The threat or use of weapons of mass destruction, in particular nuclear weapons, which are indiscriminate in effect and are of a nature to cause destruction of human life on a catastrophic scale is incompatible with respect for the right to life and may amount to a crime under international law. States parties must take all necessary measures to stop the proliferation of weapons of mass destruction, including measures to

---

\* Rutgers University School of Law, member of the Board of Advisors. Based on the author's Human Rights Day address, New York, 10 December 2018, under the auspices of Lawyers Committee on Nuclear Policy and the Sorensen Center for International Peace and Justice, CUNY Law School, at Bahá'í International Office.

1 *International Covenant on Civil and Political Rights*, opened for signature 16 December 1966, 999 UNTS 171 (entered into force 23 March 1976) ("*ICCPR*").
2 Ibid art 6(1).
3 Ibid art 6(2), (4), (5), (6). Para (3) provides that
   When deprivation of life constitutes the crime of genocide, it is understood that nothing in this article shall authorize any State Party to the present Covenant to derogate in any way from any obligation assumed under the provisions of the Convention on the Prevention and Punishment of the Crime of Genocide.
4 Human Rights Committee, *General Comment No 36 (2018) on Article 6 of the International Covenant on Civil and Political Rights, on the Right to* Life, UN Doc CCPR/C/GC/36 (30 October 2018) ("*GC 36*"). Article 40 *ICCPR* deals with State-reporting obligations and the power of the HRC to make "general comments". See below n 39.

prevent their acquisition by non-state actors, to refrain from developing, producing, testing, acquiring, stockpiling, selling, transferring and using them, to destroy existing stockpiles, and to take adequate measures of protection against accidental use, all in accordance with their international obligations. [273] They must also respect their international obligations to pursue in good faith negotiations in order to achieve the aim of nuclear disarmament under strict and effective international control. [274] and to afford adequate reparation to victims whose right to life has been or is being adversely affected by the testing or use of weapons of mass destruction, in accordance with principles of international responsibility. [275][5]

What follows addresses two main themes exemplified by the HRC's *GC 36*.[6] One is the way in which international law and the practice of international

---

5   Ibid [66]. The relevant footnotes read:
    273 See Treaty on the Non-Proliferation of Nuclear Weapons, 1 July 1968, 729 UNTS 161; Comprehensive Test Ban Treaty, 10 Sept. 1996, Treaty on the Prohibition of Nuclear Weapons, 7 July 2017 (not yet in force); Convention on the Prohibition of the Development, Production and Stockpiling of Bacteriological (Biological) and Toxin Weapons and on their Destruction, 10 April 1972, 1015 UNTS 163; Convention on the Prohibition of the Development, Production, Stockpiling and Use of Chemical Weapons and on their Destruction, 3 Sept 1992, 1974 UNTS 45.
    274 General Comment 14, para. 7. Cf. Legality of the Threat or Use of Nuclear Weapons, 1996 ICJ 226, 267.
    275 Concluding Observations: France (2015), para. 21.
6   For other commentary on para [66], see Alyn Ware, "UN Human Rights Committee Concludes that the Threat or Use of Nuclear Weapons Violates the Right to Life", *Unfold Zero* (Web Page, 23 November 2018) <http://www.unfoldzero.org/un-human-rights-committee-condemns-the-threat-or-use-of-nuclear-weapons-and-other-wmd/>; Daniel Rietiker, "Threat and Use of Nuclear Weapons Contrary to Right to Life, Says UN Human Rights Committee", *Association of Swiss Lawyers for Nuclear Disarmament* (Web Page, 7 November 2018) <https://safna.org/2018/11/07/threat-and-use-of-nuclear-weapons-contrary-to-right-to-life-says-un-human-rights-committee/>; Ryan Goodman, Christof Heyns and Yuval Shany, "Human Rights, Deprivation of Life and National Security: Q&A with Christof Heyns and Yuval Shany on General Comment 36", *Just Security* (Web Page, 4 February 2019) <https://www.justsecurity.org/62467/human-life-national-security-qa-christof-heyns-yuval-shany-general-comment-36/> (note that Shany was the HRC's final reporter for *GC 36*, having been preceded by the late Sir Nigel Rodley, and Heyns is a member of the Committee); Fionnuala Ni Aoláin, "Gendered Security and the Right to Life: Analysis of the UN Human Rights Committee's General Comment", *Just Security* (Web Page, 8 February 2019) <https://www.justsecurity.org/62475/fionnuala-ni-aolain-gender-comment-36-post/>; Janina Dill, "General Comment 36: A Missed Opportunity?", *Just Security* (Web Page, 11 February 2019) <https://www.justsecurity.org/62473/general-comment-36-missed-opportunity/>; Ryan Goodman, "Human Rights and US Military Operations in Foreign Countries: The Prohibition on Arbitrary Deprivation of Life", *Just Security* (Web Page, 19 February 2019) <https://www.justsecurity.org/62630/

bodies such as the HRC develop by accretion and cross-fertilisation from disparate areas of material. The remarks on this theme represent a sketch of the intellectual history of the ideas on nuclear weapons in the *GC 36*, adopted, as is the HRC's practice, by consensus.[7] Nuclear weapons are dangerous to human beings and other living things, and to the very survival of Spaceship Earth itself. How to put that in legal language?

The second theme is institutional. The proposition is that if someone sets up a constitutional document, whether as a structure for government or as, say, an international bill of rights, it will take on a life of its own, both procedurally and substantively. This is especially true if one devises a body such as a court or a committee to oversee such a document in some way – that body will be creative and develop the instrument in ways in which the founders may never have dreamed. If you build it, they will come!

This is the third time that the HRC has addressed the right to life. In its (page-and-a-half) *General Comment No 6* of 1982,[8] it insisted, abstractly, that it is a "right which should not be interpreted narrowly", that "war and other acts of mass violence continue to be a scourge of humanity and take the lives of thousands of innocent human beings every year", that the "protection against arbitrary deprivation of life ... is of paramount importance", that states should take "specific and effective measures to prevent the disappearance of individuals",[9] and it encouraged progress towards abolishing or limiting the application of the death penalty.

Complementing this in its *General Comment No 14* of 1984, entitled *"Nuclear Weapons and the Right to Life"*,[10] the HRC discussed the dangers of nuclear weapons. It then offered some suggestions, in language less emphatic than that now contained in *GC 36*:

---

international-human-rights-law-u-s-military-operations-foreign-countries-prohibition-arbitrary-deprivation-life/>.

7    The development of the HRC's practice on art 40, and especially its General Comments, is well elaborated in Manfred Nowak, *UN Covenant on Civil and Political Rights: CCPR Commentary* (Norbert P Engel, 2nd rev ed, 2005) 712–752. Nowak notes that the French and Austrian experts on the Committee came close to breaking consensus on the Committee's first foray into nuclear weapons in 1984, but ultimately came aboard: at 749. Consensus has continued as a *modus operandi*. See Human Rights Committee, CCPR *General Comment No 14: Article 6 (Right to Life)*, 23rd sess (9 November 1984).

8    Human Rights Committee, CCPR *General Comment No 6: Article 6 (Right to Life)*, 16th sess (30 April 1982).

9    The question of disappearances loomed large on the international agenda at the time: Maureen R Berman and Roger S Clark, "State Terrorism: Disappearances", (1982) 13(3) *Rutgers Law Journal* 531. Disappearances are noted again in *GC 36*.

10   CCPR *General Comment No 14: Article 6 (Right to Life)* (n 7).

3. While remaining deeply concerned by the toll of human life taken by conventional weapons in armed conflicts, the Committee has noted that, during successive sessions of the General Assembly, representatives from all geographical regions have expressed their growing concern at the development and proliferation of increasingly awesome weapons of mass destruction, which not only threaten human life but also absorb resources that could otherwise be used for vital economic and social purposes, particularly for the benefit of developing countries, and thereby for promoting and securing the enjoyment of human rights for all.

4. The Committee associates itself with this concern. It is evident that the designing, testing, manufacture, possession and deployment of nuclear weapons are among the greatest threats to the right to life which confront mankind today. This threat is compounded by the danger that the actual use of such weapons may be brought about, not only in the event of war, but even through human or mechanical error or failure.

5. Furthermore, the very existence and gravity of this threat generates a climate of suspicion and fear between States, which is in itself antagonistic to the promotion of universal respect for and observance of human rights and fundamental freedoms in accordance with the Charter of the United Nations and the International Covenants on Human Rights.

6. The production, testing, possession, deployment and use of nuclear weapons should be prohibited and recognized as crimes against humanity.

7. The Committee accordingly, in the interest of mankind, calls upon all States, whether Parties to the Covenant or not, to take urgent steps, unilaterally and by agreement, to rid the world of this menace.[11]

---

11   Philippe Sands invoked this *Comment* in his argument for Solomon Islands in the *Nuclear Weapons Advisory Opinion* proceedings, which was reproduced in Roger S Clark and Madeleine Sann (eds), *The Case against the Bomb: Marshall Islands, Samoa, and Solomon Islands before the International Court of Justice in Advisory Proceedings on the Legality of the Threat or Use of Nuclear Weapons* (Rutgers University, 1996) 277. In *Legality of the Threat or Use of Nuclear Weapons (Advisory Opinion)* [1996] ICJ Rep 226 ("*Nuclear Weapons Advisory Opinion*"), the International Court of Justice ("ICJ") ignored the *General Comment* but accepted, at 240 [25], that "the protection of *the International Covenant of Civil and Political Rights* does not cease in times of war" and that "[i]n principle the right not arbitrarily to be deprived of one's life applies also in hostilities". It continued: "[t]he test of what is an arbitrary deprivation of life, however, then falls to be determined by the applicable *lex specialis*, namely the law applicable in armed conflict which is designed to regulate the conflict of hostilities": at 240 [25]. The extent to which a *lex specialis* forces art 6 from the field is highly debated. Moreover the ICJ did insist, at 266 [105](2)(E), that "the use of nuclear weapons would generally be contrary to the rules of international law applicable

Unlike the 1984 *Comment No 14*, which related solely to nuclear weapons, the 2018 version, now 23 pages, covers the whole range of the HRC's concerns about the right to life. Using extensive footnotes, the HRC traces the *GC 36*'s content from many sources, including: others of its general comments; its concluding observations on states' reports; its views issued under the *Optional Protocol to the Convention*;[12] other human rights, environmental and laws-of-war treaties; material emerging from other treaty bodies; material from the United Nations ("UN") General Assembly, the World Health Organisation, the European Court of Human Rights, the Inter-American Court of Human Rights, and the African mechanisms on human and peoples' rights; instruments produced under the auspices of what is now the UN Office on Drugs and Crime ("UNODC"); material from Special Rapporteurs and other mechanisms; and material from the International Criminal Tribunal for the former Yugoslavia ("ICTY") and the International Tribunal for Rwanda ("ICTR").

*GC 36* begins with some general philosophical points. The right to life is described as "the supreme right from which no derogation is permitted even in situations of armed conflict". "It is most precious for its own sake as a right that inheres in every human being, but it also constitutes a fundamental right whose effective protection is the prerequisite for the enjoyment of all other human rights and whose content can be informed by other human rights". "The right to life", reiterating what it said in the *General Comment No 14*, "is a right which should not be interpreted narrowly". *GC 36* also contains detailed provisions on abortion, safeguards surrounding assisted suicide, safeguards on the imposition of the death penalty, enforced disappearance, special protections for the lives of children, environmental degradation, climate change and unsustainable development (described as "some of the most pressing and serious threats to the ability of present and future generations to enjoy the right to life"), and the use of force in armed conflict (including through autonomous weapons systems). The *Comment* concludes with the striking proposition (new in the context of art 6) that state parties "engaged in acts of aggression as

---

in armed conflict, and in particular the principles and rules of humanitarian law", and, at 267 [105](2)(F), that "[t]here exists an obligation to pursue in good faith and bring to a conclusion negotiations leading to nuclear disarmament in all its aspects under strict and effective international control". On the relationships between human rights law and the law of armed conflict, see Boyd van Dijk, "Human Rights in War: On the Entangled Foundations of the 1949 Geneva Conventions" (2018) 112(4) *American Journal of International Law* 553.

12   *Optional Protocol to the International Covenant on Civil and Political Rights*, opened for signature 19 December 1966, 999 UNTS 171 (entered into force 23 March 1976) ("*Optional Protocol to the ICCPR*").

defined in international law, resulting in the deprivation of life, violate ipso facto article 6".[13]

Each sentence of the material dealing with nuclear weapons packs several ideas together, all of them having intellectual antecedents.

The first sentence opens with the reference to threat or use of weapons of mass destruction. The term "weapons of mass destruction" has substantial rhetorical force but is not a legal term of art and it has no basis in any treaty definition. The term seems to have been coined initially as a way to describe the mass-bombing attack that destroyed Guernica during the Spanish Civil War.[14] That usage became solidified in the very first resolution of the UN General Assembly in 1946, which created a Commission to make "specific proposals", inter alia, "for the elimination from national armaments of atomic weapons and of all other major weapons adaptable to mass destruction".[15] The emphasis there was on nuclear weapons, although biological and chemical ones were encompassed also. *GC 36* contains footnote references to the later treaties of 1972 and 1992 on those topics.[16] The term "threat or use" finds its origin in the question asked by the General Assembly in requesting an *Advisory Opinion* on the

---

13   It states, moreover, at [70], that:
  States parties engaged in acts of aggression as defined in international law, resulting in deprivation of life, violate ipso facto article 6 of the Covenant. At the same time, all States are reminded of their responsibility as members of the international community to protect lives and to oppose widespread or systematic attacks on the right to life, [281] including acts of aggression, international terrorism, genocide, crimes against humanity and war crimes, while respecting all of their obligations under international law. States parties that fail to take all reasonable measures to settle their international disputes by peaceful means might fall short of complying with their positive obligation to ensure the right to life.
  The Committee's footnote [281] to this material references *2005 World Summit Outcome*, GA Res 60/1, UN Doc A/RES/60/1 (15 September 2005) paras 138–139. For other developments on aggression and the International Criminal Court, see Treasa Dunworth, "International Criminal Law and International Humanitarian Law" (2017) 15 *New Zealand Yearbook of International Law* 229, 231.

14   *The Times* (London, 28 December 1937) 9.

15   *Establishment of a Commission to Deal with the Problems Raised by the Discovery of Atomic Energy*, GA Res 1(I), UN Doc A/RES/1(I) (24 January 1946) para 5(c).

16   *Convention on the Prohibition of the Development, Production and Stockpiling of Bacteriological (Biological) and Toxin Weapons and on their Destruction*, opened for signature 10 April 1972, 1015 UNTS 163 (entered into force 26 March 1975) ("*Biological Weapons Convention*"); *Convention on the Prohibition of the Development, Production, Stockpiling and Use of Chemical Weapons and on their Destruction*, opened for signature 13 January 1993, 1975 UNTS 45 (entered into force 29 April 1997) ("*Chemical Weapons Convention*").

legality of nuclear weapons from the International Court of Justice ("ICJ").[17] The ICJ insisted that "[i]f an envisaged use of weapons would not meet the requirements of humanitarian law, a threat to engage in such use would also be contrary to law".[18] "Threat" does not, on the other hand, appear in the *Rome Statute of the International Criminal Court*, or, in spite of some desultory discussion during the drafting[19] and some tentative musings by the International Law Commission,[20] on the crime of aggression, which became part of the Court's *Statute* in July of 2018.[21]

When, however, in July 2017, the HRC was preparing its first reading version of *GC 36*, the word "threat" was seating itself in the *Treaty on the Prohibition of Nuclear Weapons* ("*TPNW*").[22] The HRC placed "threat" in brackets at that point and several subsequent submissions supported the removal of those brackets, now having the *TPNW* to rely on. The use of the term "indiscriminate effect" is a reference to the laws of armed conflict. The phrase "of a nature to cause destruction of human life on a catastrophic scale" is also an echo of the similar notion in the 1899 *Hague Convention* ("of a nature to cause superfluous

---

17  *Nuclear Weapons Advisory Opinion* (n 11). The question asked by the GA was: "[i]s the threat or use of nuclear weapons in any circumstance permitted under international law?". See also *Charter of the United Nations* art 2(4), which obligates states to "refrain in their international relations from the threat or use of force against the territorial integrity or political independence of any state, or in any other manner inconsistent with the Purposes of the United Nations".

18  *Nuclear Weapons Advisory Opinion* (n 11) 257 [78]. For use of the concept of a threat in other instruments, see also *Protocol Additional to the Geneva Conventions of 12 August 1949, and relating to the Protection of Victims of International Armed Conflicts (Protocol I)*, signed 12 December 1977, 1125 UNTS 3 (entered into force 7 December 1978), which renders it illegal for states "to order that there shall be no survivors, *to threaten an adversary therewith* or to conduct hostilities on this basis" (art 40), and requires them to refrain from "acts or threats of violence the primary purpose of which is to spread terror among the civilian population" (art 51(2)). *Rome Statute of the International Criminal Court*, opened for signature 1998, 2187 UNTS 3 (entered into force 1 July 2002) art 8(1)(b)(xii) forbids states from "[d]eclaring that no quarter shall be given", a form of threat.

19  Assembly of States Parties to the International Criminal Court, *Informal Inter-Sessional Meeting of the Special Working Group on the Crime of* Aggression, Doc No Doc ICC-ASP/5/SWGA/INF 1 9–10, 5 September 2006.

20  "Draft Code of Crimes against the Peace and Security of Mankind" [1991] II(2) *Yearbook of the International Law Commission* 79, 96 (art 16).

21  Dunworth (n 13).

22  *Treaty on the Prohibition of Nuclear* Weapons, opened for signature 20 September 2017 (not yet in force) art 1(d) ("*TPNW*"), under which each party "undertakes never under any circumstances to ... use or threaten to use nuclear weapons or other nuclear explosive devices". For more on the *TPNW*, see Dunworth (n 13) 229.

injury").[23] The phrase "respect for the right to life" combines the content of article 6 of the ICCPR with article 2's reference to respecting and ensuring the rights contained in the ICCPR.[24] The use of the word "incompatible" is a stronger statement than the ICJ's proposition that nuclear weapons are "scarcely reconcilable" with the laws of armed conflict.[25] The assertion that the threat or use "may amount to a crime under international law"[26] is both tentative and ambiguous. Unlike, for example, the General Assembly resolution in 1946 that asserted bluntly that "genocide *is* a crime under international law",[27] the critical word here is "may". Does "may" mean that some cases are crimes and some are not?[28] Or, is it an acknowledgement that the law is not quite there yet? And, is this a reference to individual criminal responsibility or to some notion of state criminal responsibility? Note, in this respect, that it had not been possible to include a prohibition of the employment of nuclear weapons in the *Rome Statute*.[29]

[23] *Convention (II) with respect to the Laws and Customs of War on Land and its Annex: Regulations concerning the Laws and Customs of War on Land*, signed 29 July 1899, 189 CTS 429 (entered into force 4 September 1900) art 23(e).

[24] In *ICCPR* (n 1) art 2(1), each party
undertakes to respect and ensure to all individuals within its territory and subject to its jurisdiction the rights recognized in the present Covenant without distinction of any kind, such as race, color, sex, language, religion, political or other opinion, national or social origin, property, birth or other status.

[25] *Nuclear Weapons Advisory Opinion* (n 11) 262 [95]:
Thus, methods and means of warfare, which would preclude any distinction between civilian and military targets or which would result in unnecessary suffering of combatants, are prohibited. In view of the unique characteristics of nuclear weapons, to which the Court has referred above, the use of such weapons in fact seems scarcely reconcilable with respect for such requirements.

[26] *CCPR General Comment No 14: Article 6 (Right to Life)* (n 7) uses the term "crime against humanity" rather than "crime under international law", consistently with *The Urgent Need for a Treaty to Ban Nuclear Weapons Tests under Effective International Control*, GA Res 1653(XVI), UN Doc A/RES/1653(XVI) (8 November 1961), whose para 1 (d) asserts that "[a]ny State using nuclear and thermo-nuclear weapons is to be considered as violating the *Charter of the United Nations*, as acting contrary to the laws of humanity and as committing a crime against mankind and civilization".

[27] *The Crime of Genocide*, GA Res 96(I), UN Doc A/RES/96(I) (11 December 1946) (emphasis added).

[28] Relevant here is the ICJ's remark that only mass killings with the necessary specific intent amount to genocide ("[i]n the view of the Court, it would only be possible to arrive at such a conclusion after having taken due account of the circumstances specific to each case"): *Nuclear Weapons Advisory Opinion* (n 11) 240 [26].

[29] See generally, Roger S Clark, "The Rome Statute of the International Criminal Court and Weapons of a Nature to Cause Superfluous Injury or Unnecessary Suffering, or which Are Inherently Indiscriminate", in John Carey, William V Dunlap and R John Pritchard (eds),

The second sentence begins by addressing the non-proliferation of all weapons of mass destruction, not only nuclear ones, and the measures which all parties to the ICCPR "*must take*". The footnote refers to the 1968 *Treaty on the Non-Proliferation of Nuclear Weapons* ("*NPT*"), the *Comprehensive Nuclear-Test-Ban Treaty*, the *TPNW* and the biological and chemical weapons conventions.[30] The phrase "including measures to prevent their acquisition by non-state actors" is a direct use of the term "non-state actors", which is probably a blunter version of the *TPNW*'s wording of "transfer to any recipient whatsoever".[31] The obligation to refrain from developing, producing, testing, and the like is essentially the list of prohibitions in the *TPNW*.[32] The obligation to "destroy existing stockpiles" goes beyond what the nuclear powers have accepted, and is a bone of contention for them. The reference to taking "adequate measures of protection against accidental use" sits a little strangely with an obligation to destroy existing stockpiles, as does the phrase "all in accordance with their international obligations". Is this a reference to customary obligations being enshrined in the *GC 36*? Or, do different parties to the *ICCPR* have different obligations, depending on which weapons treaties they have ratified?

The third sentence contains two notions. One is that parties "must also respect their international obligations to pursue in good faith negotiations in order to achieve the aim of nuclear disarmament under strict and effective international control". I take this as a reference both to the treaty obligation under art VI of the *NPT* and to the corresponding customary law obligation to the same effect, which is asserted in the *Nuclear Weapons Advisory Opinion*.[33] The nuclear powers have failed dismally in fulfilling that obligation, and the effort by the Marshall Islands to enforce it in the ICJ was rejected by a bare majority of the court on procedural grounds, based on jurisprudence that is frankly incoherent.[34]

---

*International Humanitarian Law: Challenges* (Transnational Publishers, 2004) 259. Mexico persists in a lonely quest to include nuclear weapons by amendment to the Statute: Assembly of States Parties to the International Criminal Court, *Report of the Working Group on Amendments*, Doc No ICC-ASP/15/24, 16–24 November 2016.

30   *Biological Weapons Convention* (n 16); *Chemical Weapons Convention* (n 16).
31   *TPNW* (n 22) art 1(b).
32   Ibid art 1(a), although the treaty is drafted using the infinitive form of the verb rather than the gerunds used by the *GC 36*.
33   *Treaty on the Non-Proliferation of Nuclear Weapons*, signed 1 July 1968, 729 UNTS 161 (entered into force 5 March 1970); *Nuclear Weapons Advisory Opinion* (n 11).
34   Roger S Clark, "Pacific Island States and International Humanitarian Law", in Suzannah Linton, Tim McCormack and Sandesh Sivakumaran (eds), *Asia-Pacific Perspectives on International Humanitarian Law* (Cambridge University Press, 2019, forthcoming) at nn 90–112 (discussing *Obligations concerning Negotiations relating to Cessation of the Nuclear*

The other is the obligation "to afford adequate reparation to victims whose right to life has been or is being adversely affected by the testing or use of weapons of mass destruction, in accordance with principles of international responsibility". Victim assistance and environmental remediation is an important aspect of the TPNW,[35] but this is not where the footnote to this sentence refers. Rather, it cites the HRC's 2015 *Concluding Observations* concerning France.[36] The relevant section in these observations notes that some 98.3% of claims relating to damage suffered during the French tests in Moruroa and Fangataufa between 1966 and 1996 were rejected, and urges something more effective.[37] Article 6 of the TPNW speaks of "assistance" to those under a state party's jurisdiction who are affected by the use or testing of nuclear weapons. This is exactly the situation in which the inhabitants of French Polynesia found themselves. The *GC 36*'s reference to "reparation" is perhaps a little stronger than the TPNW's mention of "assistance", and the word "victims" would surely include people in neighbouring states or those involved militarily in testing activities.

Keep that thought about the French *Concluding Observations* in mind as we turn to the procedural theme. Article 40 is the primary "enforcement" provision

---

*Arms Race and to Nuclear Disarmament (Marshall Islands v United Kingdom)* (*Preliminary Objections*) [2016] ICJ Rep 833; *Obligations concerning Negotiations relating to Cessation of the Nuclear Arms Race and to Nuclear Disarmament (Marshall Islands v India)* (*Jurisdiction of the Court and Admissibility of the Application*) [2016] ICJ Rep 255; *Obligations concerning Negotiations relating to Cessation of the Nuclear Arms Race and to Nuclear Disarmament (Marshall Islands v Pakistan)* (*Jurisdiction of the Court and Admissibility of the Application*) [2016] ICJ Rep 552).

35   TPNW (n 22) art 6.
36   Human Rights Committee, *Concluding Observations on the Fifth Periodic Report of France*, UN Doc CCPR/C/FRA/CO/5 (17 August 2015) [21].
37   Needless to say, France is not the only nuclear power to be less than fulsome in nuclear reparations. The United States never properly funded the compensation of victims in the Marshall Islands. The United Kingdom was reluctant to recompense its casualties, including its own military and military from Fiji, Australia and New Zealand: Tilman Ruff, "The Humanitarian Impact and Implications of Nuclear Test Explosions in the Pacific Region", (2015) 97(899) *International Review of the Red Cross* 775, 778; Sue Roff, *Hotspots: The Legacy of Hiroshima and Nagasaki* (Continuum International Publishing Group, 1995); Matthew Bolton, *Addressing Humanitarian and Environmental Harm from Nuclear Weapons: Kiritimati (Christmas) and Malden Islands* (Report, May 2018); Matthew Bolton, *Addressing Humanitarian and Environmental Harm from Nuclear Weapons: Kirisimasi (Christmas and Malden Island) Veterans* (Report, May 2018); Dimity Hawkins, *Addressing Humanitarian and Environmental Harm from Nuclear Weapons: Monte Bello, Emu Field and Maralinga Test Sites* (Report, October 2018).

in the *ICCPR*.[38] It requires state parties to make reports which are to be examined by the HRC. The Committee is empowered to make "General Comments" based on the reports.[39] "General comments", as the *Covenant* was being finalized in the mid-1960s, was consistent with the human rights practice of the United Nations: with a few exceptions like South Africa, name no names. Some general themes could be drawn from state reports. Pretty soon, those pesky non-governmental organisations ("NGOs") began to furnish material or counter-reports to the members of the human rights committees, especially to the HRC and the Committee on the Elimination of Racial Discrimination ("CERD"). This became a significant cottage industry – and Committee members read them.[40] It took a few years, but eventually the point was accepted that the members of the Committee could make some quite specific comments on the basis of the contents of, or omissions in, the reports and on the dialogue with States. Don't you love the bland title, "*Concluding Observations*"? Meanwhile, general comments took on a life of their own.

This is demonstrated dramatically by GC 36. The Committee had begun the process of drafting it in 2015, with a half day of general discussion in which governments and NGOs participated. It must have then received much informal input over the next year or so, after which it produced a first reading draft in July 2017 and invited public comments. The formal response was stunning. The HRC's website, maintained by the Office of High Commissioner for Human Rights (OHCHR), contains 23 comments by states, seven by UN organizations, specialized agencies, and experts, 33 by academics and other professionals,

---

38  Other enforcement procedures are not universally applicable to all parties, as is the case with art 40. Article 41 of the *ICCPR* is an opt-in provision that permits the Committee to hear allegations by a state, which itself accepts the article, that other states also accepting it are acting in breach of their obligations. Fifty of the 172 parties to the Covenant have accepted this power, but the procedure has never been initiated. Few states are prepared to use such procedures for fear of the diplomatic costs and the danger that skeletons in their own cupboards will be revealed. The *Optional Protocol to the ICCPR* (n 12) has 116 parties. It enables individual complaints to be made to the Committee and has generated much useful "case law" or "jurisprudence".

39  *ICCPR* (n 1) art 40(4) provides: "[t]he Committee shall study the reports submitted by the States Parties to the present Covenant. It shall transmit it reports, and such general comments as it may consider appropriate, to the States Parties …".

40  For some New Zealand practice in this respect, see discussion of shadow reports under *the International Convention on the Elimination of all Forms of Racial Discrimination*, opened for signature 21 December 1965, 660 UNTS 195 (entered into force 4 January 1969) in Shea Elizabeth Esterling, "International Human Rights Law", (2017) 15 *New Zealand Yearbook of International Law* 152, 157.

three from national institutions, and 107 from NGOs.⁴¹ How else to describe this than as a massive legislative lobbying effort? Many of the comments were single-issue ones, like those that Daniel Rietiker and John Burroughs prepared for the International Association of Lawyers against Nuclear Arms and the Swiss Lawyers for Nuclear Disarmament, which obviously focused on the nuclear issue,⁴² or submissions for and against the right to abortion. The New Zealand government, returning to issues that take up several paragraphs in art 6, argued that, as result of the development of the law, capital punishment should now be regarded as per se contrary to the prohibition of torture and of cruel, inhuman, or degrading treatment or punishment in art 7 of the *ICCPR*.⁴³ Others, especially governments, addressed a whole range of themes. The United States submissions, for example, covered twenty single-spaced pages. *GC 36* emerged from this in its current form, a true "committee job".

---

41   The submissions are collected at "General Comment No 36 on Article 6 of the International Covenant on Civil and Political Rights – Right to Life", *Office of the High Commissioner for Human Rights* (Web Page) <https://www.ohchr.org/EN/HRBodies/CCPR/Pages/GC36-Article6Righttolife.aspx>. One especially interesting submission was from Peace Movement Aotearoa, which noted that it had participated in the 2015 half day or general discussion and made submissions then, and again in 2017 on nuclear weapons, unmanned weapons systems, lethal autonomous weapons systems, militarization and the right to life, indigenous peoples' rights and economic, social and cultural rights.

42   The Association of Swiss Lawyers for Nuclear Disarmament made two sets of comments, one before the first reading draft and one after. The first encouraged expanding on what was then a fairly brief reference to nuclear weapons: "The Incompatibility of WMDs with the Right to Life (Article 6 ICCPR) – a Submission to the UN Human Rights Committee", *Association of Swiss Lawyers for Nuclear Disarmament* (Web Page, 8 September 2016) <https://safna.org/2016/09/08/the-incompatibility-of-wmd-to-the-right-to-life-article-6-iccpr-a-submission-to-the-un-human-rights-committee/>. In the later one they encouraged the retention of the bracketed words "threat" at the beginning of the paragraph and the reference to "reparation" at the end: "Threat or Use of Weapons of Mass Destruction and the Right to Life: Follow-up Submissions to the UN Human Rights Committee on draft General Comment no. 36", *Association of Swiss Lawyers for Nuclear Disarmament* (Web Page, 5 October 2017) https://safna.org/2017/10/05/threat-or-use-of-weapons-of-mass-destruction-and-the-right-to-life-follow-up-submissions-to-the-un-human-rights-committee-on-draft-general-comment-no-36/. This ultimately occurred. They also argued, unsuccessfully, for adding the word "lawful" between "necessary" and "measures" in the phrase "must take all necessary measures to stop the proliferation …". See also Daniel Rietiker, *Humanization of Arms Control Paving the War for a World Free of Nuclear Weapons* (Routledge, 2018).

43   See "Observations of New Zealand on the Human Rights Committee's Draft General Comment No 36 on Article 6 of the International Covenant on Civil and Political Rights, on the Right to Life", *Office of the High Commissioner for Human Rights* (Observations, 5 October 2017) https://www.ohchr.org/EN/HRBodies/CCPR/Pages/GC36-Article6Righttolife.aspx.

A final thought. What legal weight does the *GC 36* have? As the considered opinion of the body charged with the supervision of the *ICCPR*, it must have some significance. Words like "authoritative"[44] or "authentic" interpretation come to mind. General Comments must be a standard against which individual state reports can be assessed by Committee members.[45] Most players in the *GC 36* drama avoided such epistemological issues and concentrated on their particular points. Yet the United States took the offensive. It challenged the authority of the HRC to adopt some parts of this general comment, by arguing that "States Parties to the *ICCPR* have not given authority to the Human Rights Committee or to any other entity to fashion or otherwise determine their treaty obligations", and that[46]

> many of the Committee's more ambitious opinions appear to reflect an attempt to fill what it may consider to be gaps in the reach and coverage of the Covenant…. If one believes there to be gaps in a treaty, the proper approach to take under international treaty law is to amend the treaty to fill those gaps. It is for each Party to decide for itself, as an exercise of its sovereignty, whether it will be bound by what are, in fact, new treaty obligations.

This is by no means a majority position. A British academic surveyed the wide spectrum of views on the "legal relevance" of the Comments:

> Some commentators attach no legal value to them or regard them only as valuable indications of the content of rights and the steps that state

---

44   Nowak (n 7) writes of the "authoritative and universal character of these interpretations": at 749.

45   See Human Rights Committee, *Guidelines for the Treaty-Specific Document to be Submitted by State Parties under Article 40 of the International Covenant on Civil and Political Rights*, UN Doc CCPR/C/2009/1 (22 November 2010), which refers to General Comments as part of the framework governing state reports. See, e.g., reference in the entry for Article 6 (at p. 7) to GC 14 of 1984.

46   "Observations of the United States of America on the Human Rights Committee's Draft General Comment No 36 On Article 6 — Right to Life", *Office of the High Commissioner for Human Rights* (Observations, 6 October 2017) <https://www.ohchr.org/EN/HRBodies/CCPR/Pages/GC36-Article6Righttolife.aspx>. The United States and the United Kingdom have previously contested the obligatory nature of the Committee's opinions on the validity of reservations made by particular states: "Observations by the Governments of the United States and the United Kingdom on Human Rights Committee General Comment No 24(52) relating to Reservations", *Institute for International Law and Justice* (Observations) <http://www.iilj.org/wp-content/uploads/2016/08/US-and-UK-Responses-to-the-General-Comment.pdf>.

parties could or should undertake to ensure implementation, as useful signposts, or as important aids for interpretation. According to others, General Comments have "practical authority" because they represent an important body of experience in considering matters from the angle of the respective treaty. Many commentators, however, accept that General Comments have considerable legal weight. They suggest that a committee is the most authoritative interpreter of the treaty it monitors. They view the treaty body's output as more than mere recommendations. Some even regard General Comments as "authoritative interpretations" of the rights of a treaty. General Comments also contribute to the formation of customary international law by helping to shape opinio juris and state practice.[47]

Don't you love ambiguity?

---

47  Kerstin Mechlem, "Treaty Bodies and the Interpretation of Human Rights", (2009) 42(3) *Vanderbilt Journal of Transnational Law* 905, 929–930 (footnote omitted). Mechlem argues that given the normative significance of Comments, the treaty bodies should pay more attention to sound legal methodology in formulating them, notably using the interpretive framework of arts 31 and 32 of the *Vienna Convention on the Law of Treaties*, signed 25 May 1969, 1155 UNTS 331 (entered into force 27 January 1980). In the only occasion that I have found where the International Court of Justice mentioned a General Comment, it did not address the Comment's juridical status but noted "the development of the principle of equality of access to courts and tribunals ... seen in the significant differences between the two General Comments [in 1984 and 2007] by the Human Rights Committee on Article 14, paragraph 1, of the *International Covenant on Civil and Political Rights* of 1966". Art 14(1) requires that "[a]ll persons shall be equal before the courts and tribunals". The ICJ obviously saw the Comments as reflecting developments in customary law: *Judgment No 2867 of the Administrative Tribunal of the International Labour Organization upon a Complaint Filed against the International Fund for Agricultural Development* (Advisory Opinion) [2012] ICJ Rep 10, 27 [39].

*The South Pacific*

# Pacific Islands Forum 2018

*Tony Angelo\**

The 49th Pacific Islands Forum ("the Forum") was held in Yaren, Nauru from 3 to 6 September 2018.

The Forum was attended by representatives of 18 states of the region in addition to the presence of Tokelau as an associate member and a large number of representatives of regional and international organisations. The Leaders also met with the 18 Forum Dialogue Partners and hosted special sessions with civil society and private sector representatives.

The meeting was overshadowed to a large degree by the restrictions imposed by Nauru's government on media reporting. These restrictions related closely to the issues surrounding the refugee camp in Nauru. Another distraction at the time of the event, in New Zealand at least, was the publicity given to the special flight arranged to get the New Zealand Prime Minister to Nauru.

The press controversy had an early response on 3 July 2018 from the Forum Secretariat. It was noted in that press statement[1]

> The Pacific Islands Forum also vigorously defends the right of any sovereign country to make its own lawful decisions about the ways in which it chooses to govern itself. While Nauru as a sovereign state has stated its position and concerns about media reporting, the Pacific Islands Forum has always stood by the principles of free and open press. This also means a responsibility by the press to be factual in its reporting.

After the Forum, politicians were at pains to criticise the media for the focus on the distractions rather than on the significance of the very fact of the leaders meeting and on the new security agreement which was signed, the Boe Declaration.[2] Indeed, it is clear from the *Forum Communiqué*[3] that the security

---

[*] Professor of Law, Victoria University of Wellington, New Zealand.
[1] "Statement from Pacific Islands Forum Secretariat Regarding Media and the 2018 Pacific Islands Forum in Nauru", *Pacific Islands Forum Secretariat* (Statement, 3 July 2018) <https://www.forumsec.org/statement-from-pacific-islands-forum-secretariat-regarding-media-and-the-2018-pacific-islands-forum-in-nauru/>.
[2] "Boe Declaration on Regional Security", *Pacific Islands Forum Secretariat* (Declaration, 5 September 2018) <https://www.forumsec.org/boe-declaration-on-regional-security/>.
[3] Pacific Islands Forum Secretariat, *Forty-Ninth Pacific Islands Forum: Yaren, Nauru* (Forum Communiqué No PIFS (18) 10, 6 September 2018).

agreement had pride of place among the regular agenda items of fisheries, the ocean and West Papua.

The Boe Declaration is promoted as a complement to the Biketawa Declaration.[4] The Boe Declaration defines an expanded concept of security in clause vii. The emphasis is on human security, environmental matters, transnational crime and cyber security. The Boe Declaration primarily records affirmations of common understandings but contains a commitment in clause viii to:

>...strengthening our respective national security approaches by:
> a. developing our national security strategies: and
> b. strengthening national security capacity including through training.

Paragraphs 13 and 14 of the *Communiqué* noted the need for an implementation plan and that such a plan would be developed by November 2018. It was further agreed that progress on implementation would be reviewed in mid-2019 by the Forum Troika (Nauru, Samoa, and Tuvalu).[5]

This call for action echoed the remarks of the Fiji Minister of Defence and National Security on 18 June 2018 in the course of the pre-Forum workshop on the Boe Declaration. He said that he "would like to see clear actionable statements" about collecting and sharing security information in the Pacific region.[6] In the same speech, he indicated that Fiji was already proceeding with a review of its national security and defence position.

The Boe Declaration is very broadly framed; it may however be interpreted in a number of ways. At the time of discussions among Forum countries before the meeting in Nauru, *The Australian* (6 July 2018) devoted much space to comment on the draft document. On its front page, the main headline was "Pacific Pact to Counter China Push". Page six devoted half a page to analysing some comparative military data relevant to "military might" in the Asia-Pacific region. The data began in regard to Russia and China, but had no figures for France or the United States.

There was also a substantial comment on page 15 under the heading "China's Challenge in our Pacific Neighbourhood". That comment ended with a quote from the Australia's foreign minister at the time, Julie Bishop. She is reported as having said that Australia wished to be the "partner of choice" for is-

---

4  "Biketawa Declaration", *Pacific Islands Forum Secretariat* (Declaration, 28 October 2000) <https://www.forumsec.org/biketawa-declaration/>.
5  Pacific Islands Forum Secretariat (n 3) [14].
6  Ratu Inoke Kubuabola, "Opening Remarks" (Speech, Pacific Islands Forum Members Workshop on the Biketawa Plus Security Declaration, 18 June 2018).

land nations: "Travelling to Micronesia, Palau, Marshall Islands again sends a very clear message that we regard the Pacific as our part of the world, this is our region where we can make a difference".

In the context of the security declaration, it was noted in paragraph 26 of the *Forum Communiqué* that securing the region's maritime boundaries is a key issue for security in the region. The leaders committed themselves to "progressing the resolution of outstanding maritime boundary claims".

The *Forum Communiqué* noted in paragraph 15 that "climate change presents the single greatest threat to the livelihood, security and wellbeing of Pacific people".

At their meeting, the leaders of the smaller island states supported a decision to request the International Law Commission to place the topic of "sea level rise in relation to international law on its long term programme of work, as well as its active programme of work in order to examine the international law implications of sea level rise as a matter of extreme urgency".[7]

Wallis and Futuna was admitted as an associate member of the Forum.

Another significant matter (presented in annex 2 of the *Communiqué*) was a revised scale of contributions to the Forum budget. The new scale will reduce the contribution of each of Australia and New Zealand to 24.5% of budget need by 2021. The next biggest contributor would be Papua New Guinea with an 11.1% contribution. The eight smallest member contributions will be 1.5% of the budget. The members' contributions together are designed to meet 51% of the primary budget, which is the budget which allows the Secretariat to discharge its core functions. Further budgetary provision will be funded by donors. It was also agreed that there will be a triennial review of membership contributions, beginning in 2021.

The *Pacific Agreement on Closer Economic Relations Plus* ("PACER Plus")[8] was not among the topics mentioned in the *Forum Communiqué*. This is notable, particularly because there was a PACER Plus signatories' meeting on 12 and 13 July 2018.

The Pacific Islands Forum for 2019 will be hosted by Tuvalu.

---

7 "Summary of Decisions for the 28th Smaller Islands States Leaders Meeting", *Pacific Islands Forum Secretariat* (Summary of Decisions, 3 September 2018) <https://www.forumsec.org/summary-of-decisions-for-the-28th-smaller-islands-states-/>.

8 *Pacific Agreement on Closer Economic Relations Plus and Associated Side Letter*, opened for signature 14 June 2017, [2017] ATNIF 42 (not yet in force).

*The Year in Review*

# International Human Rights Law

*Cassandra Mudgway\* and Lida Ayoubi\*\**

## 1  Overview

In 2018, Aotearoa New Zealand continued to work on the protection and promotion of human rights both at the international and domestic levels. It was an active year regarding New Zealand's work with human rights treaty bodies. New Zealand received concluding observations from the Committees on the Elimination of Discrimination against Women and on Economic, Social and Cultural Rights. Additionally, New Zealand submitted follow-up comments to the Committee on Elimination of Racial Discrimination and received a List of Issues from the Committee on the Rights of Persons with Disabilities.

As an observer State, New Zealand actively engaged with the work of the Human Rights Council through the introduction and sponsorship of resolutions, and by taking part in interactive dialogues on human rights issues across the world. At the domestic level, the Human Rights Commission continued its work on ensuring that New Zealand works towards meeting its obligations under international human rights law. This piece provides an overview of the activities of New Zealand in 2018 on the international and domestic fronts.

## 2  Periodic Reports to Treaty Bodies

### 2.1  *Concluding Observations of the Committee on Economic, Social and Cultural Rights*

In May 2018,[1] the Committee on Economic, Social and Cultural Rights (ESC Committee) considered New Zealand's fourth periodic report, covering the period from January 2011 to May 2017, on the implementation of the *International Covenant on Economic, Social and Cultural Rights* ("*ICESCR*"). The report was accompanied by a series of shadow reports from Non-Governmental Organisations ("NGOs") including, inter alia, Action for Children and Youth Aotearoa & Child Poverty Action Group, the Human Rights Foundation, the Independent

---

\*   Lecturer, Auckland University of Technology Law School.
\*\*  Lecturer, Auckland University of Technology Law School.
1   Committee on Economic, Social and Cultural Rights, *Concluding Observations on the Fourth Periodic Report of New Zealand*, UN Doc E/C.12/NZL/CO/4 (1 May 2018).

Monitoring Mechanism for the UNDRIP, and Peace Movement Aotearoa, as well as a report by the New Zealand Human Rights Commission in its capacity as a National Human Rights Institution ("NHRI").

In its concluding observations, the ESC Committee noted its appreciation to the New Zealand delegation.[2] It commented on the positive measures New Zealand has taken in implementing provisions of ICESCR since its previous periodic report. These included: the creation and adoption of the *Migration Exploitation Prevention Strategy*; an amendment to the *Immigration Act 2015* (introducing a new offence on exploitation of temporary migrant workers); and a raft of political commitments, such as prioritising the reduction of child poverty, the increase of minimum wages, plans to reform both the education and mental health systems, and a commitment to address the housing crisis.[3]

However, the Committee expressed principal areas of concern, most notably an overall lack of economic, social and cultural rights being enshrined in legislation – despite recommendations made by the Constitutional Advisory Panel in 2013 – and suggested that these recommendations be adopted.[4] Additionally, it recommended that the government fully incorporate the provisions of the Convention, taking into account compliance with the *New Zealand Bill of Rights Act 1990* ("NZBORA") and the *Treaty of Waitangi* ("TOW").[5]

The remainder of the observations discuss the advances and gaps relating to New Zealand's implementation of specific rights and obligations under the ICESCR. Notable concerns focused on gaps in economic, social and cultural rights of certain groups of people, such as women, Māori, Pasifika and people with disabilities. The following summary highlights some of those concerns and consequential recommendations.

The ESC Committee expressed concern for the TOW's lack of legal enforceability, including the non-binding nature of Waitangi Tribunal decisions (which are also ignored by the government), and the failure to ensure Māori participation and consultation in relevant decision-making concerning, for example, their rights to the customary and traditional use of land and water.[6] It recommended that the government take immediate steps, in consultation with Māori, to implement the recommendations and proposals of the Constitutional Advisory Panel and the *2016 Matike Mai Aotearoa Report*.[7] Further, the ESC Committee recommended the government implement decisions of the

---

2  Ibid [2].
3  Ibid [3].
4  Ibid [5], [6(b)].
5  Ibid [6(a)], [6(c)].
6  Ibid [8].
7  Ibid [9(a)], [9(d)].

Waitangi Tribunal and make the necessary legislative changes to implement the *UN Declaration on the Rights of Indigenous Peoples ("UNDRIP")*.[8]

In a similar vein, the Committee noted with concern the prevalence of unconscious bias towards Māori across all areas of life, such as in education, health, and social services.[9] It recommended a comprehensive strategy to understand and address this unconscious bias at all levels of government, supported by the necessary training, education and monitoring mechanisms.[10] The Committee drew the government's attention to its General Comment No 20 on non-discrimination in economic, social and cultural rights.[11]

The Committee welcomed the establishment of the Ministry for Children in 2017 in efforts to address child abuse, but expressed concern about the high levels of domestic violence, including child abuse, and gendered violence, especially for Māori women and girls.[12] It further noted with concern the abuse of children in state care, including historic abuse which had not yet been investigated, and recommended a Royal Commission of Inquiry into these abuses.[13] Additionally, the Committee recommended introducing a comprehensive and cross-cutting strategy to eliminate family violence and intensify its efforts to address such violence.[14]

The government was commended for its efforts in introducing measures to address the protection of rights of persons with disabilities, including measures to improve data collection under the *Human Rights Act 1993 ("HRA")* in 2016.[15] However, the Committee expressed concern that such persons are significantly disadvantaged in their enjoyment of economic, social and cultural rights in comparison with the general population and called on the government to improve those conditions, for example, by implementing the *New Zealand Disability Strategy* and *Action Plans*.[16]

Although the ESC Committee welcomed measures taken to reduce unemployment in New Zealand, it noted with concern the increase of underemployment, especially among Māori and Pasifika.[17] It also noted that women and disabled persons were more likely to be unemployed and that a high number

---

8   Ibid [9(b)], [9(c)].
9   Ibid [10].
10  Ibid [11].
11  Ibid.
12  Ibid [12].
13  Ibid [12], [13(e)].
14  Ibid [13(a)]–[13(b)].
15  Ibid [19].
16  Ibid [20].
17  Ibid [23].

of young people were not employed, in training or in education.[18] It recommended the government to "step up" its efforts and implement targeted measures to address these issues, specifically among certain groups including Māori, Pasifika, women, people with disabilities, and youth.[19] It drew attention to its General Comment No 18 on the right to work. Although the Committee noted with approval the government's plan to gradually increase the minimum wage, it expressed concern about provisions under the *Minimum Wage Act 1983* which left people with disabilities vulnerable to being paid less than minimum wage.[20] It urged the government to amend the *Minimum Wage Act* accordingly.[21]

The Committee expressed concern about the prevailing lack of just and fair working conditions for migrant workers, noting the practices of excessive hours, non-payment or underpayment of wages, and high incidences of workplace death.[22] It recommended the government address these issues through adopting the necessary measures so that migrant workers enjoyed the same rights as the general population, drawing attention to its General Comment No 23.[23] The Committee commended the government for the lowest gender pay gap in the OECD, however, expressed concern that women were still overrepresented in part-time, casual, or low paid employment affecting both the wage gap and their potential pension benefits.[24] It urged the government to intensify efforts to diversify women's working opportunities and adopt the necessary measures to do so: including, adopting into statute the principle of equal pay for work of equal value, awareness-raising, temporary special measures and promotion of flexible work.[25] Regarding social security, the ESC Committee expressed concern about the practice of excessive sanctions against beneficiaries, particularly those with children and recommended an assessment of such practices with a view to reform.[26]

The ESC Committee noted with approval the government's recent commitments to sustained reduction of child poverty, but expressed concern about the overrepresentation of Māori and Pasifika children and children with

---

18 Ibid.
19 Ibid [24].
20 Ibid [25].
21 Ibid [26].
22 Ibid [27].
23 Ibid [28(a)], [29].
24 Ibid [30].
25 Ibid [31].
26 Ibid [34]–[35].

disabilities living in poverty.[27] It recommended that the government strengthen its efforts to tackle child poverty and that such a strategy is well resourced (in financial and human terms).[28] The government was commended for the adoption of the *KiwiBuild* programme, but the Committee noted a number of prevailing concerns regarding housing, such as: the overrepresentation of certain groups (Māori, Pasifika, and persons with disabilities) experiencing housing deprivation and overcrowding; unaffordable housing; the increase in homelessness; unsafe rental housing and the shortage of social and emergency housing.[29] It recommended adopting a human rights-based housing strategy, and to redouble efforts to regulate the private housing market, such as through rent controls and enforcement of minimum standards for rental housing.[30]

The Committee noted with approval the government's efforts to address mental health through an independent inquiry into mental health and addiction services, however, expressed concern about the inadequate response of such services to the rights and needs of certain groups, such as persons with disabilities and prisoners.[31] It recommended that the government ensure the availability of adequate services, including community-based care and in prisons.[32]

Regarding the right to education, the ESC Committee took note of the progress made by the government so far, but expressed concern about certain groups (Māori and Pasifika) who persistently achieve lower outcomes in secondary school and tertiary education and higher rates of stigma from disciplinary measures in secondary school.[33] It also noted with concern the low number of Māori teachers and teachers who speak te reo Māori.[34] The Committee urged the government to reform the education system with a view to adopting culturally appropriate programmes, consulting with Māori and Pasifika groups, and investing in Māori teachers and the Māori language in schools.[35] It also recommended the adoption of a zero-tolerance policy for bullying and harassment in schools and implementing effective protection measures for

---

27  Ibid [37]–[38].
28  Ibid.
29  Ibid [39].
30  Ibid [40].
31  Ibid [46].
32  Ibid [47].
33  Ibid [48].
34  Ibid.
35  Ibid [49].

victims.[36] It drew attention to its General Comment No 13 on the right to education.[37]

The Committee urged the government to ratify the following treaties: the *Optional Protocol to ICESCR*; the *International Convention on the Protection of Rights of All Migrant Workers and Members of their Families*; and the *International Convention for the Protection of All Persons from Enforced Disappearance*.[38] The Committee called for follow-up on recommendations in paragraphs 13(a), 31(b) and 40 within 18 months. Submissions for the fifth periodic report will be received in March 2023.[39]

### 2.2 Concluding Observations of the Committee on the Elimination of Discrimination against Women

In July 2018,[40] the Committee on the Elimination of Discrimination against Women (CEDAW Committee) considered New Zealand's eighth periodic report, covering the period from March 2012 to March 2016, on the implementation of the *Convention on the Elimination of All Forms of Discrimination against Women* ("*CEDAW*"). The report was accompanied by a series of shadow reports from NGOs, including, inter alia, the New Zealand Prostitutes Collective, the Abortion Law Reform Association, Pacific Women's Watch, and the National Council of Women, as well as a report by the New Zealand Human Rights Commission in its capacity as a NHRI.

In its concluding observations, the CEDAW Committee commended New Zealand on its "high level" delegation which included Jan Logie, the Parliamentary Under-Secretary to the Minister of Justice (Domestic and Sexual Violence Issues).[41] The CEDAW Committee commented on positive measures New Zealand has implemented since its previous periodic review, including, inter alia, the introduction of the *Harmful Digital Communications Act 2015* and the *Vulnerable Children Act 2014*,[42] the establishment of the Under-Secretary position on Domestic and Sexual Violence Issues,[43] a *National Pasifika Disability Plan*,[44]

---

36  Ibid.
37  Ibid.
38  Ibid [51]–[52].
39  Ibid [56]–[57].
40  Committee on the Elimination of Discrimination against Women, *Concluding Observations on the Eighth Periodic Report of New Zealand*, UN Doc CEDAW/C/NZL/CO/8 (20 July 2018).
41  Ibid [3].
42  Ibid [4(a)]–[4(b)].
43  Ibid [5(a)].
44  Ibid [5(b)].

legalisation of same-sex marriage,[45] introduction of a second *National Plan of Action (2015–2019)*,[46] and the accession to the *Optional Protocol of the Convention on the Rights of Persons with Disabilities*.[47]

However, the CEDAW Committee signalled principal areas of concern. Although New Zealand has established greater visibility of public-facing information relating to CEDAW, the Committee was concerned that the Convention is absent from consideration among the judiciary and that there is a general lack of support given to civil society organisations for women.[48] The Committee called on the New Zealand government to: raise public awareness of rights of women under CEDAW;[49] sensitise public officials and related personnel to rights under CEDAW;[50] and to provide financial support to relevant civil society organisations.[51]

The remainder of the observations discuss the advances and gaps relating to New Zealand's implementation of specific rights and obligations under CEDAW. Notable concerns focused on gaps in data collection, the legal framework and (lack of) allocated resources regarding the protection and enforcement of rights of particular groups of women who suffer intersecting (and sometimes systemic) oppression, which include: Māori women; Pasifika women; Asian women; migrant and refugee women; women with disabilities; LGBTQI communities; and rural women. The following summary highlights some of those concerns and consequential recommendations.

The CEDAW Committee noted that, although sex discrimination is prohibited under the NZBORA, discrimination based on gender identity, gender expression, or sex characteristics are not and the government was urged to consider adding these to the grounds of discrimination listed in the HRA.[52] While noting the efforts the government has made to combat negative gender stereotypes and harmful practices, the Committee was concerned with the persistence of cyberbullying, especially harmful and persistent with respect to women with disabilities and LGBTQI communities.[53] It recommended specific data

---

45  Ibid [5(c)]; Marriage (Definition of Marriage) Amendment Act 2013 (NZ).
46  *Concluding Observations on the Eighth Periodic Report of New Zealand*, UN Doc CEDAW/C/NZL/CO/8 (n 40) [5(e)].
47  Ibid [6].
48  Ibid [9]–[10].
49  Ibid [10(a)].
50  Ibid [10(b)].
51  Ibid [10(c)].
52  Ibid [11]–[12].
53  Ibid [23(a)].

collection on this issue.⁵⁴ Specific data collection was also recommended to fill the gap of information about harmful traditional practices, such as female genital mutilation, early and forced marriage, dowry payments, polygamy, and crimes of so-called honour.⁵⁵ The CEDAW Committee expressed concern about the performance of unnecessary surgical procedures on intersex children before the age of consent and recommended that the government prohibit such practices or other medical treatment on intersex people.⁵⁶

The CEDAW Committee welcomed the government's initiatives to address gender-based violence against women, including the introduction of workplace protections for victims and increased funding for front-line services.⁵⁷ However, the Committee noted a long list of concerns about the high rates of domestic violence and violence against women in New Zealand, including the absence of a national comprehensive strategy to eliminate such violence.⁵⁸ Other concerns raised included the lack of resources in prevention strategies, prevailing negative attitudes and lack of culturally sensitive approaches in the judiciary, law enforcement, and social welfare services, and the particular vulnerability of certain groups of women (such as disabled women, Māori and Pasifika women, migrant women, and transgender women).⁵⁹ The Committee recommended first and foremost the creation and adoption of a comprehensive national plan to address gender-based violence against women in accordance with General Recommendation No 35.⁶⁰ In addition, the government was urged to modify legislation to provide protections for disabled women from abusive caregivers, strengthen gender sensitivity training for judges as well as law enforcement and social welfare personnel and that this should be guided by victim-centred and culturally appropriate guidelines.⁶¹

The Committee noted New Zealand's efforts to address human trafficking by introducing new legislation, such as the *Organised Crime and Anti-Corruption Act 2014*, and establishing an inter-agency working group to combat trafficking.⁶² However, the Committee expressed concern regarding the lack of protection of migrant women under current legislation, such as the negative implication of the *Prostitution Reform Act 2000* s 19, which prohibits migrant women

---

54  Ibid [24(a)].
55  Ibid [23(b)].
56  Ibid [23(c)], [24(c)].
57  Ibid [25].
58  Ibid.
59  Ibid [25(a)]–[25(j)].
60  Ibid [26(a)].
61  Ibid [26(c)]–[26(f)].
62  Ibid [27].

from working in prostitution and thus exposes them to exploitation and/or trafficking.[63] The Committee recommended that the government amend the legislative framework to remove such negative impacts on migrant women and introduce new measures to provide adequate protection and support to victims of trafficking.[64]

The increase of the number of women in Parliament, including the recent appointment of a female Prime Minister in 2017, was welcomed by the Committee.[65] However, the CEDAW Committee expressed concern about the lack of women in leadership roles in other sectors, and recommended temporary special measures, such as quotas, to achieve equal representation of women and men in both private and public sectors.[66] With regard to education, the Committee acknowledged New Zealand's efforts to increase opportunities for women and girls in male dominated areas of study, especially in science, technology, engineering and mathematics ("STEM").[67] The Committee noted concerns regarding, inter alia, the lack of culturally sensitive, age-appropriate and comprehensive sex and sexuality education in school curricula, and recommended the introduction of such measures.[68]

The government was commended for the introduction of gender pay principles and the pay equity settlement for aged and disability care workers.[69] However, the Committee expressed concerns about persistent discrimination against certain groups of women, including Māori, Pasifika, disabled women and young women, who suffer higher rates of unemployment and a wider pay gap than Pākehā women.[70] The government was called to urgently address the working conditions of these groups and adopt new legislation based on the Joint Working Group recommendations and *Pay Equity Principles* and apply these across both the private and public sectors.[71] Furthermore, the CEDAW Committee noted the persistence of sexual harassment and sexual abuse of women in the workplace and recommended an examination of the organisational culture in workplaces to combat root causes of sexual harassment and sexual abuse.[72]

---

63  Ibid [27(a)]–[27(b)].
64  Ibid [28(a)]–[28(c)].
65  Ibid [29].
66  Ibid [30].
67  Ibid [31].
68  Ibid [31(b)], [32(b)].
69  Ibid [33].
70  Ibid [33(a)], [33(c)].
71  Ibid [34(a)], [34(c)].
72  Ibid [35]–[36].

The Committee recommended decriminalisation of abortion and to instead treat abortion as a health issue, and acknowledged the Minister of Justice's planned review of abortion law.[73] Rights of certain groups of women were explicitly discussed. These included rural women, Māori women and ethnic minorities, and migrant women. For example, the Committee expressed concern regarding the high levels of poverty and gender-based violence against rural women, as well as the disproportionate effect of climate change on such women due to a lack of access to information and consultation.[74] The Committee recommended the government urgently alleviate poverty and introduce modern technology to rural areas.[75] Additionally, the government was urged to adopt all legislative measures, including temporary special measures, to address the intersecting harms faced by Māori women.[76]

The CEDAW Committee recommended that New Zealand ratify the *Convention on the Protection of the Rights of All Migrant Workers and Members of their Families* and the *International Convention for the Protection of all Persons from Enforced Disappearances*.[77] The Committee called for follow-up on recommendations in paras 20, 26(a), 40(a) and 48(a) within two years. Submissions for the ninth periodic report will be received in July 2022.[78]

2.3 *Submission from New Zealand on follow-up to the Concluding Observations of the Committee on the Elimination of Racial Discrimination*

On 22 and 23 August 2017, the Committee on the Elimination of Racial Discrimination ("CERD Committee") requested the New Zealand government to follow up on three of its recommendations from its concluding observations regarding the Treaty of Waitangi Settlement process:[79] these included the implementation of the *Wai 262 decision*, inquiry into abuse of children and adults with disabilities in state care, and efforts to reduce the number of Māori and Pasifika children in state care.

---

73  Ibid [39], [40(a)].
74  Ibid [41].
75  Ibid [42].
76  Ibid [43] and [44].
77  Ibid [54].
78  Ibid [55]–[56].
79  Committee on the Elimination of Racial Discrimination, *Concluding Observations on New Zealand's Twenty-First and Twenty-Second Periodic Reports*, UN Doc CERD/CO/NZL/21-22 (22 September 2017).

The New Zealand government provided the following information to the CERD Committee in September 2018:[80] The government noted that since the concluding observations a further two settlements have been completed with two claimant groups (Ngāti Hei and Ngāti Rangi).[81] The government further noted that the settlement process is to enhance the ongoing partnership between claimant Māori groups, the Crown and all others and is to be completed within the terms of the *ToW* and treaty principles.[82] Detailed information was shared about the settlement process.[83]

As regards the implementation of *Wai 262*, no formal policies have been adopted in response.[84] However, the government commented on the number of measures which informally respond to the report, including *Maihi Karauna (Crown Strategy) for Māori Language Revitalisation*, launched in August 2018.[85] Additionally, the government noted the establishment of co-governance arrangements for natural landmarks of particular cultural and spiritual significance to Māori.[86]

With regards to child abuse in state care, the government pointed to the recent establishment of a Royal Commission of Inquiry into Historical Abuse in State Care, with a key focus on the differential harm caused to Māori and Pasifika groups, LGBTQI communities and persons with mental health issues.[87] Lastly, the government illustrated its commitment to reducing numbers of Māori and Pasifika in state care through the establishment of Oranga Tamariki: Ministry for Children.[88]

### 2.4 *List of Issues Prior to Submission of the Combined Second and Third Periodic Reports of the Committee on the Rights of Persons with Disabilities*

On 23 March 2018, the Committee on the Rights of Persons with Disabilities ("CRPD Committee") submitted its list of issues for New Zealand prior to the

---

80 Committee on the Elimination of Racial Discrimination, *Concluding Observations on the Twenty-First and Twenty-Second Periodic Reports of New Zealand – Addendum: Information Received from New Zealand on Follow-Up to the Concluding Observations*, UN Doc CERD/C/NZL/CO/21-22/Add.1 (17 September 2018).
81 Ibid [3].
82 Ibid [7].
83 Ibid [10], see also Table 1.
84 Ibid [13].
85 Ibid [14].
86 Ibid [16].
87 Ibid [22].
88 Ibid [29].

next periodic report under the Convention.[89] The Committee requested information regarding progress on implementation of rights and obligations under the Convention, including any legislative changes, policies adopted, awareness-raising activities, or any enforcement mechanisms put in place, as well as the resources allocated to fully implement provisions of the *Convention on the Rights of Persons with Disabilities*. The list of issues is structured thematically, according to general and specific provisions. The CRPD Committee seeks progress made or data collected with respect to the following rights and obligations: equality and non-discrimination; women with disabilities; children with disabilities; awareness-raising; accessibility; equal recognition before the law and access to justice; liberty and security of the person; freedom from torture; exploitation, violence and abuse against people with disabilities; personal mobility; freedom of expression and opinion; access to information; respect for home and family; education; health; rehabilitation; employment; adequate standards of living; participation in political and public life; participation in cultural life; and recreation, leisure and sport.

### 2.5 *Human Rights Committee Jurisprudence*

In *Miller and Carrol v New Zealand*,[90] the authors, two prison inmates sentenced to preventative detention, alleged violations of *International Covenant on Civil and Political Rights* ("ICCPR") arts 2, 9, 10 and 14(1). The Human Rights Committee ("HRC") adopted its *Views for Communication No 2502/2014* on 7 November 2017 (made available 19 November 2018).

Both authors had been sentenced to preventative detention for rape (in separate events). In both cases the authors alleged the following: (i) that they had been declined rape-oriented rehabilitation treatment prior to their initial appearance before the Parole Board (10 years after sentencing), thereby hindering their ability to gain parole; (ii) that continued preventative detention after the minimum period for parole had ended was arbitrary and excessive; (iii) that, after being conditionally released, Carrol being recalled to prison within a month without reasons and detained for a further 13 years was excessive and arbitrary; (iv) that being unable to work "outside the wire" due to their automatic status as "high risk" for a period of time aggravated conditions of

---

[89] Committee on the Rights of Persons with Disabilities, *List of Issues prior to Submission of the Combined Second and Third Periodic Reports of New Zealand*, UN Doc CRPD/C/NZL/QPR/2-3 (23 March 2018).

[90] Human Rights Committee, *Views Adopted by the Committee under Article 5(4) of the Optional Protocol, Concerning Communication No 2502/2014*, UN Doc CCPR/C/119/D/2502/2014 (19 November 2018) ("Miller and Carrol v New Zealand").

their detention; and, finally, (v) that the Parole Board was not independent, fair or impartial.

After consideration of New Zealand's submissions and the authors' replies, the HRC made the following finding on admissibility: that claims made under ICCPR art 2 were not admissible because these were general obligations which could not give rise to independent claims under the *Optional Protocol to the ICCPR ("OP-I")*.[91] The remainder of the claims were found to be admissible under the *OP-I*.

On the merits, the HRC made the following findings: that a failure to provide rape-specific rehabilitation treatment during the authors' preventative detention was not a breach of arts 9(4) and 10(3) because they were both offered and participated in a range of different rehabilitation treatments, both before their initial parole period and throughout the remainder of their detention.[92] The authors' continued preventative detention following a punitive term of imprisonment raised "serious concerns" for the HRC and it considered the length of their punitive detention (20 years and 16 years), together with the failure of the state to alter the punitive nature of their detention, a violation of arts 9(1) and 10(3).[93] The recall of Carrol without reasons other than "posing a risk to society", along with length of detention after the fact (13 years), were considered excessive and a breach of art 9(1).[94] Being unable to work "outside the wire" was not considered a breach of arts 9(1), 10(1) and 10(3), because both authors had opportunities to return to such work after the policy ended, but were prevented from doing so because of their own actions.[95] Lastly, the Parole Board was not considered a "court" for the purposes of ensuring the authors' rights to challenge the legality of their preventative detention under art 9(4).[96] New Zealand failed to show that judicial review of the lawfulness of detention was available to the authors according to requirements under art 9(4). Therefore, the HRC did not examine the authors' claims under art 14(1).[97]

Overall, the HRC found violations of arts 9(1), 9(4) and 10(3) with respect to each author.

---

91    Ibid [7.3].
92    Ibid [8.2].
93    Ibid [8.5]–[8.6].
94    Ibid [8.9].
95    Ibid [8.12].
96    Ibid [8.15].
97    Ibid [8.16].

## 3 Engagement with Charter Bodies

### 3.1 Universal Periodic Report

In November 2018, New Zealand submitted its *National Report* to the Human Rights Council ahead of its third universal periodic report ("UPR").[98]

### 3.2 New Zealand Activities in the Human Rights Council

Following its record of active participation in the Human Rights Council, New Zealand continued to contribute to the work of the Council in 2018. In the 37th session, the Minister of Justice, Andrew Little, delivered a statement to the Human Rights Council.[99] Together with Mexico, New Zealand introduced and sponsored a draft resolution on equality for persons with disabilities and their right to access to justice[100] which was adopted by the Council.[101] New Zealand also engaged in the Council's annual interactive debate on the rights of persons with disabilities.[102]

As part of the Council's work in its 37th session on the deteriorating situation of human rights in the Syrian Arab Republic, New Zealand co-sponsored a draft resolution[103] which, after some amendments, was adopted by the Council. As part of the resolution, New Zealand, along with several other countries, issued statements condemning the violations of international humanitarian law and abuses of international human rights law occurring in Syria.[104] New Zealand, as an observer State, also participated in the interactive dialogue with the Independent International Commission of Inquiry on the Syrian Arab

---

[98] Human Rights Council, *National Report Submitted in Accordance with Paragraph 5 of the Annex to Human Rights Council Resolution 16/21: New Zealand*, UN Doc A/HRC/WG.6/32/NZL/1 (13 November 2018).

[99] Human Rights Council, *Report of the Human Rights Council on its Thirty-Seventh Session*, UN Doc A/HRC/37/2 (14 June 2018) [34] (*"Thirty-Seventh Session Report"*).

[100] *Thirty-Seventh Session Report*, UN Doc A/HRC/37/2 (n 99) [277]. See Human Rights Council, *Equality and Non-Discrimination of Persons with Disabilities and the Right of Persons with Disabilities to Access to Justice*, UN Doc A/HRC/37/L.35 (20 March 2018).

[101] Human Rights Council, *Resolution Adopted by the Human Rights Council on 23 March 2018: Equality and Non-Discrimination of Persons with Disabilities and the Right of Persons with Disabilities to Access to Justice*, UN Doc A/HRC/RES/37/22 (6 April 2018).

[102] *Thirty-Seventh Session Report*, UN Doc A/HRC/37/2 (n 99) [123(b)], [178(b)].

[103] *Thirty-Seventh Session Report*, UN Doc A/HRC/37/2 (n 99) [46]. See Human Rights Council, *The Deteriorating Situation of Human Rights in Eastern Ghouta, in the Syrian Arab Republic*, UN Doc A/HRC/37/L.1 (2 March 2018) (*"Human Rights in Eastern Ghouta"*).

[104] *Thirty-Seventh Session Report*, UN Doc A/HRC/37/2 (n 99) [73]. See *Human Rights in Eastern Ghouta*, UN Doc A/HRC/37/L.1 (n 103).

Republic,[105] and co-sponsored a resolution on the human rights situation in the Syrian Arab Republic.[106]

On the matter of protection of human rights in humanitarian situations, New Zealand was a co-sponsor of a resolution put forward by Bulgaria focusing on the protection of the rights of the child.[107] The Council adopted the resolution.[108] Furthermore, New Zealand co-sponsored additional draft resolutions on a range of human rights issues. These included resolutions on the role of good governance in the promotion and protection of human rights,[109] freedom of religion or belief,[110] rights of national or ethnic, religious and linguistic minorities,[111] cultural rights and the protection of cultural heritage,[112] and the implementation of the 2030 Agenda for Sustainable Development.[113] All of these draft resolutions were adopted by the Council.[114]

---

105  *Thirty-Seventh Session Report*, UN Doc A/HRC/37/2 (n 99) [355(b)]. See Human Rights Council, *Report of the Independent International Commission of Inquiry on the Syrian Arab Republic*, UN Doc A/HRC/37/72 (1 February 2018).

106  *Thirty-Seventh Session Report*, UN Doc A/HRC/37/2 (n 99) [394]. See also Human Rights Council, *The Human Rights Situation in the Syrian Arab Republic*, UN Doc A/HRC/37/L.38 (19 March 2018); Human Rights Council, *Resolution Adopted by the Human Rights Council on 23 March 2018: The Human Rights Situation in the Syrian Arab Republic*, UN Doc A/HRC/RES/37/29 (9 April 2018).

107  *Thirty-Seventh Session Report*, UN Doc A/HRC/37/2 (n 99) [267]. See Human Rights Council, *Rights of the Child: Protection of the Rights of the Child in Humanitarian Situations*, UN Doc A/HRC/37/L.33 (20 March 2018).

108  Human Rights Council, *Resolution Adopted by the Human Rights Council on 23 March 2018: Rights of the Child: Protection of the Rights of the Child in Humanitarian Situations*, UN Doc A/HRC/RES/37/20 (6 April 2018).

109  *Thirty-Seventh Session Report*, UN Doc A/HRC/37/2 (n 99) [217]. See Human Rights Council, *The Role of Good Governance in the Promotion and Protection of Human Rights*, UN Doc A/HRC/37/L.15 (19 March 2018).

110  *Thirty-Seventh Session Report*, UN Doc A/HRC/37/2 (n 99) [227]. See Human Rights Council, *Freedom of Religion or Belief*, UN Doc A/HRC/37/L.20 (16 March 2018).

111  Human Rights Council, *The Rights of Persons Belonging to National or Ethnic, Religious and Linguistic Minorities*, UN Doc A/HRC/37/L.25 (20 March 2018).

112  *Thirty-Seventh Session Report*, UN Doc A/HRC/37/2 (n 99) [255]. See Human Rights Council, *Cultural Rights and the Protection of Cultural Heritage*, UN Doc A/HRC/37/L.30 (19 March 2018).

113  *Thirty-Seventh Session Report*, UN Doc A/HRC/37/2 (n 99) [287]. See Human Rights Council, *Promotion and Protection of Human Rights and the Implementation of the 2030 Agenda for Sustainable Development*, UN Doc A/HRC/37/L.37 (20 March 2018).

114  Human Rights Council, *The Role of Good Governance in the Promotion and Protection of Human Rights*, UN Doc A/HRC/RES/37/6 (9 April 2018); Human Rights Council, *Resolution Adopted by the Human Rights Council on 22 March 2018: Freedom of Religion or Belief*, UN Doc A/HRC/RES/37/9 (9 April 2018); Human Rights Council, *Resolution Adopted by the Human Rights Council on 22 March 2018: The Rights of Persons Belonging to National or Ethnic, Religious and Linguistic Minorities*, UN Doc A/HRC/RES/37/14 (9 April 2018);

Similarly, after its introduction by Denmark, New Zealand co-sponsored the draft resolution on the negative impact of corruption on the right to be free from torture and other cruel, inhuman or degrading treatment or punishment,[115] which was later adopted by the Council.[116] New Zealand also showed its support of Armenia's draft resolution on prevention of genocide through co-sponsorship[117] and joined the Council's debate on the promotion of truth, justice, reparation, guarantees of non-recurrence and prevention of genocide.[118]

Another draft resolution that received New Zealand's co-sponsorship[119] was an instrument reaffirming the UN Member States' commitment to effectively address and counter the world drug problem with regard to human rights.[120] Further on the theme of international cooperation, New Zealand joined the states co-sponsoring a resolution on provision of technical assistance and capacity-building for Mali[121] and Libya[122] in the field of human

---

Human Rights Council, *Resolution Adopted by the Human Rights Council on 22 March 2018: Cultural Rights and the Protection of Cultural Heritage*, UN DOC A/HRC/RES/37/17 (9 April 2018); Human Rights Council, *Resolution Adopted by the Human Rights Council on 23 March 2018: Promotion and Protection of Human Rights and the Implementation of the 2030 Agenda for Sustainable Development*, UN Doc A/HRC/RES/37/24 (13 April 2018).

115  *Thirty-Seventh Session Report*, UN Doc A/HRC/37/2 (n 99) [263]. See Human Rights Council, *The Negative Impact of Corruption on the Right to be Free from Torture and Other Cruel, Inhuman or Degrading Treatment or Punishment*, UN Doc A/HRC/37/L.32 (19 March 2018).

116  Human Rights Council, *Resolution Adopted by the Human Rights Council on 23 March 2018: The Negative Impact of Corruption on the Right to be Free from Torture and Other Cruel, Inhuman or Degrading Treatment or Punishment*, UN Doc A/HRC/RES/37/19 (9 April 2018).

117  *Thirty-Seventh Session Report*, UN Doc A/HRC/37/2 (n 99) [296]. See also Human Rights Council, *Prevention of Genocide*, UN Doc A/HRC/37/L.44 (19 March 2018); Human Rights Council, *Resolution Adopted by the Human Rights Council on 23 March 2018: Prevention of Genocide*, UN Doc A/HRC/RES/37/26 (6 April 2018).

118  *Thirty-Seventh Session Report*, UN Doc A/HRC/37/2 (n 99) [158(a)].

119  *Thirty-Seventh Session Report*, UN Doc A/HRC/37/2 (n 99) [315]. See Human Rights Council, *Contribution to the Implementation of the Joint Commitment to Effectively Addressing and Countering the World Drug Problem with Regard to Human Rights*, UN Doc A/HRC/37/L.41 (19 March 2018).

120  Human Rights Council, *Resolution Adopted by the Human Rights Council on 23 March 2018: Contribution to the Implementation of the Joint Commitment to Effectively Addressing and Countering the World Drug Problem with Regard to Human Rights*, UN Doc A/HRC/RES/37/42 (4 April 2018).

121  *Thirty-Seventh Session Report*, UN Doc A/HRC/37/2 (n 99) [1087]. See also Human Rights Council, *Technical Assistance and Capacity-Building for Mali in the Field of Human Rights*, UN Doc A/HRC/37/L.14 (16 March 2018); Human Rights Council, *Resolution adopted by the Human Rights Council on 23 March 2018: Technical Assistance and Capacity-Building for Mali in the Field of Human Rights*, UN Doc A/HRC/RES/37/39 (5 April 2018).

122  *Thirty-Seventh Session Report*, UN Doc A/HRC/37/2 (n 99) [1098]. See also Human Rights Council, *Technical Assistance and Capacity-Building to Improve Human Rights in Libya*,

rights. New Zealand was also one of the co-sponsors of the draft resolution[123] for the convening of a high-level intersessional discussion in April 2018 to celebrate the centenary of Nelson Mandela and his life and legacy.[124]

New Zealand engaged in the debate on various reports delivered to the 37th session, including the annual report of the UN High Commissioner for Human Rights,[125] the country-specific reports introduced by the Deputy UN High Commissioner for Human Rights,[126] the reports of the Chairpersons of the Commission for Human Rights in South Sudan[127] and of the Independent International Fact-Finding Mission on Myanmar,[128] as well as the report of the High Commissioner on the situation of human rights in Libya.[129]

Furthermore, as part of the Council's review of the work of its special procedures mandate holders, New Zealand joined the debate on the reports of the Special Rapporteurs on the situation of human rights in the Democratic

---

UN Doc A/HRC/37/L.45 (21 March 2018); Human Rights Council, *Resolution Adopted by the Human Rights Council on 23 March 2018*, UN Doc A/HRC/RES/37/41 (13 April 2018).

123  *Thirty-Seventh Session Report*, UN Doc A/HRC/37/2 (n 99) [248]. See Human Rights Council, *High-Level Intersessional Discussion Celebrating the Centenary of Nelson Mandela*, UN Doc A/HRC/37/L.26 (19 March 2018).

124  Human Rights Council, *Resolution Adopted by the Human Rights Council on 22 March 2018: High-Level Intersessional Discussion Celebrating the Centenary of Nelson Mandela*, UN Doc A/HRC/RES/37/15 (9 April 2018).

125  *Thirty-Seventh Session Report*, UN Doc A/HRC/37/2 (n 99) [81(a)]. See Human Rights Council, *Annual Report of the United Nations High Commissioner for Human Rights*, UN Doc A/HRC/37/3 (26 January 2018).

126  *Thirty-Seventh Session Report*, UN Doc A/HRC/37/2 (n 99) [94(a)], [1075(b)] and [1085(a)]. See Human Rights Council, *Annual Report of the United Nations High Commissioner for Human Rights on the Activities of the Office of the High Commissioner in Guatemala*, UN Doc A/HRC/37/3/Add.1 (9 February 2018); *Annual Report of the United Nations High Commissioner for Human Rights on the Situation of Human Rights in Honduras: Note by the Secretariat*, UN Doc A/HRC/37/3/Add.2 (20 March 2018); *Annual Report of the United Nations High Commissioner for Human Rights on the Situation of Human Rights in Colombia: Note by the Secretariat*, UN Doc A/HRC/37/3/Add.3 (9 February 2018); *Question of Human Rights in Cyprus: Report of the Office of the United Nations High Commissioner for Human Rights*, UN Doc A/HRC/37/22 (9 February 2018); *Promoting Reconciliation, Accountability and Human Rights in Sri Lanka: Report of the Office of the United Nations High Commissioner for Human Rights*, UN Doc A/HRC/37/23 (25 January 2018); *Situation of Human Rights in the Islamic Republic of Iran: Report of the Secretary-General*, UN Doc A/HRC/37/24 (26 February 2018).

127  *Thirty-Seventh Session Report*, UN Doc A/HRC/37/2 (n 99) [360(b)]. See Human Rights Council, *Report of the Commission on Human Rights in South Sudan*, UN Doc A/HRC/37/71 (14 March 2018).

128  *Thirty-Seventh Session Report*, UN Doc A/HRC/37/2 (n 99) [369(b)].

129  Ibid [1071(b)].

People's Republic of Korea,[130] Myanmar,[131] and Iran.[132] Subsequently, New Zealand joined the states sponsoring resolutions on the situation of human rights in the Democratic People's Republic of Korea,[133] Iran,[134] South Sudan,[135] and Myanmar.[136] New Zealand also co-sponsored a draft resolution emphasising the need for greater co-operation with the Office of the United Nations High Commissioner for Human Rights in Georgia.[137]

In the 38th session, New Zealand made a statement following the report of the UN High Commissioner for Human Rights on the activities of his Office.[138] On issues relating to women and minorities, New Zealand participated in the interactive dialogue with the panellists discussing the role of women in the information and communication technologies (ICTs) sector,[139] the Special

---

130  Ibid [373(b)]. See Human Rights Council, *Report of the Special Rapporteur on the Situation of Human Rights in the Democratic People's Republic of Korea*, UN Doc A/HRC/37/69 (9 March 2018).

131  *Thirty-Seventh Session Report*, UN Doc A/HRC/37/2 (n 99) [377(b)]. See Human Rights Council, *Report of the Special Rapporteur on the Situation of Human Rights in Myanmar: Note by the Secretariat*, UN Doc A/HRC/37/70 (9 March 2018).

132  *Thirty-Seventh Session Report*, UN Doc A/HRC/37/2 (n 99) [382(b)]. See Human Rights Council, *Report of the Special Rapporteur on the Situation of Human Rights in the Islamic Republic of Iran*, UN Doc A/HRC/37/68 (12 March 2018).

133  *Thirty-Seventh Session Report*, UN Doc A/HRC/37/2 (n 99) [389]. See also Human Rights Council, *Situation of Human Rights in the Democratic People's Republic of Korea*, UN DOC A/HRC/37/L.29 (20 March 2018); Human Rights Council, *Resolution Adopted by the Human Rights Council on 23 March 2018: Situation of Human Rights in the Democratic People's Republic of* Korea, UN Doc A/HRC/RES/37/28 (9 April 2018).

134  *Thirty-Seventh Session Report*, UN Doc A/HRC/37/2 (n 99) [407]. See also Human Rights Council, *Situation of Human Rights in the Islamic Republic of Iran*, UN Doc A/HRC/37/L.39 (20 March 2018); Human Rights Council, *Resolution Adopted by the Human Rights Council on 23 March 2018: Situation of Human Rights in the Islamic Republic of Iran*, UN Doc A/HRC/RES/37/30 (13 April 2018).

135  *Thirty-Seventh Session Report*, UN Doc A/HRC/37/2 (n 99) [414]. See also Human Rights Council, *Situation of Human Rights in South Sudan*, UN Doc A/HRC/37/L.40 (20 March 2018); Human Rights Council, *Resolution Adopted by the Human Rights Council on 23 March 2018: Situation of Human Rights in South Sudan*, UN Doc A/HRC/RES/37/31 (13 April 2018).

136  *Thirty-Seventh Session Report*, UN Doc A/HRC/37/2 (n 99) [419]. See also Human Rights Council, *Situation of Human Rights in Myanmar*, UN Doc A/HRC/37/L.43 (20 March 2018); Human Rights Council, *Resolution adopted by the Human Rights Council on 23 March 2018: Situation of Human Rights in Myanmar*, UN Doc A/HRC/RES/37/32 (9 April 2018).

137  *Thirty-Seventh Session Report*, UN Doc A/HRC/37/2 (n 99) [1092]. See also Human Rights Council, *Cooperation with Georgia*, UN Doc A/HRC/37/L.27 (16 March 2018); Human Rights Council, *Resolution Adopted by the Human Rights Council on 23 March 2018: Cooperation with Georgia*, UN Doc A/HRC/RES/37/40 (9 April 2018).

138  Human Rights Council, *Report of the Human Rights Council on its Thirty-Eighth Session*, UN Doc A/HRC/38/2 (24 August 2018) [31(a)] ("*Thirty-Eighth Session Report*").

139  Ibid [51(a)].

Rapporteur on violence against women,[140] the Working Group on the issue of discrimination against women in law and in practice,[141] and the Independent Expert on protection against violence and discrimination based on sexual orientation and gender identity.[142] Further in relation to rights of women, New Zealand co-sponsored draft instruments on the elimination of all forms of discrimination against women and girls,[143] the elimination of violence against women and girls in digital contexts,[144] and the elimination of female genital mutilation.[145]

---

140  *Thirty-Eighth Session Report*, UN Doc A/HRC/38/2 (n 138) [97(b)]. See Human Rights Council, *Report of the Special Rapporteur on Violence against Women, Its Causes and Consequences on Online Violence against Women and Girls from a Human Rights Perspective: Note by the Secretariat*, UN Doc A/HRC/38/47 (18 June 2018); Human Rights Council, *Report of the Special Rapporteur on Violence against Women, Its Causes and Consequences on Her Mission to Australia: Note by the Secretariat*, UN Doc A/HRC/38/47/Add.1 (17 April 2018); Human Rights Council, *Report of the Special Rapporteur on Violence against Women, its Causes and Consequences on Her Mission to the Bahamas*, UN Doc A/HRC/38/47/Add.2 (25 May 2018).

141  *Thirty-Eighth Session Report*, UN Doc A/HRC/38/2 (n 138) [107(a)]. See Human Rights Council, *Report of the Working Group on the Issue of Discrimination against Women in Law and in Practice*, UN Doc A/HRC/38/46 (14 May 2018); Human Rights Council, *Report of the Working Group on the Issue of Discrimination against Women in Law and in Practice on its Mission to Samoa*, UN Doc A/HRC/38/46/Add.1 (14 May 2018); Human Rights Council, *Report of the Working Group on the Issue of Discrimination against Women in Law and in Practice on its Mission to Chad*, UN Doc A/HRC/38/46/Add.2 (8 May 2018).

142  *Thirty-Eighth Session Report*, UN Doc A/HRC/38/2 (n 138) [63(b)]. See Human Rights Council, *Report of the Independent Expert on Protection against Violence and Discrimination Based on Sexual Orientation and Gender Identity: Note by the Secretariat*, UN Doc A/HRC/38/43 (11 May 2018); Human Rights Council, *Report of the Independent Expert on Protection against Violence and Discrimination Based on Sexual Orientation and Gender Identity on His Mission to Argentina*, UN Doc A/HRC/38/43/Add.1 (9 April 2018).

143  *Thirty-Eighth Session Report*, UN Doc A/HRC/38/2 (n 138) [136]. See also Human Rights Council, *Elimination of All Forms of Discrimination against Women and Girls*, UN Doc A/HRC/38/L.1/Rev.1 (3 July 2018); Human Rights Council, *Resolution Adopted by the Human Rights Council on 5 July 2018: Elimination of All Forms of Discrimination against Women and Girls*, UN Doc A/HRC/RES/38/1 (16 July 2018).

144  *Thirty-Eighth Session Report*, UN Doc A/HRC/38/2 (n 138) [168]. See also Human Rights Council, *Accelerating Efforts to Eliminate Violence against Women and Girls: Preventing and Responding to Violence against Women and Girls in Digital Contexts*, UN Doc A/HRC/38/L.6 (2 July 2018); Human Rights Council, *Resolution Adopted by the Human Rights Council on 5 July 2018: Accelerating Efforts to Eliminate Violence against Women and Girls: Preventing and Responding to Violence against Women and Girls in Digital Contexts*, UN Doc A/HRC/RES/38/5 (17 July 2018).

145  *Thirty-Eighth Session Report*, UN Doc A/HRC/38/2 (n 138) [179]. See also Human Rights Council, *Elimination of Female Genital Mutilation*, UN Doc A/HRC/38/L.9 (2 July 2018); Human Rights Council, *Resolution Adopted by the Human Rights Council on 5 July 2018: Elimination of Female Genital Mutilation*, UN Doc A/HRC/RES/38/6 (20 July 2018).

New Zealand also co-sponsored resolutions on human rights on the Internet,[146] human rights in the context of HIV and AIDS,[147] peaceful protests,[148] civil society and human rights,[149] business and human rights,[150] the situation of human rights in Belarus,[151] and the contribution of the Human Rights Council to the prevention of human rights violations.[152]

Discussing human rights in certain countries, New Zealand was part of the debate ensuing the report of the Special Rapporteur on the situation of human rights in Myanmar,[153] the reports on the Democratic Republic of the Congo[154]

---

146   *Thirty-Eighth Session Report*, UN Doc A/HRC/38/2 (n 138) [184]. See also Human Rights Council, *The Promotion, Protection and Enjoyment of Human Rights on the Internet*, UN Doc A/HRC/38/L.10/Rev.1 (4 July 2018); Human Rights Council, *Resolution Adopted by the Human Rights Council on 5 July 2018: The Promotion, Protection and Enjoyment of Human Rights on the Internet*, UN Doc A/HRC/RES/38/7 (17 July 2018).

147   *Thirty-Eighth Session Report*, UN Doc A/HRC/38/2 (n 138) [187]. See also Human Rights Council, *Human Rights in the Context of HIV and AIDS*, UN Doc A/HRC/38/L.12 (3 July 2018); Human Rights Council, *Resolution Adopted by the Human Rights Council on 5 July 2018*, UN Doc A/HRC/RES/38/8 (18 July 2018).

148   *Thirty-Eighth Session Report*, UN Doc A/HRC/38/2 (n 138) [196]. See also Human Rights Council, *The Promotion and Protection of Human Rights in the Context of Peaceful Protests*, UN Doc A/HRC/38/L.16 (29 June 2018); Human Rights Council, *Resolution Adopted by the Human Rights Council on 6 July 2018*, UN Doc A/HRC/RES/38/11 (16 July 2018).

149   *Thirty-Eighth Session Report*, UN Doc A/HRC/38/2 (n 138) [208]. See also Human Rights Council, *Civil Society Space: Engagement with International and Regional Organizations*, UN Doc A/HRC/38/ L.17/Rev.1 (4 July 2018); Human Rights Council, *Resolution Adopted by the Human Rights Council on 6 July 2018: Civil Society Space: Engagement with International and Regional Organizations*, UN Doc A/HRC/RES/38/12 (16 July 2018).

150   *Thirty-Eighth Session Report*, UN Doc A/HRC/38/2 (n 138) [228]. See also Human Rights Council, *Business and Human Rights: Improving Accountability and Access to Remedy*, UN Doc A/HRC/38/ L.18 (2 July 2018); Human Rights Council, *Resolution Adopted by the Human Rights Council on 6 July 2018: Business and Human Rights: Improving Accountability and Access to Remedy*, UN Doc A/HRC/RES/38/13 (18 July 2018).

151   *Thirty-Eighth Session Report*, UN Doc A/HRC/38/2 (n 138) [258]. See also Human Rights Council, *Situation of Human Rights in Belarus*, UN Doc A/HRC/38/L.7 (29 June 2018); Human Rights Council, *Resolution Adopted by the Human Rights Council on 6 July 2018: Situation of Human Rights in Belarus*, UN Doc A/HRC/RES/38/14 (16 July 2018).

152   *Thirty-Eighth Session Report*, UN Doc A/HRC/38/2 (n 138) [299]. See also Human Rights Council, *The Contribution of the Human Rights Council to the Prevention of Human Rights Violations*, UN Doc A/HRC/ 38/L.19/Rev.1 (4 July 2018); Human Rights Council, *Resolution Adopted by the Human Rights Council on 6 July 2018: The Contribution of the Human Rights Council to the Prevention of Human Rights Violations*, UN Doc A/HRC/RES/38/18 (17 July 2018).

153   *Thirty-Eighth Session Report*, UN Doc A/HRC/38/2 (n 138) [253(b)].

154   *Thirty-Eighth Session Report*, UN Doc A/HRC/38/2 (n 138) [878(b)]. See Human Rights Council, *Situation in Kasaï: Report of the United Nations High Commissioner for Human Rights*, UN Doc A/HRC/38/31 (3 July 2018).

and Ukraine,[155] the report of the Independent Expert on the situation of human rights in the Central African Republic,[156] and the Independent International Commission of Inquiry on the Syrian Arab Republic.[157] On Syria, New Zealand was also a co-sponsor of a resolution on the human rights situation in this country.[158]

In the last session of the Council in 2018,[159] and following its practice in the previous meetings, New Zealand made a statement on the update of the High Commissioner for Human Rights on the activities of her Office.[160] New Zealand also made statements during the debate on the annual report of the High Commissioner for Human Rights and the reports of the Office of the High Commissioner and the Secretary-General.[161]

In the 39th session, New Zealand sponsored a resolution on preventable maternal mortality and morbidity and human rights in humanitarian settings.[162] New Zealand further co-sponsored resolutions on a wide range of issues, including the promotion and protection of human rights in the Bolivarian Republic of Venezuela,[163] the situation of human rights of Rohingya Muslims and other minorities in Myanmar,[164] the human rights situation in

---

155  *Thirty-Eighth Session Report*, UN Doc A/HRC/38/2 (n 138) [887(b)].
156  Ibid [895(b)].
157  Ibid [235(b)].
158  Ibid [272]. See also Human Rights Council, *The Human Rights Situation in the Syrian Arab Republic*, UN Doc A/HRC/38/L.20 (2 July 2018); Human Rights Council, *Resolution Adopted by the Human Rights Council on 6 July 2018: The Human Rights Situation in the Syrian Arab Republic*, UN Doc A/HRC/RES/38/16 (19 July 2018).
159  Human Rights Council, *Report of the Human Rights Council on its Thirty-Ninth Session*, UN Doc A/HRC/39/2 (23 November 2018) ("*Thirty-Ninth Session Report*").
160  Ibid [29(b)].
161  Ibid [145(b)].
162  Ibid [187]. See also Human Rights Council, *Preventable Maternal Mortality and Morbidity and Human Rights in Humanitarian Settings*, UN Doc A/HRC/39/L.13/Rev.1 (26 September 2018); Human Rights Council, *Resolution Adopted by the Human Rights Council on 27 September 2018: Preventable Maternal Mortality and Morbidity and Human Rights in Humanitarian Settings*, UN Doc A/HRC/RES/39/10 (5 October 2018).
163  *Thirty-Ninth Session Report*, UN Doc A/HRC/39/2 (n 159) [42]. See also Human Rights Council, *Promotion and Protection of Human Rights in the Bolivarian Republic of Venezuela*, UN Doc A/HRC/39/L.1/Rev.1 (26 September 2018); Human Rights Council, *Resolution Adopted by the Human Rights Council on 27 September 2018: Promotion and Protection of Human Rights in the Bolivarian Republic of Venezuela*, UN Doc A/HRC/RES/39/1 (3 October 2018).
164  *Thirty-Ninth Session Report*, UN Doc A/HRC/39/2 (n 159) [49]. See also Human Rights Council, *Situation of Human Rights of Rohingya Muslims and Other Minorities in Myanmar*, UN Doc A/HRC/39/L.22 (25 September 2018); Human Rights Council, *Resolution Adopted by the Human Rights Council on 27 September 2018: Situation of Human Rights of*

Yemen,[165] Burundi,[166] and Syria,[167] the safety of journalists,[168] equal participation in political and public affairs,[169] human rights and indigenous peoples,[170] national human rights institutions,[171] and assistance to Somalia in the field of human rights.[172]

---

*Rohingya Muslims and Other Minorities in Myanmar*, UN Doc A/HRC/RES/39/2 (3 October 2018).

165 *Thirty-Ninth Session Report*, UN Doc A/HRC/39/2 (n 159) [57]. See also Human Rights Council, *Human Rights Situation in Yemen*, UN Doc A/HRC/39/L.21 (24 September 2018); Human Rights Council, *Resolution Adopted by the Human Rights Council on 28 September 2018: Human Rights Situation in Yemen*, UN Doc A/HRC/RES/39/16 (5 October 2018).

166 *Thirty-Ninth Session Report*, UN Doc A/HRC/39/2 (n 159) [246]. See also Human Rights Council, *Situation of Human Rights in Burundi*, UN Doc A/HRC/39/L.15/Rev.1 (27 September 2018); Human Rights Council, *Resolution Adopted by the Human Rights Council on 28 September 2018: Situation of Human Rights in Burundi*, UN Doc A/HRC/RES/39/14 (5 October 2018).

167 *Thirty-Ninth Session Report*, UN Doc A/HRC/39/2 (n 159) [254]. See also Human Rights Council, *The Human Rights Situation in the Syrian Arab Republic*, UN Doc A/HRC/39/L.20 (25 September 2018); Human Rights Council, *Resolution Adopted by the Human Rights Council on 28 September 2018: The Human Rights Situation in the Syrian Arab Republic*, UN Doc A/HRC/RES/39/15 (8 October 2018).

168 *Thirty-Ninth Session Report*, UN Doc A/HRC/39/2 (n 159) [161]. See also Human Rights Council, *The Safety of Journalists*, UN Doc A/HRC/39/L.7 (21 September 2018); Human Rights Council, *Resolution Adopted by the Human Rights Council on 27 September 2018*, UN Doc A/HRC/RES/39/6 (5 October 2018).

169 *Thirty-Ninth Session Report*, UN Doc A/HRC/39/2 (n 159) [200]. See also Human Rights Council, *Equal Participation in Political and Public Affairs*, UN Doc A/HRC/39/L.14/Rev.1 (26 September 2018); Human Rights Council, *Resolution Adopted by the Human Rights Council on 28 September 2018: Equal Participation in Political and Public Affairs*, UN Doc A/HRC/RES/39/11 (5 October 2018).

170 *Thirty-Ninth Session Report*, UN Doc A/HRC/39/2 (n 159) [220]. See also Human Rights Council, *Human Rights and Indigenous Peoples*, UN Doc A/HRC/39/L.18/Rev.1 (27 September 2018); Human Rights Council, *Resolution Adopted by the Human Rights Council on 28 September 2018: Human Rights and Indigenous Peoples*, UN Doc A/HRC/RES/39/13 (5 October 2018).

171 *Thirty-Ninth Session Report*, UN Doc A/HRC/39/2 (n 159) [900]. See also Human Rights Council, *National Human Rights Institutions*, UN Doc A/HRC/39/L.19/Rev.1 (27 September 2018); Human Rights Council, *Resolution Adopted by the Human Rights Council on 28 September 2018: National Human Rights Institutions*, UN Doc A/HRC/RES/39/17 (8 October 2018).

172 *Thirty-Ninth Session Report*, UN Doc A/HRC/39/2 (n 159) [985]. See also Human Rights Council, *Assistance to Somalia in the Field of Human Rights*, UN Doc A/HRC/39/L.17 (24 September 2018); Human Rights Council, *Resolution Adopted by the Human Rights Council on 28 September 2018: Assistance to Somalia in the Field of Human Rights*, UN Doc A/HRC/RES/39/23 (8 October 2018).

Together with other states, New Zealand participated in the interactive dialogues with the Independent International Commission of Inquiry on Syria,[173] the Commission on Human Rights in South Sudan,[174] the Independent International Fact-Finding Mission on Myanmar,[175] the Deputy High Commissioner reporting on human rights in Yemen,[176] and the Special Rapporteur on the situation of human rights in Cambodia.[177]

## 4  Activities of the New Zealand Human Rights Commission

As a longstanding NHRI, the New Zealand Human Rights Commission ("NZHRC") works to protect and promote human rights and harmonious relations in New Zealand. The UN Office of the High Commissioner for Human Rights and the Global Alliance of NHRIs has accredited the Commission with "A" status, being the highest recognition of independence that an NHRI can achieve. As such, the Commission has the right to speak at relevant UN Human Rights Council and committee sessions.

The Commission released its annual report for the year ending in 30 June 2018, transmitting a copy of the report to the Minister of Justice.[178] As part of New Zealand's commitment to the UN Human Rights Council, the Commission

---

173  *Thirty-Ninth Session Report*, UN Doc A/HRC/39/2 (n 159) [232(b)]. See also Human Rights Council, *Report of the Independent International Commission of Inquiry on the Syrian Arab Republic*, UN Doc A/HRC/39/65 (9 August 2018).

174  *Thirty-Ninth Session Report*, UN Doc A/HRC/39/2 (n 159) [237(b)]. See Human Rights Council, *Situation of Human Rights in Myanmar*, UN Doc A/HRC/RES/37/32 (n 136).

175  *Thirty-Ninth Session Report*, UN Doc A/HRC/39/2 (n 159) [241(b)]. See Human Rights Council, *Report of the Independent International Fact-Finding Mission on Myanmar*, UN Doc A/HRC/39/64 (12 September 2018).

176  *Thirty-Ninth Session Report*, UN Doc A/HRC/39/2 (n 159) [932(b)]. See Human Rights Council, *Situation of Human Rights in Yemen, Including Violations and Abuses Since September 2014: Report of the United Nations High Commission for Human Rights Containing the Findings of the Group of Eminent International and Regional Experts and a Summary of Technical Assistance Provided by the Office of the High Commissioner to the National Commission of Inquiry*, UN Doc A/HRC/39/43 (17 August 2018).

177  *Thirty-Ninth Session Report*, UN Doc A/HRC/39/2 (n 159) [941(b)]. See Human Rights Council, *Report of the Special Rapporteur on the Situation of Human Rights in Cambodia: Note by the Secretariat*, UN Doc A/HRC/39/73 (15 August 2018); Human Rights Council, *Report of the Special Rapporteur on the Situation of Human Rights in Cambodia*, UN Doc A/HRC/39/73/Add.1 (7 September 2018).

178  New Zealand Human Rights Commission, *Annual Report 2017/2018* (Report, November 2018) ("*NZHRC Annual Report*").

also released its updated National Plan of Action.[179] The Commission made several submissions on new legislation and policy proposals, for instance, on the *Child Poverty Reduction Bill*, the *End of Life Choices Bill*, and the *Privacy Bill*.[180]

At the invitation of the UN Special Rapporteur on Adequate Housing, the Commission provided feedback on the Rapporteur's 2018 draft thematic report.[181] This feedback was then included in the Rapporteur's final report[182] and published on the web page of the Office of the High Commissioner for Human Rights.[183]

At the 9th Commonwealth Sports Ministers Meeting, the Commission prepared a briefing paper that called for a greater recognition of sport as a human right and its importance for achieving the 2030 Sustainable Development Goals.[184] The Commission and its staff also attended the ESC Committee's review of the New Zealand's fourth periodic report under the ICESCR,[185] the 11th Conference of State Parties on the CRPD,[186] and the 62nd session of the Commission on the Status of Women.[187] As the Chair of the New Zealand Independent Monitoring Mechanism for CRPD, the Commission met with the CRPD Committee by video conference.[188]

Throughout 2018, the Commission also facilitated gatherings for submissions to the CEDAW Committee's review of the New Zealand periodic report and New Zealand's third UPR review before the UN Human Rights Council.[189] Finally, on the rights of indigenous peoples, the Commission co-hosted an

---

179 New Zealand Human Rights Commission, "National Plan of Action", *New Zealand's National Plan of Action* (Web Page) <https://npa.hrc.co.nz/>.
180 *NZHRC Annual Report* (n 178) 8, 18–20, 32.
181 Ibid 24.
182 Human Rights Council, *Report of the Special Rapporteur on Adequate Housing as a Component of the Right to an Adequate Standard of Living, and on the Right to Non-Discrimination in this Context: Note by the Secretariat*, UN Doc A/HRC/37/53 (15 January 2018).
183 New Zealand Human Rights Commission, "Request for contributions: Designing and implementing effective human rights-based housing strategies", Submission to the Special Rapporteur on adequate housing as a component of the right to an adequate standard of living, 2018.
184 *NZHRC Annual Report* (n 178) 26.
185 Ibid 29. See Committee on Economic, Social and Cultural Rights, *Concluding Observations on the Fourth Periodic Report of New Zealand*, UN Doc E/C.12/NZL/CO/4 (n 1).
186 *NZHRC Annual Report* (n 178) 30.
187 Ibid 31.
188 Ibid 30.
189 Ibid 29.

event to celebrate the 10th anniversary of the *UNDRIP*,[190] and participated at an expert workshop of the UN Expert Mechanism on the Rights of Indigenous Peoples.[191]

---

190  Ibid 29.
191  Ibid 30.

# Indigenous Peoples' Rights under International Law

*Fleur Te Aho*[*]

## 1 Introduction

This note reviews New Zealand state practice regarding Indigenous peoples' rights under international law in 2018 and traces key international developments concerning those rights. New Zealand participated in discussions in international fora regarding Indigenous peoples and their rights, including before the annual session of the United Nations ("UN") Expert Mechanism on the Rights of Indigenous Peoples ("EMRIP") where New Zealand's commitment to develop, with iwi, a national plan of action for the UN Declaration on the Rights of Indigenous Peoples ("UNDRIP")[1] prompted EMRIP to agree a country engagement mission to New Zealand for 2019. Indigenous peoples were referenced in texts advancing the Convention on Biological Diversity ("CBD")[2] and other treaties. Negotiations continued on an international instrument to protect Indigenous peoples' genetic resources ("GR"), traditional knowledge ("TK") and traditional cultural expressions ("TCE") under the auspices of the World Intellectual Property Office ("WIPO"). The UN human rights treaty bodies maintained their attention to Indigenous rights – the Committee on Economic, Social and Cultural Rights ("CESCR") and the UN Committee on the Elimination of Discrimination against Women ("CEDAW") were both critical of the human rights situation of Māori in their reviews of New Zealand. National developments of international significance included the decision in *Ngāti Whātua Ōrākei Trust v Attorney-General*.[3]

---

[*] University of Auckland. Ngāti Mutunga and English.
[1] *United Nations Declaration on the Rights of Indigenous Peoples*, GA Res 61/295, UN Doc A/RES/61/295 (13 September 2007).
[2] *Convention on Biological Diversity*, opened for signature 5 June 1992, 1760 UNTS 79 (entered into force 29 December 1993).
[3] *Ngāti Whātua Ōrākei Trust v Attorney-General* [2018] NZSC 84.

## 2 Developments in Relation to International Resolutions, Recommendations and Other Forms of Non-Binding or Soft Law Instruments

### 2.1 *Indigenous Peoples' Participation in the UN*

The President of the UN General Assembly ("GA") held an informal interactive hearing with Indigenous peoples on the margins of the 17th session of the Permanent Forum on Indigenous Issues ("PFII") "to reflect on possible further measures necessary to enhance the participation of indigenous peoples' representatives and institutions in relevant United Nations meetings on issues affecting them".[4] It was the first of three informal interactive hearings on the topic in preparation for the GA's resumption of consideration of this issue at its 75th session. New Zealand has been supportive of efforts to improve Indigenous participation in the UN.[5]

### 2.2 *2030 Agenda for Sustainable Development*

The Ministerial Declaration of the 2018 High Level Political Forum ("HLPF"), connected to the 2030 Agenda for the Sustainable Development Goals ("SDGs"), contains only one short reference to Indigenous peoples. It stresses "that the commitment to leave no one behind is at the core of the 2030 Agenda" and identifies Indigenous peoples as one of those "whose needs are reflected in the 2030 Agenda".[6] The HLPF was on the theme "transformation towards sustainable and resilient societies" and reviewed progress towards six of the SDGs (SDGs 6, 7, 11, 12, 15 and 17), all of which are of importance to Indigenous peoples. During the HLPF, New Zealand expressed its support for the SDGs, stating that "[a]t home and internationally, New Zealand is committed to a deep and transformative sustainable development agenda that directly reflects the

---

4 Miroslav Lajčák, The President of the General Assembly, "Letter to All Representatives of Indigenous Peoples", *United Nations* (Letter, 9 April 2018) 3 <https://www.un.org/development/desa/indigenouspeoples/wp-content/uploads/sites/19/2018/04/20180409193004.pdf>.
5 Ibid 4. For background see Te Aho "Indigenous Peoples' Rights under International Law" 2017 (15) *New Zealand Yearbook of International Law* 166.
6 Economic and Social Council, *Ministerial Declaration of the High-Level Segment of the 2018 Session of the Economic and Social Council on the Annual Theme "From Global to Local: Supporting Sustainable and Resilient Societies in Urban and Rural Communities", Ministerial Declaration of the 2018 High-Level Political Forum on Sustainable Development, Convened under the Auspices of the Economic and Social Council, on the Theme "Transformation towards Sustainable and Resilient Societies"*, UN Doc E/HLS/2018/1 (1 August 2018) [11].

SDGS".⁷ Positively, several of the Voluntary National Reviews, which outline state progress on implementation of the SDGS, made reference to Indigenous peoples and efforts to secure their enjoyment of the SDGS, including those concerning Australia, Canada and Mexico.⁸

## 3    Developments in Relation to International Treaties

### 3.1    *UN Framework Convention on Climate Change*

Three climate change conferences were held under the auspices of the UN Framework Convention on Climate Change ("UNFCCC") in 2018, with New Zealand participating in each. Of relevance to Indigenous peoples, at the 24th Conference of the Parties ("COP24") the parties agreed to establish the Local Communities and Indigenous Peoples' Platform Facilitative Working Group (the "Working Group").⁹ The Working Group seeks to operationalise and facilitate the work of the Local Communities and Indigenous Peoples' Platform (the "Platform"). The Platform is concerned with enhancing the engagement of Indigenous peoples and local communities in the UNFCCC process, strengthening their efforts to respond to climate change and facilitating the sharing of their mitigation and adaptation practices. The Working Group consists of 14 members, made up of equal numbers of representatives of state parties and Indigenous peoples (with provision for representatives of local communities in the future too).¹⁰ Agreement on the launch of the Working Group followed an open multi-stakeholder workshop on implementing the Platform's functions at the 48th session of the Subsidiary Body for Scientific and Technological

---

7   Craig J Hawke, Permanent Representative of New Zealand to the United Nations, "High Level Political Forum on sustainable development – New Zealand statement", *New Zealand Foreign Affairs and Trade* (Web Page, 20 July 2018) <https://www.mfat.govt.nz/en/media-and-resources/ministry-statements-and-speeches/high-level-political-forum-on-sustainable-development-new-zealand-statement/>.

8   Australian Government, *Report on the Implementation of the Sustainable Development Goals* (Report, 2018); Government of Canada, *Canada's Implementation of the 2030 Agenda for Sustainable Development: Voluntary National Review* (Report, 2018); Federal Government of Mexico, *Voluntary National Review for the High-Level Political Forum on Sustainable Development: Basis for a Long-Term Sustainable Development Vision in Mexico* (Report, 2018).

9   United Nations Framework Convention on Climate Change Conference of the Parties, *Report of the Conference of the Parties on its twenty-fourth session, held in Katowice from 2 to 15 December 2018 Addendum Part two: Action taken by the Conference of the Parties at its twenty-fourth session* (Report, Advance version FCCC/CP/2018/10/Add.1, 19 March 2019) "Decision 2/CP.24 Local Communities and Indigenous Peoples Platform" 9–11 [1].

10  Ibid [3]–[4]. For background see Te Aho (n 5).

Advice ("SBSTA").[11] In addition, "[t]he SBSTA noted the importance of indigenous and traditional knowledge in relevant aspects of scientific data and research and in communication at the science–policy interface"[12] and the Subsidiary Body for Implementation and the SBSTA "took note of the importance of issues", including Indigenous peoples, "and encouraged Parties to take them into consideration when making submissions and during the KJWA [Koronivia joint work on agriculture] workshops".[13]

In February, the Green Climate Fund ("GCF") Board adopted its Indigenous People' Policy (the "Policy").[14] The Policy contains strong references to the UNDRIP and other international instruments of relevance to Indigenous peoples' rights.[15] The guiding principles for the Policy include the following:

(a) *Develop and implement free, prior and informed consent.* GCF will ensure and require evidence of the effective consultation and application of free, prior and informed consent through appropriate procedures and in particular through their representative institutions whenever consideration is being given to GCF-financed activities that will affect indigenous peoples' lands, territories, resources, livelihoods and cultures or require their relocation as described in section 7.2;

(b) *Respect and enhance the rights of indigenous peoples to their lands, territories and resources.* All GCF activities will fully respect and support indigenous peoples' rights related to land, territories and resources, and rights related to cultural and spiritual heritage and values, traditional knowledge, resource management systems and practices, occupations and livelihoods, customary institutions, and overall well-being;

(c) *Recognize key international human rights and principles.* All GCF activities will respect the principles set forth in UNDRIP and other

---

11   United Nations Framework Convention on Climate Change, *Report of the Multi-Stakeholder Workshop: Implementing the Functions of the Local Communities and Indigenous Peoples Platform* (Report, 8 November 2018).
12   United Nations Framework Convention on Climate Change Subsidiary Body for Scientific and Technological Advice, *Report of the Subsidiary Body for Scientific and Technological Advice on the First Part of its Forty-Eighth Session, Held in Bonn from 30 April to 10 May 2018* (Report, FCCC/SBSTA/2018/4, 3 July 2018) [51].
13   Ibid [61].
14   Green Climate Fund, *Decisions of the Board – nineteenth meeting of the Board, 26 February – 1 March 2018* (Report, GCF/B.19/43, 16 March 2018) [42], annex XI.
15   Ibid annex XI [1], [7], [11(f)], [22(c)].

relevant international and regional instruments relating to the rights of indigenous peoples and individuals, including, where applicable but not limited to, ILO Convention No. 169, the International Covenant on Economic, Social and Cultural Rights, and the International Convention on the Elimination of All Forms of Racial Discrimination;...[16]

Indigenous organisations involved in GFC processes, such as Tebtebba, have welcomed the adoption of the Policy.[17]

## 4  Overseas Developments of International Significance

### 4.1  *Bill to Harmonise Canadian Law with the UNDRIP before the Senate*

In Canada, Bill C-262, which seeks to harmonise Canadian law with the UNDRIP, was adopted in its third reading by the House of Commons in May 2018 and is currently before the Senate for approval.[18] The Bill requires the Canadian Government, "in consultation and cooperation with indigenous peoples in Canada", to "take all measures necessary to ensure that the laws of Canada are consistent" with the UNDRIP and to "develop and implement a national action plan to achieve the objective" of the UNDRIP, with annual reporting obligations to Parliament.[19]

## 5  National Developments of International Significance

### 5.1  *Supreme Court Finds Treaty Settlement Decisions are Judicially Reviewable*

In *Ngāti Whātua Ōrākei Trust v Attorney-General*[20] the Supreme Court held that Crown decision-making regarding Treaty of Waitangi ("Treaty") settlement

---

16  Ibid annex XI [22(a)–(c)].

17  "IPs Welcome Adoption of GCF's Indigenous Peoples Policy, Call It a Step in the Right Direction", *Tebtebba: Indigenous Peoples' International Centre for Policy Research and Education* (Web Page, 28 February 2018) <http://www.tebtebba.org/index.php/content/432-ips-welcome-adoption-of-gcfs-indigenous-peoples-policy-call-it-a-step-in-the-right-direction>.

18  "Bill C-262" *Parliament of Canada* (Web Page, 2018) <http://www.parl.ca/DocumentViewer/en/42-1/bill/C-262/third-reading>.

19  Bill C-262: An Act to Ensure that the Laws of Canada are in Harmony with the United Nations Declaration on the Rights of Indigenous Peoples 2018 (C) cls 4–6.

20  *Ngāti Whātua Ōrākei Trust v Attorney-General* [2018] NZSC 84.

negotiations is judicially reviewable, limiting the principle of non-interference with parliamentary proceedings (as agreed settlements are enacted in legislation and, accordingly, subject to parliamentary approval). The decision could also result in changes to the Crown's policy for dealing with overlapping iwi (nations) claims in Treaty settlements.[21]

## 5.2   Waitangi Tribunal Finds Crown Breaches of Self-Determination

In its pre-publication version of Parts I and II of *Te Mana Whatu Ahuru*, the report on the claims of the iwi and hapū (extended kinship groups) of Te Rohe Pōtae (the King Country),[22] the Waitangi Tribunal found major breaches of the principles of the Treaty that impacted the exercise of the tino rangatiratanga (in general terms, the self-determination and autonomy) of the iwi and hapū of Te Rohe Pōtae. The Tribunal recommends that "the Crown acts, in conjunction with Te Rohe Pōtae Māori or the mandated settling group or groups in question, to put in place means to give effect to their rangatiratanga", and outlines minimum conditions that must be met in that regard.[23]

## 5.3   Revised Trans-Pacific Partnership Agreement Legislation Enacted

In 2018 the Trans-Pacific Partnership Agreement Amendment Act 2018 was enacted enabling New Zealand to ratify the Comprehensive and Progressive Agreement on Trans-Pacific Partnership ("CPTPP"), a revised version of the Trans-Pacific Partnership Agreement ("TPPA"). Concerns have been raised that the CPTPP retains many of the issues with the original TPPA, including that the Government failed to engage with Māori for more effective protection for the Treaty of Waitangi within the agreement.[24]

## 5.4   Royal Commission of Inquiry into Abuse in Care

The Government established the Royal Commission of Inquiry into Historical Abuse in State Care and in the Care of Faith-based Institutions (the "Royal Commission"), the largest inquiry of its kind in New Zealand. The abuse of children in care has disproportionately affected Māori. The Royal Commission

---

21    "Landmark Case Will Help Reshape Way Government Deals with Iwi Interests", *Chapman Tripp* (Publication, 20 September 2018) <https://www.chapmantripp.com/publications/landmark-case-will-reshape-way-government-deals-with-iwi-interests>.

22    Waitangi Tribunal, WAI 898 – *Te Mana Whatu Ahuru: Report on Te Rohe Pōtae Claims, Pre-publication version, Parts I and II* (Report, 5 September 2018).

23    Ibid xii.

24    See, eg, Jane Kelsey, Submission to the Foreign Affairs, Defence and Trade Committee on the revised Trans-Pacific Partnership Agreement, Otherwise Known as the Comprehensive and Progressive Agreement on Trans-Pacific Partnership (17 April 2018) [13], [63]–[77].

will be an important vehicle for understanding the abuse experienced by Māori and others and how effective current systems are at protecting against abuse.[25]

## 6 International Oversight of New Zealand's Compliance with Indigenous Peoples' Rights

### 6.1 *UN Committee on Economic, Social and Cultural Rights*

The CESCR, in its 2018 concluding observations on New Zealand, raised far-reaching concerns regarding the human rights situation of Māori. For example, it criticised the domestic insecurity of the Treaty of Waitangi; "the limited efforts that have been made to ensure meaningful participation of Māori in decision-making concerning laws that impact their rights, including land and water rights"; the "entrenched unconscious bias towards Māori in education, health, justice and social services"; and disparities for Māori in employment, housing, health and education.[26] The CESCR's recommendations included that New Zealand, in partnership with Māori, "implement the recommendations of the Constitutional Advisory Panel regarding the role of the Treaty of Waitangi within its constitutional arrangements, together with the proposals put forward in the 2016 Matike Mai Aotearoa report"; "[d]evelop a national strategy to bring legislation and public policy into line" with the UNDRIP; "[t]ake effective measures to ensure compliance with the requirement of obtaining the free, prior and informed consent of indigenous peoples"; and "introduce a government-wide strategy" to combat unconscious bias against Māori.[27]

### 6.2 *UN Committee on the Elimination of Discrimination against Women*

CEDAW identified a host of concerns regarding the ongoing disadvantage experienced by Māori women and offered wide-ranging recommendations to address them. Its recommendations included that New Zealand recognise "the special needs of Maori women and girls" in the development of culturally

---

25   Sir Anand Satyanand, "Terms of Reference following Consultation: the Royal Commission of Inquiry into Historical Abuse in State and Non-State Care" (Terms of Reference, 2018) <https://www.abuseinstatecare.royalcommission.govt.nz/vwluResources/Terms-of-Reference-from-Chair-to-Minister-of-Internal-Affairs-29-May-2018/$file/Terms-of-Reference-from-Chair-to-Minister-of-Internal-Affairs-29-May-2018-a.pdf>.

26   Committee on Economic, Social and Cultural Rights, *Concluding Observations on the Fourth Periodic Report of New Zealand*, UN Doc E/C.12/NZL/CO/4 (1 May 2018) [8], [10], [23], [39], [44], [48].

27   Ibid [9(a)], [9(c)], [9(e)], [11].

appropriate guidelines to respond to violence; "[t]ake measures to reduce poverty and improve the economic empowerment" of Māori women; "adopt all necessary legislation, including temporary special measures and awareness-raising measures, necessary to combat intersecting forms of discrimination against women"; and "provide alternatives to detention to reduce the high number of Māori women detainees".[28]

## 7  Discussion of International Issues Related to Indigenous Peoples in International Fora

### 7.1  UN Expert Mechanism on the Rights of Indigenous Peoples

At its 11th session EMRIP presented its study and advice on Indigenous peoples and free, prior and informed consent ("FPIC")[29] and reported back on its country engagement mission with Finland under its new revised mandate.[30] New Zealand welcomed the study, repeated its standard statement of qualified support for the UNDRIP, and remarked of FPIC that:

> New Zealand has developed, and will continue to develop, its own distinct processes and institutions that afford opportunities to Maori for such involvement in decision-making processes that affect their rights, interests and aspirations. These range from requirements to consult with Maori recognised in statutory frameworks to more general public law obligations on decision-makers to take the Treaty principles into account as relevant considerations.[31]

During the session, representatives of the Iwi Chairs Forum's Independent Monitoring Mechanism on the UNDRIP ("IMM"), who were present at EMRIP to deliver their fourth monitoring report on the UNDRIP, were critical of New

---

28  Committee on the Elimination of Discrimination against Women, *Concluding Observations on the Eighth Periodic Report of New Zealand*, UN Doc CEDAW/C/NZL/CO/8 (25 July 2018) [26(e)], [38(c)], [44].

29  Expert Mechanism on the Rights of Indigenous Peoples, *Free, Prior and Informed Consent: a Human Rights-Based Approach*, UN Doc A/HRC/39/62 (10 August 2018).

30  Expert Mechanism on the Rights of Indigenous Peoples, *Country Engagement Mission (10–16 February 2018) – Finland: Advisory Note* (28 March 2018).

31  Te Puni Kōkiri, "Item 4: Study and Advice on Free, Prior and Informed Consent (FPIC)", *Indigenous Peoples' Centre for Documentation, Research and Information* ("*Docip*") (July 2018) <http://cendoc.docip.org/collect/cendocdo/index/assoc/HASH01ec/fc38e8f6.dir/EM18TPK40709.pdf>.

Zealand's failures to respect the FPIC principle, including regarding seabed mining, water allocation, trade agreements and constitutional transformation.[32] New Zealand did acknowledge that, while it had taken initiatives to align with the UNDRIP, "there are also areas where there is more to be done".[33]

In what turned out to be a productive exchange, New Zealand stated that following EMRIP it would "consider proposals to develop a work programme on a national plan of action, strategy or other measures on the Declaration", that would include engagement with the IMM, Māori generally, other interested parties and the EMRIP experts.[34] Representatives of the IMM seized upon this and indicated that they would like to invite the EMRIP experts to New Zealand in order to assist with the development of that national plan of action, remarking "[c]learly there is interest from Māori as well as the NZ government to engage with the EMRIP".[35] The tactic was effective – EMRIP subsequently advised that it would conduct a country engagement mission to New Zealand in April 2019 to support the IMM and the government in their development of the national plan of action.

### 7.2   *Permanent Forum on Indigenous Issues*

During the PFII's 17th session the PFII considered the theme "Indigenous peoples' collective rights to lands, territories and resources". In its report the PFII identified New Zealand as amongst those states who have taken steps to provide legal recognition for Indigenous peoples' rights to their lands, territories and resources. The PFII remarked that it "welcomes this progress,

---

[32]  TeHuia Bill Hamilton, "Statement from the Aotearoa Independent Monitoring Mechanism", *Docip* (2018) <http://cendoc.docip.org/collect/cendocdo/index/assoc/HASH01cf/05092bd5.dir/EM18HAMILTON40709.pdf>; TeHuia Bill Hamilton, "Statement from the Aotearoa Independent Monitoring Mechanism", *Docip* (2018) <http://cendoc.docip.org/collect/cendocdo/index/assoc/HASH01a9/ee5df7of.dir/EM18HAMILTON70711.pdf>. See also Rangipare Ngaropo "Item 10 Intervention Speech", *Docip* (2018) <http://cendoc.docip.org/collect/cendocdo/index/assoc/HASHb44d/4e367f89.dir/EM18NGAPORO100712.pdf>.

[33]  Te Puni Kōkiri, "11th Session of the Expert Mechanism on the Rights of Indigenous Peoples Item 7 United Nations Declaration on the Rights of Indigenous Peoples: Good Practices and Lessons Learned", *Docip* (2018) <http://cendoc.docip.org/collect/cendocdo/index/assoc/HASH01c4/6924fc8e.dir/EM18NEWZEALAND70711.pdf>.

[34]  Te Puni Kōkiri, "11th Session of the Expert Mechanism on the Rights of Indigenous Peoples Item 3: Country engagement", *Docip* (2018) <http://cendoc.docip.org/collect/cendocdo/index/assoc/HASH01a9/c93f93f0.dir/EM18NEWZEALAND30710.pdf>.

[35]  Tracey Whare, "EMRIP 2018: Agenda item 3: Country Engagement: Statement of the Iwi Monitoring Mechanism", *Docip* (2018) <http://cendoc.docip.org/collect/cendocdo/index/assoc/HASH7b57/30cc0471.dir/EM18WHARE30710.pdf>.

although there remains a wide gap between formal recognition and actual implementation".[36]

In response, New Zealand stated that it "recognises the relationship of indigenous peoples to lands, territories and natural resources noting that this relationship is fundamental to identity, culture and wellbeing".[37] It highlighted its Treaty settlement process and resource management reforms, but noted that "New Zealand also acknowledges the need to address historic barriers to Māori making choices and decisions to develop their own future through their whenua (land)".[38]

Māori present during the session also raised issues regarding the mass imprisonment of Māori, structural racism in the criminal justice system and plans to build a mega-prison.[39] In its report, the PFII expressed concern at the high rates of imprisonment of Indigenous peoples in the Pacific, including New Zealand.[40]

### 7.3 *Convention on Biological Diversity Conference of the Parties*

Indigenous peoples were referenced repeatedly in decisions taken at the 14th Conference of the Parties ("COP14") to the CBD, where New Zealand was an active participant. For example, COP14 invited "Parties to strengthen collaboration with indigenous peoples'[41] and urged action to achieve the Aichi Biodiversity Targets, including through the effective participation of Indigenous peoples and by drawing on Indigenous knowledge.[42] COP14 also invited:

> Parties, when implementing the 2030 Agenda for Sustainable Development, to mainstream traditional knowledge, innovations and practices, including those on customary sustainable use of biodiversity, into the

---

36  Permanent Forum on Indigenous Issues, *Report on the Seventeenth Session (16–27 April 2018)*, UN ESCOR, 17th sess, Supp No 3, UN Doc E/2018/43*-E/C.19/2018/11* (2018) [7].

37  New Zealand representative, "Item 8: Discussion on the Theme "Indigenous Peoples" Collective Rights to Lands, Territories and Natural Resources", *Docip* (2018) <http://cendoc.docip.org/collect/cendocdo/index/assoc/HASH0124/415b2837.dir/PF18NewZealand080417_pdf>.

38  Ibid.

39  Julia Amua Whaipooti, "Address to the UNPFII 2018, Agenda Item 11", *Docip* (2018) <http://cendoc.docip.org/collect/cendocdo/index/assoc/HASH753e/dc30c297.dir/PF18Whaiputti110420.pdf>.

40  Permanent Forum on Indigenous Issues (n 36) [99].

41  Conference of the Parties to the Convention on Biological Diversity Fourteenth Meeting, *Updated Assessment of Progress Towards Selected Aichi Biodiversity Targets and Options to Accelerate Progress* (Draft decision, CBD/COP/14/L.2, 21 November 2018) [9].

42  Ibid annex [2(h)–(i)].

implementation of all relevant Sustainable Development Goals with the full and effective participation of indigenous peoples and local communities and with their prior and informed consent or free, prior and informed consent or approval and involvement, as appropriate, and consistent with national legislation and circumstances, and in accordance with international obligations …[43]

Further, in relation to Article 8(j) of the CBD, decisions at COP14, inter alia, encouraged "Parties to engage with indigenous peoples and local communities in the implementation of the Convention", including in the preparation of national reports and action plans.[44] To that end, the Executive Secretary, subject to the availability of resources, was requested "to extend appropriate assistance that enables representatives of indigenous peoples and local communities to participate effectively in broader discussions and processes under the Convention" related to Article 8(j).[45]

### 7.4 *World Intellectual Property Office*

WIPO's Intergovernmental Committee on Intellectual Property and Genetic Resources, Traditional Knowledge and Folklore ("IGC") continued its drafting of an international legal instrument to appropriately protect GR, TK and TCE. It held two sessions on GR[46] and two on TK/TCE.[47] Unusually, New Zealand did not participate in the sessions, although references were made to its efforts

---

[43] Conference of the Parties to the Convention on Biological Diversity Fourteenth Meeting, *Other Matters Related to Article 8(J) and Related Provisions* (Decision, CBD/COP/DEC/14/14, 30 November 2018) [1].

[44] Conference of the Parties to the Convention on Biological Diversity Fourteenth Meeting, *Integration of Article 8(j) and Provisions Related to Indigenous Peoples and Local Communities in the Work of the Convention and its Protocols* (Decision, CBD/COP/14/17, 30 November 2018) [4].

[45] Ibid [13].

[46] World Intellectual Property Office Intergovernmental Committee on Intellectual Property and Genetic Resources, Traditional Knowledge and Folklore, *Thirty-Fifth Session Geneva, March 19 to 23, 2018: Report Adopted by the Committee* (Report, WIPO/GRTKF/IC/35/10, 25 June 2018) ("WIPO IGC 35th Session"); World Intellectual Property Office Intergovernmental Committee on Intellectual Property and Genetic Resources, Traditional Knowledge and Folklore, *Thirty-Sixth Session Geneva, June 25 to 29, 2018: Report Adopted by the Committee* (Report, WIPO/GRTKF/IC/36/11, 10 December 2018).

[47] World Intellectual Property Office Intergovernmental Committee on Intellectual Property and Genetic Resources, Traditional Knowledge and Folklore, *Thirty-Seventh Session Geneva, August 27 to 31, 2018: Report Adopted by the Committee* (Report, WIPO/GRTKF/IC/37/17, 10 December 2018) ("WIPO IGC 37th Session"); World Intellectual Property Office Intergovernmental Committee on Intellectual Property and Genetic Resources, Traditional

to better protect GR, TK and TCE by the Chair during the latter two sessions.[48] The same Chair also referenced the UNDRIP. At the 37th session he remarked that the UNDRIP:

> was principle-based and guided Member States on how they should support the rights of indigenous peoples. In a way, the work of the IGC was about operationalizing the aspirations of indigenous peoples in that declaratory statement. He recalled Article 31 which was an unambiguous statement.[49]

Further, in a new move to progress the text, and to help support the constraints on Indigenous participation in its drafting (which has long been the subject of criticism), the IGC included Indigenous peoples' representatives in a formal ad hoc expert group to facilitate negotiations that met for the first time before the IGC's 36th session.[50]

## 8 Developments Contributing to Customary International Law or of Particular Relevance to New Zealand

The bodies monitoring state compliance with the core human rights treaties, in particular the Committee on the Elimination of Racial Discrimination and the Human Rights Committee, continued to offer criticism of the situation of Indigenous peoples and recommendations to improve their position, including for protection of their land rights.[51] Recommendations regarding Indigenous peoples' rights also featured in the Human Rights Council's Universal Periodic Review process, for example, regarding Indigenous peoples' lands and the FPIC principle.[52]

---

Knowledge and Folklore, *Thirty-Eighth Session Geneva, December 10 to 14, 2018: Initial Draft Report* (Report, WIPO/GRTKF/IC/38/16 Prov, 8 February 2019) ("WIPO IGC 38th Session").

48   WIPO IGC 37th Session (n 47) [41]; WIPO IGC 38th Session (n 47) [47].
49   WIPO IGC 37th Session (n 47) [41]. See also WIPO IGC 38th Session (n 47) [47].
50   WIPO IGC 35th Session (n 46) [312].
51   See, eg, Committee on the Elimination of Racial Discrimination, *Concluding Observations on the Combined Twenty-Second and Twenty-Third Periodic Reports of Peru*, UN Doc CERD/C/PER/CO/22-23 (23 May 2018) [12], [13], [16], [17]-[35], [38]-[41]; Human Rights Committee, *Concluding observations on the fourth periodic report of Guatemala*, UN Doc CCPR/C/GTM/CO/4 (7 May 2018) [8]-[11], [36]-[39].
52   See, eg, Human Rights Council, *Report of the Working Group on the Universal Periodic Review: Canada*, UN Doc A/HRC/39/11 (11 July 2018) [142.252], [142.2555] (Russian Federation), [142.254] (Holy See).

# International Economic Law

*An Hertogen*\*

## 1    Introduction

Despite the continuing threats to the world trade system posed by President Trump's trade wars against China as well as against allies such as Canada and the European Union ("EU"), and by the appointments crisis at the Appellate Body of the World Trade Organization ("WTO"), New Zealand remained committed in 2018 to strengthening the rules-based framework. As this review will illustrate, we see this through its active support of WTO negotiations, including those regarding reform of the Appellate Body, as well as in its active pursuit of regional free trade agreements that secure market access across the world.

## 2    Preferential Trade Negotiations

Preferential or free trade agreements ("PTAs") continued to be high on the agenda in 2018, with two ratification milestones in October 2018. On 24 October 2018, New Zealand became the first signatory to ratify the *Pacific Agreement on Closer Economic Relations Plus* ("*PACER-Plus*").[1] The next day the *Comprehensive and Progressive Agreement for Trans-Pacific Partnership Amendment Act 2018* received royal assent. The Act entered into force on 30 December 2018,[2] at the same time as the *Comprehensive and Progressive Agreement for Trans-Pacific Partnership* ("*CPTPP*") for New Zealand, Australia, Canada, Japan, Mexico, and Singapore.[3] The *CPTPP*'s ratification was the culmination of significant activity during 2018, starting with the signature on 8 March 2018 of the revised version of the *Trans-Pacific Partnership Agreement* by the 11 parties[4] that remained after the United States' withdrawal. The agreement was reported back to Parliament's Foreign Affairs, Defence and Trade Select Committee

---

\*  University of Auckland.
1  *Pacific Agreement on Closer Economic Relations Plus*, signed 14 June 2017 (not yet in force).
2  *Comprehensive and Progressive Agreement for Trans-Pacific Partnership Amendment Act 2018 Commencement Order 2018.*
3  With respect to Viet Nam, the *CPTPP* entered into force on 14 January 2019. The other signatories have, at the time of writing, yet to ratify the agreement.
4  Australia, Brunei-Darussalam, Canada, Chile, Japan, Malaysia, Mexico, Peru, Singapore, Viet Nam, and New Zealand.

on 24 May 2018, followed a month later by the introduction of the *Trans-Pacific Partnership Agreement (CPTPP) Amendment Bill*. This Bill amended the *Trans-Pacific Partnership Agreement Amendment Act 2016* to reflect the CPTPP's suspension of 22 United States-favoured items in the *Trans-Pacific Partnership*.[5] The CPTPP became New Zealand's first PTA with Japan, Mexico, and Canada, and it will be New Zealand's first PTA with Peru, 60 days after Peru completes its ratification process.

A number of the CPTPP signatories have been negotiating other PTAs with New Zealand. The four members of the Pacific Alliance (Chile, Colombia, Mexico and Peru) have continued to negotiate a PTA with New Zealand, as well as parallel agreements with Australia, Canada and Singapore. Five negotiating rounds and two meetings of Trade Ministers took place in 2018,[6] although an agreement has yet to be concluded despite the original intention of achieving this in 2018.[7] There is also an overlap between the parties to the CPTPP and the ongoing negotiations to consolidate the six respective FTAs of the Association of Southeast Asian Nations ("ASEAN")[8] with Australia, China, India,[9] Japan, Korea and New Zealand into the *Regional Comprehensive Economic Partnership* ("*RCEP*"). Six more negotiation rounds took place in 2018, bringing the total number of rounds to 24 by the end of 2018.[10] Seven chapters have by now been concluded,[11] bringing closer the goal of finishing negotiations in 2019.

---

5  For a comparison between both Agreements, see "CPTPP vs TPP", *New Zealand Foreign Affairs and Trade: Manatū Aorere* (Web Page) <https://www.mfat.govt.nz/en/trade/free-trade-agreements/free-trade-agreements-in-force/cptpp/understanding-cptpp/tpp-and-cptpp-the-differences-explained>.

6  "Timeline for Negotiations", *New Zealand Foreign Affairs and Trade: Manatū Aorere* (Web Page) <https://www.mfat.govt.nz/en/trade/free-trade-agreements/agreements-under-negotiation/new-zealand-pacific-alliance-free-trade-agreement/timeline-for-negotiations/>.

7  An Hertogen, "International Economic Law" (2017) 15 *New Zealand Yearbook of International Law* 177, 180.

8  The ASEAN members are Brunei-Darussalam, Cambodia, Indonesia, Laos, Malaysia, Myanmar, the Philippines, Singapore, Thailand, and Viet Nam.

9  Officially, India and New Zealand are still negotiating a bilateral FTA, but there have been no further negotiating rounds since February 2015: "New Zealand-India FTA", *New Zealand Foreign Affairs and Trade: Manatū Aorere* (Web Page) <https://www.mfat.govt.nz/en/trade/free-trade-agreements/agreements-under-negotiation/india/>.

10  "Next steps and timeline", *New Zealand Foreign Affairs and Trade: Manatū Aorere* (Web Page) <https://www.mfat.govt.nz/en/trade/free-trade-agreements/agreements-under-negotiation/regional-comprehensive-economic-partnership-rcep/next-steps-and-timeline/>.

11  "Joint Leaders' Statement on the Regional Comprehensive Economic Partnership (RCEP) Negotiations", *New Zealand Foreign Affairs and Trade: Manatū Aorere* (Joint Statement,

In addition, New Zealand has held bilateral negotiations to update its existing FTAs with two RCEP negotiating parties. First, New Zealand and Singapore negotiated a Protocol[12] to their 2000 *Agreement on a Closer Economic Partnership* ("NZSCEP"),[13] in order to update the original Agreement to reflect current PTA practice. A side letter will govern any potential conflicts between the NZSCEP and the other preferential trade agreements, including the CPTPP.[14] The Protocol's signature is expected in 2019.[15] The update of the PTA with China has progressed after three more rounds in 2018,[16] but a closing date is not yet in sight.[17]

A major new addition to New Zealand's suite of PTAs, if concluded, would be the proposed agreement with the EU, as New Zealand does not yet have preferential access to the EU market, despite it being one of New Zealand's most important trading partners. Negotiations were formally launched in June 2018, after the European Council's May 2018 approval of the European Commission's negotiating mandate.[18] New Zealand has also made a summary of its

---

14 November 2018) <https://www.mfat.govt.nz/assets/FTAs-in-negotiations/RCEP/04-RCEPSUMMIT2-Leaders-Joint-Statement_FINAL.pdf>.

12  The texts of the Protocol and its Annexes are available at "CEP Text", *New Zealand Foreign Affairs and Trade: Manatū Aorere* (Web Page) <https://www.mfat.govt.nz/en/trade/free-trade-agreements/free-trade-agreements-in-force/nz-singapore-closer-economic-partnership/cep-text/>.

13  *Agreement between New Zealand and Singapore on a Closer Economic Partnership*, signed 14 November 2000, [2001] NZTS 1 (entered into force 1 January 2001).

14  "Side-Letter Confirming the Relationship between the Protocol and New Zealand's Existing Free Trade Agreements with Singapore", *New Zealand Foreign Affairs and Trade: Manatū Aorere* (Letter) <https://www.mfat.govt.nz/assets/FTAs-agreements-in-force/Singapore-FTA/CEPUpgrade-Protocol-all-chapters-and-annexes/Side-letter-confirming.pdf>.

15  "Protocol to Amend the Agreement between Singapore and New Zealand on a Closer Economic Partnership and Associated Instruments: National Interest Analysis", *New Zealand Foreign Affairs and Trade: Manatū Aorere* (National Interest Analysis, October 2018) <https://www.mfat.govt.nz/assets/FTAs-agreements-in-force/Singapore-FTA/Singapore-CEP-Upgrade-FINAL-NIA.pdf>.

16  "Next steps and timeline", *New Zealand Foreign Affairs and Trade: Manatū Aorere* (Web Page) <https://www.mfat.govt.nz/en/trade/free-trade-agreements/agreements-under-negotiation/nz-china-fta-upgrade/timeline/>.

17  Sam Sachdeva, "MFAT Boss Defends NZ-China Relationship", *Newsroom* (News Article, 14 December 2018) <https://www.newsroom.co.nz/2018/12/13/362531/mfat-boss-defends-nz-china-relationship>.

18  "Negotiating Directives for a Free Trade Agreement with New Zealand", *Council of the European Union* (Negotiating Directives, 25 June 2018) <https://data.consilium.europa.eu/doc/document/ST-7661-2018-ADD-1-DCL-1/en/pdf>.

negotiating objectives available online.[19] Two negotiating rounds followed in July[20] and October 2018,[21] and the parties have confirmed the EU's original goal of completing the agreement by the end of 2019.[22] After the two 2018 rounds, the parties reported agreement on the text on trade in goods, rules of origin, customs and trade facilitation, technical barriers to trade, services, and dispute settlement.[23] Most of the text is drawn from existing EU texts.[24] New Zealand's text proposals on good regulatory practice and regulatory cooperation, sanitary and phytosanitary measures, the Treaty of Waitangi exception, and competition and consumer protection have been released to the public.[25] Potential roadblocks in these discussions are market access for agricultural goods, given the highly regulated state of the EU market in this area, and geographical indicators used by the EU that will affect various New Zealand foodstuffs.[26]

---

19  "Summary of Negotiating Objectives", *New Zealand Foreign Affairs and Trade: Manatū Aorere* (Web Page) <https://www.mfat.govt.nz/assets/FTAs-in-negotiations/EU-FTA/Information-package/EU-NZ-FTA-summary-of-negotiating-objectives.pdf>.

20  "EU-New Zealand Free Trade Agreement Negotiations: Report on the First Round of Negotiations in Brussels, 16–20 July 2018", *New Zealand Foreign Affairs and Trade: Manatū Aorere* (Web Page) <https://www.mfat.govt.nz/assets/FTAs-in-negotiations/EU-FTA/EU-NZ-FTA-public-report-on-first-round.pdf> ("1st Round Report"); "Report of the First Round of Negotiations for a Free Trade Agreement between the European Union and New Zealand: 16–20 July 2018, Brussels", *European Commission* (Web Page) <http://trade.ec.europa.eu/doclib/docs/2018/july/tradoc_157183.pdf>.

21  "EU-New Zealand Free Trade Agreement Negotiations: Report on the Second Round of Negotiations in Wellington, 8–12 October 2018", *New Zealand Foreign Affairs and Trade: Manatū Aorere* (Web Page) <https://www.mfat.govt.nz/assets/Uploads/EU-NZ-FTA-public-report-on-second-round.pdf> ("2nd Round Report"); European Commission, "Report on the Second Round of Negotiations for a Free Trade Agreement between the European Union and New Zealand: 8–12 October 2018, Wellington", *European Commission* (Web Page) <http://trade.ec.europa.eu/doclib/docs/2018/october/tradoc_157478.pdf>.

22  "Timeline for Negotiations", *New Zealand Foreign Affairs and Trade: Manatū Aorere* (Web Page) <https://www.mfat.govt.nz/en/trade/free-trade-agreements/agreements-under-negotiation/eu-fta/timeline-for-nz-eu-negotiations/>.

23  1st Round Report (n 20).

24  The proposed text is available online: "EU-New Zealand Trade Agreement negotiations", *European Commission* (Web Page, 13 December 2018) <http://trade.ec.europa.eu/doclib/press/index.cfm?id=1867>.

25  "OIA Released New Zealand Text Proposals in EU-NZ FTA", *New Zealand Foreign Affairs and Trade: Manatū Aorere* (Web Page) <https://www.mfat.govt.nz/assets/Uploads/OIA-26378-Release-material.pdf>. The text on Competition and Consumer Protection is based on the text agreed to between the EU and Chile. The subsidies negotiating text has been withheld so as to not prejudice other negotiations.

26  2nd Round Report (n 21).

The ambitious timeline for the EU's negotiations with New Zealand, as well as its parallel negotiations with Australia, can be interpreted as the EU trying to get ahead of the United Kingdom ("UK") before Brexit.[27] New Zealand has started the first preparatory steps for negotiations of a PTA with the UK, but negotiations cannot start as long as the UK remains an EU member since the EU has the exclusive competence to negotiate trade agreements under EU law.[28] When Brexit comes to pass, whether the UK will be able to negotiate a deal with NZ will depend on the shape of the UK's future relationship with the EU. If the UK enters into a customs union with the EU, it will still not have an independent trade policy.

In contrast to negotiations with the EU and the preparations for potential negotiations with the UK, negotiations with the Eurasian Customs Union remain suspended. In 2017, the coalition agreement between the Labour and New Zealand First parties, at the latter's request, referred to restarting these talks, which had been suspended in response to the Crimea crisis. This led to a diplomatic kerfuffle when the EU's Ambassador to New Zealand was reported to have stated that the prospect of restarting the talks could pose a threat to the EU negotiations.[29] Eventually, any reopening of the talks was shelved after the Skripal poisoning incident.[30]

Finally, aside from the negotiations of individual agreements, the government also launched its *Trade for All* agenda in 2018. Described as a "step back from looking at any individual trade agreement and instead consider trade policy in general, what we are currently doing, and what's best for New Zealand",[31] and originally known as the *New Progressive and Inclusive Trade*

---

27  Daniel Boffey, "EU Talks with Australia and New Zealand Deal Blow to UK Free Trade Plans", *The Guardian* (online, 22 May 2018) <https://www.theguardian.com/politics/2018/may/22/eu-trade-talks-australia-new-zealand-brexit-commonwealth>.

28  Interestingly, the UK floated the idea of becoming a party to the CPTPP, but this is unlikely to happen following Australian opposition due to the UK not being a Pacific nation: see Jamie Smyth, "Australia to Fast-Track UK Trade Pact in Event of No-Deal Brexit", *The Financial Times* (online, 17 February 2019) <https://www.ft.com/content/ac8918d8-30e0-11e9-8744-e7016697f225>.

29  Matt Nippert, "Winston Peters' Plans to Reopen Trade with Russia Raises Alarm from Europe", *The New Zealand Herald* (online, 4 November 2017) <https://www.nzherald.co.nz/business/news/article.cfm?c_id=3&objectid=11940045>.

30  Sam Sachdeva, "EU Approves Launch of NZ Trade Talks", *Newsroom* (News Article, 23 May 2018) <https://www.newsroom.co.nz/2018/05/22/110908/eu-approves-launch-of-nz-trade-talks>.

31  "Trade For All Agenda", *New Zealand Foreign Affairs and Trade: Manatū Aorere* (Web Page) <https://www.mfat.govt.nz/en/trade/nz-trade-policy/trade-for-all-agenda/>.

Agenda ("NPITA"),[32] the aim is to ensure that New Zealand's trade policy delivers for all New Zealanders, including for women, Māori, and in the regions, and is compatible with other societal values.[33] Although the *Trade for All* process has not yet been concluded, it aligns with the inclusion of the Treaty of Waitangi exception in the CPTPP and in the EU-New Zealand negotiations, as well as with a trade and gender chapter also being negotiated as part of the latter.[34] The process so far has involved a public consultation,[35] as well as the creation of a Trade for All Advisory Board with 23 members drawn from business, civil society, and academia, chaired by former diplomat David Pine. The Board will report directly to the Minister of Trade and Export Growth in 2019.[36]

## 3  World Trade

### 3.1  *New Zealand and the WTO Negotiations*

In 2018, New Zealand continued its involvement in negotiations on issues it had pushed during the 11th Ministerial Conference in Buenos Aires in 2017. A first issue has been fisheries subsidies that lead to overfishing as well as subsidies that contribute to illegal, unreported and unregulated ("IUU") fishing. The aim is to develop an agreement in 2019, in order to meet the 2020 deadline set out in the United Nation's Sustainable Development Goals.[37] To this end, the WTO's Negotiating Group on Rules in April 2018 agreed to a work programme for 2018–19, with a first cluster of meetings taking place in May,[38]

---

32  Cabinet Economic Development Committee, "Trade for All: Update", *New Zealand Foreign Affairs and Trade: Manatū Aorere* (Minute of Decision, June–July 2018) <https://www.mfat.govt.nz/assets/Uploads/Trade-for-All-Update-Cabinet-paper.pdf> ("Trade for All Update").

33  Cabinet Business Committee, "A New Progressive and Inclusive Trade Agenda", *New Zealand Foreign Affairs and Trade: Manatū Aorere* (Minute of Decision, February 2018) <https://www.mfat.govt.nz/assets/Uploads/A-New-Progressive-and-Inclusive-Trade-Agenda-redacted-doc.pdf>.

34  2nd Round Report (n 21).

35  A summary of feedback is available: Public Voice, "Summary of Feedback", *New Zealand Foreign Affairs and Trade: Manatū Aorere* (Web Page, December 2018) <https://www.mfat.govt.nz/assets/Uploads/Trade-for-All-Summary-of-Feedback.pdf>.

36  Trade for All Update (n 32) pt 6. The Advisory Board's website is <https://www.tradeforalladvisoryboard.org.nz>.

37  "Sustainable Development Goal 14: Conserve and Sustainably Use the Oceans, Seas and Marine Resources for Sustainable Development", *United Nations* (Web Page) <https://sustainabledevelopment.un.org/sdg14>.

38  "WTO Members Complete First Cluster of Meetings for Fisheries Subsidies Negotiations since MC11", *World Trade Organization* (Web Page, 17 May 2018) <https://www.wto.org/english/news_e/news18_e/fish_18may18_e.htm>.

June[39] and July 2018.[40] The first two meetings concentrated on subsidies leading to overfishing, whereas the latter dealt with IUU fishing. Work intensified during the second cluster of meetings from September to December 2018,[41] leading to a streamlined negotiating text for 2019.[42]

New Zealand is also a driving force behind efforts to limit fossil fuel subsidies through WTO action. The phasing-out of these subsidies was discussed at the WTO's Committee on Trade and Environment in June 2018,[43] but further progress has yet to be made.

Another matter arising from the 11th Ministerial Conference is e-commerce. At the Ministerial Conference, New Zealand signed up to a statement proposing exploratory work for a WTO agreement on trade-related aspects of electronic commerce.[44] Negotiations did not start until early 2019,[45] but much time was spent in 2018 on exploratory work.[46] The briefing by the Ministry of Foreign Affairs and Trade ("MFAT") to the Minister for Trade and Export Growth indicates that NZ's areas of priority in the negotiations are: privacy and protection of personal information; consumer protection; paperless trading; continuation of the customs duties moratorium; and protection against spam.[47]

---

39 "WTO Members Focus on Subsidies for Fishing in Overexploited Stocks at June Meetings", *World Trade Organization* (Web Page, 11 June 2018) <https://www.wto.org/english/news_e/news18_e/fish_11jun18_e.htm>.

40 "WTO Members Take up Disciplines on Subsidies to IUU Fishing at July Meetings", *World Trade Organization* (Web Page, 26 July 2018) <https://www.wto.org/english/news_e/news18_e/fish_26jul18_e.htm>.

41 *Negotiating Group on Rules Fisheries Subsidies Work Programme September–December 2018*, WTO Doc TN/RL/30 (31 July 2018) (Communication from the Chair).

42 *Negotiating Group on Rules Fisheries Subsidies Working Document*, WTO Doc TN/RL/W/274/Rev.6 (14 November 2018) (Communication from the Chair).

43 *Committee on Trade and Environment: Report of the Meeting Held on 28 June 2018*, WTO Doc WT/CTE/M/65 (21 September 2018) (Note by the Secretariat).

44 *Joint Statement on Electronic Commerce*, WTO Doc WT/MIN(17)/60 (13 December 2017) (Joint Ministerial Statement).

45 *Joint Statement on Electronic Commerce*, WTO Doc WT/L/1056 (25 January 2019) (Communication).

46 "WTO e-commerce Negotiations", *New Zealand Foreign Affairs and Trade: Manatū Aorere* (Web Page) <https://www.mfat.govt.nz/en/trade/our-work-with-the-wto/wto-e-commerce-negotiations/>. Further background is in the briefing to the Minister of Trade and Export Growth: see "Proactive Release", *New Zealand Foreign Affairs and Trade: Manatū Aorere* (Briefing, 18 February 2019) <https://www.mfat.govt.nz/assets/Trade/WTO-e-commerce-Proactive-Release.pdf> ("Briefing to the Minister").

47 Briefing to the Minister (n 46) [14].

The negotiations for plurilateral agreements on trade in services (often referred to as "TiSA") and on an environmental goods agreement remained suspended in 2018.[48]

### 3.2 New Zealand and WTO Dispute Settlement

As reported last year,[49] New Zealand prevailed in the WTO Panel and Appellate Body decisions regarding its complaint against Indonesia's import restrictions on beef, but parties had yet to agree on a reasonable time to comply with the report. In 2018, the parties agreed that Indonesia would have until 22 July 2018 to make the most of the required changes, whereas it would have until 22 June 2019 to make the necessary changes to measures that make importations dependent upon the sufficiency of the domestic supply to satisfy domestic demand.[50] Indonesia implemented the first group of changes before the deadline.[51]

New Zealand is also involved as a third party in a number of proceedings. The first concerns the challenges brought by the United States and Australia against measures maintained by the Canadian Government and the Canadian provinces of British Columbia, Ontario, Quebec and Nova Scotia governing the sale of wine. These cases are still in the consultations stage. New Zealand has a direct interest in these measures given that Canada is its highest value-per-litre market, with 2016 exports reportedly worth $107 million.[52] A second case is *Korea – Radionuclides*, in which Japan challenged Korea's import ban and additional testing and certification requirements for certain Japanese food products, following the Fukushima nuclear accident, under the *SPS Agreement*.[53]

---

48  For more on this, see Hertogen (n 7) 184.
49  Ibid 185.
50  *Indonesia – Importation of Horticultural Products, Animals and Animal Products*, WTO Doc WT/DS477/19 WT/DS478/19 (19 June 2018) (Communication from New Zealand and the United States).
51  *Indonesia – Importation of Horticultural Products, Animals and Animal Products*, WTO Doc WT/DS477/21 WT/DS478/22 (18 January 2019) (Status Report Regarding Implementation of the DSB Recommendations and Rulings by Indonesia).
52  "Current WTO Disputes", *New Zealand Foreign Affairs and Trade: Manatū Aorere* (Web Page) <https://www.mfat.govt.nz/en/trade/trade-law-and-dispute-settlement/current-disputes/>.
53  *Marrakesh Agreement Establishing the World Trade Organization*, opened for signature 15 April 1994, 1867 UNTS 3 (entered into force 1 January 1995) ("*Marrakesh Agreement*") Annex 1A.

The panel circulated its report in early 2018 and Korea subsequently appealed in April 2018.[54]

Two long-running cases in which New Zealand was involved as a third party have concluded. The first is the *US — Tuna II* case, in which Mexico challenged measures regarding the eco-labelling of dolphin-safe tuna products. The case is now in the compliance stage, with both the United States and Mexico having previously filed further proceedings, and Mexico having appealed[55] a 2017 compliance panel report that affirmed US compliance. In December 2018 the Appellate Body circulated its reports.[56] The second is the plain packaging case brought against Australia by Cuba, Honduras, the Dominican Republic, and Indonesia. News reports in 2017 had already signalled that Australia's plain packaging legislation for tobacco products had survived the legal challenges.[57] However, official confirmation did not arrive until 28 June 2018 when the Panel circulated its report.[58]

Looming large over the future of the WTO's Appellate Body is the refusal by the United States to appoint new members of the Appellate Body when the current terms expire. At the time of writing, only three out of the usual seven members remain, which is the minimum required to hear a case. Two of them will see their terms expire in December 2019. New Zealand has been part of efforts to reach a solution. In November 2018, New Zealand co-sponsored a

---

54   Panel Report, *Korea – Import Bans, and Testing and Certification Requirements for Radionuclides*, WTO Doc WT/DS495/R (22 February 2018); *Korea – Import Bans, and Testing and Certification Requirements for Radionuclides*, WTO Doc WT/DS495/8 (9 April 2018) (Notification of Appeal by Korea). The Appellate Body's report was circulated and adopted in April 2019, and is thus outside the scope of this review: Appellate Body Report, *Korea – Import Bans, and Testing and Certification Requirements for Radionuclides*, WTO Doc WT/DS495/AB/R (11 April 2019, adopted 29 April 2019).

55   *United States – Measures Concerning the Importation, Marketing and Sale of Tuna and Tuna Products – Recourse to Article 21.5 of the DSU by the United States – Second Recourse to Article 21.5 of the DSU by Mexico*, WTO Doc WT/DS381/45 (1 December 2017) (Notification of Appeal by Mexico).

56   Appellate Body Report, *United States – Measures Concerning the Importation, Marketing and Sale of Tuna and Tuna Products*, WTO Doc WT/DS381/AB/RW/USA, WT/DS381/AB/RW2 (14 December 2018). The first report was adopted by the Dispute Settlement Body in early 2019: see *United States – Measures Concerning the Importation, Marketing and Sale of Tuna and Tuna Products – Appellate Body Report and Panel Report Pursuant to Article 21.5 of the DSU*, WTO Doc WT/DS381/49/Rev.1 (17 January 2019) (Action by the Dispute Settlement Body).

57   Hertogen (n 7) 186–187.

58   Panel Report, *Australia – Certain Measures Concerning Trademarks, Geographical Indications and Other Plain Packaging Requirements Applicable to Tobacco Products and Packaging*, WTO Doc WT/DS435/R, WT/DS441/R, WT/DS458/R, WT/DS467/R (28 June 2018, adopted 27 August 2018).

communication to the General Council[59] proposing a set of amendments to existing procedures, such as an amendment to the Dispute Settlement Understanding ("DSU")[60] that would allow outgoing Appellate Body members to continue appeals for which the hearing took place during their term; an amendment to ensure more consultation and transparency, as well as mechanisms to enable an appeal to be decided within the 90-day timeframe of article 17.5 DSU; a proposal to clarify the extent to which the Appellate Body can interpret municipal law, particularly if this goes against the Panel's interpretation; an amendment to article 17.12 DSU to clarify that the Appellate Body can only address issues if necessary to resolve the dispute; and the creation of a communication channel where WTO Members could voice concerns about systemic issues and jurisprudence outside the context of a specific dispute, so as to avoid unwanted de facto precedents. The WTO's General Council agreed in December to launch an informal process to aim for a resolution in 2019. Whether or not an agreement can be reached that restarts Appellate Body appointments remains to be seen, as it is not clear whether the United States is serious about addressing these concerns or whether the concerns mask a deeper agenda to undermine the dispute settlement system altogether.

## 4   Conclusion

As in 2017, 2018 saw a continuing emphasis by the New Zealand government on protecting the rules-based trading system at both the global and the regional level. However, 2018 was a transitional year, during which much work happened without yet leading to final results. It will be interesting to see what 2019 brings: Which PTAs will be successfully concluded and under which terms? Will the appointments crisis at the Appellate Body be resolved? What will happen to the legal challenges against the United States' steel tariffs and against the retaliatory tariffs taken by economies targeted by the steel tariffs – all cases in which New Zealand has reserved its third-party rights? One can expect New Zealand to continue to promote the rules-based system, but whether the rules-based system survives will ultimately be decided by factors beyond New Zealand's control.

---

59  *Communication from the European Union, China, Canada, India, Norway, New Zealand, Switzerland, Australia, Republic of Korea, Iceland, Singapore and Mexico to the General Council*, WTO Doc WT/GC/W/752 (26 November 2018).

60  *Marrakesh Agreement* (n 53) Annex 2 *Understanding on Rules and Procedures Governing the Settlement of Disputes*.

# International Environmental Law

*Vernon Rive**

1      Introduction

The 2018 calendar year covered by this report was the first full year for the new government formed in October 2017, led by the New Zealand Labour Party in coalition with the New Zealand First Party and with a confidence-and-supply agreement with the Green Party of Aotearoa. With the co-leader of the Green Party James Shaw holding the position of Minister for Climate Change – the first New Zealand Green Party politician to hold that office – it was not surprising that major steps were taken during the year towards a fundamental reform of New Zealand climate change regulation, including a nationwide consultation exercise in relation to a Zero Carbon Bill and the establishment of an Interim Climate Change Committee. As detailed in this report, New Zealand actively participated in international negotiations on climate change, including at the 24th conference of parties to the *United Nations Framework Convention on Climate Change* in Katowice, Poland, where the *Paris Rulebook*, a detailed set of provisions designed to operationalise the 2015 *Paris Agreement*, was largely concluded.

At the domestic level, the government continued to refine its central policy instrument for climate change mitigation (the *Emissions Trading Scheme* ["ETS"]), published an important report on the development of a more robust framework for adaptation to climate change and, controversially, implemented a ban on new offshore oil and gas exploration.

Biodiversity protection featured prominently at the international and domestic levels. New Zealand representatives attended a significant meeting of parties to the *Convention on Biological Diversity* ("CBD") in Sharm El-Sheikh, Egypt, while developing the political and policy foundation for a new national biodiversity strategy, work on which is likely to continue through 2019 and 2020, in parallel with international negotiations towards a new global biodiversity framework to be finalised in October 2020.

Other notable developments during the year covered in this report include: the formal launch of a United Nations working group examining a proposed "Global Pact for the Environment"; ongoing work by New Zealand officials towards a meaningful response to repeated statements of international concern

* Auckland University of Technology School of Law.

over the threatened status of Hector's and Māui dolphins; ministerial announcements and initial steps towards a comprehensive review of New Zealand's domestic resource management legislation and institutional framework; a widely publicised ban on single-use plastic bags in the retail sector; and the signing and (after the passage of domestic implementing legislation) ratification of the *Comprehensive and Progressive Trans-Pacific Partnership Agreement* ("CPTPP"), a "mega-regional" trade agreement with a number of important environmental features discussed below.

As with previous reports, this overview does not address 2018 developments connected with fisheries, the marine environment and Antarctica. Those matters are covered in the reviews of Joanna Mossop and Alan Hemmings.

## 2 International Developments

### 2.1 *Global Pact for the Environment*

Scholars and policymakers have voiced concerns about the negative consequences of the ongoing fragmentation of international environmental law for many years.[1] In part to address issues of fragmentation, and in part to promote the creation of a legally binding framework of international environmental law principles, civil society representatives, scholars and legal experts produced a *White Paper Towards a Global Pact for the Environment* ("*Global Pact*") in 2017.[2] Its authors described the document as promoting a "third generation of fundamental rights" – the rights associated with the protection of the environment, following the 1966 United Nations ("UN") *International Covenant on Civil and Political Rights* and *International Covenant on Economic, Social and Cultural Rights*.[3]

Principles put forward in the White Paper included the right to an ecologically sound environment and the corresponding duty falling upon "every State

---

1  On fragmentation of international law generally, see Martti Koskenniemi, *Fragmentation of International Law: Difficulties Arising from the Diversification and Expansion of International Law: Report of the Study Group of the International Law Commission*, UN Doc A/CN4/L682 (13 April 2006). On issues of fragmentation and international environmental law, see, eg, Karen Scott, "International Environmental Governance: Managing Fragmentation through Institutional Connection" (2011) 12(1) *Melbourne Journal of International Law* 177; Harro Van Asselt, "Managing the Fragmentation of International Environmental Law: Forests at the Intersection of the Climate and Biodiversity Regimes" (2011) 44(4) *New York University Journal of International Law & Politics* 1205.
2  Club des Juristes, *Toward a Global Pact for the Environment* (White Paper, September 2017).
3  Ibid 4.

or international institution, every person, natural or legal, public or private" to "take care of the environment". Other principles – already familiar from their inclusion and articulation in previous international instruments – [4] included obligations to integrate environmental protection into national and international policies and activities, sustainable development, intergenerational equity, prevention of harm, precaution, liability to remediate damage and the "polluter-pays" doctrine. The Paper also proposed a range of procedural rights, including: public participation; access to environmental justice; and state obligations to promote education, training, research and innovation.

On 10 May 2018, the UN General Assembly launched a process to investigate the feasibility of developing a legally binding international instrument from the 2017 *White Paper*.[5] The first step in this process was the tabling in the General Assembly of "a technical and evidence-based report that identifies and assesses possible gaps in international environmental law and environment-related instruments with a view to strengthening their implementation".[6] That report was formally submitted to the General Assembly at its 73rd session in November 2018.[7] The second step was the establishment of an "ad hoc open-ended working group" to advance the initiative.[8] The working group held its first meeting in September, co-chaired by Francisco António Duarte Lopes, Portuguese Permanent Representative to the UN, and Amal Mudallali, Lebanese Permanent Representative to the UN.[9]

The *Global Pact* initiative has received widespread support at the civil society level,[10] among some scholars,[11] and, of course, from its lead state sponsor,

---

4  These include (but are not limited to): Report of the United Nations Conference on the Human Environment: Stockholm, 5–16 June 1972, UN Doc A/CONF.48/14 (16 June 1972) 2 and Corr 1 [1.2] (Principle 2), [1.8] (Principle 8), [1.19] (Principle 19) and [1.21] (Principle 21); World Charter for Nature, GA Res 37/7, UN Doc A/RES/37/7 (28 October 1982) [II.6–8],[III.14–15]; Rio Declaration on Environment and Development, UN Doc A/CONF.151/26 (vol I) (14 June 1992) 8 Principles 2, 3, 4, 10, 13 and 15.
5  *Towards a Global Pact for the Environment*, GA Res 72/277, A/RES/72/277 (14 May 2018).
6  Ibid para 1.
7  Gaps in International Environmental Law and Environment-related Instruments: Towards a Global Pact for the Environment: Report of the Secretary-General, UN Doc A/73/419 (30 November 2018).
8  *Towards a Global Pact for the Environment* (n 5) para 2.
9  Report of the Ad Hoc Open-ended Working Group Established Pursuant to General Assembly Resolution 72/277 of 10 May 2018 Entitled "Towards a Global Pact for the Environment", UN Doc A/AC.289/2 (22 October 2018).
10  Club des Juristes (n 3) 23.
11  For example, M Grooten and REA Almond, *Living Planet* (Report, 2018) 7; (and more guardedly) Christina Voigt, "How a "Global Pact for the Environment" Could Add Value to

France.¹² However, it faces considerable challenges in coming to fruition in light of state opposition¹³ and scholarly scepticism towards the feasibility (or, indeed, desirability) of producing an international instrument which purports to translate soft-law hortatory principles into a legally binding form.¹⁴ It remains to be seen whether the 2018 UN General Assembly resolution and initial steps towards a negotiating process result in concrete outputs able to materially respond to fragmentation and other concerns noted above.

### 2.2   Biodiversity and Conservation

#### 2.2.1   Sharm El-Sheikh United Nations Biodiversity Conferences

Despite a plethora of international initiatives directed towards biodiversity protection,¹⁵ a major global assessment in 2018 by the World Wide Fund for Nature confirmed that biodiversity loss had continued at alarming rates, and was predicted to have significant ecological, cultural and economic consequences if not urgently addressed.¹⁶ The assumption of executive power by Jair Bolsonaro in Brazil provoked expressions of concern over an expected weakening of legal protection mechanisms for the Amazon and other parts of Brazil,

---

International Environmental Law" (2019) 28(1) *Review of European, Comparative & International Environmental Law* 13.

12   Club des Juristes (n 3) 3.

13   See, eg, Peter Doran, Laura Bullon-Cassis and Natalie Jones, "Summary of the First Substantive Session of the Ad Hoc Open Ended Working Group towards a Global Pact for the Environment: 14–18 January 2019" (2019) 35(1) *Earth Negotiations Bulletin* 1, 3–4 (providing a summary of general statements on behalf of UN members in relation to the *Global Pact* initiative, recording reservations and/or outright opposition on the part of: the US, Argentina, Cuba, Iran, the Philippines, Russian Federation, Egypt, Mexico and others).

14   Louis J Kotzé and Duncan French, "A Critique of the Global Pact for the Environment: A Stillborn Initiative or the Foundation for *Lex Anthropocenae*?" (2018) 18(6) *International Environmental Agreements: Politics, Law and Economics* 811; Susan Biniaz, "The UNGA Resolution on a "Global Pact for the Environment": A Chance to Put the Horse before the Cart" (2019) 28(1) *Review of European, Comparative & International Environmental Law* 33.

15   For example, *Decision Adopted by the Conference of Parties to the Convention on Biological Diversity: The Strategic Plan for Biodiversity 2011–2020 and the Aichi Biodiversity Targets* (UNEP/CBD/COP/DEC/X/2, 29 October 2010); *Transforming Our World: the 2030 Agenda for Sustainable Development*, GA Res 70/1, UN Doc A/RES/70/1 (21 October 2015) 24–25 ("Protect, restore and promote sustainable use of terrestrial ecosystems, sustainably manage forests, combat desertification, and halt and reverse land degradation and halt biodiversity loss").

16   Grooten and Almond (n 11) 7 (Living Planet Index shows an overall decline of vertebrate species of 60% in population sizes between 1970 and 2014).

which contains 20.8% of the world's plant species, 17.6% of its birds, 13.6% of its amphibians and 11.8% of its mammals.[17]

Against that backdrop, parties to the CBD met for their 14th conference of the parties in Sharm El-Sheikh, Egypt, from 13–29 November 2018 ("*CBD COP14*"). Representatives of international and non-governmental organisations, civil society, and academics also participated in discussions. Two associated biodiversity-oriented conferences took place alongside CBD COP14: namely, the ninth conference of the parties serving as the meeting of the parties to the *Cartagena Protocol on Biosafety* and the third meeting of the parties to the *Nagoya Protocol on Access to Genetic Resources and the Fair and Equitable Sharing of Benefits Arising from their Utilisation*.

Significant themes which were the subject of negotiations at the 2018 biodiversity conferences of the parties ("COPs") included: the implications and management of synthetic biology (including genome editing and gene drives); digital sequence information on genetic resources; and proposed arrangements for the post-2020 international biodiversity protection framework.[18] As a signatory to the Sharm El-Sheikh declaration *Investing in Biodiversity for People and Planet* adopted by ministers and heads of delegation on 15 November 2018, the New Zealand Conservation Minister Eugenie Sage affirmed New Zealand's commitment to continue accelerating efforts towards achievement of the 2010 *Aichi Biodiversity Targets* and development of the post-2020 global biodiversity framework.[19]

#### 2.2.2 International Whaling Commission on Māui Dolphins

As observed in the *Year in Review* for the 2017 calendar year in this publication, the status of the International Union for Conservation of Nature ("IUCN") red-listed critically endangered Māui Dolphin subspecies of Hector's dolphin has been the subject of significant concern for the International Whaling Commission's ("IWC") Scientific Committee for many years.[20] The April-May 2018 IWC *Report of the Scientific Committee* reiterated statements made in earlier reports "as it has [observed] repeatedly in the past, that existing management measures

---

17  Jonathan Watts, "Jair Bolsonaro's Rise to Power Casts Shadow over UN Environment Conference", *The Guardian* (Web Page, 18 November 2018) <https://www.theguardian.com/world/2018/nov/18/jair-bolsonaro-election-sparks-fears-for-brazil-biodiversity>.

18  See generally Elsa Tsioumani et al, "Summary of the UN Biodiversity Conference: 13–29 November 2018" (2018) 9(725) *Earth Negotiations Bulletin* 1.

19  "Conservation Minister to Visit UK and Egypt" (Media Release, New Zealand Government, 3 November 2018).

20  Josephine Toop, "Year in Review: International Environmental Law" (2017) 15 *New Zealand Yearbook of International Law* 189, 191.

in relation to bycatch mitigation fall short of what has been recommended...". In its report, the Scientific Committee urged the New Zealand Government "to commit to specific population increase targets and timelines for Māui Dolphin conservation".[21]

### 2.2.3 Convention on Wetlands ("Ramsar Convention")

In October 2018, parties to one of the oldest multilateral environmental agreements – the *Ramsar Convention* –[22] met in Dubai, United Arab Emirates, under the theme "Wetlands for a Sustainable Urban Future". New Zealand was represented at and participated in the conference, which adopted 25 resolutions, including an Australian-sponsored (and New Zealand-supported) resolution titled *Promoting Conservation, Restoration, and Sustainable Management of Coastal Blue Carbon Ecosystems*.[23] "Blue carbon" had not previously been defined in any binding international instrument. It was described in the resolution as "the carbon captured by living organisms and coastal (e.g., mangroves, salt marshes and sea grasses) and marine ecosystems and stored in biomass and sediments".[24] A number of parties at the Dubai conference expressed concerns at the prospect of "blue carbon" ecosystems being explicitly managed under the *Ramsar* regime because of potential conflict with initiatives and negotiations under the *United Nations Framework Convention on Climate Change* ("UNFCCC") and *Paris Agreement*.[25] In the event, the resolution was passed with an explicit caveat recording that not all parties endorsed the resolution's definition of "blue carbon" nor recognised the *Ramsar Convention* as the competent forum to address climate change-related aspects of wetland protection.[26]

---

21 International Whaling Commission, *Report of the Scientific Committee of the IWC* (No IWC/67/Rep01(2018), 25 May 2018) 69.
22 *Convention on Wetlands of International Importance Especially as Waterfowl Habitat*, opened for signature 2 February 1971, 996 UNTS 245 (entered into force 21 December 1975) ("Ramsar Convention").
23 13th Meeting of the Conference of the Contracting Parties to the Ramsar Convention on Wetlands: "Wetlands for a Sustainable Urban Future" Dubai, United Arab Emirates, 21–29 October 2018 (Conference Report, 2018) [149]–[150].
24 Teya Penniman, Natalie Jones and Asterios Tsioumanis, "Summary of the Thirteenth Meeting of the Conference of the Parties to the Ramsar Convention on Wetlands: 22–29 October 2018" (2018) 17(48) *Earth Negotiations Bulletin* 1, 13.
25 13th Meeting of the Conference of the Contracting Parties to the Ramsar Convention on Wetlands: "Wetlands for a Sustainable Urban Future" (n 23) [50].
26 Teya Penniman, Natalie Jones and Asterios Tsioumanis (n 25) 13.

## 2.3 Climate Change

The 2018 calendar year exhibited a continued pattern of worldwide warming, and was assessed by the US National Aeronautics and Space Administration and the National Oceanic and Atmospheric Administration as the world's fourth warmest year on record since 1880.[27] January 2018 was New Zealand's hottest month on record, with a mean temperature 3.1°C higher than the 1981–2010 January average, according to the National Institute of Water and Atmospheric Research.[28] Extreme weather events during 2018 included wildfires in California, major flooding in East Africa and destructive cyclones in different parts of the globe.[29]

2018 was an important year in international climate change negotiations. Informed by the content of the Intergovernmental Panel on Climate Change's ("IPCC") *Special Report on the Impacts of Global Warming of 1.5°C*,[30] parties to the UNFCCC and *Paris Agreement* engaged between January and December 2018 in an informal stocktake process, which had commenced in 2017, known as the *Talanoa Dialogue*. Negotiations also progressed on a detailed set of rules and modalities necessary to operationalise the *Paris Agreement* in the form of the *Paris Rulebook*, which culminated in the two-week 24th conference of the parties to the UNFCCC in Katowice, Poland ("COP24").

The IPCC *Special Report* was produced in response to a decision taken at UNFCCC COP21.[31] As Mike Hulme has noted, this was significant because, firstly, the IPCC was "being asked to 'identify a level' to which annual emissions should be reduced by 2030 to offer the prospect of just 1.5 °C of warming", and, secondly, because the impacts of a 1.5 °C warming would be relevant to

---

27  "2018 Fourth Warmest Year in Continued Warming Trend, According to NASA, NOAA", *NASA: Global Climate Change* (Web Page, 6 February 2019) <https://climate.nasa.gov/news/2841/2018-fourth-warmest-year-in-continued-warming-trend-according-to-nasa-noaa/>.

28  "Climate Summary for January 2018", *NIWA* (Web Page, 1 February 2018) <https://www.niwa.co.nz/climate/monthly/climate-summary-for-january-2018>.

29  See Kelly Levin and Dennis Tirpak, "2018: A Year of Climate Extremes", *World Resources Institute* (Web Page, 27 December 2018) World Resources Institute <https://www.wri.org/blog/2018/12/2018-year-climate-extremes>.

30  Ove Hoegh-Guldberg, Daniela Jacob and Michael Taylor "Impacts of 15°C Global Warming on Natural and Human Systems" in Intergovernmental Panel on Climate Change, *Global Warming of 1.5°C: The Impacts of Global Warming of 1.5°C above Pre-industrial Levels and Related Global Greenhouse Gas Emission Pathways, in the Context of Strengthening the Global Response to the Threat of Climate Change, Sustainable Development, and Efforts to Eradicate Poverty* (Special Report, 2018).

31  *Decision 1/CP.21: Adoption of the Paris Agreement*, UN Doc FCCC/CP/2015/10/Add.1 (29 January 2016) [21].

discussions about the *Warsaw International Mechanism for Loss and Damage*.[32] Predictably, the IPCC concluded that climate-related risks would be lower with global warming of 1.5°C rather than 2°C.[33] The difference is especially relevant to low-lying island states in the Pacific and elsewhere, given that limiting global average temperature rise to 1.5°C would result in a slower rate of sea level rise which "enables greater opportunities for adaptation in the human and ecological systems of small islands, low-lying coastal areas and deltas".[34] Of particular note was the IPCC finding that, in order to restrict global average temperatures to 1.5°C, emissions would need to decline by approximately 45% from 2010 levels by 2030, and reach net zero by around 2050.[35]

The *Talanoa Dialogue* was launched at 2017's COP23 by the Fijian presidency pursuant to *Decision 1/CP.21* para 20, under which parties agreed to convene a facilitative dialogue "to take stock of the collective efforts of Parties in relation to progress towards the long-term goal" of the *Paris Agreement*. "Talanoa" is a Fijian term for a process of "inclusive, participative, and transparent dialogue".[36] The initiative took place in 2018 in two stages. The first was a preparatory phase which took place between January and December involving analysis, discussions and production of policy inputs. The second political phase occurred at COP24 in Katowice in December. The process culminated with the *Talanoa Call for Action* accompanied by a synthesis report of relevant policy inputs.[37]

To the disappointment of some participants in the *Talanoa Dialogue* and many observers, it was not apparent that the process led to a discernible effect on decisions taken at COP24.[38] It remains to be seen whether the Talanoa

---

32   Mike Hulme, "1.5 °C and Climate Research After the Paris Agreement" (2016) 6(3) *Nature Climate Change* 222, 222.
33   Ove Hoegh-Guldberg, Jacob and Taylor (n 30) 177.
34   Valérie Masson-Delmotte et al, "Summary for Policymakers" in Intergovernmental Panel on Climate Change, *Global Warming of 1.5°C: The Impacts of Global Warming of 1.5°C above Pre-industrial Levels and Related Global Greenhouse Gas Emission Pathways, in the Context of Strengthening the Global Response to the Threat of Climate Change, Sustainable Development, and Efforts to Eradicate Poverty* (Special Report, 2018).
35   Ibid 12.
36   Presidencies of COP22 and COP23, *Talanoa Dialogue: Approach* (Informal Note, 16 November 2017) 1.
37   Presidents of COP23 and COP24, *Talanoa Call for Action* (Call for Action, 12 December 2018); Presidencies of COP23 and COP24 *Talanoa Dialogue for Climate Action* (Synthesis of the Preparatory Phase, 19 November 2018).
38   The final COP decision records an invitation to "consider the outcome, inputs and outputs of the Talanoa Dialogue in preparing their nationally determined contributions and in their efforts to enhance pre-2020 implementation and ambition", *Preparations for the Implementation of the Paris Agreement and the First Session of the Conference of the Parties*

process and outputs will have any impact on the content of finalised nationally determined contributions, as the first commitment period under the *Paris Agreement* approaches.

State delegates to COP24 were faced with the very challenging task of bridging major differences on a host of substantive and procedural issues in the *Paris Rulebook* negotiations. Going into the conference, the draft *Rulebook* covered 236 pages with approximately 3,000 bracketed items for resolution.[39] Differences in position reflected long-standing points of contention within the UNFCCC framework which had not been conclusively settled by the 2015 *Paris Agreement* and the accompanying COP decision. Unresolved issues included: the extent to which differentiation between developed and developing members should be reflected in rules and modalities; differing perspectives on the need for common requirements for accounting, reporting and other aspects of transparency; the desire for clearer information and firm commitments on financing and other assistance from developed country members; and procedures for market and non-market-based flexibility mechanisms.

In the event – contrary to the expectations of many commentators – compromises were reached on enough of the outstanding issues to enable the *Paris Rulebook* to be substantially confirmed, allowing the Polish presidency to declare that the "1,000 little steps countries took together" would "move us one step further to realizing the ambition enshrined in the *Paris Agreement*".[40] Key decisions included:[41] agreement on a substantially common framework for presentation of nationally determined contributions including accounting approaches, common timeframes and provision for voluntary reporting of adaptation measures within Nationally Determined Contributions; finalisation of a set of rules and modalities for a transparency framework for action and support; agreement on the broader approach to be taken for formal global stocktakes under Article 14 of the *Paris Agreement*; agreement on information to be provided by developed country member and other members on finance in

---

*Serving as the Meeting of the Parties to the Paris Agreement*, UN Doc FCCC/CP/2018/L.27 (14 December 2018) para 37. This was a weaker outcome than many had hoped for: see, eg, Jennifer Allan et al, "Summary of the Katowice Climate Change Conference: 2–15 December 2018" (2018) 12(747) *Earth Negotiations Bulletin* 1, 33.

[39] "COP24: Key Outcomes Agreed at the UN Climate Talks in Katowice", *Carbon Brief* (Web Page, 16 December 2018) <https://www.carbonbrief.org/cop24-key-outcomes-agreed-at-the-un-climate-talks-in-katowice>.

[40] Jennifer Allan et al (n 38) 33.

[41] See generally ibid and *Preparations for the Implementation of the Paris Agreement and the First Session of the Conference of the Parties Serving as the Meeting of the Parties to the Paris Agreement* (n 38).

accordance with art 9.5; and procedures for operation of a committee to facilitate implementation and promote compliance.

At COP24, the New Zealand Minister of Climate Change James Shaw was appointed as a co-facilitator of negotiations on the particularly contentious issue of negotiations on *Paris Agreement* art 6 ("Cooperative Approaches", including the *Paris Agreement* term for international emissions trading – "Internationally Transferred Mitigation Outcomes" – together with markets and non-market approaches to cooperative action). In negotiations, New Zealand adopted a strong stance on the need for environmental integrity (including, but not limited to, the avoidance of double counting) in any international cooperative mechanisms including, contentiously, rules for "corresponding adjustments in connection with transfers of mitigation outcomes and emission reductions".[42] But despite the efforts of Minister Shaw and other facilitators, agreement was not able to be reached on art 6 arrangements. The final COP outcome decision on this point deferred the outstanding issues to the 25th Conference of Parties in 2019.[43]

## 2.4   The Pacific

New Zealand attended the 49th Pacific Islands Forum 3–6 September 2018, providing one of the largest contributions to the event's budget.[44] The 2018 meetings were held in Yaren, Nauru, under the theme "Building a Strong Pacific". At the event, Forum leaders endorsed the first Quadrennial Pacific Sustainable Development Report, documenting progress in the Pacific Islands area which will also act as the Sustainable Development Report towards the United Nations 2030 Sustainable Development Goals. Key topics for discussion included the need for collective action on climate change, fisheries management, oceans and waste management.

In 2018 the Cook Islands signed the *United Nations Treaty on the Prohibition of Nuclear Weapons*,[45] following in the footsteps of other member countries, including New Zealand, which signed and ratified the treaty in 2017.

---

42  *Preparations for the Implementation of the Paris Agreement and the First Session of the Conference of the Parties Serving as the Meeting of the Parties to the Paris Agreement* (n 38) 17.
43  Matters Relating to Article 6 of the Paris Agreement and Paragraphs 36–40 of Decision 1/CP.21, UN Doc FCCC/CP/2018/L.28 (14 December 2018) para 3.
44  Pacific Islands Forum Secretariat, *Forty-Ninth Pacific Islands Forum: Yaren, Nauru* (Forum Communiqué, No PIFS(18)10, 5 September 2018) 13.
45  "The Cook Islands accedes to the Treaty on the Prohibition of Nuclear Weapons (TPNW)", *United Nations Regional Centre for Peace and Disarmament in Asia and the Pacific* (Web Page, 4 September 2018) <http://unrcpd.org/news-item/the-cook-islands-accedes-to-the-treaty-on-the-prohibition-of-nuclear-weapons-tpnw/>.

### 2.5 *WTO and International Trade*

Throughout 2018, the World Trade Organisation ("WTO") continued to face operational and other challenges to its ongoing status and role as the pre-eminent multilateral institution overseeing international trade arrangements.[46] Despite those challenges, trade disputes, including disputes involving environmental issues, continued to be referred to the WTO Dispute Settlement Mechanism ("DSM"). Continuing a trend of referrals to the DSM of disputes concerning renewable energy technology and initiatives, in August 2018 China requested consultations with the United States ("US") "concerning certain measures allegedly adopted and maintained by the governments of certain US states and municipalities in relation to alleged subsidies or alleged domestic content requirements in the energy sector".[47]

During 2018, WTO members continued to consider two reform initiatives for the international disciplining of environmentally harmful subsidies in which New Zealand has played a major role. Discussions occurred within the WTO Committee for Trade and the Environment on a New Zealand-led project to introduce binding fossil fuel subsidy disciplines to the WTO, the subject of a *Fossil Fuel Subsidies Joint Ministerial Statement* tabled at the 11th Ministerial Conference in Buenos Aires in December 2017.[48] Negotiations also progressed (haltingly) on contentious fisheries subsidies reform proposals throughout 2018. At the final (29th) informal meeting of the year, heads of WTO member delegations "declared their commitment to intensify negotiations on fisheries subsidies in the new year to meet the end-2019 target for an agreement".[49]

Outside of the WTO regime, the most significant multilateral trade initiative with environmental implications for New Zealand was the signing and ratification of the CPTPP, a revamped form of the former *Trans-Pacific Partnership Agreement* following the withdrawal of the US in 2017.[50] The CPTPP contains a chapter (20) on the environment, addressing (amongst other matters): high-level commitments to "environmental protection and effective enforcement of

---

46   See, eg, Bradly J Condon, "Captain America and the Tarnishing of the Crown: The Feud Between the WTO Appellate Body and the USA" (2018) 52(4) *Journal of World Trade* 535.

47   WTO Secretariat, "DS563: United States — Certain Measures Related to Renewable Energy", *World Trade Organization* <https://www.wto.org/english/tratop_e/dispu_e/cases_e/ds563_e.htm>.

48   *Report of the Meeting Held on 28 June 2018*, WTO Doc WT/CTE/M/65 (21 September 2018) (Note by the Secretariat).

49   "WTO Members Voice Commitment to Intensify Fisheries Subsidies Negotiations in 2019", World Trade Organization (Web Page, 20 December 2019) <https://www.wto.org/english/news_e/news18_e/fish_20dec18_e.htm>.

50   *Comprehensive and Progressive Agreement for Trans-Pacific Partnership*, opened for signature 8 March 2018, [2018] ATS 23 (entered into force 30 December 2018).

environmental laws"; implementation of existing obligations arising from multilateral environmental agreements; ozone protection; preservation of the marine environment; public participation; trade and biodiversity; environmental goods and services; and institutional arrangements for consultations, review and implementation of the chapter's commitments and dispute resolution. Article 20.16 also introduces detailed rules on fisheries subsidies which build on existing (generic) subsidy disciplines within the WTO *Agreement on Subsidies and Countervailing Measures*.

## 3 National Developments

### 3.1 *Biodiversity and Conservation*

#### 3.1.1 New Zealand Biodiversity Strategy – 2018 Goals

In the *New Zealand Biodiversity Action Plan 2016–2020*,[51] a number of goals were set for 2018, including: the promulgation of a *National Environmental Standard for Plantation Forestry* ("*NES-PF*");[52] new legislation to protect native plant species and control exports;[53] and legislation to protect marine life.[54] The first of these goals was met when the *Resource Management (National Environmental Standards for Plantation Forestry) Regulations 2017* came into effect on 1 May 2018 (see more information on Plantation Forestry in the subsection below).[55] The government also made progress on the goal to strengthen legislative protection of marine life. The Conservation (Indigenous Freshwater Fish) Amendment Bill passed its first reading in September 2018 and is currently at the Select Committee Stage.[56]

#### 3.1.2 A New Biodiversity Strategy

New Zealand's existing *Biodiversity Strategy* is set to expire in 2020. In October 2018, the Minister of Conservation announced the government's intention to commence work on a new strategy,[57] having obtained Cabinet approval to the

---

[51] Department of Conservation, *New Zealand Biodiversity Action Plan 2016–2020* (National Strategy, September 2016).
[52] Ibid 22.
[53] Ibid 29.
[54] Ibid 30.
[55] *Resource Management (National Environmental Standards for Plantation Forestry) Regulations 2017* (NZ) LI 2017/174.
[56] Conservation (Indigenous Freshwater Fish) Amendment Bill (NZ).
[57] "New National Biodiversity Strategy Needed" (Media Release, New Zealand Government, 9 October 2018).

terms of reference and a timeline for the development of a new *National Biodiversity Strategy*.[58] Cabinet agreed that a new strategy is needed to reflect, among other things, developments since the existing strategy was prepared, including the impacts of climate change, changes in the science sector such as the establishment of the *New Zealand Biological Heritage National Science Challenge* and new programmes like *Predator Free 2050*, and the development of a draft *National Policy Statement on Indigenous Biodiversity*.

As part of progress towards a new *Biodiversity Strategy* in 2018, the Department of Conservation ("DOC") sought public input on the content and approach to biodiversity protection and management in New Zealand.[59] According to the 2018 approved timeline, the government intended to present a final document to Cabinet for approval in December 2019, although it acknowledged the need for the new strategy to satisfy the requirements of a new global biodiversity framework scheduled to be confirmed at a conference of parties to the CBD in October 2020.[60] It seems likely that a revised strategy will not be in place until late 2020 at the earliest.

### 3.1.3 Māui Dolphins

As noted above, in April–May 2018, the Scientific Committee of the IWC expressed grave concerns about the plight of the Māui dolphins in New Zealand in light of a dramatic drop in species numbers.[61]

In 2007 New Zealand implemented the *Hector's and Maui's Dolphin Threat Management Plan* which was scheduled for review in 2018.[62] Over the course of the year, DOC officials held two stakeholder forums – one in the South Island and one in the North Island – and in July convened a Risk Assessment Workshop to "identify, analyse and evaluate all anthropogenic threats to Hector's and Māui dolphins, and identify those that pose the greatest risk to achieving management objectives".[63] A panel report resulting from the July 2018 Risk

---

58   Office of the Minister of Conservation, *Development of a New National Biodiversity Strategy* (Cabinet Paper, 2018).
59   "Help Design Our Proposal for New Zealand's Next Biodiversity Strategy", *Department of Conservation* (Web Page, 2018) <https://dxcprod.doc.govt.nz/get-involved/have-your-say/all-consultations/2018/new-zealand-biodiversity-strategy/>.
60   Office of the Minister of Conservation (n 58) 9–10.
61   International Whaling Commission (n 21) 69.
62   "Review of the Hector's and Maui Dolphin Threat Management Plan", *Department of Conservation* (Web Page) <https://www.doc.govt.nz/our-work/our-work-with-maui-dolphin/hectors-and-maui-dolphin-threat-management-plan/review/>.
63   Department of Conservation and Fisheries New Zealand, *Hector's and Māui Dolphin Threat Management Plan Review: Risk Assessment Workshop, 9–13 July 2018* (Terms of Reference, 2018) 2.

Assessment Workshop contained a substantial number of technical recommendations which contributed to ongoing threat management consultation and draft strategies intended to continue into 2019.[64]

### 3.2 *Climate Change*

#### 3.2.1 Greenhouse Gas Inventory

In April 2018, the Ministry for the Environment published a substantial report on New Zealand's greenhouse gas emissions from 1990–2016 which also served to fulfil New Zealand's reporting requirements under the UNFCCC and *Kyoto Protocol*.[65] *New Zealand's Greenhouse Gas Inventory 1990–2016* reported that, since 1990, the country's gross emissions had increased by 20%, with major contributions from agricultural sources (principally methane resulting from enteric fermentation from dairy cattle); road transport from increased fuel use; chemical industry and food processing (carbon dioxide) from increased production due to economic growth and population increase; agricultural soils from increased fertiliser use; and industrial and household refrigeration and air-conditioning systems. The report also noted that, over the period 2015–16, the general upward trend in gross emissions had slightly reversed (a 2.4% decrease), although that decrease was more than offset by an 8% land-use change (mainly because of an increase in the harvest rate of planted forests).[66]

#### 3.2.2 Progress Towards a Zero Carbon Act

The documentation of a continued substantial rise in gross emissions from 1990 to 2016 in the 2018 *Inventory* (despite a series of international emissions reductions commitments under the UNFCCC, *Copenhagen Accord* and *Paris Agreement*, and the operation of the *New Zealand ETS* from 2008) was cited as a reason for "urgent action ... at a level not previously contemplated" by the Minister of Climate Change in a release commenting on the new figures.[67] During 2018, consistent with campaign promises to introduce legislation cementing a government commitment to a net zero-emissions target by 2050, the government continued consultation and policy development on a proposed Zero Carbon bill, to be introduced in 2019.

---

64  Barbara Taylor, Mike Lonergan and Randall Reeves, *Hector's and Māui Dolphin Threat Management Plan Review, Risk Assessment Workshop, 9–13 July 2018* (Panel Comments and Recommendations, 2 August 2018).
65  Ministry for the Environment, *New Zealand's Greenhouse Gas Inventory: 1990–2016* (Report, 2018).
66  Ibid 1.
67  "Latest Greenhouse Gas Figures Show a Rise in Emissions" (Media Release, 12 April 2018).

A significant step towards a proposed new legal and institutional framework for domestic climate change mitigation and adaptation was the establishment on 1 May 2018 of the Interim Climate Change Committee ("ICCC"). The ICCC was tasked with providing independent evidence and analysis on issues in accordance with the terms of reference approved by Cabinet in April 2018,[68] with the intention that its work be handed over to the statutory Climate Change Commission once established under the proposed zero-carbon legislation. Under its terms of reference, the ICCC's primary deliverables were reports on two matters: firstly, surrender obligations if agricultural methane and nitrous oxide emissions were to enter into the *New Zealand ETS*; and second, planning for the transition to 100% renewable electricity by 2035. Over the course of 2018, the ICCC was engaged in technical analysis and undertook stakeholder consultations with over 200 organisations and individuals as it progressed work on the two projects noted above.

In June 2018, the Ministry for the Environment released a discussion document titled *Our Climate Your Say: Consultation on the Zero Carbon Bill*, which provides background information on, and a summary of proposals for, the Zero Carbon Bill. The discussion document was part of an extensive consultation process which included an online engagement portal, and a series of public events held around the country between June and July. Over 15,000 individuals and organisations made submissions on the document, providing feedback (among other matters) on: the nature of the 2050 emissions reductions target; treatment of biogenic methane within the target; the role and function of the Climate Change Commission; and the scope of the legislative and institutional framework (in particular, whether adaptation to climate change should be addressed alongside mitigation measures).

A summary of submissions was published in October 2018. It recorded that: an overwhelming majority (91%) of submitters considered that the net zero target should cover all gases (including biogenic methane); the Climate Change Commission's role should include advice on and monitoring of New Zealand's progress towards its goals (in the view of 97% of submissions); and that the legislative framework should cover adaptation (in the view of 92% of submissions). The results of submissions, together with other policy and technical input (including, notably, a substantial report by the newly appointed Parliamentary Commissioner for the Environment, Simon Upton)[69] were considered

---

68   Office of the Minister for Climate Change for Cabinet Environment, *Interim Climate Change Committee Terms of Reference and Appointment* (Cabinet Paper, April 2018).

69   Parliamentary Commissioner for the Environment, *A Zero Carbon Act for New Zealand: Revisiting Stepping Stones to Paris and Beyond* (Report, March 2018).

by the government in its ongoing development of the Zero Carbon Bill, scheduled for introduction to Parliament in 2019.

### 3.2.3 New Zealand Emissions Trading Scheme and its Review

During 2018, the government continued a long-running *Review of the Emissions Trading Scheme* underway since 2015. In December 2018, the Minister of Forestry Shane Jones announced what he described as "the first set of improvements to the *Emissions Trading Scheme*", focusing on the forestry sector with the aim of creating stronger incentives for afforestation, including: adding a category of "permanent forests" to the ETS (replacing the former *Permanent Forestry Sink Initiative*); and other changes "geared towards helping reduce both complexity and barriers to forest owners being part of the ETS".[70] The changes were implemented through the *Climate Change (Emissions Trading Scheme) Amendment Regulations 2018*, to be followed by additional (and more substantive) changes to the ETS in 2019.

### 3.2.4 Adaptation Technical Working Group

In May 2018, the New Zealand Adaptation Technical Working Group presented to the Minister for Climate Change a report and set of recommendations which build on previous analysis and a "stock-take" released in December 2017.[71]

Since 2004, local authorities have had an explicit mandate to consider and respond to issues of climate change adaptation under the *Resource Management Act 1991*.[72] However, despite a series of non-statutory guideline documents issued by the government, concerns have been expressed for many years at the lack of a clear, nationally coordinated framework for climate change adaptation in New Zealand. A key recommendation of the Working Group was the creation of a regularly updated national adaptation action plan in conjunction with a national climate change risk assessment which prioritises adaptation actions.[73] The Working Group also recommended the establishment of governance arrangements to support long-term adaptation action, and that these actions be reflected in the Zero Carbon Bill "to give a consistent and clear legislative mandate for climate change adaptation".[74] The Group also recommended that councils have particular regard to adapting to the effects of

---

70  "ETS Forestry Improvements to Create More Benefits for New Zealand" (Media Release, New Zealand Government, 12 December 2018).
71  Climate Change Adaptation Technical Working Group, *Adapting to Climate Change in New Zealand* (Recommendations, May 2018).
72  See Resource Management (Energy and Climate Change) Amendment Act 2004 (NZ).
73  Ibid 8, 9.
74  Ibid 48.

climate change when implementing the *National Policy Statement for Freshwater Management*.[75]

As noted above, the government consulted on the inclusion of adaptation measures (including through the proposed institutional framework) as part of its overall Zero Carbon Bill consultation, and received strong support for those proposals through submissions on the proposed Bill.

### 3.2.5 Ban on New Offshore Oil and Gas Exploration

On 12 April 2018, the Prime Minister announced that the government would be banning future offshore oil and gas exploration as "an important step to address climate change and create a clean, green and sustainable future for New Zealand".[76] The immediate effect of the announcement was to restrict the Block Offer 2018 (the mechanism by which the government awards new exploration permits) to new exploration on land in Taranaki only. The government indicated that officials would commence work on a review of the *Crown Minerals Act 1991* "to ensure the Act is consistent with this announcement" and that the government would "review its approach to onshore exploration in the next parliamentary term".[77]

Predictably, environmental groups reacted positively to the announced ban on new offshore fossil fuel exploration.[78] National MPs Jonathan Young and Todd Muller, on the other hand, described the situation as a "decision [which] is devoid of any rationale. It certainly has nothing to do with climate change. These changes will simply shift production elsewhere in the world, not reduce emissions".[79]

The government subsequently introduced legislation to give statutory effect to the announced ban in the form of the Crown Minerals (Petroleum) Amendment Bill 2018 which was passed on 7 November 2018 with support from Labour, New Zealand First and the Green Party, whilst being opposed by the National and Act parties. The Bill received Royal Assent on 12 November 2018, and on 13 November 2018, the *Crown Minerals (Petroleum) Amendment Act 2018* ("*Amendment Act*") came into force.[80] Under the amended legislation, oil and

---

75  Ibid 49.
76  "Planning For the Future: No New Offshore Oil and Gas Exploration Permits" (Media Release, New Zealand Government, 12 April 2018).
77  New Zealand Government, *Oil and Gas Exploration* (Fact Sheet, 2018).
78  See, eg, Greenpeace International, "New Zealand Places Historic Ban on All New Offshore Oil and Gas Exploration" (Media Release, 11 April 2018).
79  Jonathan Young, "Gas and Petroleum Decision is Economic Vandalism" (Media Release, New Zealand National Party, 12 April 2018).
80  *Crown Minerals (Petroleum) Amendment Act 2018* (NZ).

gas companies may continue to implement existing permits, but there is no legal scope for the issuing of new permits for offshore exploration.[81] The *Amendment Act* also contains particular provisions restricting access to conservation land in Taranaki.[82]

### 3.3 Resource Management Legislation

#### 3.3.1 Resource Management Act 1991 Reform

In October 2018, the Minister for the Environment David Parker announced the government's intention to undertake a major review of the New Zealand resource management system and legislation. The announcement followed Cabinet's approval of a proposed two-stage perform process involving firstly, a set of amendments in the form of "a narrowly-focused Bill", which would: remove certain ministerial regulation-making powers; remove preclusions on public notification and appeals for particular resource consent applications; reinstate the presumption that subdivision is restricted unless expressly permitted by a plan rule, national environmental standard or resource consent; and reinstate the option for councils to require financial contributions to support development. The Stage 1 bill would also "introduce a number of relatively simple changes to, in particular, improve consenting, fresh water management, enforcement and Environment Court operations".[83] The second stage of the reform process would involve "a more comprehensive review of the resource management system" including consideration of the regulation of climate change issues and urban tree protection.[84] Also to be addressed in the Stage 2 process would be housing and urban growth issues aimed at "addressing the planning system settings and fundamentals of land supply, development capacity, and infrastructure provision".[85]

The reform proposals build on a number of comprehensive reviews of New Zealand's resource management legislation and institutional framework, including reports by the Environmental Defence Society, New Zealand Productivity Commission, Local Government New Zealand and other groups. The second stage of reform is expected to attract close interest of stakeholders and

---

81  *Crown Minerals Act 1991* (NZ) s 23A(2), inserted by *Crown Minerals (Petroleum) Amendment Act 2018* (NZ) s 5.
82  Crown Minerals Act 1991 (NZ) s 50A, inserted by Crown Minerals (Petroleum) Amendment Act 2018 (NZ) s 9.
83  Office of the Minister for the Environment, Proposed Resource Management Amendment Bill: Stage 1 of a Resource Management System Review (Cabinet Paper, 9 October 2018) 2.
84  Ibid 12–14.
85  Ibid 4.

commentators given the government's open acknowledgement that reform proposals will cover all aspects of the now 28-year-old *Resource Management Act 1991*, including: the purpose and principles in Part 2; and the possibility of separating urban resource management regulation under a distinct legislative regime from non-urban environmental and planning issues.

### 3.3.2 Plantation Forestry

The *Resource Management (National Environmental Standards for Plantation Forestry) Regulations 2017* came into force on 1 May 2018, meeting one of New Zealand's goals set for 2018 in the *National Biodiversity Strategy*.[86]

Promulgation of a *National Environmental Standard for Plantation Forestry* ("NES-PF") introduces a nationally consistent regulatory regime for forestry activities, in most (but not all) cases, replacing a collection of (not always consistent) rules and policies contained in district and regional council plans. An explanatory document released in conjunction with the NES-PF stated that, while "local variation has offered some benefits, it has unnecessarily increased costs and operational complexity for the forestry sector, particularly for forests that cross council boundaries".[87]

The NES-PF covers a number of core plantation forestry activities, including afforestation, earthworks, river crossings, forest quarrying, harvesting and replanting. The regulations provide for the majority of forestry activities as permitted activities, provided that specific conditions, designed to avoid significant adverse environmental effects, are met. Where permitted activity conditions are not able to be met, foresters are required to apply for resource consents.

### 3.4 *Other Developments in Environmental Law and Policy*

#### 3.4.1 Waste and Packaging

In July 2018, the Parliamentary Commissioner for the Environment Simon Upton published an online resource titled *Biodegradable and Compostable Plastics in the Environment*, following an enquiry into claims for the promotion of certain biodegradable, degradable or compostable plastics "said to be environmentally friendly".[88] Upton's public observations on waste and plastics disposal

---

86   *Resource Management (National Environmental Standards for Plantation Forestry) Regulations 2017* (NZ) 2017/174.
87   Ministry for the Environment and Ministry for Primary Industries, *National Environmental Standards for Plantation Forestry* (Overview of the Regulations, August 2017) 1.
88   "Biodegradable and Compostable Plastics in the Environment", *Parliamentary Commissioner for the Environment* (Web Page, July 2018) <https://www.pce.parliament.nz/publications/biodegradable-and-compostable-plastics-in-the-environment>.

followed signing of a "New Zealand Plastic Packaging Declaration" by local and international businesses, signalling industry commitment to only using reusable, recyclable or compostable packaging by 2025.[89]

Upton's online resource included statements of concern not only around the amount of plastic being produced annually in New Zealand, but also in respect of products held out or certified as "compostable" despite the fact that they, having been tested in *commercial* composting conditions, will not necessarily biodegrade in home compost heaps.[90]

In conjunction with Upton's online release of the enquiry outcome, the Commissioner wrote to the Associate Minister for the Environment Eugenie Sage "to urge [her] and [her] officials to take the lead in lifting consumer and business understanding about claims of biodegradability made in respect to many single-use plastics".[91] In his letter, the Commissioner encouraged the Associate Minister to "consider the overarching hierarchy of policy goals that govern a waste policy" and noted his intention to "maintain a watching brief in this area".

On 24 November 2018, following a five-week public consultation process, the Associate Minister announced a decision to implement a "mandatory phase-out of single-use plastic shopping bags in New Zealand", effective from mid-2019. That policy announcement was followed by the promulgation of the *Waste Minimisation (Plastic Shopping Bags) Regulations 2018*, confirmed by order in council on 17 December 2018. The central reg 5 provides that a retailer "must not sell plastic shopping bags for the purpose of distributing goods sold by the retailer in New Zealand".[92]

### 3.4.2 Ozone Protection

The major development in 2018 concerning ozone protection was the implementation of the *Ozone Layer Protection Amendment Regulations*,[93] drafted to bring New Zealand legislation in line with the *Kigali Amendment to the Montreal Protocol on Substances that Deplete the Ozone Layer* adopted by New Zealand in October 2016 ("*Kigali Amendment*").[94] A key focus of the *Kigali Agreement* is to transition away from the use of hydrofluorocarbons ("HFCS")

---

89   "Action on Plastic Announced on World Environment Day" (Media Release, 5 June 2018).
90   "Biodegradable and Compostable Plastics in the Environment" (n 88).
91   Letter from Simon Upton to Eugenie Sage, 5 July 2018.
92   *Waste Minimisation (Plastic Shopping Bags) Regulations 2018* (NZ) 2018/270.
93   *Ozone Layer Protection Amendment Regulations 2018* (NZ) 2018/255.
94   *Amendment to the Montreal Protocol on Substances that Deplete the Ozone Layer*, opened for signature 15 October 2016 (entered into force 1 January 2019).

which, as well as having a small impact on ozone depletion, have a harmful effect on the climate as they are greenhouse gases.[95]

Regulations 7A to 7K impose strict control on HFCs, providing that there will be no bulk importation of HFCs without a permit. Part 1(2) of Schedule 1AA sets out the maximum allocation of HFCs that will be allowed in 2020 and 2021 respectively.[96]

The entry into force of the *Ozone Layer Protection Amendment Regulations 2018* on 18 February 2019 will enable New Zealand to formally ratify the *Kigali Amendment* (intended for October 2019) so that the instrument will enter into force for New Zealand on 1 January 2020.[97]

### 3.5 Trade

On 24 October 2018, the Trans-Pacific Partnership Agreement (CPTPP) Amendment Bill completed its third reading, receiving Royal Assent on 25 October 2018.[98] The purpose of the legislation was to enable New Zealand to ratify the CPTPP, signed in March 2018.

As noted above, the CPTPP entered into force on 30 December 2018, following New Zealand's ratification on 25 October 2018 and Governor General's making of the Comprehensive and Progressive Agreement for Trans-Pacific Partnership Amendment Act 2018 Commencement Order 2018, bringing into force provisions implementing the CPTPP from 30 December 2018.[99]

### Acknowledgements

Vernon Rive expresses his gratitude to AUT Law (Honours) student Jaime Rodger for research assistance in relation to this contribution.

---

95 "Why the Rules for HFCs Changed", *Environmental Protection Authority* (2019) <https://www.epa.govt.nz/industry-areas/hazardous-substances/hfcs/why-rules-have-changed/>.
96 *Ozone Layer Protection Amendment Regulations 2018* (NZ) (n 93) regs 7A–7K.
97 Ministry of Foreign Affairs and Trade, "Amendment to the Montreal Protocol on Substances that Deplete the Ozone Layer, Kigali 15 October 2016", *New Zealand Treaties Online* (Web Page) <https://www.treaties.mfat.govt.nz/search/details/p/213/780>.
98 "Trans-Pacific Partnership Agreement (CPTPP) Amendment Bill", *New Zealand Parliament* (Web Page) <https://www.parliament.nz/en/pb/bills-and-laws/bills-proposed-laws/document/BILL_78569/trans-pacific-partnership-agreement-cptpp-amendment-bill>.
99 *Comprehensive and Progressive Agreement for Trans-Pacific Partnership Amendment Act 2018 Commencement Order 2018* (NZ).

# Law of the Sea and Fisheries 2018

*Joanna Mossop**

## 1 Introduction[1]

2018 was a very busy year for ocean-related matters in New Zealand. The government undertook a number of initiatives in relation to the marine environment, ratified International Maritime Organisation conventions, updated legislation on the exercise of powers against drug smugglers and implemented new rules to minimise the risk of alien invasive species entering New Zealand through its ports.

## 2 Continental Shelf Outer Limits

New Zealand submitted the coordinates of its claimed continental shelf beyond 200 nautical miles to the Commission on the Limits of the Continental Shelf ("CLCS") in 2006. Recommendations were received from the CLCS in 2008. On 13 September 2018, the *Continental Shelf Order* established the outer limits of the extended continental shelf according to the recommendations from the CLCS.[2] According to *United Nations Convention on the Law of the Sea* ("*UNCLOS*") art 76(8),[3] "the limits of the shelf established by a coastal State on the basis of [the CLCS] recommendations shall be final and binding". New Zealand and Australia signed a treaty in 2004 in respect of the overlapping continental shelves in the vicinity of Norfolk Island and Macquarie Island.[4] There is an area to the north of New Zealand where New Zealand's continental shelf overlaps with claims of Fiji and Tonga. New Zealand will need to negotiate this boundary with Tonga and Fiji. The *Continental Shelf Order* and New Zealand's deposit with the United Nations ("UN")[5] note that they are

---

\* Victoria University of Wellington.
1 The author is grateful to the Ministry of Foreign Affairs and Trade for its input to this Year in Review contribution.
2 Continental Shelf Order 2018 (NZ) 2018/135.
3 *United Nations Convention on the Law of the Sea*, opened for signature 10 December 1982, 1833 UNTS 3 (entered into force 16 November 1994).
4 *Treaty Between the Government of Australia and the Government of New Zealand Establishing Certain Exclusive Economic Zone and Continental Shelf Boundaries*, signed 25 July 2004, [2006] ATS 4 (entered into force 25 January 2006).
5 18 December 2018, M.Z.N.140.2018.LOS.Rev.

without prejudice to the outcome of future continental shelf delimitation negotiations.

## 3 International Maritime Organisation Treaty Action

In 2017, New Zealand passed legislation[6] to enable it to implement the protocols to the *Convention for the Suppression of Unlawful Acts against the Safety of Navigation* and its *Protocol for the Suppression of Unlawful Acts against the Safety of Fixed Platforms Located on the Continental Shelf*.[7] New Zealand ratified both 2005 *Suppression of Unlawful Acts* ("SUA") protocols[8] on 26 February 2018 and they came into force for New Zealand on 27 May 2018. New Zealand declared that both protocols will also enter into force in respect of Tokelau.

New Zealand also acceded to the *Protocol of 2003 to the International Convention on the Establishment of an International Fund for Compensation for Oil Pollution Damage 1992* ("*Supplementary Fund Protocol*").[9] The *Supplementary Fund Protocol* raises the compensation payable to New Zealand in the event of a spill from an oil tanker from approximately $377 million to $1.4 billion.[10] The accession occurred on 29 June 2018 and the protocol took effect on 29 September 2018. New Zealand declared that the accession does not extend to Tokelau. Legislation implementing the *Supplementary Fund Protocol* was passed in May 2017 and received royal assent on 15 December 2017.[11]

---

6   *Maritime Crimes Amendment Act 2017* (NZ).
7   *Convention for the Suppression of Unlawful Acts against the Safety of Maritime Navigation*, signed 10 March 1988, 1678 UNTS 221 (entered into force 1 March 1992); *Protocol to the Convention of 10 March 1988 for the Suppression of Unlawful Acts against the Safety of Fixed Platforms Located on the Continental Shelf*, signed 10 March 1988, 1678 UNTS 304 (entered into force 1 March 1992).
8   International Maritime Organization, *Protocol of 2005 to the Convention for the Suppression of Unlawful Acts against the Safety of Maritime Navigation* (No LEG/CONF.15/21, 1 November 2005); *Protocol of 2005 to the Protocol for the Suppression of Unlawful Acts against the Safety of Fixed Platforms Located on the Continental Shelf* (No LEG/CONF.15/22, 1 November 2005).
9   *Protocol of 2003 to the International Convention on the Establishment of an International Fund for Compensation for Oil Pollution Damage 1992*, opened for signature 16 May 2003, [2006] IETS 13 (entered into force 3 March 2005).
10  Ministry of Transport, *Protocol of 2003 to the International Convention on the Establishment of an International Fund for Compensation for Oil Pollution Damage, 1992* (Supplementary Fund Protocol) (National Interest Analysis, May 2014) [22].
11  *Maritime Transport Amendment Act 2017* (NZ).

## 4     Maritime Powers Extension Act 2018 ("MPEA")

The MPEA amended two Acts[12] to provide a basis in New Zealand domestic law for the enforcement and prosecution of drug offences in waters beyond New Zealand's territorial sea. The MPEA further implements New Zealand's obligations under UNCLOS art 108 and *United Nations Convention against Illicit Traffic in Narcotic Drugs and Psychotic Substances*[13] art 17 to cooperate in the suppression of drug trafficking. Under these provisions, New Zealand can take "appropriate measures" in its exclusive economic zone and the high seas against foreign vessels engaged in drug trafficking, if the flag state gives authorisation.

Prior to the enactment of the MPEA, New Zealand domestic legislation did not provide clear legal authority for the New Zealand Customs Service ("Customs") to interdict vessels beyond the contiguous zone (24 nautical miles from shore), even if they were New Zealand vessels or New Zealand was acting with the permission of the flag state. The goal of the MPEA is to clarify in domestic law the powers of law enforcement agencies to board, search and take enforcement action in international waters against drug smugglers.[14]

According to the new schedule 5A of the *Customs and Excise Act 2018*, customs officers may board and undertake an initial inspection of a ship beyond New Zealand's territorial sea if they have reasonable cause to suspect that the ship is involved in drug smuggling or a person on board is a drug smuggler. If the officer has reasonable cause to believe that a person on a ship is involved in the commission of a drug smuggling offence, the officer may undertake a full search and arrest a person.[15] However, the powers only apply to a foreign ship if the flag state has consented to the exercise of the powers.[16] The exception is if the foreign ship is arrested following hot pursuit under UNCLOS art 111.[17] These provisions ensure that the powers will be exercised consistently with international law, including UNCLOS art 92.

The new provisions of the *Misuse of Drugs Act 1975* create new criminal offences relating to the smuggling of illicit drugs outside New Zealand.[18]

---

12    *Customs and Excise Act 2018* (NZ) and *Misuse of Drugs Act 1975* (NZ).
13    *United Nations Convention against Illicit Traffic in Narcotic Drugs and Psychotic Substances*, opened for signature 20 December 1988, 1582 UNTS 95 (entered into force 11 November 1990).
14    New Zealand Customs Service, *Maritime Powers Extension Bill: Initial Briefing to the Foreign Affairs, Defence and Trade Committee* (Select Committee Briefing, 21 March 2019).
15    *Customs and Excise Act 2018* (NZ) sch 5A.
16    Ibid sch 5A.
17    Ibid sch 5A.
18    *Misuse of Drugs Act 1975* (NZ) ss 12D–12F.

Prosecutions under these provisions may only take place with the consent of the Attorney-General and, where the smuggling took place aboard a foreign ship, with the consent of its flag state.[19]

The MPEA entered into force on 1 October 2018.

## 5  The Impact of Sea-level Rise on Maritime Zones

In 2018, the New Zealand Cabinet endorsed an *Action Plan on Pacific Climate Change-Related Migration*.[20] Among the five "early actions" was an instruction for the Ministry of Foreign Affairs and Trade to develop a strategy for New Zealand in championing the progressive development of international law to protect coastal state rights to maritime zones in the face of sea-level rise.[21] In response, officials have been instructed to consider the problem caused by shifting baselines and in particular consider how to ensure that Pacific Island countries retain existing rights to their maritime zones in the context of climate change. The commitment to engaging in the issue is seen as reflecting New Zealand's support for a rules-based order including UNCLOS as well as equity concerns.[22]

## 6  Protection of the Marine Environment

### 6.1  *New Biofouling Regulations*

In 2018, New Zealand introduced stringent biofouling regulations aimed at vessels entering port after leaving the territorial sea of another state.[23] The requirement is that the operator of any vessel arriving in port has the obligation to ensure the vessel has a clean hull.[24] Prior to arriving in New Zealand, a vessel operator must submit a Biofouling and Ballast Water Declaration including

---

19   Ibid s 28A and sch 5A s3(1).
20   Office of the Minister of Foreign Affairs, *Pacific Climate Change-Related Displacement and Migration: a New Zealand Action Plan* (Cabinet Paper) <https://www.mfat.govt.nz/assets/Uploads/Redacted-Cabinet-Paper-Pacific-climate-migration-2-May-2018.pdf>.
21   Ibid 11–12.
22   Victoria Hallum, "Sea-Level Rise and International Law" (Public Lecture, Beeby Colloquium on International Law, 30 November 2018).
23   Ministry for Primary Industries, *Biofouling on Vessels Arriving to New Zealand* (Craft Risk Management Standard, 15 November 2018).
24   Ibid 5. See also Ministry for Primary Industries, *Craft Risk Management Standard for Biofouling* (Guidance Document, 6 April 2018).

details about the vessel's antifouling coating and evidence that one of the three management options to meet the standard have been done.[25] These are: cleaning of the hull before visiting New Zealand or immediately on arrival; continual maintenance using best practice; or application of approved treatments to the hull.[26] Based on the information provided, the Ministry for Primary Industries conducts an assessment to assign a risk category for the vessel.[27] Vessels may be inspected on arrival.[28] If the vessel is not in compliance with the *Biofouling Standard*, it may be directed to rectify the biofouling or to leave New Zealand.[29] International vessels are prohibited from cleaning their hulls in New Zealand waters.[30] If the vessel will remain in New Zealand for more than 20 days, a stricter standard for biofouling applies.[31]

It seems that New Zealand is the first country to apply such stringent controls on biofouling, and the authority to do so is based on its ability to impose conditions for entering its ports. The *Guidance Document* for New Zealand's *Biofouling Standard* refers to the International Maritime Organization's *2011 Guidelines for the Control and Management of Ships' Biofouling to Minimize the Transfer of Invasive Aquatic Species* as examples of best practice.[32]

### 6.2 New Zealand–Chile Cooperative Arrangement on Albatrosses

In November 2018, the New Zealand and Chilean ministers of foreign affairs signed a cooperative arrangement aimed at protecting the endangered antipodean albatross.[33] These seabirds are at risk of being caught on longlines used by the fishing fleet in the Pacific. The arrangement establishes a partnership between the ministries of conservation and fisheries in Chile and New Zealand.[34] Under the arrangement, the parties will develop an action plan to develop priority research and conservation activities and report to the Advisory

---

25  Ministry for Primary Industries, Craft Risk Management Standard for Biofouling (n 24) 8.
26  *Biofouling on Vessels Arriving to New Zealand* (n 24) 5.
27  *Craft Risk Management Standard Guidance Document,* (n 25) 8–9.
28  Ibid 9.
29  Ibid 11.
30  Ibid 11.
31  Ibid 21.
32  Ibid 6, referring to International Maritime Organization, *2011 Control and Management of Ships' Biofouling to Minimize the Transfer of Invasive Aquatic Species* (Guidelines No MEPC 62/24/Add.1, 15 July 2011).
33  "Chile and NZ Arrangement to Protect Seabirds" (Media Release, New Zealand Government, 19 November 2018).
34  Ibid.

Committee of the Agreement for the Conservation of Albatrosses and Petrels.[35] The states will also cooperate through regional fisheries management organisations to improve measures to prevent such birds being caught on fishing lines.[36]

## 7 Fisheries

### 7.1 *South Pacific Regional Fisheries Management Organisation ("SPRFMO")*

One of the unique features of the *Convention on the Conservation and Management of High Seas Fishery Resources in the South Pacific Ocean* ("SPRFMO *Convention*")[37] is its limitation on objections and a timely dispute settlement process. Under the SPRFMO *Convention*, decisions may be taken by a three-fourths majority vote on matters of substance if consensus cannot be reached.[38] The ability of a non-consenting state to object to the new conservation and management measure is limited under art 17. A member of the SPRFMO Commission can only object to a decision becoming binding on it for two reasons: either, that the decision unjustifiably discriminates in form or in fact against the member of the Commission; or the decision is inconsistent with the SPRFMO *Convention* or other relevant international law.[39] If a member wishes to object it must specify the grounds for its objection and adopt alternative measures "that are equivalent in effect to the decision to which it has objected".[40] A Review Panel is then established which considers whether the objection has met the requirements under the SPFFMO *Convention* and whether the alternative measures are equivalent in effect to the decision to which the objection has been presented.[41] Depending on the Panel's conclusion, the alternative measures may be confirmed, the Panel may recommend modifications, the Commission may meet to consider the decision in light of the Panel's findings,

---

35  John Cooper, "Chile and New Zealand to Produce a Joint Action Plan for the Endangered Antipodean Albatross", *Agreement on the Conservation of Albatrosses and Petrels* (Web Page, 10 December 2018) <https://acap.aq/en/news/latest-news/3175-chile-and-new-zealand-to-produce-a-joint-action-plan-for-the-endangered-antipodean-albatross>.
36  "Chile and NZ Arrangement to Protect Seabirds" (above n 33).
37  *Convention on the Conservation and Management of High Seas Fishery Resources in the South Pacific Ocean*, opened for signature 14 November 2009, [2012] ATS 28 (entered into force 24 August 2012) ("SPRFMO Convention").
38  Ibid art 16(2)(b).
39  Ibid art 17(2)(c).
40  Ibid art 17(2)(b).
41  Ibid art 17(5)(a), (e).

or the objecting party can initiate dispute settlement procedures.[42] Only one previous objection has gone through this process, an objection by Russia in 2013.

In 2018, Ecuador entered an objection against a conservation and management measure on Chilean jack mackerel, arguing that it should have received a greater allocation on the basis that it is a developing coastal state and that it was unable to fully participate in a crucial meeting which decided on prior allocations.[43] It argued that it needed a substantial increase in allocation to develop a fishery for jack mackerel.[44] New Zealand, as a member of the Commission, provided a written memorandum and made oral submissions in the hearing in addition to other members. Ecuador and the Chairperson of the Commission agreed to nominate Professor Don MacKay of New Zealand to chair the Review Panel. The decision of the Review Panel was released on 5 June 2018, only two weeks after the hearing.

The Panel did not uphold Ecuador's claim that the failure to allocate additional catch was inconsistent with *UNCLOS* or the *Agreement for the Implementation of the Provisions of the United Nations Convention on the Law of the Sea of 10 December 1982 Relating to the Conservation and Management of Straddling Fish Stocks and Highly Migratory Fish Stocks* ("UN Fish Stocks Agreement 1995").[45] Although both agreements require consideration of the needs of developing states, the Panel considered that the *SPRFMO* Commission had a wide margin of discretion in how to determine the allocation of catch.[46] In the circumstances, Ecuador could not demonstrate that the Commission had failed to consider its position as a developing state.[47] Similarly, the Panel found that the decision did not unjustifiably discriminate against Ecuador.[48] It found that Ecuador's request for additional total allowable catch ("TAC") was made late but was still considered by the Commission.[49] Additionally, the mere fact that Ecuador is a developing country does not determine the matter as many of the

---

42  Ibid annex II. See also Joanna Mossop, "Law of the Sea and Fisheries" (2009) 7 *New Zealand Yearbook of International Law* 336.
43  Objection by the Republic of Ecuador to a Decision of the Commission of the South Pacific Regional Fisheries Management Organisation (CMM 01-2018) (Findings and Recommendations of the Review Panel) (Permanent Court of Arbitration, Case No 2018-13, 5 June 2018) [43].
44  Ibid [43].
45  Ibid [129].
46  Ibid [95].
47  Ibid [97].
48  Ibid [109].
49  Ibid [107].

members are also developing states.[50] The Panel concluded that Ecuador's proposal to increase its catch of jack mackerel was not equivalent in effect to the management measure.[51] However, this was not the end of the matter. The Panel also made a number of suggestions about how Ecuador's concerns could be met in the future, including the need to consider ways in which Ecuador's aspirations to develop a jack mackerel fishery could be facilitated.[52] Thus, although Ecuador failed to convince the Panel that it should be allowed an increased TAC in 2018, the process may ultimately facilitate an increased catch in the future.

## 8  Whaling

At the September meeting of the International Whaling Commission in Brazil, New Zealand made a statement in support of the IWC and the *Governance Review* process.[53] Among other things, the statement opposed the resumption of commercial whaling and expressed support for a commitment to non-lethal whale research.[54] It called on Japan to cease lethal research in the Southern Ocean and North Pacific and instead rely on non-lethal research methods.[55] New Zealand expressed disappointment that Japan chose to harvest whales within the Ross Sea region's Marine Protected Area.[56] It also called on Iceland and Norway to cease commercial whaling.[57]

New Zealand was a co-sponsor of a draft resolution on ghost gear entanglement.[58] Following discussions, *Resolution 2018–3* was adopted by consensus. The resolution encourages states and other actors to work towards development of best practices and removal of debris, directs the Scientific Committee and the Conservation Committee to continue work on ghost gear and impacts on cetaceans, urges states to report relevant information on ghost gear, agrees

---

50   Ibid [108].
51   Ibid [118].
52   Ibid [122]–[128].
53   Ministry of Foreign Affairs and Trade, *New Zealand: IWC 67 Is the Commission's Opportunity to Step Up Its Global Leadership on Whale and Dolphin* Conservation (Opening Statement, 10 September 2018).
54   Ibid 2.
55   Ibid 2–3.
56   Ibid 2–3.
57   Ibid 3.
58   IWC-67, Resolution 2018-3: Resolution on Ghost Gear Entanglement among Cetaceans (Resolution No IWC/67/11 Rev2, September 2018).

to seek collaboration and cooperation with other initiatives and invites parties to join the IWC's *Global Whale Entanglement Response Network*.[59]

Following Japan's announcement that it was withdrawing from the IWC (which took effect on 30 June 2019), the Foreign Minister issued a press release welcoming the announcement that Japan will cease whaling in the Southern Ocean, but also expressing disappointment that Japan was leaving the Commission with an intention to resume commercial whaling within its exclusive economic zone.[60]

---

59   Ibid.
60   Winston Peters, "NZ Disappointed at Japan's Decision to Leave International Whaling Commission" (Media Release, New Zealand Government, 26 December 2018).

# The Antarctic Treaty System

*Alan D Hemmings**

## 1     Introduction

The key Antarctic Treaty System ("ATS")[1] events of 2018 were, as is usual, its two annual diplomatic meetings: the Antarctic Treaty Consultative Meeting ("ATCM") and the Meeting of the Commission for the Conservation of Antarctic Marine Living Resources ("Commission"). These diplomatic meetings include the main sessions of the advisory bodies, the Committee for Environmental Protection ("CEP") and the Scientific Committee for the Conservation of Antarctic Marine Living Resources ("SC-CAMLR"), established under the relevant international instruments.[2] The ATCM received reports from seven Intersessional Contact Groups ("ICGS") operating through electronic means between the 40th and 41st ATCMS (six through Working Papers ("WPs"), one through an Information Paper ("IP")). ICGs are now variously named and constituted: some are "informal"; others are given terms of reference; some are established for a particular intersessional period between ATCMS; some are labelled "subsidiary groups"; others are "open-ended" and some report only to the CEP. No Meeting of Experts was held between these ATCMs.

In relation to the Commission, and following usual practice, three intersessional meetings of Working Groups of the SC-CAMLR (Ecosystem Monitoring and Management; Statistics, Assessments and Modelling; and Fish Stock Assessment) and a meeting of the Subgroup on Acoustic Survey and Analysis Methods were again held during 2018. The *Convention for the Conservation of Antarctic Marine Living Resources* ("*CCAMLR*") Independent Stock Assessment Review for Toothfish held a meeting in the United Kingdom ("UK") in June 2018. The UK also hosted a Workshop on Spatial Management in July 2018. New

---

\*  Gateway Antarctica, University of Canterbury.
1  "'Antarctic Treaty system' means the Antarctic Treaty, the measures in effect under that Treaty, its associated separate international instruments in force and the measures in effect under those instruments": Protocol on Environmental Protection to the Antarctic Treaty, opened for signature 4 October 1991, 30 ILM 1455 (entered into force 14 January 1998) ("Madrid Protocol") art 1.
2  Ibid arts 11, 12; Convention for the Conservation of Antarctic Marine Living Resources, opened for signature 5 May 1980, 1329 UNTS 47 (entered into force 7 April 1982) ("CCAMLR") arts XIV, XV.

Zealand was, seemingly, an active and significant participant across all the major issues before the ATS institutions.

In 2018, the most significant fact of ATS activity was the truncated ATCM, occasioned by the inability of the anticipated host state to meet its undertaking. As a result, only part of the usual workload of the annual meeting could be met. Discussion of Marine Protected Areas ("MPAS") continued within the Commission, but with no immediate indications that further designations will be possible in the short term.

## 2      1959 Antarctic Treaty[3]

The 41st ATCM[4] was convened in Buenos Aires, Argentina, 13–18 May 2018.[5] Argentina was not due to hold the ATCM for some decades, since it had last hosted it (the 34th ATCM) in 2011. ATCMs are ordinarily rotated through the Consultative Parties, in a rough alphabetical sequence (in relation to the English language formulation of their names). At the 40th ATCM in Beijing in 2017, Ecuador had agreed to host the ATCM in its capital Quito in June 2018.[6] It proved unable to do so, following the adoption of *Decree 135*,[7] addressing austerity measures, promulgated by the President in September 2017.[8] Therefore, at short notice, a much truncated meeting (three rather than eight days) was scheduled in the Argentine capital, where the Secretariat of the *Antarctic Treaty* is based. At the opening of the meeting, the Chair[9]

> noted the unusual circumstances that led to this condensed ATCM XLI–CEP XXI, and thanked the Delegation of Argentina and the Antarctic Treaty Secretariat for organising the meetings in such a short time frame.

---

3   Antarctic Treaty, opened for signature 1 December 1959, 402 UNTS 71 (entered into force 23 June 1961).
4   ATCMs address the full range of obligations under both the Antarctic Treaty and the Madrid Protocol, and the presently more limited reporting obligations under the Convention for the Conservation of Antarctic Seals, opened for signature 1 June 1972, 1080 UNTS 175 (entered into force 11 March 1978).
5   Antarctic Treaty Secretariat, *Final Report of the Forty-First Antarctic Treaty Consultative Meeting* (Buenos Aires, 2018).
6   Antarctic Treaty Secretariat, *Final Report of the Fortieth Antarctic Treaty Consultative Meeting* (Buenos Aires, 2017) [422].
7   *Final Report of the Forty-First Antarctic Treaty Consultative Meeting* (n 5) [29].
8   *Decreto 135* [Decree 135] (Ecuador) 1 September 2017 <https://www.eltelegrafo.com.ec/images/cms/EdicionImpresa/2017/Septiembre/30-09-17/decreto-135.pdf>.
9   *Final Report of the Forty-First Antarctic Treaty Consultative Meeting* (n 5) [7].

The Chair emphasised that this was not a normal or ordinary meeting, and should not be seen as setting a precedent for future Meetings.

The Executive Secretary noted that the change of venue "resulted in a net cost to the Secretariat of approximately USD 110,000".[10] There was, unsurprisingly, some discussion of the lessons and implications of a party being unable to host a meeting, and the arrangement of alternatives at short notice, and the meeting agreed to establish an Intersessional Contact Group ("ICG") on Organisational Aspects of the ATCM, convened by Argentina, with the following terms of reference:[11]

> 1. to examine the implications and lessons learned from the organisation of ATCM XLI and CEP XXI, including:
>
> Impact on ATCM and CEP matters as they relate to ensuring efficient governance of Antarctica or the maintenance of the Antarctic Treaty System;
>
> Impact on the Secretariat's resources.
>
> 2. To consider options for how best to manage future scenarios where, because of exceptional circumstances, the organisation of the ATCM and CEP does not follow existing practice of rotation through the Consultative Parties, (unless rotation exchange has been previously arranged) including, for example:
>
> The usefulness of the submission of an IP by the Host Country of the next ATCM during the previous meeting, and the contents of it;
>
> Anticipation, regularity and deadlines for the submission of (informal) progress reports by the Host Country to the Antarctic Treaty Secretariat regarding the organisation of the ATCM;
>
> Consider the merits of creating a guarantee fund (possibly with special contribution by the next ATCM host country) to bear the cost of any extraordinary expenses assumed by the ATS required by the organisation of an ATCM in a country other than the one originally agreed;
>
> Any possible implications for ATCM or CEP Rules of Procedure;
>
> Any possible guidance for handling any future such scenarios; and
>
> Except in cases of force majeure, the possibility of measures taken with regard to the Parties not abiding by the commitment to organise the ATCM (e.g. payment of an extra fee to compensate for unforeseen expenses, losing rights on the next two ATCMs, etc.).

---

10   Ibid [41].
11   Ibid [30].

This was plainly an atypical ATCM. However, it was still cast as an ATCM, whereas on the previous occasion (the 2000 meeting) when the anticipated host was ultimately unable to host the event and the meeting was held elsewhere (a five-day meeting in The Hague), it was designated as a "Special Consultative Meeting".[12] The tone of the discussion in the meeting and its establishment of an ICG, which would report back to the next ATCM, indicates that parties are now concerned about ensuring continuity of operation given the heavy technical workload that characterises the annual ATCM and its CEP advisory body. This work enables the decision-making upon which operational practice is dependent, and in some cases (such as environmental evaluation) may be necessary to ensure compliance with legal obligations.

The 41st ATCM conducted its work through the usual three entities – the CEP and two Working Groups: Working Group 1 on Policy, Legal and Institutional Issues and Working Group 2 on Operations, Science and Tourism. However, whilst the CEP met as a body, the main part of the ATCM was conducted in plenary, with the Chairs of each Working Group chairing agenda items assigned to these in turn.

The United States, as Depository Government for the *Antarctic Treaty* and the *Madrid Protocol*, advised the accession of Turkey to the *Madrid Protocol*. There are now 53 parties to the former and 40 to the latter.[13]

For the ninth successive year (and perhaps unsurprisingly given the circumstances of this meeting), all six of the legally-binding Measures adopted related to protected areas or historic sites and monuments (this year, all concerned Antarctic Specially Protected Areas). Only one of these Measures was related to the region of particular interest to New Zealand,[14] the Ross Sea region that New Zealand claims as the Ross Dependency. This was *Measure 6 (2018), Antarctic Specially Protected Area No 172 (Lower Taylor Glacier and Blood Falls, McMurdo Dry Valleys, Victoria): Revised Management Plan*, which was tabled by the United States.[15]

Three administrative Decisions ("D") were adopted: (D1) Secretariat Report, Programme and Budget; (D2) Renewal of the Contract of the Secretariat's

---

12  Netherlands, *Final Report of the Twelfth Antarctic Treaty Special Consultative Meeting* (The Hague, 2000).
13  United States, "Report of the Depository Government of the Antarctic Treaty and its Protocol in accordance with Recommendation XIII-2" (Information Paper No 6, 2018).
14  All of the others were in the Antarctic Peninsula.
15  United States, "Revised Management Plan for Antarctic Specially Protected Area (ASPA) No 172 Lower Taylor Glacier and Blood Falls, McMurdo Dry Valleys, Victoria Land" (Working Paper No 10, 2018).

External Auditor; and (D3) Multi-Year Strategic Work Plan for the Antarctic Treaty Consultative Meeting.

Five hortatory Resolutions ("R") were adopted: (R1) Site Guidelines for Visitors; (R2) Guidelines for the Assessment and Management of Heritage in Antarctica; (R3) Revised Guide to the Presentation of Working Papers Containing Proposals for Antarctic Specially Protected Areas, Antarctic Specially Managed Areas or Historic Sites and Monuments; (R4) Environmental Guidelines for Operation of Remotely Piloted Aircraft Systems (RPAS) in Antarctica; and (R5) SCAR's Environmental Code of Conduct for Terrestrial Scientific Field Research in Antarctica.

Reflecting the reduced circumstances of the ATCM, there were fewer Measures, Decisions and Resolutions adopted, down from the respective seven, six and six which were adopted in 2017.[16]

There was a marked reduction in the number of substantive papers (WPs and IPs) tabled at the 41st ATCM: 35 WPs and 73 IPs, compared to the 47 and 175 respectively at the 40th ATCM. New Zealand tabled fewer meeting papers than usual: three WPs and three IPs. The three IPs comprised two tabled by New Zealand alone,[17] one of which was a notice of intent to conduct a Comprehensive Environmental Evaluation ("CEE") – the highest level of environmental impact assessment mandated under the *Madrid Protocol*, and which involves international review of the Draft CEE – for the redevelopment of Scott Base; the other was on regional scale environmental management. The third IP, tabled with ATCM Observer the Scientific Committee for Antarctic Research ("SCAR"), related to the Antarctic Environments Portal that New Zealand leads.[18]

Of the three WPs, two were tabled by a number of parties including New Zealand, and only one by New Zealand alone. The last was the five-yearly management plan review conducted by New Zealand for the Antarctic Specially Protected Area on Mount Erebus designated in 1997 to keep inviolate the site

---

16   See Alan D Hemmings, "Year in Review: The Antarctic Treaty System" (2017) 15 *New Zealand Yearbook of International Law* 218, 219–220.

17   New Zealand, "Notice of intention to prepare a Comprehensive Environmental Evaluation for redevelopment of Scott Base" (Information Paper No 15, 2018); New Zealand, "Supporting the regional-scale analysis of Antarctica: A tool to enable broader-scale environmental management" (Information Paper No 22, 2018).

18   New Zealand and SCAR, "Antarctic Environments Portal: Progress Report" (Information Paper No 3, 2018).

of the 28 November 1979 crash of Air New Zealand Flight 901. The review "concluded that the current management provisions remain appropriate to protect the values of the Area and that no changes to the management plan are required".[19] On this basis, the CEP advice to the ATCM was that the Management Plan for this Antarctic Specially Protected Area ("ASPA") (and two others) "remained in force with the next reviews to be initiated in 2023".[20]

New Zealand was one of seven states tabling a WP on harmonisation of marine protection initiatives across the ATS, and introduced the WP.[21] This

> recommended that the CEP establish an ICG to support harmonisation of marine protection initiatives across the Antarctic Treaty System. The ICG would be tasked with identifying options, within its mandate, to contribute to the Ross Sea Region Marine Protected Area (RSRMPA) as well as capturing related broader issues raised.[22]

It was agreed that New Zealand would lead the informal intersessional work and report back to the next CEP meeting in 2019.[23]

In the third WP, New Zealand with 13 other states and SCAR proposed a joint SCAR/CEP workshop on the Antarctic Protected Area system.[24] This WP was introduced by Australia,[25] the proposal was strongly supported by the CEP, which agreed with the workshop terms of reference provided in the WP,[26] and the Czech Republic offered to host the workshop in Prague prior to the commencement of the CEP at the next ATCM.[27]

---

19 New Zealand, "Review of Management Plan for ASPA No 156, Lewis Bay, Mount Erebus, Ross Island" (Working Paper No 15, 2018).
20 *Final Report of the Forty-First Antarctic Treaty Consultative Meeting* (n 5) [104].
21 Belgium, Chile, France, Germany, Netherlands, New Zealand and United States, "Harmonisation of Marine Protection initiatives across the Antarctic Treaty system (ATS)" (Working Paper No 12, 2018).
22 *Final Report of the Forty-First Antarctic Treaty Consultative Meeting* (n 5) [154].
23 Ibid [160].
24 Argentina, Australia, Belgium, Chile, China, Czech Republic, France, Germany, Japan, New Zealand, Norway, Russian Federation, SCAR, United Kingdom and United States, "Proposal for a Joint SCAR/CEP Workshop on further developing the Antarctic Protected Area System" (Working Paper No 16, 2018).
25 *Final Report of the Forty-First Antarctic Treaty Consultative Meeting* (n 5) [127].
26 Ibid [128].
27 Ibid [129].

## 3 1980 Convention on the Conservation of Antarctic Marine Living Resources

The regular 2018 (37th) Meeting of the Commission was held at the CCAMLR Secretariat in Hobart, Tasmania, Australia 22 October – 2 November 2018.[28] Commission decisions are adopted as "Conservation Measures".[29]

The Ministry of Foreign Affairs and Trade describes New Zealand as having "a particular interest in the exploratory toothfish fisheries in the Ross Sea",[30] and this is the primary area of fisheries activity by New Zealand operators. The Ross Sea is divided between CCAMLR Statistical Subareas 88.1 and 88.2.[31] For the 2018–19 season, New Zealand vessel activity was, again, confined to these two subareas.

In Subarea 88.1 the precautionary catch limit ("PCL") for the 2018–19 season was set at 3,157 tonnes across 24 vessels – identical in both respects to the 2017–18 season. The 24 vessels were apportioned as a maximum of three New Zealand, one Australian, one Japanese, five South Korean, four Russian, one Spanish, five Ukrainian, three UK and one Uruguayan flagged vessels. Of the total PCL, 2,628 tonnes were set for areas outside the Ross Sea Region MPA; 464 tonnes in the Special Research Zone of the MPA; and a further 65 tonnes assigned to New Zealand for the Ross Sea Shelf Survey.[32]

For Subarea 88.2, as in 2017, an overall PCL figure is not provided in the Conservation Measure itself, and is complicated by the fact that "the precautionary catch limits for Statistical Subarea 88.2 small-scale research units ('SSRUS') A–B are included in" the catch limits of *Conservation Measure 41-09* (2018) attaching to Subarea 88.1 and addressed above. Whilst such an aggregation presumably makes some sense for operational purposes, it is rather opaque in terms of policy assessment. Whatever that figure is, a further 1,000 tonnes catch is sanctioned across "Research Blocks" 1–4 and SSRU H in the Conservation Measure for 88.2.[33] This PCL is spread across 23 vessels (compared to 21 in

---

28  CCAMLR Secretariat, *Report of the Thirty-Seventh Meeting of the Commission* (Hobart, 2018).
29  CCAMLR Secretariat, *Schedule of Conservation Measures in Force 2018/19* (Hobart, 2018).
30  "The Antarctic Treaty System", Ministry of Foreign Affairs and Trade <https://www.mfat.govt.nz/en/environment/antarctica/the-antarctic-treaty-system>.
31  CCAMLR Secretariat, "Convention Area" <https://www.ccamlr.org/en/organisation/convention-area>. See particularly the map showing Statistical Areas at <https://www.ccamlr.org/en/system/files/CCAMLR-Convention-Area-Map.pdf>.
32  CCAMLR Conservation Measure 41-09 (2018): Limits on the Exploratory Fishery for Dissostichus mawsoni in Statistical Subarea 88.1 in the 2018/19 season.
33  Commission for the Conservation of Antarctic Marine Living Resources, Conservation Measure 41-10 (2018): Limits on the Exploratory Fishery for Dissostichus mawsoni in Statistical Subarea 88.2 in the 2018/19 season.

2017–18) comprising a maximum of three New Zealand, one Australian, five South Korean, four Russian, five Ukrainian, three UK and two Uruguayan flagged vessels.[34]

New Zealand tabled four papers in the Commission and none in the Scientific Committee. In the latter, there appears to be a trend towards fewer papers by Commission Members as states, and more papers by individual scientists, Working and Expert Groups and Workshop reports, so the New Zealand situation is not necessarily an issue. The Commission papers included three solely by New Zealand: one was an investigation report on late removal of fishing gear following fishery closure notification;[35] the second was a report of CCAMLR inspections undertaken from the vessel *HMNZS Otago*;[36] and the third was its report as the CCAMLR Observer at the annual meeting of the Commission for the Conservation of Southern Bluefin Tuna.[37] A fourth paper, on a mechanism to support implementation of the proposed General Capacity Building Fund, was tabled jointly with Australia, Norway, the Republic of Korea and the UK.[38]

MPAS continued as a focus at this Commission meeting, discussed under the heading of "Spatial Management", which had also been the subject of the Workshop earlier noted. The discussions considered research and monitoring of the two existing MPAS (the South Orkney Islands Southern Shelf MPA; and the Ross Sea Region MPA), and proposals for new MPAS. The latter include the proposals for: (1) an East Antarctica MPA; (2) a Weddell Sea MPA; (3) an Antarctic Peninsula MPA; and (4) MPAS in the sub-Antarctic areas of the Atlantic and Indian Ocean. Whilst the discussions were extensive, extending over 14 pages of the Commission's *Final Report*,[39] no substantive development of any of these proposals occurred, and the ambivalence of some Commission Members in relation to MPA designations, which became evident in the course of the Ross Sea MPA process, remains an issue.

---

34   Ibid.
35   New Zealand, "New Zealand investigation reports into late removal of fishing gear following the fishery closure notifications" (CCAMLR-XXXVII/BG/33, 2018).
36   New Zealand, "CCAMLR Inspections Undertaken by New Zealand from HMNZS Otago during 2017/18" (CCAMLR-XXXVII/BG/34, 2018).
37   New Zealand, "Report from the CCAMLR Observer (New Zealand) to the 25th Annual Meeting of the Commission for the Conservation of Southern Bluefin Tuna (CCSBT) (Nouméa, New Caledonia, 15–16 October 2018)" (CCAMLR-XXXVII/BG/49, 2018).
38   Australia, New Zealand, Norway, the Republic of Korea and the United Kingdom, "A proposal for a mechanism to support the implementation of the proposed General Capacity Building Fund" (CCAMLR-XXXVII/02 Rev. 1, 2018).
39   CCAMLR Secretariat, *Report of the Thirty-Seventh Meeting of the Commission* (Hobart, 2018) [6.1]–[6.69].

## 4  New Zealand Legislative Activity

No substantive legislative activity relating to Antarctica occurred during 2018. The *Antarctica (Environmental Protection: Liability Annex) Amendment Act 2012* (NZ) has not yet entered into force.[40]

---

[40]  See Alan D Hemmings, "Year in Review: The Antarctic Treaty System" (2016) 14 New Zealand Yearbook of International Law 287, 296–297.

# International Criminal Law and Humanitarian Law

*Treasa Dunworth\**

## 1     Introduction

As anticipated, New Zealand ratified the *Treaty on the Prohibition of Nuclear Weapons*[1] in 2018, becoming the 18th state, and the fourth state in the Pacific region (joining Palau, Samoa and Vanuatu), to do so. The treaty is discussed further in the review on security by Anna Hood.[2] 2018 saw no further developments on the crime of aggression in New Zealand, either in terms of moves towards ratification or preparations to implement domestic legislation. Nor was the issue mentioned in New Zealand's statement to the International Criminal Court's ("ICC") Assembly of States Parties in December.[3] This was despite the fact that, on 17 July 2018, the jurisdiction of the ICC over the crime of aggression was activated.[4]

In contrast, there was a clear indication from New Zealand as to its intentions regarding the "weapons crimes" in the *Rome Statute of the International Criminal Court* ("*Rome Statute*"). New Zealand voted for three further weapons-related crimes to be added to the ICC's jurisdiction and announced that it would move to ratify all the weapons amendments now pending.[5] This is discussed more fully in Part 2 below. Part 3 considers the work of the government's *Inquiry into Operation Burnham* – established under the *Inquiries Act 2013* to examine allegations of wrongdoing by the New Zealand Defence Force in Afghanistan.

## 2     The Weapons Crimes in the Rome Statute

As explained in a previous Review, at the 2010 Review Conference of the *Rome Statute*, three weapons-related crimes were added as war crimes to the

---

\*     University of Auckland.
1     *Treaty on the Prohibition of Nuclear Weapons*, opened for signature 20 September 2017 (not yet in force).
2     Anna Hood, "International Law and Security" (2018) 16 *New Zealand Yearbook of International Law*.
3     Victoria Hallum, "New Zealand Statement" (Statement, 17th Session of the Assembly of States Parties to the Rome Statute of the International Criminal Court, 6 December 2018).
4     Assembly of States Parties to the Rome Statute, *Activation of the Jurisdiction of the Court over the Crime of Aggression*, Doc No ICC-ASP/16/Res.5, 13th plen mtg, 14 December 2017.
5     Hallum (n 3).

*Statute*.⁶ These 2010 amendments essentially took the three weapons crimes (the use of poison or poisonous weapons, asphyxiating poisonous or other gases or liquids, and expanding bullets) that had originally been included as war crimes for international armed conflict and reproduced them in the context of non-international armed conflict. The imbalance between the two categories of conflict (international armed conflict and non-international armed conflict) was an anomaly in any event, so this balancing up was long overdue and appeared to be relatively uncontentious. Despite this, over the years, New Zealand has taken no steps to ratify those amendments, or even to bring the amendments through the parliamentary oversight procedures.

In 2017, three further crimes, in both international and non-international conflicts, were adopted into the *Rome Statute* by amendments.⁷ These were: the crime of using biological weapons; the crime of using weapons designed to injure with fragments that escape detection by x-rays; and the crime of using laser weapons specifically designed to cause blindness.⁸ The use of all these types of weapons is well accepted as being subject to strong treaty prohibitions⁹ and is also prohibited as a matter of customary international law.¹⁰ Accordingly, it seems intuitive to support their inclusion as war crimes

---

6   Treasa Dunworth, "International Criminal Law and International Humanitarian Law" (2016) 14 *New Zealand Yearbook of International Law* 298.

7   Assembly of the States Parties to the Rome Statute, *Resolution on Amendments to Article 8 of the Rome Statute of the International Criminal Court*, Doc No ICC-ASP/16/Res.4, 12th plen mtg, 14 December 2017.

8   Ibid annexes I, II, III, respectively.

9   For biological weapons: *Convention on the Prohibition of the Development, Production and Stockpiling of Bacteriological (Biological) and Toxin Weapons and on their Destruction*, opened for signature 10 April 1972, 1015 UNTS 163 (entered into force 26 March 1975). For weapons causing non-detectable fragments: *Protocol on Non-Detectable Fragments (Protocol I) to the Convention on Prohibitions or Restrictions on the Use of Certain Conventional Weapons Which May be Deemed to be Excessively Injurious or to Have Indiscriminate Effects (with Protocols I, II and III)*, opened for signature 10 April 1981, 1342 UNTS 137 (entered into force 2 December 1983). For laser weapons: *Additional Protocol to the Convention on Prohibitions or Restrictions on the Use of Certain Conventional Weapons Which May Be Deemed to Be Excessively Injurious or to Have Indiscriminate Effects (Protocol IV, Entitled Protocol on Blinding Laser Weapons)*, adopted 13 October 1995, 1380 UNTS 370 (entered into force 30 July 1998).

10  See the International Committee of the Red Cross's rules 73 ("Biological Weapons"), 79 ("Weapons Primarily Injuring by Non-Detectable Fragments") and 86 ("Blinding Laser Weapons"): Jean-Marie Henckaerts and Louise Doswald-Beck (eds), *Customary International Humanitarian Law* (International Committee of the Red Cross and Cambridge University Press, 2005) vol 1, 256–258, 275–277, 292–296.

in the *Rome Statute*. Unsurprisingly, then, at the Assembly of States Parties in December 2018, New Zealand announced that it would soon move to ratify both the still-outstanding 2010 amendments (repeating the three original crimes in the context of non-international armed conflict) along with the 2017 amendments.[11] However, the statement sounded a note of caution, saying:[12]

> New Zealand considers that at this point in the Court's history there is a need to consolidate and focus on the existing crimes within the Court's jurisdiction, rather than States Parties seeking to expand the crimes covered by the Statute. None of the challenges facing the Court today are to do with a shortage of crimes to pursue. For this reason, while we welcomed the War Crimes Amendments adopted at the Assembly last year, we share the view of many in this room that at this point the Assembly should be cautious about adding further new crimes to the Rome Statute, particularly those that criminalise new categories of weapons.

Thus, New Zealand would appear to be taking a pragmatic approach to the question of incrementally adding to the list of crimes in the *Rome Statute*. In my view, such an approach is valid, because I agree that from an institutional point of view it would be good for the ICC to consolidate and focus on its existing jurisdiction, rather than engaging in a continual expansion of jurisdiction, however worthy the crimes are of inclusion in the *Rome Statute*. However, my concerns about expanding the categories of weapons are deeper than questions about the ICC's capacity and the need to consolidate its work. Rather, as I will explain, in my view, the original formulation of the weapons-based crimes in the *Rome Statute* was ill-conceived, and constituted a flawed (although perhaps necessary) compromise. This incremental approach, whereby further crimes are being added in a piecemeal manner, not only fails to address the original flaw, but in fact perpetuates the underlying problem.

The original formulation of the weapons-based crimes in the *Rome Statute* came in three provisions set out in art 8(2)(b) of the *Statute* (and applying only to international armed conflict), being:

(xvii) employing poison or poisoned weapons;

(xviii) employing asphyxiating, poisonous or other gases and all analogous liquids, materials or devices;

---

11  Victoria Hallum (n 3).
12  Ibid.

(xix) employing bullets which expand or flatten easily in the human body, such as bullets with a hard envelope which does not entirely cover the core or is pierced with incisions.

In addition, there was one catch-all provision in art 8(2)(b)(xx) which makes it a crime to use weapons that are of a nature to cause "superfluous injury or unnecessary suffering or which are inherently indiscriminate", provided that these methods are already the subject of a comprehensive prohibition and that these weapons have been included by amendment in an annex to the *Statute*. There has never been agreement to include any weapons in the annex, and so it is widely understood that art 8(2)(b)(xx) is essentially moribund.

Although the only ones included in the *Rome Statute* originally, these three crimes were far from being the only weapons of concern. In fact, during the Rome negotiations, there had been considerable support for a so-called "generic formula" approach, particularly from within the African Group.[13] This would have meant that the provision dealing with weapons would be stated in very general terms, using language drawn from the general principles of international humanitarian law (such as "inherently indiscriminate", "causing superfluous injury and unnecessary suffering", and so on) and it would fall for the ICC to decide whether any use of a particular weapon constituted a war crime in a particular instance. Importantly, no specific weapons would have been mentioned in the *Statute* and the generic provision would thus have had a potentially broad scope.

An alternative approach – and the one that was ultimate adopted – was to list specific weapons, the use of which would be a crime. While this had the advantage of greater certainty (especially important in the criminal law context), it opened up a debate as to what weapons should be included in the *Rome Statute*, the use of which would then be criminal. At the heart of the difficulty with this approach was the vexed question of nuclear weapons. If there is any weapon which is inherently indiscriminate and destined to cause superfluous injury and unnecessary suffering, the argument goes, it is a nuclear weapon. And indeed, this was the position of many states. However, the political reality was that nuclear weapons were not going to be included in the *Statute* due to opposition of all of the states in possession of nuclear weapons and their allies.[14] And so, Rome delivered a narrow specific approach asserting ju-

---

13  Roger Clark, "Building on Article 8(2)(b)(xx) of the Rome Statute of the International Criminal Court: Weapons and Methods of Warfare" (2009) 12(3) *New Criminal Law Review* 366.

14  For an account of the different positions during negotiations, see William A Schabas, *The International Criminal Court: A Commentary on the Rome Statute* (Oxford University Press, 2nd ed, 2016) 277–284. See also Elaina I. Kalivretakis, "Are Nuclear Weapons above the

risdiction over just the three crimes with an ineffectual nod to the generic formula in art 8(2)(b)(xx). In other words, the compromise meant that nuclear weapons escaped the jurisdiction of the ICC, much to the dismay of many states, but the alternative was – potentially – no *Rome Statute* at all.

Seen in this light, it becomes clear that each time the *Rome Statute* is amended to expand the list of weapons-related crimes, without addressing the question of nuclear weapons, it perpetuates and reinforces the imbalance between the states in possession of nuclear weapons and their allies, on the one hand, and the majority of other states, on the other. In adding three further weapons to the criminalised list (in both types of armed conflict), the parties to the *Rome Statute* are perpetuating this division. Taking the amendments at their face value, there seems to be merit in expanding the ICC's jurisdiction to cover the use of already-prohibited weapons. However, in my view, there is a more fundamental principle at stake and that is that we should be careful about implicitly condoning the use of nuclear weapons by leaving them off the list of crimes that fall within the jurisdiction of the ICC.

## 3   The Burnham Inquiry

After several years of public calls for an inquiry to be established to consider the allegations being raised about Special Air Service actions in Afghanistan, the new Labour-led government established the *Operation Burnham Inquiry* (the "*Inquiry*") in April 2018.[15] The *Inquiry*, established under the *Inquiries Act 2013*, is tasked with examining "allegations of wrongdoing by NZDF forces in connection with Operation Burnham and related matters".[16]

Established in April, it did not really start work in earnest until May 2018, and then had some key preliminary matters to deal with, namely, determining the process to be followed in managing classified information and whether the procedure adopted by the *Inquiry* should be inquisitorial or adversarial. The one public hearing that was convened in November focused on the processes to be followed in the *Inquiry*.[17] As such, by the end of 2018, the *Inquiry* had yet

---

Law: A Look at the International Criminal Court and the Prohibited Weapons Category" (2001) 15(2) *Emory International Law Review* 683.

15   Treasa Dunworth, "International Criminal Law and International Humanitarian Law" (2017) 15 *New Zealand Yearbook of International Law* 223, 227–229.
16   New Zealand Government, *Terms of Reference: Government Inquiry into Operation Burnham and Related Matters* ("*Terms of Reference*").
17   New Zealand Government, "Hearing 21–22 November 2018", *Inquiry into Operation Burnham* (Web Page, 21 June 2019) <https://operationburnham.inquiry.govt.nz/>.

to embark on its substantive work. Unsurprisingly then, the *Inquiry*'s term, which was initially one year, was subsequently extended to the end of 2019.

Considered in international terms, this *Inquiry* forms part of a much broader movement towards greater scrutiny of the deployment and actions of troops. This move reflects a concern that is a feature of the international law system since the 2003 Iraq War and the unleashing of the war on terror. However, even when seen in this context, it is also evident that this particular inquiry is relatively constrained in its scope. Clearly, a tightly constrained, short-term inquiry was envisaged, given its limited budget and the relatively short time frame initially granted.[18] However, while the *Terms of Reference* are clearly focused on Operation Burnham,[19] the reference to "and related matters" in para 5 may provide some room to expand the scope of the *Inquiry*'s work, and therefore its duration.

Convening the *Inquiry* was a legal obligation, when one considers New Zealand's international humanitarian law obligations. As a state party to the four *Geneva Conventions*, New Zealand has an obligation to "respect and ensure respect for" international humanitarian law.[20] It is also important to note the so-called "grave breaches" regime of the four *Geneva Conventions 1949*, which selects particularly serious crimes of international concern (such as the wilful killing of civilians, torture, and so on), and imposes on state parties to the *Conventions* the obligation to prosecute those who commit these serious crimes. It is appropriate to note that the *Inquiry* has no power to determine the liability (criminal or otherwise) of any person.[21] Rather, the *Inquiry* is to simply report its findings and any recommendations to the Minister.[22] Nevertheless, the *Inquiry* is an important (though perhaps not sufficient) step towards New Zealand observing its obligations to ensure respect for this body of law.

One contentious issue which arose almost immediately was the process by which the *Inquiry* ought to review and manage classified information. In September, the *Inquiry* issued its preliminary view as to the appropriate pro-

---

18  12 months from the date of the establishment of the Inquiry, *Terms of Reference* (n 16) [20].
19  Ibid [6]–[7].
20  *First Geneva Convention for the Amelioration of the Condition of the Wounded and Sick in Armed Forces in the Field*, signed 12 August 1949, 75 UNTS 3 (entered into force 21 October 1950); *Second Geneva Convention for the Amelioration of the Condition of Wounded, Sick and Shipwrecked Members of Armed Forces at Sea*, signed 12 August 1949, 75 UNTS 85 (entered into force 21 October 1950); *Third Geneva Convention Relative to the Treatment of Prisoners of War*, signed 12 August 1949, 75 UNTS 135 (entered into force 21 October 1950); *Fourth Geneva Convention Relative to the Protection of Civilian Persons in Time of War*, adopted 12 August 1949, 75 UNTS 287 (entered into force 21 October 1950).
21  *Terms of Reference* (n 16) [13]. See also *Inquiries Act 2013* (NZ) s 11(1).
22  *Terms of Reference* (n 16) [6.5].

cess, deciding that it would adopt and comply with the government's *Protective Security Requirements*.[23] This meant that there would be limits on the information available to the non-Crown parties appearing before the *Inquiry*, and corresponding limits on their right to cross-examine. To ameliorate that, the *Inquiry* appointed Ben Keith, a barrister and former Deputy Inspector-General of Intelligence and Security, to provide advice and assistance to the *Inquiry*.[24] The *Inquiry* formally adopted that provisional view in its *Ruling* in December.[25]

Another contentious preliminary issue that faced the *Inquiry* almost immediately was whether it should adopt an inquisitorial or an adversarial approach in its work.[26] This debate was closely aligned to the question of how public the work of the *Inquiry* should be, and so the parties were again split between support for an inquisitorial approach (the Crown) and an adversarial approach (the non-Crown parties). The *Inquiry* decided to adopt a mixed method,[27] that is, one that is "mainly inquisitorial but may have elements of traditional adversarial processes where that is appropriate".[28]

As the year came to a close, the *Inquiry* announced its decision to hold a series of public hearings organised in the course of 2019 around a series of substantive questions facing the *Inquiry*: the nature of New Zealand's deployment in Afghanistan; the process adopted for setting the *Rules of Engagement*; issues concerning detention and transportation of detainees in Afghanistan; and the processes followed regarding the predetermined and offensive use of lethal force against specified individuals other than in direct battle.[29]

---

23  New Zealand Government, *A Government Inquiry into Operation Burnham and Related Matters* (Minute No 4, 14 September 2018) ("*Burnham Inquiry: Minute No 4*").
24  Ibid [27].
25  New Zealand Government, *A Government Inquiry into Operation Burnham and Related Matters* (Minute No 1, 10 July 2018).
26  *Burnham Inquiry: Minute No 4* [34]–[91].
27  Ibid [75]–[77].
28  Ibid [76].
29  "How the Government Inquiry into Operation Burnham Will Proceed" (Media Release, New Zealand Government, 21 December 2018).

# International Law and Security

*Anna Hood**

## 1  Introduction

If anyone were to take a cursory glance at the international law and security issues that arose for New Zealand in 2018, they could be forgiven for concluding that there was nothing particularly controversial that emerged. However, digging behind the headlines and taking a deeper look, it becomes apparent that there were in fact some important issues that arose during the year, which are likely to generate debate for years to come. Significantly, the Prime Minister made comments that were supportive of the illegal use of force by the United States ("US"), United Kingdom ("UK") and France in Syria and that may well provide ammunition for those wanting to broaden the grounds for the use of force in international law. Further, New Zealand ratified the *Treaty on the Prohibition of Nuclear Weapons* ("*TPNW*") without amending its domestic nuclear legislation. This report will consider both of these issues in detail before turning to briefly note a number of other international law and security issues that arose over the course of the year.

## 2  Did New Zealand Sanction an Illegal Use of Force in Syria and Possibly Endorse a New Doctrine of Humanitarian Intervention?

One of the most significant international law and security matters that occurred in New Zealand in 2018 was something that received relatively little attention at the time, especially with respect to its international legal ramifications. The matter was Prime Minister Jacinda Ardern's response to the airstrikes carried out by the US, UK and France against Syria.[1]

On 14 April 2018, the US, UK and France launched 103 missiles at Syria in retaliation for the fact that the Assad regime had deployed chemical weapons

---

\*  University of Auckland.
1  "PM on Syria Strikes: 'Time to Return to the Table'", *Radio NZ* (Web Page, 14 April 2018) <https://www.rnz.co.nz/news/political/355058/pm-on-syria-strikes-time-to-return-to-the-table>.

a week earlier in Damascus and killed 80 civilians.² After the airstrikes had taken place, Ardern gave a press conference where she stated that New Zealand would have preferred it if the military action had been undertaken with the consent of the United Nations ("UN") Security Council but, given that this route had not been possible (because Russia had threatened to veto any Security Council resolution authorising the use of force against the Assad regime), the actions of the western states were "understandable" and New Zealand "accept[ed]" why those states had taken the steps they did.³

Ardern's comments attracted some attention in the New Zealand press.⁴ Commentators and politicians initially noted that the comments were rather "ambiguous" but tended to show at least some level of support for the airstrikes.⁵ Discussions then turned to focus on the political ramifications of the comments, with some believing that they were problematic because they showed a lack of independent foreign policy and because military interventions are "disastrous",⁶ while others asserted that the comments were not strong enough and that the Prime Minister should have backed the airstrikes more fully without mentioning a role for the UN Security Council.⁷

What was missing from the public commentary was any analysis of the international legal consequences of Ardern's comments. This was somewhat

---

2   Graham Russell and Patrick Greenfield, "Strikes on Syria: What We Know So Far", *The Guardian* (Web Page, 14 April 2018) <https://www.theguardian.com/world/2018/apr/14/air-strikes-in-syria-what-we-know-so-far>.
3   "PM on Syria Strikes: 'Time to Return to the Table'" (n 1).
4   For a general overview of the discussion, see Bryce Edwards, "Political Roundup: NZ's Fraught Balancing Act on Syria Bombing", *NZ Herald* (Web Page, 17 April 2018) <https://www.nzherald.co.nz/nz/news/article.cfm?c_id=1&objectid=12034295>.
5   See, eg, Edwards (n 4); Chris Trotter, "Prime Minister Jacinda Ardern Has a Bob Each Way on Bombing Syria", *Stuff* (17 April 2018) <https://www.stuff.co.nz/national/politics/103140145/prime-minister-jacinda-ardern-has-a-bob-each-way-on-bombing-syria>; Keith Locke, "Ardern Wrong to "Accept" US-Led Air Strikes on Syria. The Greens Get it Right", *The Daily Blog* (16 April 2018) <https://thedailyblog.co.nz/2018/04/16/adern-wrong-to-accept-us-led-air-strikes-on-syria-the-greens-get-it-right/>; Golriz Ghahraman, "Bombing Syria Will Never Bring Peace. NZ Must Stand Up Against Ad Hoc Violence", *The Spinoff* (14 April 2018) <https://thespinoff.co.nz/politics/14-04-2018/bombing-syria-will-never-bring-peace-nz-must-stand-up-against-ad-hoc-violence/>; Martyn Bradbury, "Painting Jacinda Out as a War Criminal", *The Daily Blog* (17 April 2018) <https://thedailyblog.co.nz/2018/04/17/painting-jacinda-out-as-a-war-criminal/>; Dan Satherley, "NZ Should Support US-Led Strikes on Syria, UN is Useless – Simon Bridges", *Newshub* (16 April 2018) <https://www.newshub.co.nz/home/politics/2018/04/nz-should-support-us-led-strikes-on-syria-un-is-useless-simon-bridges.html>.
6   Trotter (n 5); Ghahraman (n 5); Locke (n 5).
7   Bradbury (n 5); Satherley (n 5).

surprising as this was a case where the Prime Minister's comments had particular significance for the development of international law. To understand what their significance was, it is necessary to provide some background information about the legality of the western powers' airstrikes and then to return to the particular comments made by Ardern.

Prima facie, the US, UK and France's airstrikes against Syria were illegal. Traditionally under international law, states can only use force against another state in three circumstances: if they have the consent of the target state;[8] if they have the authorisation of the UN Security Council;[9] or if they are acting in self-defence.[10] In this case, none of these conditions was satisfied.[11] However, a number of states (lead by the UK) as well as some academics asserted that the strikes should be understood as legal because they gave rise to a new international legal ground for the use of force: humanitarian intervention.[12] Over the last 25 years there have been numerous attempts to develop the doctrine of humanitarian intervention (which holds that states can use force against another state where civilians are facing severe humanitarian suffering) at international law.[13] It has, however, been a highly controversial doctrine and, at least until April 2018, there had been no agreement in the international community that it should be recognised as a permissible ground for the use of force.[14]

However, the actions of the US, UK and France offered a fresh opportunity for the doctrine to take hold. While the US, UK and France claiming that they were acting on the grounds of humanitarian intervention would not have been enough alone for the doctrine to be recognised as a new rule of international law, it might have been sufficient if the claims had been supported (or at least not rejected) by other states around the world.[15]

With this context set out, the significance of Ardern's comments that the airstrikes were "understandable" and that New Zealand "accept[ed]" them becomes apparent. While the comments do not explicitly endorse the actions taken by the US, UK and France, they do not clearly denounce them and can

---

8   Christine Gray, "The Use of Force and the International Legal Order" in Malcolm Evans (ed) *International Law* (Oxford University Press, 4th ed, 2014) 618, 626–627.
9   Charter of the United Nations art 42.
10  Charter of the United Nations art 51.
11  Michael Scharf, "Striking a Grotian Moment: How the Syria Airstrikes Changed International Law Relating to Humanitarian Interventions" (2019) 19(2) *Chicago Journal of International Law* 1, 8.
12  Ibid 3 and 22; Alonso G Dunkelberg et al, "Mapping States' Reactions to the Syria Strikes of April 2018", *Just Security* (Web Page, 22 April 2018) <http://perma.cc/R8BS-DMX9>.
13  Gray (n 8) 623–626; Scharf (n 11) 10–19.
14  Ibid.
15  Scharf (n 11) 23–24.

be read as being implicitly supportive of them. It is therefore possible that they could be interpreted as New Zealand backing the doctrine of humanitarian intervention or, at the very least, acquiescing to its use in this particular situation.

As it stands, there are not currently enough states that support the doctrine of humanitarian intervention to enable a conclusion to be made that it has become a rule of international law.[16] However, academic research published since April 2018 indicates that there is growing support for this controversial doctrine.[17] It is concerning to think that New Zealand may be counted amongst those states that now support humanitarian intervention as a rule of international law despite the fact there has been no national discussion or debate about this very serious matter. The rules that restrict the use of force amongst states are some of the most important in the international system, and there are good reasons for ensuring that the exceptions to the prohibition on the use of force remain very narrow. What is more, the doctrine of humanitarian intervention has been the subject of some very serious critiques. There is a lot of scepticism about its ability to actually protect civilians as it purports to do, and there is great concern about the propensity for it to be abused.[18] In light of these facts, there is a need for a much larger national discussion about whether we should support the transformation of the doctrine into an international legal rule and I urge the Prime Minister to think carefully before she "accept[s]" or expresses "understand[ing]" for any similar situations that may arise in the future.

## 3 New Zealand's Ratification of the Treaty on the Prohibition of Nuclear Weapons and Its Failure to Update its Domestic Nuclear Legislation

On 1 August 2018, New Zealand ratified the *TPNW*.[19] The *TPNW* contains the most comprehensive limitations on nuclear weapons in history, including a prohibition on states parties from developing, testing, producing, manufacturing,

---

16  There were multiple states that spoke out against the legality of the 14 April 2018 use of force: see, eg, Scharf (n 11) 23–27; Dunkelberg (n 11).
17  See generally Scharf (n 11).
18  See, eg, Anne Orford, *Reading Humanitarian Intervention* (Cambridge University Press, 2003).
19  iCAN Aotearoa New Zealand, "New Zealand Ratifies Nuclear Ban Treaty", *Scoop* (Web Page, 1 August 2018) <http://www.scoop.co.nz/stories/PO1808/S00020/new-zealand-ratifies-nuclear-ban-treaty.htm>.

acquiring, possessing, stockpiling, transferring, receiving, using or threatening to use, stationing, installing or deploying nuclear weapons or other nuclear explosive devices.[20] While there is much to celebrate about New Zealand becoming a state party to this treaty and it fits well with our strong nuclear-free identity, we have not yet taken the necessary steps to ensure that our domestic legislation implements all aspects of the treaty. What is more, there appears to be little public awareness of the fact that our laws do not adequately encompass the different provisions of the treaty.

In the lead-up to ratification, the Foreign Affairs, Defence and Trade Committee (the "Committee") conducted an examination of the *TPNW* and whether New Zealand would need to pass legislation to ensure that our domestic laws were in compliance with it.[21] The Committee concluded that no legislation would be needed for ratification stating that:

> We understand that New Zealand already complies with the key obligations of the treaty, and can ratify it without any change to legislation. This country's existing policies and laws – in particular the New Zealand Nuclear Free Zone, Disarmament, and Arms Control Act 1987 – provide an acceptable basis for implementing the treaty.[22]

The Committee's conclusion is to a certain extent understandable because for a long time the *New Zealand Nuclear Free Zone, Disarmament and Arms Control Act 1987* has been heralded as one of the strongest, most comprehensive pieces of legislation in the world dealing with nuclear weapons issues.[23] New Zealand has long been seen as a leader in the anti-nuclear movement, and thus it might be expected that our laws already covered the ideas set out in the *TPNW*. However, the 1987 Act was passed in response to very particular nuclear matters: first, the need to create legislation that implemented the *South Pacific Nuclear Weapons Free Zone Treaty*;[24] and, secondly, the need to respond to the concerns that arose in the mid-1980s about the United States sending nuclear powered

---

20   *Treaty on the Prohibition of Nuclear Weapons*, opened for signature 20 September 2017, 729 UNTS 161 (not yet in force) ("*TPNW*") art 1.
21   Foreign Affairs, Defence and Trade Committee, New Zealand Parliament, *International Treaty Examination of the Treaty on the Prohibition of Nuclear Weapons* (Report, July 2018).
22   Ibid 3.
23   "History of NZ Legislation", *Disarmament and Security Centre* (Web Page, 2018) <http://www.disarmsecure.org/nuclear-free-aotearoa-nz-resources/history-of-nz-legislation>.
24   This treaty appears in annex 1 of the New Zealand Nuclear Free Zone, Disarmament, and Arms Control Act 1987 (NZ).

and/or nuclear weapons-carrying ships and aircraft to New Zealand.[25] Consequently, while it was progressive for its time and placed a number of limitations on New Zealand's involvement with nuclear weapons, it did not set out the comprehensive array of measures that are encompassed in the TPNW.

In this short piece, I do not intend to document all of the ways that New Zealand's legislation fails to implement the TPNW. I will, however, provide some examples of where gaps exist.[26] To start with, TPNW art 1(f) prohibits states parties from "seek[ing] or receiv[ing] any assistance, in any way, from anyone to engage in any activity prohibited to a State Party under this Treaty". There is no equivalent provision in the New Zealand Nuclear Free Zone, Disarmament, and Arms Control Act 1987. The Act prohibits New Zealand citizens and people ordinarily in New Zealand from doing things such as "manufactur[ing], acquir[ing], or posess[ing], or hav[ing] control over, any nuclear explosive device"[27] and from "aid[ing], abet[ting], procur[ing] any person to manufacture, acquire, possess, or have control over any nuclear explosive device".[28] But it does not stop someone for seeking assistance or receiving assistance to undertake these activities. Thus, if someone in New Zealand asked another person for help to acquire nuclear weapons but did not receive that help, or received that help but was ultimately unsuccessful in their quest to get hold of the weapons, they would be in violation of the TPNW but not New Zealand's 1987 Act.

A second way that the New Zealand legislation falls short of complying with the TPNW is that it does not have a provision that adequately captures art 1(g) of the TPNW. That article provides that states parties cannot "[a]llow any stationing, installation or deployment of any nuclear weapons or other nuclear explosive devices in its territory or at any place under its jurisdiction or control". The closest the 1987 Act comes to this is in s 6 where it provides

---

25  New Zealand Nuclear Free Zone, Disarmament, and Arms Control Act 1987 (NZ) ss 9–11 are specifically targeted at this issue.

26  When considering the differences between the New Zealand Nuclear Free Zone, Disarmament, and Arms Control Act 1987 and the TPNW, it is important to note that there are some occasions where the Act and the Treaty use different language but cover the same concepts. For example, the TPNW outlaws the "use" of nuclear weapons in art 1(d), while the New Zealand legislation does not. The New Zealand act does, however, outlaw "control" over nuclear weapons in s 5(1)(a) and (2)(a). Arguably, it is not possible to "use" nuclear weapons without having "control" over them, so anyone who used nuclear weapons would be found to be in violation of the 1987 Act.

27  New Zealand Nuclear Free Zone, Disarmament, and Arms Control Act 1987 (NZ) s 5(1)(a), (2)(a).

28  New Zealand Nuclear Free Zone, Disarmament, and Arms Control Act 1987 (NZ) s 5(1)(b), (2)(b).

"[n]o person shall emplant, emplace, transport on land or inland waters or internal water, stockpile, store, install or deploy any nuclear explosive device in the New Zealand Nuclear Free Zone". The problem with s 6 is that, while the words in it are broad enough to cover the ideas of "stationing, installation or deployment" in *TPNW* art 1(g), it does not provide sufficient geographic coverage. The "New Zealand Nuclear Free Zone" is defined in s 4 of the Act as "all land, territory, and internal waters within the territorial limits of New Zealand; and the internal waters of New Zealand; and the territorial sea of New Zealand; and the airspace above the[se] areas specified". This does not cover any potential territory that New Zealand at some stage may have "under its jurisdiction or control". Thus, if New Zealand were to ever exercise control over territory in another state (for example, during an armed conflict or occupation, or perhaps under an arrangement with its dependent territory of Tokelau) and it allowed the stationing, installation or deployment of nuclear weapons or nuclear explosive devices on that territory, it would not be in contravention of the 1987 Act but would be in violation of the *TPNW*.

A further example of a disconnect between the 1987 Act and the *TPNW* is that the *TPNW* bans states from "threaten[ing] to use nuclear weapons or other nuclear explosive devices"[29] and from "assist[ing], encourag[ing] or induc[ing]" states from threatening to use nuclear weapons or nuclear explosive devices[30] but no such prohibitions appear in the New Zealand legislation.

In closing, it is important to note that just because New Zealand's nuclear-free legislation does not cover all of the principles set out in the *TPNW*, it does not mean that New Zealand is currently in breach of the *TPNW*. It is possible for a dualist state such as New Zealand to be in compliance with international treaties without domestic implementing legislation. However, to lower the risk of New Zealand ever being in violation of the *TPNW*'s provisions in the future and to ensure that there are domestic avenues available for concerned individuals to challenge any problematic practices that may arise in the future, it would be advisable for the government either to amend the existing nuclear legislation or pass a new piece of legislation so that the *TPNW*'s provisions are clearly implemented in domestic law.

The prospect of New Zealand doing anything that comes close to violating the prohibitions on nuclear weapons activities in the *TPNW* may seem remote given the country's 30-year commitment to being nuclear free. But recently questions about whether Rocket Lab's activities could be connected to the US

---

29   *TPNW* (n 20) art 1(d).
30   Ibid art 1(e).

nuclear programme have arisen.³¹ While we do not currently have enough information to ascertain how to answer these questions, the fact that they have emerged shows that New Zealand's strong anti-nuclear stance should not be taken for granted and steps need to be taken to ensure that our anti-nuclear legislation is as comprehensive as possible.

## 4    Matters in Brief

Outside of the Prime Minister's comments over the use of force in Syria and the concerns relating to whether New Zealand's anti-nuclear legislation adequately captures all of the *TPNW*'s provisions, a number of other international law and security matters arose in 2018. None of them was particularly controversial, but each of them will be mentioned here briefly to ensure they are captured for the benefit of future researchers:

– New Zealand enacted the *Brokering (Weapons and Related Items) Controls Act 2018* on 21 May 2018. The Act helps to ensure New Zealand's compliance with the *Arms Trade Treaty* by setting up a registration and permit system for people and entities in New Zealand that want to broker arms and military equipment.³²

– In 2017, the New Zealand company Pacific Aerospace Ltd was found guilty of violating United Nations Security Council sanctions by indirectly sending aircraft parts to North Korea.³³ In 2018, Pacific Aerospace was fined $74 805 for this contravention.³⁴

– In 2018, the United States withdrew from the Joint Comprehensive Plan of Action ("JCPOA" or "Iran Nuclear Deal").³⁵ New Zealand, however, "remain[ed] a firm supporter of the JCPOA, which we consider critical to

---

31    See, eg, Ollie Neas, "'She'll Be Right' Attitude to Rocket Lab Putting Nuclear Free NZ at Risk, Experts Say", *The Spinoff* (Web Page, 17 May 2019) <https://thespinoff.co.nz/business/17-05-2019/shell-be-right-attitude-to-rocket-lab-putting-nuclear-free-nz-at-risk-experts-say/>.

32    Victoria Hallum, "International Law Year in Review" (Speech, Australia and New Zealand Society of International Law Annual Conference, Wellington, 5–6 July 2018, 30 August 2018).

33    See Anna Hood, "International Law and Security 2017" (2017) 15 *New Zealand Yearbook of International Law* 236, 239–240.

34    Hallum (n 32).

35    Mark Landler, "Trump Abandons Iran Nuclear Deal He Long Scorned", *New York Times* (Web Page, 8 May 2018) <https://www.nytimes.com/2018/05/08/world/middleeast/trump-iran-nuclear-deal.html>.

reducing the risk of nuclear proliferation in the Middle East region and globally".³⁶
- In September 2018, New Zealand extended its deployment of the New Zealand Defence Force for military training to Iraq and Afghanistan. The government also renewed its involvement with three peacekeeping missions: the United Nations Mission in South Sudan, the United Nations Truce Supervisions Organisation in the Golan Heights and Lebanon and the Multinational Force and Observers in the Sinai Peninsula, Egypt.³⁷

---

36  Nicole Robertson, "New Zealand Statement to the International Atomic Energy Agency" (Speech, International Atomic Energy Agency General Conference 2018, 19 September 2018).

37  New Zealand Government, "New Zealand to Extend NZDF Deployments to Iraq and Afghanistan and 3 Peacekeeping Missions" (Media Release, 17 September 2018).

*New Zealand State Conduct*

# Treaty Action and Implementation

*Mark Gobbi*\*

## 1 Overview

This article documents governmental activity undertaken to implement New Zealand's international obligations during the current interval.[1] It concludes that the level of activity in the current interval, relative to the previous interval,[2] decreased for the judicial, parliamentary, and executive branches. This overview summarises that activity and compares it with the activity undertaken during the previous interval.

### 1.1 *Parliamentary Activity*

#### 1.1.1 Acts of Parliament

During the current interval, Parliament enacted 35 Bills with implications for New Zealand's international obligations. Thirty-one simply amended Acts that had implemented treaties, one improved compliance with treaties that had already been implemented, and three implemented new treaties. Twenty-nine of these Bills involved multilateral agreements, four involved bilateral agreements, and two involved a code.

In terms of Acts, this level of activity is less than during the previous interval. During the previous interval, Parliament enacted 43 Bills with implications for New Zealand's international obligations. Thirty-five simply amended Acts that had implemented treaties, six improved compliance with treaties that had already been implemented, and two implemented new treaties. Thirty-nine of these Bills involved multilateral agreements, three involved bilateral agreements, and one involved a code.[3]

---

\* The author is currently serving as Parliamentary Counsel in New Zealand's Parliamentary Counsel Office. However, the views expressed herein are the author's own and may not be attributed to the Parliamentary Counsel Office or the Attorney-General.
1 The current interval began on 1 July 2017 and ended on 30 June 2018.
2 The previous interval began on 1 July 2016 and ended on 30 June 2017.
3 Mark Gobbi, "Treaty Action and Implementation" (2017) 15 *New Zealand Yearbook of International Law* 243, 253–263.

### 1.1.2 Treaty Examination Reports

During the current interval, the House of Representatives considered six select committee reports on treaties (six agreements in all). Five reports brought matters to the attention of the House. Public submissions featured in three of these reports, and none warranted a government response.[4]

In terms of reports, this level of activity is less than during the previous interval (two less reports). In terms of agreements examined, this level of activity is also less than during the previous interval (four less agreements). During the previous interval, the House of Representatives considered eight select committee reports on treaties (10 agreements in all). Five reports brought matters to the attention of the House. Public submissions featured in three of these reports, and none warranted a Government response.[5]

## 1.2 *Executive Activity*

### 1.2.1 Regulations

During the current interval, the executive made 35 regulations relevant to New Zealand's international obligations. Two of these regulations implemented a bilateral agreement, one implemented recommendations, one implemented standards, and 31 implemented multilateral agreements. Eleven concerned environmental agreements, eight dealt with civil aviation, six concerned resolutions of the United Nations ("UN") Security Council, four involved taxes, two concerned the courts, two dealt with financial markets, one dealt with money laundering, and one concerned work safety.

This level of activity is less than the level of activity that took place during the previous interval. During the previous interval, the executive made 43 regulations relevant to New Zealand's international obligations. Three of these regulations implemented a bilateral agreement, three implemented recommendations, three implemented standards, and 34 implemented multilateral agreements. Twenty concerned environmental agreements, eight dealt with civil aviation, six concerned trade, three involved land transport, two dealt with money laundering, one dealt with social welfare, one dealt with food, one dealt with intellectual property, and one adopted resolutions of the UN Security Council.[6]

---

4 See *Standing Orders of the House of Representatives 2017* ord 252.
5 Mark Gobbi, "Treaty Action and Implementation" (2017) 15 *New Zealand Yearbook of International Law* 243, 244, 251–253.
6 Ibid 244, 263–275.

### 1.2.2    Treaty Actions

During the current interval, the executive was involved in 19 treaty actions with respect to nine multilateral agreements and 10 bilateral agreements. Of the nine multilateral agreements (nine actions), the executive ratified three, acceded to three, signed two, and accepted one. Of the 10 bilateral agreements (10 actions), the executive signed two. Eight came into force.

This level of activity is less than the level of activity that took place during the previous interval. During the previous interval, the executive was involved in 44 treaty actions with respect to seven multilateral agreements and 28 bilateral agreements. Of the seven multilateral agreements (11 actions), the executive ratified one, accepted two, and acceded to one. Seven came into force. Of the 28 bilateral agreements (32 actions), the executive signed 12. Twenty came into force.[7]

### 1.2.3    Periodic Reports

New Zealand is required to provide periodic reports to the UN regarding its compliance with the following human rights treaties: the *International Covenant on Civil and Political Rights* (1966); the *International Convention on the Elimination of All Forms of Racial Discrimination* (1965); the *International Covenant on Economic, Social and Cultural Rights* (1966); the *Convention on the Elimination of All Forms of Discrimination against Women* (1979); the *Convention against Torture and Other Cruel, Inhuman or Degrading Treatment or Punishment* (1984); the *Convention on the Rights of the Child* (1989); and the *Convention on the Rights of Persons with Disabilities* (2006).[8]

During the current interval, the executive submitted New Zealand's fourth periodic report in respect of the *Covenant on Economic, Social and Cultural Rights* (1966).[9] New Zealand also submitted a reply to a list of issues and questions in relation to its eighth periodic report in respect of the *Convention on the Elimination of All Forms of Discrimination against Women* (1979).[10]

---

7    Ibid 244–245, 248–251.
8    For an online record of New Zealand's periodic reporting under these agreements, see "Reporting Status for New Zealand", *United Nations Human Rights: Office of the High Commissioner* (Web Page) <http://tbinternet.ohchr.org/_layouts/TreatyBodyExternal/Countries.aspx?CountryCode=NZL&Lang=EN>; "International Human Rights", *Ministry of Justice* (Web Page, 20 March 2017) <https://www.justice.govt.nz/justice-sector-policy/constitutional-issues-and-human-rights/human-rights/international-human-rights/>.
9    For a copy of this report, see Committee on Economic, Social and Cultural Rights, *Fourth Periodic Report Submitted by New Zealand under Articles 16 and 17 of the Covenant, Due in 2017*, UN Doc E/C.12/NZL/4 (6 October 2017).
10   For a copy of this reply, see Committee on the Elimination of Discrimination against Women, *List of Issues and Questions in Relation to the Eighth Periodic Report of New Zealand*, UN Doc CEDAW/C/NZL/Q/8/Add.1 (16 April 2018).

In terms of periodic reports, this level of activity is the same as the level of activity that took place during the previous interval. During the previous interval, the executive submitted New Zealand's eighth periodic report in respect of the *Convention on the Elimination of All Forms of Discrimination against Women* (1979).[11]

### 1.3 Judicial Activity

During the current interval, the judiciary delivered 81 judgments that referenced New Zealand's international obligations. Eleven of these judgments were reported in the New Zealand Law Report series; the Supreme Court delivered three, the Court of Appeal delivered five, and the High Court delivered three. Seventy were reported in other series; the Supreme Court delivered two, the Court of Appeal delivered nine, the High Court delivered 51, the Family Court delivered four, and the District Court delivered four. None were unreported.

Of these 81 judgments, 11 dealt with family law, 10 with refugees, seven with civil procedure, five with administrative law, five with judicial review, four with criminal law, four with prisoners' rights, three with the Bill of Rights, three with costs, three with immigration, three with deportation, two with social security, two with customs, two with extradition, two with torts, two with accident compensation, two with sentencing, one with evidence, one with criminal procedure, one with legal aid, one with intellectual property, one with fisheries, one with resource management, one with defamation, one with charity law, one with land law, one with employment law, and one with media law.

These 81 judgments referred to 27 different international instruments (one of which does not have New Zealand as a party), of which 25 are multilateral agreements and two are UN statements of principles. In total, these judgments have 118 references.

In these cases, the most frequently cited international agreements are the *International Covenant on Civil and Political Rights* (1966) (33 references), the *United Nations Convention on the Rights of the Child* (1989) (15 references), the *United Nations Convention relating to the Status of Refugees* (1951) (11 references), *The Hague Convention on the Civil Aspects of International Child Abduction* (1980) (eight references), the *European Convention for the Protection of Human Rights and Fundamental Freedoms* (1950) (seven references), the *Universal Declaration of Human Rights* (1948) (six references), the *United Nations Convention*

---

11   Mark Gobbi, "Treaty Action and Implementation" (2017) 15 *New Zealand Yearbook of International Law* 243, 245.

*Against Torture and Other Cruel, Inhuman or Degrading Treatment or Punishment* (1984) (six references), the *Optional Protocol to the Convention on the Rights of Persons with Disabilities* (2006) (six references), the *International Covenant on Economic, Social and Cultural Rights* (1966) (four references), and four other instruments are referenced twice and 14 others are referenced once.

In terms of the number of judgments delivered, the level of activity is less than the activity that took place during the previous interval. During the previous interval, the judiciary delivered 106 judgments that referenced New Zealand's international obligations. Twenty of these judgments were reported in the New Zealand Law Report series; the Supreme Court delivered four, the Court of Appeal delivered 10, and the High Court delivered six. Eighty-six were reported in other series; the Supreme Court delivered one, the Court of Appeal delivered seven, the High Court delivered 52, the Family Court delivered 12, the Employment Court delivered five, the District Court delivered three, the Youth Court delivered two, the Human Rights Review Tribunal delivered three, and the Privy Council delivered one. None were unreported.

Of these 106 judgments, 20 dealt with family law, 15 with criminal law, 13 with deportation, eight with refugee law, seven with employment law, five with immigration law, four with prisoners' rights, four with civil procedure, three with extradition, three with taxation, three with accident compensation, two with Māori land, two with aviation law, two with evidence law, two with social security, two with the *New Zealand Bill of Rights Act 1990*, two with judicial review, two with discrimination law, two with copyright law, one with insolvency, one with equity, one with local government, one with defamation, and one with constitutional law.

These 106 judgments referred to 36 different international instruments (one of which does not have New Zealand as a party), of which 34 are multilateral agreements and two are model laws. In total, these judgments have 154 references.

In these cases, the most frequently cited international agreements are the *International Covenant on Civil and Political Rights* (1966) (37 references), the *United Nations Convention on the Rights of the Child* (1989) (23 references), *The Hague Convention on the Civil Aspects of International Child Abduction* (1980) (11 references), the *United Nations Convention relating to the Status of Refugees* (1951) (eight references), the *European Convention for the Protection of Human Rights and Fundamental Freedoms* (1950) (eight references), the *International Covenant on Economic, Social and Cultural Rights* (1966) (eight references), the *United Nations Convention Against Torture and Other Cruel, Inhuman or Degrading Treatment or Punishment* (1984) (six references), the *Universal Declaration of Human Rights* (1948) (six references), the *Vienna Convention on the*

*Law of Treaties* (1969) (four references), the *Berne Convention for the Protection of Literary and Artistic Works* (1886 as amended 1971) (three references), the *United Nations Convention on the Rights of Persons with Disabilities* (2006) (three references), the *United Nations Declaration on the Rights of Indigenous Peoples* (2007) (three references), while three other instruments are referenced twice and 17 others are referenced once.[12]

### 1.4 Conclusion

During the current interval, each of the three branches of government contributed to the implementation of New Zealand's international obligations. The level of activity for the current interval decreased relative to the previous interval for the judiciary, Parliament, and the executive. Nevertheless, international agreements continue to be an important source of law in New Zealand.

## 2 Treaty Action

This Part sets out the treaty actions taken by the executive during the current interval. It lists the agreements that New Zealand has signed, ratified, accepted, approved, or acceded to, or that entered into force for New Zealand. It also sets out the reports on treaties that the executive tabled in the House during the current interval.

### 2.1 *Executive Treaty Action*[13]
#### 2.1.1 Multilateral Treaties

*Treaty on the Prohibition of Nuclear Weapons*, opened for signature 20 September 2017 (not yet in force): signed by New Zealand on 20 September 2017.

*International Convention on Standards of Training, Certification and Watchkeeping for Fishing Vessel Personnel*, signed 7 July 1995 (entered into force 29 September 2012): acceded to by New Zealand on 4 December 2017.

*Convention on Registration of Objects Launched into Outer Space*, signed 12 November 1974, 1023 UNTS 15 (entered into force 15 September 1976): acceded to by New Zealand on 23 January 2018.

International Maritime Organization, *Protocol of 2005 to the Protocol for the Suppression of Unlawful Acts against the Safety of Fixed Platforms Located on*

---

12   Ibid 246–247, 275–288.
13   See Ministry of Foreign Affairs and Trade, *Annual Report 2017–18* (Report No A.1 AR, 2018) 107–108. See also Ministry of Foreign Affairs and Trade, "Search Treaties", *New Zealand Treaties Online* (Web Page) <www.treaties.mfat.govt.nz/>.

*the Continental Shelf*, Doc No LEG/CONF.15/22, International Conference on the Revision of the SUA Treaties, 1 November 2005: ratified by New Zealand on 26 February 2018.

International Maritime Organization, *Protocol of 2005 to the Convention for the Suppression of Unlawful Acts against the Safety of Maritime Navigation*, Doc No LEG/CONF.15/21, International Conference on the Revision of the SUA Treaties, 1 November 2015: ratified by New Zealand on 26 February 2018.

*Comprehensive and Progressive Agreement for Trans-Pacific Partnership*, signed on 8 March 2018, [2018] ATS 23 (entered into force 30 December 2018): signed by New Zealand on 8 March 2018.

*Amendments to the Treaty on Fisheries between the Governments of Certain Pacific Island States and the Government of the United States of America*, signed December 3 2016: accepted by New Zealand on 18 April 2018.

*Multilateral Convention to Implement Tax Treaty Related Measures to Prevent Base Erosion and Profit Shifting*, signed 7 June 2017, [2019] ATS 1 (entered into force 27 June 2018): ratified by New Zealand on 27 June 2018, entered into force in respect of New Zealand on 1 October 2018.

*Protocol of 2003 to the International Convention on the Establishment of an International Fund for Compensation for Oil Pollution Damage 1992*, opened for signature 16 May 2003, [2006] IETS 13 (entered into force 3 March 2005): acceded to by New Zealand on 29 June 2018.

2.1.2  Bilateral Treaties

*Third Protocol to the Convention between the Government of New Zealand and the Government of the Republic of India for the Avoidance of Double Taxation and the Prevention of Fiscal Evasion with Respect to Taxes on Income*, signed 26 October 2016 (entered into force 7 July 2017): entered into force in respect of New Zealand on 7 September 2017.

*Agreement between the Government of New Zealand and the Government of the Commonwealth of Dominica on the Exchange of Information with respect to Taxes and Tax Matters*, signed 16 March 2010 (entered into force 7 September 2017).

*Agreement between the Government of New Zealand and the Government of the Republic of San Marino on the Exchange of Information with Respect to Taxes*, signed 1 April 2016 (entered into force 8 September 2017).

*Agreement between the Government of New Zealand and the Government of the United States of America for the Sharing of Visa and Immigration Information*, signed 4 May 2017 (entered into force 2 October 2017).

*Protocol to amend Annex 3 of the Thailand–New Zealand Closer Economic Partnership*, signed 24 July 2017 (entered into force 13 November 2017).

*Agreement relating to Science, Research and Innovation Cooperation between the Government of Australia and the Government of New Zealand*, signed 17 February 2017 (entered into force 27 November 2017).

*Agreement between the Government of Bermuda (as authorised by) the Government of the United Kingdom of Great Britain and Northern Ireland and the Government of New Zealand on the Exchange of Information with Respect to Taxes*, signed 16 April 2009: entered into force in respect of New Zealand on 15 December 2017.

*Agreement between the Government of New Zealand and the Government of Papua New Guinea regarding the Status of Visiting Forces and Defence Co-operation*, signed 7 March 2018 (entered into force 22 August 2018).

*Agreement in the Form of an Exchange of Letters between the European Union and New Zealand pursuant to Article XXIV:6 and Article XXVIII of the General Agreement on Tariffs and Trade (GATT) 1994 relating to the Modification of Concessions in the Schedule of the Republic of Croatia in the Course of its Accession to the European Union*, signed 13 March 2018 (entered into force 1 October 2018).

*Agreement between the European Union and New Zealand on Cooperation and Mutual Administrative Assistance in Customs Matters*, signed 3 July 2017 (entered into force on 1 May 2018).

### 2.2 *Reports on Treaties Tabled in the House of Representatives*

2.2.1 Reports Where No Substantive Matters were Drawn to the Attention of the House

Education and Science Committee, New Zealand Parliament, *International Treaty Examination of the Regional Co-operative Agreement for Research, Development and Training related to Nuclear Science and Technology, 2017* (Report, 7 July 2017)

2.2.2 Reports Where Substantive Matters were Drawn to the Attention of the House

Foreign Affairs, Defence and Trade Committee, New Zealand Parliament, *International Treaty Examination of the Treaty on the Prohibition of Nuclear Weapons* (Final Report, 2 July 2018) [24 submissions, 8 heard]

> The Committee noted that New Zealand law need not change its laws to ratify the treaty as they are already consistent with the treaty. While the treaty aligns with New Zealand's goal of a nuclear weapon-free world, the states that currently possess nuclear weapons do not support the treaty and did not participate in its creation (United States, Russia,

United Kingdom, France, China, India, Pakistan, Israel, and North Korea).

Foreign Affairs, Defence and Trade Committee, New Zealand Parliament, *International Treaty Examination of the Comprehensive and Progressive Agreement for Trans-Pacific Partnership* (Final Report, 24 May 2018) [427 submissions, 69 heard]

> The Committee noted that New Zealand signed the agreement for strategic, commercial, and sustainability reasons. It also noted that some submitters expressed the view that a genuinely independent cost-benefit analysis as well as a human rights impact analysis is needed. Some submitters expressed the view that the agreement provides disincentives for the New Zealand government to act in the interests of New Zealanders when those interests conflict with the interests of certain international investors.

Finance and Expenditure Committee, New Zealand Parliament, *International Treaty Examination of the Multilateral Convention to Implement Tax Treaty Related Measures to Prevent Base Erosion and Profit Shifting* (Final Report, 22 February 2018)

> The Committee noted that the convention is a core part of New Zealand's policy response to base erosion and profit shifting and the Organisation for Economic Co-operation and Development's ("OECD") recommendations. It also noted that New Zealand should take all steps it can to ensure compliance with tax legislation and expressed its support for the convention.

Finance and Expenditure Committee, New Zealand Parliament, *International Treaty Examination of the Second Protocol to Amend the Agreement for the Avoidance of Double Taxation and the Prevention of Fiscal Evasion with respect to Taxes on Income with the Government of the Hong Kong SAR of the PRC* (Final Report, 22 February 2018)

> The Committee noted that the purpose of the protocol is to amend the Hong Kong double tax agreement to facilitate automatic exchanges of information between New Zealand and Hong Kong in respect of certain tax matters. The change would bring Hong Kong's double tax agreement in line with virtually all other jurisdictions under the *Multilateral*

Convention on Mutual Administrative Assistance in Tax Matters (1988, as amended).

Economic Development, Science and Innovation Committee, New Zealand Parliament, *International Treaty Examination of the Marrakesh Treaty to Facilitate Access to Published Works for Persons Who are Blind, Visually Impaired, or Otherwise Print Disabled* (Report, 7 July 2017)

> The Committee noted that 90% of all written material published worldwide is unavailable in a format that meets the needs of those who are blind or have a print disability. The Committee noted that the treaty will allow New Zealanders to import copyrighted works in accessible format like braille, large print, and audio books from other counties that have ratified the treaty.

## 3 Legislation Related to New Zealand's International Obligations

This Part sets out the legislation dealt with during the current interval that concerns New Zealand's international obligations. It is divided into two sections, the first listing the Acts that were enacted and the second listing the regulations that were made.

### 3.1 *Acts of Parliament*

Acts of Parliament relating to New Zealand's international obligations are identified as: (3.1.1) Acts simply amending legislation that has implemented treaties; (3.1.2) Acts improving compliance with treaties that have already been implemented; or (3.1.3) Acts implementing new treaty obligations.

3.1.1 Acts Simply Amending Legislation that Implemented Treaties
*Anti-Money Laundering and Countering Financing of Terrorism Amendment Act 2017*

This Act amends the *Anti-Money Laundering and Countering Financing of Terrorism Act 2009*, which implements the recommendations of the Financial Action Task Force (established in 1989) from its *Mutual Evaluation Report* on New Zealand (October 2009).

*Broadcasting (Election Programmes and Election Advertising) Amendment Act 2017*

This Act amends the *Broadcasting Act 1989*, which implements the International Chamber of Commerce's *International Code of Advertising Practice* (1987).

### Children, Young Persons, and Their Families (Oranga Tamariki) Legislation Act 2017

This Act renames the *Children, Young Persons, and Their Families Act 1989* as the *Oranga Tamariki Act 1989*. The act implements the *Arrangement between New Zealand and Australian States and Territories regarding the Transfer of Children Subject to Child Protection Orders* (2000).

### Commerce Amendment Act 2018

This Act amends the *Commerce Act 1986*, which implements the *Trans-Tasman Mutual Recognition Arrangement* (1998).

### Commerce (Cartels and Other Matters) Amendment Act 2017

This Act amends the *Commerce Act 1986*, which implements the *Trans-Tasman Mutual Recognition Arrangement* (1998).

### Conservation (Infringement System) Act 2018

This Act amends the *Conservation Act 1987*, which implements the *Convention on Wetlands of International Importance especially as Waterfowl Habitat* (1971) and the *Convention for the Protection of the World Cultural and Natural Heritage* (1972). The Act also amends the *Marine Mammals Protection Act 1978*, which implements the *Convention on the Prevention of Marine Pollution by Dumping of Wastes and other Matter* (1972). The Act also amends the *Trade in Endangered Species Act 1989*, which implements the *Convention on International Trade in Endangered Species of Wild Fauna and Flora* (1973).

### Crown Minerals (Petroleum) Amendment Act 2018

This Act amends the *Crown Minerals Act 1991*, which implements the *Convention on Wetlands of International Importance especially as Waterfowl Habitat* (1971).

### Domestic Violence – Victim's Protection Act 2018

This Act amends the *Employment Relations Act 2000*, which implements the International Labour Organization's ("ILO") *Convention 11* (1921): *Right of Association (Agriculture)*, the ILO's *Convention 14* (1921): *Weekly Rest (Industry)*, the ILO's *Convention 22* (1926): *Seamen's Articles of Agreement*, the ILO's *Convention 32* (1932): *Protection against Accidents (Dockers)*, and the ILO's *Convention 122* (1964): *Employment Policy*. The Act also incorporates the principles underlying the ILO's *Convention 87* (1948): *Freedom of Association* and the ILO's *Convention 98* (1949): *Right to Organise and Bargain Collectively*.

The Act also amends the *Human Rights Act 1993*, which implements the *Universal Declaration of Human Rights* (1948), the ILO's *Convention 97* (1949): *Migration for Employment*, the ILO's *Convention 100* (1951): *Equal Remuneration*, the *Convention relating to the Status of Refugees* (1951) [arts 2 and 4], the ILO's *Convention 111* (1958): *Discrimination (Employment and Occupation)*, the *Convention on the Elimination of All Forms of Racial Discrimination* (1965), the ILO's *Convention 122* (1964): *Employment Policy*, the *International Covenant on Civil and Political Rights* (1966), the *International Covenant on Economic, Social and Cultural Rights* (1966), the *Optional Protocol to the International Covenant on Civil and Political Rights* (1966), the *Convention on the Elimination of All Forms of Discrimination against Women* (1979), and the *United Nations Convention on the Rights of Persons with Disabilities* (2006).

### Education Amendment Act 2018
This Act amends the *Education Act 1989*, which implements the ILO's *Convention 10* (1921): *Minimum Age (Agriculture)*, the ILO's *Convention 58* (1936): *Minimum Age (Sea)*, the ILO's *Convention 59* (1937): *Minimum Age (Industry)*, the *Convention against Discrimination in Education* (1960), and the ILO's *Convention 122* (1964): *Employment Policy*.

### Education (National Education and Learning Priorities) Amendment Act 2018
This Act amends the *Education Act 1989*, which implements the ILO's *Convention 10* (1921): *Minimum Age (Agriculture)*, the ILO's *Convention 58* (1936): *Minimum Age (Sea)*, the ILO's *Convention 59* (1937): *Minimum Age (Industry)*, the *Convention against Discrimination in Education* (1960), and the ILO's *Convention 122* (1964): *Employment Policy*.

### Education (Teaching Council of Aotearoa New Zealand) Amendment Act 2018
This amends the *Education Act 1989*, which implements the ILO's *Convention 10* (1921): *Minimum Age (Agriculture)*, the ILO's *Convention 58* (1936): *Minimum Age (Sea)*, the ILO's *Convention 59* (1937): *Minimum Age (Industry)*, the *Convention against Discrimination in Education* (1960), and the ILO's *Convention 122* (1964): *Employment Policy*.

### Education (Tertiary Education and Other Matters) Amendment Act 2018
This Act amends the *Education Act 1989*, which implements the ILO's *Convention 10* (1921): *Minimum Age (Agriculture)*, the ILO's *Convention 58* (1936): *Minimum Age (Sea)*, the ILO's *Convention 59* (1937): *Minimum Age (Industry)*, the *Convention against Discrimination in Education* (1960), and the ILO's *Convention 122* (1964): *Employment Policy*.

*Electoral (Integrity) Amendment Act 2018*
This Act amends the *Electoral Act 1993*, which implements the *International Covenant on Civil and Political Rights* (1966) arts 21 and 25 and the *Convention on the Elimination of All Forms of Discrimination against Women* (1979) Pt 1 and art 7.

*Electronic Interactions Reform Act 2017*
This Act amends the *Births, Deaths, Marriages, and Relationships Registration Act 1995*, which implements the *International Covenant on Civil and Political Rights* (1966) art 24.

The Act also amends the *Marriage Act 1955*, which implements the *Convention relating to the Status of Refugees* (1951) art 12, the *International Covenant on Economic, Social and Cultural Rights* (1966) art 10, the *Convention on the Rights of the Child* (1989), and the *Convention on the Elimination of All Forms of Discrimination against Women* (1979) art 16.

The Act also amends the *Commerce Act 1986*, which implements the *Trans-Tasman Mutual Recognition Arrangement* (1998).

The Act also amends the *Copyright Act 1994*, which implements the *Berne Convention for the Protection of Literary and Artistic Works* (1896, as amended in 1971), the *Universal Copyright Convention* (1952), the *Agreement on Trade-Related Aspects of Intellectual Property Rights* (1994), the *Madrid Agreement concerning the International Registration of Marks* (1989), the *Nice Agreement concerning the International Classification of Goods and Services for the Purposes of the Registration of Marks* (1957, as amended in 1979), and the *Singapore Treaty on the Law of Trademarks* (2006).

The Act also amends the *Fair Trading Act 1986*, which implements the *United Nations Guidelines for Consumer Protection* (1985) and annex 14 of the *Free Trade Agreement between the Government of New Zealand and the Government of the People's Republic of China* (2008), which sets out the *Agreement between the Government of New Zealand and the Government of the People's Republic of China on Cooperation in the Field of Conformity Assessment in Relation to Electrical and Electronic Equipment and Components* (2008).

The Act also amends the *Patents Act 2013*, which implements the *Budapest Treaty on the International Recognition of the Deposit of Microorganisms for the Purposes of Patent Procedure* (1977, as amended in 1980), the *Patent Cooperation Treaty* (1984), the *Regulations under the Patent Cooperation Treaty* (1992), the *Agreement on Trade-Related Aspects of Intellectual Property Rights* (1994), and the *Arrangement between the Government of Australia and the Government of New Zealand relating to Trans-Tasman Regulation of Patent Attorneys* (2013).

The Act also amends the *Trade Marks Act 2002*, which implements the *Convention for the Protection of Industrial Property* (1883), the *Agreement on Trade-Related Aspects of Intellectual Property Rights* (1994), *Madrid Agreement concerning the International Registration of Marks* (1989), the *Nice Agreement concerning the International Classification of Goods and Services for the Purposes of the Registration of Marks* (1957, as amended in 1979), and the *Singapore Treaty on the Law of Trademarks* (2006).

This Act also amends the *Conservation Act 1987*, which implements the *Convention on Wetlands of International Importance especially as Waterfowl Habitat* (1971) and the *Convention for the Protection of the World Cultural and Natural Heritage* (1972).

*Enhancing Identity Verification and Border Processes Legislation Act 2017*

This Act amends the *Privacy Act 1993*, which implements the *Recommendation of the Council of the Organisation for Economic Co-operation and Development concerning the Protection of Privacy and Transborder flows of Personal Data* (1980).

The Act also amends the *Births, Deaths, Marriages, and Relationships Registration Act 1995*, which implements the *International Covenant on Civil and Political Rights* (1966) art 24.

The Act also amends the *Corrections Act 2004*, which implements the *United Nations Standard Minimum Rules for the Treatment of Prisoners* (1955, as amended in 1977) and the *Convention on the Rights of the Child* (1989).

The Act also amends the *Immigration Act 2009*, which implements the ILO's *Convention 97* (1949): *Migration for Employment*, the *Convention relating to the Status of Refugees* (1951), the *Covenant on Civil and Political Rights* (1966), the *Protocol relating to the Status of Refugees* (1967), the *Convention against Torture and Other Cruel, Inhuman and Degrading Treatment or Punishment* (1984), the *Convention against Transnational Organised Crime* (2000), the *Protocol against the Smuggling of Migrants, by Land, Sea and Air, supplementing the Convention against Transnational Organised Crime* (2000), and the *Protocol to Prevent, Suppress and Punish Trafficking of Persons, Especially Women and Children, supplementing the Convention against Transnational Organised Crime* (2000).

The Act also amends the *Intelligence and Security Act 2017*, which implements the *Convention on the Physical Protection of Nuclear Material and Nuclear Facilities* (1980) and the *Convention on the Marking of Plastic Explosives for the Purpose of Detection* (1991).

The Act also amends the *Land Transport Act 1998* (which implements the *Convention on Road Traffic* (1949)), the *Mental Health (Compulsory Assessment and Treatment) Act 1992* (which implements the *Universal Declaration of Human Rights* (1948)), and the *Sentencing Act 2002* (which implements the *Convention on the Physical Protection of Nuclear Material and Nuclear Facilities* (1980) and the *Convention on the Marking of Plastic Explosives for the Purpose of Detection* (1991)).

### *Exclusive Economic Zone and Continental Shelf (Environmental Effects) Amendment Act 2018*

This Act amends the *Exclusive Economic Zone and Continental Shelf (Environmental Effects) Act 2012*, which implements the *Convention on the Prevention of Marine Pollution by Dumping Wastes and Other Matter* (1972), the *International Convention for the Prevention of Pollution from Ships* (1973), the *United Nations Convention on the Law of the Sea* (1982), the *Convention on Biological Diversity* (1993), and the *Protocol to the Convention on the Prevention of Marine Pollution by Dumping Wastes and Other Matter* (1996, as amended in 2006).

### *Films, Videos, and Publications Classification (Interim Restriction Orders) Amendment Act 2017*

This Act amends the *Films, Videos, and Publications Classification Act 1993*, which implements the *Convention for the Suppression of the Circulation of, and Traffic in, Obscene Publications* (1923), the *Protocol to Amend the Convention for the Suppression of the Circulation of, and Traffic in, Obscene Publications* (1947), the *International Covenant on Civil and Political Rights* (1966) arts 3, 15, and 19, the *Convention on the Elimination of All Forms of Discrimination against Women* (1979) art 5, and the ILO's *Convention 182* (1999): Worst Forms of Child Labour.

### *Land Transport Amendment Act 2017*

This Act amends the *Land Transport Act 1998*, which implements the *Convention on Road Traffic* (1949).

### *Maritime Crimes Amendment Act 2017*

This Act amends the *Maritime Crimes Act 1999*, which implements the *Convention for the Suppression of Unlawful Acts against the Safety of Maritime Navigation* (1988).

### *Maritime Powers Extension Act 2018*

This Act amends the *Customs and Excise Act 2018*, which replaces the *Customs and Excise Act 1996*, which implements the *Customs Convention on the Temporary Importation of Private Road Vehicles* (1954), the *Customs Convention on*

*Containers* (1972), the recommendations of the Financial Action Task Force (established in 1989) from its *Mutual Evaluation Report* on New Zealand (October 2009), the *Protocol of Amendment to the International Convention on the Simplification and Harmonization of Customs Procedures* (1999), and the *Free Trade Agreement between the Government of New Zealand and the Government of the People's Republic of China* (2008).

This Act also amends the *Misuse of Drugs Act 1975*, which implements the *Single Convention on Narcotic Drugs* (1961), the *Convention on Psychotropic Substances* (1971), the *Protocol Amending the Single Convention on Narcotic Drugs* (1972), the *Convention on the Physical Protection of Nuclear Material and Nuclear Facilities* (1980), the *Convention against Illicit Traffic in Narcotic Drugs and Psychotropic Substances* (1988), the recommendations of the Financial Action Task Force (established in 1989) from its *Mutual Evaluation Report* on New Zealand (October 2009), and the *Convention on the Marking of Plastic Explosives for the Purpose of Detection* (1991).

### Maritime Transport Amendment Act 2017

This Act amends the *Marine Transport Act 1994*, which implements the *International Convention for the Unification of Certain Rules of Law relating to Bills of Lading* (1924), the *Protocol to Amend the International Convention for the Unification of Certain Rules of Law relating to Bills of Lading* (1968), the *Convention on Civil Liability for Oil Pollution Damage* (1969), the *International Convention on Tonnage Measurement of Ships* (1969), the *International Convention on the Establishment of an International Fund for Compensation for Oil Pollution Damage* (1971), the *Convention on the Prevention of Marine Pollution by Dumping of Wastes and other Matter* (1972), the *Protocol relating to Intervention on the High Seas in Cases of Pollution by Substances other than Oil* (1973), the *International Convention for the Prevention of Pollution from Ships* (1973), the *Convention on Limitation of Liability for Maritime Claims* (1976), the *Protocol relating to the International Convention for the Prevention of Pollution from Ships* (1978), the *International Convention on Standards of Training, Certification and Watchkeeping for Seafarers* (1978), the *Protocol to the International Convention for the Unification of Certain Rules of Law relating to Bills of Lading* (1979), the *United Nations Convention on the Law of the Sea* (1982), the *International Convention on Salvage* (1989), the *Protocol to Amend the Convention on Limitation of Liability for Maritime Claims* (1996), the *Protocol to the Convention on the Prevention of Marine Pollution by Dumping Wastes and Other Matter* (1996, as amended in 2006), and the *Protocol of 1996 to Amend the Convention on the Limitation of Liability for Maritime Claims* (1976).

### Minors (Court Consent to Relationships) Legislation Act 2018

This Act amends the *Care of Children Act 2004*, which implements the *International Covenant on Civil and Political Rights* (1966), the *International Covenant on Economic, Social, and Cultural Rights* (1966), and the *Convention on the Civil Aspects of International Child Abduction* (1980).

The Act also amends the *Marriage Act 1955*, which implements the *Convention relating to the Status of Refugees* (1951) art 12, the *International Covenant on Economic, Social and Cultural Rights* (1966) art 10, the *Convention on the Rights of the Child* (1989), and the *Convention on the Elimination of All Forms of Discrimination against Women* (1979) art 16.

The Act also amends the *Citizenship Act 1977* (which implements the ILO's *Convention 82* (1947): *Social Policy (Non-Metropolitan Territories)*), the *Family Courts Act 1980* (which implements the *Convention on the Elimination of All Forms of Discrimination against Women* (1979) art 3), and the *Oranga Tamariki Act 1989* (which implements the *Arrangement between New Zealand and Australian States and Territories regarding the Transfer of Children Subject to Child Protection Orders* (2000)).

### Misuse of Drugs (Medicinal Cannabis) Amendment Act 2018

This Act amends the *Misuse of Drugs Act 1975*, which implements the *Single Convention on Narcotic Drugs* (1961), the *Convention on Psychotropic Substances* (1971), the *Protocol Amending the Single Convention on Narcotic Drugs* (1972), the *Convention on the Physical Protection of Nuclear Material and Nuclear Facilities* (1980), the *Convention against Illicit Traffic in Narcotic Drugs and Psychotropic Substances* (1988), the recommendations of the Financial Action Task Force (established in 1989) from its *Mutual Evaluation Report* on New Zealand (October 2009), and the *Convention on the Marking of Plastic Explosives for the Purpose of Detection* (1991).

### National Animal Identification and Tracing Amendment Act 2018

This Act amends the *National Animal Identification and Tracing Act 2012*, which implements the World Organisation for Animal Health's *Terrestrial Animal Health Code* Ch 4.2.

### Parental Leave and Employment Protection Amendment Act 2017

This Act amends the *Parental Leave and Employment Protection Act 1987*, which implements the ILO's *Convention 111* (1958): *Discrimination (Employment and Occupation)*.

*Reserve Bank of New Zealand (Monetary Policy) Amendment Act 2018*
This Act amends the *Reserve Bank of New Zealand Act 1989*, which implements the recommendations of the Financial Action Task Force (established in 1989) from its *Mutual Evaluation Report* on New Zealand (October 2009).

*State Sector and Crown Entities Reform Act 2018*
This Act amends the *State Sector Act 1988*, which implements the ILO's *Convention 111* (1958): *Discrimination (Employment and Occupation)*.

*Statutes Amendment Act 2018*
This Act amends the *Anti-Money Laundering and Countering Financing of Terrorism Act 2009, Biosecurity Act 1993, Care of Children Act 2004, Child Support Act 1991, Companies Act 1993, Crown Proceedings Act 1950, Customs and Excise Act 2018, Domestic Violence Act 1995, Exclusive Economic Zone and Continental Shelf (Environmental Effects) Act 2012, Family Proceedings Act 1980, Films, Videos, and Publications Classification Act 1993, Fisheries Act 1996, International Finance Agreement Amendment Act 1966*, which amends the *International Finance Agreements Act 1961, Oranga Tamariki Act 1989, Policing Act 2008, Protection of Personal and Property Rights Act 1988*, and *Public Finance Act 1989*, all of which implement international obligations.

*Tariff (PACER Plus) Amendment Act 2018*
This Act amends the *Tariff Act 1988*, which implements the *General Agreement on Tariffs and Trade* (1947 and 1997), the *Agreement between New Zealand and Singapore on Closer Economic Partnership* (2001), the *New Zealand–Thailand Closer Economic Partnership Agreement* (2005), the *Trans-Pacific Strategic Partnership Agreement among Brunei Darussalam, Chile, New Zealand, and Singapore* (2005), the *Free Trade Agreement between the Government of New Zealand and the Government of the People's Republic of China* (2008), the *Malaysia–New Zealand Free Trade Agreement* (2009), the *Agreement Establishing the ASEAN–Australia–New Zealand Free Trade Area* (2009), the *New Zealand–Hong Kong, China Closer Economic Partnership Agreement* (2010), and the *Free Trade Agreement between New Zealand and the Republic of Korea* (2015).

*Telecommunications (New Regulatory Framework) Amendment Act 2018*
This Act amends the *Telecommunications Act 2001*, which implements the *International Telecommunication Convention with Annexes, Final Protocol, and Additional Protocols I to VII, and Annexed Radio Regulations* (1932), and the *Constitution of the Asia–Pacific Telecommunity* (1979).

*Tribunals Powers and Procedures Legislation Act 2018*
This Act amends the *Copyright Act 1994*, which implements the *Berne Convention for the Protection of Literary and Artistic Works* (1896 as amended 1971), the *Universal Copyright Convention* (1952), the *Agreement on Trade-Related Aspects of Intellectual Property Rights* (1994), the *Madrid Agreement concerning the International Registration of Marks* (1989), the *Nice Agreement concerning the International Classification of Goods and Services for the Purposes of the Registration of Marks* (1957, as amended in 1979), and the *Singapore Treaty on the Law of Trademarks* (2006).

The Act also amends the *Education Act 1989*, which implements the ILO's *Convention 10* (1921): *Minimum Age (Agriculture)*, the ILO's *Convention 58* (1936): *Minimum Age (Sea)*, the ILO's *Convention 59* (1937): *Minimum Age (Industry)*, the *Convention against Discrimination in Education* (1960), and the ILO's *Convention 122* (1964): *Employment Policy*.

The Act also amends the *Human Rights Act 1993*, which implements the *Universal Declaration of Human Rights* (1948), the ILO's *Convention 97* (1949): *Migration for Employment*, the ILO's *Convention 100* (1951): *Equal Remuneration*, *Convention relating to the Status of Refugees* (1951) arts 2 and 4, the ILO's *Convention 111* (1958): *Discrimination (Employment and Occupation)*, the *Convention on the Elimination of All Forms of Racial Discrimination* (1965), the ILO's *Convention 122* (1964): *Employment Policy*, the *International Covenant on Civil and Political Rights* (1966), the *International Covenant on Economic, Social and Cultural Rights* (1966), the *Optional Protocol to the International Covenant on Civil and Political Rights* (1966), the *Convention on the Elimination of All Forms of Discrimination against Women* (1979), and the *United Nations Convention on the Rights of Persons with Disabilities* (2006).

The Act also amends the *Health Act 1986*, which implements the *Convention for the Constitution of the World Health Organisation* (1946), the *Protocol concerning the Office International d'Hygiène Publique* (1946), the *Health and Safety in Employment Act 1992*, the ILO's *Convention 12* (1921): *Workmen's Compensation (Agriculture)*, the ILO's *Convention 10* (1921): *Minimum Age (Agriculture)*, the ILO's *Convention 32* (1932): *Protection against Accidents (Dockers)*, the ILO's *Convention 134* (1970): *Prevention of Accidents (Seafarers)*, the *Health Benefits (Reciprocity with Australia) Act 1999*, and the *Agreement on Medical Treatment* (1986).

The Act also amends the *Immigration Act 2009*, which implements the ILO's *Convention 97* (1949): *Migration for Employment*, the *Convention relating to the Status of Refugees* (1951), the *International Covenant on Civil and Political Rights* (1966), the *Protocol relating to the Status of Refugees* (1967), the *Convention Against Torture and Other Cruel, Inhuman and Degrading Treatment or Punishment*

(1984), the *Convention against Transnational Organised Crime* (2000), the *Protocol against the Smuggling of Migrants, by Land, Sea and Air, supplementing the Convention against Transnational Organised Crime* (2000), and the *Protocol to Prevent, Suppress and Punish Trafficking of Persons, especially Women and Children, supplementing the Convention against Transnational Organised Crime* (2000).

The Act also amends the *Maritime Transport Act 1994*, which implements the *International Convention for the Unification of Certain Rules of Law relating to Bills of Lading* (1924), the *Protocol to Amend the International Convention for the Unification of Certain Rules of Law relating to Bills of Lading* (1968), the *Convention on Civil Liability for Oil Pollution Damage* (1969), the *International Convention on Tonnage Measurement of Ships* (1969), the *International Convention on the Establishment of an International Fund for Compensation for Oil Pollution Damage* (1971), the *Convention on the Prevention of Marine Pollution by Dumping of Wastes and other Matter* (1972), the *Protocol relating to Intervention on the High Seas in Cases of Pollution by Substances other than Oil* (1973), the *International Convention for the Prevention of Pollution from Ships* (1973), the *Convention on Limitation of Liability for Maritime Claims* (1976), the *Protocol relating to the International Convention for the Prevention of Pollution from Ships* (1978), the *International Convention on Standards of Training, Certification and Watchkeeping for Seafarers* (1978), the *Protocol to the International Convention for the Unification of Certain Rules of Law relating to Bills of Lading* (1979), the *United Nations Convention on the Law of the Sea* (1982), the *International Convention on Salvage* (1989), the *Protocol to Amend the Convention on Limitation of Liability for Maritime Claims* (1996), and the *Protocol to the Convention on the Prevention of Marine Pollution by Dumping of Wastes and other Matter* (1996, as amended in 2006).

This Act also amends the *Prisoners and Victims Claims Act 2005*, which implements the *Universal Declaration of Human Rights* (1948), the *Convention relating to the Status of Refugees* (1951), the *Convention on the Elimination of All Forms of Racial Discrimination* (1965), the *International Covenant on Civil and Political Rights* (1966), the *Optional Protocol to the International Covenant on Civil and Political Rights* (1966), and the *Convention on the Elimination of All Forms of Discrimination against Women* (1979).

The Act also amends the *Social Security Act 2018*, which amends the *Social Security Act 1964*, which implements the ILO's *Convention 44* (1934): *Unemployment Provision*, the ILO's *Convention 122* (1964): *Employment Policy*, and the *Convention on Social Security between the Government of the United Kingdom of Great Britain and Northern Ireland and the Government of New Zealand* (1969).

### 3.1.2 Acts Improving Compliance with Treaties Already Implemented
*Employment Relations Amendment Act 2018*

This Act amends the *Employment Relations Act 2000*. The departmental disclosure statement in the explanatory note of the Bill as introduced states that it will

> provide a positive contribution to New Zealand's compliance with International Labour Organisation (ILO) Convention 98 on the Right to Organise and Collective Bargaining. This includes employees making an informed and free choice, preventing discrimination based on union membership and providing a fairer framework for collective bargaining to take place.

### 3.1.3 Acts Implementing New Treaties
*Brokering (Weapons and Related Items) Control Act 2018*

Section 3(b) states that a purpose of this Act is to "support New Zealand's commitments under the Arms Trade Treaty". The *Arms Trade Treaty* ("ATT") is a multi-lateral treaty that entered into force on 24 December 2014. New Zealand signed the ATT on the 3 June 2013 and ratified it on 2 September 2014.

*Comprehensive and Progressive Agreement for Trans-Pacific Partnership Amendment Act 2018*

This Act makes the changes necessary for New Zealand to ratify the *Comprehensive and Progressive Agreement for Trans-Pacific Partnership* (2018). The Agreement also requires New Zealand to accede to the *Berne Convention* (1886), *WIPO Copyright Treaty* (1996), and the *WIPO Performers and Phonograms Treaty* (1996).

*Outer Space and High-altitude Activities Act 2017*

This Act implements the *Agreement between the Government of New Zealand and the Government of the United States of America on Technology Safeguards*

---

[14] This list of regulations does not include commencement orders for Acts that implement international obligations. See, e.g., *Customs and Excise Act 2018 Commencement Order 2018* 2018/148, *Hazardous Substances and New Organisms Amendment Act 2015 Commencement Order 2017* 2017/232, and *Maritime Crimes Amendment Act 2017 Commencement Order 2018* 2018/56.

*Associated with United States Participation in Space Launches from New Zealand Technology Safeguards Agreement* (2016) ("*TSA*"). The TSA enables the transfer of United States rocket technology to New Zealand and its use and secure management in New Zealand.

The Act also implements the *Convention on Registration of Objects Launched into Outer Space* (1975) (the "*Registration Convention*"), which the New Zealand government has agreed to accede to. The *Registration Convention* requires a state party to establish a register of all objects sent into orbit or space. This Act contains a regulation-making power that will enable a register of space objects to be established.

### 3.2 Regulations

This section sets out the regulations made during the current interval that relate to New Zealand's international obligations.[14]

1  *Antarctica (Environmental Protection) Act (Schedule 2) Order 2018*

This order is made under *Antarctica (Environmental Protection) Act 1994* s 55 (2)(a). The 1994 Act sets out, in sch 2, the text of the *Protocol on Environmental Protection to the Antarctic Treaty* (1991). Annex II of that protocol has been amended by various measures of the consultative parties to the *Antarctic Treaty*. This order replaces annex II of that protocol with the current text of that annex, updated to reflect those amendments.

2  *Anti-Money Laundering and Countering Financing of Terrorism (Class Exemptions) Notice 2018*

This is a notice made under *Anti-Money Laundering and Countering Financing of Terrorism Act 2009* s 157(1), having regard to ss 157(3) and 158 of the principal Act. This notice publicises the class exemptions granted by the Minister of Justice. Pt 3 of the schedule creates an exemption for managers of specified retirement schemes from ss 10 to 71 of the Act in relation to services provided in respect of the specified retirement scheme. Paragraph 11(d) states that this exemption is consistent with New Zealand's international obligations as a member of the Financial Action Task Force and the Asia/Pacific Group on Money Laundering.

3  *Customs Export Prohibition Order 2017*

This order is made under *Customs and Excise Act 1996* s 56, and prohibits the exportation of various goods under the Act without the relevant ministerial or official consent. Clause 6 of the order states that the exportation of goods or electronic publications that are a military end-use is prohibited if the country of destination is subject to a UN Security Council arms embargo and the subject of regulations under *United Nations Act 1946* s 2.

4    *Customs Export Prohibition (Toothfish) Order 2018*
These regulations are made under *Customs and Excise Act 1996* s 56. This order prohibits the exportation of two species of toothfish unless the toothfish is covered by an appropriately completed catch document. Those documents are required by the catch documentation scheme for toothfish under *Conservation Measure 170/XVIII*. This conservation measure was adopted by the Commission for the Conservation of Antarctic Marine Living Resources in 1999, under *Convention on the Conservation of Antarctic Marine Living Resources* (1982) art IX.

5    *Customs Import Prohibition (Toothfish) Order 2018*
These regulations are made under *Customs and Excise Act 1996* s 54. This order prohibits the importation of two species of toothfish unless the toothfish is covered by an appropriately completed catch document. Those documents are required by the catch documentation scheme for toothfish under *Conservation Measure 170/XVIII*. That conservation measure was adopted by the Commission for the Conservation of Antarctic Marine Living Resources in 1999, under *Convention on the Conservation of Antarctic Marine Living Resources* (1982) art IX.

6    *District Court (Access to Court Documents) Rules 2017*
These rules are made under *Criminal Procedure Act 2011* s 386(1) and *District Court Act 2016* s 228. Clause 4 includes *International Crimes and International Criminal Court Act 2000* pts 4 to 6, which implements the *Rome Statute of the International Criminal Court* (1998), within the definition of "criminal proceeding" for the purpose of these rules. Parts 4 to 6 relate to the arrest and surrender of persons to the ICC, domestic procedures for other types of co-operation, and the enforcement of penalties.

7    *Double Taxation Relief (India) Amendment Order 2017*
This order is made under *Income Tax Act 2007* s BH 1. This order gives effect to the *Third Protocol to the Convention between the Government of the Republic of India and the Government of New Zealand for the Avoidance of Double Taxation and the Prevention of Fiscal Evasion with Respect to Taxes on Income* (2016). The agreement will come into force in accordance with art 3 of the protocol.

8    *Double Tax Agreements (Multilateral Convention to Implement Tax Treaty Related Measures to Prevent Base Erosion and Profit Shifting) Order 2018*
This order is made under *Income Tax Act 2007* s BH 1. The order gives effect to the *Multilateral Convention to Implement Tax Treaty Related Measures to Prevent Base Erosion and Profit Shifting* (2017). This order provides the full text of the convention. The convention is a multilateral agreement developed by the OECD in conjunction with more than 100 jurisdictions. It sits

alongside New Zealand's existing bilateral double tax agreements ("BDTAS") and modifies them to the extent provided in the convention, based on the positions taken by BDTA partners in their respective lists of reservations and notifications.

9   *Double Tax Agreements (San Marino) Order 2017*

This order is made under *Income Tax Act 2007* s BH 1. This order gives effect to the *Agreement between the Government of New Zealand and the Government of the Republic of San Marino on the Exchange of Information with Respect to Taxes* (2016). The order provides the full text of the agreement.

10   *Financial Advisers (Overseas Custodians – Assurance Engagement) Exemption Notice 2018*

This notice is made by the Financial Markets Authority pursuant to *Financial Advisers Act 2008* s 148. This notice exempts certain overseas custodians from the requirements in *Financial Advisers (Custodians of FMCA Financial Products) Regulations 2014* regs 9 and 10 to obtain an assurance engagement from a New Zealand auditor that covers the New Zealand assurance engagement matters specified in reg 10.

The securities regulators in the jurisdictions listed in the schedule are signatories to the *International Organization of Securities Commissions Multilateral Memorandum of Understanding concerning Consultation and Cooperation and the Exchange of Information* (2002). The audit regulators in those jurisdictions are signatories to the *International Forum of Independent Audit Regulators Multilateral Memorandum of Understanding concerning Co-operation in the Exchange of Information for Audit Oversight* (2015). The Financial Markets Authority will be able to seek assistance from relevant regulators if enforcement issues arise.

11   *Financial Markets Conduct (Overseas Custodians – Assurance Engagement) Exemption Notice 2018*

The notice is made by the Financial Markets Authority pursuant to *Financial Markets Conduct Act 2013* s 556. This notice exempts certain overseas custodians from the requirement in *Financial Markets Conduct Regulations 2014* reg 87 to obtain an assurance engagement from a New Zealand auditor that covers the New Zealand assurance engagement matters specified in reg 88.

The securities regulators in the jurisdictions listed in the schedule are signatories to the *International Organization of Securities Commissions Multilateral Memorandum of Understanding concerning Consultation and Cooperation and the Exchange of Information* (2002). The audit regulators in those jurisdictions are signatories to the *International Forum of Independent Audit Regulators Multilateral Memorandum of Understanding concerning Co-operation in the Exchange of Information for Audit Oversight* (2015).

12   *Fisheries (High Seas Fishing Notifications – North East Atlantic Fisheries Commission) Amendment Notice 2018*

This notice is made under *Fisheries Act 1996* s 113C. It amends the *Fisheries (High Seas Fishing Notifications – North East Atlantic Fisheries Commission) Notice 2009*. The amendment updates the list of international conservation and management measures that have been adopted by the North East Atlantic Fisheries Commission.

13   *Fisheries (High Seas Fishing Notifications – South Pacific Regional Fisheries Management Organisation) Amendment Notice 2018*

This notice is made under *Fisheries Act 1996* s 113C. It amends the international conservation and management measures listed in the *Fisheries (High Seas Fishing Notifications – South Pacific Regional Fisheries Management Organisation) Notice 2013*.

14   *Fisheries (High Seas Fishing Notifications: Western and Central Pacific Fisheries Commission) Amendment Notice 2018*

This notice is made under *Fisheries Act 1996* s 113C. It amends the *Fisheries (High Seas Fishing Notifications: Western and Central Pacific Fisheries Commission) Notice 2009*, which gives notice of a host of international conservation and management measures that the Commission has adopted. This amendment replaces the schedule to update the list of international conservation and management measures that have been adopted by the Western and Central Pacific Fisheries Commission.

15   *Fisheries (High Seas Fishing Notifications – Commission for the Conservation of Southern Bluefin Tuna) Amendment Notice 2017*

This notice is made under *Fisheries Act 1996* s 113C. It amends the *Fisheries (High Seas Fishing Notifications – Commission for the Conservation of Southern Bluefin Tuna) Notice 2009*. The amendments update the list of international conservation and management measures that have been adopted by the Commission for the Conservation of Southern Bluefin Tuna, including measures adopted in 2017.

16   *Health and Safety at Work (Hazardous Substances) Amendment Regulations 2017*

These regulations are made under *Health and Safety at Work Act 2015* ss 211, 212 and 218 and make corrections and other minor amendments to the *Health and Safety at Work (Hazardous Substances) Regulations 2017*. Regulation 42 amends reg 16.30 (requirements for UN approved containers) by inserting new reg 16.30(4A), which makes clear that WorkSafe can perform the functions of a competent authority under the *UN Model Regulations – UN Recommendations on the Transport of Dangerous Goods Model Regulations* (1999), incorporated by reference into reg 16.30.

17    *Senior Courts (Access to Court Documents) Rules 2017*

These rules are made under *Criminal Procedure Act 2011* s 386(1) and *Senior Courts Act 2016* s 148. Clause 4 includes *International Crimes and International Criminal Court Act 2000* pts 4 to 6 within the definition of "criminal proceeding" for the purpose of these rules. Parts 4 to 6 relate to the arrest and surrender of person to ICC, domestic procedures for other types of co-operation, and the enforcement of penalties.

18    *Tax Administration (Reportable Jurisdictions for Application of CRS Standard) Amendment Regulations 2018*

These regulations are made under *Tax Administration Act 1994* s 226D and amend the *Tax Administration (Reportable Jurisdictions for Application of CRS Standard) Regulations 2017*. The principal regulations prescribe overseas territories to be reportable jurisdictions for the purposes of the *Common Reporting Standard* ("*CRS*"), the *Common Standard on Reporting and Due Diligence for Financial Account Information*, which is part of the *Standard for Automatic Exchange of Financial Account Information in Tax Matters* (2014). Croatia and Indonesia have recently completed implementation of the standard and are now added as reportable jurisdictions for reporting periods beginning on or after 1 July 2017.

19    *United Nations Sanctions (Democratic People's Republic of Korea) Amendment Regulations 2017*

These regulations are made under *United Nations Act 1946* s 2 and amend the *United Nations Sanctions (Democratic People's Republic of Korea) Regulations 2017*. These regulations give effect to three additional resolutions of the UN Security Council: resolution 2356 (2017), resolution 2371 (2017), and resolution 2375 (2017).

20    *United Nations Sanctions (Democratic People's Republic of Korea) Amendment Regulations 2018*

These regulations are made under *United Nations Act 1946* s 2 and amend the *United Nations Sanctions (Democratic People's Republic of Korea) Regulations 2017*. These regulations, which impose additional sanctions on the Democratic People's Republic of Korea (DPRK), give effect to UN Security Council Resolution 2397 (2017).

21    *United Nations Sanctions (Libya) Regulations 2018*

These regulations are made under *United Nations Act 1946* s 2(1). These regulations give effect to resolution 1970 (2011), resolution 1973 (2011), resolution 2009 (2011), resolution 2095 (2013), resolution 2146 (2014), resolution 2174 (2014), resolution 2213 (2015), resolution 2278 (2016), resolution 2292 (2016), and resolution 2362 (2017). These are resolutions of the UN Security Council that relate to Libya.

22   *United Nations Sanctions (Mali) Regulations 2018*
These regulations are made under *United Nations Act 1946* s 2. These regulations give effect to resolution 2374 (2017) by the UN Security Council under the *Charter of the United Nations* (1945) ("*UN Charter*"). These are resolutions of the UN Security Council that relate to Mali.

23   *United Nations Sanctions (Somalia) Regulations 2018*
These regulations are made under *United Nations Act 1946* s 2(1). These regulations give effect to resolution 733 (1992), resolution 1356 (2001), resolution 1425 (2002), resolution 1725 (2006), resolution 1744 (2007), resolution 1772 (2007), resolution 1844 (2008), resolution 2036 (2012), resolution 2111 (2013), resolution 2142 (2014), resolution 2182 (2014), resolution 2184 (2014), resolution 2244 (2015), resolution 2317 (2016), and resolution 2385 (2017). These are resolutions of the UN Security Council that relate to Somalia.

24   *Various Civil Aviation Rules*
Section 30 of the *Civil Aviation Act 1990* empowers the Minister to make rules for the designation, classification and certification of aircraft, pilots, crew members and other services, for the setting of standards, specifications, restrictions and licensing requirements, the conditions of operation of foreign aircraft and international flights to, from, or within New Zealand, and for a number of other purposes. Many of these rules incorporate international standards or implement international obligations. The following amendment rules were made during the current interval:

*Part 1: Definitions and Abbreviations Amendment 2018 (Amendment 54)*
This rule amends *Civil Aviation Rules* pt 1, which sets out the definitions and abbreviations used in these rules. It implements aspects of the *Convention on International Civil Aviation* (1944), the *Agreement between the Australian and New Zealand Governments on Mutual Recognition of Aviation-Related Certification* (2007), and the International Civil Aviation Organization's ("ICAO") *Technical Instructions for the Safe Transport of Dangerous Goods by Air*. The amendments provide new definitions and abbreviations related to amendment 30 to pt 91.

*Part 12: Accidents, Incidents, and Statistics Amendment 2017 (Amendment 10)*
This rule amends *Civil Aviation Rules* pt 12, which prescribes rules for: notification, investigation, and reporting of accidents and incidents; preservation of aircraft, aircraft contents, and aircraft records following an accident or serious accident; and reporting of aircraft operating and statistical data. It implements aspects of the *Convention on International*

*Civil Aviation* (1944). The amendments introduce a requirement for freight-only operators to provide data to the Civil Aviation Authority of New Zealand ("CAA") showing the tonnage of freight carried by the operator.

*Part 66: Air Traffic Services Personnel Licences and Ratings Amendment 2018 (Amendment 6)*

This rule amends *Civil Aviation Rules* pt 66, which prescribes the rules governing the issue of aircraft maintenance licences, certificates, and ratings, and the privileges and limitations of those licences, certificates, and ratings. It implements aspects of the *Convention on International Civil Aviation* (1944). The amendments are consequential ones resulting from amendment 30 to pt 91.

*Part 91: General Operating and Flight Rules Amendment 2018 (Amendment 30)*

This rule amends *Civil Aviation Rules* pt 91, which forms the basis of general operating and flight rules for the New Zealand aviation environment. It implements aspects of the *Convention on International Civil Aviation* (1944) and the ICAO's *Technical Instructions for the Safe Transport of Dangerous Goods by Air*. The amendments provide for the transition from secondary surveillance radar to Automatic Dependent Surveillance Broadcast ("ADS-B") OUT as the primary source of data for surveillance in New Zealand.

*Part 125: Air Operations – Medium Aeroplanes Amendment 2017 (Amendment 22)*

This rule amends *Civil Aviation Rules* pt 125, which prescribes the operating requirements for air operations conducted by a holder of an Airline Air Operator Certificate. It implements aspects of the ICAO's *Technical Instructions for the Safe Transport of Dangerous Goods by Air*. The amendments enable a performance-based set of options for determining landing distance calculation procedures and requires certain passenger operations to have sufficient electrical supply to land safely in an emergency.

*Part 129: Foreign Air Transport Operations – Certification Amendment 2018 (Amendment 8)*

This rule amends *Civil Aviation Rules* pt 129, which prescribes the operating requirements for air operations conducted by a holder of an Airline Air Operator Certificate. It implements the *Convention on International Civil Aviation* (1944) and the *Agreement between the Australian and New Zealand Governments on Mutual Recognition of Aviation-Related*

*Certification* (2007). The amendments adopt part of ICAO's amendment 40 to *Convention on International Civil Aviation* (1944) pt 1 of Annex 6, relating to the location of aircraft in distress and the carriage of emergency locator transmitters ("ELTs") to give operators a choice of systems and a potential reduction in the number of ELTs to be carried on these international flights.

*Part 135: Air Operations – Helicopters and Small Aeroplanes Amendment 2017 (Amendment 23)*

This rule amends *Civil Aviation Rules* pt 135, which prescribes the operating requirements for air operations conducted by a holder of an airline air operator certificate or a general aviation air operator certificate. It implements aspects of the ICAO's *Technical Instructions for the Safe Transport of Dangerous Goods by Air*. The amendments enable a performance-based set of options for determining landing distance calculation procedures.

*Part 172: Air Traffic Service Organisations – Certification Amendment 2018 (Amendment 13)*

This rule amends pt 172 of the *Civil Aviation Rules*, which prescribes the certification requirements for the issue of an aviation document for organizations currently providing, or intending to provide, any air traffic service. It implements aspects of the *Convention on International Civil Aviation* (1944). The amendments are consequential ones resulting from amendment 30 to pt 91.

25   *Various Land Transport Rules*

Part 11 of the *Land Transport Act 1998* provides for the making of rules with respect to various aspects of land transport. Many of these rules incorporate international standards or implement international obligations. None of the amendments made during the current interval affected New Zealand's international obligations.

26   *Various Marine Protection Rules*

Section 386(1) of the *Maritime Transport Act 1994* provides for the making of rules for the purposes of implementing New Zealand's obligations under any marine protection convention, of enabling New Zealand to become a party to a convention, protocol or agreement relating to the protection of the marine environment, and of implementing international practices and standards relating to the protection of the marine environment that the International Maritime Organization recommends. The following rules were made during the current interval:

*Marine Protection Rules: Amendments to Ballast and Harmful Substances Provisions 2018*

Part 300 of the *Marine Protection Rules* implements aspects of the *Convention for the Control and Management of Ships' Ballast Water and Sediments* (2004) and the *Convention on the Law of the Sea* (1982). The amendments, among other things, clarify the instances when discharge of ballast water is permitted and when discharge of ballast water and sediment is harmful.

*Marine Protection Rules Various Amendments (Changes to related Conventions) 2017*

These amendments update *Marine Protection Rules* pts 100, 120, 121A, 121B, 122, 123B, 125, 130A, 140, 141, 142A, 142B, 143, and 170, which implement aspects of various international obligations, particularly those found in the *Convention for the Prevention of Pollution from Ships* (1973, as amended).

27  *Various Maritime Rules*

Section 36(1) of the *Maritime Transport Act 1994* provides for the making of rules for the purposes of the implementation of technical standards, codes of practice, performance standards and other requirements of certain conventions. Section 36(1)(u) of the Act provides for the making of rules for prescribing or providing for such matters as may be necessary to enable New Zealand to become a party to any international convention, protocol, or agreement relating to maritime transport as may be recommended by the International Maritime Organization. The following rule was made during the current interval:

*Maritime Rules Part 40 Series Amendment 2017*

This series of amendments amend *Maritime Rules* pts 40C, 40D, 40E, and 43 to improve safety outcomes, remove outdated and conflicting requirements, or reduce the cost of compliance. Part 40 and its brethren implement aspects of the *Convention for Safe Containers* (1972, as amended), the *Convention for the Prevention of Pollution from Ships* (1973, as amended), the *Convention for the Safety at Sea* (1974, as amended), the *Protocol Relating to the Torremolinos International Convention for the Safety of Fishing Vessels* (1993), and IMO Resolution A.706(17).

*Maritime Rules Various Amendments (Changes to related to Conventions) 2017*

These amendments update *Maritime Rules* pts 24C, 31, 32, 40B, 42A, and 46, which implement aspects of various international obligations, including those found in the *Convention on Standards of Training, Certification and Watchkeeping for Seafarers* (1978, as amended), the *Convention for the Safety of Life at Sea* (1974, as amended), the *Convention for the Prevention of Pollution from Ships* (1973, as amended), the *Convention for Safe Containers* (1972, as amended), the *Protocol relating to the Convention for the Safety of Life at Sea* (1978), the IMO's *Code of Safe Practice for Ships Carrying Timber Deck Cargoes*, the IMO's *Code of Safe Practice for Solid Bulk Cargoes*, and the IMO Assembly's Resolution A.1047(27) (Principles of Safe Manning).

## 4 Judicial Decisions Related to New Zealand's International Obligations

This Part sets out the reported and unreported judicial decisions rendered during the current interval that concern New Zealand's international obligations. It divides the reported cases into those cases reported in the New Zealand Law Reports ("NZLR") and those cases reported in other series. It also identifies the international agreements that were referenced and sets out the distribution of these references among the various courts.

### 4.1    *Reported Cases*
#### 4.1.1    NZLR Cases

*Attorney-General v Smith* [2018] 2 NZLR 899 (Court of Appeal): an *NZBORA* case that cites the *International Covenant on Civil and Political Rights* (1966) and the *European Convention for the Protection of Human Rights and Fundamental Freedoms* (1950).

*Brown v New Zealand Basing Ltd* [2018] 1 NZLR 245 (Supreme Court): an employment law case that cites the *Convention on the Law Applicable to Contractual Obligations* (1980).

*Chamberlain v Minister of Health* [2018] 2 NZLR 771 (Court of Appeal): a social security case that cites the *Convention on the Rights of Persons with Disabilities* (2006) and the *Optional Protocol to the Convention on the Rights of Persons with Disabilities* (2006).

*Chatfield & Co Ltd v Commissioner of Inland Revenue* [2018] 2 NZLR 385 (High Court): an administrative law case that cites the *Vienna Convention on the Law of Treaties* (1969).

*Chief Executive of New Zealand Customs Service v DB Breweries Ltd* [2017] 3 NZLR 613 (Court of Appeal): a revenue and customs case that cites the *General Agreement on Tariffs and Trade* (1947).

*Chisnall v Chief Executive, Dept of Corrections* [2018] 1 NZLR 83 (Supreme Court): a criminal practice and procedure case that cites the *International Covenant on Civil and Political Rights* (1966).

*Durie v Gardiner* [2018] 3 NZLR 131 (Court of Appeal): a defamation case that cites the *European Convention for the Protection of Human Rights and Fundamental Freedoms* (1950).

*Fahey v R* [2018] 2 NZLR 392 (Court of Appeal): a criminal law case that cites the *International Covenant on Civil and Political Rights* (1966).

*Hartono v Minister for Primary Industries* [2018] 1 NZLR 857 (Supreme Court): a fisheries case that cites the *United Nations Convention on the Law of the Sea* (1982) and the *International Convention relating to the Arrest of Seagoing Ships* (1952).

*Kim v Minister of Justice* [2017] 3 NZLR 823 (High Court): an extradition case that cites the *International Covenant on Civil and Political Rights* (1966), the *United Nations Convention against Torture and Other Cruel, Inhuman or Degrading Treatment or Punishment* (1984), the *United Nations Convention on the Rights of the Child* (1989), and the *European Convention for the Protection of Human Rights and Fundamental Freedoms* (1950).

*King v Attorney-General* [2017] 3 NZLR 556 (High Court): a tort law case that cites the *International Covenant on Civil and Political Rights* (1966).

4.1.2     Cases Reported in Other Series that Reference International Obligations

*AA (Zimbabwe) v Refugee and Protection Order* [2018] NZHC 2523: a refugee law case that cites the *United Nations Convention relating to the Status of Refugees* (1951), the *International Covenant on Civil and Political Rights* (1966), and the *United Nations Convention against Torture and Other Cruel, Inhuman or Degrading Treatment or Punishment* (1984).

*AH v Immigration and Protection Tribunal* [2017] NZHC 1880: a deportation case that cites the *United Nations Convention relating to the Status of Refugees* (1951), the *International Covenant on Civil and Political Rights* (1966), the *United Nations Convention against Torture and Other Cruel, Inhuman or Degrading Treatment or Punishment* (1984), and the *United Nations Convention on the Rights of the Child* (1989).

*Allen v Wade* [2017] NZFC 5189: a family law case that cites *The Hague Convention on the Civil Aspects of International Child Abduction* (1980).

*AR v Immigration and Protection Tribunal* [2017] NZAR 1524 (High Court): a refugee law case that cites the *United Nations Convention relating to the Status of Refugees* (1951).

*Attorney-General v Taylor* [2017] NZSC 104: an *NZBORA* case that cites the *International Covenant on Civil and Political Rights* (1966), the *Optional Protocol to the International Covenant on Civil and Political Rights* (1966), and the *European Convention for the Protection of Human Rights and Fundamental Freedoms* (1950).

*Awatere v R* [2018] NZHC 883: a criminal law case that cites the *European Convention for the Protection of Human Rights and Fundamental Freedoms* (1950).

*AX (Afghanistan) v Immigration and Protection Tribunal* [2017] NZHC 2840: a refugee law case that cites the *United Nations Convention relating to the Status of Refugees* (1951), the *International Covenant on Civil and Political Rights* (1966), and the *United Nations Convention against Torture and Other Cruel, Inhuman or Degrading Treatment or Punishment* (1984).

*AX (Afghanistan) v Immigration and Protection Tribunal* [2018] NZHC 52: a costs application that cites the *United Nations Convention relating to the Status of Refugees* (1951).

*AX (Afghanistan) v Immigration and Protection Tribunal* [2018] NZCA 290: a refugee law case cites the *United Nations Convention relating to the Status of Refugees* (1951), the *International Covenant on Civil and Political Rights* (1966), and the *Universal Declaration of Human Rights* (1948).

*Azoulay v Nelson* [2017] NZFC 7713: a family law case that cites *The Hague Convention on the Civil Aspects of International Child Abduction* (1980).

*Bahri v Adoption Services* [2017] NZFC 8164: a family law case that cites *The Hague Convention on Protection of Children and Co-operation in Respect of Intercountry Adoption* (1980).

*Balajadia v R* [2018] NZCA 483: a criminal law case that cites the *United Nations Declaration of Basic Principles for Victims of Crime and Abuse of Power* (1985).

*BC (Philippines) v Immigration and Protection Tribunal* [2018] NZHC 2722: a refugee law case that cites the *United Nations Convention relating to the Status of Refugees* (1951), the *International Covenant on Civil and Political Rights* (1966), and the *United Nations Convention against Torture and Other Cruel, Inhuman or Degrading Treatment or Punishment* (1984).

*BD (India) v Legal Aid Tribunal* [2018] NZHC 2542: an appeal from a decision of the Legal Aid Tribunal that cites the *United Nations Convention relating to the Status of Refugees* (1951).

*Benjamin Morland Easton v New Zealand Police* [2018] NZCA 411: a practice and procedure case (application for leave to bring second appeal against conviction and sentence) that cites the *Universal Declaration of Human Rights* (1949).

*Biggs v Biggs* [2017] NZHC 3170: a civil procedure case that cites the *United Nations Convention on the Rights of the Child* (1989).

*BP v Refugee and Protection Officer* [2017] NZHC 3529: a refugee law case that cites the *International Covenant on Civil and Political Rights* (1966).

*BP (South Africa) v Refugee and Protection Officer* [2017] NZHC 3259: a practice and procedure case (application for leave to appeal, or for judicial review of, immigration and refugee decision) that cites the *International Covenant on Civil and Political Rights* (1966).

*BR (Bangladesh) v Chief Executive of the Ministry of Business, Innovation and Employment* [2018] NZCA 267: an immigration and refugee law case that cites the *United Nations Convention relating to the Status of Refugees* (1951).

*Brook Valley Community Group Inc v The Trustees of the Brook Waimarama Sanctuary Trust* [2018] NZRMA 51 (High Court): a resource management case that cites the *Convention on Biological Diversity* (1992).

*Cavanagh v Cavanagh* [2017] NZFLR 701 (High Court): a family law case that cites the *International Covenant on Civil and Political Rights* (1966) and the *United Nations Convention on the Rights of the Child* (1989).

*Chamberlain v Attorney-General* [2017] NZAR 1271 (High Court): a judicial review that cites the *United Nations Convention on the Rights of Persons with Disabilities* (2006) and the *International Covenant on Civil and Political Rights* (1966).

*Chief Executive of the Minister of Business, Innovation and Employment v Singh* [2018] NZAR 434 (High Court): an immigration law case that cites the *United Nations Convention on the Rights of the Child* (1989).

*Chord v Commissioner of Police* [2017] NZDC 18584: a criminal law case that cites the *International Covenant on Civil and Political Rights* (1966).

*CO v Chief Executive, Ministry of Business Innovation and Employment (MBIE)* [2018] NZHC 442: a judicial review case that cites the *International Covenant on Civil and Political Rights* (1966) and the *International Covenant on Economic, Social and Cultural Rights* (1966).

*COL v LRR* [2018] NZHC 2902: a family law case that cites *The Hague Convention on the Civil Aspects of International Child Abduction* (1980).

*Crockett v Accident Compensation Corporation* [2018] NZACC 11 (District Court): an accident compensation case that cites *United Nations Convention on the Rights of Persons with Disabilities* (2006).

*Crockett v Accident Compensation Corporation* [2018] NZHC 2432: an accident compensation case that cites the *United Nations Convention on the Rights of Persons with Disabilities* (2006).

*Cunliffe v Marsh* [2018] NZHC 948: an application for an interlocutory injunction that cites the *United Nations Convention on the Rights of the Child* (1989).

*DB Breweries Ltd v Chief Executive of New Zealand Customs Service* [2017] NZSC 156: a revenue and customs case that cites the *General Agreement on Tariffs and Trade* (1947).

*Dean v Associate Minister of Immigration* [2018] NZHC 2455: an administrative law case that cites the *International Covenant on Civil and Political Rights* (1966) and the *International Covenant on Economic, Social and Cultural Rights* (1966).

*Dennis v Chief Executive of Ministry of Business, Innovation and Employment* [2018] NZHC 2169: an application for judicial review that cites the *United Nations Convention on the Rights of the Child* (1989).

*Department of Corrections v Thorpe* [2017] NZHC 2559: a sentencing case (application for an extended supervision order) that cites the *International Covenant on Civil and Political Rights* (1966).

*Devi v Chief Executive Officer of the of Ministry of Business, Innovation and Employment* [2018] NZHC 362: an immigration law case that cites the *United Nations Convention on the Rights of the Child* (1989).

*Dickson-Johansen v Accident Compensation Corporation* [2018] NZACC 36 (District Court): an application for costs that cites the *United Nations Convention on the Rights of Persons with Disabilities* (2006).

*Dotcom v District Court at North Shore* [2018] NZCA 442: an extradition case that cites the *Treaty on Extradition between New Zealand and the United States of America* (1970)

*Easton v New Zealand Police* [2018] NZCA 411: an application for leave to appeal case that cites the *Universal Declaration of Human Rights* (1948).

*Eight Mile Style, LLC v New Zealand National Party* [2017] NZHC 2603: an intellectual property law case that cites the *Universal Copyright Convention* (1952).

*Re Family First New Zealand* [2018] NZHC 2273: a charity law case that cites the *Universal Declaration of Human Rights* (1948), the *International Covenant on Economic, Social and Cultural Rights* (1966), and the *United Nations Convention on the Rights of the Child* (1989).

*Gardiner v Chief Executive of the Department of Corrections* [2017] NZAR 1348 (High Court): a tort law case that cites the *International Covenant on Civil and Political Rights* (1966).

*Genge v Chief Executive, Dept of Corrections* [2018] NZHC 1447: a prisoners' rights case that cites the *International Covenant on Civil and Political Rights* (1966).

*Genge v Chief Executive, Dept of Corrections* [2018] NZHC 1827: a prisoners' rights case that cites the *United Nations Standard Minimum Rules for the Treatment of Prisoners* (1955).

*Genge v Visiting Justice at Christchurch Men's Prison* [2017] NZHC 3168: a prisoners' rights case that cites the *United Nations Standard Minimum Rules for the Treatment of Prisoners* (1955) and the *International Covenant on Civil and Political Rights* (1966).

*Genge v Visiting Justice at Christchurch Men's Prison* [2018] NZHC 1457: a prisoners' rights case that cites the *Universal Declaration of Human Rights* (1948) and the *International Covenant on Civil and Political Rights* (1966).

*Goundan v Immigration and Protection Tribunal* [2018] NZHC 1756 (High Court, Van Bohemen J): an immigration and refugee law case that cites the *International Covenant on Civil and Political Rights* (1966).

*Grande Meadow Developments Ltd v Clark Road Developments Ltd (No 2)* [2018] NZHC 1394: a civil procedure case that cites the *United Nations Commission on International Trade Law Model Law on International Commercial Arbitration* (1985).

*Green v White* [2018] NZHC 3249: a family law case that cites *The Hague Convention on the Civil Aspects of International Child Abduction* (1980).

*G v R* [2018] NZHC 2587: a family law case that cites the *United Nations Convention on the Rights of the Child* (1989).

*H v R* [2017] NZHC 2617: a family law case that cites *The Hague Convention on the Civil Aspects of International Child Abduction* (1980).

*H v Refugee and Protection Officer* [2017] NZAR 1518 (High Court): a refugee law case that cites the *United Nations Convention relating to the Status of Refugees* (1951) and the *Protocol relating to the Status of Refugees* (1967).

*H v Refugee and Protection Officer* [2018] NZCA 188: a refugee law case that cites the *United Nations Convention relating to the Status of Refugees* (1951), the *Protocol relating to the Status of Refugees* (1967), the *International Covenant on Civil and Political Rights* (1966), and the *United Nations Convention against Torture and Other Cruel, Inhuman or Degrading Treatment or Punishment* (1984).

*Haddock v Thames-Coromandel District Council* [2017] NZHC 1926: a land law case that cites the *Universal Declaration of Human Rights* (1948).

*Hai v Minister of Immigration and Border Protection* [2017] NZHC 2028: a deportation (leave to appeal) case that cites the *International Covenant on Civil and Political Rights* (1966), the *United Nations Convention on the Rights of the Child* (1989), and the *International Covenant on Economic, Social and Cultural Rights* (1966).

*Harrison v Chief Executive, Ministry of Social Development* [2017] NZHC 2041: an administrative law case that cites the *United Nations Convention on the Rights of Persons with Disabilities* (2006).

*Heinz Wattie's Ltd v Ministry of Business, Innovation and Employment* [2018] NZAR 1613 (High Court): an administrative law case that cites the *Agreement on Trade-Related Aspects of Intellectual Property Rights* (1994).

*Henry v Minister of Justice* [2018] NZHC 2831: an application for judicial review that cites the *United Nations Principles relating to the Status of National Institutions* (1993).

*IA v RRN* [2017] NZFLR 659 (High Court): a family law case that cites the *United Nations Convention on the Rights of the Child* (1989).

*J v Attorney-General* [2018] NZHC 1209: a social security case that cites the *International Covenant on Civil and Political Rights* (1966) and the *United Nations Convention on the Rights of Persons with Disabilities* (2006).

*Jeffries v Chief Executive of the Department of Corrections* [2018] NZCA 272: a sentencing case that cites the *European Convention for the Protection of Human Rights and Fundamental Freedoms* (1950).

*Kamo v Minister of Conservation* [2018] NZAR 1334 (High Court): an NZBORA case that cites the *International Covenant on Civil and Political Rights* (1966).

*Kelly v Police* [2017] NZHC 1611: an evidence case that cites the *International Covenant on Civil and Political Rights* (1966).

*Kruger v Winkel* [2017] 31 FRNZ 268 (Family Court): a family law case that cites *The Hague Convention on the Civil Aspects of International Child Abduction* (1980) and the *United Nations Convention on the Rights of the Child* (1989).

*Kumar v Immigration and Protection Tribunal* [2018] NZHC 2928: a deportation (leave to appeal) case that cites the *International Covenant on Civil and Political Rights* (1966) and the *United Nations Convention on the Rights of the Child* (1989).

*Langdon v Wyler* [2017] NZHC 2535: a family law case that cites *The Hague Convention on the Civil Aspects of International Child Abduction* (1980).

*Li v Chief Executive of the Ministry of Business, Innovation and Employment* [2018] NZAR 265: (High Court): a judicial review (deportation) case that cites the *International Covenant on Civil and Political Rights* (1966).

*Matua v Minister of Immigration* [2018] NZHC 2078: an immigration law case that cites *International Covenant on Civil and Political Rights* (1966).

*NZME Publishing Ltd v R* [2018] NZCA 363: a media law case that cites the *Convention on the Rights of the Child* (1990).

*Prescott v District Court* [2018] NZHC 485: an application for costs by lay litigant that cites the *International Covenant on Civil and Political Rights* (1966).

*Re Haden* [2018] NZDC 14986: an administrative law case that cites the *United Nations Convention against Corruption* (2003).

*SG v DSG* [2018] NZFLR 762 (High Court): a civil procedure case that cites *The Hague Convention on the Civil Aspects of International Child Abduction* (1980).

### 4.2 Unreported Cases

Owing to the advent of various electronic case law services and the timing of this publication, unreported judicial decisions rendered during the current interval that concern New Zealand's international obligations are rare. This interval has none.

4.3   *Distribution of References to International Agreements among Various Courts, NZLR Cases, Other Reported Cases, and Unreported Case*[15]

| *International obligations* | NZLR | *Other* | *Unrep* | *All* | *Total* |
|---|---|---|---|---|---|
| *International Covenant on Civil and Political Rights*, opened for signature 16 December 1966, 999 UNTS 171 (entered into force 23 March 1976) | SC:1<br>CA:2<br>HC:2 | SC:1<br>CA:2<br>HC:24<br>DC:1 | | SC:2<br>CA:4<br>HC:26<br>DC:1 | 33 |
| *Convention on the Rights of the Child*, opened for signature 20 November 1989, 1577 UNTS 3 (entered into force 2 September 1990) | HC:1 | CA:1<br>HC:12<br>FC:1 | | CA:1<br>HC:13<br>FC:1 | 15 |
| *Convention relating to the Status of Refugees*, signed 28 July 1951, 189 UNTS 137 (entered into force 22 April 1954) | | CA:3<br>HC:8 | | CA:3<br>HC:8 | 11 |
| *The Hague Convention on the Civil Aspects of International Child Abduction*, opened for signature 25 October 1980, 1343 UNTS 89 (entered into force 1 December 1983) | | HC:5<br>FC:3 | | HC:5<br>FC:3 | 8 |

15   Key: SC = Supreme Court, CA = Court of Appeal, HC = High Court, DC = District Court, FC = Family Court, * = New Zealand is not a party to this convention.

| International obligations | NZLR | Other | Unrep | All | Total |
|---|---|---|---|---|---|
| *European Convention for the Protection of Human Rights and Fundamental Freedoms*, signed 11 April 1950, 213 UNTS 221 (entered into force 3 September 1953) | CA: 2<br>HC: 1 | SC: 1<br>CA: 2<br>HC: 1 | | SC: 1<br>CA: 4<br>HC: 2 | 7 |
| *Universal Declaration of Human Rights*, GA Res 217A (III), UN GAOR, UN Doc A/810 (10 December 1948) | | CA: 3<br>HC: 3 | | CA: 3<br>HC: 3 | 6 |
| *Convention against Torture and Other Cruel, Inhuman or Degrading Treatment or Punishment*, opened for signature 10 December 1984, 1465 UNTS 85 (entered into force 26 June 1987) | HC: 1 | CA: 1<br>HC: 4 | | HC: 5<br>CA: 1 | 6 |
| *Optional Protocol to the Convention on the Rights of Persons with Disabilities*, opened for signature 30 March 2007, 2518 UNTS 283 (entered into force 3 May 2008) | CA: 1 | HC: 3<br>DC: 2 | | CA: 1<br>HC: 3<br>DC: 2 | 6 |
| *International Covenant on Economic, Social and Cultural Rights*, opened for signature 19 December 1966, 993 UNTS 3 (entered into force 3 January 1976) | | HC: 4 | | HC: 4 | 4 |

| International obligations | NZLR | Other | Unrep | All | Total |
|---|---|---|---|---|---|
| *Convention on the Rights of Persons with Disabilities*, opened for signature 30 March 2007, 2515 UNTS 3 (entered into force 3 May 2008) | CA: 1<br>HC: 1 | | | CA: 1<br>HC: 1 | 2 |
| *General Agreement on Tariffs and Trade*, signed 30 October 1947, 55 UNTS 194 (entered into force 1 January 1948) | CA: 1 | SC: 1 | | SC: 1<br>CA: 1 | 2 |
| *Protocol relating to the Status of Refugees*, opened for signature 31 January 1967, 606 UNTS 267 (entered into force 4 October 1967) | | CA: 1<br>HC: 1 | | CA: 1<br>HC: 1 | 2 |
| *Standard Minimum Rules for the Treatment of Prisoners*, ESC Res 663 C (XXIV) (31 July 1957, adopted 30 August 1955) | | HC: 2 | | HC: 2 | 2 |
| *Vienna Convention on the Law of Treaties*, signed 25 May 1969, 1155 UNTS 331 (entered into force 27 January 1980) | HC: 1 | | | HC: 1 | 1 |
| *United Nations Convention on the Law of the Sea*, signed 10 December 1982, 1833 UNTS 3 (entered into force 16 November 1994) | SC: 1 | | | SC: 1 | 1 |

# TREATY ACTION AND IMPLEMENTATION

| International obligations | NZLR | Other | Unrep | All | Total |
|---|---|---|---|---|---|
| *International Convention relating to the Arrest of Seagoing Ships*, signed 10 May 1952, 439 UNTS 193 (entered into force 24 February 1956) | SC: 1 | | | SC: 1 | 1 |
| *Optional Protocol to the International Covenant on Civil and Political Rights*, opened for signature 19 December 1966, 999 UNTS 171 (entered into force 23 March 1976) | | SC: 1 | | SC: 1 | 1 |
| *United Nations Declaration of Basic Principles for Victims of Crime and Abuse of Power*, GA Res 40/34, UN Doc A/RES/40/34 (29 November 1985) | | CA: 1 | | CA: 1 | 1 |
| *Convention on Biological Diversity*, opened for signature 5 June 1992, 1760 UNTS 79 (entered into force 29 December 1993) | | HC: 1 | | HC: 1 | 1 |
| *Convention on Protection of Children and Co-operation in respect of Intercountry Adoption*, opened for signature 29 May 1993, 32 ILM 1139 (entered into force 1 May 1995) | | FC: 1 | | FC: 1 | 1 |

| International obligations | NZLR | Other | Unrep | All | Total |
|---|---|---|---|---|---|
| *Treaty on Extradition between New Zealand and the United States of America*, signed 12 January 1970, 791 UNTS 253 (entered into force 8 December 1970) | | CA: 1 | | CA: 1 | 1 |
| *Universal Copyright Convention*, signed 6 September 1952, 216 UNTS 132 (entered into force 16 September 1955) | | HC: 1 | | HC: 1 | 1 |
| United Nations Commission on International Trade Law, UNCITRAL *Model Law on International Commercial Arbitration* (21 June 1985) | | HC: 1 | | HC: 1 | 1 |
| *Marrakesh Agreement Establishing the World Trade Organization*, opened for signature 15 April 1994, 1867 UNTS 3 (entered into force 1 January 1995) annex 1C ("*Agreement on Trade-Related Aspects of Intellectual Property Rights*") | | HC: 1 | | HC: 1 | 1 |
| *Principles relating to the Status of National Institutions*, GA Res 48/134, UN Doc A/RES/48/134 (20 December 1993) | | HC: 1 | | HC: 1 | 1 |

TREATY ACTION AND IMPLEMENTATION

| International obligations | NZLR | Other | Unrep | All | Total |
|---|---|---|---|---|---|
| United Nations Convention against Corruption, GA Res 58/4, UN Doc A/58/422 (14 December 2005, adopted 9 December 2003) | | DC: 1 | | DC: 1 | 1 |
| Convention on the Law Applicable to Contractual Obligations, [1980] OJ L 266/1 | SC: 1 | | | SC: 1 | 1 |
| Totals | 18 | 100 | 0 | 118 | 118 |

## 5 Update of Master List of Implementing Acts

This Part updates the master list of implementing Acts set out in Part 5 of "In Search of International Standards and Obligations Relevant to New Zealand Acts" (2007) 4 *New Zealand Yearbook of International Law* 366–93 (as amended).[16] The master list entries should be amended as follows:

### 5.1 New Entries
Add the following entries in their appropriate alphabetical order:

---

16  For previous amendments to the master list, see Mark Gobbi, "Treaty Action and Implementation" (2017) 15 *New Zealand Yearbook of International Law* 243, 293; Mark Gobbi, "Treaty Action and Implementation" (2016) 14 *New Zealand Yearbook of International Law* 311, 355; Mark Gobbi, "Treaty Action and Implementation" (2015) 13 *New Zealand Yearbook of International Law* 295, 335–336; Mark Gobbi, "Treaty Action and Implementation" (2014) 12 *New Zealand Yearbook of International Law* 247, 286; Mark Gobbi, "Treaty Action and Implementation" (2013) 11 *New Zealand Yearbook of International Law* 285, 326–328; Mark Gobbi, "Treaty Action and Implementation" (2012) 10 *New Zealand Yearbook of International Law* 261, 302–303; Mark Gobbi, "Treaty Action and Implementation" (2011) 9 *New Zealand Yearbook of International Law* 351, 386; Mark Gobbi, "Treaty Action and Implementation" (2010) 8 *New Zealand Yearbook of International Law* 283, 328–329; Mark Gobbi,

*Brokering (Weapons and Related Items) Control Act 2018*
Arms Trade Treaty (2013)
***Comprehensive and Progressive Agreement for Trans-Pacific Partnership Amendment Act 2018***
*Comprehensive and Progressive Agreement for Trans-Pacific Partnership* (2018)
***Outer Space and High-Altitude Activities Act 2017***
*Agreement between the Government of New Zealand and the Government of the United States of America on Technology Safeguards Associated with United States Participation in Space Launches from New Zealand Technology Safeguards Agreement* (2016)
*Convention on Registration of Objects Launched into Outer Space* (1975)

5.2    **Changes to Entries**
None

6    **Update of Master List of Implementing Regulations**

This Part updates the master list of implementing regulations set out in Part 5 of "In Search of International Standards and Obligations relevant to New Zealand Regulations" (2007–2008) 5 *New Zealand Yearbook of International Law* 327–72 (as amended).[17] The master list should be amended as follows:

[17] "Treaty Action and Implementation" (2009) 7 *New Zealand Yearbook of International Law* 381, 424–431; Mark Gobbi, "Treaty Action and Implementation" (2008) 6 *New Zealand Yearbook of International Law* 379, 418–420; Mark Gobbi, "Treaty Action and Implementation" (2007–2008) 5 *New Zealand Yearbook of International Law* 279, 326.

For previous amendments to the master list, see Mark Gobbi, "Treaty Action and Implementation" (2017) 15 *New Zealand Yearbook of International Law* 243, 296–300; Mark Gobbi, "Treaty Action and Implementation" (2016) 14 *New Zealand Yearbook of International Law* 311, 355–358; Mark Gobbi, "Treaty Action and Implementation" (2015) 13 *New Zealand Yearbook of International Law* 295, 336–339; Mark Gobbi, "Treaty Action and Implementation" (2014) 12 *New Zealand Yearbook of International Law* 247, 287–290; Mark Gobbi, "Treaty Action and Implementation" (2013) 11 *New Zealand Yearbook of International Law* 285, 328–332; Mark Gobbi, "Treaty Action and Implementation" (2012) 10 *New Zealand Yearbook of International Law* 261, 303–306; Mark Gobbi, "Treaty Action and Implementation" (2011) 9 *New Zealand Yearbook of International Law* 351, 386–389; Mark Gobbi, "Treaty Action and Implementation" (2010) 8 *New Zealand Yearbook of International Law* 283, 330–335; Mark Gobbi, "Treaty Action and Implementation" (2009) 7 *New Zealand Yearbook of International Law* 381, 425–431; Mark Gobbi, "Treaty Action and Implementation" (2008) 6 *New Zealand Yearbook of International Law* 379, 421–423.

## 6.1 New Entries

Add the following entries in their appropriate alphabetical order:

**Antarctica (Environmental Protection) Act (Schedule 2) Order 2018** *LI 2018/85*
*Antarctica (Environmental Protection) Act 1994* s 55(2)(a)
*Protocol on Environmental Protection to the Antarctic Treaty*, opened for signature 4 October 1991, 30 ILM 1455 (entered into force 14 January 1998)
**District Court (Access to Court Documents) Rules 2017** *2017/186*
*Criminal Procedure Act 2011* s 386(1); *District Court Act 2016* s 228
*Rome Statute of the International Criminal Court*, opened for signature 1998, 2187 UNTS 3 (entered into force 1 July 2002)
**Double Tax Agreements (*Multilateral Convention to Implement Tax Treaty Related Measures to Prevent Base Erosion and Profit Shifting*) Order 2018**
*Income Tax Act 2007* s BH 1
*Multilateral Convention to Implement Tax Treaty Related Measures to Prevent Base Erosion and Profit Shifting*, signed 7 June 2017, [2019] ATS 1 (entered into force 27 June 2018)
**Double Tax Agreements (San Marino) Order 2017** *2017/209*
*Income Tax Act 2007* s BH 1
*Agreement between the Government of New Zealand and the Government of the Republic of San Marino on the Exchange of Information with Respect to Taxes*, signed 1 April 2016 (entered into force 8 September 2017).
**Financial Markets Conduct (Overseas Custodians – Assurance Engagement) Exemption Notice 2018** *2018/9*
*Financial Advisers Act 2008* s 148
*Multilateral Memorandum of Understanding concerning Consultation and Cooperation and the Exchange of Information*, adopted May 2002
*Multilateral Memorandum of Understanding concerning Co-operation in the Exchange of Information for Audit Oversight*, adopted 30 June 2015
**Health and Safety at Work (Hazardous Substances) Regulations 2017** *LI 2017/131*
*Health and Safety at Work Act 2015* ss 211, 212, 213, 218
*UN Recommendations on the Transport of Dangerous Goods Model Regulations* (1999)
**Marine Protection Rules: Amendments to Ballast and Harmful Substances Provisions 2018**
*Maritime Transport Act 1994* s 386
*United Nations Convention on the Law of the Sea*, signed 10 December 1982, 1833 UNTS 3 (entered into force 16 November 1994)

*Convention for the Control and Management of Ships' Ballast Water and Sediments,* signed 13 February 2004 (entered into force 8 September 2007)
***Senior Courts (Access to Court Documents) Rules 2017 2017/193***
*Criminal Procedure Act 2011* s 386(1); *Senior Court Act 2016* s 148
*Rome Statute of the International Criminal Court,* opened for signature 1998, 2187 UNTS 3 (entered into force 1 July 2002)
***Tax Administration (Reportable Jurisdictions for Application of* CRS *Standard) Regulations 2017 2019/34***
*Tax Administration Act 1994* s 226D
Organisation for Economic Co-operation and Development, *Standard for Automatic Exchange of Financial Account Information in Tax Matters* (21 July 2014)
***United Nations Sanctions (Mali) Regulations 2018 2018/32***
*United Nations Act 1946* s 2
SC Res 2374, UN Doc S/RES/2374 (5 September 2017)

6.2     *Changes to Entries*

**Anti-Money Laundering and Countering Financing of Terrorism (Class Exemptions) Notice 2014 LI 2014/142**
Replace with the following item:

***Anti-Money Laundering and Countering Financing of Terrorism (Class Exemptions) Notice 2018 2018/101***
*Anti-Money Laundering and Countering Financing of Terrorism Act 2009* s 157(1)
Recommendations issued by the Financial Action Task Force (established in 1989) in the following report: Financial Action Task Force and Asia-Pacific Group on Money Laundering, *Anti-Money Laundering and Combating the Financing of Terrorism: New Zealand* (Mutual Evaluation Report, October 2009).

**Civil Aviation Rules 2007: Part 91**
Add the following item:

*Convention on International Civil Aviation,* signed 7 December 1944, 15 UNTS 295 (entered into force 4 April 1947) annex 18 (*"Technical Instructions for the Safe Transport of Dangerous Goods by Air"*)

**Customs Export Prohibition Order 2014 LI 2014/256**
Replace with the following item:

*Customs Export Prohibition Order 2017* 2017/213
    *Customs and Excise Act 1996* s 56
    *Treaty Banning Nuclear Weapon Tests in the Atmosphere, in Outer Space and Under Water*, signed 5 August 1963, 480 UNTS 43 (entered into force 10 October 1963)
    *Treaty on the Non-Proliferation of Nuclear Weapons*, signed 1 July 1968, 729 UNTS 161 (entered into force 5 March 1970)
    *Treaty on the Prohibition of the Emplacement of Nuclear Weapons and Other Weapons of Mass Destruction on the Sea-bed and the Ocean floor and in the Subsoil Thereof*, signed 11 February 1971, 955 UNTS 115 (entered into force 18 May 1972)
    *Convention on the Prohibition of the Development, Production and Stockpiling of Bacteriological (Biological) and Toxin Weapons and on their Destruction*, opened for signature 10 April 1972, 1015 UNTS 163 (entered into force 26 March 1975)
    *South Pacific Nuclear Free Zone Treaty*, signed 6 August 1985, 1445 UNTS 177 (entered into force 11 December 1986)
    *Convention on the Prohibition of the Development, Production, Stockpiling and Use of Chemical Weapons and on their Destruction*, opened for signature 13 January 1993, 1975 UNTS 45 (entered into force 29 April 1997)
    The order also prohibits the exportation of certain conventional weapons to countries subject to UN Security Council arms embargoes and regulations made under *United Nations Act 1946* s 2.

**Customs Export Prohibition (Toothfish) Order 2015** LI 2015/65
Replace with the following item:

*Customs Export Prohibition (Toothfish) Order 2018* LI 2018/58
    *Customs and Excise Act 1996* s 56
    *Convention on the Conservation of Antarctic Marine Living Resources*, opened for signature 1 August 1980, 1329 UNTS 47 (entered into force 7 April 1982)
    Commission for the Conservation of Antarctic Marine Living Resources, *Conservation Measure 170/VIII* (as amended)

**Customs Import Prohibition (Toothfish) Order 2015** 2015/64
Replace with the following item:

*Customs Import Prohibition (Toothfish) Order 2018* LI 2018/57
    *Customs and Excise Act 1996* s 54

*Convention on the Conservation of Antarctic Marine Living Resources*, opened for signature 1 August 1980, 1329 UNTS 47 (entered into force 7 April 1982)

Commission for the Conservation of Antarctic Marine Living Resources, *Conservation Measure 170/VIII* (as amended)

**Double Taxation Relief (India) Order 1986 SR 1986/336**
Add the following item:

*Third Protocol to the Convention between the Government of New Zealand and the Government of the Republic of India for the Avoidance of Double Taxation and the Prevention of Fiscal Evasion with Respect to Taxes on Income*, signed 26 October 2016 (entered into force 7 July 2017)

**Maritime Rule Part 40D: Amendment 2012**
Add the following item:

International Maritime Organization, *Resolution A.706(17): World-Wide Navigational Warning Service*, Doc No A 17/Res.706, 2 December 1991

**United Nations Sanction (Democratic People's Republic of Korea) Regulations 2006 SR 2006/382**
Replace with the following item:

*United Nations Sanctions (Democratic People's Republic of Korea) Regulations 2017 2017/74*
United Nations Act 1946 s 2
SR Res 1718, UN Doc S/RES/1718 (14 October 2006)
SR Res 1874, UN Doc S/RES/1874 (12 June 2009)
SR Res 2087, UN Doc S/RES/2087 (22 January 2013)
SR Res 2094, UN Doc S/RES/2094 (7 March 2013)
SR Res 2270, UN Doc S/RES/2270 (2 March 2016)
SR Res 2321, UN Doc S/RES/2321 (30 November 2016)
SR Res 2356, UN Doc S/RES/2356 (2 June 2017)
SR Res 2371, UN Doc S/RES/2371 (5 August 2017)
SR Res 2375, UN Doc S/RES/2375 (11 September 2017)
SR Res 2397, UN Doc S/RES/2397 (22 December 2017)

**United Nations Sanctions (Libya) Regulations 2011 SR 2011/77**
Replace with the following item:

*United Nations Sanctions (Libya) Regulations 2018* 2018/69
United Nations Act 1946 s 2
SR Res 1970, UN Doc S/RES/1970 (26 February 2011)
SR Res 1973, UN Doc S/RES/1973 (17 March 2011)
SR Res 2009, UN Doc S/RES/2009 (16 September 2011)
SR Res 2095, UN Doc S/RES/2095 (14 March 2013)
SR Res 2146, UN Doc S/RES/2146 (19 March 2014)
SR Res 2174, UN Doc S/RES/2174 (27 August 2014)
SR Res 2213, UN Doc S/RES/2213 (27 March 2015)
SR Res 2278, UN Doc S/RES/2278 (31 March 2016)
SR Res 2292, UN Doc S/RES/2292 (14 June 2016)
SR Res 2362, UN Doc S/RES/2362 (29 June 2017)


**United Nations Sanctions (Somalia) Regulations 1992 SR 1992/42**
Replace with the following item:

*United Nations Sanctions (Somalia) Regulations 2018* 2018/68
United Nations Act 1946 s 2
SR Res 733, UN Doc S/RES/733 (23 January 1992)
SR Res 1356, UN Doc S/RES/1356 (19 June 2001)
SR Res 1425, UN Doc S/RES/1425 (22 July 2002)
SR Res 1725, UN Doc S/RES/1725 (6 December 2006)
SR Res 1744, UN Doc S/RES/1744 (21 February 2007)
SR Res 1772, UN Doc S/RES/1772 (20 August 2007)
SR Res 1844, UN Doc S/RES/1844 (20 November 2008)
SR Res 2036, UN Doc S/RES/2036 (22 February 2012)
SR Res 2111, UN Doc S/RES/2111 (24 July 2013)
SR Res 2142, UN Doc S/RES/2142 (5 March 2014)
SR Res 2182, UN Doc S/RES/2182 (24 October 2014)
SR Res 2184, UN Doc S/RES/2184 (12 November 2014)
SR Res 2244, UN Doc S/RES/2244 (23 October 2015)
SR Res 2317, UN Doc S/RES/2317 (10 November 2016)
SR Res 2385, UN Doc S/RES/2385 (14 November 2017)


### Acknowledgements

The sterling research work of Kerran Cobb and Sam Collins, who gathered the material found in Parts 3 and 4, is gratefully acknowledged.

# Book Reviews

⁘

Margaret Bedggood, Kris Gledhill and Ian McIntosh (eds) *International Human Rights Law in Aotearoa New Zealand*. Thomas Reuters, 2017, 1060 pp ISBN: 9781988504292, 226.80 NZD + GST

Margaret Bedggood, Kris Gledhill and Ian McIntosh (along with 13 other authors) have created a significant piece of work. In this book, the authors collectively provide an overview of international human rights law and each chapter, to varying degrees, explores how such human rights frameworks have been implemented, or should be implemented, in New Zealand (NZ). Apart from a few select chapters, engagement with NZ law is seemingly light, often following lengthy discussion of *international* human rights frameworks. For some, this cursory treatment of the NZ system may reflect the reality of NZ's cursory implementation of international human rights norms, particularly of cultural and social rights. However, others may be left wanting. Because this book acts as a general text, it does not purport to make any particular argument. However, there are plenty of chapters which engage with current debates in relation to specific areas of human rights law, without firmly taking a position. Therefore, *International Human Rights Law in Aotearoa New Zealand* should be one's first point of call on the topics that it covers, and those topics are comprehensive.

This book is purposely split up into themes: Chapters 1–3 provide context and are a must-read for anyone teaching, researching or practicing in the area of human rights in NZ; Chapters 4–7 examine the relevant international legal frameworks; Chapters 8–16 explore specific classes of human rights; and, in the back half of the book, Chapters 17–20 discuss emerging rights.

Andrew Geddis opens the book with a philosophical discussion – where do human rights come from and why did the international framework develop the way that it did? Chapter 1 begins with the British, French and American revolutions. This of course ignores conceptions of human rights which developed outside of a western context; however, the focus of the book is on the international "human rights project" and its implementation in NZ. Due to the historical context of NZ, which was a British colony, it is arguably appropriate to limit discussion in this way (Mamari Stephens addresses part of this gap in Chapter 3). Nevertheless, Geddis does provide a light critique of the predominance of the western view of rights as applied universally throughout the chapter. This chapter explores the concepts of natural law and liberalism as the dominant philosophical underpinnings of the human rights project and further discusses the negative implications of the individualisation of human rights (such issues are picked up by other authors in later chapters). This chapter also tracks the historical development of the international human rights framework through various political and social struggles. These include abolition, women's suffrage, worker's rights and decolonisation after the two world wars. Geddis rounds out the chapter with an overview of the "three generations" of rights: political and civil rights; social and cultural rights; and collective development rights. The latter two categories are highlighted as being controversial in present day, particularly for NZ.

Keeping within the theme of contextualising, Chapter 2 explores the common law tradition in NZ and how this converges with the development (and implementation) of human rights. Paul Rishworth provides a brief overview of the constitutional history of NZ, addressing the fact that our legal system is inherited from Britain through colonialism and the implications of having an unwritten constitution on the role of the judiciary. Rishworth explains that the common law has been vital for human rights in NZ in various ways; for example, through checking the power of the executive, the interpretation of the *NZ Bill of Rights Act 1990* ("*NZBORA*") and the interpretation of principles derived from the *Treaty of Waitangi*. Although Rishworth notes poor implementation of social and cultural rights in NZ, the author is not altogether pessimistic and illustrates the potential importance of judicial review in enforcing such rights.

Mamari Stephens re-contextualises human rights in NZ through the lens of Māori jurisprudence in Chapter 3. The chapter is not framed within the question of how universal human rights can be applied to Māori communities; rather, the author frames discussion around the extent to which existing Māori values and practices may translate those rights. In what ways can universal human rights contribute to or develop tikanga Māori? This chapter takes time explaining the key concepts of Māori jurisprudence and the impact of colonialisation on these concepts: for example, whakapapa and whanaungatanga, mana, tapu and noa, tikanga and rangatiratanga. Stephens stresses the importance of the transferral of cultural knowledge for the survival of Māori jurisprudence (done through hui rūnanga). This chapter then explores the interrelationship between Māori thought and rights, and the relationship between Eurocentric human rights, specifically the universality of rights and state neutrality, and principles of Māori jurisprudence. Stephens then discusses the potential conflict and resolution between the two using illustrative scenarios. The chapter rounds out with an argument for a long-term solution to manage these tensions and avoid irreversible change or extinction of tikanga Māori.

The book then shifts from the context of NZ back to the international in Chapters 4–7. Natalie Baird introduces the international human rights framework in Chapter 4 with an overview of the United Nations ("UN") treaty system, the Human Rights Council and various regional human rights mechanisms. In Chapter 5, Claire Breen provides an introductory overview of the interrelationship between human rights and the law of armed conflict (and international criminal law). Following on from the historical discussions in Chapters 1 and 4, Breen explores the beginnings of human rights and international criminal law after World War II and the creation of the UN. This chapter then discusses the influence of human rights on the interpretation and application of international humanitarian law, particularly after the creation of the International Criminal Court. Chapter 5 ends with some comments on NZ's implementation of international criminal law and the law of armed conflict, noting that the newest international crime of aggression (contained in the *Kampala Amendments to the Rome Statute of the International Criminal Court*) has yet to be adopted into domestic law.

Chapter 6 surveys state obligations to implement and enforce human rights under the core international treaties: these include the *International Covenant on Civil and Political Rights*, *International Covenant on Economic, Social and Cultural Rights*, the *International Convention on the Elimination of All Forms of Racial Discrimination*, the *Convention on the Elimination of All forms of Discrimination against Women*, the *Convention on the Rights of the Child* and the *Convention on the Rights of Peoples with Disabilities*. Kris Gledhill identifies potential barriers to implementation and enforcement (for example, extraterritoriality) and provides an overview of remedies. This chapter then considers the extent to which NZ has implemented and enforced such rights domestically, examining the NZBORA, the *Human Rights Act 1993* ("HRA") and the role of the judiciary.

In Chapter 7, Breen and Margaret Bedggood outline the international rights to equality and non-discrimination and explain the extent to which these rights have been realised in NZ. This chapter is broken up by groups protected by international equality rights, which include: colour, race, nationality, ethnicity, or language; gender; age; migrant workers; disability; and sexual orientation. While noting that comprehensive anti-discrimination laws exist domestically (for example, under the HRA, the NZBORA and the work of the Human Rights Commission), significant gaps still exist, and these issues are made clear by the authors. Such issues and gaps include the prevailing oppression of Māori and Pasifika groups, the persistence of domestic abuse, child poverty, the continued exploitation of migrant workers (particularly on foreign flagged ships) and the lack of adequate protection of transgender people.

The next nine chapters discuss particular rights. These chapters follow the similar structural formula of: (a) outlining the international legal documents which govern these rights; (b) discussing the key concepts underpinning those rights; and then (c) explaining how these rights have been implemented in NZ (if at all). As a reference tool, this similar structure is useful in enabling the reader to find key information swiftly. The following provides a brief summation of these chapters.

Chapter 8 explores the fundamental rights: the right to life (or death) and the right to liberty and security of the person (covering torture, slavery, forced labour, and modern-day slavery). This chapter also reviews current gaps in NZ legislation; however, the authors are optimistic about the future development of these rights domestically.

Chapter 9 covers the links between human rights and refugee law. This chapter also examines the experience of refugees in NZ and, further, the negative impact of politicising refugees. Although the chapter ends on a hopeful note in regard to the UN General Assembly *Declaration for Refugees and Migrants* in 2016, recent events in NZ suggest continued politicisation and challenges ahead.[1]

Chapter 10 concerns a bundle of rights around privacy, autonomy and family life. Paul Roth explores the protection of familymarriage rights, and the various ways in which NZ protects individual privacy. This includes an in-depth discussion of mass surveillance and big data. Petra Butler explores democratic and political rights such as freedom of expression, the right to vote and freedom of assembly and association in Chapter 11. The right to a fair trial is examined in Chapter 12 which surveys, inter alia, the presumption of innocence, equality of arms and appeals in criminal trials. Chapter 13 outlines the labour movement and the solidification of workplace rights through the

---

1 Michelle Nichols, "UN Refugee Chief warns New Zealand Massacre the Result of Toxic Politics", *Reuters* (Web Page, 9 April 2019) <https://www.reuters.com/article/us-un-refugees-newzealand-shooting/u-n-refugee-chief-warns-new-zealand-massacre-the-result-of-toxic-politics-media-idUSKCN1RL28S>.

development and influence of the International Labour Organisation. This chapter is concerned with the right to work, the right to just and favourable working conditions and the rights to trade unions and social security. NZ's poor implementation of economic, social and cultural rights is specifically called out in Chapter 14, which concerns the right to an adequate standard of living. As well as examining "adequate standard of living" as a whole, the chapter breaks this topic down into separate rights to food, clothing, housing and health.

Chapter 15 analyses the right to culture, language and education. This chapter is unique here as it directly engages with the historical (colonial) context of NZ, not just the legal one, and, at well over 100 pages, is the most comprehensive. As well as outlining the relevant international frameworks, this chapter explores the varying influence that the *Treaty of Waitangi* has had across these three rights. However, the impact of the *Treaty of Waitangi* on the right to education has been one of policy only. Like Chapter 14, Mamari Stephens is explicit regarding the failure, and indeed reluctance, of NZ to implement these rights. Finally, Chapter 16 explores the rights of indigenous peoples. Claire Charters reviews the development of such rights and the scholarly disagreement concerning the influence of the individualisation of rights, which has been created from a solely western perspective, on the rights of indigenous peoples. This chapter also explores the *UN Declaration on the Rights of Indigenous Peoples* ("UNDRIP") and its relevance in NZ for Māori. Charters ends the chapter with a comment on the potential constitutional reforms required to fully implement such rights, including the possibility of a entrenching the *Treaty of Waitangi* under a written constitution.

The remaining chapters of the book offer insight into emerging issues in human rights that are of growing importance internationally as well as domestically. Chapter 17 provides an overview of the intersection between intellectual property ("IP") and human rights as well as the key scholarly tensions surrounding this topic. After explaining the interrelationship, Lida Ayoubi illustrates three ways in which the IP and human rights intersection is relevant in NZ: patents and the human rights to health (impact of the commercial incentive of patients to access to medicine); IP and mātauranga Māori (potential for appropriation of traditional knowledge and cultural expression); and copyright and access to books for the visually impaired.

Chapter 18 explores the role of human rights in maintaining international peace and security, with particular emphasis on (UN) peace operations and counter-terrorism. A key issue discussed regarding peace operations is the reach of human rights obligations extraterritorially. Claire Breen utilises NZ's contributions in Cambodia and Afghanistan peace operations as case studies to illustrate the influences of, and gaps in, human rights law. The chapter then turns to counter-terrorism and details the tension between human rights and the broad goals of counter-terrorism laws, particularly in NZ. Breen ends with a comment on current human rights fatigue in the face of global violence and the real concern of the erasure of human rights from peace and security measures.

Chapter 19 concerns environmental rights and examines the various arguments for their existence. Ceri Warnock explores the need for a rights-based approach to environmental management in NZ. With the threat of climate change looming, and in light of its expected future consequences for a small island nation such as NZ, this chapter is a must-read.[2] Lastly, Chapter 20 outlines the various issues relating to private international law and human rights. This chapter explores the circumstances in which NZ courts may breach international human rights obligations when they deny giving effect to foreign laws and judgments. Additionally, Maria Hook argues that private international law potentially conflicts with human rights obligations relating to access to justice. Although mostly optimistic about the state of NZ's legal framework regarding these issues, Hook examines notable limitations, such as the public policy exception to applying foreign laws and judgments and the doctrine of *forum (non) conveniens*.

The book lacks a concluding chapter, which may leave some readers feeling incomplete without a final discussion regarding where the editors see the future for NZ human rights law. However, as this is a reference book, rather than a collection of essays, it is perhaps more appropriate to leave these questions to individual chapters (subject to future editions).

At over 1000 pages, *International Human Rights Law in Aotearoa New Zealand* is certainly not a casual read. Instead, this book aims to be a resource for those "wishing to promote further and better utilisation of ... human rights standards". This book is thus recommended for academics (who research or teach human rights law), students, practitioners and policymakers. It will certainly be a much reached-for book in this academic's collection.

*Cassandra Mudgway*[*]

---

[2] See generally, Ministry for the Environment and Stats NZ, *Environment Aotearoa 2019* (April 2019).

[*] Lecturer, Auckland University of Technology Law School.

Hannah Harris *The Global Anti-Corruption Regime: The Case of Papua New Guinea*
[Routledge, 2019, xiii + 252 pp, ISBN 9781138298927 (hardback), 115 GBP]

Hannah Harris's path-breaking study explores the effectiveness of the global anti-corruption framework, and in particular the *United Nations Convention against Corruption* ("UNCAC"),[1] through a case study of Papua New Guinea ("PNG"). The book steers a path between two potentially conflicting realities. Harris understands that corruption is a complex concept that is easily hijacked for ulterior purposes by external state actors wishing to achieve their foreign policy and economic goals in developing countries like PNG. But she is also aware that graft and corruption are significant problems in PNG, as is recognised by both local civil society and government.

Harris's analysis rests heavily on Nadelmann and Andreas's[2] five-stage model for the evolution of global prohibition regimes (14): an initial stage during which the target activity is deemed legitimate, a de-legitimation stage, a dissemination stage and a criminalisation stage. In the final stage, the now-prohibited action is suppressed. In simple terms, Harris's thesis is that the global anti-corruption framework, at least as far as it operates in PNG, is stuck in fourth gear — it gets to criminalisation but never to suppression. The PNG case study is used to explore why this has occurred.

Before she does so, however, in Chapter one Harris engages in a well-theorised account of the evolution of the global anti-corruption system, leading to the development of the UNCAC. She is aware of the problem that constructing the crime of corruption through law constructs the social reality of corruption (28), and that there are intrinsic problems, which could bluntly be described as being of a neo-colonial kind, in the transfer of norms developed in metropolitan countries to countries like PNG. She notes that action against transnational crime in the South Pacific has largely been the result of the activities of more powerful neighbours seeking to protect themselves from the threat of crime emanating from island states, rather than a consequence of concern about the conditions in those states (32). Corruption may be different in that corrupting influences often come from metropolitan states and thus

---

[1] *United Nations Convention against Corruption*, opened for signature 9 December 2003, 2349 UNTS 41 (entered into force 14 December 2005).
[2] Ethan A Nadelmann, "Global Prohibition Regimes: The Evolution of Norms in International Society" (1990) 44(4) *International Organization* 479; Peter Andreas and Ethan Nadelmann, *Policing the Globe: Criminalization and Crime Control in International Relations* (Oxford University Press, 2006).

implicate potentially powerful individuals in those states. Undertaking a thorough survey of the literature, she shows a coalescence of ideas around four risk factors for the building of prohibition regimes (34): diversity among the target states, links to organised crime, an obsession with criminalisation as a solution to all problems and the limits of a universal and consistent approach. These disruptive factors produce enormous variance in prohibition regimes. Perhaps the most important research question she asks is how the expression of the anti-corruption regime in PNG — including the manifestation of these risk factors in different degrees — feeds back into insights in regard to UNCAC and the global anti-corruption regime (38).

The UNCAC itself is set out in Chapter 2 against the background of the theoretical framework set up in Chapter 1. The consensus that corruption is so threatening stands in nice opposition to the non-participation of Pacific states in the process of the development of the Convention (61). Her analysis of the treaty provisions themselves makes up the bulk of the chapter, in which she provides a useful concise guide to the treaty. Importantly she shows how the focus on criminalisation in the treaty was complemented in the first cycle of review, which focused on criminalisation and international cooperation (88).

Chapter 3 then shifts this tale of corruption and anti-corruption to the region, where Harris sets the regional scene in what constitutes a very informative introduction to those unfamiliar with the region. The asymmetry of the relationship between Australia and New Zealand, on the one hand, and the 15 island states who make up the other members of the Pacific Islands Forum, on the other, is highlighted. One striking fact is how corruption really only came onto the South Pacific agenda in parallel with the rise of the global anti-corruption regime (96) and yet is now paradoxically considered endemic, suggesting long-term entrenchment. Another factor which has increased global concern about corruption has been the significant increase in the flow of aid to the region. Anti-corruption is clearly linked to the development agenda. She sets out how the regional institutions have mediated between the UNCAC and states in the region. The net result is heavy external influence combined with poor local influence or interest (110). One unexplored question is how the nature of these regional institutions reflects, in itself, the hesitant nature of local compliance.

In Chapter 4 the book gets into the case study of PNG. In order to achieve fifth gear the UNCAC must achieve local support and enforcement across diverse contexts, and in this regard the incredible tribal, linguistic and political complexity of PNG provides perhaps the ultimate test for such a global prohibition regime. Harris shows how the legal response has been relatively sophisticated, at least on paper (131). She shows that even fourth gear is difficult to get into purely as a technical exercise of law on paper because of the staggering challenges that modern law-making faces in a place like PNG (144). Yet, when looked at more closely, the cracks begin to show. The debacle around the establishment and then disbandment of the anti-corruption "Task Force Sweep" by the Prime Minister, who was subject to its enquiries, is an object lesson in the limitations of the normative strength of anti-corruption measures in PNG (137).

Chapter 5 digs a little deeper, based on interviews of key local and foreign players in anti-corruption in PNG. There is too much here to summarise in this review, but Harris does illustrate comprehensively that UNCAC has had limited actual impact (155). Personally, I found the transformation of the hard legal nature of the obligations in the minds of local and United Nations officials into a soft policy document particularly interesting because of what it says about the nature of these large framework treaties when seen from the national perspective (157). But sometimes the story is one of simple non-enforcement, predatory foreign investment, lack of political will, turf wars among law enforcement agents, lack of cooperation.... It's a familiar tale. Harris draws from this the insight that critics of prohibition regimes should not overestimate the impact of these regimes at a national level; indeed, these hard-edged international norms appeared to defuse under local conditions, pointing to the obvious but difficult-to-answer question: is this softness a result of local flexibility or local defection?

Chapter 6 further explores the UNCAC in the context of the PNG case study, by bringing back the theoretical framework she introduced in Chapter one. Although it is challenging to synthesise the many different views into a single point of view, Harris characterises UNCAC as playing a supporting role rather than a central role in the fight against corruption in PNG and suggests that perhaps globally, it is a flexible framework leading to diverse interpretations at the national level.

Overall Harris provides readers interested in anti-corruption with a rich and detailed story which makes a significant contribution to the existing literature. She has gathered material from a range of available sources to give a nuanced picture of the operation of UNCAC in PNG. Refreshingly, she does not become obsessed with failure, unlike many foreign critics of PNG. Getting stuck in fourth gear is a common problem for prohibition regimes like that used against corruption. They face two challenges: the appearance of adherence and the non-reality of that adherence, on the one hand, and the fact that actual reform is inappropriate to the domestic context, on the other. For Harris, treaty frameworks such as the UNCAC are powerful tools, but they must engage in a dynamic way with the local context. Harris drives home the point that only if they gain and maintain local legitimacy and avoid co-optation by external political actors or manipulation by local corrupt governments will they ever get out of fourth into fifth.

*Neil Boister**

---

\* Professor and Head of School of Law, University of Canterbury, New Zealand.

Harmen van der Wilt & Christophe Paulussen (eds) *Legal Responses to Transnational and International Crimes: Toward an Integrative Approach*. [Edward Elgar Publishing, 2017, 336 pp, ISBN 9781786433985, 90 GBP]

This book brings together a blue-ribbon assortment of international law scholars, all of whom work at the interesting and troubled cross-roads which is the book's substantive subject matter: namely, the intersection of international and transnational crime, and thus of its legal fields of study (international criminal law ("ICL") and transnational criminal law ("TCL")). Through 14 essays on a variety of topics, they tackle different skeins of what they identify (in my view, correctly) as the most pressing practical and analytical point regarding crime that is internationalised in any way. This point is that, through the forces and trends which gave rise to globalisation, crime in the early 21st century is becoming more vertically and horizontally integrated than ever before, on a global scale.

It is a most timely discussion. For those in criminal law-making and enforcement – and those who study it – it is difficult to overstate the importance of this development. This is not just a matter of magnification of "classic" organised crime gangs which diversify their operations through fraud, prostitution, illegal gambling, etc., but rather a massive expansion in fluidity of organization and operational flexibility. The convergence is as startling as it is logical: rebel groups who fund attacks on civilian populations via trafficking in wildlife parts, minerals, and humans, enlisting the assistance of organised gangs; terrorist attacks carried out by specialist cybercrime flotillas; and gangland chieftains in one state who use piracy-generated booty to corrupt public officials in a second state, with profits laundered in a third.

This 21st-century crime operates within an international legal system still tied to practically impervious adherence to the territorial sovereignty of states, whose members adhere to localised (even parochial) notions of what constitutes crime and how it should be combatted, and where efforts at international cooperation are silo-ised, lopsided and incomplete. And as co-editor Christophe Paulussen's foreword notes, the friction and frustration created has come to the attention of various United Nations ("UN") agencies and other international bodies, which are sounding the alarm regarding the nexus between organised crime and terrorism in particular.[1] Indeed, as this book

---

[1] Christophe Paulussen, "Preface" in Harmen van der Wilt and Christophe Paulussen (eds), *Legal Responses to Transnational and International Crimes: Toward an Integrative Approach* (Edward Elgar Publishing, 2017) ix–xi.

review was being prepared, the UN Security Council issued a resolution that, while nominally focused on the convergence of organised crime and terrorism, is practically a manifesto calling on states to implement and integrate the interstate cooperative machinery already in place to address a host of transnational crimes.[2]

As Professor van der Wilt explains in the masterfully-written thematic first chapter, the transnational nexus and integration of crime demands a fresh conversation around a new set of questions. The central inquiry of that conversation, at least in this collection, is whether states should take an "integrative approach"[3] that throws down the distinction between international crimes and transnational crimes, and which reforms the distinction between supranational and domestic enforcement mechanisms in a way that allows for the most practical and efficacious use of both. In terms of the collection of essays itself, Professor van der Wilt captures its contours quite accurately:

> A number of the chapters address specific crimes and investigate whether these crimes would qualify to be "upgraded" to a supranational level of law enforcement. Other contributors have reflected more generally on the pros and cons of the direct and indirect enforcement model in relation to the special nature of transnational crimes. The reader should not expect a clear-cut and commonly held conclusion. Apart from reflecting personal preferences, the chapters demonstrate that "the most appropriate solution" may differ from crime to crime. The objective of this work is rather to increase our understanding of the ways in which crime and criminal law enforcement are interrelated.[4]

It is first interesting to note that, in proposing as their starting point that the lines may be blurring between international criminal law *stricto sensu* and transnational criminal law, the authors in this collection begin (more or less) from the proposition that the two are analytically and practically distinct from each other. This is an entirely defensible and correct proposition, though it is

---

2   SC Res 2482, UN SCOR, 8582nd mtg, UN Doc S/RES/2482 (19 July 2019).
3   Harmen van der Wilt, "Legal Responses to Transnational and International Crimes: Towards an Integrative Approach?" in Harmen van der Wilt and Christophe Paulussen (eds), *Legal Responses to Transnational and International Crimes: Toward an Integrative Approach* (Edward Elgar Publishing, 2017) 3.
4   Ibid 5.

certainly one of fairly recent vintage[5] as it rests largely on the 21st-century work of Professor Neil Boister, the doyen of transnational criminal law.[6] Boister's contribution here is a chapter entitled "Responding to Transnational Crime: the Distinguishing Features of Transnational Criminal Law",[7] in which he sketches out the various characteristics and systemic implements of TCL as well as pointing out its travails in the areas of coherence and legitimacy.

Boister is also the first author (in terms of the chapters' numerical order) to launch a considered view on one of the central questions that seems to occupy several of the authors in this volume: should some transnational crimes be added to the subject matter jurisdiction of the International Criminal Court ("ICC")? This idea, which permeates the ICL literature, receives, in my view, an appropriate amount of cold water thrown over it by Boister, who posits that the incoherence of the TCL order can only work mischief if parts of it are transplanted into the fairly constrained and politically contentious ICC regime.[8] In fact, while this is very much a personal view, not enough cold water is thrown over this question in the collection, as in light of the expensive, top-heavy nature and limited effectiveness of the ICC it should be viewed as a dead letter already. The authors who do deal with it are both cautious and skeptical as to how it should be answered. In Chapter 5,[9] Inez Braber constructs a careful and nuanced argument for inclusion of terrorism within the subject matter jurisdiction of the ICC that explicitly responds to arguments to the contrary, while in Chapter 10[10] Dirk van Leeuwen makes a cautious and principled argument

---

5    On this point, I am in respectful disagreement with Professor van der Wilt, whose survey in his chapter proposes a case for TCL as a field having coalesced earlier: ibid 4.
6    See Neil Boister, *An Introduction to Transnational Criminal Law* (Oxford University Press, 2nd ed, 2018).
7    Neil Boister, "Responding to Transnational Crime: the Distinguishing Features of Transnational Criminal Law" in Harmen van der Wilt and Christophe Paulussen (eds), *Legal Responses to Transnational and International Crimes: Toward an Integrative Approach* (Edward Elgar Publishing, 2017) 27.
8    Ibid 44–45.
9    Inez Braber, "Terrorism as a New Generation Transnational Crime: Prosecuting Terrorism at the International Criminal Court" in Harmen van der Wilt and Christophe Paulussen (eds), *Legal Responses to Transnational and International Crimes: Toward an Integrative Approach* (Edward Elgar Publishing, 2017) 92.
10   Dirk van Leeuwen, "Prosecuting Money Laundering at the ICC: Can it Stop the Funding of International Criminal Organisations?" in Harmen van der Wilt and Christophe Paulussen (eds), *Legal Responses to Transnational and International Crimes: Toward an Integrative Approach* (Edward Elgar Publishing, 2017) 181.

against such upgrading for the crime of money laundering. Alejandro Chehtman takes on[11] a more substance-oriented branch of the inquiry: should terrorism be considered an international crime? His answer: sometimes, specifically when state authorities are involved and domestic enforcement machinery will necessarily be inadequate. Héctor Olásalo[12] and Guilio Nessi[13] provide similar takes on organised crime and corruption, respectively.

The other essays in the collection represent a mixed bag of perspectives on various aspects of a central question: how should we understand transnational and international crime, and how do we enforce against it? On the topic of cybercrime, for example, Professor Ilias Bantekas[14] takes a fascinating deep dive into the dissonance between how cybercrime offences are framed from a substantive and law enforcement point of view, and how data and technological infrastructure are actually manifest in the physical world, while Nicolò Bussolati[15] uses the example of politically-motivated cyberattacks to explore transnational and domestic European cybercrime suppression efforts. Marta Bo[16] comes squarely at the classification question as regards piracy, concluding that it is a transnational rather than international crime and proposing regional enforcement mechanisms as an effective means of suppression.

---

11  Alejandro Chehtman, "Terrorism and the Conceptual Divide between International and Transnational Criminal Law" in Harmen van der Wilt and Christophe Paulussen (eds), *Legal Responses to Transnational and International Crimes: Toward an Integrative Approach* (Edward Elgar Publishing, 2017) 107.

12  Héctor Olásalo, "Is International Criminal Law an Appropriate Mechanism to Deal with Organized Crime in a Global Society?" in Harmen van der Wilt and Christophe Paulussen (eds), *Legal Responses to Transnational and International Crimes: Toward an Integrative Approach* (Edward Elgar Publishing, 2017) 50.

13  Guilio Nessi, "Transnational Prosecution of Grand Corruption and Its Discontent" in Harmen van der Wilt and Christophe Paulussen (eds), *Legal Responses to Transnational and International Crimes: Toward an Integrative Approach* (Edward Elgar Publishing, 2017) 168.

14  Ilias Bantekas, "Cybercrime and Its Sovereign Spaces: an International Law Perspective" in Harmen van der Wilt and Christophe Paulussen (eds), *Legal Responses to Transnational and International Crimes: Toward an Integrative Approach* (Edward Elgar Publishing, 2017) 128.

15  Nicolo Bussolati, "Domestic and International Legal Approaches to the Repression of Politically Motivated Cyber-Attacks" in Harmen van der Wilt and Christophe Paulussen (eds), *Legal Responses to Transnational and International Crimes: Toward an Integrative Approach* (Edward Elgar Publishing, 2017) 146.

16  Marta Bo, "Piracy at the Intersection between International and National: Regional Enforcement of a Transnational Crime" in Harmen van der Wilt and Christophe Paulussen (eds), *Legal Responses to Transnational and International Crimes: Toward an Integrative Approach* (Edward Elgar Publishing, 2017) 71.

The latter point is also picked up by Professor Charles Jalloh,[17] who provides a useful account of the subject matter jurisdiction of the new criminal chamber of the African Court of Justice and Human and People's Rights – "the first regional criminal court to be contemplated anywhere in the world".[18] Exploring established typologies of international and transnational crimes and analysing the African court's offences in light of them, Jalloh challenges their usefulness in the African context and briefly proposes a more nuanced approach allowing offences to escape their silos – "permeability", in his view, being a good thing.[19] Regionality is also the theme of the chapter by Sander Wirken and Hanna Bosdriesz,[20] who examine criminalised and state-sponsored violence in Mexico and the Northern Triangle, criticizing traditional ICL as being "of limited relevance"[21] to such problems and examining localised and regional responses that emphasise the enforcement of human rights norms.

Most welcome to this reader are two pieces on the protection (or lack thereof) of the procedural and civil rights of defendants within international and transnational criminal processes, a pressing but most neglected topic. Maria Laura Ferioli[22] examines defendant rights within the ICC system against the overall backdrop of the protection of human rights in transnational criminal cooperation processes, while Professor Sabine Gless[23] provides a new chapter in her brilliant ongoing work[24] to conceptualise "the theoretical underpinnings

---

17   Charles Cherner Jalloh, "The Distinction between 'International' and 'Transnational' Crimes in the African Criminal Court" in Harmen van der Wilt and Christophe Paulussen (eds), *Legal Responses to Transnational and International Crimes: Toward an Integrative Approach* (Edward Elgar Publishing, 2017) 272.
18   Ibid 274.
19   Ibid 301.
20   Sander Wirken & Hanna Bosdriesz, "Privatisation and Increasing Complexity of Mass Violence in Mexico and Central America: Exploring Appropriate International Responses" in Harmen van der Wilt and Christophe Paulussen (eds), *Legal Responses to Transnational and International Crimes: Toward an Integrative Approach* (Edward Elgar Publishing, 2017) 245.
21   Ibid 246.
22   Maria Laura Ferioli, "Safeguarding Defendants' Rights in Transnational and International Cooperation" in Harmen van der Wilt and Christophe Paulussen (eds), *Legal Responses to Transnational and International Crimes: Toward an Integrative Approach* (Edward Elgar Publishing, 2017) 203.
23   Sabine Gless, "*Ne bis in idem* in an International and Transnational Criminal Justice Perspective – Paving the Way for an Individual Right?" in Harmen van der Wilt and Christophe Paulussen (eds), *Legal Responses to Transnational and International Crimes: Toward an Integrative Approach* (Edward Elgar Publishing, 2017) 220.
24   See, eg, Sabine Gless, "Transnational Cooperation in Criminal Matters and the Guarantee of a Fair Trial: Approaches to a General Principle" (2013) 9(4) *Utrecht Law Review* 90.

that can provide for an adequate and appropriate legal position of the individual facing prosecution"[25] in TCL matters. Contrasting the strong but limited protection in ICL for *ne bis in idem* (the right not to be tried twice for the same conduct) with the lack of a corresponding right in transnational cooperation, she advocates for its establishment as a firm principle of TCL in a powerful and principled way.

Even above all of its other salutary qualities, there is one pre-eminent reason to commend this book to readers (which I do), and that is its thoughtful explication of the explicit point on which the project that produced it was based. To wit: the landscape of international and transnational crime, which existing typologies attempt to define and deal with, is shifting rapidly in a globalised world, and both our scholarly and enforcement-oriented legal modelling must shift with it. As a legal conversation, it could hardly be more important, and this collection will undoubtedly help to ignite further inquiry.

*Robert J. Currie\**

---

25  Gless (n 23) 241.
\*   Professor of Law, Schulich School of Law, Dalhousie University.

Printed in the United States
By Bookmasters